THE STATISTICAL ACCOUNT OF SCOTLAND

General Editors: Donald J. Withrington and Ian R. Grant

VOLUME XVI

BANFFSHIRE, MORAY & NAIRNSHIRE

THE
STATISTICAL ACCOUNT OF SCOTLAND

GENERAL EDITORS' INTRODUCTION

The *Statistical Account of Scotland* has been used by generation after generation of social historians enquiring into the local or national affairs of Scotland in the later 18th century. It is an unrivalled source, and historians of other countries, as well as their sociologists, geographers and natural scientists, have long regretted having no similar body of evidence available to them. Sir John Sinclair, determinedly cajoling the parish ministers of the Established Church to respond to his long list of over 160 queries, intended his statistical enquiry to enable the country, and its government, not only to assess its current state but to prepare better for a better future—"ascertaining the quantum of happiness enjoyed by its inhabitants and the means of its future improvement", moral as well as economic or political. The quality of the returns he received was generally good and was often excellent, and the parochial reports provided the Scots of the 1790s with a uniquely valuable analysis of their own times: the same reports provide us today with an incomparable view of Scotland two centuries ago, through the sharp eyes and the often sharp words of men who knew their localities very well indeed.

However, the original *Account*, printed in twenty-one volumes in the course of the 1790s, is difficult and often exasperating to use. Sinclair published the parish returns just as they came in to him; therefore the reports for one county or for part of one county may be scattered throughout a dozen volumes or more. Readers of the original printing must have the index in volume xx in order to search out easily the particular returns they want, and even then they may overlook the supplementary replies eventually published in volume xxi. Furthermore, Sinclair's indexes of subjects and persons in volume xxi are woefully inadequate.

In this new edition we have brought together the parish returns in groupings by county and have printed them in alphabetical order, thus avoiding a major difficulty in using the earlier compilation. This new arrangement will not only assist those who wish to use the *Account* as a whole, it will also be especially useful to local historians and to others engaged in local or regional researches with an historical basis: and the new format makes much easier a direct comparison of the Sinclair *Account* with the *New Statistical Account*, published by counties in 1845. So large is the volume of material for Aberdeenshire and Perthshire, however, that these counties have required two volumes each in this reissue. And we have decided to gather together in one volume all the returns from western island parishes, in the Inner and Outer Hebrides and in Bute, rather than leave them scattered among the returns from mainland Ross-shire, Inverness-shire and Argyll: these have a coherence in themselves which would be lost if placed with their respective counties.

Each of the twenty volumes in this reissue is being edited by a scholar who contributes an introduction showing the significance of the *Statistical Account* reports for the region and assessing their importance for modern historical and other social studies. Each volume will also contain an index (of the more important topics discussed in the returns, but not of persons or places) which will make the *Account* more accessible to and more immediately useful to all students, not least to pupils in schools where Scottish local studies are being introduced or extended. We are grateful to James Hamilton for his help in preparing the indexes.

We believe that the significantly improved format of this reissue will make more widely useful, and more widely used, an already acknowledged vital work of standard reference.

Ian R. Grant   Donald J. Withrington

THE

STATISTICAL ACCOUNT

OF

SCOTLAND

1791 – 1799

EDITED BY SIR JOHN SINCLAIR

VOLUME XVI

BANFFSHIRE, MORAY & NAIRNSHIRE

With a new introduction by
DONALD J. WITHRINGTON

EP Publishing Limited
1982

This is volume XVI of a reissue in twenty volumes of *The Statistical Account of Scotland*, originally published between 1791 and 1799. In this reissue all the parish accounts for individual counties are printed together for the first time, with a new introduction and index in each volume.

Volume I of this reissue carries a general introduction by Donald J. Withrington.

ISBN 0 7158 1000 6 (set)
0 7158 1016 2 (vol. XVI)

Printed in Great Britain by
The Moxon Press Ltd
Ben Rhydding, Ilkley
West Yorkshire

CONTENTS

NAIRNSHIRE

INTRODUCTION

'Few parishes in Scotland afford less subject for statistical enquiries than this of Botriphnie', wrote the Rev. Alexander Angus – unnecessarily apologetic – to Sir John Sinclair about the year 1792,[1] as a prelude to seven pages of concise, careful and valuable analysis of a parish in which he had already been minister for 18 years and where he was to remain for a further 37. So assured was he of having so little to contribute, indeed, that within another two or three years he sent in four more pages to fill out his initial account! Mr. Angus's gentle seriousness and purposefulness is paralleled in nearly all the parish reports which are gathered together in this volume: only a handful out of 49 are both short and generally uninformative. The vast majority are wide-ranging and enlightening in their comments, with some writers having gone to enormous trouble in searching out very precise details – about the parish population, its produce and its imports, its crops and its social concerns.

We are, of course, dependent on the truthfulness and reliability of the contributors of these accounts – something which, when it came to answers to such sensitive questions as those about the character and characteristics of the parishioners, was clearly understood by some ministers. The Rev. George Gordon, of Mortlach, who probably wrote his account after he had been translated to the East Church in Aberdeen in 1793, was aware of the temptations involved:[2] 'It here obviously occurs, that a minister may be induced, from various motives, to go to the extreme of truth, on the favourable side for his flock. His regard for them may blind and mislead him; or, by condemning them, he may think that he obliquely condemns himself; at least, if another did it, he might perhaps be led too readily to think so. Few chuse to depreciate their own importance; few to diminish the happy effects of their pastoral care; and fewer still are inclined to

1. Botriphnie, 99.
2. Mortlach, 334.

render themselves ungracious.' Yet in most instances, saving those where a writer clearly believes it better to say nothing at all on a sensitive point than to be judged as partial or graceless, it is hard not to be very impressed by the matter-of-factness and directness of these accounts (and by the care which has been given to the task Sir John gave his correspondents).

Impressions apart, it is worth noting how well most of our writers must have known their parishes and their parishioners. Out of 48 known contributors, 17 had already been for more than 15 years in the charges on which they reported and no fewer than 35 (including those 17) had served five years and more, by the time Sinclair initiated his enterprise in 1789 – 90. Only 13 of our writers held recent appointments — not that being an incomer necessarily meant that a minister's report would be meagre and without detailed knowledge: true, some were, such as those for Alves or Knockando or Rothes, but the Rev. John Dunbar produced 43 pages on Dyke and Moy while the Rev. George Donaldson (writing his second account, having already contributed a report on the parish he had just left, Kennethmont in Aberdeenshire) left us 36 informative pages on Rathven. Before we leave this commentary on the writers of our accounts, it may be worth noting how long most of them served their parishes. We have already seen that Mr. Angus of Botriphnie was to hold office there for 55 years, yet his is not the longest record of service: it is matched by Mr. John Grant in Abernethy and Kincardine (1765 – 1820) and both are just surpassed by Mr. William Leslie of St. Andrews Lhanbryde who was the first minister of that united parish (1788 – 1839) but had already been in the ministry at St. Andrews since 1783, to give him 56 years in the locality. In all, five of our contributors remained for more than 50 years in their parishes (George Cruikshank of Rothes; Abercromby Gordon at Banff, including a period as missionary at Portsoy, in addition to the three others noted above); 16 held office for 40 – 49 years; 11 stayed on for 30 – 39 years; nine remained for 20 – 29 years and another five for 10 – 19 years. Thus 46 out of the known 48 contributors either had already (in 35 cases) long been in their parishes or otherwise were to have to live with their public comments on them for many years to come; and the two exceptions were not going to escape very far – being translated from Edinkillie to Forres[1] and from Keith to Fordyce.[2] Thus the reader's general impression of the aptness and knowledgability of the accounts which follow is underlined by the extraordinary record of long service by the writers in their localities. As a postscript to this discussion of length of appointment, it may be added that Mr. Thomas Wilson who served Gamrie for 47 years from 1771 to 1818 was preceded by his father in that parish and then followed by his son – a total of 123 years (1732 – 1855) in which the family held the cure; and in Inverkeithney Mr. John Milne (1767 – 1809) also succeeded his father and was also followed in turn by a son, to give no fewer than 137 years of continuous service (1721 – 1858).

One account, or part-account, was apparently not written by the minister. The first contribution from Duffus was, rather mysteriously, attributed to a 'friend to statistical enquiries', yet it was clearly written in 1792 – 93 and was not so late in being presented that Sir John Sinclair would have sent one of his agents to act as substitute-contributor for the local minister. Indeed that minister, who had been in Duffus since 1778 and would live until 1803, provided a second account which was published in the final volume in 1799 – with no note in it to resolve our puzzlement. The only parish account – that is, sole contribution – about whose author there is no clear information is that for Spynie. This seems to have been prepared in 1792 – 93, at a time when the parish was in the throes of a dispute over the rights to the presentation to the benefice – the eventual minister, Mr. Alexander Brown school-master of Bellie since 1779, was actually presented by the Duke of Gordon in 1790 but was not ordained until September 1793. In the event, the account published by Sir

1. Rev. John MacDonnel was only at Edinkillie for 15 months but contributed 13 helpful pages on that parish; he wrote a 9-page and reasonably informed account of Forres within two years of going there in 1792.
2. Rev. Alexander Humphrey went to Fordyce in 1792, having been an assistant at Keith since 1789: his predecessor at Fordyce, Rev. James Lawtie who had been there since 1747 died in 1791, but had sent in a long account of the parish just before his death. Humphrey seems to have written his lengthy account of Keith in 1791 but sent it in after he had transferred to Fordyce.

John Sinclair was signed by the 'Rev. Abraham Gordon, Minister,' someone who is not to be found in any of the volumes of the *Fasti Ecclesiae Scoticanae*: the writer, whoever he was, seems to have been very well versed for his task, the account containing — as well as much informative comment on contemporary Spynie — an abundance of historical evidence which drew on original sources, in chartularies, registers and sheriff court records.

The three counties which lie within the area covered by this volume — Nairnshire, Moray or Elginshire, and Banffshire — form a roughly triangular-shaped wedge running southwards from the shores of the Moray Firth into the mountainous lands of upper Strathspey. The district is bounded by a north-facing coastline some 70 miles in length, leading into a wide coastal plain, then to hillier country with deep valleys and finally — some 40 miles or so from the coast — edging into a region which juts into the Cairngorms. It comprises four parishes of Nairnshire, nineteen in Moray (excluding Cromdale, the account of which is reprinted in the Inverness-shire volume of this edition) and twenty-six in Banffshire (including the 'anomaly' of St. Fergus, a parish on the coast to the north of Peterhead, widely separated from the remaining parishes of its civil county yet tied to it by history and tradition).[1]

Within the landmass of the area included in our counties, there are three generally distinctive districts: (i) the low-lying lands of the coastal plain, including eighteen Banffshire parishes, twelve in Moray and two in Nairnshire;[2] (ii) twelve parishes which occupy higher ground, separating the plain from the mountainous interior — six in Banffshire, five in

1. Banffshire in this volume retains St. Fergus, still in that county in the *New Statistical Account* published in 1845, but also 'loses' to Aberdeenshire the parish of King Edward, lying on the coast between Gamrie and Banff, whose account appears in volume 15 of this reprint.
2. Alvah, Banff, Bellie, Boharm, Boyndie, Cullen, Deskford, Fordice, Forglen, Gamrie, Grange, Inverkeithny, Keith, Marnoch, Ordiquhill, Rathven, Rothiemay, St. Fergus; Alves, Drainy, Duffus, Dyke and Moy, Elgyn, Forres, Kinloss, Rafford, St. Andrew's, Lhanbryd, Speymouth, Spynie, Urquhart; Auldearn, Nairn.

Moray and two in Nairnshire;[1] finally, (iii) five parishes which are more evidently high land and remote, three in Banffshire and two in Moray.[2] In matters of economy, in social and cultural characteristics, they may be seen as distinctive – but we should beware of making too simple or direct contrasts between them. Even in respect of population, its increase or decrease between Webster's census of 1755 and the *Statistical Account* returns or those made in the census of 1800 – 01, while the division of parishes into those three groupings is helpful, it also brings questions to be resolved:

		Banff	Moray	Nairn	Total	Total population in		
		± %age	± %age	± %age	± %age	1755	1790s	1801
Low lying	1755—1790s	+ 9.2	– 12.7	+ 4.3	0.0	53955	53885	52408
	1755—1801	+ 5.2	– 14.2	– 0.9	– 2.9	(70.9%)	(71.4%)	(72.3%)
Higher	1755—1790s	– 7.7	+ 15.3	+ 6.3	+ 2.0	15445	15757	14018
	1755—1801	– 22.1	– 4.0	+ 19.1	– 9.2	(20.3%)	(20.9%)	(19.3%)
Highest	1755—1790s	– 11.1	– 16.7	—	– 14.0	6713	5775	6036
	1755—1801	– 13.1	– 7.2	—	– 10.1	(8.8%)	(7.7%)	(8.3%)

The table shows that there was no notable change, from one count of population to the next, in the proportionate numbers of the inhabitants living in the different geographic areas. But why did coastal Moray lose population throughout the later eighteenth century while the Banffshire lowland plain increased in numbers? Why did the 'middle' area of Moray increase in population in the decades before 1790, yet diminish in the following decade, while the similar Banffshire parishes lost population throughout the period and the two Nairnshire parishes increased theirs?

The population tables in the Appendix, detailing changes parish by parish, show that not *all* lowland Moray parishes declined in population – but only Forres (a thriving and expanding market town) and Speymouth (with its village at Garmouth expanding to serve its own harbour, for export of timber floated down the Spey, and also the shipbuilding centre at nearby Kingston) showed large increases, and did so for

1. Botriphnie, Gartly, Glass, Inveraven, Mortlach; Birnie, Dallas, Edenkeillie, Knockandow, Rothes; Ardclach, Calder.
2. Aberlour, Cabrach, Kirkmichael; Abernethy and Kinchardine, Duthil and Rothiemurchas.

obvious enough reasons. The other lowland Moray parishes
– even Elgin – all show large decreases, from a variety of
causes: the enlargement of farms in a period of agrarian
reform and improvement, with landlords sometimes putting
an embargo on subletting (often expressly forbidden in the
improving leases which were offered to tenants),[1] limitation
on the supply of peat for use in domestic fires (a vital matter
when coal could be scarce and was expensive),[2] lack of
employment in new manufacturing enterprises,[3] the activities
of press gangs,[4] tenants' lack of capital in an era of substantially
rising rents and inflation.[5] Some Banffshire parishes shared
this loss of population: Alvah, we learn, needed the establishment of a village to retain in the parish those who were
removed from crofts and cottages; Grange lost many inhabitants who went south to well-paid labour there; in
Deskford the population declined as the lairds restricted lime-
burning in order to preserve peat for domestic use; Inverkeithney was affected by scarcity of fuel and by a reduction
in the number of tenancies granted by the landlords.[6] But
why, it may be asked, did Elgin parish and burgh decrease in
population? The minister's report is not conclusive. There is
much comment, as in other reports, about very large increases
in rents and in labourers' wages. In a very general commentary on the causes of depopulation, local factors seem to include
– the drawing off of men to the army, navy and merchant
service, decreasing numbers of marriages or late marriages because of the 'luxury and expense of living' and the
fears of labourers and tenants about settling down in an age
of engrossment of farms, the decline in woollen manufacture
and glove-making, and incitement to emigrate in order to make
a fortune.[7]

Where in contrast, did the overall increase in population in
lowland Banffshire come from? The numbers of inhabitants
in the trading town of Banff had risen substantially since 1782,

1. e.g. Spynie, 694.
2. e.g. Alves, 458n; Speymouth, 677.
3. e.g. Dyke and Moy, 560.
4. e.g. Elgyn, 607.
5. e.g. Drainy, 495.
6. Alvah, 12; Grange, 213n; Deskford, 140; Inverkeithny, 245.
7. Elgyn, 607–609.

offsetting a decrease in the country part of the parish.[1] The fishing village of Whitehills in Boyndie parish, the burgh of Cullen and the village of Portknockie – with Cullen a substantial weaving centre, having 65 looms for linen and 7 looms for stockings, as well as being an expanding fishing town, the fishing stations in Gamrie parish and in Rathven; the quickly-growing settlements at New Keith and Newmill in the parish of Keith (weaving and manufactures expanding here, not fishing) – all these retained and increased their population.[2] It is worth noting how many of these expanding parishes show a definite, even considerable, majority of women in their communities – as men went to sea or into the army or to the south for work; and many seaboard parishes saw an influx of highland women who came for employment in the fishing industry, for example.[3]

There is indeed a great deal of evidence of the importance to an area of an existing village or a new settlement, to which displaced tenants and cottagers could go to find work or at least to find accommodation. The town of Nairn seems to have been especially attractive: it rose in population from 600 in 1755 to 1100 in the 1790s, its cheap and readily available supplies of peat and of 'vivres' making it 'thronged with foreigners', while neighbouring Auldearn (village-less) lost population quite heavily with its young men 'flocking to the manufacturing towns'.[4] To have a new village or town in the parish was, in the 'middle' as well as in the lowland area, a means of holding or increasing population: thus Rothes drew in large numbers to its new village, even though it did not provide any extensive manufacturing employment until distilleries were placed there in the early nineteenth century; and in the highland area of Banffshire the new village of Tomintoul proved to have the same attraction, both for per-

1. Banff, 40 – 41.
2. Boyndie, 112; Cullen, 123; Gamrie, 188 – 189; Rathven, 369 – 371; Keith, 253 – 254.
3. There was a distinct majority of women in all three of the districts we have designated, in the 28 parishes which made the information available, not only in those on the coast. Only Keith and Nairn had more men than women among their inhabitants. The proportions of women to men were as follows: mountainous parishes, 53%:47%; upland parishes, 54½%:45½%; lowland parishes, 52½%:47½%.
4. Nairn, 751 – 752; Auldearn, 720.

manent residents and for many 'foreign beggars', yet Cabrach and Aberlour — without the stabilising agency of a new town or new village — lost many inhabitants and produced the overall decreases in population in upper Banffshire.[1] Army service in fencible regiments, enlargement of farms, 'the opportunity afforded young adventurers to traverse the field of fortune', are said to account for the overall decrease in population in the two parishes in the Moray highlands: neither Duthil nor Abernethy contained village settlements – and, while the minister of Duthil was anxious about the fact that villages were 'too frequently nurseries of political disquisition', he recognised their utility in offering 'sufficient employment in their native country' and so reducing the drain of emigration.[2]

'Middle area' parishes in Moray generally increased in population, as did both Cawdor and Ardclach in Nairnshire: only Birnie in Moray diminished in numbers throughout the years 1755 and 1800, the minister blaming engrossment of farms and some emigration to America.[3] There is notable contrast between these districts of Moray and Nairn and the hilly areas of mid-Banffshire: Mortlach still lacked a town or village and lost population; the enlargement of farm holdings and restrictions on subletting decreased numbers in Botriphnie and Gartly; in Botriphnie and Mortlach fewer agricultural labourers were employed (for, as their wages increased, tenants more and more used their sons and daughters instead of 'annual servants' in farm work); in Glass, after the dearth of 1782 – 83, many cottars left to gain employment in manufacturing towns.[4] Whereas the Moray parishes seemed to have plenty of peat – for sale as well as for domestic use – and tended to retain a structure of small farms in which a lively cottage industry in spinning and weaving survived, while there was some migration to the south of Scotland and to Aberdeen as well to neighbouring parishes with towns or villages, it was not sufficient to produce an overall decline, at least until the later 1790s.

1. Rothes, 635; Kirkmichael, 278 – 279, 285; Cabrach, 119; Aberlour, 4.
2. Duthil, 524.
3. Birnie, 464.
4. Botriphnie, 103 – 104; Gartly, 195; Mortlach, 328; Glass, 198.

Introduction

Thus neighbouring counties, with apparently similar geographical characteristics, could have quite distinctive population trends: so too could neighbouring parishes within a single area. The reforming initiative of landowners, the potential and actual capability of a parish or even a portion of a parish to provide sufficient fuel and food for its inhabitants, the extension of fisheries or manufactures, the susceptibility of parishioners to pressures to emigrate or to enlist in the services were all among the factors which produced an often surprising diversity in matters of population.

Agriculture provided a livelihood for the vast majority of inhabitants in our three counties and remained the most crucial factor in the stability or instability of population. Apart from a very few coastal communities in which some of the inhabitants supported themselves entirely from their fishing activities, all depended directly on farming, to a greater or lesser extent. Let us therefore look at the state of farming in the three geographical areas we have outlined.

The accounts, in dealing – often quite expansively – with the state of agriculture in the various parishes, give a clear indication of the specialisms which varying farming practices could and did incorporate. Thus, in the five 'mountainous' parishes in the southern extremity of our area, Aberlour was 'calculated rather for grain than for pasture'; in Cabrach, it was said, the inhabitants did not depend more for subsistence on the produce of the land than on sales of sheep and cattle, but once the seed was in they 'mind little else but their cattle'; in Kirkmichael, particularly in the hilly borderlands of the parish, the pasturing of sheep and cattle was dominant 'with sheep, at present, their staple commodity'; in Abernethy 'all depends on the returns from cattle, sheep, wool, butter and cheese for paying rent'; in Duthil the 'only articles of export are black cattle and sheep'; in Rothiemurcas the great predominance of sheep is obvious.[1] These distinctions are reflected in other comments too. Thus Aberlour, with its mixed grain and stock economy, 'not only supplies itself but sells oats, meal and barley, sometimes to the highlands, and

1. Aberlour, 3; Cabrach, 115; Kirkmichael, 284; Abernethy and Kincardine, 439; Duthil and Rothiemurchas, 514, 522.

sometimes for exportation' even though it was at a considerable distance, over poor roads, from the coast; in Cabrach the upper (Aberdeenshire) part of the parish 'seldom produces sufficiency of grain for itself', while the lower (Banffshire) part produced a sufficiency 'and about 200 bolls' – which was sold to neighbouring distilleries while the other group of inhabitants had to seek supply elsewhere; in Kirkmichael it was said that the land seldom produced a sufficiency to support its inhabitants and the minister estimated that the potato crop provided them with a full two months' subsistence each year.[1] While Duthil and Rothiemurcas could apparently supply its parishioners 'abundantly with provisions', the minister of Abernethy and Kincardine reported that the produce of corn and potatoes never maintained the inhabitants and often fell far short. Some inhabitants often needed to buy meal for as much as six months in the year (hence making more crucial than elsewhere the demand for and prices of the cattle, sheep, etc., which they sold, therefore, not only to meet the rent but to pay for necessary subsistence).[2]

The writers all expected that they would have to comment on the impact of improving ideas and policies. Their reports note some characteristic signs of improvement – the introduction of turnips and potatoes, of cabbages, of clover and sown grasses. Here again there was a variety of experience to be explained. Aberlour, rather surprisingly, had only just introduced both turnips and potatoes, in small quantities; Duthil had only a few acres of turnips but extensive planting of potatoes; and in Cabrach turnips thrived throughout the parish, but suffered from lack of enclosures, while potatoes were mentioned as 'the most uncertain crop'. In Kirkmichael turnips and potatoes alone signalled any kind of general improvement (save for the increased size and diminished number of farms in its central valleys) – and, as we have seen, the potato had become there a vital element in the diet of the inhabitants; in the supplementary report on Duthil, the potato was recommended particularly as cattle feed ('beef fed on turnips is far inferior in quality to that on potatoes') and also for being of greatest benefit 'for the kitchen'; in Abernethy

1.   Aberlour, 4; Cabrach, 119; Kirkmichael, 284.
2.   Abernethy and Kincardine, 438 – 439; Duthil and Rothiemurchas, 514.

potatoes were listed in crops whose returns were described as 'precarious'.[1] Sown grasses, meanwhile, were evidently part (but still quite a small part) of the Aberlour system, implying that some form of rotation was in vogue in some places there; in Cabrach, we are merely told that grass was sown with success; in Kirkmichael, in a countryside apparently well provided with natural pasture, the minister reported that no artificial grass could be raised – arguing that this was impossible without enclosures, and that the introduction of enclosures would mean getting rid of sheep (the essential item in the economy) and would also be particularly expensive in that parish.[2] Duthil reported the existence of 'but a few enclosures' and also of much popular opposition to them, the 'cattle having been accustomed to range promiscuously through the year, except in the summer season and while the corns are on the ground' – Duthil planted few turnips, and no doubt the inhabitants feared for their cattle in winter if they could not roam the whole parish.[3] In Abernethy only five farms were in any degree of improvement, those with the 'best climate', and the minister almost immediately warns against making too much of this by noting that 'run-ridge still takes place in a great part of the parish' and declaring that 'the farms are generally in no better state than they were 100 years ago'. Of Kirkmichael it was said that 'for the improvements of agriculture and manufactures the country is ill calculated' and that 'the inhabitants follow the practice of their ancestors'.[4] Thus, there were improvements of a kind, often meagre: and all but the minister of Aberlour were concerned to declare that only the most rudimentary change had yet taken place in the traditional agricultural system.

Much, of course, in this matter of agrarian improvement depended on the initiative and energy of the landlords or their factors, although the responsiveness of tenants was always crucial. In these five 'mountainous' parishes, the Grants owned most of the lands in Aberlour, Abernethy and Kincardine

1. Aberlour, 4; Cabrach, 114; Kirkmichael, 284; Duthil and Rothiemurchas, 513, 528; Abernethy and Kinchardine, 437.
2. Aberlour, 4; Cabrach, 114; Kirkmichael, 284.
3. Duthil and Rothiemurchas, 513–514.
4. Abernethy, 437–438; Kirkmichael, 284.

Introduction

and Duthil and Rothiemurcas, while the Duke of Gordon owned Cabrach and Kirkmichael. The Grants seem, from our accounts, to have been the more active in promoting change. But the Duke had only recently dissolved the tacksman system in Cabrach and Kirkmichael and had begun to issue direct leases, albeit only for nineteen years, to the tenants – leases which could provide a new and more immediate means of prompting preferred developments. Any general policy of improvement on the Gordon lands, however, if it were to be applied to the parishes of Cabrach and Kirkmichael, would be very expensive indeed, and it would assuredly diminish returns from rent for some years. But the Duke of Gordon was already very heavily, and expensively, committed elsewhere: as Victor Gaffney noted in his detailed study of the founding of the Kirkmichael village, Tomintoul, 'in the Gordon estates at large a "ca' canny" policy had to be adopted in view of the Duke's costly undertakings nearer home...on the enlargement of Gordon Castle, the re-siting of Fochabers, the endless acres of plantation and the high standard of the ducal farms'.[1] The remote highland parts of the estate would therefore have to wait. As we shall see, the variations in landlords' policies in respect of different parishes in different parts of their estates are sometimes as notable as the general distinctions in policy and practice between different landlords.[2] Let us turn now to the upland parishes.

In the 'middle' and hilly areas of our three counties, there was again a varied response to improving ideas and policies. In Edinkillie, we are told, 'farming is in a very wretched state in this part of the country'; and in neighbouring Ardclach 'the

1. Victor Gaffney, *The Lordship of Strathavon: Tomintoul under the Gordons* (Aberdeen, 1960), 177 – 182.
2. There could be more than economic considerations at work in that determined aggregation of estates which was so much a feature in our three counties in the latter half of the 18th century. The Earls of Fife and Findlater, and the Duke of Gordon too, were political rivals; ownership of land brought with it the prospect of manufacturing votes for use at general elections – and hence purchase of land (and sometimes exchanges of lands) might be made for essentially political purposes. There was then not always a desire to improve these lands quickly, for their major and immediate value was political – and what seem rather puzzling variations in estate policy may therefore appear in distinct or disjointed sections of the same estate.

method of labouring seems to have undergone little alteration for centuries'. Dallas meanwhile reported some large enclosures of planted firs and, interestingly, a group of carpenters in the parish who made stakes or palings for cattle-folds and for enclosing fields – but the minister gave no hint of any more general enclosures there: indeed, he was to report that the crops were generally insufficient to sustain the inhabitants or their cattle from one year's end to the next. In the same stretch of country, in Knockando, the lands were said to be unenclosed, with little encouragement to change existing practices. In Dallas and Edinkillie potatoes were widely grown for family use – an important supplement to the diet, as no doubt they were also in Ardclach and Knockando where potatoes were merely listed among the principal crops. In Dallas turnips were grown for domestic use too; the crop in Knockando was probably more extensive and intended for winter feeding for cattle and/or sheep, just as was the 'little artificial grass' which both Dallas and Knockando grew. Thus in this particular area of Moray and Nairnshire there was little advance in improvements: among the reasons noted for this were the facts that the farms were very small (Edinkillie), that there were few leases and also so barren a soil that farmers were forced to rear as many cattle as possible on it (Ardclach).[1]

Enclosures were not by any means 'complete' anywhere in this middle area. 'Opulent' tenants in Cawdor were making moves that way; in Mortlach, on several farms, a good deal was being done 'by dykes and hedges'. Yet, there, leases were offputtingly short and winter herding was not 'relished' – so that there were difficulties facing those who wished to fence off land for turnips and clover. In Botriphnie only two farms were enclosed and grew much sown grass, apparently, but – apart from a straightening of the ridges in the old run-rig system, showing that a single-crop field structure had not been introduced yet – little else had been achieved: even so, 'much more grain than is needed' was grown and a high return was obtained from the sale of black cattle, so that little impetus to push on with improvements was to be found. Nor, so

1. Edenkeillie, 582–583; Ardclach, 712–713; Dallas, 472, 474; Knockandow, 623–624.

it seems, had Gartly made much advance with enclosures: this parish had many acres in turnips and sown grasses and, with surpluses in grain and other crops being produced, there was no doubt little stimulus to make further and possibly upsetting changes.[1]

Where the older system of farming 'worked', while it may have been adapted slightly to introduce the more amenable and acceptable kinds of improvement but not greatly altered in essentials, and where it could be altered without much disturbance or expense to the tenants; where there was no or no significant landlord leadership; where a useful concentration of tenants' holdings could be made to form something like 'fields' (as in Botriphnie, Dallas or Gartly) in which a more concentrated cropping of grass or turnips could be carried on with the added possibilities of introducing such novelties as horse-hoeing – then it seems that little more was done to carry through extensive enclosures, so as not to restrain the winter wanderings of the cattle and sheep that were so vital to the economy of these 'middle' parishes. Sources of income additional to those from farming could also weaken the drive to more radical improvements. Thus, the inhabitants of Dallas and Edinkillie could survive the 'wretchedness' of their farms because they were well placed to sell large amounts of peat for fuel in the nearby towns of Elgin and Forres – as well as sell spun flax and other cottage products to merchants or manufacturers there. It was said of Edinkillie, indeed, that 'almost every man in the parish is a cartwright', in addition to his farming commitments, and that he sold the results of his industry at neighbouring burgh markets. For the parishioners of Gartly the same kind of market, for peats and other goods, was readily available in Huntly.[2]

The 'middle' area parishes grew good crops of barley, oats, pease, some rye; and some wheat was produced in Birnie and Mortlach.[3] The parishes all kept numerous black cattle, which were the real mainstay of the family incomes, and many

1. Calder, 735; Mortlach, 329; Botriphnie, 100; Gartly, 194.
2. Botriphnie, 100; Dallas, 473; Edenkeillie, 584; Gartly, 194.
3. Birnie, 463; Mortlach, 329.

also had large flocks of sheep – especially Cawdor, Dallas, Knockando, Inveraven and Gartly, while in Mortlach 'some very good sheepwalks' had been formed.[1] Plantations in the moorlands of the area, though reducing the grazing land, still kept large natural pastures widely available. There was, it seemed, a reasonable enough balance in the local economies, in good times at least – precarious as it might turn out to be in times of crisis; is it surprising that there seemed, therefore, to be no very great reason to change in this 'middle' region, especially when long leases were seldom given and the sizes of holdings were relatively small?

Let us turn next to the parishes of the lowland plain and divide them, for the purpose of this part of our enquiry, into two groups: fourteen inland parishes without immediate access to the coast, and seventeen parishes which bordered the Moray Firth together with the detached coastal parish of St. Fergus.

In the inland grouping, only Rothiemay provided a very positive statement about enclosures – 'well advanced here compared to neighbouring parishes' is the rather ambiguous comment. Alvah and Rafford remarked that 'few have begun to enclose' and in Rafford, indeed, 'exhausted fields' were let out to the poor in parcels, rent free, to manure, trench, plant and reap. In Grange, Marnoch and Forglen, and in Rafford again, only the mains farms of resident heritors or of their factors (or farms directly in their own hands) .had adopted enclosures: the parishes of Keith and Ordiquhill, and several hundreds of acres near Elgin, were reputed to be all but unenclosed.[2]

In Spynie, larger farms – still in open fields – which had been rented out to gentlemen had introduced some form of rotation, including turnips and sown grasses, but 'on the smaller, none of the modern improvements have yet been

1. Calder, 734 – 735; Dallas, 473; Knockandow, 623; Inveraven, 240; Gartly, 194; Mortlach, 331.
2. Rothiemay, 398 – 399; Alvah, 10; Rafford, 630; Grange, 217 – 218; Marnoch, 316 – 317; Forglen, 168; Keith, 247; Ordiquhill, 358; Elgyn, 604 – 605; also Deskford, 135 – 136.

adopted'; there was an abundance of stone available for constructing dykes or 'stone fences', but it was not used to any extent. In Alvah there had been the introduction of sown grasses (grown mainly for sale), of winter herding on grass and turnips, and much planting of woods by the Earl of Fife; hedges had also been tried, to mark enclosures, but without success; earthen (feal) dykes did not last, and stone dykes were expensive. Dyking stone was readily to hand in Ordiquhill, yet agriculture there was 'still in its infancy', lacking the long leases that would tempt tenants to drain and enclose. Short leases and the smallness of holdings restrained enclosures at Deskford, yet there hedges were being tried and were thriving – while, on the other hand, an attempt to improve a large area of moorland had failed and it had been put into small plots. At Keith, rotation including green crops was being tried but was hindered by the lack of enclosures; at Grange, a new rotational system including green crops was in operation when the famine of 1782 struck – and since that time the tenants would only grow grain (partly for export by sea) so that 'agriculture is in a worse state here than it was 10 years ago'. In Forglen, it seems, rotation was having a good effect; in Boharm some helpful consolidation of farms was taking place; in Marnoch, however, once extensive farms had been 'parcelled out and let in crofts' so as to provide the immediate security of a considerable increase in rent to the landlords there.[1]

What do we see happening in this lowland but inland area, then? There was, clearly, widespread adoption of some form of rotation, including sown grasses and/or turnips, more notably and effectively on the farms of 'tenants of some rank' rather than those of the poorer sort. There was evidence of winter herding, often practised with difficulty in open fields, with little more than rudimentary ditching or turf dykes to restrain 'promiscuous' grazing. There was certainly a range of crops – with wheat as well as barley, oats, pease, beans in the Moray parishes (and in Alvah and Botriphnie in Banffshire), plus flax, grass grown for hay and sometimes intended for sale, as well as the expected crops of turnips, cabbages and

1. Spynie, 689; Alvah, 10; Ordiquhill, 357; Deskford, 136 – 137; Keith, 249; Grange, 212 – 214; Forglen, 168; Boharm, 92; Marnoch, 316.

potatoes. In Boharm the minister was concerned in case too concentrated a cropping of grain brought problems – it was not uncommon for much of a crop to be lost, indeed for much not to ripen properly, because of the onset of severe weather in late autumn.[1] In Inverkeithney the high grain and cattle prices were tempting farmers not to sublet but to take more and more land into their own hands.[2] Almost every parish in the district grew far more grain than it needed for the sustenance of its own inhabitants – and did so intentionally, for export of the surplus through the Moray Firth ports. In St. Andrews Lhanbryde the local demand for oatmeal had been reduced as the parishioners used increasingly large quantities of potatoes; in Elgin, too, great quantities of potatoes were grown, partly at least for export to Newcastle and other towns in the south.[3] Horse-hoeing had been introduced in Spynie and Deskford and improved the quality, if not the yields, of the crops.[4] In Spynie, too, the taking-in of mosses for plantation with trees cut back on the available pasture, which would support only a few sheep where once every tenant had had 'a stock'; and in Grange the landlord's removal of the old commonty land from pasture meant that 'cattle and sheep dwindled away': only Rafford, Ordiquhill, St. Andrews Lhanbryde and Forglen retained sheep in any quantity, whereas the rearing of cattle was widely maintained – and no doubt prompted the moves to introduce root and green crops into somewhat more elaborate rotations than the ancient one.[5] But it all seems rather haphazard, without any very clear direction nor according to any firmly-enacted policies, even for such basic questions as that of deciding the most prudent length of a lease with which to promote improvement. The account for St. Andrews Lhanbryde makes it clear enough, however, that in general the mere granting of long leases was not sufficient in itself – direction was needed and had to be sustained. According to the comments in this group of parish accounts, remarkably little landlord direction was being given.

1. Boharm, 92–93.
2. Inverkeithny, 245.
3. St. Andrew's Lhanbryd, 648; Elgin, 595.
4. Spynie, 690; Deskford, 140.
5. Spynie, 693; Grange, 213n; Rafford, 627; Ordiquhill, 360; St. Andrew's Lhanbryd, 642; Forglen, 169.

Introduction

When we look at the agricultural state of the coastal parishes, we can find better evidence of that most dramatic signal of improvement – enclosed fields separated from each other by dykes or hedges or fences or ditches, as part of a tidy system of farming which incorporated careful rotations and concentrated cropping. Three parishes out of 18 are definite about the existence of enclosures – in Gamrie 'much was accomplished' under improving leases from the Earl of Fife and in Banff there were 'stone fences' and excellent crops, with Lords Banff and Findlater sharing a zest for enclosure; in Cullen there was movement of population from farms which the Earl of Findlater was enclosing.[1] Yet, even in what was called by a perceptive contemporary the 'champaign country' of lowland Moray, in a period when the same writer was to claim that the Banffshire plain was even more fertile and more apt for improvement than the Moray one, the marks of any really extensive changes in the area are not easily found.[2] Thus in Bellie, Speymouth and Urquhart there was little evidence of enclosure, except around Gordon Castle at Fochabers; the farms were reckoned too small, field stones for dyking were not readily available and cattle wandered at will throughout the parish in winter. To the west, along the Moray coast, this tale continues. The minister of Drainie states that modern improvements of all kinds were 'only in their infancy'; only the lands at 'gentlemen's seats' had been enclosed at Duffus – elsewhere agriculture was in 'a very low state', and the parish was 'totally open'.[3] The Kinloss account gives no information at all, nor does that for Forres; but in Dyke and Moy the soil was 'much exhausted by an early culture and incessant cropping', some small patches of sown grass were enclosed 'by stakes and palings by the poorer sort' and elsewhere clover and rye grass were sown 'in open fields'.[4] Further west again, in the two Nairnshire parishes, we find no enclosures, and no encouragement to enclose in Auldearn where the ten-

1. Gamrie, 189 – 190; Banff, 22 – 23; Cullen, 125.
2. See James Donaldson's two county agricultural surveys, also promoted by Sir John Sinclair as president of the Board of Agriculture: *General View of the Agriculture of the County of Elgin or Moray*...(London, 1794), 3; and *General View of the Agriculture of the County of Banff, with Observations on the Means of its Improvement* (Edinburgh, 1794), 3 – 4.
3. Bellie, 82; Speymouth, 656; Urquhart, 699 – 700; Drainy, 483; Duffus, 491.
4. Dyke and Moy, 534, 540 – 541.

ants were 'tenacious of antiquated practices'; in Nairn only two or three farms were fenced in, the farms in general were too small and, with as many as ten heritors in the parish, the impulse to enclose was weak.[1]

The detached Banffshire parish of St. Fergus, where many farmers had as much as one-third of their holdings in grass, had – perhaps surprisingly – 'no specific signs of enclosures', but three- or four-year rotations were in vogue as was the winter feeding of cattle on turnips; even so, the minister concludes that 'improvements have made but little progress yet' although the 'mode of farming has much changed' – and leaves us to ponder on his definition of 'improvements'.[2] Some of the Banffshire parishes fronting the Moray Firth, in addition to Banff, Cullen and Gamrie, had clearly been moving towards a reasonably thorough improved state. Alves had made 'rapid progress'; in Fordyce some farms seem to have begun to be enclosed; there is a strong likelihood that enclosures were known in Boyndie and Forres. Yet here, as in other districts, it is not safe to generalise too much; for in Rathven, a parish abounding with corn for export, where outfield was hardly known, where improvement was certainly in progress, nonetheless 'short leases and what is here termed runrigging are hurtful to the farmer'.[3]

It was in Banffshire, however, that the improving movement began in our area, with one or two·of the local ministers and Lord Findlater in the van. The stimulus to improve seems still, in the 1790s, to be stronger in Banffshire than in either Moray or Nairnshire, and generally more marked on the properties of Lords Banff or Findlater than, say, on those of the Duke of Gordon (save, perhaps, in the matter of the planting of trees).[4] Progress generally was more evident in the coastal

1. Auldearn, 722; Nairn, 743.
2. St. Fergus, 411 – 412.
3. Alves, 455; Fordice, 152 – 153; Boyndie, 111; Forres, 611; Rathven, 394.
4. The main plantations were of firs, but hardwoods were frequently planted (partly for decorative purposes) around the heritors' own houses; Fife and Findlater maintained very large nurseries for seedlings. These were not the only trees to be grown, however, for there are frequent references in the accounts to the planting of orchards for all kinds of fruit – cf. Aberlour and Kinchardine, 4; Dyke and Moy, 530; Dallas, 472; Edenkeillie, 581.

parishes than elsewhere in the three counties, for instance in the introduction of ploughing with horses rather than oxen and the parallel appearance of the lighter English plough. Among the other signs was the taking-in of common lands into tillage or into forest (e.g. in Fordyce), a development which reduced the numbers of sheep which could be maintained unless, as happened in a few parishes (e.g. Banff and Gamrie), a much more specialist sheep-farming was adopted.[1] But the overwhelming concentration of effort was on grain, with a more-or-less fixed rotation being widely introduced, all in the attempt to increase the crop returns and the profit. Wheat was, in this group of coastal parishes, a much more popular grain crop and, with other varieties of corn, was exported in substantial quantities – some to highland or inland distilleries, most to markets in the south of the country. Lime was easily available and vast amounts were quarried and burned in Fordyce and were brought in from Keith.[2] Other manures that were readily obtained included seaweed, shell-sand (either local or imported from Sunderland) and marl. The very availability and accessibility of lime and other fertilizers tended indeed to emphasise still more in these parishes the concentration on grain, to the point that it could weaken the maintenance of steady rotations and could lead to over-cropping. Turnips were quite generally grown, mostly for cattle feed, together with cut hay from sown grasses; the growing of grass, for sale as hay, was a notable feature. (In one parish[3] it was apparently customary to sow barley and grass seed together: while this did not affect the returns from the barley, it provided an especially good return of hay and straw for winter feeding.) Potatoes were grown in the parish of Banff as feed for horses and were also, as in Fordyce, sold and exported; but generally elsewhere they were grown for human consumption locally. Even in parishes which had very considerable surpluses of grain for export, the potato had become an essential element in the diet of poorer tenants, cottagers and labourers of all kinds. In Drainie and in Auldearn, we read, the crop 'served as subsistence for the poor for at

1. Fordice, 152; Banff, 24; Gamrie, 184.
2. Fordice, 148; Keith, 247.
3. Inveraven, 52.

least a third of the year'; in Nairn it would supply the 'common people' for as much as two-thirds of the year; and the parishes of Bellie, Dyke, Rathven and Urquhart all draw attention to the potato as having a vital and increasing part to play in the subsistence of the labouring and poorer classes.[1]

Another commodity that was vital to subsistence, and to at least a modest comfort in living, was fuel. Without adequate supplies, of peat or wood or coal, it was impossible to maintain population and there might be quite severe restrictions on manufacturing. In coastal or near-coastal parishes, easily accessible from a port, it was certainly possible to obtain coal. There was a steady traffic in coal between Moray Firth harbours and ports in the Firth of Forth and north-east England: thus the exporting of surplus potatoes from Banff to Sunderland and other Northumbrian ports may be explained by the fact that the main purpose of the connection was to bring coals north. The tax on sea-transported coal, a frequent complaint in parish accounts written before 1794, made it a less attractive substitute for peat than it might otherwise have been. With government at last convinced to withdraw that tax, the ministers of a number of parishes looked forward to a new era in manufacturing enterprise (especially, but not only, in the preparation of lime as a fertiliser) in areas to which coal could be easily carried at reasonable cost. This hope was sometimes frustrated by the wretched state of the roads in the 1790s, not least those leading directly to and from the ports. Also, it was anticipated, tenants and farm servants would be increasingly relieved of the need to spend all summer and early autumn in casting and carrying peats and would then be able to concentrate time and effort on working the land. Nonetheless, according to reports written in the later as well as the earlier 1790s, peat was still usually the main and often the only fuel. Lack of peat, and particular difficulties in obtaining peat from other sources, always had the most serious consequences – it was a direct stimulus to emigration (as in Alves) to other north-east parishes which had manufacturing villages or to farms or towns in the south or overseas.

1. Banff, 22; Fordice, 152; Drainy, 482 – 483; Auldearn, 723; Bellie, 82; Dyke and Moy, 82; Rathven, 364; Urquhart, 700.

Introduction

Some of our ministers report that they had no, or hardly any, peat deposits left at all – Drainie, Duffus, Dyke in Moray; Fordyce (where the lime-works no doubt depended on coals imported via Portsoy) and Mortlach in Banffshire; and the parish of Nairn. Mortlach bought much burnt lime from neighbouring Cabrach and probably peats too from its 'inexhaustible moss'; Nairn had 'excellent peat brought in' and, with such ready access to firing, great numbers of poor were enticed to settle in the town.[1] Peat stocks were 'wearing out' elsewhere, in a good many parishes – in Urquhart, Speymouth, Alves and Rafford in the Moray plain; in Gamrie, Forglen and Inverkeithney in the Banffshire lowlands and in Botriphnie in the hill country of the same county.[2] Kirkmichael, although in the highlands of Banffshire, had no great quantity of good peat and the mosses were in any case at considerable distances from the main area of settlement; Rathven, though on the coast, seemed to have few anxieties over fuel – no doubt from access to imported coal as much as from the availability of local mosses.[3] As we have seen, Edinkillie not only supplied itself with peat but gave much work and income to its parishioners in selling cartloads of the fuel at the market in the town of Forres; similarly, Rothiemay supplied Huntly, and Dallas provided peats twice a week to both Elgin and Forres.[4] Deskford reported that it had such large peat mosses that many poor were attracted to settle there – becoming such a drain on the resource that the heritors had then to restrict lime-burning in order to preserve stocks.[5] The parishes of Birnie and Ardclach as well as Dallas in upland Moray and Nairnshire all took part in a widespread traffic in peat.[6] One thing is plain: the opportunity to cast and sell peats, or to work at limestone quarries and at limekilns fired by peat, allowed cottagers, labourers and the poorer tenants an additional and welcome means of paying their rents.

1. Drainy, 482; Duffus, 496; Dyke and Moy, 562; Fordice, 161; Mortlach, 332; Nairn, 751 – 752; Cabrach, 113 – 114.
2. Urquhart, 698; Speymouth, 677; Alves, 457 – 458; Rafford, 630 – 631; Gamrie, 191; Forglen, 181; Inverkeithny, 244 – 245; Botriphnie, 108.
3. Kirkmichael, 285n; Rathven, 310.
4. Rothiemay, 397 – 398; Dallas, 473 – 474.
5. Deskford, 136.
6. Birnie, 467; Ardclach, 713.

Introduction

Returns from working the land were by no means always sufficient to meet these rentals – rentals which had doubled on average in the last 20 or 30 years of the 18th century. In Dallas, the minister reported, the crops which had been grown since 1778 had not been sufficient to maintain both the inhabitants of the parish and their cattle – it was the sale of fuel and of plaids worked by the wives which provided the money required to pay the landlords.[1] The returns from the spinning of wool or yarn, from the wages earned in summer labour on farms in the south of Scotland, even from the trunks and boughs of ancient fir trees dug up from local mosses and sold as especially valuable fuel or as 'lights', all helped to pay the rent:[2] it was frequent indeed to find in the accounts some evidence of smaller tenants and cottagers being unable to meet their financial responsibilities directly from farm produce – the industry of their wives and daughters at home, or of their sons and daughters away from home, was often crucial. But many parishes did provide grain surpluses, hay crops for sale, turnips and potatoes which were taken to market as were black cattle and/or sheep, and did have wool or flax and butter and cheese for sale, all producing that vital balance in the local economy which would meet the landlords' demands. In fact, however, there were relatively few parishes in our area in which money rents alone were demanded; usually rent was asked for at two terms, money at Martinmas and produce (victual) at Candlemas; quite often it was asked for in victual alone, wheat or barley or oatmeal. These rental structures had an important effect on the state of agriculture in the localities and also on the state of the parishioners. Poorer tenants could be obliged to sell their corn, under value, to obtain money for the November payment of rent.

In the parish of Fordyce in Banffshire, tenants along the coast paid large victual rents and, in order to maximise the returns from planting grain, preserved and extended their arable land and had therefore to find grazing lands in the upper part of the parish for their cattle in summer. When there

---

1. Dallas, 472
2. Kirkmichael, 290; in one parish (Fordice, 153) a species of 'white moss' was found to be useful to the poor as a means of lighting.

was a partial conversion of victual rent into money and when sown grasses were able to be introduced in the coastal area, it was possible to change this practice – and move towards a more improved agriculture.[1] Nairn rents had 'of old' been paid in victual, but by the 1790s had mostly been converted into money; in Gamrie and in Rothiemay, the Earl of Fife had also ended victual rents; in Alves where the inhabitants had 'till lately' paid most of their rents in wheat, money-rents had been largely substituted; in Dyke small proportions of rent formerly paid in victual were demanded in money and 'at different times augmented'.[2] If landlords took their rents only in victual or substantially in victual, then the returns they obtained could fluctuate considerably as grain prices fluctuated from year to year; if they took their rents only in money, they saved themselves from the chore of storing and selling grain or meal but could lose out in respect of long-term leases as inflation reduced rent-values. Therefore, the temptation was to retain a mixed victual – money rent or to convert to money rents and at intervals increase them (adding to these immediate returns by opening up tenancies to the highest bidders when leases fell in, and not attempting to be 'tender' to the existing tenants or their families).

In Botriphnie and Keith in Banffshire, and in St. Andrews Lhanbryde in Moray, part-victual part-money rents were being taken; and in Rathven a similar structure of rent was probably employed.[3] In Spynie where the Earl of Fife was apparently offering a conversion to money rents, at 12s. or 12s. 6d. per boll, the minister nonetheless commented that 'generally in the whole parishes of the country, the landlords drew a victual rent', and that in his own parish 'grain, including pease and beans, is the article on which the tenants chiefly depend for the payment of their rents' – but this may mean that they actually paid in money which was gained from their own marketing of their produce.[4] In Duffus, however, it is clear that rents were still chiefly taken in grain, so that

1. Fordice, 151, 160.
2. Nairn, 744; Gamrie, 190; Rothiemay, 400; Alves, 455, 457; Dyke and Moy, 544.
3. Botriphnie, 101; Keith, 255; St. Andrew's Lhanbryd, 641.
4. Spynie, 691n.

'great quantities...are raised and exported, and the rearing of black cattle is neglected'. But the same writer, as we have seen, also noted 'the low state' of farming in Duffus and the lack of enclosures there, and in Spynie only the gentlemen's lands had been much improved.[1] Since Gamrie, Rothiemay and Dyke – all with money rents – were reported to be 'advancing' in agriculture, did conversion to money rentals tend to prompt improvements while an insistence on victual rents, in part or more particularly in whole, tend to suppress or frustrate agrarian reform?

In rural parishes, while tenants and farmservants and the male day-labourers were all heavily engaged in agricultural work or in such related activities as winning and leading peats, women in the households spent much time in spinning wool and/or flax (home-grown or imported), in knitting stockings, and in weaving coarse cloths for domestic use or rather better-quality plaids for sale. These activities all brought in money which helped to pay the rent: without the returns from the industry of the wives many smaller tenants, cottagers and day-labourers with families could not have made ends meet. The menfolk could take part in work at the loom in winter-time; cottagers, often not able to find employment in farm labour for the whole year, helped to support themselves by working as part-time tradesmen. Ministers of rural parishes, describing the occupations of their parishioners, sometimes clearly make the distinction between full-time craftsmen, e.g. masons, who in the course of the year often travelled widely to offer their expertise in neighbouring parishes or in the south of Scotland, and the part-timers who picked up locally what they could in the off-season from husbandry.

In such rural parishes and in those which contained burghs, alike, the spinning of wool and more especially the spinning of linen yarn was universal throughout the three counties – from Abernethy and Kirkmichael in the highlands to Fordyce or Bellie on the coast: it was particularly mentioned in the reports from Birnie and Botriphnie, Drainie and Edinkillie,

---

1. Duffus, 509; Spynie, 691 – 692

Glass and Grange, Forglen and Forres (although here it was judged to have been in decline since 1784), Keith and Rathven, St. Andrews Lhanbryde and St. Fergus.[1] Weaving was also very widespread – in some measure in the 'middle' district of Banffshire (linen at Botriphnie and Grange, and at Keith but in decline with the introduction of cotton) and more extensively in the lowland plain: Ardclach and Dyke produced plaidings and Bellie stockings in Nairnshire and Moray, and in Banffshire there was production of silk, cotton and worsted stockings and also linen cloth in Banff, of hemp cloth (including nets and sailcloth) at Buckie in Rathven, linen in Fordyce and St. Fergus, and there were (as we saw earlier) as many as 65 looms working linen and damask and 7 more for stockings in Cullen.[2]

Bleachfields – to bleach linen yarn and cloth – were also established at Banff, at Deskford where business was reducing as the yarn trade gave way to cotton, at Keith and St. Fergus.[3] The entire textile enterprise at Banff was quite substantial: a considerable thread and linen manufacture, which had previously employed 60 hecklers, 400 spinners, 200 twisters and 40 bleachers, had been largely supplanted by stocking manufacturing – employing 560 people working 150 'improved' frames – with only 20 weavers left in a much contracted linen trade.[4] Bellie had 'an eminent weaver- businessman' who made cotton and worsted stockings, waistcoats and breeches.[5] Connections within the textile business were countrywide: the merchants who bought the spun thread or cloth might be local, from Banff or Huntly or Keith or Fraserburgh or Aberdeen, but they could just as well be from Edinburgh or Glasgow or Paisley or be based in the north of England – the goods mainly carried in sloops which worked from coastal stations in the parishes of Banff, Drainie, Duffus, Gamrie, Rathven and Nairn.

1. Birnie, 464; Botriphnie, 106 – 107; Drainy, 477; Edenkeillie, 583; Glass, 109; Grange, 219 – 220; Forglen, 173; Forres, 617 – 618; Keith, 252 – 253; Rathven, 368 – 369; St. Andrew's Lhanbryd, 640; St. Fergus, 414 – 415.
2. Botriphnie, 102; Grange, 219 – 220; Keith, 252 – 253; Ardclach, 713; Dyke and Moy, 546; Bellie, 83; Banff, 52 – 53; Rathven, 368; Fordice, 159; St. Fergus, 415; Cullen, 124.
3. Banff, 52; Deskford, 141; Keith, 253; St. Fergus, 414
4. Banff, 52.
5. Bellie, 83.

Trading was an important element in the activities of these harbours or inlets; but fishing was on the whole more significant. Bellie and Speymouth, at the outflow of one of the finest salmon rivers, were very active in salmon fishing and export: over 130 were employed by the English company to which the Duke of Gordon had contracted his Spey fishings (at £1500 per year) in Bellie; from there and from Banff and Speymouth much salmon was sent south to London, in ice or boiled or salted.[1] The fishertowns in Rathven – East and West Buckie, Portessie, Findochtie, Portknockie – all took part in salmon fishing at some part of the year, as did fishermen at Dyke and Nairn. The minister at Gamrie records that salmon was cured in Macduff, being pickled there and sent to London, to France and to Spain.[2] Lobsters and crabs were also fished for the lucrative London market – Cullen and Fordyce (which adds limpets and periwinkles) were particularly active here.[3] White fish of great variety were sold in the hinterland parishes in our three counties from the string of fishertowns along the Moray Firth – but the main traffic seems to have been with Leith and the Firth of Forth ports, and with other east-coast Scottish ports: much of this fish, no doubt, was cured by salting or was dried.[4] The Dyke account mentions seal-fishing.[5] The minister at Nairn, where the number of boats had fallen because 'greater encouragement has removed several to other parts of the kingdom' claimed that fish had become very much scarcer locally after 1782 and that it became necessary sometimes to go to the coasts of Sutherland and Caithness; we are told that '7 large boats' from Burghead in the parish of Duffus 'are hired to the fishing on the west coast'.[6] The four fishing stations in Rathven sent boats to the Caithness fishery in August and September of each year, fished for cod between October and February and also took part in lobster-catching

---

1.   Bellie, 83 – 84; Speymouth, 667 – 668; Banff, 49.
2.   Rathven, 373, 375; Dyke and Moy, 547 – 548; Nairn, 748 – 750; Gamrie, 185 – 186.
3.   Cullen, 123; Fordice, 146; see also Drainy, 478, and Duffus, 494.
4.   The minister of Rathven (373) notes exports of dried fish as far afield as to Jamaica.
5.   Dyke and Moy, 548.
6.   Nairn, 748; Duffus, 493.

in Caithness and other fishings nearer home.[1] White fish were also the quarry of fishermen based in Cullen (where cured cod, ling, etc. were sold in the south in exchange for hemp, wool and salt); in Fordyce at Portsoy and Sandend (where, as in Banff, boatbuilding was carried on); in Gamrie at Macduff, Crovie and Gardenstown; in St. Fergus; in Boyndie at the village of Whitehills; in Drainie at Lossiemouth and Stotfield; and in Kinloss.[2] The Duffus account noted that there was no good, safe harbour from Buchan Ness to Inverness, a concern echoed in the reports from Rathven and Nairn: but we find that a new harbour was being built at Macduff and the erection of piers was mooted for Burghead (in Duffus itself) and for Buckie, Findochtie and Nairn.[3]

Textiles and fishing apart, there was great variety in industries and manufactures in the three counties. Sawmilling was to be found in Abernethy, Boharm and Speymouth and 'dealing in timber' at Dyke.[4] Freestone quarrying was emphasised as an important occupation in Alves, Drainie, at Burghead, and in Spynie.[5] There were tobacco manufacturies in Bellie and Spynie; the town of Banff contained a brickworks, a tileworks, a candle and soap works (there was a soapery in Elgin too), a rope and sail factory.[6] Distilleries were widespread, particularly in the 'middle' parishes; breweries were noticed in Banff and St. Fergus among others.[7] Tanneries were working in Keith and Elgin – in Elgin the making of high-quality leather gloves was said to be in decline but there were no fewer than 55 shoemakers in the town.[8] The commerce of Elgin was worrying to its minister – forty or fifty years before, trade had been mostly with Holland 'but now the trade is chiefly with London, Leeds, Manchester, Birmingham, Newcastle, Carron etc. etc. for the import-

1. Rathven, 369 – 376.
2. Cullen, 123; Fordice, 146 – 147; Banff, 48; Gamrie, 185, 188 – 189; St. Fergus, 409 – 410; Boyndie, 112; Drainy, 478 – 479; Kinloss, 619.
3. Duffus, 494 – 495; Rathven, 376 – 379; Nairn, 752 – 753.
4. Abernethy and Kinchardine, 431; Boharm, 90 (referring to Boat of Brigg); Dyke and Moy, 536 – 537.
5. Alves, 457; Drainy, 484; Duffus, 488; Spynie, 688.
6. Bellie, 83; Spynie, 694; Banff, 53 – 54; Elgyn, 599.
7. See index to text.
8. Keith, 253; Elgyn, 599 – Forres, 612, reports 56 shoemakers in that parish.

ation of manufactured articles, rather more than the country can well afford... There are now 44 shops opened in this town, principally for the sale of imported goods'.[1] In this respect Elgin seems to have been little different from the only other major town nearby, Forres. It had no marked manufacturing base – nothing to speak of, in comparison with Banff, for example – but contained '60 merchants and shopkeepers'; still offering market facilities for a considerable area between Inverness and Elgin (Nairn had a mere 16 merchant shops, 'only 6 or 8 anything considerable'), its trading area had actually been contracting. The Forres shops 'were formerly principally supported by travelling and vending their goods in all the villages and market towns to the west and north, particularly Sutherland, Caithness and Ross, and as far as Orkney. But this intercourse is in a great measure now rendered unnecessary, as in all those countries they have got stationary shopkeepers who can retail their goods nearly upon as low terms as the merchants of Forres.'[2] It is small wonder that, recognising the market potential in our three counties and those to the north, and wishing to expand the local economy and retain population, a good many of the writers of our accounts plead for energetic introduction of manufactures. Apart from harbour-villages and fishing stations on the coast, there were very few other village-settlements which were likely to provide an expanding industrial and commercial base without a considerable drive being applied. Villages were not judged useful only as places in which there could be full-time employment for displaced cottagers. The need for farm labour at busy times of the year, and the desire to avoid employing expensive farm servants on annual or half-year contracts, could both be met from a pool of villager-craftsmen: thus the minister of Fordyce hoped to see 'villages scattered up and down the country where day-labourers could be hired'.[3]

In 1782 there was widespread failure of the grain harvest in Scotland. In the north-east there was not only severe rain in

1. Elgyn, 598.
2. Forres, 612; Nairn, 748.
3. Fordice, 165.

the late summer, which ruined the oats crop, but also very early frosts and snowstorms which devastated the wheat and barley. Frost and snow also seriously affected the potato crop on which so many would have depended otherwise: in Banff much fever was caused, it was said, by the immoderate use of bad potatoes.[1] The dearth was particularly severe in the mountainous parishes: grain and meal had to be sent in, by the landowners and by government, in 1782 and 1783 and seems to have warded off any deaths directly attributable to starvation. The wretchedness of the times caused emigrations, temporary as well as permanent, to North America and to towns and villages in Scotland where manufactures were carried on, work was available and food could be got. The minister of Birnie, indeed, in a general comment on the famine wrote that if the war with the American colonists had not ended then 'thousands would have perished for want of bread': the end of hostilities released supplies of meal which would have gone to the army and also made it easier for the distressed to cross the Atlantic.[2]

In the upland parishes of the three counties the impact of the bad weather was more variable. While Ardclach in Nairnshire suffered badly from scarcity, next-door Cawdor – usually able to export grain — found its situation 'not so ill as in many places'.[3] Elsewhere Dallas, Botriphnie, Glass and Mortlach were all badly hit, so badly in Mortlach that its inhabitants were still suffering in 1788 — the year in which emigration from the parish reached its height.[4] In the lowland parishes this variability was even more marked. St. Fergus, Speymouth, Drainie, Rathven and St. Andrews Lhanbryde all got in their crops without much damage to them and had grain to spare for their upland neighbours, and the parishioners of Rathven 'bettered their circumstances' from the very high prices which their exports were able to command.[5] Only one coastal parish, Nairn – perhaps be-

---

1. Banff, 43.
2. Birnie, 466 – 467.
3. Ardclach, 712; Calder, 735.
4. Dallas, 472; Botriphnie, 102, 108; Glass, 198; Mortlach, 340.
5. St. Fergus, 413; Speymouth, 651 – 652; Drainy, 482; Rathven, 366n; St. Andrew's Lhanbryd, 640.

cause of that great influx of poor into the town which we have already noted — needed supplies of meal from the government.[1] The other lowland parishes which required assistance included Alvah, Forglen and Rothiemay; also Grange where the Earl of Fife provided 'excellent grain' but only for ready money, so that 'not many' were able to take up the offer; and Keith where those who occupied new farms would only have been able to subsist for six weeks or three months at most without aid and where hundreds in the parish were on short allowance for some time after 1782.[2] This famine was not the last to hit the area: Forglen's harvest in 1793 'was as bad as any', a judgment said to be 'true of parishes over three-quarters of the country'; for the minister of Banff, writing his account rather later than most, it was the year 1795 which produced an 'alarming deficiency of crop'.[3] Dearth in the later 18th century demonstrated time and again local dependence on local crops; it also showed that, with government coming to the aid of churches and heritors in the 1780s and afterwards, widespread famine did not necessarily lead directly to deaths from privation. But one immediate and direct impact of the famine years of 1782 – 83 was clear in many parishes, on the funds available to support the poor — for their numbers often rose alarmingly. Sometimes the capital as well as the interest of invested monies had to be disbursed in order to save needy parishioners and others from starvation — not so much in individual payments perhaps as in buying imported meal at severely inflated prices for distribution.[4]

Support of the pomple — but contained '6h Sir John Sinclair had particularly drawn the attention of his contributors. And in the long aftermath of the famine of 1782 – 83, with intermittent bad years in the decade that followed, poor relief was a topic given much attention and space by our writers. A parish was enabled by parliament, if it wished, to adopt a scheme of legal assessment, a compulsory local taxation based

1. Nairn, 745.
2. Alvah, 11; Forglen, 175; Rothiemay, 404; Grange, 214 – 215; Keith, 260 – 261.
3. Forglen, 169; Banff, 25 – 26.
4. See, for example, Aberlour, 6.

on valuation of property. No parish in our three counties did so, even temporarily, according to the reports; instead, they retained the system of depending on voluntary givings at the church door, supplemented by the proceeds of disciplinary fines, fees for use of the mortcloth, etc., with further supplementation from the charity of individuals. The minister of Speymouth made this comment:[1] 'Poor's rates are not known in this part of the country, and perhaps the poor are on a proper footing. The supplies granted from the session funds and by the private charity of the people at large are sufficient to preserve the poor from want; and there is less danger of abuse and of encouraging idleness. In populous cities where the conditions of the poor cannot generally be so well known, and in countries in a different situation, poor's rates are no doubt very proper and even necessary.'

In our parishes it seems to have been anticipated that, in the first instance, the local poor would be the responsibility of their families, the kin-group, and then of their friends and neighbours; only when these sources of support failed, as in times of severe distress, or in cases where there was no kin and the poor man or woman was 'friendless', would he or she be accepted as a public responsibility and be enrolled on the poor's list.[2] In fact, the roll was often extended beyond these groups, and it was customary in many parishes for occasional and non-enrolled poor to be relieved from the church funds.[3] At Keith the listed poor were restricted to those unable to leave their beds and their houses to beg support from the parishioners. In Birnie the aged and infirm, not the housebound, were expected to travel – beyond the parish – to entreat support from the charitable (while those who could not go so far from home were to be given meal and fuel by their fellow-parishioners).[4] In the mountainous areas of Abernethy and Kirkmichael, complaints were levelled against the government tax on leather since it put the making or purchase of a decent pair of shoes beyond the reach of the poor

1. Speymouth, 633n.
2. 'When old, if their children be not both dutiful and successful, (the inhabitants) need help from the poor's funds' (Fordice, 155).
3. Dyke and Moy, 553.
4. Keith, 257; Birnie, 466.

highlander; the minister of Kirkmichael commented that his parishioners 'will derive one advantage' from the tax, for 'it will eliminate the number of beggars by confining them in winter in their booths to die at leisure, without the trouble of exposing them, as the Scythian Alani did their infirm, to the frozen blasts of their bleak mountains'.[1] That that particular group of poor would, and indeed should, wander for their support was a commonplace expectation, but they were not always welcome.

Some parishes seem to have attracted especially large numbers of travelling beggars (or beggars who attempted to remain 'stationary' in order to obtain settlement rights there). An abundance of easily-obtained peat could bring them in, as at Deskford; Nairn seems to have been inundated by stranger poor seeking employment. Parishes such as Banff with a reputation for open-heartedness and with substantial sums in mortified funds (with interest to be distributed to the poor) tempted the wanderer. At Keith there was a 'great influx of highlanders', probably settled on heathland being gradually taken into cultivation or attracted by the possibilities of employment in the manufactures of New Keith and Newmill, which ranged throughout it and the neighbouring parishes 'and are a great encroachment on what is truly the property of the native poor'.[2]

The Mortlach minister was keen to emphasise that disbursements from the parish's poor funds, for the enrolled or for the temporary poor, were intended 'for assistance and not support'.[3] Often the sums given out in official relief by the church were mere pittances, but we should remember that they were not usually, and were not normally meant to be, the sole support of the pauper; these sums were to be 'topped up' from the kindly and charitable attentions of fellow-countrymen. And where there was a 'better sort of people' who had the wherewithal to be ready with their charity,

1. Abernethy and Kinchardine, 443; Kirkmichael, 277 – 278.
2. Deskford, 139; Nairn, 751 – 752; Banff, 32 – 34 (where it is noted that to 'do good' to the poor, however undeserving they may seem to be, is a prime Christian responsibility); Keith, 257.
3. Mortlach, 340.

where there was profit to be made on surplus produce and there was something (however little) to spare on Christian relief, where there was stability in the local economy and where non-resident local landowners did not leave poor relief only to the tenants (as happened at Abernethy),[1] then the traditional, voluntary system seemed to work reasonably well. The major threats to its success came from sudden and severe economic upset (poor harvest, decline in trade) and from the depredations of the 'professional' vagabonds – 'vagrants, thieves, pickpockets going about under the pretence of begging'. The enforcement of the law against these sorners hardly took place – and they not only survived but seem to have been allowed, even grudgingly, charitable support.[2] Indeed, what is remarkable in the accounts as they deal with questions of poor relief is the all but constant reference to the open-handedness of the parishioners: 'the people are, all over this county, disposed to every kind of humane and generous action' (St. Andrews Lhanbryde); the people are 'remarkable' for their charity (Cullen); 'very charitable to the poor and, in cases of distress, very much disposed to acts of humanity' (Speymouth); even highland parishes, with evidence of widespread poverty, report instances of generosity by the poor to the poorer.[3] Poverty was everywhere to be seen and, traditionally, it was everywhere to be relieved: the strolling vagabond apart, the beggar was recognised as someone that the community should care for, little as that care might amount to. Bad times could hit hard and they could hit nearly everyone; one helped when one could and received when one had to. The relief of poverty, just like the relief of ignorance through parochial schooling, was undoubtedly a community responsibility: something which was accepted as an obligation on all, of whatever religious persuasion. The fact that the Established Church had a leading part to play in the organisation of schooling and poor relief caused little disturbance among dissenting groups.[4]

1. Abernethy and Kincardine, 440
2. Forglen, 174 – 175; see also Kirkmichael, 285
3. St. Andrew's Lhanbryd, 642; Cullen, 130; Speymouth, 675
4. It is interesting that in the predominantly Catholic district of Glenlivet the priest organised a separate relief system from the collections taken at the chapel for his own congregation, but Protestants and Catholics alike shared the funds for the poor which came from the interest on mortified money (Inveraven, 238).

Some ministers in the remoter highland districts had considerable numbers of Roman Catholics in their parishes (e.g. 384 out of a population of 1276 in Kirkmichael), but reported no antagonisms arising from this fact; in Cabrach, indeed, relationships between the various religionists were good and brought frequent intermarriages which led, apparently, to the halving of the numbers of Catholics there – and convinced the minister heartily to support a gentle and accommodating attitude to the sectaries in the parish.[1] There was much Roman Catholicism too in northern Banffshire: in Cullen, in Banff itself where there was an RC chapel, in Bellie where 'very considerable numbers' of Catholics (and a good many in Speymouth) lived cordially with Established and seceder Presbyterians and some Episcopalians, in Fordyce which noted that it had a resident Catholic priest, in Keith where we know that Methodism had also taken root, in Marnoch and Mortlach, in Rathven where there was an RC chapel for the long-standing Catholic community in the Enzie, and in Inveraven which included in its bounds the traditionally Catholic district of Glenlivet containing a 'mass house' and priest and at Scalan the seminary for training Scottish priests.[2] There was a fair scattering of Episcopalians and Episcopal chapels in Banffshire elsewhere than in Bellie and Speymouth: in Banff, Fordyce (with 'a considerable number' and a non-juring clergyman), Keith, Marnoch, Rathven (with a clergyman serving two chapels) and St. Fergus. But there were comparatively few Episcopalians in Moray or Nairnshire, apart from those who supported two chapels in Elgin.[3] Only Mortlach of the parishes in the 'middle' upland district and the highland area reported Protestant sectaries other than Episcopalians, but things were very different in the lowlands.[4]

1. Kirkmichael, 272, 279; Cabrach, 117
2. Cullen, 125; Banff, 31; Bellie, 85; Speymouth, 653; Fordice, 151; Keith, 251–252; Marnoch, 318; Mortlach, 334; Rathven, 383n; Inveraven, 234–236
3. Banff, 31; Fordice, 151; Keith, 251; Marnoch, 318; Rathven, 383n; St. Fergus, 414
4. Mortlach. 334.

Introduction

In the Moray and Nairn plain, there was a seceder meeting house in Elgin and a largish group of seceders in St. Andrews Lhanbryde (as well as a chapel for an independent preacher, curiously enough supported by the town council and session of Elgin, for some 30 people who remained in the Established Church but had withdrawn from attendance at the parish kirk); there were almost 100 Antiburghers in Auldearn and several families of them in Nairn and in Urquhart; the Duffus minister, in reporting a few Antiburghers and also a small non-juring Episcopalian congregation in that parish, argued that 'till commerce and manufactures arrive, to put money in the purses of the lower ranks, we cannot expect that multiplicity of religious opinions, and diversity of worship, which mercantile wealth in a special manner produces'.[1] Does the incidence of secession in Banffshire, much more varied in its religious affiliations, bear out this assertion?

The fact that there was a group of seceders in Rothiemay, with its few weavers and wrights and millers, would not in itself do so — but there were also large and active seceder congregations in the more significantly commercial and manufacturing parishes of Keith, Fordyce and Banff: a total of 133 dissenters in Keith, a minister of the Relief Church serving at Portsoy in Fordyce, and as many as 400 in the Relief congregation in Banff.[2] The appearance of dissent was certainly of concern to some of the parish ministers; but in the 1790s it was the association of dissent with radicalism which was really worrying — there was much doubting the loyalty and attachment to government of those who, not being of the Establishment, were judged to be anti-Establishment, pro-French, would-be revolutionaries. Thus the Abernethy minister is thankful that his parishioners were free from contact with the 'itinerant fanatics' that infected the coastal lands and with the 'political pamphlet writers'. The Duffus minister is at pains to note that his seceder and non-juring

---

1. St. Andrew's Lhanbryd, 640; Auldearn, 719; Nairn, 746; Urquhart, 705; Duffus, 495.
2. Rothiemay, 402; Keith, 252; Fordice, 151; Banff, 31.

parishioners were nonetheless 'well affected to government' and showed this by attending the parish church when they had no services of their own to attend. In Forglen there were 'no evil men seeking only rebellion' and the 'absurd system of France is universally detested'. In Banff, for all that it was such a centre of dissent, a few copies of Tom Paine's *Age of Reason* had been in circulation, yet had done 'little harm' in disturbing religious affiliations or in extending the influence of 'the sophistry of sceptical writers'.[1] Three accounts – those for Boharm, Rathven and Forglen – go out of their way to applaud the policies of Henry Dundas at Westminster, in improving the conditions of living in Scotland by removing the taxes on coal and salt, for example, or by 'increasing the independence of the judges...on whom the administration of justice among the poor so much depends'.[2]

Schooling was widely available throughout the three counties, although not always of the quality which the writers of the accounts wished it to be. Considering the reports on all parishes, we have no information at all about schools in ten instances – Aberlour in the highland area; Knockando and Rothes in the uplands; Kinloss, Spynie, Alvah, Boharm, Boyndie, Gamrie and Inverkeithney in the coastal plain. Fortunately, William Barclay's *The Schools and Schoolmasters of Banffshire* (Banff, 1925), in which the author draws mostly on church records, allows us to fill in some of these gaps. Thus we know that Aberlour had a parochial school with £20 of stipend and about 30 scholars in winter; that Boharm school had only a 'wretched' salary which, no doubt, accounted for the fact that it had no fewer than four schoolmasters from 1786 to 1794; and that Inverkeithney's master in 1786 – 1815 was a Peter Morrison who was followed in that post by his son, the two eventually completing a total of 70 years' service to the parish.[3] However, Barclay has nothing direct to say about Alvah, Boyndie or Gamrie in the 1790s: Boyndie had a parochial school in 1801 with 40 pupils and teaching the

---

1. Abernethy and Kinchardine, 444; Duffus, 508; Forglen, 181 – 182; Banff, 74.
2. Boharm, 98; Rathven, 389; Forglen, 181.
3. Barclay, *op. cit.,* 151.

'usual branches'; all we know about Gamrie is that there was a school in Macduff 'for some time after 1768'.[1] There is no information from other sources about the two Moray parishes, Kinloss and Spynie; yet it would be strange indeed if, when other smaller, remoter, poorer and less populous parishes had schools, that these two (and Alvah, Boyndie and Gamrie) were without masters. Hence, 44 out of the 49 parishes were certainly provided with a modicum of schooling and it seems likely that the remaining five had the usual legal provision too.

But the maintenance of one parochial or burgh school was not the limit of what was supplied in the education of many parishes. The Society in Scotland for Propagating Christian Knowledge (SSPCK) was active in the area. Abernethy, Duthil (two), and Kirkmichael had Society schools while Cabrach had had its one removed in 1779; in our 'middle' district there were SSPCK schools in Inveraven, Dallas, Mortlach ('taken away lately'), Edinkillie and Ardclach (and a female spinning school under SSPCK auspices there besides); in the lowlands there were Society schools in Bellie, Speymouth, Fordyce, Marnoch, Rathven (two there, one in Buckie and the other in the Enzie) and recently one in Grange ('now withdrawn').[2]

Nor were these public parochial and SSPCK schools always the only extent of what was provided. In the Cabrach, deprived of its Society school in Doveranside, 'to remedy this in some degree (the people there) hire a countryman to teach their children to read and write in winter, the only time they can dispense with them from herding their cattle'.[3] But it is in the account for Dyke and Moy that we can, perhaps, gain the best view of what a reasonably-sized and reasonably-populous parish, with a well-scattered population (there were only three very small villages in the parish), could secure in

1. *Ibid.,* 124, 278.
2. Abernethy and Kinchardine, 440; Duthil and Rothiemurchas, 514, 522; Kirkmichael, 274 – 275; Cabrach, 117; Dallas, 474 – 475; Mortlach, 353; Edenkeillie, 585; Ardclach, 715; Bellie, 86; Speymouth, 662; Fordice, 161; Marnoch, 318; Rathven, 384 – 385; Grange, 223.
3. Cabrach, 117.

educational provision.[1] The contributor of that account
gives more detail, than do most of his colleagues in similar en-
tries, about the two public schools in the parish: there was a
parochial school whose master received a stipend from
heritors and tenants according to law, plus the interest on
1000 merks in a parochial fund and the income from his fees
– for teaching English, writing, arithmetic, Latin, mensuration and landsurveying, geometry, book-keeping – as well as
the small salary and fees for his work as session clerk; and
there was a 'woman school' whose mistress had the interest
from 2500 merks of invested money but who was not making
of the school the success it had once been – 'There was once
a great resort from Caithness, Sutherland, Ross etc. to this
boarding school, where young gentlewomen were taught
reading, knitting stockings, marking, plain and coloured
seams, and music by the mistress; and writing and arithmetic
by the parochial schoolmaster. Many daughters of men of property were educated here, without referring for accomplishments
anywhere else.' This comprises the information in the section
on schooling in the Dyke and Moy account, concentrating, as
do nearly all others, on the 'official' schools; but in the list
of occupations he includes in a commentary on population, the
author enters no fewer than nine 'private teachers' and one
private tutor. No doubt the private teachers taught ABC schools
on adventure in corners of the parish at some distance from
the parochial and female schools. How many of the other
parishes may have had a substantial provision of private schooling, to supplement what was offered in parochial and other
official schools, but their ministers limited discussion in their
reports only to those official and legal schools?

The parishes which contained burghs (Banff, Cullen, Elgin,
Forres, Nairn) all had well-established Latin grammar schools
under the management of their town councils, usually in close
association with the local kirk sessions.[2] How widely were
classics taught? Only two parishes in the upland district refer
specifically in the accounts to Latin being offered to their

1. Dyke and Moy, 553 – 554.
2. Banff, 57; Cullen, 126; Elgin, 601 – 602; Forres, 614 – 615; Nairn, 744 – 745.

pupils, Botriphnie and Cawdor, but it is very likely that Latin was also taught in Ardclach, Mortlach (which had four bursaries available to its pupils for their support at King's College in Old Aberdeen), Inveraven and Glass.[1] At least half of the parishes in the lowland district also certainly offered instruction in the classics, and there can be little doubt that most had (or aspired to obtain) Latin grammar masters for their schools.[2] Among the non-burghal parishes, in addition to Dyke and Moy, only Bellie, Speymouth and Fordyce appear to have taught any of the modern or commercial subjects – in all three cases here, the sole subject was book-keeping. Again it is to be suspected that such studies were available elsewhere but many of the contributors to the *Account* did not bother to go into detail about the curricula that were offered.[3] However, the writer of the Fordyce account describes how, in addition to the parochial school, the SSPCK school at Portsoy – also funded by the Countess Dowager of Findlater – had a master who was permitted to add about £7 per year to his salary 'by teaching those who are able to pay for reading, writing, arithmetic, book-keeping and navigation'; furthermore, there was another school at Portsoy for boys, with 20 – 30 pupils, and 'through the rest of the parish... four schools for girls where reading, sewing and knitting of stockings are taught'.[4] In Speymouth, as well as the parochial and SSPCK schools, two more schools were supported by the Duke of Gordon while 'two or three women' taught to read; and in St. Fergus 'some' private schools supplemented (or rather withdrew pupils from) the parochial school.[5]

The five burgh-parishes all attempted to deal, in their own ways, with the pressures of increasing population and also the demands for a wider curriculum than the 'standard' offering of English, arithmetic and Latin.[6] Cullen was the smallest of

1. Botriphnie, 109; Calder, 736; Ardclach, 715; Mortlach, 339 – 340; Inveraven, 237 – 238; Glass, 198.
2. 18 out of 32 at the very least: Alves, Bellie, Drainie, Dyke and Moy, Elgin, Forres, Rafford, Speymouth in Moray; Auldearn, Nairn in Nairnshire; Alvah, Banff, Cullen, Fordice, Keith, Marnoch, Rathven, St. Fergus in Banffshire.
3. Bellie, 86; Speymouth, 662; Fordice, 160.
4. Fordice, 160 – 161.
5. Speymouth, 662 – 663; St. Fergus, 418.
6. Cullen, 126; Nairn, 744 – 745; Banff, 57 – 59, and see Barclay, *op. cit.*, 61; Forres, 614 – 615; Elgyn, 602.

the five and found it could make do with its burgh grammar school, extending the subjects taught to include book-keeping, plus a girls' school with a salaried mistress who taught reading and sewing, and two other schools taught on adventure which gave instruction in reading and the principles of Christianity. Nairn, another quite compact parish, seems to have had only two public schools and no adventure schools at all: there was a school for girls with a salaried teacher and the grammar school, 'in a very flourishing condition for many years', where 'every branch of education which now makes such a noise in the academies, is taught... to perfection'. The Nairn grammar school, with its curriculum incorporating a range of modern subjects, was not used only by the local population: 'Gentlemen from all quarters of the country, and some from England, send their children to be educated here.' In Banff, unlike in Nairn, the town council and parishioners had in 1786 formally converted the existing public schools into an academy and had managed to attract to the rectorship of the new foundation the well-known Dr. George Chapman who had previously been at Dalkeith and then at Dumfries. A native of Alvah, Chapman had already moved north to open a very high-class academy in Inchdrewer Castle where he had among his pupils James, 4th Earl of Findlater, and his brother. Chapman remained at Banff from 1786 to 1792, before moving to Edinburgh to set up as a printer, long enough to settle the academic structure of the school – dividing it into three departments whose teaching the rector shared with four assistants: (i) a classical school, teaching Latin and Greek, geography and the principles of rhetoric, clearly intended for those who had it in mind to go on to university studies; (ii) a commercial school, with instruction in writing, arithmetic, book-keeping, mensuration, algebra, practical geometry and navigation; and (iii) a languages school, which included teaching in English, French, etc. In addition to the academy, Banff town council and session supported a charity school for poor children from the town and the country part of the parish; there were also two English schools taught on adventure and two boarding schools for 'young ladies', one set up by two English-women and the other taught in part by 'a qualified governess from Edinburgh'.

This provision of schools was well matched in Forres. There, at the burgh school, Latin, Greek, French 'and the various branches of mathematics' were taught 'with great success' – and boarding at the school could be had for £20 per year. There was also boarding for young ladies at a school which, unlike those at Banff, was supported by a salary from the town council: it offered needlework, music 'and other parts of female education'. In addition to these establishments, the council funded an English school, quite separate from the grammar school, and also gave donations to 'those who keep private schools, to encourage them'. With some pride, the minister of Forres judged that there was not 'a more eligible place for the education of youth anywhere'. The Elgin council and the Elgin parishioners had been much slower in moving to meet the new demands, and only in June 1791 had come up with a proposal to 'enlarge the plan of education', intending 'to add Greek, French, geography, book-keeping, land surveying and drawing' to the subjects already taught in the existing grammar school and music school. A subscription was organised for the founding of an academy, but this was not to open for another ten years.

'The price of education in this town, as in every other part of Scotland, is very low,' wrote the minister of Forres, and that is borne out by the level of fees demanded for the standard subjects, those necessary to able poor boys who wished to make their way to university (as they were reported to be doing from the parishes of Dyke and Moy, Nairn, Fordyce, Grange and Mortlach).[1] A master could certainly increase his income by teaching the 'modern' subjects for which much higher fees were permitted; otherwise, with inflation reducing fixed stipends – fixed as long ago as 1696 – his only hope was to persuade the heritors to increase that stipend, something which heritors and indeed parliament proved very reluctant to do. The writers of our accounts, therefore, frequently refer to the much too low incomes which could be obtained by parochial schoolteachers, and often notice the results – well qualified masters could not be attracted to take

1.   Forres, 615; Dyke and Moy, 558; Nairn, 745; Fordice, 150; Grange, 211; Mortlach, 339.

up vacant posts, Latin was becoming not so universally available as it once had been, and was also not so generally demanded by parents, there were too frequent changes of master in poorly-paid schools, and 'mere schoolboys' or 'bankrupt tenants, even less qualified,' were to be found teaching. Yet, in reviewing the whole range of schooling available in the three counties, it is still difficult not to be impressed by the sheer numbers of schools, and by the variety in curricula, that were to be found in all districts.

What else of interest and importance do these accounts tell us or let us glimpse from a distance of two hundred years? In an age of fundamentally unscientific medicine, matters of health produced many curious reactions. Superstition abounded, not least in respect of illness or the warding off of illness: it was particularly rife in Kirkmichael, for instance.[1] The use of mineral or chalybeate springs for all manner of ailments was common, and becoming more prevalent: the parishes of Ordiquhill, Banff, Gamrie, Dallas, Keith and Mortlach (both claiming an equivalence with the much-used waters at Peterhead), St. Andrews Lhanbryde and Kirkmichael (where the spring was held to be superior to the Pananich Wells on Deeside) all announced their having 'medicinal wells'; at the Well of Boyndie in Banff, indeed, it was reported that the serious-minded sick would take as much as three gallons of the water in one day![2] The minister of Banff blamed the admission of potatoes into the diet for the considerable increase in stomach troubles: to Dallas and to Cabrach there was much resort in summer by those 'tender people' who wished to try goats' milk as an aid to stomach ailments.[3] Apart from these troubles and smallpox, which could still be fatal but was much lessened in its impact on the population by the greater 'reconciliation' to inoculation (as in Banff, Cullen, Forglen, Mortlach, and a hope that the inhabitants would soon lose their prejudice against it in Ardclach and Abernethy), the most common forms of illness were certainly rheumatism and

1. Kirkmichael, 299 et seq.
2. Ordiquhill, 356; Banff, 45 – 46; Gamrie, 186; Dallas, 473; Keith, 249 – 250; Mortlach, 323; St. Andrew's Lhanbryd, 638; Kirkmichael, 270.
3. Banff, 43; Dallas, 473; Calder, 734.

pulmonary troubles of one kind or another — undoubtedly caused or made worse by the coldness and dampness of the houses in which so many parishioners lived.[1] Physicians or surgeons were seldom called to sick people and were not widely available anyway – 'no doctor has found it worthwhile to settle in this parish', remarks the Rathven account.[2] Greater cleanliness is noted here and there (e.g. Cullen) as a factor in improving health – perhaps bringing about the reduction in incidence of the 'itch' (in Duffus) but leaving us unsure why 'the progress of scrofula' in Elgin should have been so 'alarming'.[3]

The Kirkmichael minister tells us that doctors were seldom called to that parish because the inhabitants could not afford to pay fees to both doctors *and* lawyers, and expands greatly on the topic of the litigious character of his parishioners. Curiously enough, other accounts which comment on this matter welcome a change in the other direction – there was 'hardly a law suit' in Cullen and only a few in Cabrach, and the minister of Mortlach was glad that, with a sheriff-substitute no longer sitting in Keith, his people had lost their old readiness to take counsel's opinion for every little slight they suffered.[4] Several ministers remark on the reduction in public drunkenness – Ardclach, Banff, Keith ('taverns are now nearly deserted') and Fordyce (where the writer still felt obliged now and again, however, to go out after dinner to break up 'drinking companies'); more frequent still, however, were comments about the increase in dram-drinking, instead of beer-drinking, and its danger for health and morals[5] – just as there were similar doubts voiced at the great increase in tea drinking in the area.[6] Other signs of expanding 'civilisation' are widely mentioned – the use of carts

1. Banff, 44; Cullen, 122; Forglen, 177; Mortlach, 353; Ardclach, 714; Abernethy and Kinchardine, 430.
2. Rathven, 363.
3. Cullen, 122; Duffus, 490 — but in the additional account for this parish (505), the minister ranks scrofula as 'the only notable local disease' with its cause either the usual diet of fish and pease-meal or its inheritance from Oliver Cromwell's soldiers in the previous century; Elgyn, 604; see also Keith, 253.
4. Kirkmichael, 286; Cullen, 130; Cabrach, 118; Mortlach, 345.
5. Ardclach, 713; Banff, 74; Keith, 261; Fordice, 164; Bellie, 86; Mortlach, 344; Duthil and Rothiemurchas, 520.
6. Mortlach, 344; Kirkmichael, 308.

instead of creels, postchaises instead of horses; the great changes in dress that had taken place since mid-century – imported hats instead of bonnets, fine cloths for suits and gowns instead of homemade stuffs, etc.; the coming to an end of the worst of the old lowland vs. highland prejudices; the large numbers of watches and clocks which were to be found; the phasing out of public penance for moral and other misdemeanours at the stool of repentance in the church; the generally visible but only gradual improvement in housing – still very poor and mean in some parishes, however, if in others 'neat' stone-walled and slate-roofed accommodation was being built.

Among all the complaints, all but universal indeed, against the very swift rise in the cost of living in the later 18th century, there were also indications that for people in some parishes that increase had been matched at least by improved incomes from agriculture or manufactures. In Boharm, the inhabitants enjoyed the 'necessaries and many of the comforts of life'; in Rathven, they were 'well clothed, well fed, decently lodged... and have a reasonable share of the comforts and conveniences'. In Birnie the people were 'cheerful, though poor', in Aberlour and Cawdor they seemed 'satisfied with their condition'.[1] One major complaint, which drew no placatory comments at all from any of our writers, was related, however, to the cost of living – or at least to one particularly upsetting factor in its rise: we find a concerted attack in all areas on the vastly increased wages demanded, and got, by farm servants. As cottagers and smaller tenants were removed from the land, and as the unit-size of farms in many parishes was enlarged, the remaining tenants found themselves increasingly dependent on hired labour for working the fields and stock, particularly at harvest. The attractions of work in farms in the south of Scotland or of working in manufacturing villages or towns led to a great scarcity of farm servants; and these servants determinedly refused more than a six-month contract, were always ready to move to another master who would pay a little more, and managed to force landlords and tenants to pay them increasingly high wages. It was

1. Boharm, 96; Rathven, 391; Birnie, 467; Aberlour, 6; Calder, 736 – 737; see also Urquhart, 705.

generally claimed that these wages had doubled in twenty years – in Speymouth, it was said, they had trebled in that time. Minister after minister mentions their 'prodigious' rise (Duthil), the 'most extravagant pitch they had reached' (Mortlach), their 'progression beyond all precedent' (Rathven).[1] The bitterness to be found in the comments stems, it seems, from two results of the strong bargaining position which the servants were in. Firstly, 'ordinary', though not 'opulent', farmers were unable to afford them and yet still had to pay – threatening the tenants with a decline into poverty or bankruptcy, stimulating their emigration, forcing them to withdraw their children early from school to work the farm more cheaply. Secondly, the 'domineering insolence' of the hired servants was socially upsetting in a period of great political sensitivity (cf. French revolutionary times) – they were breaking the traditional mould of rural society. The minister of Kirkmichael, always ready with a sharply observed and caustic comment, did not spare the new-style farm servants in his account:[2]

'The short term of engagement, wages immoderately high, inspire them with a pride, insolence and indifference that could frequently require a meek and patient spirit to brook. Nice in the choice of their food to squeamishness, it must neither fall short nor exceed that exact proportion of cookery which their appetites can relish. Care too must be taken that no offence shall be offered them. They must sleep in the morning as long, and go to bed at night as soon, as their pleasure dictates. Expostulations are opposed by rudeness...'

To smaller tenant farmers, tied down by increased rents, under the nagging anxiety of short leases, suffering the still-widespread feudal services demanded by the landlords, the freedom which had thus come to the farm servants through the changing economic structure seemed appallingly unjust while they struggled, often ineffectively, to make ends meet. The Duthil minister shared with others a desire to see servants' wages more directly regulated (e.g. by the county com-

1. Speymouth, 664; Duthil and Rothiemurchas, 516; Mortlach, 340; Rathven, 387.
2. Kirkmichael, 277n.

missioners of supply), and the servants themselves having to present certificates as to their character and morals from previous employers at a new engagement – anything to change a situation where 'they stroll about idly in summer, living on the previous half year's earnings, knowing that farmers must pay the highest terms at harvest'.[1] It is perhaps not surprising after all that the Keith account remarks that 'tradesmen and manufacturers appear more cheerful, and seem happier, than the farmers and the tenants'.[2]

But there would be some leisure time, even for the hard pressed small farmer and cottager – though not much perhaps, according to the minister of St. Andrews Lhanbryde who judged that some of the lower ranks were too poor and beaten down by their hand-to-mouth existence to indulge themselves. Other accounts, however, refer to opportunities for dancing on Christmas and New Year's days, to the festivities at penny weddings (not complained of by the minister); at Birnie the bagpipes and the violin were major diversions from the harshness of life.[3] As for the inhabitants of Tomintoul,[4] 'all of them sell whisky and all of them drink it; when disengaged from this business, the women spin yarn, kiss their inamoratos, or dance to the discordant sounds of an old fiddle'. For the better-off, there were other diversions than the drinking party, the tavern, the tippling-house or the inn – though no doubt they shared in these too. In Banff, for example, that resort of 'genteel, opulent and respectable families', there was golf and riding on the extensive town links, dancing assemblies once a fortnight in the winter season, 'academical concerts of music', a circulating library which had easy access by sea to London for the latest books and periodicals, 'Sock and Buskin' visitors to entertain them in the summer (early versions of the pierrot show, no doubt) – and, if they joined the Turriff hunt, they could chase foxes in Forglen woods.[5] If they strayed on their journeyings as far as the village of Tomintoul in Kirkmichael, they could always

1. Duthil and Rothiemurchas, 515.
2. Keith, 262.
3. St. Andrew's Lhanbryd, 642; Keith, 261; Drainy, 485; Birnie, 467.
4. Kirkmichael, 279.
5. Banff, 65; Forglen, 179.

join the locals in the best inn there, 'at the sign of the horns', and meet Mrs. Mackenzie, of whom the always entertaining Mr. Grant has much to say.[1] She had begun 'her career of celebrity' as a camp follower with a regiment in Flanders in 1745 at the age of 14, 'caressing and caressed', attaching herself to a 'noble personage high in the military department'. Thereafter she was to marry and find her way, with a soldier-husband, to the war in America in 1756 – then, 'after a variety of vicissitudes in Germany, France, Holland, England, Ireland, Scotland, America and the West Indies, her anchor is now moored on dry land in the village of Tammtoul', meantime adding '24 children to the aggregate of general births, besides some homunculi that stopped short in the passage'.

Clearly this lady, though remarkable, was not the only character of note in our three counties; the accounts suggest a good deal of knowledge, personal or second-hand, of the 'outside world', of places and events at great distances from the particular localities in which the inhabitants of Banffshire, Moray and Nairnshire lived in the 1790s.[2] In this, and in many other aspects, the parish accounts which are printed here provide a valuable antidote to any too-ready presumptions that we might make about these Scots of the later 18th century.

DONALD J. WITHRINGTON
Senior Lecturer in Scottish History
University of Aberdeen

1. Kirkmichael, 279n – 280n.
2. See the intriguing note by the minister of Fordice (159) about local recruitment for one continental army: 'more lately, when the King of Prussia was collecting his tall men, the incumbent has not heard that he obtained any from this corner; but he got some from the contiguous parish of Rathven'.

APPENDIX

BANFFSHIRE

†OSA date	Parish	1755	Population in 1790s	1801	Percentage Change 1755/1790s	1755/1801
1790 – 1	Aberlour	1010	'920'	815	− 9	− 19
1790 – 1	Alvah	1161	'1070'[1]	1057	− 8	− 9
1797	Banff	3000	3510	3571	+ 17	+ 19
1791 – 3	Bellie	1730	1919	1802	+ 11	+ 4
1794 – 5	Boharm	'1435'[2]	1294	1161	− 9	− 19
1796	Botriphnie	953[3]	630	589	− 34	− 38
1797	Boyndie	994	1260	1122	+ 27	+ 13
1791 – 2	Cabrach	960	700	684	− 27	− 29
1791	Cullen	900	1214	1076	+ 35	+ 20
1790 – 1	Deskford	940	752	610	− 20	− 35
1782	Fordyce	3212	'3425'[4]	2747	+ 7	− 14
1793 – 4	Forglen	607	'600'[5]	605	− 1	0
1790 – 1	Gamrie	2083	'3000'	3052	+ 44	+ 47
1793	Gartly	1328	1800[6]	958	+ 36	− 28
1791	Glass	1000	970	793	− 3	− 21
1791	Grange	1797	1572[7]	1529	− 13	− 15
1779	Inveraven	2464	'2176'[8]	2107	− 12	− 14
1793	Inverkeithney	571	460	503	− 19	− 12
1791	Keith	2683	3057[9]	3284	+ 14	+ 22
1791 – 3	Kirkmichael	1288	1276	1332	− 1	+ 3
1790	Marnoch	1894	1960	1687	+ 3	− 11
1792	Mortlach	2374	1918[10]	1876	− 19	− 21
1791 – 2	Ordiquhill	666	517	510	− 22	− 23
1792 – 3	Rathven	2898	3524	3901	+ 22	+ 35
1792 – 7	Rothiemay	1190	1125	1061	− 5	− 11
1793	St. Fergus	1271	1240[11]	1270	− 2	0
		40409	41889	39702	+ 4	− 2

Appendix

MORAY

†OSA date	Parish	Population in 1755	1790s	1801	Percentage Change 1755/1790s	1755/1801
1792 – 3	Abernethy & Kincardine	1670	1769	1627[12]	+ 6	– 3
1793	Alves	1691	1111	1049	– 34	– 38
1792	Birnie	525	402[13]	366	– 23	– 30
1788	Dallas	700	'888'[14]	818	+ 27	+ 17
1791	Drainie	1174	1040	1057	– 11	– 10
1792 – 3	Duffus	1679	1500	1339	– 11	– 20
1790 – 1	Duthil & Rothiemurcas	1785	1110[15]	1578	– 38	– 12
1793	Dyke & Moy	1826	1529[16]	1492	– 16	– 18
1792 – 3	Edinkillie	1443	1800	1123	+ 25	– 22
1791 – 2	Elgin	6306	4534	4345	– 28	– 31
1791	Forres	1993	2987[17]	3114	+ 50	+ 56
1789 – 90	Kinloss	1191	1031	917	– 13	– 23
1791 – 2	Knockando	1267	'1500'[18]	1432	+ 18	+ 13
1791	Rafford	1313	1072	1030	– 18	– 22
1790 – 1	Rothes	'1346'[19]	'1500'	1521	+ 11	+ 13
1791 – 3	St. Andrew's Lhanbryde	1132[20]	777	799	– 31	– 29
1791	Speymouth	994	1347	1236	+ 36	+ 24
1792 – 3	Spynie or New Spynie	865	602	843	– 30	– 3
1793	Urquhart	1110	1050	1023	– 5	– 8
		30010	27549	26709	– 8	– 11

NAIRNSHIRE

†OSA date	Parish	Population in 1755	1790s	1801	Percentage Change 1755/1790s	1755/1801
1790 – 1	Ardclach	1163	1186[21]	1256	+ 2	+ 8
1796	Auldearn	1951[22]	1406	1401	– 28	– 28
1790 – 1	Cawdor	882	'987'[23]	1179	+ 12	+ 34
1792 – 3	Nairn	1698	'2400'	2215	+ 41	+ 30
		5694	5979	6051	+ 5	+ 6

SUMMARY TABLE

	Population in 1755	1790s	1801	Percentage Change 1755/1790s	1755/1801
Banffshire	40409	41889	39702	+ 4	– 2
Moray	30010	27549	26709	– 8	– 11
Nairnshire	5694	5979	6051	+ 5	+ 6
	76113	75417	72462	– 1	– 5

Appendix

Notes:

* The totals in this table are for entire parishes, even though in some instances substantial areas of the parishes lay in contiguous counties: thus, for example, Gartly is entered as being in Banffshire, although the greater extent of the parish (and the majority of the population) was actually situated in Aberdeenshire. Such parishes as Gartly or Duthil have been allotted to particular counties according to their listings in the *New Statistical Account* in order to make it as easy as possible to compare the two *Accounts*.

† The dates given in this first column indicate, as nearly as possible, the actual year in which the counts of population were made. The particular parish account often gives this information: failing that, the date shown is either that indicated by Sinclair at the start of each volume of the published *Accounts* or is the date of publication of the appropriate volume in the 1790s. A figure within quotation marks in the listed populations for the 1790s indicates that the minister estimated rather than made a particular count of the number of inhabitants in his parish.

1 In 1782 an exact count of parishioners amounted to 1070, 'which is very nearly the present state of it'.

2 A large portion of the parish of Dundorcas was annexed to Boharm in 1782 and is included in the figures returned in the 1790s and 1801: the Boharm population numbered 835 in Webster's census and to this roughly one-half (600) of the Dundorcas figure of 1194 has been added. (See note 19.)

3 The minister, noting that the population of the parish in 1774 was recorded as 700, concludes that the 1755 figure is in error, being too high — but we have no means of estimating by how much.

4 In 1782 'a tolerably exact numeration was made and...amounted to about 3425. The population since that period has rather increased than diminished.'

5 In 1782, 1783 and 1784 the population was given, respectively, as 577, 544 and 573; in 1788 it was 613 and 'since that time it has been about 600'.

6 The account records 2000 inhabitants in 1783.

7 The decline in population in the 1790s was very recent: the population is given as 1980 in 1780, 1875 in 1782, 1760 in 1784 and 1598 in 1789.

8 The account gives no figure for the 1790s but records 2244 inhabitants in 1779: 2176 is the average of that figure and the 2107 recorded in 1801.

9 In 1783 a count of population indicated a total of 3583 inhabitants.

10 There were 2169 inhabitants in 1782.

11 In 1775 the population numbered 1254.

12 The 1801 census omitted the Inverness-shire portion of the united parish for which an estimated population of 700 seems reasonable.

13 In 1781 a total of 460 inhabitants was recorded.

14 There was a population of 917 in 1788.

15 Webster gives only the combined total for both of the united parishes: in 1790 – 1 Duthil contained 830 inhabitants and Rothiemurcas 280; in 1801 these figures had risen respectively to 1113 and 465.

16 In 1788 the population was 1564.

17 There was a total of 2793 in 1774.

18 As well as making this estimate, the minister commented that 'the population is rather less than about 25 years ago'.

19 Dundorcas was divided in 1782, and annexed partly to Boharm and partly to Rothes. In 1755 the Rothes population was given as 746, and to this has been added 600 — roughly half of the Dundorcas population of 1194. (See note 2.)

20 The figure comprises 690 inhabitants in St Andrew's and 442 in 'Longbride'.

21 The inhabitants in 1781 numbered 1167.

22 The minister, writing in 1796, doubted the validity of Webster's figure of 1951, on the grounds that his predecessor in 1754 had claimed a population of only 1600: but did this last figure represent the total inhabitants or only the 'examinables' in the congregation?

Appendix

23 The minister's return noted some '850 above the age of six' in the population. Sir John Sinclair, using an unknown method of estimating, suggested 1062 as the appropriate total. But, if we follow the formula which Webster used in 1755, the best estimate of population would be $36 \div 31 \times 850$, that is 987.

BANFFSHIRE

MORAY FIRTH

ABERDEENSHIRE

MORAY

INVERNESS–SHIRE

KEY TO PARISHES

1. Bellie
2. Rathven
3. Cullen
4. Deskford
5. Fordyce
6. Boyndie
7. Banff
8. King Edward, Aberdeenshire
9. Gamrie
10. Alvah
11. Forglen
12. Marnoch
13. Ordiquhill
13. Inverkeithney
15. Rothiemay
16. Grange
17. Keith
10. Boharm
19. Botriphnie
20. Glass
21. Gartly
22. Cabrach
23. Inveraven
24. Mortlach
25. Aberlour
26. Kirkmichael
27. St Fergus

PARISH OF ABERLOUR.

(County of Banff.)

By the Rev. Mr James Thomson.

Name, Situation, Extent, Surface and Soil.

T HE ancient name of this parish was *Skirduſtan*, ſo
called from its tutelary ſaint, Duſtan. Its modern
name is *Aberlour*, derived from its local ſituation; being
ſituated at the mouth of a noiſy burn, where it diſcharges
itſelf into the Spey. It lies in the weſtern part of the
county of Banff, about 20 computed miles W. of the coun-
ty-town, 10 S. of Elgin, and 12 S. E. of Forres. It
gives name to the preſbytery to which it belongs, being
the preſbytery-ſeat; and pertains to the Synod of Murray.
The figure of the pariſh reſembles a wedge, being broader at the weſt end, and growing gradually narrower
towards the E. Its length from E. to W. is about 6
Scotch miles; its breadth from S. to N. at the weſt end,
about 5 Scotch miles; about the middle, between 2 and 3,
but at the eaſt end it will not exceed an Engliſh mile.
It is bounded on the S. and S. E. by the pariſh of Mort-
lack, from which it is ſeparated by a ſmall rivulet and a
range of hills called the Convals; it is bounded on the E.
by the pariſh of Boharm, from which it is divided by a
ſmall

fmall river called Fiddich; on the N. by the parifh of
Rothes, from which it is feparated by the river Spey;
on the N W. by the parifh of Knockandow, from which
it is alfo feparated by the river Spey; and on the W.
and S W. by the parifh of Inveraven, from which it is
divided by a hill called the Drum of Carron, the fmall
water of Tarvey, and the hill of Allachoynachan, upon
which the battle between the Earls of Argyle and Huntly,
commonly called the battle of Glenlivat, was fought.
The appearance of the parifh is various; that part of it
which lies N W. N. and E. and runs along Spey and Fiddich, is flat; that which lies towards the S E. and
S W. is hilly. In the middle of the parifh ftands the
high mountain of Belrinnes, from the top of which you
can, in a clear day, fee as far S. as the Grampian hills, and
as far N. and E. as the mountains of Rofs, Sutherland and
Caithnefs. The foil towards the river is light, and when
you dig to any depth, a ftratum of fand. That which is
towards the hills is deep, and a clay bottom. But both the
one and the other are abundantly fruitful when properly
clutivated.

Rivers, &c.—Befides the Spey and Fiddich, there are
a good number of fmall rivulets or burns, which abound
with trout and eel, as do Spey and Fiddich; in the former of which confiderable numbers of falmon ufed to be
caught; and for a liberty of catching them with rods,
dikes or cairns, the tenants, along the river-fide, paid to
their refpective heritors a certain yearly rent, which was
called water-rent. But, of late years, the quantity of falmon caught within the bounds of this parifh is greatly diminifhed, in confequence of a procefs between the Duke of
Gordon and the upper heritors, wherein it was found,
that the Duke had a title to raife cruives acrofs the river,
under

under certain regulations, and with what they call the Sunday's ſleep; the few that are ſtill caught are ſold within the pariſh, in the beginning of the ſeaſon, at 4 d. the lb. and not below 2 d. at any ſeaſon. Within theſe 24 years paſt, there have been more frequent overflowings of the Spey, than are remembered before that, by the oldeſt man alive, and whereby the adjacent fields have been much damaged. In September 1768, eſpecially, the river roſe about 18 feet perpendicular above the channel, overflowed the fields, carried along with its ſtream the cut corn, and large trees torn up by the roots, buried the corn which was not cut under a bed of ſand above 30 inches deep, and left the ſalmon dead on the fields, at the diſtance of above 100 yards from the bed of the river. There have been ſundry extraordinary ſwellings of the river ſince that time, but never to ſuch a prodigious pitch, although the rains have been greater, and of longer duration, in the low country ; from which it has been concluded, that the inundation in 1768 was occaſioned by water-ſpouts on the hills.

Produce.—Though the pariſh is rather calculated for grain than for paſture, it rears ſufficient black cattle, ſheep and hogs ; not only ſupplying itſelf, but ſending to market. Some of the beſt farmers alſo bring up horſes fit for ſaddle and draught ; and although the diſtrict cannot be ſaid to be famous for breeding horſes, black cattle or ſheep of ſuperior qualities, yet there are, of each kind, ſome raiſed, which are eſteemed very handſome, and well ſhaped, for which the owners draw for horſes from L. 15 to L. 20 Sterling ; for cows from L. 5 to L. 9 Sterling, for oxen from L. 8 to L. 12, and for ſheep ten guineas the ſcore. And as the pariſh has theſe uſeful animals, it wants not thoſe that are noxious ; ſuch as, foxes, badgers,
otters,

otters, &c. It is alfo ftored with fowls and birds. Being a highland country, abounding with woods, and almoft furrounded with hills, there are muirfowls, patridges, plovers, fnipes, lapwings, cormorants, hawks,
magpies, and woodcocks at their feafon ; fometimes
eagles are feen upon Belrinnes, and fome of their feathers
are found there ; the night owl alfo fhows itfelf. The
migratory birds are the cuckoo, which appears in the
beginning of April, and difappears in Auguft ; the lapwing, about the month of March, and is feldom feen
after the end of July ; the fwallow about the firft of
June, and difappears in the end of July ; the wood-
cock about October, and is fcarce feen after April.—The
parifh produces grain of all forts, with any due culture ;
and not only fupplies itfelf, but fells oats, meal and
barley, fometimes to the highlands, and fometimes for
exportation. It has alfo abundance of barren timber, efpecially oak, allar and birch, which grow naturally in large
woods, and fome plantations of firs are lately planted. There
are alfo fruit-trees, fuch as apple, pear, cherry trees, &c.
in fome gardens. Turnip and potatoes begin now to be
raifed on every farm, though, being but lately introduced,
in fmall quantities. The practice of planting cabbage in
the fields has not got in here ; nor is it likely that it will
be introduced foon, as almoft all the fields are without
any fence ; and winter herding is not practifed. There
is alfo fome flax raifed, but no hemp; and no great quantities of fown grafs.

Population.—According to Dr Webfter's ftate of the population, the number of inhabitants was 1010. There are,
at prefent, about 920 fouls ; about 450 males, and 470 females. The births and deaths bear not the ordinary proportion to the population. By fumming up the baptifms
and

and burials for 20 years, it appears, that the baptiſms are, at an average, 25, deaths 13, and marriages 8. Though there are ſcarce any remarkable for longevity, yet the people are generally healthy, and, a few excepted, who are carried off by ſmall pox and conſumptions, arrive at the age of 70, 80, and not a few at 84. The whole are of the Eſtabliſhed Church, except about 10 or 11, who are Roman Catholics. The inhabitants, except a very few ſervants and cottagers who come from Strathſpey and Badenoch, are natives, deſcended from anceſtors who have lived in the pariſh for many generations ; and as there are very few who come from other places, ſo there are as few who leave the pariſh : For ſince the year 1782, when there were whole families emigrating from the neighbouring pariſhes to North America, none, except a few aſpiring young men, who have had a more liberal education than their neighbours, have left this pariſh, and gone, ſome to London, ſome to the Weſt India Iſlands. There is but one reſiding heritor.

Church, Stipend, Poor, &c.—The church ſeems to be very old, and was repaired in 1786. The ſtipend till the year 1772 was only L. 50 ; but at that period the Earl of Fife, as patron, without any application from the incumbent, or any in his name, with a generoſity worthy of his Lordſhip, propoſed an augmentation of the ſtipend, and deſired the incumbent to name what augmentation he thought the miniſter of Aberlour ought to have ; who, with the advice of the preſbytery, propoſed L. 8 : 6 : 8 Sterling, of money, with 18 bolls of oat-meal, at 8 ſtone the boll, which his Lordſhip agreed to, and obtained a decreet, without any expence to the incumbent : So that, at preſent, the ſtipend is L. 58 : 6 : 8 of money, and 18 bolls

of

of meal, with about a litttle more than 5 acres of arable
ground for a glebe, little more than an acre of grafs, a
manfe, garden and offices. The funds for the poor are
not great, though the number on the poor's roll is confiderable, there being juft now about 30. There is a mortification of 3¼ bolls of meal, at 9 ftone the boll, payable
yearly off a fmall farm. One hundred merks, befides,
were mortified by a farmer of the name of M'Erron ;
another hundred merks by one of the name of Green;
both which fums, with any favings made in years of
plenty, are lent out upon intereft, and amount now to
about L. 80 Sterling of capital. The annualrent of this,
with the above mentioned mortified meal, the weekly collections, amounting to about 2 s. Sterling, at an average,
each Sabbath, with the produce of the mort-cloth, and
any fines for immoralities, are all the funds for affifting this
numerous roll. Indeed, in 1782, it was neceffary, by reafon of the fcarcity, to diminifh the capital ; but fince that
time it has been raifed to what it is at prefent.

Price of Provifions and Labour.—The prices of victuals
and clothing are greatly raifed within thefe 20 years paft.
Meal, which before that period, would have been bought
at 8 s. 4 d. the boll, now fells at 11 s. or 12 s. ; beef, which
formerly fold at 1¼ d. a-pound, now gives 3 d. or 4 d. ;
eggs, which were bought at 1 d. for 14, coft now 1¼ d.
for 12 ; and fifh, which would have been bought at 5 d.
the dozen, now coft 1 s. ; fo in proportion with refpect
to every fort of provifions. The fame proportion holds
with refpect to clothes and fhoes ; yet the people feem fatisfied with their condition, live very comfortably, being
generally very induftrious, and receive a proportional high
price for any commodity they bring to market ; and the
                                                labouring

labouring people and servants have nearly double the wages of what they had about 20 years ago. A day-labourer gets his victuals and 6 d. a-day, at any season; in harvest, 10 d. and 1 s. A man-servant, who can only drive a cart-horse, is allowed L. 4 yearly; and he who can plow and sow, gets L. 5 or L. 6. A woman-servant gets L. 2 a-year.

PARISH OF ALVAH,

(COUNTY OF BANFF.)

By the Rev. Mr GEORGE SANGSTER.

Situation, Surface, &c.

THE parish of Alvah is situated in the presbytery of Turriff, and Synod of Aberdeen. Its form is irregular; extending in length about 6 English miles, and at its greatest breadth to nearly the same distance, but in other places to only 3 or 2. On the N. and N. W. it is bounded by the parish of Banff; on the S. W. by Marnoch; on the S. by Forglen; on the S. E. by Turriff; and on the E. and N. E. by King Edward and Gamery. The river Dovern enters this parish about a mile below Forglen, the seat of Lord Banff, and after many beautiful windings through a very fertile valley, leaves it about 2 miles from the sea. It abounds with salmon, trout, and eel, and is frequented by wild ducks, widgeons, teals, herons, &c. On the E. bank lie the estates of Dunlugas and Inrichney, separated by the intervention of a part of the parish of King Edward; and on the W. the lands of Mountblairie, Auchinbadie, Sandlaw, and a small part of

the

the barony of Alvah. About half a mile below the church, the river is contracted by 2 ſteep and rugged precipices, which are commonly denominated the Craigs of Alvah, where it meaſures about 50 feet in depth. The ſcenery, which is naturally bold and picturefque, has been greatly embelliſhed by its noble proprietor, the Earl of Fife, by thriving plantations, and a magnificent arch, which unites both ſides of the river, and forms an eaſy communication between the oppoſite parts of his Lordſhip's extenſive park. The fruitful haughs along the banks of the river are ſubject to frequent inundations, which, in ſummer and harveſt, make dreadful depredations among the corns. This inconvenience is more eſpecially felt in the neighbourhood of the rocks of Alvah, which, during a flood, check the rapidity of the ſtream, and make the water flow backward for nearly 2 miles, and ſpread more than a quarter of a mile over the adjacent fields. As we recede from the river toward the W. the country becomes more hilly and barren. Of theſe eminences, one of the moſt conſpicuous is the Hill of Alvah, which riſes from the bed of the river to a very great height, and ſerves as a common landmark to mariners, on their approach to the coaſt. The majeſtic appearance of this mountain, which is ſomewhat increaſed by the view of the church, manſe, ſchool, and a farm-ſtead on its E. brow, is thus deſcribed by an indigenous poet.

Erigit ad nubes hic ſe mons Alvius ingens,
Oſtentatque procul conſpicienda juga.
Hic quoque Templa Deûm ſurgunt in monte locata
Sublimi; ſurgit Pieridumque domus.

Agriculture, &c.—The air of this pariſh is in general dry and healthy. Its ſoil, along both ſides of the river, is very fertile; deep on the haughs, and more ſhallow on the declivities.

declivities. Nor are there wanting fruitful fields on the upper grounds, interfperfed amongft the rough paftures and
heath, which ftill occupy a very confiderable part. The
crops which are commonly cultivated are oats, barley, and
peas; and on fome of the richer and more fheltered fpots,
wheat has been tried with fuccefs. Turnip, for 20 years
paft, has been fown in the fields; and clover and rye-grafs
have become a conftant part of the rotation. Feeding for
the butcher is carried on by a few; but rearing young
cattle has of late years been found a more lucrative branch,
and by confequence more generally practifed. As farms
are not commonly let by the acre, it cannot be faid with
accuracy what value is put upon each. The beft arable
ground may rent about L. 1, or perhaps fomewhat higher;
a ftill greater quantity about 15 s. and much more about
12 s. or 10 s. and even below that value. There are only
a few farms inclofed, nor does that mode of melioration
keep pace with the other fpecies of improvement. Hedges
do not thrive, unlefs in places which are fheltered, as well
as fertile. Feal or earthen fences have been found of fhort
duration, and ftone fences are expenfive. But, though inclofures are not fo frequent as might be wifhed, the practice
of herding in winter is general; fo that the turnip and
fown graffes fuftain little detriment from ftraggling cattle.
Several of the farms are already brought to a very high
degree of cultivation, and others are advancing by gradual
progrefs to a like ftate of improvement. About the year
1747, the minifter began to bring home his peats in carts,
valued each at 4 s. 6 d. Before that period the fuel was
carried in creels, and the corns in curracks; two implements of hufbandry which, in this corner, are entirely dif-
ufed. The ftraw brechem is now fupplanted by the leather
collar, the rafhen theets by the iron traces; and more is
now

now expended on a ſingle cart, than would then have purchaſed both cart and horſe. The ſize of farms is increaſing, and of conſequence their number diminiſhes. We
account one of from L. 30 to L. 50 rent, a middle ſized
farm. There are a few above that rent, but many more
below it.—This pariſh, unleſs in very bad years, produces
much more grain than is neceſſary for the ſubſiſtence of its
inhabitants. Beſides the farm-victual, which amounts to a
very conſiderable part of the rent, there are large quantities, both of meal and barley, annually ſold by the farmers
for the ſupply of the neighbouring town of Banff, and for
exportation. In 1782 the crop was ſo defective, that, according to the computation of inſpectors, there was not
grain within the pariſh ſufficient to ſupply it beyond the
month of April. By the attention and generoſity of the
heritors, and the bounty of Government, with L. 40 from
the funds of the pariſh, the poorer ſort were ſupplied. The
moſt curious fact relating to that alarming period was, that
the oats on the earlier grounds, which ripened, were plump,
and were found on trial to yield abundance of excellent
meal, did not vegetate when ſown next year; whereas the
oats on late grounds, which were green, and neither filled
nor ripened, ſprang up with vigour. As this was not found
out till too late, it proved of the greateſt detriment to the
ſucceeding crop. The ſeed, which had been bought up at
an enormous expence, miſgave; what might have greatly
contributed to the ſupport of families, was unprofitably
caſt into the ground; and what might have been profitably
ſown, was ſent to the mill, where it made but a ſcanty
return.

Population.—The numbers returned to Dr Webſter
were 1161. As there are no pariſh regiſters previous to
the

the year 1720, the ancient ftate of its population cannot be afcertained. From the records fince that period, it fhould feem that population is upon the decline.

Births, Marriages and Burials, for three different periods, viz.

$$
\begin{array}{lll}
\text{7 years fucceeding 1ft Jan. 1720.} & \left\{\begin{array}{l} \text{Births, 214.} \quad \text{Aver. } 30\frac{4}{7} \\ \text{Mar.} \quad 32. \quad\quad\text{—} \quad 4\frac{4}{7} \\ \text{Bur. (no regift.)} \end{array}\right. \\[2em]
\text{1ft Jan. 1750.} & \left\{\begin{array}{l} \text{Births, 137.} \quad\quad\text{—} \quad 19\frac{4}{7} \\ \text{Mar.} \quad 44. \quad\quad\text{—} \quad 6\frac{2}{7} \\ \text{Bur.} \quad 52. \quad\quad\text{—} \quad 7\frac{3}{7} \end{array}\right. \\[2em]
\text{1ft Jan. 1780.} & \left\{\begin{array}{l} \text{Births, 113.} \quad\quad\text{—} \quad 16\frac{1}{7} \\ \text{Mar.} \quad 43. \quad\quad\text{—} \quad 6\frac{1}{7} \\ \text{Bur.} \quad 62. \quad\quad\text{—} \quad 8\frac{6}{7} \end{array}\right.
\end{array}
$$

The marriages are reftricted to thofe where the hufband was a refidenter; from the idea, that girls married out of the parifh do not contribute to its population: But left this fhould be deemed erroneous, it may be proper to notify, that the average of all, who were married during the firft period, was $7\frac{1}{7}$; during the fecond, $9\frac{3}{7}$; and during the third, $9\frac{4}{7}$. In the year 1782, the number of parifhioners, on an exact furvey, was found to amount to 1070; which is very nearly the prefent ftate of it. Some years before it was rather greater. One principal caufe of depopulation in this parifh is, the eagernefs of fome improvers to take all their land under their own management; by which means mechanics, and even day-labourers are deprived of their crofts; and, as there are no villages within the parifh, betake themfelves to other places, where they can find accommodation. Why the fame number of marriages doth not produce an equal number of births as in former times, is left to more intelligent heads to explain? There have been no extraordinary inftances

ftances of longevity of late. Only one man has reached
100, and a few are on the verge of 90 years. The inhabitants are moftly employed in agriculture. There are feveral weavers and wrights, a few fmiths and tailors, and
often not one fhoemaker. They are regular attenders of
the Eftablifhed Church ; nor do the Diffenters, of whatever denomination, exceed 8 or 10.

Heritors, Stipend, Poor, &c.—The property of the parifh belongs at prefent to 5 heritors, of whom only 1 refides. The manfe was built in 1764. The church is very
old, and in bad repair. The ftipend is 58 bolls 2 firlots
2 pecks oat-meal ; 5 bolls 2 firlots bear ; L. 600 Scots,
with 50 merks for communion-elements. The glebe confifts of between 6 and 7 acres, of which the rough meadow ground has been drained and cultivated by the prefent incumbent, and the whole inclofed.—The yearly collections amount to about L. 15 or L. 16, which, with the
intereft of L. 120, and L. 1, 10 s. the rent of fome feats in
the area of the church, conftitute the whole funds for the
maintenance of the poor.

Wages and Prices.—The wages of fervants and mechanics, and the price of provifions have rifen rapidly within
thefe few years. The yearly wages of a man fervant
may be rated at L. 5, or L. 5, 10 s. ; and of a woman at
L. 2. A labourer earns 8 d. a-day. The price of beef,
mutton, poultry, &c. is regulated entirely by the weekly
market in Banff, of which an account will be given in the
report from that parifh.

Roads and Bridges.—The principal roads were made by
the ftatute-work, and are kept in repair by the fame
means.

means. It is commonly exacted in kind; but when commutations in money are more convenient for the people, they are accepted. Of late years, bridges have been built over the moſt dangerous paſſes, to the great accommodation and ſafety of travellers; and it is hoped, that, as ſoon as the funds can afford, more will be erected. Turnpikes are unknown in this corner of the country, and would undoubtedly be unacceptable at firſt; though the experience of their advantages might in time reconcile us. It muſt indeed be allowed, that, as the reſort on our roads is but little, they are not ſo neceſſary as on thoſe that are more frequented.

Antiquities.—There are few or no antiquities in this pariſh worthy of a place in hiſtorical records. At the farm of Bog of Mountblairie are the remains of an old caſtle, ſituated in a ſwamp now overgrown with alder, and ſaid to have been built by the Earl of Buchan; and on an eminence above it, the ruins of a chapel, adjoining to which is a well, famed of old for its ſovereign charms, but now fallen into diſrepute. Within theſe few years there was an iron laddle; and many ſtill alive remember to have ſeen the impending boughs adorned with rags of linen and woollen garments, and the ciſtern enriched with farthings and boddles, the offerings and teſtimonies of grateful votaries, who came from afar to this fountain of health. At the foot of the hill of Alvah, towards the north, is another ſpring, which paſſes by the name of Com's or Colm's well, in honour, very probably, of the renowned Saint of Icolumkil.

PARISH OF BANFF.

(County of Banff, Synod of Aberdeen, and Presbytery of Fordyce.)

By the Rev. Mr Abercromby Gordon.

Name.

THE town of Banff gives name to the county and parish, in which it is situated. Its etymology is variously stated, and indeed seems of little importance to trace.

By some, the name is said to be of Gaelic extraction, signifying a place surrounded with high ground; but this interpretation apears too vague and general, and cannot well be applied to a situation partly open to the sea.

Banff was a part of the ancient thanedom of Boin, whence the name seems to be derived. In some old charters it is spelled Boineffe and Baineffe. The district of Boin has probably received its name from a conspicuous mountain in the neighbourhood of Cullen, called the Binn. On

the

the fouth fide of this hill, at Darbrich, the forrefter had
his dwelling; and it is well known that the forreftry and
thanedom territory extended thence to the borough lands
of Banff, divided only by the water of Boindie *·

Situation and Extent.—The fituation of this parifh is
fomewhat peninfular, being bounded by the river Doveran on the eaft, which divides it from the parifh of Gamery; and by the water of Boindie on the weft, feparating it
from the parifh of that name. On the fouth, it is bounded
by part of the parifh of Alva; and on the north, by the
Murray Frith.

It belongs to the prefbytery of Fordyce, and to the fynod and commiffariot of Aberdeen. This parifh forms an
irregular oblong figure, ftretching from north to fouth-weft
above fix miles; and in breadth meafures from one and an
half to two and an half miles. It may contain about 12
fquare miles, and 7680 acres.

Surface and Soil.—The furface is in general beautifully
unequal, and rifes gradually to the fouth-weft. The nature
and quality of the foil are no lefs various. There are all
forts, the rich fertile loam, the deep ftrong clay, the light
fandy field, and the thin gravelly bottom.

Sea-coaft and Rivers.—The fea coaft, for half-a-mile weftward of the harbour, is bold and rocky.

Towards the water of Boindie it forms a fine fandy
beach, adjoining which is the links †, affording an excellent

---

* The following etymology is hazarded: Boiny or Boindie is faid, in the
Gaelic, to fignify a little hill, and in this parifh there are a great number of
knolls, mounts and rifing grounds.

† An extenfive down or plain by the fea fide, is known in Scotland by
the name of links.

lent field for the healthful exercifes of riding and the golf.

The only river is the Doveran, which has its fource in Aberdeenſhire, and, winding through many fruitful and highly cultivated plains, falls into the fea at Banff.

State of Property, Valued and Real Rents.—The Earl of Findlater, the Earl of Fife, and Lord Banff, are the principal proprietors ; of whom, Lord Fife is the only refiding heritor.

The valued rent of the landward part of the pariſh is L. 2313 Scots. The real rent, including the falmon-fiſhing and town's lands, is eftimated at L. 4500 Sterling.

Burgh.—The town is fituated at the influx of the river Doveran, on a fine declivity, opening to the eaft and foutheaft; commanding various and delightful profpects. From the floping road, on the oppofite fide the river, the variegated fcenery which opens to the view is highly gratifying, and never fails to attract the attention of ftrangers.

The noble manfion of the Earl of Fife, the fpacious lawn and extenfive pleafure-grounds in his Lordſhip's park, the fmooth flowing Doveran, with its ftately bridge, the town and caftle of Banff, the bay, harbour and ſhipping, are the ftriking objects which at once prefent themfelves to the eye, and charm every traveller of tafte.

Banff is an ancient royalty, and the capital of the county. In conjunction with Elgin, Cullen, Inverury, and Kintore, it fends a Commiffioner to Parliament.

At what precife period it was erected into a royal burgh cannot be afcertained. According to tradition, it was in the reign of Malcolm Canmore. It is, however, certain, that Malcolm IV. called the Maiden, was at Banff, A. D. 1163.

William

William the Lyon gives a toft and garden in the burgh
of Banff to his chaplain Archibald Douglas, bishop of Moray, A. D. 1165 ; and similar gifts are made to him in the
towns of Invernefs, Nairn, and Cullen, all royal burghs at
this period.

King Robert Bruce confirms the privileges of royalty,
and King Robert II. 7th October 1372, also confirms the
fame, and fuch other privileges and liberties as were enjoyed by the town of Aberdeen.

Thefe grants were followed by confirmations from King
James VI. and Charles II.

Municipal government, &c.—The town is governed by
a provoft, four bailies and twelve counfellors. Eight of
the old council are re-elected, and the new counfellors are
chofen annually out of the merchant guild-brethren.

The annual revenue of the burgh amounts to L. 300
Sterling, arifing chiefly from feu-duties, rents of lands,
fhore-dues and petty cuftoms.

Alienation of Lands and Fifhings.—Such was the diftreffed
fituation of the burgeffes, A. D. 1470, that, having no
power to increafe their revenues but by leafe alone, the
managers of the town, without fraud, and upon their great
aith, with confent of all and fundry neighbours of Banff, let
out to certain burgeffes, for 19 years, the whole of their
falmon-fifhings, confifting of 12 nets, for the " infefting
" and fundanation makkin of a perpetual chaplenary *, to
" fing in the Peil-heife † of the burgh, for our Sovereign
                                                    " Lord

---

* Public Records.

† Pool-haven, where formerly boats and fmall craft were generally
moored. It is now the burying-ground, and was the fite of the old
church.

" Lord the King and Queen, their predeceffors and fuccef-
" fors ; for all Chriftiane foules ; for the theiking of the
" kirk with fclate, and the bigging of the tolbuthe, and for
" quhat the burgh has not fubftance." Similar leafes were
probably granted until the year 1581, when George Ogilvie of Dunlugas, provoft, and his coadjutors in office, refolved to feu to perpetuity. To this effect they obtained a
charter from James II. of Scotland, dated May 9. 1581.
The preamble bears, that, " for the advantage of the burgh *,
" the council had been in ufe of granting leafes of their
" property to the refiding burgeffes ; that thefe leafes were
" now expired, and that the nobility in the neighbourhood
" feeing the fame, and hoping to acquire the profits, did
" trouble and moleft the peace of the town, and gave no
" reft to the people : therefore," &c. &c.

This charter was renewed on the King's attaining the
age of 25 years, *mutatis mutandis*.

Having thus obtained a right to let out their property to
perpetuity, the guardians proceeded to exercife their powers.
John Baird, provoft, and the bailies of the town, (two of
whom could not write), were among the commiffioners appointed *ad hunc effectum*. Accordingly, A. D. 1595, " be-
" caufe of the warres and troubles, the darth of the coun-
" try, and fcantinefs of victual, with exorbitant ftents and
" taxations for fupporting the warres, the public warkes, and
" uphading of the kirk, tolbuthe, and calfies, &c. ; for re-
" meid whereof, this empower to fet, fell and feu, the com-
" mon land and falmon-fifhings of the burgh, to merchant-
" burghers, and actual refidenters."

Thefe magiftrates and commiffioners, in confequence of
their inftructions, did accordingly let out to perpetuity, for
a fmall annual feu-duty, the greater part of their lands, and
the whole of their falmon-fifhings.

In

* Public Records.

In the above-mentioned charter of 1592, the King, in order to preſerve the government of the town pure from any
mixture of *ariſtocracy*, gives power to the council to diſpoſe of their property to *reſiding burgeſſes and their heirs-
male only*. Had this arrangement been cautiouſly executed,
the intentions of the original granters might have been accompliſhed ; but it is evident, that the ancient governors, if
not too attentive to their own intereſt, were at leaſt ſomewhat negligent of the advantages of future generations.
Thus did the meaſure defeat its own purpoſe, and produced
the conſequences they wiſhed to avoid ; for though the
neighbouring nobility have not moleſted the peace and quiet
of the inhabitants, they have got poſſeſſion of the property,
as the Earl of Fife has purchaſed near three-fourths of the
whole, and the Earl of Findlater and Lord Banff a conſiderable part of the remainder. It was the remark of Dean
Swift, which the preſent ſituation of this burgh ſtrongly
confirms, that " great changes and alienations of property
" have created new and great dependencies."

Duff Houſe and Park.—Duff Houſe, the principal ſeat of
the Earl of Fife, and the beautiful ſcenery of his Lordſhip's
park, are well known to the touriſt, and deſcribed in the
journals of ſeveral celebrated travellers.

The houſe is a large quadrangular building, planned and
executed by the late celebrated Mr Adam.

The architecture is ſuperb, but the deſign is not yet
completed. The original plan, which is truly magnificent,
may be ſeen in Wolf's Vitruvius.

Duff Houſe contains ſeveral very elegant apartments, in
which is a great profuſion of paintings, chiefly portraits.
Thoſe particularly noticed by Mr Pennant, are, Frances
Ducheſs of Richmond, a full length, in black, painted in
1633,

1633, by Vandyck. Fine heads of Charles I. and his Queen. A head of Duff of Corfindae. There are likewife a few paintings by Sir Jofhua Reynolds, and other eminent mafters.

The library is a fpacious room, near 70 feet in length, and extending through the whole breadth of the building. The books are numerous, and well felected. In a fmall apartment adjoining, is a cabinet, containing an extenfive collection of Roman and Britifh coins, medals, &c.

Lord Fife's park and furrounding plantations meafure 14 miles in circumference.

The park is bounded by the two bridges of Banff and Alvah, and contains within its circuit a part of two counties, and four parifhes *. The pleafure grounds are laid out with much tafte and elegance. The walks are of great extent and variety, fome winding beautifully along the banks of the Doveran, and others leading off, in different directions, to wide and diftant plantations.

About three miles from the houfe, where the river is confiderably narrowed by the lofty and impending craigs of Alvah, a majeftic arch is thrown acrofs, which is highly picturefque. Here the view which prefents itfelf is peculiarly wild and romantic. The fine windings of the river, the rugged fcenery on either fide, the overhanging woods, and,

> ——————— the precipice abrupt,
> Projecting horror on the blacken'd flood,
>
> THOMSON.

form a landfcape truly grand, and worthy the pencil of a Claude Lorraine.

Agriculture

* Counties of Aberdeen and Banff, and the parifhes of Banff, Gamrie, Alvah and King Edward.

Agriculture and Improvements.—The ſtate of agriculture in this pariſh continued ſtationary for almoſt a century preceding 1754.

This fact is confirmed, by confidering that the land rent ſuffered little or no change during the above period. From the proven rental in the former decreet of ſtipend, it appears, that the lands belonging to the town paid no advance of rent from 1635 to 1729.

The extenſive paſturage of the Gallow-hill, the property of the town, was then rented at the pitiful ſum of 10 merks yearly.

In 1754, the town-council feued out theſe grounds to the inhabitants at 10 s. *per* acre, with a reſerve to them of buying up the feu-duty at 25 years purchaſe.

Induſtry, ſuperior culture, the advantages of ſea-weed, and vicinity to the town, have now rendered what was originally barren, fertile and productive.

Theſe lands are regularly ſubdivided, and incloſed with ſubſtantial ſtone fences, may be let from L. 2 to L. 3 an acre, and produce excellent crops of all kinds. A few fields adjoining the town are rented ſo high as L. 5 and L. 6 *per* acre. Theſe are chiefly occupied by gardeners, who raiſe pot-herbs and other vegetables for the ſupply of the inhabitants.

About 40 years ago, potatoes and turnips were cultivated, as rare vegetables, in the garden, and were not brought to market. Now, cattle are chiefly fed by turnip; potatoes are frequently given to horſes, and are ſold in great abundance by the gardeners, and in the weekly markets, at 6 d. and 7 d. a peck, of 32 lbs weight.

It is a curious fact, that on the introduction of this uſeful root, the great landholders were alarmed leſt it ſhould be the means of depreciating the value of grain, the ſtaple

commodity

commodity of the country. The effect, however, has been the reverse; grain of all kinds being, for some years past, in greater demand, and at higher prices, than at any former period.

Prior to the year 1754, the practice of winter-herding was little known. No sooner was the harvest completed, than the whole country became one great common, and every farmer considered he had an undoubted right to pasture his flocks on his neighbour's fields. In those days, even the best farms were generally divided into what is called out-field and infield; and both were wasted by an injudicious mode of cropping. From this torpid state the farmer was roused by the spirited exertions of the late Earl of Findlater, who happily introduced a new system of farming in this country. His Lordship, during his residence in the Castle of Banff, having taken one of his farms into his own possession, determined to cultivate it after the most approved methods then known in the kingdom. With this view, he engaged an active and experienced overseer from England, to whom he devolved the management of this farm, and in a few years improved it in a stile and manner unknown in this country *.

To conquer the power of habit, and eradicate ancient prejudices, is often a fruitless attempt, and is a task peculiarly difficult in effecting agricultural improvements. Such, however, was the influence of his Lordship's eminent example as a farmer, joined to the judicious encouragement which he afforded his tenants, that, in a few years, a spirit of industry and enterprise pervaded all ranks of proprietors and farmers in this country, and produced a striking improvement in the soil and appearance of this parish and neighbourhood.

Lord

* See Agricultural Report of this county, by Mr Donaldson.

Lord Findlater was alſo the firſt who introduced, on a large ſcale, the practice of fallow, and the uſe of lime, ſowing graſs-ſeeds, turnip and other green crops; improvements now generally adopted, and with great ſucceſs. His Lordſhip's improvements, with the general mode of farming practiſed in this corner, will be found more fully detailed' in the Agricultural Reports of this county.

Farms.—The farms moſt remarkable for beauty, extent and improvement, in this pariſh, are, Colleonard and Boindie Hills, belonging to Lord Findlater, and Blairſhinnoch, the property of Lord Banff. The firſt of theſe was one of Lord Findlater's experimental farms. It lies on a gentle declivity, opening to the ſouth, and commands a variety of pleaſing proſpects. The fields are laid out with much taſte and judgment, incloſed and ſubdivided with hedge-rows and belts of thriving wood. It bears a ſtriking reſemblance to a fine Engliſh farm, and to thoſe who remember its former appearance, it ſeems altogether a new creation. The farm of Blairſhinnoch contains about 400 acres, and is generally a productive field.

Boindie Hills is chiefly occupied as a ſheep farm, and proves a very lucrative poſſeſſion to Mr Milne, affording excellent paſture to a flock of 200 to 300 ſheep, chiefly of Engliſh breed, and of the largeſt ſize.

Nor, in this account, muſt we omit the little farm of Cowden Knows *, diſtant about a mile from the town, and juſtly celebrated for its rural beauty.

Attracted by its wild and ſimple ſcenery, the preſent tenant has choſen this *ferme ornée* as a ſummer retreat.

From

---

* This is not ſuppoſed to be the ſcene of the plaintive Scots ballad.

From his clay-built cottage, fituated on a rifing ground, there is an extenfive view of the Murray Frith, of the lofty mountains of Sutherland and Caithnefs, and various woodland profpects.

This favoured fpot is preferved quite in the paftoral ftile.

" Here no rude ploughman fide-long lays the glebe,
" —————————— Nor fower ftalks
" With meafur'd fteps, —————————
" Nor harrow follows, harfh, to fhut the fcene."

THOMSON.

The prefent occupier afpires not to the extravagant praife which Dean Swift beftows on the man " who makes " one ear of corn to grow where there was none before."

————— Juvat arva videre
Non raftris hominum, non ulli obnoxia curæ.

VIRG. GEORG.

Prices of grain, &c. at different periods.—Meal was fold, by contract for feven years, at 8 s. 6 d. *per* boll, commencing with crop 1758; at 9 s. for the fame period, commencing with crop 1764; and at 9 s. 6 d. from 1767. Ten fhillings was confidered a reafonable price for a contract of feven years, commencing 1768. The medium price of meal, for 20 years preceding 1782, was 11 s. 7½ d.; and from that year to 1795, about 13 s. 2 d.

For fome years paft, oats have been fold at 1 s. 1 d. and 1 s. 2 d. *per* ftone weight *. Meal and barley have given proportionably high prices. Such was the alarming deficiency

---

* The boll of oats fometimes weighs 14½, 15, and fometimes 16 ftones.

ency of crop 1795, that meal was ſold in this pariſh at 21 s.
a boll of eight ſtones Dutch weight, and barley at 25 s. *.

Implements

* Barley of a good kind generally weighs from 18 to 20 ſtones *per*
boll.

Owing to the late injudicious opening of the ports for importation, and
the threatening of a farther depreſſion of the diſtilleries, there is at preſent
an extraordinary ſtagnation in the ſale of grain, which muſt be attended
with the moſt ſerious conſequences to the farmer.

In ſeaſons of plenty, the impolicy of opening the ports for importation
muſt be obvious to the humbleſt capacity. When prices are low, in conſequence of ſuch plenty, a bounty ought to be given upon exportation; and
that bounty ought to be continued until the price riſes to a certain height.

" There muſt be ſomething very ſeductive, or very profitable, in the im-
" portation of foreign grain; for all the laws that have hitherto been made
" to prevent it, have been evaded; and yet, except the importer, it is
" clearly againſt the intereſt of every other perſon in the kingdom: for it
" is deſtructive of our own agriculture; and we have ſeen, from certain evi-
" dence, that it raiſes the price of grain upon the conſumer.

" While the ancient laws laid the country open to the importation of fo-
" reign grain, by injudicious duties or reſtrictions upon our own produce,
" our farmers were diſpirited; a great part of the ſoil lay without culture;
" the price of grain was conſequently high; and population was reſtrain-
" ed.

" When the reſtrictions were not only removed, but bounties given upon
" the exportation of our excreſcent ſtock, by the acts of 1688 and 1700,
" the happieſt effects were immediately experienced: Theſe laws acted like
" magic; our agriculture immediately roſe, as from the dead; population in-
" creaſed; and inſtead of eating the bread of foreign nations, we not only
" maintained all our own people, at a lower rate than was ever known before,
" but the kingdom received an immediate addition of riches and ſtrength,
" from the money brought in, from the increaſe of ſhipping, and from the
" people employed in raiſing and exporting the ſurplus of our produce:
" A ſtate of proſperity which continued without interruption for above
" half a century after the Union. No ſooner was importation again en-
" couraged, than our agriculture languiſhed, our exportation declined, and
" the prices of grain roſe."

" Importation of foreign grain acts like a mole under ground; we know
" nothing of its operations but by the heaps which its raiſes; and when
" theſe heaps come to cover an 8th, an 18th, or even a 475th part of our
" own ſoil, it is high time to turn them down."

The

Implements of Hufbandry.—In no branch of agriculture has there been a more ftriking and effential improvement than in the conftruction of the implements of hufbandry. Carts were not ufed in this parifh till the year 1728, when Mr Duff of Corfindae, then refiding in Banff, introduced them, having procured two " *timber carts*," at the price of 5 s. each. The creel or curroch was then the common vehicle in ufe. Grain, meal, and lime for exportation, were brought hither on horfeback, from the moft inland parts of the country.

The only plough then ufed, was what is known by the name of the old Scottifh plough, in its rudeft form. Now, carriages, ploughs, harrows, and the various utenfils of hufbandry, of the moft approved and modern conftruction, are either imported from Leith, or manufactured in this country. Thefe are generally painted; a practice which has both ornament and utility to recommend it *.

Nurfery.—Adjoining the farm of Colleonard, there is a nurfery of confiderable extent, conducted by Mr Reid. It was begun about 30 years ago, and has of late been greatly enlarged

The above facts and obfervations are taken from " An Inquiry into the
⁜ Corn Laws and Corn Trade of Great Britain, and their influence on the
" Profperity of the Kingdom ; by the late Alexander Dirom, Efq; of Muir-
" efk."
Mr Dirom was amply qualified for the inveftigation of thefe important fubjects. He was particularly acquainted with the ftate of this county, having long refided in Banff.

* The ingenious Bifhop of Llandaff, in his Chemical Effays, obferves,
" Since the fame piece of wood has different weights, when dry, and when
" foaked with water, the covering carts, ploughs, and other hufbandry gear
" ufually made of afh, with a coarfe kind of paint which will keep out the
" rain, is a practice full as ferviceable in leffening the weight of the im-
" plement which is to be moved by the ftrength of man or horfe, as in
" preferving the wood from decay."

enlarged and improved. It occupies between 15 and 20 acres, and contains all the variety of fruit and foreſt trees, ever-green and flowering ſhrubs, flower roots and plants, which are in demand in this climate.

A gentleman in this neighbourhood, Mr Garden of Troup, in the courſe of three or four years, has planted from Mr Reid's nurſery, the immenſe number of one million nine hundred thouſand trees, beſides what he procured from other quarters, and the greater part in a thriving ſtate *.

Woods, &c.—It is generally ſuppoſed, that a conſiderable part of this pariſh, towards the ſouth-weſt, has been covered with woods, and belonged to the ancient foreſt of Boin. A ſimple diſtich, which tradition has handed down, confirms this opinion :

> From Culbirnie † to the ſea,
> You may ſtep from tree to tree.

There is ſtill in poſſeſſion of a farmer in that quarter, an oak tree, 30 feet long, which was dug up in the neighbourhood of his farm.

Since the decay or demolition of that foreſt, there were very few trees in this diſtrict, till the year 1756, when Lord Fife began his plantations. Theſe are now of great extent and variety, and in a flouriſhing ſtate.

The woods on Lord Findlater's eſtates in this pariſh are likewiſe thriving, and of conſiderable extent.

All theſe plantations add greatly to the decoration of the country, to the comfort of the poor, and to the facility of every branch of induſtry.

Eccleſiaſtical

* In theſe plantations a balm of Gilead fir, laſt ſeaſon, advanced 20 inches in height.

† Culbirnie, a farm about three miles diſtant from the ſea.

Ecclefiaftical State.—From the public records it appears, that the kirk of Banff was rebuilt by the town-council in the year 1471, when Sir James Ogilvie of Defkford was provoft. They endowed a chaplain, with ten merks of ftipend, befides a living out of the common fund. Before this period, the chaplainry of St Mary, of the order of Carmelites, was the only other eftablifhment of worfhip in the royalty.

The parifhes of Banff and Inverboindie continued united till the year 1634, when Mr Alexander Seton, then minifter of Banff, brought an action * of valuation and modification of the teinds againft the heritors, by which the union was declared void, and each holden to be a feparate parifh, and diftinct congregation.

The firft minifter of this parifh, after its disjunction from Boindie, was Mr Alexander Seton. He died 1679, and was fucceeded by Mr Patrick Innes, minifter of Defkford, who died *anno* 1699. His fucceffor in office was Mr William Hunter, minifter of Tyrie. In 1712, Mr Hunter being fufpended from preaching, upon his refufal of the abjuration oath, the church was fupplied by the brethren of the neighbourhood. The following year he returned to his charge, and died 1716. Mr James Innes was admitted in December 1716, and died September 1753. In December following, Mr Robert Trail, minifter at Kettins, was admitted; and in October 1761, was preferred to the Divinity Chair

---

* The Earl of Airly, Lord Defkford, and the other heritors, unanimoufly fubmitted the terms of the disjunction, and amount of ftipend, to Patrick Archbifhop of Glafgow, and John Bifhop of Rofs. Accordingly, thefe arbiters fettled the boundaries of the two parifhes, and fixed the *quantum* of ftipend payable to each minifter, at $3\frac{1}{2}$ chalders of victual, and 350 merks of money, with the vicarage teinds *ipfa corpora.* This judgment was confirmed by the Lords Commiffioners of Teinds.

Chair in the Univerſity of Glaſgow. He was ſucceeded by
Mr Andrew Skene, miniſter of Keith, who died at Bath, in
December 1792.

The preſent incumbent, Mr Abercromby Gordon, was
admitted in Auguſt 1793.

The pariſh church was built in the years 1789 and 1790,
after the model of the new church at Dundee ; of which
Mr Pennant ſays, " It is built in a ſtile that does credit to
" the place, and ſhews an enlargement of mind in the Pref-
" byterians, who now begin to think that the Lord may be
" praiſed in beauty of holineſs."

The body of the church meaſures 80 feet in length, and
50 of breadth, within the walls. It is of proportionable
height. Four Ionic columns ſupport the galleries, which
form five ſides of an octagon, and are high and ſpacious.
The church is elegantly finiſhed within, and, excluſive of
roomy paſſages, will contain 1500 perſons. The pulpit is
perhaps raiſed to an incommodious height, being an aſcent
of 21 ſteps. Some of my brethren, accuſtomed to a more
humble *roſtrum*, decline officiating in ſo elevated a ſituation, and are ready to exclaim with the poet,

> ——————————— How fearful
> And dizzy 'tis, to caſt one's eyes ſo low !
> ——————————— I'll look no more,
> Leſt my brain turn, and the deficient ſight
> Topple down headlong.   SHAKESPEARE.

The roof is a curious and maſſy ſtructure. It has ten principal couples, whoſe beams extend the whole width of the
houſe, and ſupport the cieling. The couples are ſtrongly
bound with iron, having 700 pounds weight on each.

The ſpire ſtill remains in an unfiniſhed ſtate, which gives
the whole building a heavy and awkward appearance. It
is intended, however, to reſume the work next ſeaſon. The

The church has already coft L. 2400. The old church was taken down only laft year, excepting an ancient vaulted aifle, on the fouth fide, now a burying place of Lord Banff's family.

By a late decree of augmentation, the minifter's ftipend is 60 bolls barley, 52 bolls meal, L. 63 Sterling money. In this are included the vicarage tithes converted, and L. 5 as the allowance for communion-elements.

The glebe, which confifts of feven and one half acres, is a beautiful and fertile field, immediately adjoining the town.

The manfe was fubftantially repaired about three years ago, and is a comfortable refidence. For this purpofe, and for rebuilding the garden-walls, the heritors moft cheerfully granted L. 250, with an annual allowance to the prefent minifter of L. 10, for upholding thefe repairs.

The garden contains nearly half an acre of ground, and is a moft productive fpot.

The Earl of Findlater is patron. The Magiftrates alfo claim the right of patronage, and have been in habit of formally protefting againft his Lordfhip's prefentation. It is apprehended, however, that fuch proteft can be of no avail in preferving their rights, unlefs made before the prefentation is received and fuftained by the prefbytery, a mode which has not been attended to in this inftance.

Banff is not a collegiate charge, though the numbers of the people would require, and the funds in the parifh are fufficient to endow, a fecond minifter. Befides the Eftablifhed Church, there are three places of worfhip in this town, the Epifcopal chapel, the church of Relief, and a Roman Catholic meeting-houfe.

From the ftatement of the Reverend Mr Skinner, late minifter of St Andrews Chapel, the numbers in his charge amount nearly to 300. Formerly they were divided, and

belonged

belonged partly to the communion of the Church of England, and partly to the Epifcopal Church of Scotland. But in the year 1792, when a bill paffed in Parliament, relieving the laity of the latter perfuafion from thofe forfeitures, penalties and difabilities, to which they had long been fubjected, both congregations, with a few exceptions, united under the fpiritual jurifdiction of the Bifhop of Aberdeen.

The chapel is conveniently fituated, neat and commodious, and has a well-toned fmall organ.

The poor are admitted to the benefit of the public funds of the parifh; in return for which, an annual collection is made in the chapel on Chriftmas evening, which the clergyman diftributes indifcriminately to the poor of other perfuafions.

The church of Relief was built in the year 1780, is fituated in the Seatown, and is a very commodious edifice. The congregation, which is numerous, is compofed partly of families refiding in Banff, and partly of people from neighbouring parifhes.

The numbers from this town and parifh, according to a communication of their minifter, are as follows :

From the town,	- -	360
Country diftrict,	- -	40
Total,	- -	400

Of thefe are faid to be examinable, 330.

The poor of this congregation likewife fhare in the benefit of the general funds; and a public collection is occafionally made in their church, for the relief of the poor at large, which is ufually committed to the difpofal of the parifh minifter.

Thofe

Thofe attending the Roman Catholic meetinghoufe from this parifh, according to the ftatement of their clergyman, are in number 96 ; of which, 74 are examinable.

Poor.—The funds for the maintenance of the numerous poor in this parifh are confiderable.

The permanent funds, valuing two inclofures of land at 25 years purchafe, amount to nearly L. 900 Sterling, including L. 200 allotted for the fupport of the poor's fchool.

Intereft of money, - -	L. 27	0 0
Land rent - -	14	0 0
Weekly collections for 1797, -	98	18 0
Penalties from delinquents, -	3	0 0
	L. 142	18 0

Poor who receive occafionally, -	60
Poor on the quarterly roll, - -	80
Ditto on the weekly roll, - -	10
Total, - - -	150

The poor on the quarterly roll receive from 2 s. 6 d. to 5 s. each ; thofe on the weekly lift are generally allowed 1 s. each.

Previous to the quarterly diftribution, an edict is regularly read from the precentor's defk, requiring the attendance of heritors, magiftrates, &c.

Befides the ordinary weekly collections, there is generally an annual voluntary fubfcription, for the relief of poor families during the rigour of winter *.

Here

* This feafon the Ladies have generoufly fubfcribed a fum for a falary to a fick-nurfe, for attending the poor during illnefs.

Here is a ſmall hoſpital or bede-houſe, which affords lodging to eight poor decayed women. It has no other endowment than what is derived from the parochial funds, and the donations of charitable individuals *.

In few places are the poor ſupplied with more liberality than in Banff. Hence the great number of this deſcription who reſort hither from neighbouring pariſhes, and become ſtationary. At the ſame time, it may be remarked, that here, as in moſt other towns, indigence is often marked with the appearance of greater wretchedneſs than in country villages, or the ſolitary cottage.

Thoſe who are entruſted with the management of the poor's funds, have too frequent cauſe to obſerve, and to lament, that our charitable contributions, intended as the reward of merit, or the refuge of misfortune, are ſometimes, and unavoidably, beſtowed on the indolent, the intemperate, and the undeſerving, whether natives or ſtrangers. But, " to do the beſt, (obſerves an eloquent writer), can " ſeldom be the lot of man ; it is ſufficient if, when oppor- " tunities are preſented, he is ready to do good. How " little virtue could be practiſed, if beneficence were to " wait always for the moſt proper objects, and the nobleſt " occaſions ; occaſions that may never happen, and objects " that may never be found."

Antiquities.—Few remains of antiquity are to be ſeen in this pariſh, to attract obſervation. Of theſe few, the old religious houſes merit a place in this account.

Here

* Mr George Smith, a native of this county, lately bequeathed L. 1000 Sterling to the Magiſtrates of Banff, for the expreſs purpoſe of building an hoſpital or infirmary. The money becomes ſoon payable, and ſuch an uſeful inſtitution will prove a moſt ſubſtantial benefit to this part of the country, ſo far diſtant from the Infirmary at Aberdeen.

Here was a convent of Carmelites, or White Friars, confecrated to the Virgin Mary. This order of mendicant friars derived their origin and name from Mount Carmel, in Syria. St Lewis, King of France, returning from Afia, brought along with him fome of this fect, whom he eftablifhed in Paris. They were afterwards divided into 32 provinces, of which Scotland was the 13th. They were denominated White Friars, from their exterior drefs. It feems probable, that a convent of thefe Carmelites was eftablifhed in Banff, by Alexander III.; although the firft Sovereign grant refpecting it on record, is dated " Apud " Sconam, 1mo die Aug. 1324," confirming, &c. " Deo, " beatæ Mariæ Virgini, et religiofis fratribus ordinis de " Monte Carmelite, capellam beatæ Mariæ juxta villam " de Banff, una cum doto ad eandem capellam pertinente, " ad ædificandam ibidem ecclefiam, et alios domos fui or- " dinis, et ad inhabitandum Dom. locum eum fratribus " ejufdem ordinis, prefenti pontifice ejufdem fratribus fpe- " cialiter eft conceffum : præterea, damus et concedimus " hac prefta carta noftra, confirm. fratribus ibidem Deo " fervientibus, et pro fervituris, illam davatum terræ *, " cum pertinentiis quæ ad dictam capellam ante prefentem " collationem noftram pertinere folebant, ad inveniendum " panem, vinum, et ceram, ad cultum Domini ibidem di- " vinius exercendum."

The habit of the order was white, and on the lower part of their mantle were feveral rolls of ftuff. But this habit being difagreeable to the people, Pope Honorius IV. or- dered them to change their garb. Accordingly, they laid

afide

---

* This is the fine plain called the Daw-haugh, on which Duff Houfe ftands. This field, together with fandy hills, &c. made a davoch of land, fuppofed to contain 416 acres. *Vide Statiftical Report of Rhynie.*

aside the bands or rolls from their mantle, and wore afterwards a white cloak, above a grey or tawny gown.

The arms they assumed was a representation of the Virgin Mary, and of our Saviour, elevated on a temple; and below, the figure of a Carmelite, in his pontificals, and in a kneeling posture.

Sir Walter Ogilvie of Denlugas, eager to acquire an addition of landed property, laid in his claim, before the Reformation, for a gift of this religious convent, and obtained a grant thereof, *anno* 1544 *. The family of Denlugas retained possession of these heritages till 1630, when they became the property of the Earl of Airly, and in 1690 were purchased by the Laird of Bracco, ancestor of Lord Fife. The superiority, with the feu-duties, were gifted by James VI. to the King's College of Aberdeen, and bought from them, in 1752, by the Earl of Fife.

Two of the Carmelite cells are still to be seen, near the old church, in a pretty entire state.

The beautiful green mount in Lord Fife's park, and another of inferior size, situated in the middle of the town, formed a part of the Carmelites territory. These mounts appear to have been chiefly the work of art, and are supposed to be the labours of pennance enjoined by the fraternity.

On the mount in Duff House park, are still to be remembered the ruins and foundation of their chapel, around which was the consecrated ground of the sepulchre. Here many bones of the dead were found, and by the care of Lord Fife deposited in a large urn, elevated on a pedestal,

near

---

* To this grant William Smith, Prior of the Carmelites in Banff, Sir John Christofom, Prior at Aberdeen, and several other brethren, are subscribers.

near the mount. In the fame ground, on an eminence, overhanging the river, his Lordfhip has built an elegant maufoleum. It is of Gothic architecture, furrounded with fhrubbery,

" The cyprefs and the yew's funereal fhade,"

and forms a ftriking ornament to the park. The windows are of painted glafs, in cafements of ftone, and in front are placed two beautiful figures in ftatuary, emblematical of Faith and Hope.

Among the monuments in the maufoleum, is one of curious fculpture, and great antiquity, facred to the memory of John Duff of Maldavat, an anceftor of Lord Fife. It was brought hither a few years ago, together with the afhes of the deceafed, from the family burying-place, in the aifle of Cullen. In this monument is rudely fculptured the figure of a warrior in full coat of armour, with this infcription, " Hic jacet Johanes Duf. de Maldavat. et Baldavi. " obiit 2 Julii. 1404," &c *.

The monument of greateft antiquity in the church, feems to be that in Lord Banff's aifle, with the following infcription :

Ano Dni 1558. 29 Nove
Obiit. Valterus. Ogilvy. de. Dvnlvgvs. Miles.
Prepofit⁵. Huj⁵. Urbis, &c †.

Caftle

---

* The late reverend and ingenious Mr Cordiner, of this place, in the 24th number of his Remarkable Ruins, &c. in North Britain, has given an elegant delineation of this ancient monument, accompanied with a fhort defcription of it, and of the other monuments in Lord Fife's Maufoleum.

† As a fpecimen of the verfification of ancient epitaphs in this parifh, the following are fubjoined :

Lo,

Castle of Banff.—The Castle of Banff was a conftabulary of old, fuch as Cullen, Elgin, Forres, and Nairn. It was a place of ftrength, and faid to be oecafionally the refidence of the King, when vifiting this part of his dominions. In his Majefty's abfence, it was the meffuage of the thane, fheriff, or conftable, and the feat where juftice was adminiftered.

By the public records it appears, that Walter de Leflie obtained a charter, dated at Perth, 1364, of many lands, among others, of Blairfhinnoch in this parifh, for furnifhing to the King a foldier to attend him, at three head courts: "Apud Caftrum de Banffe." The office of fheriff continued annexed to the caftle till 1636, when the fheriffdom was refigned by the Earl of Buchan to Sir James Baird of Auchmedden; and the caftle to Mr Sharp, father of the Archbifhop of St Andrew's.

In 1683 Sir —— Sharp of Stonyhill difponed the Caftle of Banff to Provoft Leflie of Kininvie, from whom the family of Findlater afterwards derived their right of property.

The

Lo, here interred, lies the pretious duft of that renowned   -   *Defaced.*

   Soul faving Seton,
   Preacher in this Town,
   The Key of Knowledge,
   And Glory of the Gown.   -   -   *Date defaced.*

On John Andrew, town-clerk of Banff, *anno* 16—.
   Here lies a Man whofe Tongue and Pen
   Did what they could to profit Men,
   His life did prove moft Chriftian,
   So refts, to rife to Glore again.

In the church-yard is a handfome pyramidical monument, with an elegant infcription on white marble, to the memory of the late Admiral Gordon and his fon.

The caftle and adjoining grounds hold of the Crown blench, and pay neither cefs, ftipend, nor any burden whatever. The fheriff's office was refigned in 1681, by Baird of Auchmedden, to the Earl of Findlater, who enjoyed the right till the abolition of heritable jurifdictions in 1748.

Part of the ancient wall is yet entire; and the remains of the moat and intrenchments are ftill vifible.

Excepting a fmall adjoining houfe, the refidence of Archbifhop Sharp's father, the caftle is now a plain modern building *. Its fituation is uncommonly pleafing and romantic, and few dwellings can boaft of a greater variety of charming profpects.

In the caftle are fome good paintings and prints; particularly a picture of the celebrated Jamiefon, by his own hand. He is reprefented fitting in his painting chamber, with his hat on, and his pallet before him. On the walls of his room feem carelefsly to be hung feveral productions of his various pencil.

Near to the caftle was fituated the chaplainry of the Holy Rood, or *Sancti Crucis*, confecrated in commemoration of our Saviour's fufferings. At what period, or by what founder, this chapel was erected, no information can be derived, either from tradition or ancient record. From an old regifter of the town-council, 1544, we learn, that this religious houfe lay within the liberties of the burgh, and comprehended, " terras pifcatorias vocatas vulgariter *Fifher's Lands,*

---

* This was long the refidence of the late Countefs Dowager of Findlater, a lady not more diftinguifhed by her high rank, than by the unaffuming manners, and unwearied benevolence, which adorned her character.

She had, indeed,

——— ——— ——— a tear for pity, and a hand
Open as day to melting charity.

" *Lands*, ex boreali, et occidentali partibus montis Caſtri
" de Banff *."

The Caſtle of Inchdrewer, on the eſtate of Lord Banff, is
ſituated on a fine riſing ground, about four miles ſouth-weſt
of the town. It is ſtill entire and habitable. By the ſtile
of its architecture, it ſeems to have been built about the
time of King James IV. or V. This is the opinion of the
celebrated Groſe, who in his book of Antiquities has given
a correct view of this caſtle †.

Two fields, near the confines of this pariſh, are diſtinguiſhed by the names of Arrdane and Swordane. Whether
theſe have ever been the ſcenes of battle, and derived their
names from the arrows and ſwords of the Danes, muſt be
left to more able antiquaries to explore and determine.

Population.—The writer of this report is not poſſeſſed of
materials ſufficient to enable him to aſcertain, with preciſion,
the number of inhabitants in this pariſh at former periods.
It is obvious, however, that the great increaſe of buildings,
in different parts of the town, has occaſioned a proportionable increaſe of population.

It appears from a liſt drawn up by the late miniſter, in
the year 1782, that the numbers in the town then were
2380. By a very accurate roll made up 1797, the number is,

In the town,	-	-	2860
Country diſtrict,	-	-	650
			3510

The

* The great cauſes aſſigned for this foundation, were, " the veneration
" of the provoſts, et ad extirpandum hereſum dicti conventi, et propitio
" magni Dei, et promotam orthodoxam fidem."

† Sir George Ogilvie of Dunlugas, who was created a Baronet by King
Charles I. on 10th July 1627, in the ſame year obtained a charter under
the

The following is an abstract of marriages and births in the whole parish, from 1791 to 1797 inclusive.

Years.	Marriages.	Births.
1791	33	46
92	33	51
93	19	59
94	22	48
95	18	44
96	12	35
97	39	36
Average of marriages,	- -	$25\frac{1}{7}$
———— of births,	- -	$44\frac{5}{7}$

No authentic register of burials has been kept for several years.

It is believed that the population in the country district of the parish has rather decreased, and for which, nearly the same causes may be assigned with those detailed in various Statistical Reports.

Parents are sometimes negligent in recording the names of their children in the parish register. Since the late enrolment for the militia, when the inconvenience of such neglect was often felt, the people are become more attentive in this respect.

Longevity.—Although there are no instances of remarkable longevity in this parish, many of the inhabitants attain a good old age. A tradesman lately died, in full possession of his faculties, long past his ninetieth year. During the present

the Great Seal, of the lands of the barony of Inchdrewer. He was afterwards raised to the dignity of peerage, by the title of Lord Ogilvie of Banff, by letters patent to him and the heirs-male of his body, dated 31st August 1642.

present week, (the first of the year 1798), have died four
respectable characters, whose joint ages amounted to 314
years.—The writer of this Report baptized a child about
18 months ago, whose mother, grandmother, great grandfather, and great great grandmother, (five generations in a
direct line), are all alive.

Air, Climate, Diseases, &c.—If the situation of Banff is
considered with regard to those circumstances which have
an influence on the health of the inhabitants, there are many advantages in this view which it possesses in an eminent
degree.

The town stands on a rising ground, and the houses in
general are built on a dry hard stratum, in many places, in-
termixed with sand.

Such a situation is certainly more favourable to a free
circulation of air than a dead flat; and the dry foundation
of the houses prevents those deleterious consequences which
arise from breathing within doors a damp unwholesome at-
mosphere. From the river, flowing immediately below
the town, there are no swamps in its neighbourhood; nor
in any direction around it are there any stagnating waters,
whose noxious effluvia might prove injurious to health.
Thus, from local situation, are the inhabitants exempted
from a source of contagion, whence intermittents, and many
low fevers, derive their origin. On the other hand, as the
town lies open to the north and north-east, the cold winds
of these points, blowing immediately from the sea, renders
the inhabitants of this place liable to rheumatism, coughs,
pectoral complaints, sore throats, and inflammatory fevers.
The fevers of a different complexion, which sometimes prevail, are to be considered, upon the most probable and rational principles, as originating from irregularities in living,
from contagion, and, among the lower class of people, from
                                                      small,

fmall, confined, and often crowded houfes, where the air breathed is foul and noxious, and from inattention to cleanlinefs, particularly of bed and bed-clothes, which are too feldom wafhed, and very rarely ventilated.

Such exifting caufes will, in all fituations, have an influence in producing fevers of a malignant kind, or of altering the type of thofe which, upon their firft attack, appear inflammatory.

A reformation in regard to the above particulars, as far as it could be effected, would prove of the moft beneficial confequences.

The advantages attending local fituation would be much improved, and rendered more complete, by conducting into the town, from fprings in the neighbourhood, a fufficient fupply of good wholefome water. This meafure, though expenfive, is practicable, and its expediency is apparent from this circumftance, that the water in general, over the whole town, is more or lefs hard and brackifh.

Proper regulations eftablifhed, enforced, and uniformly maintained, for keeping the ftreets perfectly clean, and free from all baneful and putrid fubftances, would be highly conducive to health and comfort.

An infectious fever prevailed here, with unufual violence, about the year 1782. Unwholefome food, particularly an immoderate ufe of potatoes, (that year of a bad kind), were among the fecondary caufes to which this fever was afcribed.

Mr Skene, the late minifter of this parifh, a gentleman alike diftinguifhed by his great medical knowledge, and his humane gratuitous practice, wrote a fmall treatife on this fever, in form of a " Serious Addrefs to the People," &c.

This fhort addrefs, which Provoft Robinfon was at the expence of printing and publifhing, contained feveral plain fenfible inftructions refpecting the prevention and treatment of the difeafe, and points out the means by which health

may

may be preserved from every disorder of an infectious nature *.

Inoculation.—The practice of inoculation for the small-pox is by no means become general among the lower ranks. The too tender consciences of the superstitious interpose, to rob them of its salutary benefits. We tempt God, say they, by voluntarily bringing on a disease which we might possibly have escaped : We throw ourselves in the way of danger ; we distrust the Providence of Almighty God, who is all-sufficient to deliver us.

These words have, indeed, the appearance and the voice of piety, but they have nothing else. There are few of the actions of life to which the objection might not more or less apply. Does not the man, for instance, equally tempt God, who, apprehending a mortification in one of his limbs, submits to lose it by the operation of a surgeon. Perhaps the dreaded mortification might not have taken place, and the patient sacrifices his life to his timid caution. Yet no man of common sense will dispute, that the practice of amputation is salutary on the whole, and is the means of preserving many valuable lives to the community †.

Mineral

---

* Among other advices, Mr Skene strenuously recommends great attention to cleanliness, washing the chamber of the sick person with soap and hot water, and, upon recovery of the patient, that his apartment should be white-washed with lime, fresh slacked, laid on hot, and the windows opened every day.

† The deaths by the natural small-pox are generally allowed to be in the proportion of one in six, in seven at the very least, but oftener one in five.

Now, I presume it will be thought moderate to compute, that not above one in forty escape having the distemper, during the course of their lives. Let it be observed, then, in the first place, there are thirty-nine to
one

Mineral Springs.—As a matter connected with the health of the inhabitants of this place, and, under proper management, beneficial to the public at large, it may be proper to mention a powerful chalybeat spring, (the Well of Boindie), within two short miles of Banff.

In chronic cases, attended with debility and relaxation, where tonic medicines are admissible, the water is used with manifest advantage ; but, unfortunately, this well is considered by the country people at large as a Panacea, and resorted to as such by great numbers, afflicted with diseases very opposite in their natures. The result is what may naturally be inferred ; many are cured or relieved, while others return not only disappointed of expected benefit, but suffering under aggravated complaints. They sometimes, too, place as much dependence on the quantity, as on the quality, of the water. Having but little time to spare to the fashionable avocations of a watering-place, they are very diligent during their stay, and are often known to swallow

three

---

one against escaping the infection ; and then there are only five chances in favour of a person escaping with life. The whole chances in his favour, therefore, are but five and one-fortieth, or fix at most ; whereas, by authentic accounts of some late general inoculations, it appears, that out of 416 only one died. On other occasions the proportion has been one in 500. A risk scarcely to be accounted for, when we consider what different constitutions must exist among such a number of patients, and the strong probability of the death of fully that number, among so many infants, from other disorders, if inoculation had been entirely out of the question. See an admirable Sermon on the Lawfulness of Inoculation, by G. Gregory, F. A. S. author of Essays Historical and Moral.

A surgeon in the north, presuming that self-interest has a stronger hold on man than superstition, has lately opened a policy of insurance for the smallpox ! If a subscriber gives him two guineas for inoculating his child, the surgeon, in the event of the child's death, pays ten guineas to the parent. For every guinea subscribed, four guineas ; for one half guinea, two guineas ; and for a crown, one guinea.

three gallons a-day of the ſalutiferous ſtream, beſides a reaſonable potion of ſea-water.

Roads and Bridges.—The poſt-road, as far as it extends
through this pariſh, is kept in excellent repair. The roads
leading to the inland parts of the country, being leſs attended to, are not in ſuch good order. The propoſed eſtabliſhment of turnpikes muſt contribute much to the general
improvement of this country. If the line is adhered to,
which is already marked out in the ſurveyor's plan, the
new road from Banff to Turreff, though not much ſhortened
in point of diſtance, will oft beguile the traveller of his
time, by the varied and beautiful ſcenery which will occupy his attention.

The former fine bridge over the Doveran was ſwept a-
way by a violent flood in 1768. Another has ſince been
built, at the expence of Government, a little higher up the
river, where it is ſuppoſed to be leſs in danger from the riſe
of the water. It is a handſome ſtructure, conſiſting of ſeven
arches *.

Harbour and Shipping.—Of old, boats and trading veſſels
lay within the river, extending along the banks where the
bulwark now is.

We learn from tradition, that the courſe of the Doveran,
near its influx, was conſiderably more eaſtward than at preſent. It is ſaid to have emptied itſelf at the Craig of Down,
now Macduff.

The

---

* As an inſtance of the accuracy of ſome modern travellers, a large
quarto journal, lately publiſhed, informs us, that in Banff there is a fine
bridge of *nine* arches over the river *Dive*. The river is ſometimes ſpelled
Doveran, and ſometimes Deveron. In the Gaelic language it ſignifies the
Black Water, and is ſo named towards its ſource in Aberdeenſhire.

The traditional report is corroborated by some ancient grants in favour of the Earl of Buchan, in which are specified " the salmon-fishings at the mouth of the river, and in " the sea," jacentes apud Down.

That piece of low ground on the east side of the river, called the Gaws, now a part of Lord Fife's pleasure-grounds, was lately the property of the town, is still within the royalty, and, it is highly presumable, formerly lay on the west bank of the river, which divided the earldom of Buchan from the county of Banff. The river, indeed, seems frequently to have altered its course ; sometimes passing in a straight line through the beach, and at other times winding to the west, near the Castlehill, where it now runs, and which has been its channel for several years past.

The stream has sometimes been so small, as not to have currency sufficient to keep the passage open, the water oozing through the bank of gravel, and preventing the entrance and departure of the smallest boat.

Hence arose the necessity of building a harbour in a more convenient situation. It was begun so early as the year 1625, westward of the river mouth. The attempt was frequently frustrated, and as often resumed. After various interruptions, and repeated applications to Parliament, and to the Convention of Burghs *, the work was finished about the

* The Convention of Burghs appointed the Commissioners from Aberdeen, Elgin, Invernefs, &c. as a Committee, to examine and report the true state of the harbour, &c. Accordingly, these Commissioners met at Banff, and reported, " That the trade appeared for years past to increase : " That the merchants had very enterprising genius, but discouraged by the " bar on the mouth of the river, insomuch, that it often happened from " Candlemas to Martinmas the water mouth was in no condition to receive " a boat ; and that the last season, three ships, after being loaded, were " locked in by the bank of gravel, so that 20 coaches might pass in a breast " dry: And farther declared, That the place was exceedingly well situated " for

the year 1775; and is now a most useful and commodious harbour.

The shipping belonging to this port are at present 22 sail; of which 8 are brigantines, from 100 to 210 tons each; and 14 sail are sloops, chiefly of 60, 80 and 100 tons.

Vessels.	Tonnage.	No. of Men.
22	1943	137

Some of these vessels are employed in the London trade.

Shipbuilding is carried on here with success. One builder, eminent in his profession, usually employs 12 men, and has just finished a fine brigantine of 190 tons *.

Trade and Commerce.—The state of the trade and commerce of this town may be judged of from the preceding Table of the shipping, and from the following Abstract Accounts of the Imports and Exports, &c. from the 5th January 1795 to the 5th of January 1797, inclusive.

ABSTRACT

" for trade, the piers good, water deep, and access easy with northerly
" winds; adding, that, from Aberdeen to Inverness, there is not a harbour
" that any ship dared venture, when the wind blew hard from that *airth*."

At this harbour the burgesses and landholders of the town have the privilege of importing freestone and slate without payment of shore-dues; and for other articles they only pay the half of the usual allowance of harbour dues.

* The distressing intelligence has been lately received, of the total loss of one of these sloops, of 70 tons, with 6 men.

Port of BANFF.—ABSTRACT ACCOUNT of Goods imported, brought and sent Coast-ways, to and from this Port, from 5th January 1795 to 5th January 1797.

Year ending 5th January 1796.	Iron. Bars	Salmon Barrels	Butter and Cheese Cwt.	Salmon. Kitts	Meal. Quarters.	Barley. Quarters.	Oats. Quarters.	Cod & Ling fish. No.
Foreign trade inwards,	3882	- -	- -	- -	- -	- -	- -	- -
Coast trade outwards,	- -	122	434	1412	2361	2196	3490	5500
Ditto inwards,	800	- -	- -	- -	- -	- -	- -	- -
Year ending 5th January 1797.								
Foreign trade inwards,	3550	- -	- -	- -	- -	- -	- -	- -
Coast trade outwards,	- -	123	701	732	6897	255	600	54,400
Ditto inwards,	394	- -	- -	- -	370	100	79	- -

Year ending 5th January 1796.	Wheat. Quarters.	Flour. Bushels.	Wool. Cwt.	Bricks. No.	Tiles. No.	Spirits. Gallons.	Wine. Gallons.	Salt. Bushels.
Foreign trade inwards,	- -	- -	- -	- -	- -	- -	- -	- -
Coast trade outwards,	- -	- -	- -	- -	- -	- -	- -	- -
Ditto inwards,	- -	815	226	11,800	2500	5258	2426	7766
Year ending 5th January 1797.								
Foreign trade inwards,	- -	- -	- -	- -	- -	- -	- -	- -
Coast trade outwards,	170	- -	- -	5600	46,645	- -	- -	- -
Ditto inwards,	- -	995	210	2000	- -	1576	2420	8094

N. B. Very little foreign trade since the commencement of the war.

Port of BANFF.—An Account of the Quantity of English Coals and Cinders, Scots Coals and Culm, brought
Coast-ways into this Port, from the 5th January 1795 to
5th January 1797.

| | Quantities of English | | | | Quantities of Scotch | |
| | Coals. | | Cinders. | | Coals. | Culm. |
	Chalders.	Bushels.	Chald.	Bush.	Tons.	Cwt.	Chalders.
From 5th January 1795 to 5th January 1796.	1745	12	43	0	281	15	7
From 5th January 1796 to 5th January 1797.	1994	35	27	0	617	10	0

N. B. The great increase in the quantity of coals imported
in the year 1796, was occasioned by the demands from
the country, where peat, the usual fuel, had been much
destroyed by the rains of that season.

Salmon-fishing.—The Doveran is richly stored with salmon and trout, and yields a very handsome revenue to the
principal proprietor, the Earl of Fife.

In the year 1757, the late Lord Fife entered into contract with a gentleman in Aberdeen, by which he sold the
fresh salmon of the Doveran, from 29th September to 15th
May, at three halfpence a pound. The pound of salmon
now generally sells at sixpence, and early in the season at
nine-pence.

Comparative

Comparative ſtatement of the rent of the ſalmon-fiſhing at different periods:

Years.	Rent.
1713	L. 299 6 6
1729	310 13 4
1748	441 11 2
1762	600 0 0
1778	850 0 0
1795	1250 0 0

Provoſt Robinſon has long enjoyed the leaſe of the fiſhings, and generally employs from 80 to 100 men in the different departments of the trade.

The fiſhing commences 30th November, and is given up 29th September.

The various expences attending the fiſhing amount to a ſum at leaſt double of the yearly rent.

The cruives are about a mile from the ſea, and the whole extent of the river-fiſhing, including its windings, does not much exceed four miles *.

Manufactures

---

* The preſervation of ſalmon ſeems very early to have attracted the attention of the Legiſlature. Alexander II. anno 1214, enacted at Perth, upon Thurſday, " the feaſt of St Margaret, that the ſtream ſhall in all parts " be ſwo (ſo) free, that ane ſwine of the age of three years, well fed, " may turn himſelf within the ſtream round about, ſwo that his ſnout nor " tail ſhall not touch the bank or ſide of the water." Hence, probably, the firſt conſtruction of the cruives in Scotland.

The ſalmon is ſaid to breed or caſt his ſpawn in moſt rivers in the month of Auguſt. They depoſit their eggs or ſpawn in a ſafe place, in the gravel, and then leave it to their Creator's protection. Sir Francis Bacon obſerves, " the age of a ſalmon exceeds not ten years. His growth is very " ſudden, ſo that after he has got into the ſea, he becomes from a ſamlet, " not ſo big as a gudgeon, to be a ſalmon, in as ſhort a time as a goſling " becomes a gooſe."

r.

Manufactures.—The thread and linen manufactures were carried on here, a few years ago, to a very great extent.

For the thread manufacture alone 3500 mats of Dutch flax were annually imported; which, at an average of L. 3, 5 s. each, cost upwards of L. 11,000 Sterling. The operation of milling and heckling employed about 60 men. When given out to spin, it afforded employment for 4000 individuals; yielded 150,000 spindles of yarn, which circulated about L. 10,000 among the spinners. The doubling and twisting the yarn, which was done in Banff, employed about 200 women and children, and at the bleachfield, engaged the labour and attention of 40 people more. These threads, when sent to Nottingham or Leicester, were valued at L. 30,000 Sterling.

This productive and useful branch has since given place to the stocking manufacture, which is also conducted on a very extensive scale by Messrs Robinsons.

The stockings are wove on a highly improved frame, of which these gentlemen are the sole patentees.

They have 150 of these frames, for the manufacturing of silk, cotton, and worsted stockings. From the nature of the work, and the advanced state of the mechanical arts, which has necessarily abridged human labour, this manufacture does not offer employment to such numbers as the branch formerly mentioned. In the several departments of the work, however, about 560 persons of different descriptions are constantly engaged.

Young

It is a curious circumstance, and perhaps but little known, that the chief consumption of pickled salmon, when first in season, and when prices are high, is by the lowest classes of the people in London. The middle ranks, and those immediately above them, abstain generally from such indulgences until the prices are moderate. See an admirable treatise on the Police of the Metropolis, by P. Colquhoun, Esq; L. L. D. late Provost of Glasgow, and now one of the Magistrates of the Police for London.

Young men, from 14 to 16 years of age, will fometimes make 40 pairs worfted ftockings in one week, and at the ufual hours allotted to labour. Thefe ftockings generally fell at 3 s. 6 d. a pair.

The medium gain of the frame-worker may amount to 7 s. 6 d. or 8 s. a week.

The worfted is chiefly fpun on the two-handed Leicefter-fhire wheel.

A woman who is a diligent and capable fpinner, will earn from 5 s. to 6 s. weekly. The average gains are from 2 s. 6 d. to 3 s.

A confiderable quantity of the ftockings are difpofed of in wholefale, to the fhopkeepers in the town and country; but the principal market for the manufacture is London.

The linen trade is ftill continued, though on a more con-tracted fcale than formerly. This branch may now employ about 20 weavers.

Soap and Candles.—A foap and candle work, belonging to a company in Banff, employs a manager and four men, and pays annually to Government L. 5 ० Ste̦ling.

Brewery.—The brewing of ale, beer, and porter. is car-ried on here to a confiderable extent. The annual confump-tion of barley is generally 1200 bolls; and the duty to Go-vernment L. 700. The number of hands employed amount to eight. The ftrong beer has long been in high repute, and in great demand, from various and diftant parts of the country. The porter, when kept in bottle about a year, is fufficiently palatab e, and has beeen known fometimes to deceive the tafte of a connoiffeur in that wholefome be-veridge.

A

A Rope and Sail Manufacture has for some time been carried on here, though not to great extent.

Brick and T le Work.—The late Dr Saunders of this place, a gentleman of enterprising spirit, established, several years ago, a brick and tile work on his farm, about two miles from the town. It is still carried on with success, (and on an extensive plan), by his son. The work possesses great advantages from its local situation, having the command of a small harbou for the importation of coals, and for exporting part of the produce of the manufacture. Mr Saunders generally employs eight or nine men, besides an overseer.

A brickwork on a smaller scale has lately been set on foot in the vicinty of the town.

In the various branches of mechanical industry, this town can boast of several eminent workmen ; but on this article the limits of a Statistical Report do not allow of a minute detail.

Markets.—There is a regular weekly market. It is held on Friday, and is well supplied with provisions of all kinds. There are also in Banff three annual fairs.

Post-Office.—The revenue arising from the Post-Office has increased since the establishment of a daily mail. It amounts to nearly L. 800 *per annum.*

Great hopes are entertained of a still earlier dispatch of the mails from Edinburgh, a measure which would be attended with signal advantages to the towns north of the metropolis.

Banking Offices.—The Bank of Scotland, and the Banking Company in Aberdeen, have each of them established

2

a branch in this town. Meffrs Reid and Imlach, the agents, tranfact bufinefs to the extent of L. 150,000 to L. 200,000 *per annum.*

Battery.—During the late war, a fmall battery was erected on the high ground near the harbour. It is nearly of the half-moon conftruction, with turf embrafures *, and mounts two 18 pounders, and four 12 pounders, befides two field pieces.

On one fide of the gateway is fituated the ftore-houfe and powder-magazine, on the other a guard-room and officer's apartment.

Having an extenfive command of the bay, this battery might afford protection againft the depredations of a fingle privateer; but whether fuch works, thinly fcattered along the coaft, would prove of fubftantial fervice in the event of invafion, is a point fomewhat problematical †.

Military Affociations.—The Banff-fhire Volunteers confift of 16 companies, under the command of Colonel the Right Honourable the Earl of Fife, Lord-lieutenant of the county.

That

---

* The embrafure in batteries is now condemned by able engineers, and the low parapet recommended in its room, fo that the guns may be pointed in any direction within the fcope of the work.

† Colonel Dirom, a native of this town, in his ingenious " Plans for the " Defence of Great Britain," &c. obferves, " Indeed it is impoffible to " line the coaft of an extenfive country in fuch a manner with batteries, as " to protect it from an invading enemy ; for they can be placed in few fi.. " tuations in which they may not be avoided : and if otherwife, the guns " in them are generally fo unwieldy and difficult to traverfe, that they may " be approached and ftormed without much danger to the affailants. Bat- " teries ought therefore to be erected with great caution, and perhaps on- " ly in fituations ftrong by nature, where they may not eafily be furprifed " or attacked on the land-fide."

That part of the corps more particularly attached to the town of Banff, comprehends the numbers following, viz.:

Colonel,	- -	1
Lieutenant-colonel,	- -	1
Major,	- - -	1
Captains,	- -	7
1ſt Lieutenants,	- -	9
2d Lieutenants,	- -	9
Staff. { Chaplain,	- -	1
Adjutant,	- -	1
Quarter-maſter,	- -	1
Surgeon,	- -	1
Sergeants,	- -	36
Drummers,	- -	18
Rank and file,	- -	614

Total effective,   -   700

Of theſe, 4 companies are ſtationed in the town of Banff,

1 in Macduff,
1 at Rothiemay,
1 at Grange,
1 at Portſoy,
1 at Cullen.

Total,   9

The Strathalvah and Boyn Volunteers, including officers, conſiſt of   -   222

The Enzie Volunteers,   -   296

Total in the county of Banff,   -   1218

The firſt companies of the Banff Volunteers were offered and accepted in November 1794; but a certain number of men had previouſly, and from the commencement of the

preſent

prefent war, been trained to the exercife of the great guns
at the battery.

Befides the Volunteer Corps, there were returned to the
Privy Council, by the Lieutenancy of the county, upon
the 29th day of September laft, 45 men from this parifh,
as falling within the defcription comprehended in the late
Militia Act.

Schools.—The public fchools of Banff, which are entirely
under the direction of the Magiftrates, (for there is no parochial eftablifhment), were connected together, and converted into an academy, in the year 1786. The feveral
arrangements in this academy were made, and the teachers
recommended by Dr George Chapman *, formerly rector
of the Grammar-fchool at Dumfries, and who for fome
years fuperintended the eftablifhments for education in this
place.

The plan of inftruction which Dr Chapman laid down
has been ftrictly adhered to by the different teachers, and
has anfwered the expectations of all concerned. The feminary is at prefent in a flourifhing ftate.

At the annual public examination in Auguft 1797, the
number of daily fcholars amounted to 180.

The following branches of education are taught in this
academy, by the head mafter and four affiftants :

I. The Claffics, Latin and Greek, with geography, and
the principles of rhetoric.

II. Writing, arithmetic, book-keeping, menfuration, algebra, practical geometry, and navigation.

III. The French and Englifh languages, &c.

By

* Dr Chapman was born in this neighbourhood. His extenfive knowledge as a fcholar, and his merit as an author on Education, are well
known.

The

By the care and exertions of the late miniſter, a charity
ſchool was founded ſome years ago, for the poor children
of the town and pariſh. The numbers uſually attending this
ſchool are from 25 to 30 children. They are taught to
read, and inſtructed in the principles of religious knowledge. For ſecuring an annual and permanent ſalary of
L. 20 to a well qualified teacher, the ſum of L. 400 was
ſunk in the hands of the Magiſtrates. This fund was raiſed
by the voluntary contributions of the landholders, the inhabitants, and occaſional viſitants, and by appropriating, with
conſent of the heritors, L. 200 of the poor's money.

The girls attending the ſchool are furniſhed with eaſy
and profitable work, by ſpinning wool for Meſſrs Robin-
ſons ſtocking manufacture *.

The provoſt, miniſter, and rector of the academy, are the
patrons of this ſchool.

Beſides theſe, there are two Engliſh ſchools, in different
parts of the town. The teachers, having no ſtated ſalaries,
depend entirely on the fees paid by the ſcholars.

Boarding Schools for young Ladies.—Here, too, are repu-
table boarding-ſchools, for the education of young ladies.
One of theſe is conducted by Miſſes Mitchels from England,

The principles on which this academy is conducted, are contained in Dr
Chapman's Treatiſe on Education, a fifth edition of which is lately publiſhed, and much approved of by the Reviewers.

To this edition the author has given a ſhort ſupplement, containing uſeful Obſervations on two Eſſays on Education lately publiſhed. He has
ſubjoined further Thoughts on the Inſtruction neceſſary for the lower ranks
of the People ; on the appointment of Parochial Schoolmaſters, and on the
Encouragement they ought to receive.

* Beſides a ſmall fund belonging to this ſchool, there is a public annual
collection made, for defraying the expences of ſome neceſſary clothing to
the poorer children.

land, who have lately fettled here, and whofe fuperior accomplifhments fully qualify them for fuperintending fuch
an inftitution.

At the other boarding-fchool, a qualified governefs from
Edinburgh affifts in the education of the young ladies.

Comparative Statement, &c.—It may prove entertaining
to fome readers to trace the progrefs of luxury in this parifh, and mark a few of the moft ftriking changes of half a
century.

1748

A gown of linfey-woolfey was the
ufual drefs of a laird's daughter,

Veild in a fimple robe, her beft at-
tire,

Beyond the pomp of drefs.——

THOMSON.

Her mother, indeed, who was dignified with the knightly title of lady,
appeared on great occafions in a filk
gown, and fine laces, which were
confidered as part of the parapher-
nalia deftined to the fucceeding generation.

Ladies feldom wore any other than
coloured ftockings.

The town could only boaft of one
filken pair, and thefe were black.

The occupation of milliner was totally unknown.

1748. A four-wheeled carriage
was a luxury feldom enjoyed, unlefs by the nobility.

A gentleman and his wife generally rode together on the fame
horfe.

Drawing-rooms and dining par-
lours were no lefs rare than carriages.

1798

The decoration of our perfons is
now become a more general ftudy a-
mong both fexes, and all ranks. In
order to accommodate their drefs to
the capricious rules of fafhion, there
is a frequent, and fome times a needlefs, recourfe to the " foreign aid of
" ornament."

The art millinery affords employment and profit to many; and every
trading veffel from London brings a
frefh affortment of dreffes, adjufted to
the prevailing mode.

1798. Poft-chaifes are now in general ufe.

Several private gentlemen keep
their carriages.

The pad is become the exclufive
property of the country good-wife.

The minifter of the parifh muft
have his drawing-room.

Mahogany was seldom seen, save in the tea-tray, the round folding table, and the corner cup-board.

1748. When wants were fewer, and easily supplied, most of the useful articles of merchandise might be procured in the same shop. The various designations of grocer, iron-monger, and haberdasher, were little known, and almost every trader, even although he did not traffick to foreign countries, was denominated merchant.

1748. A joyous company, after dinner, have been seen quaffing the wine of a dozen bottles from a single glass.

1748. Agreeable to Queen Mary's act of Parliament, A. D. 1563, all butcher-meat was carried to market *skin and birn*, and, agreeable to custom, was sold amidst abounding filth.

1748. The annual wages of a great man's butler was about L. 8 ; his valet, L. 5 ; and his other servants, L. 3.

The farmer had his ploughman for 13 s. 4 d. in the half-year, with the allowance of a pair shoes. The wages of a maid-servant, 6 s. 8 d.

1773. When Dr Johnson honoured Banff with a visit, he was pleased to observe, that the natives were more frugal of their glass, (in windows), than the English. They will often, says the Doctor, " in houses not other-

Mahogany is a species of timber in general use for articles of furniture ; and the corner press is superseded by the splendid side-board.

1798. The several distinctions of tradesmen are better understood.

As ministers to our luxury, we have in the same street an oil man, who advertised the sale of Quin sauce, Genoa capers, and Gorgona anchovies, &c. ; a confectioner, whose bills contain the delectable names of non-pareils, ice-cream, and apricot jelly, &c. ; and a perfumer, who deals in such rare articles, as Neapolitan cream for the face, Persian dentrifice for the teeth, and Asiatic balsam for the hair.

1798. A sober party sometimes meet, whose libation consists of a solitary bottle, with a dozen glasses.

1798. There are convenient slaughter-houses apart, and meat is brought to market seemly, and in good order.

1798. The nobleman pays at least in a quadruple ratio for his servants.

The wages of a ploughman vary from L. 10 to L. 12, and of a maid-servant from L. 3 to L. 3, 10 s. *per annum.*

1798. Many of our windows are furnished with weights and pullies. We think of the necessity of ventilating human habitations, where we may enjoy the luxury of fresh air, without resorting to the contrivance

" wife mean, compofe a fquare of two
" pieces, not joining like cracked glafs,
" but with one edge laid perhaps half
" an inch over the other. Their win-
" dows do not move upon hinges, but
" are pufhed up and drawn down in
" grooves. He that would have his
" window open, muft hold it with
" his hand, unlefs, what may fome-
" times be found among good contri-
" vers, there be a nail, which he may
" ftick into a hole, to keep it from
" falling *."

of a nail, and with very little affiftance from the hand.

**Comparative Statement of the Prices of Cattle, Sheep, Pro-
vifions, &c. at the above periods.**

1748

A draught ox, L. 1 : 13 : 4.
20 Sheep, fmall fize, L. 4.
Beef and mutton, one penny, and three
halfpence a pound.
A hen, together with a dozen eggs,
4 d.
Dozen eggs, 1 d.
Goofe, 2 s. a pair.
Turkey, 3 s. ditto.
Pigeons, three halfpence ditto.
14 Haddocks, three halfpence.
Claret fold at 1 s. a bottle.

1798

L. 15, L. 20, and L. 25.
L. 12.
Beef and mutton, 5½ d. and 6 d. *per* lb.

Hen, without eggs, 1 s. and 1 s. 3 d.

4 d. and 6 d.
5 s. 6 d.
7 s.
6 d.
1 s. 6 d.
Claret fells in the tavern at 6 s.

Difadvantages.—Among the difadvantages which this
town fuffers in a commercial view, the principal feems to
be the want of a cuftomhoufe.

At prefent, no goods can be fhipped or landed, nor any
veffels fail from this port, without procuring the ufual permit

* In juftice to Dr Johnfon, let it be remembered, that he acknowledged
" thefe diminutive obfervations detract from the dignity of writing, and
" therefore he communicated them with hefitation and dread."

mit from the cuftomhoufe at Aberdeen, a diftance of 45 miles.

To obtain the permiffion of unloading, the fhipmafter, after the dangers and fatigues of a fea-voyage, has generally to encounter, what, to a feaman, is often no lefs perilous and fatiguing, the labours of a land journey on horfeback. Were a deputation granted from the Board of Cuftoms to two or more qualified perfons refiding in Banff, to tranfaét the neceffary routine of bufinefs, it would certainly tend to promote the trade and manufaétures of this place, and of the country around. The expence attending fuch eftablifhment muft be truly inconfiderable, when weighed in the fcale with the advantages which would accrue from it.

A few years ago, we had the profpeét of obtaining fuch a deputation; but, it is believed, a premature and impolitic conteft, for the emoluments of office, fruftrated the defign.

The jarring interefts of contending parties, it is hoped, will not in the fame manner interfere, to deprive us of the advantages of military barracks.

The town-council have made an offer of ground for the purpofe, contiguous to the battery, and the meafure is fraught with beneficial confequences to the community, as well as to the military who may be ftationed in this quarter.

Town-Houfe and Prifon.—Laft feafon were laid the foundations of a new town-houfe and prifon. The principal part of the work is nearly finifhed, and the whole promifes to be a moft fubftantial and commodious building. The front of the town-houfe, including the fpire, extends 71 feet. It contains, on the ground-floor, the fheriff-court room, and county record-office. On the fecond flat, are
the

the town-council room and town-clerk's office. The third
flat contains a county hall, 48 feet long, 27 feet in breadth,
and 18 feet high. In the fame flat of the back buildings,
are two drawing rooms, 19 feet wide, and 33 feet long.
On the ground floor of the back buildings are two correc-
tion houfes, 33 feet long, and 18 feet in breadth. The fecond flat contains two civil prifons, 19 feet fquare, and two
criminal cells, 12 feet fquare.

In the conftruction of the gaol, the judicious improvements of the benevolent Mr Howard have been attended
to, in thofe effential refpects, air, water, and cleanlinefs *.

Farming Society.—The Banff-fhire Farming Society was
eftablifhed in the year 1785. This inftitution was defigned
to forward improvements in agriculture, to reward induftry, and to produce unanimity and focial intercoufe between the heritors and farmers of the country, whofe mutual intereft and advantage can never be fo great as when
they are infeparable. To have alfo under their confideration the neceffary and confiftent regulations for the police
of the country, and for the prevention of litigious pleas
among the country people, who are induced either by low
advice, or inflamed by petty prejudices †.

To lay down rules anfwerable to the ftatute acts of the
country ; to prevent the deftruction of planting, inclofures,
and green crops in the fields.

To

* It is intended to have a large refervoir of water on the roof. The only
prifoner at prefent is an unhappy woman found guilty of child-murder. She
belongs to a neighbouring parifh, and her infanity was clearly proved before the Circuit Court.

† A litigious fpirit is by no means prevalent in this county. There are
only five procurators before the fheriff-court, who are refident in this town.

To lay down rules calculated on liberal principles, for the conduct which is becoming the character and defcription of the worthy farmer, that when he proceeds meritorioufly, he may be protected ; when he approves himfelf a ufeful member, he may be rewarded; and when he is the object of undeferved perfecution, that he may be fupported. Such are the laudable and profeffed defigns of this Society. It is compofed of the noblemen, and many of the refpectable gentlemen, and of the principal farmers, of this county.

The prefident of the fociety is an honorary member of the national " Board of Agriculture."

The funds of the fociety arife from admiffion fees, and a fmall annual ſtipulated exaction from each member. They have three ſtated annual meetings, generally held in the Mafon Hall of Banff.

Friendly Societies.—Befides St Andrews Lodge of Free Mafons, and the Operative Mafon Lodge, there are feveral friendly focieties eſtabliſhed in Banff.

I. Solomon's Lodge, or the Gardener Friendly Society, was inſtituted in April 1778. It confiſts of 500 members. Their funds are in a flouriſhing ſtate. They are poffeffed of houfes and lands in the town and vicinity, which yield a yearly rent of L. 80 Sterling. To the widows of decayed brethren, laſt year, they paid upwards of L. 60 Sterling.

II. The Grey-ſtone Friendly Society, was eſtabliſhed in the year 1792. The benefit of this inſtitution is not confined to any particular defcription of perfons or profeffions. Their funds, it is believed, are in a progreffive ſtate of improvement.

Thefe, and fome other focieties belonging to particular corporations, prove of fubſtantial advantage in this place,

by

by aiding the poor's funds of the parifh, and adminiftering
relief to many individuals.

Public Amufements.—During the winter feafon, there are
dancing affemblies once a-fortnight.
Occafionally we have academical concerts of mufic.
Sometimes the heroes and heroines of the Sock and Bu-
fkin favour us with a vifit, and fret a few of their fummer
hours on our little ftage.

Circulating Library.—Banff affords a choice circulating
library, which, befides the ufual *light fummer reading* of the
times, contains a felect collection of the works of eminent
writers, both ancient and modern.
From our conftant intercourfe with London by fea, we
have early accefs to the periodical and other publications of
the day.
The Reviews we generally receive from the bookfeller
here, in the courfe of the month fucceeding their publication in London.
A Book Society is at prefent forming, on a liberal plan,
to confift of 20 gentlemen.

Eminent Men.—Under this article may be mentioned the
Bairds of Auchmedden, a very ancient and refpectable family, long refident in Banff *.

1568.

* There is a tradition, that as King William the Lion was hunting in
one of the fouth-weft counties, and ftraggling from his attendants, he was
alarmed at the approach of a wild bear, and called out for affiftance.
Upon this, a gentleman of the name of Baird, who had followed the King,
came up, and had the good fortune to flay the bear. For which fignal fervice, the King made a confiderable addition to the lands he had formerly
given him, and affigned him for his coat of arms, a *boar paffant*, and for
his motto, *Dominus fecit*. It is further faid, that one foot of the animal
was

1568. George Baird being connected by marriage, and in habits of great friendſhip, with the Regent, Earl of Moray, received from him a diſpoſition, heritable and irredeemable, to the lands of Auchmedden ; the Regent aſſigning the following cauſe : " for many acts of utility and " friendſhip done to me, and many ſums of money given " out by him, in my ſervice."

1647. James Baird was bred to the law, and became a perſon of high reputation in his profeſſion. King Charles I. repoſed great confidence in him, and appointed him ſole Commiſſary of the Eccleſiaſtical Court of Scotland, an employment in thoſe days of great honour and truſt.

The King iſſued his warrant for creating him a peer, by the title of Lord Doveran ; but Mr Baird died before the patent paſſed the ſeals. He was married to the ſiſter of John Dempſter, ſo remarkable for his diſputations in the foreign ſchools.

1593. Andrew having received an univerſity education in Scotland, went over to France to finiſh his ſtudies ; became one of the beſt ſcholars in that kingdom, and was made a Profeſſor of Sciences at Lyons *.

1650. John his eldeſt ſon was alſo bred to the law, and after travelling much in foreign countries, became a man of great knowledge in his profeſſion. On the Reſtoration, he was created a Knight, and was ſoon after appointed one of

the

was brought north by an anceſtor of Baird of Ordinhuives, and is ſtill preſerved. The arms and motto are to be ſeen on an ancient monument belonging to the family of Auchmedden, in the church-yard of Banff.

* Gilbert, Andrew's brother, married the heireſs of Ordinhuives, in this county, *anno* 1573, and had by her thirty-two children, the greater part of whom lived to the age of maturity.

the Senators of the College of Juſtice, by the title of Lord Newbyth.

1658. Sir James Baird, High Sheriff of Banff, was much reſpected for his abilities, integrity, and addreſs. In 1662 he received ſeveral marks of the King's favour; among others, the following honourable declaration and acquittal, for acting in the above office during the Uſurpation.

" Whereas, We are certainly informed, that the office of " the Sheriffſhip of Our county of Banff, was, by the late " Uſurper, put upon Our lovite Sir James Baird of Auch- " medden; that he only exerciſed the ſamen during the " year of the great tranſactions of Our Reſtoration, where- " in, as the ſaid Sir James was contributive and active, ſo " We are fully ſatisfied of his conduct and loyal affection to " Our Perſon and Government, and therefore declare him " free of all cenſure, &c. &c." Superſigned CHARLES, and ſubſcribed LAUDERDALE.

Sir James was employed by the Duke of Lauderdale, to draw up a rational plan for the union of the two kingdoms. He accordingly prepared ſuch plan, which was ſo highly approved of, that the King became deſirous of carrying it into execution; but it is believed the Duke of Lauderdale, Secretary of State for Scotland, was not a ſincere friend to the meaſure *.

Of the ſame family was the celebrated Bayardo, an Italian poet, who wrote Orlando Innamorata, which Arioſto made the ground-work of his Orlando Furioſo.

This pariſh gave birth to Dr James Sharp Archbiſhop of St Andrews, and Primate of Scotland, whoſe tragical end exhibits

bits

* The account of the family of Auchmedden is collected from an old manuſcript received from Mr Roſe of Mountcoffer, to whom the writer acknowledges himſelf alſo indebted for ſeveral other communications in compiling this work.

bits a melahcholy inſtance of the furious and miſguided zeal of ancient times. He was the ſon of Mr Sharp, Sheriff-Clerk of Banff-ſhire. His mother was a daughter of the Laird of Kininvy. He was born May 1613, in the Caſtle of Banff.

He gave early proofs of a ſuperior genius, and excelled all his ſchool-fellows in the rudiments of learing.

Having completed his courſe of academical ſtudy with great applauſe, at the Univerſity of Aberdeen, he took the degree of Maſter of Arts, and was enrolled a Student of Divinity. By the intereſt of the Earl of Rothes, to whom he was related, Mr Sharp was elected one of the Profeſſors of Philoſophy in St Leonard's College, St Andrews, and ſoon after was appointed miniſter of Crail.

In that remarkable diviſion of the Preſbyterians into two parties, Public Reſolutioners and Remonſtrators, he eſpouſed the cauſe of the former. To ſuch height were their diſputes carried, as to induce the contending parties to lay their complaints before Oliver Cromwell, the Protector.

Mr Sharp being choſen Reſolutionary agent, on that occaſion acquitted himſelf with ſo much temper and dexterity, that Cromwell ſeemed convinced by the ſtrength of his arguments, and was ſo impreſſed with his inſinuating manner and addreſs, that he pleaſantly obſerved to ſome perſons near him, " This gentleman, to uſe a Scotch phraſe, " may well be ſtiled Sharp of that Ilk."

In May 1660, Mr Sharp, at the earneſt deſire of General Monk and the leading Preſbyterians in Scotland, went over to King Charles at Breda, to repreſent their conduct, and to learn his Majeſty's diſpoſition towards them.

During his abſence, he was choſen Profeſſor of Divinity in Mary's College, St Andrews; and before he left London, the

the King, as a mark of his royal favour, made him his Chaplain for Scotland, with a penfion of L. 200.

In April 1661, he accompanied the Earl of Glencairn, Chancellor, and the Earl of Rothes, Prefident of the Council, to London, to lay before the King an account of the ftate of affairs in Scotland.

In a council held at Whitehall foon after, Mr Sharp was nominated Archbifhop of St Andrews. A refolution having been formed to fill up all the other vacant fees, the choice of proper perfons was left to the new Archbifhop, who, (according to his inveterate enemy Bifhop Burnet), acted in this inftance with great moderation. One of his firft official acts, after his preferment to the Archiepifcopal See, was, obtaining a proclamation prohibiting the meeting of clergymen in prefbyteries or other church judicatories, until the Bifhops arranged a plan for their procedure.

This, and fome other rigorous meafures, raifed againft him an hoft of enemies, feveral of whom bound themfelves by folemn vow to facrifice him to the fufferings of their party. They at length accomplifhed their horrid purpofe by affaffination, attended with circumftances of favage barbarity *.

The

* The following letter from Sir William Sharp of Stonyhill, containing a detail of the fhocking circumftances attending his father's murder, was addreffed to Sir James Baird, at Banff. It is a genuine copy, and appears never to have been publifhed.

" Honoured Sir,

" THIS horrid and ftupenduous murther has fo confounded me, that I " am not able to give a fuitable return to your excellent and kind letter. " What I have learnt of that execrable deed, is, that on Friday, the 2d of " this inftant month, my worthy father croffed the water; lay at Kenno- " way all night, next morning fet out for St Andrews. Being two miles " off, 27 of thofe villainous regicides had a full view of the coach, and not " finding

The character of this prelate has been differently repreſented by different hiſtorians. While Biſhop Burnet writes of him with the pen of ſevere obloquy, another of his biographers

" finding the opportunity, divided into three parties, which took up the
" three ways he could take homewards. Nine of them aſſaulted the coach
" within two miles of this place, by diſcharging their piſtols, and ſecuring
" his ſervants. The coachman drove on for half-a-mile, until one of his
" horſes was wounded in three places, and the poſtilion wounded in the
" hand. Then they fired ſeveral ſhot at the coach, and commanded my
" deareſt father to come out, which he ſaid he would. When he had
" come out, (not being yet wounded), he ſaid, Gentlemen, I beg my life.
" No ! bloody villain, betrayer of the cauſe of Chriſt, No mercy ! Then,
" ſaid he, I aſk none for myſelf, but have mercy on my poor child, (his el-
" deſt daughter was in the coach with him), and holding out his hand to
" one of them, to get his, that he would ſpare his child, he cut him in the
" wriſt. Then falling down upon his knees, and holding up his hands, he
" prayed that God would forgive them ; and, begging mercy for his ſins
" from his Saviour, they murdered him, by ſixteen great wounds, in his
" back, head, and one above his left eye, three in his left hand, when he
" was holding them up, with a ſhot above his right breaſt, which was
" found to be powder. After this damnable deed, they took the papers out
" of his pocket, robbed my ſiſter and their ſervants of all their papers, gold
" and money ; and one of theſe helliſh raſcals cut my ſiſter in the thumb,
" when ſhe had him by the bridle, begging her father's life. God, of his
" infinite mercy ſupport this poor family, under this dreadful and unſup-
" portable caſe, and give us to know why God is thus angry with us,
" and earneſtly beg not to conſume us in his wrath, but now that his anger
" may ceaſe, and he may be at peace with us, through the blood of a re-
" conciled Saviour ; and alſo may have pity upon this poor diſtreſſed
" Church, and that he may be the laſt ſacrifice for it, as he is the firſt Pro-
" teſtant Martyr Biſhop in ſuch a way.

" Dear Sir, as my worthy father had alway a kindneſs and particular
" eſteem for yourſelf, ſon, and family, ſo I hope you will be friendly to his
" ſon, who ſhall ever continue, worthy Sir, your moſt faithful, &c. &c.

" W. Sharp."

" St Andrews, 1oth May 1679,
" ½ hour after receipt of your's.

" On Saturday next is the funeral."

graphers has drawn his character in terms of unqualified praife.

In his more humble fituation, as minifter of Crail, we are told he approved himfelf a diligent and faithful paftor, and by his mildnefs, condefcenfion, and affability, acquired the love of his people.

But a fudden elevation to great rank and power feems to have a baneful influence on the human heart, and it muft be admitted, that the Archbifhop of St Andrews did not add one to the few inftances of ftrict moderation in that dangerous fphere. In his official capacity, he was violent in the exercife of his power, and, like moft other profelytes, he became the perfecutor of his deferted brethren.

Yet his inveterate enemies are agreed in afcribing to him the high praife of a beneficent and humane difpofition. He beftowed a confiderable part of his income in miniftering to preffing indigence, and relieving the wants of filent diftrefs. In the exercife of his charity he had no contracted views. The widows and orphans of the Prefbyterian brethren richly fhared of his bounty, without knowing whence it came. He died with the intrepidity of a hero, and the piety of a Chriftian, praying for the affaffins with his lateft breath *.

The late Earl of Findlater and Seafield, a nobleman of fingular and extraordinary merit, refided for many years in the caftle of Banff. " His Lordfhip employed his ample " fortune in promoting trade, manufactures, agriculture, " and all kinds of induftry. Ever folicitous to fill his " high ftation with real dignity, and farther to qualify him-
" felf

---

* The Archbifhop's monument, in the Cathedral of St Andrews, is extremely magnificent, and his epitaph highly flattering. " The difputable " parts of his life, (fays a celebrated traveller), are fully related ; his un- " doubted charity and deeds of alms omitted."

" felf to be more extenfively ufeful to fociety, (the fole ob-
" ject of his ambition), he converfed much with, and great-
" ly honoured, men of letters, and men of ingenuity in al-
" moft every profeffion, always endeavouring to convert
" whatever knowledge he thus acquired, to the benefit and
" improvement of his country.

" His natural difpofition was calm, placid, and ferene, his
" fentiments generous and enlarged, his underftanding folid
" and manly, and his integrity fuch as could not be fha-
" ken." Lond. Chron.

He died November 3. 1770.

Under this article it may not be out of place to mention
a gentleman of Banff fingularly eminent for his good fortune in the lottery. In the Britifh and Irifh lotteries he has
acquired, by the produce of three tickets, about L. 30,000
Sterling.

Characters and Manners, &c.—To difcriminate minute-
ly the manners and characters which diftinguifh one fociety
or parifh from another; to beftow particular and appropriate praife or cenfure, feems the moft arduous attempt of the
Statiftical hiftorian.

The writer of this account enters on the delicate fubject
aware of its difficulty, yet encouraged by the fentiments of
a great moralift, that the " hiftory which draws a portrait
" of living manners, may perhaps be made of greater ufe
" than the folemnities of profeffed morality, and convey
" the knowledge of vice and virtue with more efficacy than
" axioms and definitions *.

Banff has been for feveral years the general refidence and
occafional refort of many genteel, opulent, and refpectable
families ;

* Rambler.

families ; and in few provincial towns are the inhabitants more diftinguifhed for general information, focial intercourfe, and urbanity of manners.

In their general conduct they are both " pitiful and cour-" teous ;" deferving the praife of beneficence to the poor, and hofpitality to ftrangers.

The author of this report has had frequent opportunities of remarking their liberal and ready fpirit to do good, and their willingnefs to communicate to every judicious and difinterefted charity.

In their attendance on the ordinances of divine inftitution, all ranks are highly regular and exemplary.

Such laudable attention to external obfervances, fo prevalent here, and fo generally remarked in the different Statiftical Reports, though not a certain criterion, is at leaft a ftrong prefumption, of the exiftence of internal religion among us. It is a truth, for the confirmation of which we may appeal to living hiftory, and to the conduct of a neighbouring nation, that the decay of outward forms of worfhip precedes the decay of the more " weighty matters of the " law, juftice, mercy, faith," and leads to the diffolution of all the " charities of father, fon, and brother."

In our prefent imperfect ftate, there is certain danger of religion gliding by degrees from the heart, unlefs invigorated by external ordinances, by a due obfervance of the Sabbath, by ftated calls to worfhip, and the falutary influence of example.

That difagreement in religious opinions, which generally obtains in every numerous fociety, is here attended with no perfonal hatred, or rancorous animofity. We differ quietly, and in general maintain that meeknefs and moderation which found reafon approves, and Chriftian charity commands.

The

The number of thoſe is very inconſiderable who are en‑
tangled in the ſophiſtry of ſceptical writers.

A few copies of Paine's Age of Reaſon found their way
this length; but many more copies of the learned Biſhop of
Llandaff's admirable Apology ſoon followed *. Thus the
" Bane and Antidote were both before us." The new
fangled theology of Mr Paine, however captivating by its
popular ſtyle, has done little harm, and the great body of
the people " continue in the faith grounded and ſettled."

The inhabitants are alſo entitled to their portion of nega‑
tive praiſe. Great crimes are happily uncommon; robbe‑
ries, houſe‑breaking, and ſwindling, are rarely known.
The writer has not heard of an inſtance of any perſon, a na‑
tive of this pariſh, ſuffering the ultimate of human puniſh‑
ment †.

However ungrateful the taſk, truth and impartiality re‑
quire us to delineate the back‑ground of this picture.

While here, as in every large community, there are ma‑
ny deſerving of much commendation, for the general pro‑
priety of their conduct, ſome are highly reprehenſible, for
the vices which attach to their characters.

It may be inferred, from the ſhort publication already
alluded to, that the practice of dram‑drinking, habitual
ſwearing, and that ſpecies " of converſation admitting no
" defence ‡," were vices which formerly diſgraced ſome of
the

* The celebrated ſpeech of our countryman, Mr Erſkine, in the trial of
Williams, likewiſe proves a ſtrong ſhield in defending our religion againſt
the bold attacks of Mr Paine.

† During the laſt rebellion in Scotland, a poor fellow from the country,
whoſe imprudent curioſity led him to mark, by notches on his ſtaff, the
number of Britiſh ſhips paſſing in the bay, was apprehended as a ſpy, and
hanged by the King's troops, without the formality of trial.

‡ " Immodeſt words admit of no defence,
" For want of decency is want of ſenſe."

the lower orders of the people, and it is to be feared, they are vices not altogether eradicated.

But though the intemperate are ſtill to be ſeen reeling from their nightly revels, and ſometimes from their noonday debauch, the uſe of ardent ſpirits is not ſo common as formerly.

It is apprehended, however, that this partial reformation cannot be aſcribed ſo much to the change of inclination in thoſe who were addicted to the practice, as to the ſalutary clauſes introduced in the late diſtillery laws.

Although the great majority of the people are juſtly accounted conſcientious, and honourable in their dealings, there are known ſome ſolitary inſtances of perſons, who, availing themſelves of the ignorance or good nature of a neighbour, do not heſitate to over-reach him in a bargain.

Notwithſtanding our excellent eſtabliſhments for the education of youth, it muſt be admitted, that the children of the poor are often ſuffered to follow, without controul, the bent of their own inclinations. The truth is, the care, the vigilance, and the example of the parents, are not always exerted to guide their youthful ſteps. But this is chiefly to be underſtood of the profligate poor.

The violations of certain decorum occaſion too frequently to the kirk-ſeſſion a multiplicity of unpleaſant diſcuſſion, which might be veſted with more propriety in the hands of the civil judge.

Within theſe few years, one or two inſtances of child-murder have occurred, although the unhappy mothers have hitherto eſcaped detection.

To this atrocious crime there is here no temptation, ariſing from the ſeverity of church diſcipline. The diſgrace of public penance has long ſince been aboliſhed. The reformation of delinquents is now ſought by gentler methods, by mild rebuke and admonition, while the ſeſſion endea-

vour

vour to render theſe private vices of individuals, as much
as poſſible, public benefits to the poor.

Among ranks higher in the ſcale of ſociety, there is perhaps too ſtrict a conformity to the faſhionable cuſtoms and
manners of the age ; too much attention to the pleaſures of
the table, and too much of refinement in many things which
adminiſter to luxury.

Although the limits which ſeparate harmleſs gaiety from
blameful diſſipation are ſeldom tranſgreſſed, a grave mora-
liſt, perhaps, would venture to inſinuate, that engagements in
convivial feſtivity are, at ſome ſeaſons, too inceſſant and too
laborious. He might even farther allege, that men, not always contented with a little wine for their ſtomach's ſake,
are ſometimes perſuaded to increaſe the quantity, in order,
perhaps, to " remove the natural reſerve of their manner,
" and give a proper degree of eaſe and ſpirit to their con-
" verſation."

Were honeſt Mr Umphraville to paſs the winter in this
northern burgh, he might occaſionally have reaſon to complain, that the drawing-rooms, where, in his younger days,
the ladies and gentlemen were accuſtomed to meet each
other, were now almoſt totally deſerted; and that, amidſt
the boaſted refinement of modern manners, the gentlemen
paid leſs attention to the ladies than they had done 50 years
ago *.

In politics, as in religion, there ſubſiſts among us ſome
difference of opinion, not tinctured, however, with the vi-
rulence of party ſpirit. Here, it is believed, there are
very few who may be ſaid to belong to the order of modern
Illuminati, or to the claſs of violent malecontents †

His

* Mirror.

† The general good behaviour of the people of this county, in regard to
the militia act, was ſo exemplary, as to call forth the following eulogium
from

His Majesty's late gracious declaration has happily tended to diffuse greater unanimity of sentiment.

Ascribing the failure of the negociation at Lisle to its just cause, the ambitious and vindictive spirit of our enemies, that well judged appeal is calculated to rouse the loyalty of all ranks and descriptions of the people. It must excite them to express, with united voice, their firm determination to defend that happy constitution, which, under the auspices of Divine Providence, is the distinguished source of all our blessings.

Meanwhile, the Executive Directory are entitled to the assurances of our high consideration, for their late fulminating proclamation, of the 1st Frimaire.

It is a Philippic which speaks to the feelings and patriotism of the British Nation, in language still more forcible than the manifesto from the Throne.

It is a warning voice, conveying to us this friendly counsel,

> Go call thy sons, instruct them what a debt
> They owe their ancestors, and make them swear
> To pay it, by transmitting down, entire,
> Those sacred rights to which themselves were born.
>
> Akenside.

Quadrupeds,

from the lieutenancy, at their general meeting in September last: " The " meeting cannot omit this opportunity of expressing, in terms of the high- " est approbation, the very high sense they entertain of the orderly, quiet, " and respectful behaviour of all ranks of the inhabitants of this county, " in regard to the militia business. This propriety of conduct has not been " confined to one or two districts, but, from the reports of the different de- " puty-lieutenants, has been universal throughout the county ; nor has a " single instance occurred, wherein the people have not resisted every in- " finuation to the prejudice of the act, and come forward with the most " cheerful and implicit obedience to the law."

Quadrupeds, Birds, &c.—Of indigenous animals there are none peculiar to this place. In Lord Fife's park are ſeveral varieties of the deer; and the pheaſant is found wild in many of the adjoining woods.

A maccaw, celebrated for its beautiful plumage, was brought from the Weſt Indies in 1756, and lived 27 years at Duff Houſe. His vigour was not impaired, when, in 1784, he was killed by ſome animal unknown.

In Mr Condiner's late publication of " Singular Subjeƈts of " Natural Hiſtory," are engraved ſome beautiful ſpecimens of coralline and polypus, found off the coaſt of Banff. He has annexed particular deſcriptions of each.

PARISH OF BELLIE.

(SYNOD OF MURRAY [*], PRESBYTERY OF STRATHBOGIE.)

By the Rev. Mr. JAMES GORDON.

Name, Extent, Situation, &c.

BELLIE has been imagined by fome to be the Gaelic word *Bellaidh*, fignifying " broom ;" but others, more juftly, reckon it a compound from the two Gaelic words *Beul-aith*, meaning "the mouth of the ford." This etymology is perfectly natural, as, a little above the church, there was, till the prodigious flood in 1768 deftroyed it, and opened various channels, one of the fineft fords upon the Spey. There his Royal Highnefs, with his Majefty's army, paffed with great fafety in 1746, a few days before the battle of Culloden, the Duke of Kingfton's light cavalry leading the van. A gentleman once would, jocularly, have this place Bel-lieu. Indeed, Bellie's hill is a moft beautiful fpot, commanding a delightful

[*] Fochabers is in the county of Murray, and the country part is in Banff-fhire.

lightful prospect of Gordon Castle, of the river and part of Murray, of the Murray Frith, and the mountains of Sutherland and Caithness *.

Bellie extends from S. to N., near 6 measured miles, and from E. to W. almo 4. It is bounded on the N. by the Murray Frith, and on the W. by the river Spey. A considerable part of this space, to about 4 miles from the sea, is contained within the ancient banks of this river, which are very high. What these banks enclose may be considered as the range or territory of the Spey at this place, though it has greatly shifted its channels in different periods. At Gordon castle, which is between them, but near that on the E., these banks are near a mile distant from each other. They gradually widen in their approach to the sea, and where the river falls into the frith, are near 2 miles asunder. Between the bank on the E., and the present bed of Spey, is a fine extensive plain, with many farms, and a great number of inhabitants, the river having kept near the W. side for time immemorial, though it has frequently made ravages, that have rendered many embankments and bulwarks requisite. This bank is for about a mile below Gordon castle, handsomely dressed in imitation of nature, and adorned by fine plantations of trees and shrubs, with very pleasant walks. Here is a very great number of large clusters of hollies, which have procured it the appellation of the Holly Bank, as below it is styled the

* All the old names of farms here are of Celtic origin, as *Dalachy*, the plain field ; *Auchenreath*, the field of heath ; *Auchenhalrigg*, the field of spectres or hobgoblins, &c. The Gaelic tongue, however, has long disappeared in this part of the country ; the language, in general, being that dialect of English common to the North of Scotland ; though, among all persons who pretend to any thing like education, the English language is daily gaining ground.

the Bank of Bellie. At the S. end of this charming
level ftands Gordon caftle. It has a front of 568 feet.
I will not attempt to defcribe this moft fuperb and elegant ftructure. It is well known to be one of the
nobleft palaces in Britain, and attracts the notice of all
travellers, who never fail to return highly gratified *.
Here many a coftly drain has been employed to form the
enchanting landfcape it now exhibits. There is an immenfe extent of plantation, a large park of fallow deer ;
and here we are charmed with all the melody of the
grove. Here the woodcock vifits us about the end of
October, the fieldfare in the winter, and the green plover
in the fpring. About a mile N. of Gordon caftle, and 3
miles S. of the Frith, is the church of Bellie, upon the
old eaft bank of the Spey, foon to be tranflated to Fochabers, where a very commodious, elegant church is to be
built, which will be greatly ornamental to the place.
The old manfe is in ruins, and the minifter has got an
excellent houfe in the town of Fochabers †.

Soil

* The ancient refidence here was called *Bogra-gbdbu*, or windy bog, there being
a very free circulation of air from the Frith and the W. ; and the ferry-boat is
ftill the boat of Bog. This habitation was long known all over the N., by
the name of The Bog, for an obvious reafon. Spalden, if I remember right,
feldom ufes any other term for it. The caftle had doubtlefs been built here
with a view to ftrength, by ditches and inundation, when property was not
fo effectually fecured as in our happy days, by the regular execution of
wholefome and equitable laws. I need not fay how neceffary it was in thofe
times to erect fortreffes on rocks and in marfhes.

† Fochabers is compounded of the two Gaelic words, *Foich*, a green plain,
properly a plain for rendezvous or weapon-fhaw, which was often practifed here,
and *Aber*, a bay or junction of two waters ; the burn of Fochabers here u-
niting itfelf with the Spey. Some years ago, Fochabers was removed fouthward from the vicinity of Gordon Caftle to a rifing ground, near a mile diftant, and built on a neat plan, with an extenfive fquare in the centre. It is a
burgh of barony, and has a baron bailie. A phyfician refides among us. We
have

Soil and Agriculture.—The ground, which has been recovered from the Spey, is, in general, by a very long courfe of frequent manure, and, being in fmall farms, abundantly fertile. We have a good deal of loamy foil. There is not much clay land: That upon the coaft is fandy. In general, we depend very much upon the dews of heaven. In a droughty July, our crop near the fea, though promifing, dwindles amazingly. We enjoy, however, upon the whole, a happy climate: Our agricultural fyftem has nothing very different from that of our neighbours all around. We have very few enclofures, except at Gordon caftle, (where an extenfive farm is totally enclofed), and at Auchenhalrigg. We cannot boaft much of our other modes of melioration, though we commonly do the beft we well can. The people are induftrious, and labour hard; and you will not fee any thing like a farm, where you do not behold a field of fown grafs, a piece of turnips, and fome potatoes. The potatoe is much cultivated by thofe who have but fmall fpots of ground, and proves very ufeful. The fea-weed is much ufed as manure, to the diftance of 2 or 3 miles along the coaft; and no work is fuffered to interrupt the purfuit of it. Our crops of grain confift chiefly of barley, oats, peafe, and rye *.

There

have three annual fairs, one of them for black cattle; and a weekly market for butter and cheefe, eggs, poultry, &c. but it is not much reforted to. There are feveral retail fhops, and an ordinary number of the ufual artificers. There are two goods inns, well frequented. We have a friendly fociety pretty numerous. Its funds are accumulating, and will, in a little time, anfwer very benevolent and ufeful purpofes.

* The average wages for common labourers are 6 d. a-day in winter, and 8 d. in fummer. For harveft work, women receive 6 d., and men 10 d. A common artificer gets 10 d. or 1 s. a-day. With thefe payments, they generally have their victuals. A good man fervant for the half year feldom has lefs than 3 l., and the women, for the fame period, receive about 20 s. And thefe point at continual increafe.

There are in the parifh upwards of 1000 black cattle, moftly of the common country breed, many of which are fent away in the fummer to graze, pafture grafs being fcarce upon the coaft. We have about 340 horfes, many of them rather fmall fized, and fomething above 2200 fheep, generally a mixture of the Linton breed. Gordon caftle will readily be fuppofed an exception to all thefe, where the cattle, horfes and fheep are large. Many plough with a pair of horfes. Indeed, it is the moft frequent practice, the ground being light and eafily managed: Some put a yoke or two of black cattle behind them. There are but few ploughs, comparatively; drawn by oxen entirely. A cart among the country people may generally be reckoned for every horfe: Carts drawn otherwife, are not many in comparifon.

Manufactures and Fifheries.—One manufacturer of fome eminence, has long refided on the burn of Fochabers, and manages very confiderable bufinefs in weaving ftockings of cotton, thread, and worfted, and fome pieces for waiftcoats and breeches. He alfo deals a little in the thread trade. Another, who is alfo a merchant, carries on a manufacture of lint, thread and tobacco, to fome amount. There is a capital falmon fifhery here upon the Spey, chiefly the property of the Duke of Gordon, from which his grace derives a rent of 1500l. a-year, from Meffrs. Gordon and Richardfon. It extends from Speymouth about 5 miles, and terminates in a complete row of cruives acrofs the river. There is a large lofty edifice near the fea for the gentlemen that hold the leafe. There are buildings for the overfeers, coopers, &c., and that furnifh every accommodation for the fifhery. They have got a very good ice-houfe. An hundred and

thirty

thirty men, or more, are employed in this fiſhery. There is alſo a ſalmon fiſhing upon the coaſt, called ſtell fiſhing. Some thouſands of ſalmon are ſent to London early in the ſeaſon, covered with ice : Afterward they are exported in kits ſteeped in vinegar, of which many hogſheads are yearly laid in for the purpoſe. Theſe kits contain about 36 pounds of ſalmon each. When the great city is plentifully ſupplied, and the price much reduced, it becomes convenient to ſalt the ſalmon, and to ſend them to the foreign markets. The natural effeȼt of this demand, is dearth of ſalmon here. Indeed, the expenſe of living has increaſed very conſiderably within theſe 20 years in almoſt every article. In this we are not ſingular.

Proprietors.—The Duke of Gordon is our only reſiding heritor, and, indeed, ſole proprietor of the pariſh, except of one farm belonging to the Earl of Findlater.

Population, &c.—The return to Dr. Webſter in 1755, was 1730. The pariſh of Bellie now contains 1919 fouls, viz. country part 984, and the village 935. Of theſe, there are 859 males, and 1060 females. This diſproportion has not been occaſioned by emigration, for of that we have had very few inſtances, but from the military genius exerting itſelf on particular emergencies. We have of married couples 272, and of young people about 10 years old, and under, 437, viz. 205 boys, and 232 girls. Though it be known, that a ſuperior number of males is born into the world, theſe little differences will happen in particular corners, by removals and other cauſes. For 14 years paſt, 10 couples, at a medium, have been married yearly, and 31 children regiſtered, regiftered, viz. 16 males, and 15 females. The latter article cannot be exact as to the number born in the parifh, it being difficult to bring fome, even of our own people, to infert the names of their children, with all the care that can be taken. There are in the parifh 458 dwellings ; 250 in Fochabers, and 208 in the country. The average number in thefe habitations is a little more than 4. With regard to longevity, there is nothing here peculiar. We are bleffed with a mild, pure, temperate air. Some live to 70, fome to 80 years of age, though few, in comparifon, it may be fuppofed. A few are now alive on the very borders of 90. A man died at 90 fome little time ago, and another at 108, or upwards. There are no difeafes incident, in any uncommon way, to this corner. The fifhermen, from their employment, are fometimes feized with palfies in the lower parts, and fevere rheumatifm. Thefe maladies are guarded againft by the care taken of them, and the quantity of fpirits allowed them.

Ecclefiaftical State, &c.—By far the greater part of the people are of the eftablifhed church. We have, however, a very confiderable number of Roman Catholicks, with a prieft of the church of Rome, and a large chapel.

There are a few Proteftants of the Epifcopal perfuafion ; and 4 or 5 Seceders refide among us. We all live very cordially and happily together. The body of the people, it is but juftice to fay, are of refpectable character. We have, alas ! exceptions : And what community is without fome, whofe conduct in life is matter of very ferious regret. The cuftom that prevails more and more, not in this corner alone, among the lower claffes,

of

of fubftituting dram-drinking for a draught of good beer, has a moft pernicious tendency, with regard to health and morals. The people here are, in general, of a fober, rational, religious difpofition, regular in their attendance on public ordinances, and careful of the focial duties *.

The ftipend of Bellie is 72l. 6s. 4½d., including allowances for communion elements. The glebe at Bellie was lately excambed for one at Fochabers, which meafures 13 acres of good land.

Schools and Poor.—There is a parochial fchool at Fochabers. The fchoolmafter teaches Englifh, Latin, writing, arithmetic, and book-keeping. His falary is 14 bolls meal. He has a fmall fee as feffion-clerk, the fchool dues, and payment for regiftration of baptifms and marriages. There is a fociety fchool about 3 miles from Fochabers, of the utmoft confequence to very great numbers of poor creatures, who could not poffibly attend, or be accommodated in the parifh fchool.

We have not many common beggars, yet a numerous lift of poor, among whom are diftributed the collections in the church, which (efpecially when our great family is at home) are of much benefit, the dues from the mortcloth, and the intereft of a little money. A chalder of meal is annually beftowed upon the poor about 2d February, the Marquis of Huntly's birth day. There are fome bedemen who, by an ancient provifion in the family,

---

* Near the confines of this and Rathven parifh, a neat chapel has been lately built for the itinerant minifter, who has a confiderable diftrict of this parifh as part of his charge. He has fomething from a fund collected, and accumulating, for the benefit of that miffion, in addition to his falary from the fociety, and a glebe of 8 acres. A houfe is alfo intended him.

family, receive meal and money, which give a very comfortable subsistence. They are old worn-out men. Private donations are given ; and the people, in general, are
charitably disposed.

Curiosity and Antiquity.—The only rare plant in the
parish, is the *Satyrium Repens,* which grows in plenty
within a mile of Fochabers.

There is a field of a little more than 3 acres, a little
to the N. of the church of Bellie, to which tradition has
given the name of the Danish Camp. Large remains of
the entrenchments have been preserved. It is upon the
old E. bank of the Spey, and the river had then flowed
at the bottom, which had occasioned the choice of the
post. This camp may have been connected with the
battle between the Scots and Danes, in the neighbourhood of Cullen. From the square figure of the encamp-
ment, it should rather seem to have been a Roman camp,
though it be difficult to say when the Romans were here,
unless Agricola might land a detachment in his traverse
on the coasts of Scotland.

Bridge over the Spey.—I cannot conclude this sketch of
the parish of Bellie, without taking notice of the necessity of throwing a bridge over the Spey at Fochabers.
This is, upon the most solid grounds, the ardent wish of
all who know this passage. Fochabers is a very considerable thorough-fare, and Spey is well known to be a
large and rapid river. Numberless travellers of all descriptions from every part of Britain, pass this way, who
are frequently detained by floods and boisterous winds,
and sometimes cross with danger. The post-boy is, at
times, detained, though they waft him over when they
would

would not run the riſk with any other perſon. Not long
ago, he was ſtopped 3 nights in the courſe of one week.
They ſometimes ferry over the mail, when they dare
not take the horſe into the boat. A bridge here would
be of the utmoſt conſequence to the country, in driving
cattle to and from the markets, of which many fine
droves travel this way, and are often reduced to great
hardſhips. It would be extremely beneficial in bringing
lime from Banffſhire to Murray, where it is exceedingly
wanted; and it would be of unſpeakable importance to
his Majeſty's troops, who almoſt always march by this
route; eſpecially would it be of the laſt moment, when
the public ſervice requires diſpatch. The univerſal
ſenſe of the propriety of this meaſure, has already been
ſtrongly evinced by very conſiderable ſubſcriptions, to
which, it is to be hoped, liberal additions will yet be
made. Public aid, however, is indiſpenſibly neceſſary:
and we may humbly preſume, that aid will very generouſly be granted, when the ſtate of national affairs can
properly admit of it.

PARISH OF BOHARM.

(Counties of Banff and Moray.—Presbytery of Aberlour.—Synod of Moray.)

By the Rev. Mr Francis Leslie, *Miniſter.*

Geography and Natural Hiſtory.

THE ancient name is *Bocharin ;* in the original ſignifying the bow about the cairn, or rocky hill, from its ſurrounding nearly three parts of the bottom of the mountain of Beneageen. The length, between the pariſh of Mortlich, at the weſt, and the pariſh of Bellie, at the eaſt, is from 7 to 9 Engliſh miles ; the breadth, from the pariſh of Botriphnie, at the ſouth, to the higheſt cultivated land on the mountain, northward, is from 2 to 3 Engliſh miles ; but the figure of the pariſh is ſo irregular, that theſe meaſures are to be regarded as the mean, rather than as the particular length and breadth.

The general appearance of the country may be conceived as an extenſive valley from eaſt to weſt, having all the arable land hanging on the declivities of both ſides, there being little or no plain on the banks of the brooks, which, riſing in the hills, bend their courſes to either hand ; to Fiddich, on the weſt ; and, by the eaſt, turning by the north-weſt to Spey. From this general deſcription, Airndilly, the ſeat of David M'Dowall Grant, Eſq; falls to be excepted, being delightfully

lightfully fituated on a rifing ground, above a pretty extenfive plain, half encircled by the Spey, in the fouth-weftern
end of the parifh, near to which, a little farther down the
river, lie the haughs of Kailymore, a part of the fame eftate,
fignifying the *great wood;* which epithet, in fome degree, it
ftill comparatively merits. The foil here is fandy, warm,
and fertile ; but, in general, over the reft of the parifh, it is
a ftiff, rich, deep clay, generally on a bed of lime-ftone, and
very retentive of water, with which it is too frequently fupplied, the fummit of the mountain attracting or intercepting
the clouds borne along from the ocean by the north and
north-wefterly winds, on which account the harvefts are
rather late ; and, though the air be moift, yet there is no
diftemper generally prevalent. The people are vigorous and
healthy; and feverals attain to the longeft term of human
life, there being at prefent feveral men, each 80, and one
woman accounted 100 years of age.

The water of Fiddich, turned almoft at right angles, from
an eaftern to a northern courfe, along the weft end of the
parifh, fteals in to the river Spey, which is only navigable
for floating timber down from Strath Spey, part of which is
manufactured into plank, deal, fpar, and fcantling, by two
faw-mills at the Boat of Brigg. It is hardly neceffary to notice here the excellent falmon caught in the Spey, as the
public are already fufficiently apprifed of this particular.

The charter of Moray has preferved the memorial of the
bridge over Spey at this place. Part of the foundation of
the fouthern pier ftill remains. It has been fuppofed the
bridge was of timber. Here alfo ftood *the Chapel of St Nicholas*—" *Ad receptionem Pauperum tranfeuntium.*" Both the
bridge and hofpital were extant in the year 1232 ; but few
particulars of their hiftory or deftruction remain.

It

It may be mentioned, that it is ſuppoſed practicable to build a ſtone-bridge here for about the ſum of 3000 l. Sterling, which, beſides certain conveniencies peculiar to this ſituation, would comprehend alſo all the requiſite accommodation to the public ; for, if the high-way were continued from where it joins the road between Keith and Fochabers, at the ſouth end of the laſt of theſe villages, in the ſhorteſt courſe, to the Boat of Brigg, the diſtance from Cullen to Elgin would not be increaſed above 5 Engliſh miles on the whole, on a road as firm, and leſs expoſed to depth of ſnow, than the preſent high-way from Fochabers to Elgin.

Population.—The ancient ſtate of the population of the pariſh cannot now be aſcertained, farther than that it does not appear that the number of farm-houſes, or the extent of arable land, has been any way materially altered from what they were in times very remote.

Of late years, the population has been rather on the decreaſe, owing to ſeveral ſmaller farms, on which from 2 to 6 families reſided, being reduced into a ſingle farm, and occupied by a ſingle family.

At preſent, the number of perſons amounts to 1294, of whom 588 are males, and 706 females.

They all reſide in the country, and follow the occupation of huſbandry, with the exception of the few craftſmen who are requiſite for that object, and for the more immediate accommodation of the people. There are none who have left the pariſh for want of employment ; yet a few go ſouthward in ſummer, on account of the higher wages given in that part of the kingdom.

There has never been any accurate regiſter kept of baptiſms, marriages, or burials. Theſe particulars, therefore, cannot with any ſatisfactory preciſion be aſcertained.

Productions

Productions of the Parish.—Oats, barley, and peaſe, are the
kinds of corn principally raiſed. There are fields of ſown
graſs, bearing, however, little proportion to the natural lie
graſs and common paſturage. Of the corn, there may be
about two third parts in oats, the remaining third in barley
and peaſe, in which part the potatoe and flax may be alſo
included.

The oats and peaſe are ſown from the beginning of March,
as the ſeaſon allows, to near the middle of May ; and the
barley ſeed-time is generally completed before the 1ſt of
June. The harveſt begins from about the middle of Auguſt
to the middle of September. In ſome years, of late, it has
not begun before the firſt week of October. Its concluſion,
of courſe, muſt be at different times ; and it has been, of
late, accounted early, if completed by the end of November.

On the eſtate of Airndilly, if the different banks and
clumps be regarded as a whole, there is a conſiderable extent of natural wood, in which wild cherries, plumbs, and
geens, are interſperſed. On this eſtate there are alſo extenſive plantations of fir and pine, and other foreſt trees ; and
ſimilar plantations have alſo riſen up on the eſtate of Auchluncart, and on the lands in this pariſh appertaining to the
Earl of Findlater, and which are not deſtitute of natural
wood.

The black cattle among the country tenants, though not
of great bone, are accounted handſome, and of a fine figure.
The ordinary price of a yoke of oxen may be from 8 l. to
15 l. Sterling ; and ſome have been ſold at a higher rate.
A milk cow may ſell from 3 l. or 4 l. to 6 l. Sterling ; and a
ſcore of wedders, with the fleece, from 6 l. to 9 l. Sterling.

Miſcellaneous.—It muſt be accounted a diſadvantage to the
greater part of the pariſh, that it is ſo much expoſed to rain
                                                          in

in the end of ſummer, and during the autumn ; and, from the coldneſs of the ſoil, the ſnow lies long in the ſpring, ſo that the ſeaſons are later ; much of the corn not fully ripened ; much loſt ; and much vexatious trouble in harveſt, evils to which the oppoſite ſide of the Spey are comparatively not expoſed ; while, on the other hand, the near and more eaſy acceſs to the cattle fairs during the ſummer, the abundance of natural paſture and lime-ſtone, are advantages which the neighbourhood on the north ſide of that river do not ſo amply poſſeſs.

The pariſh is at preſent poſſeſſed by 4 heritors. David M'Dowall Grant, Eſq; has the lands of Airndilly, Papeen, Newtown, Gallval, and Auchmadies. The Earl of Findlater holds the barony of Mulben, the lands of Cairnty and Muldeiry. Andrew Stewart, Eſq; writer to the ſignet, has the barony of Auchluncart. Archibald Duff of Drummuir, Eſq; has the farm of Knocan. The valued rent of the pariſh is 2840 l. Scotch. The real rent of the whole has not been aſcertained.

The Scotch is the only language ſpoken in the pariſh ; but, with a few exceptions, the names of the places belong to the Earſe tongue.

There are no funds for the ſupport of the poor, except two ſmall mortifications, amounting only to 8 l. 10 s. Sterl. together. The number of poor on the roll may amount to 17.

The ruin of the caſtle of Gallvall is the only remain of any thing that can be deemed antiquity in the pariſh. It was built fronting the eaſt, on the north ſide of the valley towards the weſtern end, where the declivity hath fallen more gently into an inclined plain, and ſhot a promontory into the deep defile, formed by the courſe of the ſtream of Aldermy ; ſnugly ſheltered from the northern blaſt, with an

enlivening

enlivening extent of arable field, rifing behind on either hand; a luxuriant landfcape, fpread weftward on the winding banks of the Fiddich, glittering through the meadows and woods, decorated by the fteady battlements of the caftles of Balvenie and Auchendown, each on its own green hill, and terminated by the fummits of the blue mountains, ranged at a diftance around, feeming to debar all irruption upon the fequeftered vales. It bore little refemblance to the other caftles of the feudal lords, whofe towers, or fquare or round, of various heights and form, projected for the protection of the intermediate walls. It appears to have been a fimple ftructure of an 119 by 24 feet within, divided by an internal wall, fo as to form two halls on the ground floor, one 65, and the other 54 feet in length. The windows were only 20 inches wide, though the walls were 8 feet thick, built up in frames of timber, for keeping in the fluid mortar which was poured into the dry ftone-wall, when raifed to a certain height. The front and corners were neatly finifhed with free-ftone from the quarries of Duffus, at the diftance of 20 miles, on the other fide of Spey, the neareft where fuch ftone could have been procured. The front and gables are now entirely broken down; but, within thefe 50 years, they ftood to the height of feveral ftories. About that period, feveral filver fpoons were found among the rubbifh, having the handle round, and hollow like a pipe; and the concave part, or fhell, perfectly circular.

This bulky fabric, which on the eaftern front had lower external accommodations, in the year 1200 was denominated Caftellum de Bucharin. It then belonged to the Frefkyns of Duffus, by whom it was no doubt built. By affuming the title *De Moravia*, from their connection with that country, they became the author of that firname. They were once poffeffed of many a fair domain in the north, namely, Duffus, Duldavie,

Duldavie, Dalvey, Inverallen, and Kirkdales, in Moray; Airndilly, Aikenwall, Boharm, Botriphnie, then Botruthin, Kinermonie, then Cere Kainermonth, in Banff shire; and in Nairn or Inverness, Brachlie, Croy, Ewan, Lunyn, and Petty, as appears by the charter of Moray, from the 1100 to 1286. At this day, they are represented, in the 20th generation, by the Duke of Atholl, Captain Sutherland of Duffus, and Mr Murray of Abercairny.

It is also by the charter of Moray instructed, that, between the year 1203 and 1222, William, the son of William Freskyn, obtained the consent of Brucius, Bishop of Moray, for building a domestic chapel, for the more commodious performance of the offices of devotion. It stood on its own consecrated burying-ground, forsaken only in the course of the last 60 years, about 50 yards from the north end of the castle; and, though only 24 by 12 feet within, must have been the parent of the present parish church, which, with several others, was erected at the private expence of James VI. for civilizing the north of Scotland, in the year 1618, at which period the parish of Airndilly may be supposed to have been annexed.

A part also of the parish of Dundurcos has been of late conjoined, and a new church erected about two miles eastward, in a situation which some suppose to be more centrical. But the stipend, after both annexations, including the allowance for communion elements, is only 75 l. 7 s. 2½ d. Sterling.

Although it is not certainly known that any man of peculiar eminence was born in the parish, yet it may be proper to notice, that Mr James Ferguson, the astronomer, received the rudiments of his education here, under the patronage of the grandfather of the present Mrs Grant of Airndilly. Mr Ferguson has himself published his life: It is only necessary
therefore

therefore here to add, that, while a little boy who could hardly read, and employed in tending the cows, the family clock was the firſt objeƈt which elicited thoſe ſparks of mechanical genius which in due time ſhone with ſuch a bright and vigorous flame.

The people, on the whole, are induſtrious, economical, obliging, and kind, according to their manners and circumſtances; very attentive to the national religion; and there is no remembrance of any having been judicially puniſhed for the violation of the laws of morality or juſtice. They appear, in general, to enjoy the neceſſaries, and many of the comforts of life, and to be contented with that ſituation in the world which has been allotted to them by Providence. There are means by which their circumſtances might be meliorated; but, it being extremely probable they will not be adopted, it may be deemed officious to enumerate them here.

The difficulty and expence of procuring hands for the operations of agriculture, and the want of all police, either conventional or legal, reſpeƈting this objeƈt, has of late been ſo heavily and univerſally felt, that perhaps any ſpeculation that might contribute to turn the attention of the more diſcerning to this intereſting objeƈt, may not be deemed entirely nugatory.

In ſo far as this grievance hath ariſen from the diminiſhed value of money in the preſent opulent age, when, as in the days of Solomon, it may be ſaid " *of ſilver, that it is not any* " *thing accounted of,*" it cannot be regarded as any cauſe of complaint; for the price of labour muſt be proportional to that of other articles : But, in ſo far as the evil ariſes from the combined fraud, the falſehood, the ſtubbornneſs, and the domineering inſolence of that rank of ſociety, it ought to be repreſſed, although in due conſiſtence with the rights

of

of men ; and much delicacy, in this regard, is no doubt requisite. It might tend, perhaps, to check the evil, were every agricultural servant, by law, obliged to produce to the master with whom he engages, and to the church-session of the parish, when required, a certificate from the master whom he left, granted before two legal witnesses, of the wages which he received, and of the discretion, fidelity, and diligence, which he maintained during the period of his preceding service ; the engaging master to forfeit equal to a quarter of year's wages, and the servant as much, to the parish fund, for every omission of such formality; to be recovered at the instance of the cashier of the session, by the warrant of one justice of the peace, or other judge ordinary, in the same summary manner in which the fines are levied on the absentees from the statute labour on the roads.

Those who have been attentive to the operation of any new law, will be able perhaps to form a judgment of the effect of such an establishment, were it so framed as to admit of equal execution in England and in Scotland. It does not appear that it could be attended with much inconvenience to either party ; and, while it would, in general, prevent imposition on the master who engages, by an exaggerated account of the wages paid by the last master, as is now so generally the case, it would, in many instances, have the effect of rendering the servant discreet and diligent during the term of his service, when so much as a quarter's wages depended on his behaviour.

Other improvements respecting diet, and the hours of labour, might be suggested ; but it is probable the effect alone of the certificate may render these unnecessary : At any rate, if regulations respecting the contract between master and servant shall be taken under the consideration of Legislature,

every

every thing of this kind will be maturely digefted, and fufficiently provided for.

By the naufeous draught of train oil in Lapland, and the more difgufting beverage of Otaheite, it may be inferred, that man cannot be fatisfied with the fimple element alone of water. From the different circumftances concomitant on the excife law in England and in Scotland, it would not be difficult to inveftigate why beer has been the prevailing drink among the peafantry of the fouthern, while ardent fpirits has fo univerfally ob ained among the fame rank in the northern end of the ifland, to which muft be attributed their afperated and contracted features, rather than to the influence of their climate.

The Secretary of State for this department, by the reftoration of its ancient families to their paternal fortunes; by increafing the independence of its Judges, particularly the Sheriff-fubftitutes, on whom the adminiftration of juftice among the poor fo much depends; by providing for the intereft of the feamen and their connections; and by the repeal of the tax on water-borne coal, hath merited more of his native country than all his predeceffors in office together. Characters fo highly refpectable are unpopular only among the blindeft of the mob. To him it would be eafy to model the law in fuch a manner, that beer, inftead of whifky, fhould in a fhort time be generally adopted by all the labouring people in Scotland; and, by this means, while he would contribute to maintain, in a high degree, the purity of the morals, and the foundnefs of the conftitutions of his countrymen, he would at the fame time expand their countenances, and improve their whole exterior form to the higheft elegance of fymmetry and beauty.

PARISH OF BOTRIPHNIE.

(County of Banff.—Presbytery of Strathbogie.—Synod of Moray.)

By the Reverend Mr ALEXANDER ANGUS.

Extent, Name, &c.

FEW parishes in Scotland afford less subject for statistical inquiries than this of Botriphnie. It is situated about 24 English miles W. from the county town, and extends from N. to S. about 4½, and from E. to W. about 3 English miles, comprehending the whole breadth of the county, being bounded by the parish of Glass, in Aberdeenshire, on the S. and on the N. by part of Dundurcas, in Moray.

The name of the parish, like most others in this part of Scotland, is probably of Gaelic origin ; but, though the present incumbent has conversed with many persons who understood that language, he could obtain no information with respect to its derivation. The greater part of the parish consists of one beautiful strath, situated between two hills to the N. and S with the small river of Isla (which takes its rise in the W. part of the parish towards Mortlach) running through the middle of it. The banks of this stream are beautifully adorned with aller and birch trees, the natural produce of the country ; several small rills, which fall into it from the hills on each side, are covered in the same manner ;

and

99

and the proprietor has made very extenſive plantations of fir
and other trees, all which add greatly to the beauty of the
country.   The fir trees towards the top of the hills are generally dwarfiſh ; but they increaſe in ſize towards the bottom,
and are generally found to thrive better in a northerly than
in a ſoutherly expoſure.

Soil, Agriculture, &c.—The ſoil is a black loam, and, in
ſome places, a ſtrong clay, and not many feet from the ſurface.   Limeſtone, of an excellent quality, is to be met with
in every field ; but it is little uſed, except for the purpoſes
of building.   Many farmers in this pariſh have tried it without ſucceſs ; and, though they do not pretend to ſay that it
hurts their fields, yet they do not find the returns from it
equal to the expence.   A gentleman, who rents a very extenſive farm, has lately uſed lime in very conſiderable quantities ; but it will require a little time fully to aſcertain its
effects.   On ground lately taken in from the heath, its influence is more perceptible.

The fields on the N. ſide of the pariſh have a good expoſure, and are of conſiderable extent, from the river to the
top of the hill ; and, for the whole length of the pariſh on
that ſide, there is hardly a break in them, except where they
are interſected by a few ſmall rills, and clumps of birch and
aller.   About every farm there are a conſiderable number of
aſh trees, which are equally ſubſervient to utility and ornament.

Except in two farms, there are no incloſures in the pariſh.
The ſtones for that purpoſe might be quarried at no great
expence.   In general, the ridges are ſtraight ; but few other
improvements in huſbandry are to be met with.   No country
anſwers better for ſown graſs ; and as rich fields of it are to
be met with here as in any part of Scotland ; but they are
                                                    confined

confined to two or three farms, and serve only to show what the country might produce, were it in the hands of persons who had abilities or encouragement to improve.

Rent, Services, &c.—The rent of the parish is upwards of 1000 l. Sterling, divided into farms of different extent, from 70 l. to 8 l. a year, partly paid in money, and partly in oatmeal. It may be proper to mention, among other causes that retard improvement, that leases are only granted for 19 years, and some for a shorter period; that besides the rent, as above specified, several services are exacted of the tenants, such as leading fuel, cutting down corn in harvest, and other exactions of a similar nature, which, if viewed in a proper light, are more hurtful to the tenant than beneficial to the proprietor.

These remains of feudal vassalage are mentioned with reluctance; and it is to be hoped, that the good sense of the proprietors will lead them to vie with one another in removing every restraint on industry, and consider it as their honour, as it is certainly their interest, to see their tenants thriving and independent. For this purpose, besides an allowance to build comfortable houses, make substantial inclosures, and plant trees and hedges, no lease should be for a shorter period than two 19 years and a life; and thirlage, and every other service, should be abolished.

Flax answers well in this parish, and considerable quantities of it are raised annually. Barley and oats are the principal produce of the country. The late harvests, for some years past, have discouraged the growth of pease; but, in ordinary years, they are very productive, both in point of corn and provender for cattle, and as an excellent preparation for a crop of barley.

The

The rent of land, when let out in ſmall parcels, is 20 s. the Scotch acre ; and, in larger farms, about 15 s. Land of an inferior quality leſs from 6 s. to 10 s. Barley harveſt begins generally about the middle of September, though oats are commonly three weeks later. An earlier ſpecies of oats has of late been introduced, which ſucceeds well on ground in good heart, and is as ſoon ready as barley.

In 1782, there was a great deficiency in the crop, owing to the froſt coming on early, and preventing the grain from coming to maturity. Had it not been for a very conſiderable importation, the conſequences muſt have been fatal. The deficiency of the ſucceeding crop aroſe entirely from the badneſs of the ſeed. Even oats that appeared little inferior in plumpneſs and colour to the produce of ordinary years, proved equally unfit for ſeed as the pooreſt grain. They looked well on their firſt coming above ground, but ſoon after totally diſappeared *.

Manufactures, &c.—In this pariſh there are 9 weavers, 3 turners, chiefly employed in making ſpinning wheels, 1 carpenter. 4 taylors, 4 ſhoemakers, 2 ſhopkeepers, and 12 maſons. The latter are not much employed within the pariſh ; but they find work in the ſouthern counties, and reſide here in the winter.

The women are employed in ſpinning linen yarn, from flax partly of their own rearing, and partly imported from Holland by the manufacturers. The latter kind is ſpun from 6 to 8 hanks in the pound, and varies in the price of ſpinning according to the demand. Flax of home growth is ſpun from 2 to 5 hanks in the pound, and is ſold at an annual

* The price of labour has increaſed much within 7 years. Men-ſervants wages are from 6 l. to 7 l. and women-ſervants about 50 s. a year. A day-labourer earns 6 d. beſides victuals.

nual fair held here in February, and bought up by manufacturers in the villages of Keith and Huntly, who fend it to Glafgow and Paifley. At prefent, it fells at 2 s. 6 d. the fpindle, or 4 hanks, which is 4 d. dearer than it was laft feafon.

A confiderable quantity of linen cloth is likewife made from flax reared in the parifh, which, after it is bleached, is fold at an annual fair held in Keith in September, and at Huntly in July.

Produce.—A great deal of money is annually received for black cattle, which have now become an object of as much importance to the farmer as corn itfelf.

Much more grain is raifed in the parifh than is fufficient for the maintainance of the inhabitants. The meal paid to the proprietors finds a market in the fouthern counties. The barley raifed by the tenants is confumed by the licenfed diftillers. The countries of Badenoch, Strathfpey, and Strathaven, generally have a demand for what meal can be fpared; and the farmer often finds his account in felling oats, which are fhipped at Garmouth or Buckie for the Frith of Forth.

Very few fheep are reared in the parifh, and thefe of a very fmall fize; and very little woollen cloth is made, except for home confumption.

Population.—The population of this parifh has decreafed about 80 fince 1774; at that period the numbers were 700, and they are now 620, of all ages. The return to Dr Webfter in 1755 was 953 fouls. This decreafe is owing to the enlargement of fome farms, and to the number of fubtenants being leffened, the farmer generally finding his account more in occupying the ground himfelf, than in letting it at a fmall advanced rent to others. The advance of wages, too, has
made

made the farmer contrive to labour with fewer ſervants. For 10 years preceding 1793, there were 66 males and 64 females baptiſed, and 41 couples married.

Eccleſiaſtical State, &c.—The church was built in 1617, and is at preſent in a very ruinous condition. There is no reſiding heritor, and the principal one is a minor, which will account for the circumſtance now mentioned. The Earl of Fife is patron. The ſtipend fixed by decreet in 1776 is 47 l. 5 s. Sterling, (including 50 merks Scotch for communion elements, and 54 bolls of oat-meal. The glebe meaſures 6 acres, including 2 acres of meadow graſs. The manſe was built in 1776. There are few diſſenters of any deſcription in the pariſh ; 1 Roman Catholic, 1 Epiſcopal, and 15 Seceders *.

There is a parochial ſchoolmaſter, whoſe ſalary is 12 bolls of meal, and 2 l. Sterling for acting as ſeſſion clerk. The boys are taught reading, writing, and accounts. It was much the faſhion formerly to inſtruct them in Latin, and ſend them to the Univerſity ; but, whatever advantage this might be to the individual, it was a loſs to the ſociety, who was thereby drained of uſeful hands, that are now more profitably employed in agriculture and manufactures.

The funds for the ſupport of the poor are, the weekly collections, the intereſt of 70 l. and the rent of a loft in the church,

* The preſent incumbent, who was ſettled in 1774, is the ſecond Preſbyterian miniſter in this place ſince the Revolution. His immediate predeceſſor, Mr Campbell, was ſettled in 1727, and died in 1773. The preceding miniſter, Mr Chalmers, was an Epiſcopal, and ſettled in 1682 ; and it is mentioned as a mark of the reſpectability of his character, and the moderation of the Preſbytery, that, notwithſtanding the heat of the times, he was permitted to enjoy his living, though he did not conform, till his death in 1727.

church, which, at an average, will amount to 10 l. yearly, by which 10 perfons receive occafional fupplies *.

Mifcellaneous Obfervations.—The people are fober, induftrious, and of good morals, and well affected to our prefent conftitution.

There are no difeafes peculiar to this country. The practice of inoculation is not yet introduced among them. In the courfe of 19 years, 8 children have died of the fmallpox. No extraordinary inftances of longevity have occurred here. Two perfons died fome years ago at the age of 90; and there are 4 now living upwards of 80.

The neighbouring hills fupply the inhabitants with peat and turf; but much of their time in fummer is confumed in preparing and leading them home. If the tax on coals be taken off, it will probably encourage the farmers to fupply themfelves with that article, and thereby they will have more time to devote to hufbandry. The roads are more attended to, and kept in better repair, by the ftatute labour, in this than in any of the neighbouring parifhes.

---

* The price of every neceffary of life has advanced very confiderably fince 1783; fome of them have nearly doubled in value. Eggs, formerly 1 d. *per* dozen, are now 2 d; hens 8 d. formerly 5 d.; butter 7 d. formerly 5 d. *per* lib. of 24 Englifh ounces; cheefe 5 s. *per* ftone; beef, mutton, and pork, from 4 s. to 5 s. *per* ftone. But the price of no article is fo much felt, and fo loudly complained of, as falt and leather, the taxes on which fall heavily on the middling and lower claffes of people.

The clergy whofe livings are fixed, fuffer particularly by the advanced price of almoft every article neceffary in a family; but, if our Judges continue to grant augmentations to minifters on the fame liberal principles they have done of late, it will in fome degree remedy this inconveniency, and is the only circumftance that can enable them to maintain that refpect in fociety which they have hitherto done.

PARISH OF BOTRIPHNIE.

(COUNTY OF BANFF.)

By the Rev. Mr ALEXANDER ANGUS.

Name, Situation, &c.

I AM entirely unacquainted with the derivation of the name Botriphnie. It is probably Gaelic; but there is no tradition remaining how long it is fince that language was fpoken in this part of the county. The extent of the parifh from north to fouth, is about 3¼ computed miles, and from eaft to weft, about 3 miles. The parifh of Mortlich lies to the weft, Glafs to the fouth, Cairney and Keith to the eaft, and the united parifhes of Boharm and Dundurcus to the north. The diftance from the fea is 9 computed miles.

The appearance of the country is hilly; but the valley is very fertile and beautifully diverfified with fmall ftreams of water, the banks of which are covered with birch and aller, the natural production of the foil. Lime-ftone is found here in great plenty, and in many places not above 2 feet from the furface; but it is little ufed in this parifh as a manure. There are few mechanics of any kind; the men are generally employed in hufbandry, the women in fpining flax; partly

the

the growth of this country, which they manufacture into coarse cloth; and partly flax imported from Holland, which is made into finer yarn; and sent from this to Paisley or Glasgow. At present, the price of spinning is low, and a woman cannot earn more than 20d, or 2s a-week.

The farmers are in general poor. Considering the state of cultivation, the land is high-rented, the best paying nearly 20s, and the inferior 10s; but, besides the fixed rent, the tenant pays the land-tax; is obliged to work so many days in harvest, to lead fuel in summer, to carry so many loads to the distance of 20 miles; a practice which has a tendency to break the spirit of the tenant, and to discourage improvement; besides, the tenants seldom having a lease for more than 19 years.

The rent of the parish is about L. 1000; of which L. 850 belongs to Mr Duff of Drummuir; L. 100 to Lord Fife, and L. 50 to Mr Stewart of Auchluncart. The church was built in 1617, and the manse in 1776. The only funds for the maintenance of the poor, are our weekly collections, which will amount yearly, to about L. 6 sterling, and L. 3 : 10, the interest of money belonging to the Kirk Session.

The minister's stipend, including the glebe of 4 acres, does not amount to more than L. 80 sterling.

The Session Records are not older than the incumbency of my predecessor, who was settled in 1728, and was the first Presbyterian minister after the Revolution. There is a register of baptisms kept pretty regularly since 1690.

The parish consists of 630 souls, of whom males 301; females 329; the number of families 150; the average number of births 14; no register of burials kept; 103 under 10 years of age; 85 between 10, and 20. There are no remarkable instances of longevity; there are only about 3 persons in the parish above 80. We have 15 Seceders; 3 Roman ca-

tholics;

tholics; and 1 of the Epifcopal church.   Population has decreafed 1782, about 100. This decreafe is owing to the poverty of the country, and the advance of rents; the poorer people retire to the villages and towns where they are employed
by the manufacturers; and many of the young men find
more encouragement in the fouthern counties.

I am perfuaded there muft have been fome miftake in
the account of the population of this parifh given to Dr Webfter in 1755.   The numbers are ftated by him at 953.

The lift I have taken is very exact, and correfponds to a
roll of examinable perfons, as far back as 1681, which I
found lately in looking over an old Seffion Regifter; the
number at that time, was 486, and it would not be too high
a calculation to fuppofe, that there might be 100 under 8
years of age.   Since I have been here, that is, from 1774,
the population has decreafed about 100.   This is owing in
fome degree, to the bad crops in 1782, and 1783, which reduced many of the farmers, and obliged others to go to the
neighbouring towns and villages.   But befides this, mofs for
fuel is becoming every day more and more fcarce; and heritors reftrict their tenants to a certain number of fubfets.
The difficulty of providing fuel is one of the greateft obftacles
to the progrefs of agriculture; while our fouthern neighbours
are employing their horfes and fervants in the different parts
of hufbandry, we are drudging from the beginning of fummer
to the end of it, in providing at beft but a very precarious
ftock of fuel for the winter.   Were the duty taken off the
coals, we fhould then be able to provide them at a much
cheaper rate than peats, and in one fixth part of the time *.

It might be mentioned as another caufe of the decreafe of
population, that the fervants wages have advanced very con-
                                                 fiderably

---

* The duty on coals carried coaft-ways, has been taken off fince this account was written.

fiderably fince 1782, and the farmers, at leaft in this parifh, employ fewer than they did before that period; and as the cattle have advanced much in their value, more of them are reared in this country, and of confequence, lefs grain is raifed, and fewer hands are neceffary for the cultivation.

School of this Parifh.—There is a legal parifh fchool; the falary of the fchoolmafter, 12 bolls of meal; L. 2 fterling as Seffion clerk; 6d for every baptifm; 1s for every marriage; and 1s 6d a quarter for every fcholar. The number of fcholars, from 20 to 30. The children are taught reading Englifh and writing; a few of them inftructed in the principles of arithmetic; but the Latin language not fo commonly taught at the parochial fchools as formerly; though in general, the fchoolmafters are fufficiently qualified for that purpofe. This is of great confequence to minifters children, as their narrow livings could not afford to board them in a town, while at the grammar fchool.

My own family is very numerous: I have 2 fons and 5 daughters; and have been married 13 years.

There is not an ale-houfe, or inn in the parifh; we have an annual fair in the month of February; where linen yarn, commonly the production of home flax, is fold; and alfo fome farming utenfils; where bargains are made for victual, and fervants are engaged.

The farmers in this corner, generally employ hired fervants; cottagers are very little employed; they are generally tradefmen, and cultivate a few acres; which they hold of the tenant, and over and above their rent, are bound for fo many days work.

PARISH OF BOYNDIE,

(County of Banff, Synod of Aberdeen, Presbytery of Fordyce).

From Materials communicated by the Rev. Mr Alexander Milne, *the Minister.*

Name, Situation, &c.

THE origin of the name is unknown. The parish is bounded by the Murray Frith on the north and north-west; by Banff on the east; by Ordiequhill on the south, and Fordyce on the west. It is of small extent, being only five English miles long, and from a mile to a mile and an half in breadth. It contains about 3000 acres, above one half of which are arable, and 400 acres are planted with wood of different kinds, but chiefly with Scotch fir.

Soil

Soil and Agriculture.—The ſoil of the pariſh is various. The agriculture is, on the whole, pretty well conducted. Though the pariſh is of ſmall extent, yet there are generally from 60 to 70 acres of turnips, and 300 acres of ſown graſs. This pariſh was one of the firſt in the north of Scotland in which the new huſbandry was attempted, and carried on with ſucceſs. The late Earl of Findlater was the author of all theſe early improvements. The farm of Craigholes was firſt improved by his Lordſhip about 1754; and after improving this farm, to ſhew what could be done, he took every method of exciting his tenants to follow his example. He gave them long leaſes of 38 years and a lifetime. A better method could not have been deviſed. The certain period of 38 years gave his tenants a ſecurity for carrying on their improvements. The uncertain period at which the leaſe terminated, naturally deterred them from ſcourging their farms when once improved, becauſe every man flatters himſelf with the hopes of a long life. From the example and the encouragement of Lord Findlater, the face of this and ſome of the neighbouring pariſhes was ſpeedily altered. But though turnip and green crops were encouraged, and flour-mills were built, yet a regular rotation of crop has not been eſtabliſhed, nor has much wheat been raiſed in this diſtrict. It is probable, however, that the high prices of flour will occaſion wheat to be raiſed in greater quantities, though for a light ſoil a crop of turnips, and another of barley, is leſs ſcourging, and generally more productive than the ſouth country practice of fallow and wheat.

Rent.—The rent of the pariſh is moſtly in victual, and varies from L. 1000 to L. 1200.

Population.

Population.—The number of inhabitants is 1260; of which there are 800 nearly in the country parish, and 460 in the sea-town of Whitehills. The population in 1755, is stated by Dr Webster at 994 souls.

Sea-town.—The town of Whitehills is chiefly inhabited by fishers. There are seven boats employed in the fishery; and they are generally very successful. The kinds of fish principally caught are cod, ling, and haddocks; and befides considerable quantities sold in the town of Banff, and in the country around, the fishers generally carry every year to the Frith of Forth cod and ling to the amount of L. 500 or L. 600.

Stipend, &c.—The minister's stipend is, in money, L. 39, and in victual, 60 bolls. The collections for the poor amount to about L. 25 yearly, including the interest of L. 200 of lent money. The schoolmaster's salary is only 9 bolls of meal.

Character of the People.—They are sober, industrious, and charitable. From the long leases, and reasonable rents of the farms in this parish, the people have not that spur to exertion which racked rents produce for a season. But they have every inducement to steady and regular industry, which improves both their bodies and their minds; and they are strangers to that despondency, lassitude, and disguft, which, after a few years unavailing exertion, take possession of the dispirited, hard-toiling, and discontented farmer, who is oppressed by a rack-rent and short lease, and at last becomes careless of every thing, when he sees, that with all his industry, he is unable to pay his landlord and maintain his family.

PARISH OF CABRACH.

(County of Banff.—Presbytery of Alford.—Synod of Aberdeen.)

By the Reverend Mr JAMES GORDON.

—————————

Name.

THE name is derived from the Gaelic language, and signifies *the Timber Mofs*: Accordingly, the parifh is full of mofs and fir. Every place within the bounds, except fuch as are new, has a name of Gaelic extract.

Boundaries, Extent, &c.—Cabrach is 30 miles diftant from the county town, viz. Aberdeen, and furrounded by a range of hills, not very high, covered with heath. The length of this parifh, at a medium, from fouth to north, is 5 miles; the breadth, from eaft to weft, 3 miles, (all computed).

Climate, Soil, Produce, &c.—In fummer the climate is pleafant enough; and, for the benefit of goats milk, is reforted to from the low country by many of weak conftitutions, or labouring under confumption, for whofe accommodation there are 4 goat whey quarters. In winter, the frofts are more intenfe, and fnow lies deeper and longer here, than in fome of the neighbouring parifhes; but from this the natives feel no inconvenience: They have an inexhauftible mofs at their

doors,

doors, and depend not more for ſubſiſtence on the produce of their fields, than on the profits of a traffic they carry on in ſheep and black cattle. The ſoil is wet, and full of ſwamps, productive enough in provender for cattle; but owing to the froſt, miſts, and hoar froſt in autumn, the annual produce of grain does not exceed the confumpt of the inhabitants.

The farmers ſow bear and birley oats only; and theſe in the upper parts of the pariſh are always more or leſs affected by the froſts, in ſo much that if the ſeaſon has not been extremely favourable, they never depend on their own bear, and but ſeldom on their birley oats for ſeed.

Sometimes one half of a field is froſted, and the other ſafe; and what is ſtill more extraordinary, the upper half of the ear has been found to be affected, while the lower was ſafe. Daily experience evinces, that the corns on the heights and eminences, run leſs riſk than thoſe on flat low grounds. For the moſt part they begin to ſow in the end of March, and reap in September and October. Potatoes are the moſt uncertain of their crops. Turnips thrive; but for want of incloſures through the whole pariſh, experiments are not tried on a large ſcale. Clover and rye-graſs have been ſown in yards with ſucceſs; cabbages are common.

Agriculture and Employments.—The mode of culture is perhaps the ſame at this day which it was a century ago. The plough in uſe is the old Scotch, drawn by 6, 8, or 10 oxen, or cows and oxen, or horſes and oxen together. The dung is, in a great meaſure, carried out in creels, on the horſes ſides, a method by which there is a great waſte of time that might be gained, 3 of theſe loads being only equal to one of a cart.

Men and women are employed, and as ſoon as the ſeed time is done, the plough and harrow are laid aſide; the farmers

mers mind little elfe but their cattle; the women, befides their ordinary domeftic affairs, are employed in providing coarfe cloths for the family, and fpinning linen yarn to the manufactories.

Neverthelefs, with all thefe peculiarities of climate and cuftoms, the tenants, efpecially within the four hills of Cabrach, are in good circumftances enough for their rank, and are thriving. Nature feems to have intended the country more for pafturage than agriculture; aware of this, the inhabitants pay their attention chiefly to fheep and black cattle. Early in the fpring, they ftock their little farms with the former, and, about Whitfunday, with the latter. During the courfe of the fummer, they are ever buying and felling at home and in markets. About the end of Auguft, they clear their towns, if the fale is brifk, of all except as many as they have provender to fupport in the winter: If the market has been bad, they keep more than their ufual number, and buy corn and ftraw for them in the neighbouring parifhes.—By thefe means they feldom meet with much lofs, nor indeed can it ever be great; their ftocks are fmall, and the circle of their trade but narrow, of courfe, the little fpeculation that is here, depending merely upon the appearance of a good grafs crop, or a demand from the fouth, is feldom attended with bad confequences, even if the crop fhould happen to be fhort. Accordingly, one year with another, they replace the capitals employed in this trade, with a fmall profit, deducting all charges.

Eftimate of Black Cattle, &c.

Black cattle bought and fold, about	L. 500
Kept in winter on each farm,	30
Sheep bought and fold,	2000
Kept in winter,	1000

Horfes

Horſes in the pariſh, all ſmall,   -   -   -   335
Black cattle, taken to hill paſture annually, at 2 s. each, 350
Black cattle, taken to infield graſs, at 5 s. Sterling each, 200

Quarries.—Thoſe who reſide in the northern parts, contiguous to Mortlach, burn and ſell annually about 4000 bolls
of lime, at 6 d. *per* boll; two firlots Aberdeen meaſure make
a boll. Lime is little uſed here as a manure, on the ſuppoſition that it turns the crop late. It is preſumed, however,
that in ſome parts it would be attended with advantage.

Beſides great numbers of lime-ſtone quarries, there is a
ſlate quarry, of a light grey colour on the Hill of the Bank;
there being little demand for the ſlates, the quarry is not in
leaſe. They are not ſold, but given *gratis.*

Forreſts.—The banks of the river Dovern, about half a
century ago, were covered with birch, although, ſince the
ſale of it, there is not a plant of wood to be ſeen there, or in
any part of the pariſh, except in Glen-Feddich, where there
are ſome old trees, and on the burn of Bank, where there
are ſome young buſhes. The Feddick, which runs into
the Spey, between Aberlour and Boharn, riſes between Cabrach and Glenlivet, and runs into Mortlach. On its banks
the Duke of Gordon has a houſe for a hunting ſeat in a beautiful romantic ſpot, but within the pariſh of Mortlach. He
has another farther up on the Black-water, in the ſame pariſh. The foreſts of Gleneddich and Black-water are ſtored
with red deer and roes; the hills all around, with innumerable flocks of muir-fowl. Here there are partridges, hares,
foxes, otters, wild ducks, and black cocks. The migratory
birds are the ſwallow, the plover, and cuckow, who appear
about the middle of April.

Church,

Church, School, and Poor.—The minifter's ftipend is 45 l.
Sterling, and the fervices; befides 2 l. 15 l. 6½ d. Sterling
for communion element money; with a glebe of 19 acres
arable, and 2 of pafture ground. The parochial fchool falary
is 5 l. 11 s. 1½ d. Sterling. The charity fchool was taken
away from Dovernfide in 1779, a want which the people
there feel much. To remedy this in fome degree, they hire
a country man to teach their children to read and write in
winter; the only time they can difpenfe with them from
herding their cattle.—The number of poor on the roll who
receive occafional fupply are 12. The weekly contributions
amount annually to 2 l. Sterling, befides a fund of 50 l. Sterling at intereft, under the management of the heritors and
kirk-feffion.

Religion, Sectaries, &c.—Befides the eftablifhed Church,
there are two chapels; one for Papifts, who are not half the
number that they were 30 years ago, and one for Seceders,
who are much on the decline. One great reafon for the
decline of both fects, is the moderation with which they are
treated all over this country. Intermarriages with Proteftant
families have been frequently obferved to bring over Papifts,
efpecially the female part, from their former perfuafion.

Character, Difeafes, &c.—The inhabitants, whofe ordinary
fize is 5 feet 10 inches, though variable from 5 feet 6 inches
to 6 feet, are induftrious, fober, and healthy; live much better, are neater and cleanlier in their dreffes and dwellings
than their predeceffors were fome generations ago, when
men and beafts lay under the fame roof. They all read and
write; are intelligent in the ordinary and even fome of the lefs
common affairs of life, beyond what could be expected from
their opportunities, and of an obliging difpofition. Notwithftanding

ſtanding the temptations inſeparable from the ſpecies of traffic they are conſtantly engaged in, in the cattle markets, they
are not addicted to drinking.—However unaccountable, in
ſuch a place, the want of inns and alehouſes may be, *there is
not one in the pariſh ;* a circumſtance perhaps not unfriendly to
health and morals; nor are the inconveniencies attending it
felt by travellers, becauſe of the hoſpitality of the people.
With all the neceſſaries, and ſome of the conveniencies of
life, they live happy and content at home. They are not in
general litigious; nor are law-ſuits frequent, which is a conſequence of their honeſty in dealings. That the natives of a
place full of moſſes, and interſperſed with ſwampy ground,
ſhould be healthy, and ſubject to no local diſtemper, may
appear a little problematical; yet, excepting a few fevers,
which are by no means frequent or fatal, the hooping cough,
meaſles, and ſmall-pox in the natural way, are the only diſeaſes known here. The moſt common diſeaſe of which they
die is old age. Of late, the conſumption has appeared in 4
inſtances; in each of them fatal, excepting one caſe. Thoſe
who died of it were attacked when at ſervice in other countries. It is not pretended to account for the healthineſs of
the people. Perhaps the great fires conſtantly burning in
their houſes, have confiderable influence in counteracting the
effects of the exhalations which are continually riſing from
the earth. Strangers, not accuſtomed to them, catch cold.

Valued Rent, Servants Wages, &c.—The valued rent in
this pariſh is 1290 l. 2 s. 10 d. Scotch.

Men ſervants gain yearly about (Sterling) -	L. 5	5	0
Women ditto - - - -		2	10	0
Geeſe are ſold at - - - -		0	2	6
Hens are ſold at - - - -		0	0	6
Butter *per* lib. - - - -		0	0	6
Cheeſe *per* quarter - - - -		0	1	0

The

The services which used to be paid to the principal tacksman were happily done away when the present leases were given by the Duke of Gordon, by getting tacks immediately from himself; the best thing he could have done to this country.

Population, &c.—The number in 1755 was 960.
Within the parish are, above 8 years of age, catechise-
able, - - - - - - 550
Children below 8 years of age, - - - 150
___
700

Each marriage, at an average, produces 4 children.

Remarks —The number of inhabitants has decreased about 200 since 1782 and 1783; at which period the householders or crofters were driven in quest of subsistence to other countries and towns, where manufactures are carried on.—The upper part of the parish in Aberdeenshire seldom produces sufficiency of grain for itself. The lower part of the parish in Banffshire produces sufficiency of grain for itself, and disposes of about 200 bolls, which would make up the deficiency in the upper part, was it not disposed of to the neighbouring distilleries. The defect is made up from other places. The state of the inhabitants then, (in 1782) when few places hereabout had enough for themselves, may be learned from this circumstance, that the *mill multures* of Cabrach amounted to a ninth part only of what they are in ordinary years; yet, by means of the indulgence of the Duke of Gordon, who allowed them to detain their rents for buying meal, and supporting their families, till they were able to pay without hurting them, and the spirited exertions of individuals, particularly John Gordon, Esq; of Craig, who imported grain of different kinds for a subsistence to the indigent poor, which

he

he gave to this and fome of the neighbouring parifhes, no body fuffered for want; but their circumftances were much impaired; there was no demand for cattle. Meal was fold at 1 s. 6 d. and 2 s. *per* peck, 9 lib. Servants fuffered moft; for every body reduced their numbers; and day-labourers got little if any employment.

So early as the 15th September 1782, there was a great fall of fnow, which laid all the corns, then hardly begun to fill, in moft places. The frofts were often intenfe, and vegetation was ftopt here.

The corns which had milky juices in the ear were totally ruined; thofe which had only watery juices wanted feafon; there were none of them perfectly full or ripe. They were therefore given moftly unthrefhed to the cattle. It was after Chriftmas before they were all cut. The meal made of what was threfhed was bad. To fome it may appear trivial, to others worthy to be remarked, that, in fpring 1783, cows had calves much earlier, and in greater numbers, than was ever remembered; a fortunate circumftance, in a year when the victual of home produce was exceffively bad, and in a place where milk is a conftituent part of ordinary fare. It was obferved, too, very truly, as to this parifh, that there was lefs ficknefs that year than ufual; a fact which the curious will, no doubt, trace up to feveral caufes.

PARISH of CULLEN.

(COUNTY OF BANFF, SYNOD OF ABERDEEN, PRESBYTERY OF
FORDYCE.)

By the Rev. MR. ROBERT GRANT.

Royalty, Extent, Climate, &c.

CULLEN, as appears from old charters, was originally
called *Inverculan,* becaufe it ftands upon the bank of
the Burn of Cullen, which, at the N. end of the town, falls
into the fea: but now it is known by the name of Cullen only. Cullen is a royal burgh, formerly a conftabulary, of
which the Earl of Findlater was hereditary conftable. The
fet, as it is called, of the council, confifts of 19, in which number are included the Earl of Findlater, hereditary prefes, 3
bailies, a treafurer, a dean-of-guild, and 13 counfellors. The
parifh extends from the fea fouthward, about 2 Englifh miles
in length, and about 1 mile in breadth. The annexed part
of the parifh of Rathven, *quoad facra,* is of extent about 3
miles in length, and 2 in breadth, forming together the figure
of a quadrant, having a ftraight line on the N. and E. and
the

the ſegment of a circle on the W. and S.   The face of the
country is neither hilly nor flat ; in general the fields have
an eaſy gentle ſlope.   The ſoil is of 3 kinds ; the greateſt
part is a fine rich loam, upon a ſoft clay bottom ; ſome fields
of a ſtrong rich clay, and a few of a light loam, upon a tilly
bottom.   As the fields in general are dry, and as the hills in
the neighbouring pariſhes of Rathven and Deſkford attract the
clouds and vapours that ariſe from the ſea, the air of this pariſh is pure and extremely wholeſome ; as a proof of this, many of the inhabitants live and enjoy comfortable health, till
far paſt 80, and ſeverals above 90 years.   And no local or epidemical diſtemper has been known to prevail in the memory
of any perſon alive.   Even the ſmall-pox, in the natural way,
is become mild, and in no proportion ſo fatal as in former
times ; but this may be owing to the greater degree of cleanlineſs among the people, and learning the modern treatment
of that loathſome diſtemper.

Agriculture.—The farms are ſmall, from 5 l. to 50l. of
rent, and the fine field about the town is let in ſmall lots, to
accommodate the inhabitants.   Although the ſoil is fit to produce any kind of grain, yet the crops generally raiſed are,
oats, barley, peaſe, beans, turnip, potatoes, ſown graſs and
fl x.   Flax ſeems to be a precarious crop upon the eaſt coaſt
of Scotland ; the ſoil and climate are too dry for it, but in a
moiſt ſeaſon there are good crops.   This obſervation might,
perhaps, be worthy the attention of landholders and farmers
in moiſter climates, where crops of corn are more precarious,
to encourage the culture of flax ; eſpecially as it is an early
crop, and fit for pulling before the ſeaſon of the mildews, ſo
fatal to grain, generally ſets in.   The average rent of the land
is from 10 s. to 2 l. 10 s. the acre.   The only plough uſed
here

here is the light Yorkſhire plough, commonly drawn by 2 horſes.

Fiſheries.—The sea affords plenty and variety of fiſhes, haddock, whiting, flounders, mackerel, holybut, turbot, cod, ling, tuſk, ſkate, dog and cat. The only ſhell-fiſh in abundance is crab and lobſter, which laſt are caught in great quantities, and of late ſent to the London market. There are two fiſhing villages, one at the north end of the town of Cullen, where there are 7 fiſhing boats; and one called Portknockies, 2 miles weſt of Cullen, in the annexed part of the pariſh of Rathven, where there are other 7 boats. Each boat has 6 men; by whoſe induſtry the town and country around are amply ſupplied with good fiſh. Beſides what is ſold daily, the fiſhers cure and dry a conſiderable quantity of cod, ling, ſkate and haddocks, which, after ſerving the country, they carry to Montroſe, Forfar, Dundee and Leith, where, beſides their oil, each man ſells at an average, 10 l. value of fiſh; and they bring home hemp, wool, and ſalt for their own uſe.

Manufactures.—Before the year 1748, the inhabitants of Cullen were as poor and idle as any ſet of people in the north. There was no induſtry, trade, nor manufacture among them: their only employment was to labour a few acres of land, and to keep tippling houſes; and often to drink with one another, to conſume the beer for want of cuſtomers. The late Earl of Findlater, that true patriot, pitying the ſituation of the people, reſolved to introduce the linen manufacture among them. And here, perhaps, it may not be improper to mention the method he adopted to promote this purpoſe. He brought 2 or 3 gentlemen's ſons from Edinburgh, who had been regularly bred there to the buſineſs, and who had ſome patrimony of their own; but, for their encouragement to ſettle ſo far

north,

north, he gave to each 600 l. free of intereſt for ſeven years;
after which, the money was to be repaid by 50 l yearly, the
remainder in their hands to be always free of intereſt. Beſides this, he built excellent weaving ſhops, and furniſhed
every accommodation at very reaſonable rates : and as his
lordſhip preſided at the Board of Truſtees at Edinburgh, he
obtained for his young manufacturers, premiums of looms,
heckles, reels, and ſpinning wheels, with a ſmall ſalary to a
ſpinning miſtreſs. So good a plan, and ſo great encouragement, could not fail of ſucceſs. In a few years, the manufacture was eſtabliſhed to the extent deſired. All the young
people were engaged in the buſineſs; and even the old found
employment in various ways by the manufactures : and thus
a ſpirit of induſtry was diffuſed over the place and neighbourhood in a very ſhort time, which ſoon appeared in their comfortable mode of living, and their dreſs. The manufacture
here, as well as in other places, has had its viciſſitudes, owing
to good or bad markets and demands ; but ſtill it continues
on the whole in a comfortable ſtate. There are in this ſmall
place 65 looms, conſtantly employed in weaving linen, ſome
few of them in weaving damaſk. The manufacturers alſo
give out a great number of webs to be woven by country
weavers in their own ſhops. There are alſo 7 ſtocking looms
conſtantly employed.

Population.—According to Dr. Webſter's report, the population then was 900. About 100 years ago, at the average
of 7 years, multiplying the baptiſms by 26, the number of
people in Cullen, and the annexed part of the pariſh of Rathven, amounted to 806. 60 years ſince, by the ſame rule, the
number was 1040, but the accuracy of the regiſters, I am a-
fraid, cannot be depended upon. By a liſt taken in 1791,
the number of ſouls in the pariſh of Cullen, and the annexed
                                                          part

part of the parifh of Rathven, amounted to 1719. Of which, in the parifh of Cullen 1214 ; of thefe, males 550, females 664. In the annexed part of Rathven 505 ; males 271, females 234. Of the above numbers in Cullen, and the annexed part of Rathven, there are under 7 years of age, males 140, females 115. The increafe of the population has been only in the town of Cullen, and in the fea-towns of Cullen and Portknockies : for during the periods of the above average-calculations, there were feveral farms well peopled, which, after that, were enclofed for the Earl of Findlater's own accommodation, and are fince uninhabited. The average of baptifms annually, is about 45, marriages 12. The bulk of the people are of the Eftablifhed religion. Before the year 1782, there was not one Catholic in the parifh, at prefent there are about 30, and 8 Epifcopalians.

Church, Stipend, School, Charitable foundations, Poor, &c.— Cullen feems originally to have been a Chapel of Eafe for the accommodation of the people of that corner of the parifh of Fordyce, and the contiguous part of Rathven ; there were 2 churches or chapels, that of St. Mary and St. Anne ; the latter was a prebend. The prefent church is compounded of the two former ; it is very old, not well lighted, and too fmall for the congregation. The Earl of Findlater and Seafield is patron. The ftipend confifts of 40 l. 18 s. 10$\frac{8}{12}$ d. in money, including 50 merks for communion elements, 2 chalders of barley and 2 chalders of meal. The glebe confifts of 4$\frac{1}{4}$ acres and fome falls ; but the minifter has no grafs, nor any allowance for it. The manfe was repaired about 7 years fince, at which time there was a complete fet of offices built and covered with flates. Lord Findlater is proprietor of the whole parifh, except fome property belonging to the town-council ; one fmall heritage, confifting of a houfe, a garden, and an acre

of

of land, and ſome few acres mortified for pious uſes *.—There
is generally a good ſchool in Cullen, where from 40 to 50
boys are taught Latin, Engliſh, writing, arithmetic, and book-
keeping ; but the ſchoolmaſter's ſalary is very ſmall : he has
only about 6 l. 10 s. a-year, the greateſt part of which ariſes
from two pious donations, to be afterward mentioned.   There
is a pretty good ſchool-houſe, and a convenient room for the
accommodation of the maſter.   School-fees for teaching Engliſh 1 s. 6 d., writing and arithmetic 2 s., and for Latin 2s 6d.
the quarter.   There is a ſchoolmiſtreſs who has a ſalary of 5l.
for teaching girls to read and ſew.   And there are generally
other two ſchools, where young children are taught to read
Engliſh, and are inſtructed in the principles of Chriſtianity.
The Earl of Findlater had a bede-houſe in the town of Cullen,
which accommodated 8 poor men, who had peats allowed
them for fuel, and each had 6½ bolls of meal yearly.   The
bede-houſe being ruinous, was lately taken down ; but the
Earl allows a houſe free of rent, and the fuel, to ſuch of the
bede-men as incline to poſſeſs it, but few of them ſeem inclined to do it ; but the meal is regularly given to poor perſons, and ſometimes divided between two poor families, which
makes it more extenſively uſeful†.—The number of poor receiving

---

* Lord Findlater has his chief ſeat of reſidence here, called Cullen houſe. It
is literally founded upon a rock, which is above 50 feet high, almoſt perpendicular, hanging over the burn of Cullen.   The ſituation of the houſe is romanti-
cally pleaſant, having a beautiful proſpect to the S., and a fine view of the Moray-frith to the N.   To the W. of the houſe there is an excellent bridge of one
arch, caſt over the burn, 84 feet wide, and 64 feet high, which makes an eaſy communication with the park and woods, where the ground admits of endleſs beauty and variety.

† William Lawtie of Myrehouſe, appointed a croft of land, with ſome houſes
and a ſum of money, with which were purchaſed ſome additional acres of land,
which pay of yearly rent for behoof of the poor, 10 bolls and an half of barley,
and 13 s. of money.   This foundation is under the management of the heirs of
the

ceiving alms is 80 ; which is very great, confidering the number of the people ; the chief reafon of this is, the liberal fupplies which they receive from the beneficence of the noble family here, makes them prefs in from all corners. As there
are

the late Rev. Mr. Lawtie of Fordyce. John Lawtie, burgefs of Cullen, bequeathed his whole property, confifting of a houfe, a fmall garden, and a croft
of land for behoof of the poor of Cullen, which pays of yearly rent to the kirk-
feffion, 1 guinea. William Leflie of Birdfbank, an heritor in the parifh, bequeathed the fum of a 1000 merks Scotch, the intereft of which, was to be applied as an encouragement to a fchoolmafter in Cullen, under direction of the
magiftrates of Cullen. This money, by a negotiation of the magiftrates, was
fettled in the hands of the Earl of Findlater, upon his agreeing to make fome
addition to it, and he thereby is become patron of the fchool, the magiftrates
and council paying 1 l. 2 s. 2 d. 6-12ths, of a farther addition, which makes the
falary in whole 5 l. Sterling yearly. A man of the name of Smith, who had a
fmall houfe, a garden, and a croft of land. left them and the rents of them as
an additional encouragement to the fchoolmafter of Cullen—the rent of the
whole is about 1 l. 10 s. yearly. John Lorimer, town-clerk of Cullen, appointed a piece of land, with 1 or 2 houfes upon it, for the education of a boy at the
fchool of Cullen, of his own name, or related to him. Befides the rent of the
houfes, the land paid, in the end of the laft century, 6 bolls charitat bear, that
is, 6 bolls, 6 pecks barley, yearly. This foundation has been very ufeful in
giving education to a number of the founder's relations ; and among others, to
a great nephew of his own, Mr. William Lorimer of St. James's parifh, London, who out of gratitude for the benefit of his own education upon his great
uncle's burfe at the fchool of Cullen, appointed by his laft will, a fum of money
fit to produce, by intereft, 1 l. Sterling yearly, to purchafe books for his great
uncle's burfar at Cullen; and alfo, 10 s. yearly to the fchoolmafter at Cullen, for
his attention to faid burfar : And further, the faid Mr. William Lorimer appointed the intereft of 200 l. Sterling, for a burfary at the Marifchal College of
Aberdeen ; and that his great uncle's burfar at Cullen, when found qualified,
fhould enjoy this burfary at the college, with the relations by his mother alternately. Mr. William Lorimer's burfary is under the direction of the mafters of
Marifchal College, and the magiftrates and church-feffion of Cullen. John
Watfon, merchant in Edinburgh, appointed the intereft of 1000 merks Scotch,
for affifting in the education of a boy at the fchool of Cullen, related to himfelf
by father or mother ; alfo, the intereft of 100 l. Scotch, to be paid to the mafter of the fchool of Cullen for the boy's education. Collector John Ogilvie of
the

are no poor's rates, the only ordinary supplies arise from the
weekly collections at the church, with the interest of some
settled money, amounting in whole to about 35 l. a-year: out
of which the session-clerk and officers fees are paid. This
would be by no means an adequate supply for such a number
of poor, if Lord Findlater did not only give 10 bolls and a firlot of meal yearly to be distributed by the church session, but
also appoint supplies of meal and money for all their exigencies, which makes their state here better than anywhere else
in the neighbourhood *.

Woods.—It may not be improper from Cullen, the principal seat of the Earl of Findlater and Seafield, to take a general view of the immense plantations of trees made by that
family. Before the year 1744, little in that way was done.
The whole country, and even about Cullen house, was naked
and destitute of cover or ornament from trees. Since the
above period, it appears by attested lists before the writer,
that the Earls of Findlater have planted upwards of 8000
Scotch

the customs at Inverness, and his son bailie William Ogilvie, merchant in Banff,
bequeathed the sum of 44 l. 9s. Sterling, the interest of which is to be applied
by the church-session of Cullen, for behoof of their poor relations, and the poor
of the parish in equal parts. James Ogilvie, formerly wadsetter of Logie, bequeathed for behoof of the poor of the parish of Cullen, the sum of 300 merks
Scotch.

 * Although the whole produce of grain in the parish is never sufficient for
the consumpt of the people, yet meal is always here in as great plenty, and as
good in quality, and as cheap, as in any part of Scotland; owing to the attention of Lord Findlater and his managers. 20 or 30 years since, eggs sold 14 for
a penny, now they are 2 d. for 12. Hens, which were sold for 4 d. each, now
give 7 d. and 8 d. Beef and mutton, which used to sell from 1 d. to 2 d. the
pound, now sell from 2½ d. to 4 d. the pound. Haddocks, which were from 1 d.
to 2d. the dozen, sell now at 7 d. and 8 d. the dozen, and other articles in proportion. The price of labour is rising so fast, that it may be said not to be settled at present.

Scotch acres, about Cullen, and in their other eftates in the counties of Banff and Moray ; and, if we allow 4000 plants, as ufual, for every Scotch acre, the number originally planted, will exceed the amazing fum of 32,000,000 of trees. All thefe plantations, which at firft were generally planted with common firs, have been, with great care and attention, properly filled up with larch, and great variety of hard wood plants, fuited to the different foils ; and all this upon ground which never returned one farthing of rent to the proprietor.

For the encouragement of thofe who have wafte ground fit for planting, I fhall beg leave to quote the following curious paragraph, from an account before me, attefted by Mr. George Brown, furveyor of land at Elgin, and factor to Lord Findlater there. " To fhow in fome degree the value of Lord Findlater's plantations, and the very rapid progrefs they make in this country near Elgin, there was a good deal cut out of one plantation of common firs, to make room for more valuable and ufeful trees ; many of thofe cut out meafured of girth 2 feet 10 inches and 3 feet, and fold at 3 d. Sterling the tree, and, in general, when fawn down the middle, are large enough for paleing and other ufes. This is a fingular inftance of wood only planted 18 years, and fhows the great wealth that will accumulate from thofe plantations."

Mountains.—There is only one remarkable mountain called the Bin-hill ; it has two tops, the one higher than the other, it lies about a mile S. W. of the town of Cullen, about two miles from the fea, and ferves as a land-mark to the fifhers. Its elevation above the fea is faid to be from 1000 to 1100 feet. It was formerly covered with heath, but is now planted with trees.

Character of the People.—The people, in general, are fober and

and induſtrious. They enjoy a reaſonable ſhare of the comforts of life, and ſeem ſtrongly attached to the place of their
abode. They have long been remarkable for their charitable
diſpoſition, not only to their poor neighbours, but alſo to
ſtrangers. They live peaceably with one another. In proof
of this, although they have town-courts at their door, and
the ſheriff-court within 8 miles of them, there is hardly ſuch
a thing as a law-ſuit heard of among them.

Advantages and Diſadvantages.—The town of Cullen, by
its ſituation, has many advantages. It lies on the poſt road,
which is kept in good repair. It has, in general, good ſchools.
It has the advantage and accommodation of a poſt-office, a
pretty good butcher market, plenty of all the neceſſaries of
life ſupplied from a rich country, on the one hand, and an
ample ſupply of all kinds of fiſh from the ſea, on the other,
with command of plenty of moſs for fuel. The diſadvantages are, a ſcanty ſupply of good water. There is not a
good ſpring in the pariſh of Cullen but one, and that lies
without the town. To the burn of Cullen, there is acceſs
only at two places, and there the roads are ſo ſteep, that it is
difficult to carry up water. The only ſupply, is a ciſtern in
the centre of the town, where water is brought in leaden
pipes from the annexed part of the pariſh of Rathven. To
accommodate the town properly, they would need at leaſt
other two ciſterns. The houſes, in general, though cheap
rented, are mean and bad; and moſt of them being placed
with their ends to the ſtreet, it offends the eye of the traveller. If Lord Findlater were either to lock up his moſſes,
or to alter the roads, and thereby render them more diſtant,
the inhabitants would ſoon be obliged to remove, except his
Lordſhip were pleaſed to make a harbour for ſhips to bring
coal, which would be far preferable to their preſent fuel. If
it

it were agreeable to his Lordſhip to erect better houſes, and to build a harbour at the ſhore, which it is believed, would not be attended with a great expenſe, Cullen would perhaps be one of the moſt comfortable and convenient places in the north of Scotland to live in.

Antiquities.—At the north end of the town of Cullen, there is a beautiful green hill, called the Caſtle-hill, hanging over the ſea, which before the uſe of cannon, was extremely well ſituated for a place of ſtrength, being inacceſſible from the north by an almoſt perpendicular high rock, and having a deep ditch in all other directions for its defence. There is no record concerning it, when, or by whom built, or when deſtroyed ; but it is evident from the calcined ſtones dug every where, that it has been deſtroyed by fire. And the only tradition concerning it is, that the town of Cullen lay at the eaſt ſide of it, and when an enemy appeared, the inhabitants carried their moſt valuable effects into the caſtle for protection ; but when the caſtle was burned, that the inhabitants removed to the preſent ſituation of the town, to be under the protection of the conſtable at Cullen houſe, the reſidence of the Earl of Findlater. Near Cullen houſe, there is the veſtige of a houſe, in which, it is ſaid, Queen Elizabeth, Queen of King Robert Bruce died. In the annexed part of the pariſh of Rathven, there is the ruin of a chapel at Farſkane, upon the ſea bank, which is ſuppoſed to have been a Chapel of Eaſe in the pariſh of Rathven, and worſhip was probably performed there by the clergymen from Cullen.

* *Royal Deaths.*—It is ſomewhat curious, that ſo far
north

---

* With regard to the death of Indulfus, there is no doubt. The accounts given of it by Buchanan, and Abercrombie in his Martial Atchievements, agree
perfectly

north as Cullen, in Lord Findlater's eftate, a King and
Queen of Scotland fhould have died, namely, King Indulfus,

perfectly with the then fituation of the country; That the King having prevented the Danes from landing at the Frith of Forth, at the Tay, and Aberdeen, upon being informed that they had unexpectedly landed at Cullen, haftened forward with his army, attacked and totally routed them, and made them
fly to their fhips; but hearing that there ftill remained a fmall body of them
together at the fide of a wood, he rafhly rufhed forward with a handful of men,
and attacked them, where he fell fighting valiantly in defence of the liberty of
his country. Upon the place where the King fell, there was, as ufual, a huge
cairn of ftones collected, which, to this day, is called the King's Cairn. It
lies a mile weft from Cullen houfe, in the annexed part of the parifh of Rathven. The ground which was formerly an open moor fit for a field of battle, is
now covered with fine trees, and around the cairn there are about 3 acres of
ground enclofed, and ufed as a nurfery for raifing young trees. A great many
of the ftones of the cairn were ufed for this enclofure, but the remainder of the
cairn is as yet very diftinct. Whether the body of King Indulfus was buried
under this cairn, or whether, according to the Scoti-chronicon, it was carried
to the Ifland of Calumb Kill or Jona, I fhall not pretend to judge; but it would
certainly be worth while to examine the bottom of the cairn, to know whether
there is any urn or ftone coffin in it, according to the cuftom of our anceftors in
thofe days. With regard to the death of Queen Elizabeth, the writer afferts
nothing pofitively; but he thinks it proper to mention the circumftances that
have come to his knowledge, which at leaft make the matter appear probable.
In the 1ft place, The tradition mentioned above, concerning the houfe in which
Queen Elizabeth is faid to have died, is very diftinct in the place. But what
tends to confirm this; 2dly, From the charter of the town of Cullen, a copy
of which is before the writer, it appears, " That Robert of Bruce, King of the
Scotch, granted and gave in gift for ever, 5l. of the money of the kingdom
(that is, 8s. and 4d. Sterling) for the fupport of a chaplain in the parifh church
of the bleffed Mary of our burgh of Cullen, always to pray for the falvation of
the foul of the moft ferene Princefs Queen Elizabeth, confort of the fame King
Robert." And, 3dly, There is a tradition that Queen Elizabeth's bowels are
erded, that is, buried in our Lady Kirk of Cullen. Now, it may be afked, if
the Queen had not died in Cullen, what could have given rife to thefe diftinct
traditions, and particularly, why would her hufband have endowed a chaplain
to pray for the falvation of her foul in the church of Cullen? But the great
queftion is, what could have brought Queen Elizabeth to Cullen? The moft
probable

fus, and Queen Elizabeth, fecond Queen of King Robert Bruce.

N U M-

probable anfwer to this is, that as fhe had a daughter married to the then Earl of Sutherland, fhe had come upon a vifit to her daughter. And as the family of Sutherland had then confiderable property in the Boyn and Enzie, probably fome friend of that family lived in this houfe, where the Queen is faid to have died. Whether the burying her bowels in the church implies the burial of the whole body, or whether the bowels only were interred in Cullen, I fhall not take upon me to determine; but I never heard of any other place for her interment.

PARISH of DESKFORD,

(COUNTY OF BANFF.)

By the Rev. Mr WALTER CHALMERS.

Name, Situation, Surface, &c.

ACCORDING to ſome, *Deiſh* ſignifies a " Linn or Lake.'' As there is a ſmall linn formed by a water-fall, a little to the north of the village, Deſkford may ſignify the ford near the linn. According to others, *Deſkford* is a corruption from *Cheſsfure*, which ſignifies " a cold ſouth," or a " cold place to the ſouthward." This alſo anſwers to the ſituation of the pariſh, as it lies ſouth from the ſea, and varies conſiderably in climate from the country along the coaſt. The worthy and ingenious Mr Lawtie, miniſter of Fordyce, thinks Deſkford a corruption from Decius's Fort. His opinion is founded upon a belief, that there was a Roman ſtation in the pariſh *. Deſkford was originally a

part

---

* Mr Lawtie has formed this opinion from Roman coins found at Deſkford; remains of foſſes and roads; ſimilarity of ſituation to ſtations in England; exact diſtance between it and the ſtation at Rothes (Tuiſſis) as mentioned in Richard's Itinerary; ancient bridge over Spey on this road; ancient name of the water of Deſkford (Cullan) which is not more different from Selina (Deſkford) than Ituna (now Fyvie) from Itheo Æſaca (now Brechin) from Eſk, Devana (now Aberdeen) from Dee, &c.

part of the pariſh of Fordyce, and was included in Cullen, when that pariſh was disjoined from Fordyce; but the preciſe period when Deſkford was erected into a ſeparate pariſh from Cullen is not diſtinctly known. It appears from a decreet of ſtipend for Fordyce, that the Union ſubſiſted in the year 1618. The pariſh of Deſkford lies in the preſbytery of Fordyce, and Synod of Aberdeen. It is bounded upon the W. and N. by the pariſh of Ruthven, on the N. E. and E. by Fordyce, and on the S. and S. W. by Grange. Its length from N. to S. may be about 5 Engliſh miles; its breadth from E. to W. variable, but the greateſt about 3 miles. The form of the pariſh is that of a ſtrath, having hills on the E. and W. and a ſmall opening to the S. and N. The fields lie in a ſloping direction from the hills towards a ſmall river or burn, which runs in the hollow, and has its banks covered with a variety of natural wood. From ſprings in the hills on each ſide of the ſtrath, deſcend through the fields various rivulets, which empty themſelves into the burn, and which are beautifully edged with natural wood. In many of theſe rivulets are water-falls, which, in ſummer floods and winter thaws, deſcend through the trees with great impetuoſity, and exhibit many romantic and pictureſque ſcenes.

Hills.—Upon the E. ſide of the ſtrath is the Green Hill, which was formerly a commonty to the tenants, and afforded a rough kind of paſture. The late Earl of Findlater, who was the patron of farming, of manufactures, and of every meaſure that tended to the improvement of his country, tried to bring it into culture. With this view, it was incloſed and divided with ditch and hedge, belts of Scotch fir and alder planted, and a complete ſet of farmhouſes built; but after conſiderable expence, and repeated trials,

trials, his Lordſhip was diſcouraged. The bleak ſituation, the bad expoſure, the wetneſs of ſoil, owing to a pan beneath it, prevented the crops from filling and ripening. The incloſures are now let annually for paſture. The hedges, by great care and attention, thrive in ſome places; but the planting in the belts does not promiſe to ſucceed. The preſent Earl of Findlater, about 10 years ago, made trial of the larix fir in one of the incloſures to N. E. It thrives at preſent, and gives encouragement to proceed in planting under its ſhelter. Upon the W. ſide of the ſtrath, is a hill called *Old More*, which affords, at a moderate diſtance, a plentiful ſupply of excellent peat and turf. The late Earl of Findlater parcelled out the ſkirts of this hill into ſmall lots, and let them at a low rent; but the people are poor, and their improvements not ſubſtantial.

Soil and Produce.—The ſoil, along the lower parts of the Strath, is generally a loam, with a bottom of ſtrong deep clay, and produces wheat, barley, oats, peas, beans, and good crops of hay. Towards the hills, it is a light black ſoil, and under it, an obſtinate pan. Owing to this pan, in ſome places, and the clay bottom in others, the fields retain the rains long; which circumſtance retards the labour in the ſpring, and renders the crops late, eſpecially in rainy ſeaſons. In favourable ſeaſons, the tenants ſell conſiderable quantities of barley and oats to merchants in Portſoy, who export them generally to the ſouth frith. In the pariſh, there are ſpots of mooriſh and waſte ground, which might be improved to advantage. One of conſiderable extent adjoining to a farm, has been lately trenched and drained, at the expence of the heritor. This is a ſubſtantial and advantageous mode of improvement. It not only gives bread

to

to the induſtrious, and beautifies the face of the country, but perhaps proves more lucrative to the landholder, than an extenſion of property. In the lower grounds, the ſoil ſeems peculiarly adapted for the growth of planting; and had the famous Dr Johnſon directed his tour through Deſkford, and deigned to pull down the blinds of his carriage *, he would have ſeen many trees not unworthy of attention from the moſt prejudiced Engliſh traveller. In an orchard adjoining to an ancient caſtle, there is particularly an aſh-tree, which meaſures in girth 24 feet 5¼ inches. It is called St John's tree, from its vicinity to a chapel of that name, to be afterwards mentioned. There is another aſh in the ſame orchard, which meaſures in girth 12 feet 3½ inches, having a ſhank 20 feet high, of nearly the ſame dimenſions. This aſh is called Young St John. There is alſo a holly tree, perhaps the largeſt of its ſpecies in this country. It meaſures, at the diſtance of 2 feet from the ground, 8 feet 4¼ inches in girth. In ſeveral places of the pariſh, hedges have been planted; and they alſo thrive amazingly, when they receive proper care and attention.— There is a quarry of limeſtone at Craibſtown, which yields lime ſuperior in ſtrength and colour to any in the neighbourhood. It is conſequently in great requeſt, and affords a profitable employment to many of the tenants, in ſummer and autumn.

Church, and ancient Caſtles.—There is no date upon the church; one pew in it bears 1627, another 1630. It is ſituated nearly in the centre of the ſtrath, and, like the generality of churches in this country, is gloomy and miſerably furniſhed.—Cloſe by it is an old caſtle, called the Tower

of

---

* It is ſaid the Doctor drew up the blinds of his carriage in paſſing through Cullen.

of Defkford, and faid to have been built by the Sinclairs, who were the immediate predeceffors of the Ogilvies in the property of the lordfhip of Defkford. It appears to have been a pretty fpacious building, in the form of a court; but there now remains only one room's length, vaulted below, with 3 ftoreys and a garret. It bears no date.—Adjoining to this tower, there was formerly a chapel, called St John's Chapel, upon one of the walls of which there is an infcription, bearing the name of Alexander Ogilvie, with the Ogilvies arms and motto, and dated 1551.—About a mile to the S. of the church, ftands the caftle of Skuth, but of late years become ruinous. It is delightfully fituated upon an eminence rifing from the burn, having a peep of the fea, and an extenfive view of the ftrath. On each fide are water-falls from the hill, defcending between rocks and fertile fields, beautifully interfperfed with natural wood. This ruin is a ftriking object to paffengers, and a beautiful vifta to the furrounding inhabitants.

Manfe.—The manfe and offices, with flated roofs, were built about 5 years ago. The heritor gave a liberal allowance, indulged the incumbent with his own plan, and every accommodation he could defire; and had the undertaker done his duty, it would have been perhaps a model of abundant and genteel accommodation; but the work, in every department, is infufficiently executed. Such inftances are too common, and they are exceedingly diftreffing, both to heritors and minifters. The heritors juftly complain of the hardfhip of incurring new expence, after recent and liberal expenditure; and minifters muft daily feel the grievance of inhabiting houfes that will not defend wind and rain. Neceffitated to apply for repairs, they are confidered as troublefome, and fometimes loaded with much unjuft

and

and illiberal abuſe. With a view to remedy theſe evils, along with the contractor, an overſeer ſhould be appointed, who ought carefully to inſpect the materials, and have a watchful eye over the work in all its ſtages. At leaſt, if this is objected to, it ought to be a clauſe in the contract, that the work is not to be judged of, nor the contract diſcharged, until the houſes have been inhabited for 12 months.

Stipend, Glebe, School, Poor, &c.—The glebe is about 4 acres arable, including the garden, with about $\frac{1}{4}$ acres of graſs-ground. The preſent ſtipend is L. 44 : 15 : $3\frac{4}{12}$ Sterling of money, with 24 bolls 1 firlot of barley, and the ſame quantity of meal at 8 s. the boll. The Earl of Find-later is patron of the church, and ſole proprietor of the pa-riſh.—The ſchoolmaſter's ſalary is L. 2 : 1 : 8 Sterling of money, payable by the heritor, and about 9 bolls 3 firlots of meal payable by the tenants. In ſummer there are generally about 30 ſcholars.—The number of poor pre-ſently on the roll is 32. This uncommonly great number may be owing to the abundance of excellent moſs, which has induced them to ſettle in its vicinity. The funds be-longing to them are, the intereſt at 5 *per cent.* of L. 1000 Scotch, the weekly collections, which may amount to L. 8 Sterling a-year, and 6 bolls of meal given annually by the heritor. Theſe afford only a ſcanty ſupply ; but ma-ny of the women are able to earn ſomething by ſpinning flax, and the men by day-labour, ſo that few if any of them beg.

Population.—The return to Dr Webſter, about 40 years ago, was 940. At preſent the number of inhabitants is 752. Males, - - - 359
Females, - - - 393
Heads of families, - - - 268
Children

Children above 8 years,	- -	171
Children under 8 years,	- - -	145
Male ſervants,	- - -	68
Female ſervants,	- - -	44
Weavers,	- - -	18
Shoemakers,	- - -	8
Tailors,	- - - -	4
Wrights,	- - -	2
Cart and Plough wrights,	- -	2
Wheel wrights,	- - -	2
Maſons,	- - -	3
Blackſmiths,	- - -	2

There are 46 perſons in the pariſh who do not properly
belong to any of the preceding deſcriptions. There are
2 Roman Catholics ; all the reſt Preſbyterians. The prevailing ſurnames in the pariſh are Reid and Lawrence.
Of each there are 9 families. The decreaſe of inhabitants
may be accounted for from there having been formerly a
great number of crofters and ſubtenants in the pariſh, who
ſubſiſted chiefly by manufacturing limeſtone. Since that
time, many of the crofts have been added to the adjacent
farms, and the tenants reſtricted to 1, 2 or 3 ſubſets, according to the extent of their poſſeſſions. A reſtriction
in the manufacturing of lime alſo ſucceeded, in order to
prevent the too rapid conſumption of moſs. Theſe circumſtances muſt have occaſioned the removal of ſeveral
families from the pariſh.

State of Farming, &c.—Improvements in farming are
making ſome progreſs. The horſe-hoeing huſbandry has
of late been introduced with ſucceſs. There were about
20,000 cabbages managed in this way laſt ſeaſon. It is
computed there were 150 acres in ſown graſs, 30 in turnips,

nips, 15 in potatoes, and 10 in lint. Though the soil in many places seems favourable for the growth of flax, it has not hitherto been extensively cultivated. The cattle are of the Scotch breed, but considerably improved in fize by the culture of green crops. These are confumed in rearing young cattle, which, from the fituation of the country, is found more profitable, than in fattening thofe that are grown. There are not many fheep, the pafture being much confined by the improvements in the hills formerly mentioned, and what remains being wet, is rather againft their profperity. Some of the Englifh breed, and of a crofs breed from them, are paftured upon the farms. Thofe which pafture on the hills are of a very fmall fize. The farms are fmall; the largeft not exceeding 100 acres arable, and the generality from 30 to 60 acres. The rent varies from L. 1, 10 s. to 2 s. the acre. The average may be 9 s. the acre. The leafes are generally for 19 years, a term by far too fhort for fpirited exertion and fubftantial improvement. The generality of the houfes are poor and uncomfortable; and no allowance granted for meliorations. There are 2 meal-mills and 1 lint-mill in the parifh. The real rent is computed to be L. 1000 Sterling a-year, including money, victual and cuftoms.

Bleachfield.—In the north end of the parifh, there is a bleachfield, rented by a manufacturer in Cullen, of about 10 acres in extent. At this field there are whitened yearly about 1500 pieces of cloth, and 1700 fpindles of thread and yarn. Owing to a deficiency of water, the machinery is frequently wrought by horfes.

Services.—It is reluctantly to be obferved, that the tenants are bound to perform many fervices, fuch as cafting,

winning

winning and leading peats, ploughing and harrowing, making hay, cutting down corns, and various carriages. Thefe
fervices, though not exacted with rigour, are detrimental
to the intereft of the tenant, and confequently to that of
the landholder.   They often occafion interruptions to urgent domeftic concerns, fometimes prevent the feafonable
cultivation of the fields, and not unfrequently hazard the
fafety of their produce.   It is aftonifhing, that heritors,
in many refpects liberal minded and indulgent to their tenants, ftill continue this pernicious veftige of feudal flavery.

Wages and Prices.—The wages of fervants ' have in-
' creafed, are increafing, and, in the opinion of the farmer,
' ought to be diminifhed.'   A capable ploughman receives
from L. 6 to L. 7 ; an inferior man-fervant L. 5 ; and a
female fervant L. 2, 2 s. a year.   Thefe gains are not now,
as formerly, laid up for future fupport and provifion, but
generally expended upon drefs, the defire of which has obtained great prevalence among them within thefe few
years.   The following wages are given to other labourers
a-day : To a man for cafting peats, 1 s. without victuals,
in harveft, to a man 10 d. and to a woman 6 d. with
victuals ; to a day-labourer 6 d. with victuals ; to a mafon
1 s. 2 d. ; to a common wright 8 d. ; and to a tailor 6 d.
with victuals.   The prices of provifions have increafed very
confiderably within thefe 30 years.   A hen, formerly
bought for 4 d. now gives from 6 d. to 8 d. ; beef and
mutton fell from $2\frac{1}{4}$ d. to $3\frac{1}{4}$ d. the pound ; haddocks,
which fold within thefe five years at 2 d. the dozen,
now give from 8 d. to 1 s.   This great and fudden rife in
value, is faid to be owing to a fcarcity of haddocks along
this coaft for two years paft.   Butter fells from 6 d. to 8 d.
the

the pound, 24 ounces; and cheese from 4 s. to 5 s. the stone weight.

Roads.—There are 2 principal roads in the parish. Like the generality of roads in this country, they have been formed originally by far too narrow; are not kept in proper repair; and, from the nature of the soil, are very uncomfortable to travellers, especially in winter and wet seasons. They are wrought in spring and autumn by statute-labour, which the people undertake with reluctance, and perform without care. Perhaps it would be better to levy the money along with the rents, and to employ labourers, under direction of an attentive and capable overseer, during the summer season.

Miscellaneous Observations.—The people are in general sober, industrious, and regular in behaviour. There is but one ale-house in the parish, and which is little frequented. Though not rich, several of them are substantial in their stations. The late unfavourable seasons, with the consequent failure of crops, have reduced their circumstances in some instances. Perhaps a total abolition of services, an extension of their leases, and an allowance for building neat and comfortable houses, would tend to meliorate their situation. In consequence of their sobriety and regularity, the people are prolific and long-lived. The wife of one of the elders brought him lately 3 daughters at one birth, who are all alive, and doing well. There are 3 families consisting of eight children each, and several of 7 and of 6. The last minister died about 10 years ago, in the 88th year of his age; and there are now living in the parish one woman aged 91, another 89, and a man 38.—The parish of Deskford is a spot universally admired, on account of its natural beauties and ancient caſtles. Its vicinity to the ſea, and various internal advantages, particularly water, wood, moſs and lime, render it one of the beſt tracks in the north of Scotland.

PARISH OF FORDICE.

(*County of Banff.*)

By the Rev. Mr JAMES LAWTIE.

Name, Situation, Extent, Soil, and Surface.

THE antient and modern name of this parifh is Fordice, it is faid to be derived from the Gaelic, and to fignify *the bleak country*. And, indeed, the upper part of the parifh may ftill be entitled to the epithet of *bleak;* but much more fo, before the woods were cut down, and the marfhes drained. Fordice is fituated in Banfffhire, in the prefbytery of Fordice, and fynod of Aberdeen.

This parifh fince Ordiquhill, Defkford, and Cullen, were detached from it after the Reformation, is nearly triangular. From the mouth of the river or burn of Boyn, on the eaft, to the Knockhill, is five miles Scots. From the Knockhill to Logie the fame number of miles on the weft. From Logie to the mouth of the burn of Boyn, near Scots Miln and Old Houfe of Boyn, alongft the fide of the fea, five miles. On the eaft it is bounded by the parifh of Boyndie, on the fouth by Ordiquhill and Grange, on the weft by Defkford, Rathven, and Cullen, on the north by the fea, or Moray Frith.

The

The general appearance of the country is rather flat, with many inequalities and riſing grounds. There are two ſmall and contiguous hills, thoſe of Fordice and Durn, about a mile ſouth from the ſea, beſides the Knockhill at the ſouth-weſt extremity, much higher than the two preceding, and which ſeparates this pariſh from part of Grange and Ordi-quhill.

The coaſt or ſhore is high and rocky, with the exception of a few bays, ſuch as thoſe of Portſoy and Sandend.

Many ſorts of fiſhes are caught on the coaſt, ling, cod, tuſk, haddock ; beſides dog, whiting, mackarel, holybut, turbot, cat, and flounder of various kinds. Lobſters, crabs, clams, limpits, and periwinkles. The principal market for the firſt four kinds was Leith and the South Frith ; but now the fiſhers ſay they ſuffer ſuch exactions at Leith, (a ſtrange policy upon an article of proviſions) that they ſeldom proceed to that market, and ſell betwixt this and the South Frith. There are corallines on the coaſts, and from ſamples taken up on the fiſhers lines or hooks, it is believed a few corals and ſponges. There are large ſhoals of herrings and conſiderable numbers of ſeals, purpoiſes, and ſometimes whales, and ſharks, ſeen on the coaſt. The lime-ſtone on the coaſt is frequently perforated by a ſpecies of ſmall muſcle, which live and grow in the ſtones. The fiſh of this kind called *pholades* in Italy, have three or four ſhells, ours, like common muſcles, only two. There might be large quantities of kelp made on the coaſt. However, the great quantity of both tangle, and belly-weed, which grows on the ſea rocks, when by ſtorms looſened and diſengaged from them, and caſt aſhore, are carefully gathered and uſed

as

as manure. Sometimes belly-weed is fhorn or cut for that purpofe by the farmers.

An intelligent boatmafter at Sandend, fays, that the courfe of the tides is from half tide to half tide, and that there are no extraordinary currents until they get above Cromarty; and the only dangerous rocks are the Skairs of Caufrey. The fifhers direct their courfe by the hills of Durn and Knockhill. There is no light-houfe; but a beacon, it is faid, would be ufeful upon the above-mentioned Skairs. Eafter and Wefter Heads of Portfoy, and Logie Head on the weft towards Cullen, and a few miles from Scarnofe, in the parifh of Rathven, are the moft remarkable head-lands. Redhyth betwixt Sandend and Portfoy, is a very ufeful and fafe creek in fome cafes, having a deep beech. A fhip from Onega, about twenty two years ago, by being run into the bay of Sandend, faved both her cargo and hands.

The hills are covered with grafs, or heath, moftly the latter. There has been a very deep mofs on the top of the Knockhill; but was never ufed, being inacceffible almoft by horfe carriages, and moftly burnt out in the dry year 1723. There is much marble (or rather jafper) at Portfoy, quarried in the ordinary manner, and manufactured into chimney-pieces, funeral-monuments, tea-cups, fun-dials, &c. Upon the firft difcovery, much of it was exported to France, and it is faid, there are two chimney pieces of it in the palace of Verfailles, and that it became fafhionable in France; but the family of Boyne overftocking the market, it went out of fafhion, and a fhip load of it lies neglected on the banks of the Seine, as a gentleman who faw and knew the ftones informed me. This quarry runs fouthward from Portfoy into the hill of Durn, and then acrofs the country to the

weft

weſt end of the hill of Fordice, and from that ſouth nearly
to the Knockhill. The hill of Durn ſeems to be one maſs
of marble, and a kind of quartz, a white ſiliceous ſtone employed in the manufacture of ſtoneware. There are likewiſe in the lower end of the pariſh, through the eſtates of
Findlater, Birkenbog, Glaſſaugh, and Durn, inexhauſtible
quarries of limeſtone ; large quantities of lime and limeſtone are tranſported. There is a weighty clumſy ſort of
ſlate in the rocks of Findlater. Hopes have been entertained of finding a coal mine near Glaſſaugh or Sandend. A-
longſt with the limeſtone there are mixtures and layers of a
black ſubſtance, like ſlate of coal. Boring was tried at
Glaſſaugh, both by the late General Abercrombie, and his
father, but no diſcovery of coal was made. The rocks on
the ſea at the eaſt ſide of the pariſh, near Craig of Boyn,
have been ſaid to conſiſt entirely of iron ſtone. The ſoil in
general is deep and fertile, but rather wet than dry, which
renders the harveſt late in a rainy harveſt. No part of the
pariſh is ſubject to inundations, except the haughs and flat
grounds, near the rivulets, where miſchief is ſometimes
done, both to corns and houſes. In ſummer 1772, ſome
houſes and a bridge were ſwept away, both at Fordice and
Glaſſaugh. The ſame happened in November 1781.

Climate and Diſtempers.—The air is rather dry than moiſt,
and in general healthy. The ravages of the ſmall-pox are
very much abated by the practice of inoculation. The moſt
prevalent diſtemper is fever, and that for the moſt part not
univerſal, but confined to particular diſtricts. It is ſometimes thought to ariſe from infection and communication
with other parts of the country ; at other times from local
ſituations, and circumſtances of the people's houſes and habits of living in particular diſtricts.

Population.

Population —The population of this parish, so far as it has been traced, was as great formerly as at present. This may appear a little problematical, considering the great number of people collected together and living in Portsoy ; but formerly there were many mosses, now exhausted, and the sides of these mosses were crouded with cottagers, who laboured a few acres of ground, had a little coarse flax of their own growth, and kept a small flock of sheep, which afforded them clothes. These people multiplied and afforded soldiers, servants, and tradesmen. The great check given to this rank of people was first the mosses being exhausted, and then some heritors limited by their leases the number of subtenants, in order to save their mosses. The return of the population of this parish to Dr Webster was 3212. In the year 1782, the police of the county required an account of the number, young and old, in the parish, in order to ascertain the quantity of meal necessary to be imported. A tolerably exact numeration was made, and then young and old, amounted to about 3425. The population since that period has rather increased than diminished.

The average of births according to the register of baptisms in 1683,—4,—5, is 104 ; in 1783,—4.—5, 55. It is believed, however, that there are as many, or nearly as many births and baptisms in the parish now as formerly, and that the difference of these two averages arises in a great measure from the inaccuracy of the baptism registers, owing to the negligence of the people, in registering their children's names. During last century, there was only one minister, and the schoolmaster was attentive to his own interest, in obliging the people to register their children. There are now several who baptize at Portsoy, a minister of the establishment,—a Seceder,—a Nonjuror who preaches every fortnight,

night,—and a Roman Catholic prieſt, who frequently ſays
maſs there. The regiſter of baptiſms commences in 1663,
and from the beginning, the average of baptiſms continues
much the ſame as the firſt mentioned average, to the end of
the century, when the ſeven years famine which then happened, reduces the number in 1699, to 70. From that
time the number riſes gradually in the regiſter to 1717,
when a Nonjuror ſettling at Portſoy, and afterwards near it,
the people became negligent in regiſtering, and have generally continued ſo, to the great loſs of many, in proving their
kindred with relations who had entered the ſeafaring line,
or ſettled abroad.

There has only very lately been a regiſter of burials; and
the average for 1784,—5,—6, is 47. But, as there is a burial place at Portſoy, this average is not very accurate.

There is no regiſter of marriages before 1722. By the a-
verage for 1729,—30,—31, about 22 men ſettled in this pariſh
married wives either within or without the pariſh,—and eight
women married from this pariſh into other pariſhes. In
1784,—5,—6, 24 men ſettled in this pariſh, married women
of this or other pariſhes, and three women were married
from this into other pariſhes. Without attending to this circumſtance, marriages might be ſtated twice; becauſe, when
the man and woman belong to different pariſhes, the publication
of the banns and regiſtration of the contract take place in both.

There are five fiſhing boats, ſix men to a boat, and a few
yawls beſides, for the boys. This rank is ſtill diminiſhing by
preſſing for the Navy ſervice, and young people going to the
merchant ſervice; likewiſe by accidents of ſhipwreck.—
There is one ſtudent at the Univerſity.—A few belonging to
this

this parish were born in England.—Great numbers are born
to the weſt of Spey. A great part of the ſervants male and
female come from other pariſhes, in queſt of more liberty,
and better wages ; particularly from the more northerly parts
of the iſland.—No nobility have reſided in this pariſh ſince
the end of laſt century, when the family of Findlater ſold
Durn. Reſident families are Birkenbog, Glaſſaugh, and
Durn ; only Sir George Abercrombie of Birkenbog, has pulled down the old family ſeat, and has not yet rebuilt it.—
There are ſix heritors.—There is a miniſter of the eſtabliſhed church at Fordice, and a preacher at Portſoy, preſented
by the preſent Lord Findlater's grandfather with L. 20 yearly ; likewiſe a Relief one, occaſionally a Nonjuror Epiſcopalian miniſter, and a Popiſh prieſt.—There is one notary, and
one meſſenger.—One ſurgeon at Portſoy, and one apothecary.—The great body of the people are Preſbyterians of the
eſtabliſhed church.—There are a few Seceders.—A conſiderable number of Epiſcopalians.—A few Papiſts.

The population of the pariſh is not very materially different from what it was 25 years ago. The decreaſe of ſubtenants by throwing many ſmall tacks into one, is balanced
by tenanting the graſs-rooms, and the increaſe of people at
Portſoy. The tenants alongſt the coaſt paid large victual
rents ; and therefore, found it convenient to have graſs farms
in the upper part of the pariſh, for ſubſiſting their cattle in
ſummer. In theſe farms the folding grounds were only
ſown. The introduction of graſs-ſeeds, and partial converſion of victual rent, have rendered this policy unneceſſary ;
and it is diſcontinued.

None have died for want ſince the 1700.—None have left
the pariſh for want of employment, except a few day-labourers,
who

who removed to the contiguous parish of Cullen, for more constant employment in Lord Findlater's works ; and a considerable number of lint-dressers dispersed into different parts upon the failure of the thread manufactory at Portsoy, a few years ago.

Cultivation and Produce, &c.—Horse ploughing has in some farms superseded the use of oxen ; sheep have greatly decreased by winter herding, and the wearing out of the commons by tillage and much feal. A great deal of oats and barley, and also a considerable quantity of wheat, are raised in this parish, especially since the erection of flour-mills. Almost every farmer has fields of turnip and potatoes ; the last are sometimes sold for exportation. The culture of field cabbage and coleworts is likewise coming into practice. The parish does surely more than supply itself with provisions, though there is, no doubt, a considerable importation of meal and flesh at Portsoy, from other parishes ; yet that must be more than balanced by exportation. Almost all the farmers raise flax for their own use, and some of them for sale ; while others let their lands for a crop to the flax-raisers at Portsoy. The sowing of grass-seeds has become very general. The rage of ploughing and raising corn had long ago destroyed the natural best pastures of the parish, except a few on the sides of burns and rising grounds, which could not be safely touched by the plough. There are, however, still remaining in some parts of the parish, what they call outfields, which may be called pasture, as they do not undergo the culture of the plough, except for two or three crops in a dozen or twenty years. The use of lime has much diminished the quantity of out-field. Wheat is generally sown in the end of harvest, pease, beans, oats, and barley, are sown from the beginning of
March

March to the end of May, according to feafons and fituations. Harveft begins in Auguft, and in early years terminates in September or beginning of October. Common or
wafte ground is every year diminifhing, being converted into
tillage by the contiguous tenants, or planted by the heritors.
There is one natural wood of alder, and feveral plantations of
fir, afh, elm, and other trees ; but fewer than might be expected from the refidence and opulence of the heritors. The
land-rent of the parifh may amount to nearly L. 4000 yearly. The valuation of this parifh is between the 8th and 9th
part of that of the whole county. The rent of fifhing boats
about L. 4 yearly each ; but from this is to be deduced the
price of a boat furnifhed once in feven years by the heritors.
About 20s. is the rent of the beft lands. From 10s. to 12s.
for thofe of inferior value. The fmall allotments to the inhabitants of villages go higher, perhaps above 40s. the acre.
The number of farms is diminifhing every year. From 80
to 100 acres is the largeft. However, a confiderable number
of fmall farms ftill remain, for furnifhing tradefmen and fervants to the country. Farms are beginning to be enclofed.
There is a white peat (under the name of *greafy clods*)
which may be called a bitumen, and fome years ago was univerfally ufed for giving light to fpinners in winter ; and is
ftill ufed by the pooreft people for that purpofe.

Language.—No language is fpoken in this parifh, except
the Scottifh or Anglo-Saxon. All the old farms feem to
have their names from the Gaelic or Erfe. *Glaffaugh*, Gray
or Green-Haugh. *Kilhillock*, Burial-Hillock. *Aird* of Portfoy, Height of Portfoy. *Durn*, Round, from its contiguous
round hill. *Auchmore*, Large Field. *Hindrought*, Bridge-
end, &c. The old Mains of Findlater, which was very extenfive, is now divided into many farms, which have all
Englifh

English names. Some farms in the upper part of the parish; which were laid waste, in the bad years, or famine, at the end of the last century, have had new and fanciful names given them, such as York, Windsor, &c.

Stipend.—The stipend (in which are 21½ bolls meal, reckoned at 10s. *per* boll) amounts to L. 71 : 10. The glebe, according to the value of contiguous lands, L. 7 : 10. Grass money L. 2. In whole L. 81. The glebe having been perfectly inclosed by the present incumbent, it may be worth something more to his successor. There is likewise L. 5 of communion-element money; but that has not been uniformly paid. The Earl of Findlater is Patron.

Poor.—The number of poor receiving alms is 97. There are three different managements for the poor at Fordice, Portsoy, and Sandend. The produce of the collections may be about L. 31 annually. Besides this, there is the interest of L. 130 of settled money, which has chiefly risen from saving on the collections, with a few small benefactions from particular persons. There is the rent of a loft in the church at Fordice, and of two mort-clothes. There are likewise penalties on delinquents; and three of our heritors dying within the last ten years, about L. 30 accrued to the poor, either by their own bequeathments, or that of their families. Some of the heritors likewise, give every year a quantity of meal to the poor of their respective estates.

Price of Provisions and Labour.—When the incumbent settled here, 43 years ago, beef, mutton, pork, and lamb, sold from 1½ d. to 2 d. *per* pound. Chickens at 2 d. the pair; hens from 5 d. to 6 d. the pair. Butter from 5 s. to 6 s. the stone, Amsterdam weight; cheese at 2 s. 6 d. *per* stone. At prefent beef fells from 2½ d. to 4 d. the pound Amfterdam weight; mutton from 2 d. to 4 d. according to the feafon; veal and lamb from 3½ d. to 6 d.; pork from 2½ d. to 3½ d.; pigs from 2 s. 6 d. to 6 s. Ducks 1 s. 6 d. the pair; hens 1 s. 4 d. to 1 s. 6 d. the pair; chickens fell at 2 d. the piece; pigeons at 2 d. the pair; turkies at 2 s. 6 d. and 3 s. each; geefe 2 s. 6 d. each. Wheat at an average may be 17 s. 6 d. the boll; fomething better than Linlithgow meafure. The heritors convert barley rent at 14 s. Oats may be reckoned from 8 s. to 12 s. the boll; peafe and beans equal to one boll oat-meal. Farmers men-fervants get from L. 2 : 10 to L. 6 : 6 annually. Maid-fervants from L. 2 to L. 2 : 10 annually. Day-labourers from 8 d. to 1 s. *per* day, without meat, with meat 6 d. a day. Moffing and harveft-work is the deareft, and perhaps a little more than the above; for a good harveft-man fometimes gets 1 s. and victuals, *per* day. Thirty or forty years ago, men-fervants got from L. 1 : 13 : 6 to L. 4 yearly; women fervants from 16 s. to 20 s.; day-labourers from 5 d. to 6 d. without meat, with meat, about 4 d. Mafter-mafons now receive about 2 s. *per* day; mafter-carpenters 1 s. 4 d. or 1 s. 6 d.; journeymen-mafons from 1 s. 4 d. to 1 s. 6 d.; journeymen-wrights from 10 d. to 1 s.; taylors get 6 d. and victuals; houfe fervant-maids from L. 2 to L. 3 : 3 yearly; men from L. 6 to L. 19 yearly. With the induftry of his wife, a day-labourer may bring up his family. As foon as they are able to work, the children are fet to fpinning, or hired out to herd. When old, if their children be not both dutiful and fuccefsful, they need help from the poor's-funds. Their food is meal of oats, barley, peafe, and beans, with potatoes, milk, greens, and fome fifh, which fome years ago, when cheap, was a great help to their living; but of late are rifing above their purchafe. They feldom can afford any flefh meat now, except at Chriftmas;

but

but formerly could afford a little through the winter. They are generally affectionate to their children, and part with more to them, than a prudent concern for old age permits.

Antiquities.—There is a triple fosse and rampart on the sides and top of the hill of Durn, which seem to have quite surrounded it. The highest, which includes the large plain on the top of the hill, seems to have been strong with a stone rampart or wall, especially at the entry or most accessible part, where it joins the hill of Fordice. It commands an extensive view of the adjacent country; and probably was used as a retreat for the people, their families, and cattle, on invasions of the Danes from the sea, or of the wild Highlanders. Hard by it, on the side of the hill of Fordice, there is a farm called *Badhuntoul.* According to Mr Pennant, in his Hebrides, *Badhun* signifies a place of refuge, and some say *Toul* signifies a burn, others a hollow; in either way it seems to justify the supposition, with respect to the intrenchments on the hill of Durn. Of predatory invasions from the Highlanders, there still remain some traditions in the parish. There is a tribe of Gregors amongst the country people, said to be the descendants of boys taken in a pursuit of the thieves. Kirktown and the Castle of Deskford in the old bounds of this parish, are supposed to have been a Roman station. Flint arrow-heads of our ancestors, called by the country people *elf arrow-heads*, have been found in this parish. There are the remains of some Druidical temples, likewise burrows or tumuli. Three of the last have been opened within these few years. One very large between Glassaugh and the sea, immediately above the bay of Sandend. It consisted of a large circular accumulation of stones, fourteen feet high, and sixty feet broad, and then covered with earth or turf. Upon breaking in at the top, there were found

found a ftone coffin of flag or flat ftones, and in it the bones of a chieftain lying in their natural order; and a deer's horn, a fymbol of the chief's being a hunter. The ftones, of which fort there were few in the neighbourhood, by the fhells of the pholades, or mufcles included in many of them, feem principally to have been brought from the fea. The quantity, diftance, and difficulty of accefs, feem to have required an army, or large diftrict of country to tranfport them. This burrow is now the fite of a wind-mill. There had been another comparatively very fmall burrow, at about a hundred paces diftance from the largeft. It had been conftructed by cafting up a trench round it, which ftill remains; but the earth of the tumulus has been long ago carried off. Another burrow was likewife broken up at Kilhillock in Findlater fome years ago. It was entirely a cairn of ftones; and in removing them for the purpofe of inclofing, an urn was found, and likewife a ftone coffin covering a fkeleton. The tenant was greatly furprifed, and, that he might not fuffer for violating burial ground, he carefully interred the bones, and the pieces of the urn, at a marked place in the inclofure. Another tumulus was likewife broken up in the contiguous farm of Brankamentum, through the curiofity of Mr Duncan of Broom, where there was found an urn containing afhes; it was very hard, and the clay well baked. In the 10th century, the Danes landed at the mouth of the burn of Cullen; King Indulfus came up, beat them, and obliged them to reembark; but was flain at the end of the engagement, in a corner of a wood, where he fell in with an unbroken party of the Danes. It is a matter of uncertainty whether the battle was fought in this parifh, or in that of Rathven on the weft of Cullen, where remains the King's Cairn, in the

midft

midſt of Lord Findlater's plantations, a little to the weſt of Cullen-Houſe, at which place, according to ſome, Indulfus fell.

Eminent Men.—It is probable that Archbiſhop Sharp was a native of this pariſh. His father was proprietor of Ordinhoves, the family eſtate in this pariſh, and afterwards removed to Banff, where, as is generally ſuppoſed from that circumſtance merely, the Archbiſhop was born. The father managed the buſineſs of the family of Findlater, and the incumbent has heard the late Earl of Findlater's father ſay, that the beſt written papers in their charter cheſt, were done by him. The late General Abercrombie of Glaſſaugh, was a native of this pariſh, and educated in it. Mr George Smith another native of this place, after ſerving as clerk in Holland, Paris, and Aleppo, found his way over land to the Eaſt Indies, was not heard of by his friends for ſeveral years, and died February laſt, on his way to Britain. He had become maſter of a very conſiderable fortune ; and, if any of his five ſiſters, or their progeny, fail to claim in five years, their ſhares come under the adminiſtration of the magiſtrates of Banff.—L 1000 to be employed for an hoſpital or infirmary at Banff or Fordice,—L. 25 yearly in augmentation of the miniſter of Fordice's ſtipend, —L. 40 yearly, to endow a ſchoolmaſter at Fordice, to teach the French and Dutch languages, with arithmetic, mathematics, and book-keeping,—and L. 25 yearly, to each of his burſars at this ſchool. Walter Ogilvie of Redhyth, a native of this pariſh, laſt century, endowed twelve burſars at the ſchool of Fordice, and eight at King's College Aberdeen. The preſentation was in the gift of Ogilvie of Boyn, but ſold by the late Inchmartin to the family of Findlater.

Findlater. Trial is appointed to be made of the proficiency of the burfars, the 4th year of their attendance, and, if they be found not qualified for a literary education, or not inclined to follow it, they get the 5th year to prepare them fo far for fome trade.

General Character of the People, &c.—There is nothing in the heighth of the people which may diftinguifh them from their neighbours in the country. Their fize cannot be called dwarfifh, but lower, probably, than it would otherwife be, owing to the boys being early put to hard work, and the girls confined to fpinning. Very few of the people reach the height of fix feet. Here it may not be improper to obferve, that Sir John Gordon of Park, about a century ago, introduced a breed of tall men into his eftate in Ordiquhill parifh, collected from different parts of Scotland ; but that their defcendants of the third generation have generally come down to the fize of the country. More lately, when the King of Pruffia was collecting his tall men, the incumbent has not heard that he obtained any from this corner ; but he got fome from the contiguous parifh of Rathven.

The people are in general difpofed to induftry. Since the failure of thread-bleaching at Portfoy, there is no manufacture of confeqence carried on within the parifh. But moft of the inhabitants raife as much flax, and weave as much linen cloth, as ferve their families. Perhaps not 1000 yards of the cloth manufactured in it, are fold out of the parifh at prefent. The manufacture of linen feems to have exifted in this parifh 300 years ago, for amongft other privileges granted to the weekly market at Fordice, by charter from the Crown, that of felling *Linteum latum et arctum*, is given in 1490. The people are rather inclined to the fea than the land fervice. However, many do not enter voluntarily, but by draughts made from the fifhing boats, and preffing from the merchant fervice. The people are in general economical and frugal ; but luxury in drefs and living are creeping in. Only one eftate in this parifh has been fold for many years, that of Durn, which fetched, it is believed, about 30 years purchafe; but much more had been offered for it a few years before. A part of Sir William Gordon of Park's unentailed eftate in this parifh, fold not long after 1746, for 40 years purchafe. The better fort of people are much dif-pofed to give charitable affiftance to the fhipwrecked; but perhaps the old feudal favage cuftom of diftreffing the fhip-wrecked, and embezzling their property, would appear, if not reftrained by law, and by the humanity of the better fort. The people enjoy the comforts and advantages of fo-ciety in a tolerable degree, and feem contented. Their ftate might be ftill bettered by long leafes, commutation of victual rent, abolition of fervices, &c. and all thefe things are coming in apace. There is one woman in prifon for theft.

School.—The number of fcholars at the parochial fchool, is, at an average, between 50 and 60. The mafter's e-moluments from the kirk-feffion, keeping the regifters, fa-lary from the parifh, and thirteen burfars, amount to L. 26. Befides this, he has fchool-fees from his other fcholars, from 1 s. to 2 s. 6 d. quarterly, according to what they are taught. Something likewife is made by teaching book keeping.

There is a fchool by fubfcription at Portfoy, the fixed fa-lary of the fchoolmafter is L. 15 ; and, as he is allowed to take in fome more fcholars than thofe fubfcribed for, about

L.

L. 5 more is made of it. The number of scholars amounts
to 30.

There is likewise a charity schoolmaster at Portsoy, for
teaching the poor. His fixed salary from the Society
for propagating Christian Knowledge is L. 8,—from the
Countess Dowager of Findlater L. 5,—and the value of L. 2
in land from Lord Findlater as a cow's grass,—L. 2 as clerk
and treasurer for the poor's funds at Portsoy, in all L. 17.
And about seven pound more may be made by teaching
those who are able to pay for reading, writing, arithmetic,
book-keeping, and navigation.

There is another school for boys at Portsoy, where from
20 to 30 are taught ; and through the rest of the parish there
are four schools for girls, where reading, sowing, and knitting of stockings are taught.

Miscellaneous Observations.—The remarkable meteor which
travelled over so great a space a few years ago, was seen here,
as also in the neighbourhood, about the same hour.—
Likewise the remarkable noise like cannon shot, heard all
over the north country in summer 1745, was heard in this
parish.

The fuel generally used in the parish is peat or turf; a
good cart load of the first costs 1 s. 3 d. of turf 8 d. Considerable quantities of English and Scots coal are imported at
Portsoy, and even bought by the tenants in the lower parts
of the parish, at a distance from the mosses. Some of the
poorer villagers pull heath and cut furze.

There is one coach and two four wheeled chaises belonging

ing to private perſons. There is a fiſhing village at Sandend. A fiſhing and trading one at Portſoy, both on the ſea
ſide. The Kirktown of Fordice, half a mile above Sandend,
which was erected into a borough of barony, by Elphingſton
Biſhop of Aberdeen, in 1499, afterwards by another Biſhop
of Aberdeen feued out to Ogilvie of Durn, is now the property of Lord Findlater. There is a ſmall village at Newmills of Boyne, about two mills from the ſea.

The bridges are few, and not all in repair ; they are moſtly conſtructed and kept up by county aſſeſſments. The great
road between Cullen and Banff is in excellent order, but the
other roads are greatly neglected ſince General Abercrombie's death. The ſtatute labour is generally exacted ; but by
the lateneſs of the harveſt, the exaction of the three laſt days
being ſometimes hindered, theſe days are frequently commuted for a day extraordinary in ſummer.

In the years 1782,—83, the pariſh fell ſhort of its ordinary produce of corn and potatoes, and, without importation,
could ſcarcely have ſupplied itſelf with feed and proviſions.
The heritors ſold their farms in the country, and encouraged importation ; Government gave ſupplies, and the
kirk-ſeſſion encroached upon their funds. The incumbent
had the curioſity to read over the ſeſſion's records, for the
laſt ten years of the laſt century, in which period happened the great famine of ſeven years, called the *Ill Years*.
An antient elder of this pariſh ſaid, that if the ſame precautions had been taken at that time, which he had
ſeen taken more lately in times of ſcarcity, the famine
would not have done ſo much hurt, nor would ſo
many have periſhed. From the records, it did not appear, that any public meaſures were purſued for the ſupply
of

of the poor, nor any thing uncommon done by the feffion, except towards the end. The common diftribution of the collections of the church, amounted only to about 1 s. 2 d. or 1 s. 4 d. weekly. The thing moft remarkable was, that for feveral years before the famine, adultery and fornication had been extremely frequent, to which the famine put an entire and fpeedy ftop.—Neither do thefe crimes feem to have abounded fo much in the parifh, fince that time. Soon after the Reformation, Popery in its outward form feems to have left the parifh entirely, but the fuperftition as to wells, fpells, charms, remained much longer; and above all, a difregard to the decent religious obfervation of Sunday. The eaft and weft fide of the parifh continued their competition at the foot-ball after divine worfhip, and a public market was held in the church-yard. Bifhop Elphingfton, when he got his village of Fordice erected into a borough of barony in 1499, and obtained the privilege of a weekly market day, thought it decent to leave out *Sabbathi*, and perhaps thought of abolifhing the practice, which probably exifted before his time. But in the renewal of the charter in 1592, to Menzies of Durn, whofe predeceffor had feued it from the Bifhop of Aberdeen, *die Sabbathi* is exprefsly inferted. This practice was only got gradually fuppreffed in the beginning of this century or end of the laft. Some people, whom the incumbent has feen, remembered the fale of oxen-yokes, fnuff, &c. upon the Sunday. The laft parcel of fnuff brought into the church-yard for fale on Sunday, was toffed out of the bag by Mr Gellie the minifter, who paid the value. The annual market called Hallow-fair, by Mr Menzies's charter, was to be held *ad Feftum Omnium Sanctorum ad All-Hallomes per fpatium octo dierum.* By Bifhop Elphingfton's charter, *in Fefto Sancti Talleritani et per octavas ejufdem;* of which faint, none of the Popifh clergy of this country, with whom

whom the incumbent has converſed, can give him any ac‐
count ; though it is plain he was once a ſaint of their
church, and had a feſtival dedicated to him. He ſeems to
have been the patron ſaint of the pariſh, and a well is ſtill
called by his name.

There are in this pariſh thirteen ale-houſes and three inns.
The number of ale-houſes is greatly diminiſhed, whereby the
morals of the people with reſpect to ſobriety and decency
are greatly mended. The ale houſes in this village, now re‐
duced to one, were very numerous, and the Sunday's drink‐
ing very great, originating from the Sunday's market ; in ſo
much that the miniſter was obliged to compound the matter,
to allow a certain time after public worſhip, and then to cauſe
ring what was called the *Drunken Bell ;* after which he viſit‐
ed the ale-houſes, and diſmiſſed any who remained in them.
This practice, however, ceaſed before the incumbent's time,
or that of his predeceſſor, though both have been obliged
to make a ſtep through the village, after dinner, and break
up drinking companies.

More cottages have fallen in the laſt ten years than have
been rebuilt ; but on the whole, the number fallen in and
not rebuilt, is abundantly compenſated by new feus taken,
and new houſes built at Portſoy.

The employing cottagers in agriculture is much diſconti‐
nued in this pariſh. The farmers think themſelves better
ſerved by hired ſervants who lodge with them, and have no
interruption by the neighbourhood of their families. Forty
years ago, moſt large farms had their cottar-man, i. e. a
cottager living near them, who held the plough, bound the
corn in harveſt, and built the ricks. This ſeemingly uſeful
                                                      member

member of a farm is difcontinued, becaufe ploughing is better and more generally underftood than formerly, and the
difficulty is not great, of finding a good ploughman to hire
at any term; however, fome of the farmers wifh for cottagers on their farms, whom they can employ incidentally, or,
what would be ftill more ufeful, to have villages fcattered
up and down the country, where day-labourers could be
hired.

PARISH OF FORGLEN.

(County of Banff, Synod of Aberdeen, Presbytery of Turriff.)

By the Rev. Mr. Robert Ballingall.

Name.

THE name of the pariſh was formerly *'T Eunan,* or *St. Eunan,* after the titular ſaint of that name, to whom the church or chapel had been dedicated. The common name now is *Forglen,* or *Foreglen,* to diſtinguiſh it from the neighbouring pariſh of Alvah, or Back Glen. For ſome time, the two pariſhes were joined, and ſupplied by one paſtor; but, before the middle of laſt century, Forglen became a ſeparate erection, and an annexation was made to it from the pariſh of Marnoch, comprehending the greater part of the eſtate of Carnouſie. The annexation of both *quoad ſacra et civilia.* At Burn-end, about half a mile to the W. of the preſent church, is to be ſeen the remains of a ſmall chapel, probably the place of worſhip in Popiſh times. For more conveniency, the church had afterwards been transferred to its preſent ſituation. On a ſtone built into

into the S. wall of it, is an infcription, in thefe terms :
*This church was re-edified by George Ogilvie, Mafter of
Banff,* 1692.

Situation and Extent.—Forglen lies on the N. fide of
the river Diveron : it is bounded on the W. by the parifh
of Marnoch, on the S. by Turriff, on the E. by Turriff
and Alvah, and on the N. by Alvah. On the S. and E.
fide the river is the boundary. Lord Banff's lands, however, crofs it in two or three different places. He has a
large alley oppofite his own houfe, on the Turriff fide ;
another below the church, by the houfe of Muirifh, and
a fmall part oppofite Boat of Muirifh. On the N. boundary, the part of the farm of Brownfide, Captain Hay's,
called the Broadmyre, is in Forglen parifh, and the reft
in Alvah.—The figure of the parifh is an oblong, not
far from regular ; only the N. E. angle is cut off by Alvah. The length, from the church to the river fide, to-
wards the S., is $3\frac{1}{2}$ Englifh miles, and the breadth $2\frac{1}{2}$ miles.
It has a S. expofure, one of the beft in the country. The
lands have a gradual flope, from the back parts of the parifh, to the river on the S. ; and there are no high hills to
occafion any inconvenience of fhade, being gentle rifing
grounds, affording a beautiful variety.

Soil.—The foil, on haugh grounds, is fandy, but produces very fine crops of grain, and very rich pafture. The
foil on braes and flats above them is richer, and yields the
fineft crops of barley and oats. Having the river on two
fides, which acts as a drain, and there being little mofs
or marfhy ground in this parifh, the harveft is early, and
the grain, in ordinary feafons, well filled and ripened. It
is now cuftomary with merchants to buy oats and barley

by

by weight. The Banffshire firlot is 32 Scotch standard pints, and the medium of a boll of oats of said measure is 14 stone Amsterdam weight; of barley 18 stone: barley, however, is often much above that; 19½ and even 20 stone: and oats often yield 8 stone of meal, besides paying mill dues.

Cultivation.—The most part of this parish is arable, and has been, at one time or other, under the plough. The lands on the river side have been, for some time past, in a state of improvement. The tenants, stimulated by the example set before them by the heritors, the late and present Lord Banff, and Captain Hay, when he resided at Carnousie, in improving their mains, had made rapid progress in cultivation. And now the same spirit has caught some young farmers, and even the old are stirring, and extending the like improvements over the rest of the parish. In the remotest parts of the parish, we have now as good husbandry, fields as well dressed, and as good grain, grass, and turnip raised, as on the river side. The principal tenants have been in the practice of sowing turnip in broad-cast chiefly, for the space of 18 or 20 years; and now the smaller ones have each their proportion of them, and of sown grass, which they find much for their profit, and is much in favour of the brute creation.—The mains, in the hands of the heritors, are of considerable extent, and well improved. There are only two large farms in the parish; the farm of Old-Town of Carnousie, of about 100l. Sterling rent, and the farms of Kirktown and Eastside, presently conjoined, of about 60l.: the rest, at a medium, rent from 20l. to 30l. There are a good many crofts for the accommodation of the servants and labourers employed by the heritors.

In

In ploughing, the farmers fom times ufe horfe ploughs, and fometimes oxen, according to the nature of the ground ; and the cattle are now yoked with collars and traces, and trained to carts and wains. The breed of cattle and horfes is much improved of late ; and alfo the fheep, of which there are feveral flocks of a larger fize, with finer wool, and giving double or triple price of the ordinary country breed. Wool is fold from feveral farms at 20s. and 21s. 4d. the ftone.

The farmers now raife flax for their own ufe *.—Peafe, oats, and barley, are fown from the beginning of March to the end of May ; and harveft begins in Auguft, and terminates, in ordinary years, in September or beginning of October. Harveft 1732, and feveral fince, have been much out of courfe ; and the laft (1793) as bad as any †.

Heritors.—The heritors of the parifh are, the Right Honourable William Lord Banff, Colonel Duff of Car-noufie,

---

* They are but learners, however : they have not yet acquired the neceffary fkill, and not reckoning the crop effential, they often lofe it, for want of a little attention to weeding and watering ; and fo come to be difcouraged by their own neglect. A night or two extraordinary, in hot weather, will rot it in the fteep. Care then fhould be taken of this, if it fhould lie a little longer on grafs.

† The feed was late laid down, owing to a cold fpring. Rains in fummer kept it in the growing ftate, and extended it to an extraordinary length ; fo that it was, perhaps, the fulleft in appearance we ever faw ; but the rain continuing after the ordinary feafon of harveft was come, prevented its ripening, and alfo lodged it. In the beginning of harveft this year, about the end of September and beginning of October, a confiderable part was got in in fafety, but rendered very light by lodging. The weather was good till the middle of October, but then the rains came back again, and fpoiled a great part of what remained in the field. Though ordinarily earlier than our neighbours, the victual was not fully fecured in this parifh when December was come. The fame was the cafe over all this quarter of the country.

noufie, and Captain Hay of Mountblairy. Only Lord Banff, who is patron, and Colonel Duff, refide in it. Colonel Duff's eftate of Carnoufie is a late purchafe from Captain Hay.

Lord Banff's houfe is called *Forglen*, and ftands on the banks of the river Diveron, on the E. fide of the parifh ; a moft beautiful fituation. Here the river takes a fine circular fweep inwards, clofe upon the houfe ; fo as, ftanding within, and looking out at the windows, to feem to run under it. The banks of the river, above and below, are covered with a variety of fine old wood, of a large fize ; confifting of afhes, elms, planes, limes, larixes, and beeches. The ground rifes gradually from the river fide, and forms a concentric circular hill in the front of the houfe. The top of the hill is planted, which fhuts the fields and houfes below finely in, and fcreens them from the winds and ftorms. In the centre, on the fide of the hill, lies the mains of Forglen. The fields are divided with ditches and hedges, and furrounded with belts of plantation in a thriving ftate. Without thefe fields, on the N. and S., are accommodated, with neat houfes and convenient crofts, all his Lordfhip's people ; grieve, gardener, and farm fervants, wright and fmith, and labourers, with their families. Thefe perform his Lordfhip's work, and have their reward, without burdening the tenants at all.—There are 500 or 600 acres, or upwards, of plantation upon the eftate, moftly executed by the late Lord Banff, to which confiderable additions have been made by the prefent Lord ; all in a thriving condition. His Lordfhip has done much of late to beautify his feat. The workmen were forry to put the firft hand to change fome of the improvements of his father, which they thought well enough, and to undo their own workmanfhip ; but the execution pleaf-

ed

ed their eye fo much, that they forgot their fympathy *.
They found this was the order of Providence.—While
they were executing thefe improvements, they were earn-
ing their own and their families bread by them. Sorry,
forry were their hearts when his Lordfhip was called a-
way to the wars. Earneft is their prayer for peace, that
he may return to them again.

On the front of the houfe, over the entry, is a coat of
arms, and above it this fentence : *Houp of reward caufis
guid fervice.* Underneath, there is this infcription : " Do
" veil, ᴀnd doubt nocht, althoch Thou be fpyit. ʜe is
" lytil guid vorth that is nocht invyit. Tak thou no Tent
" qvhat everi man tellis. Gyve you wald leive on demit,
" Gang qvhair na man dwellis." The date below, or age
of the houfe, or year of building, is 1578.

Colonel Duff's houfe, *Carnoufie,* ftands upon a rifing
ground, about an Englifh mile and a half W. from the
church, not very diftant from the river, but not in fight
of it. There are feveral confiderable plantations upon this
eftate, and a good deal of natural wood by the river fide.
The Colonel is prefently enclofing his mains. There are
no good quarries in the parifh ; they are obliged then to
ufe fuch furface ftones as they can find ; and yet with
thefe, they make the moft beautiful work of dry ftone
fence I ever faw. The ftones are all courfed ; and the
mafons fay, they make as much work that way as the
other, when their hand is in ufe ; but it requires to be
bred to it, as ordinary workmen cannot do it.

River Diveron.—This river abounds with trout, eel, and
falmon ; and both heritors have fifhings on it. Lord
Banff

* They began to remember, that there was a time to plant, and a
time to pluck up that which was planted ; a time to break down, and a
time to build up ; a time to caft away ftones, and a time to gather
them.

Banff has about 3¼ Englifh miles of the river, and Colonel Duff only one. The fifh, however, are fmall, and the fifh-ings inconfiderable. It is only when there happens a high water on Sunday, when the cruives are open, that there is a chance of a run. At other times, the fifhings below are plied fo clofe, that few can efcape.

There are three mills in the parifh : Mill of Ribra, Lord Banff's; and Mill of 'Burn-end and Mill of Car-noufie, Colonel Duff's.

Rent, Stipend, and Accommodations.—The valued rent of the parifh is about 1700l. Scotch.—The ftipend is 42 bolls of meal and 6 bolls of bear, and 45l. Sterling in money, befides 2l. 10s. for communion elements.—The manfe was built in 1683. The prefent incumbent has had his barn, kiln, ftable, and byre renewed; and is getting the wings of the manfe repaired, with the addi-tion of a kitchen and childrens room in one of them, the houfe being fmall.—The glebe is good land, but is only a few falls more than legal meafure. For pafture, the mi-nifter has a den adjoining to the glebe, and a fmall field on the banks of Diveron, annexed in 1751, by decreet of the prefbytery, to make the pafture fufficient. He has prefently no accommodation of mofs; the mofs on which he had a locality being exhaufted, and no new one yet fettled for him. There is indeed but little mofs in the parifh.

Population.—According to Dr. Webfter's report, the population in 1755 was 607. The lift of parifhioners varies from accidental caufes, by the refidence or. non-refidence of the heritors and their families. The popula-tion has increafed of late, by the divifion of fome tacks and fubfets on a large farm. In 1782, the number of fouls

fouls was 577. The lift at this time was exactly taken.
Whether the following year's lift was equally exact, I
know not, but find it fet down at 544. This being a
year of particular fcarcity of meal, perhaps t`e difference
of 33 is to be accounted for by fewer fervants being engaged by the fmaller tenants and tradefmen, and by allowing their own children to go forth to fervice. The
year following it is up again at 573, and continues about
that till 1788, when I find 613; and fince that time, it
has been about 600. The medium of fouls then of thefe
different years is, - - - 596

Of which number there are males,	282
Females, - - -	314
Examinable, - -	500
Children about 8 years, and under,	96
Average of marriages, - -	6
Baptifms, - -	11
Burials, - -	12

There are but few tradefmen and mechanicks in the
parifh. There are 5 fquare wrights, with about as many
journeymen and apprentices; 3 wheelwrights; 10 weavers; 4 fhoemakers; 2 fmiths; 1 tailor; and 2 good old
foldiers, difcharged and fuperannuated, enjoying each his
penfion, fober and induftrious, and of courfe thriving.
There is a fmith, an elder of the church, and a miller fit
to be one. There is 1 boat within the parifh, the boat of
Muirifh, belonging to Lord Banff; and another, the boat
of Afhoyle, belonging to Mr. Leflie of Donlugafs, and
lands upon it a little below the houfe of Forglen *.

Funds

* Boat of Muirifh is the only publick houfe in the parifh. There is
no manufactory of any kind. There are two or three merchants who
retail fome fmall articles, and fome of them give out lint to fpin, and
take in the yarn for manufacturers in Banff and Huntly.

Funds of the Poor.—Though the funded money does not amount to a large fum, only 65 l. Sterling, yet the poor in this parifh are as well fupplied as in moft other parifhes, owing to the liberality of the people themfelves, and the diftinguifhed charity of the heritors. The Forglen family being refident, and giving regular attendance upon the ordinances, have afforded a continual fupply to the poor and the fick. And Colonel Duff, when abroad in India, appointed a very handfome fum, in place of Sunday collection. The intereft of 65 l., then in Lord Banff's and Captain Hay's hands, at 5 per cent., with the ordinary and facramental collections, and produce of mortcloth, goes to the fupply of the poor. A meeting is held at the manfe annually, of the heritors, minifter, and elders, in the end of the year, to confider the ftate of the poor, and appoint fupplies for them. Blankets, clothes, fhoes, and other neceffaries, are purchafed for them, as they need. A fupply of meal is appointed for the year, and diftributed in equal proportions of their quantity monthly. One of the elders, in the centre of the parifh, takes charge of the diftribution. By this means, the poor are kept from wandering, there not being one belonging to the parifh that goes out of it. In times of fcarcity, upon application of the feffion, the heritors generoufly afforded the meal at the eafy rate of 10s. the boll, over and above their other charities. At other times, 2 members of the feffion, Peter Mearfon in Eaftfide, and William Robertfon in Mill of Ribra, refpectable men, and men of fubftance, furnifhed it, and afforded it alfo at eafy rates. This was a great faving to the fund. Keeping the poor thus comfortable within their own houfes, would be one happy mean to leffen iniquity, by preventing vagrants, thieves, and pickpockets, from going about under

under pretence of begging, and fave many from an untimely end. No one would grudge the real indigent their fupply; but fo many impofitions and thefts are intolerable in a land that has any regulation. In 1783, this parifh received 13½ bolls of the government meal.

Mortification in favour of the Minifter.—There is a mortification in behalf of the minifter, of 10l. Sterling, which lies in his hands, free of intereft, and is transferred to the fucceffor at entry. This is faid to be made by one of the Earls of Buchan, who had property in this parifh, in teftimony of the minifter's hofpitality, which had much pleafed him, upon honouring him with a vifit.

Mortification in favour of the Schoolmafter.—The Reverend Mr. George Bruce, minifter of Dunbar, has, within thefe two years, mortified 100l. Sterling in behalf of the fchoolmafter, through an attachment to the parifh, he himfelf having taught the fchool here in his younger days. He has required the fchoolmafter to be eftablifhed, and to be put in poffeffion of at leaft 100 merks of falary; and the heritors, to concur with him, have made it 200 merks. He requires, as a condition of tenure, that the fchoolmafter fhall read portions of fcripture to the congregation, betwixt the fecond and third bells. In cafe of neglect, the mortification to be transferred to Rothiemay, Mr. Bruce's native parifh. Lord Banff, as patron, and Colonel Duff, as next greateft heritor, and the minifter, and their fucceffors, are appointed truftees for the management. And the reverend prefbytery of Turriff are requefted by the donor to infpect the application, with power to queftion any abufe; and a copy of the deed of mortification is inferted in their records.

Lord

Lord Banff and Colonel Duff have taken the 100l. Sterling betwixt them, 50l. each, and bound themſelves to
pay the intereſt annually to the ſchoolmaſter, Mr. Mori-
ſon, and his ſucceſſors in office, at the rate of 5 per cent.
Mr. Bruce has become a rich man. How honourable
to himſelf is ſuch teſtimony of his gratitude to God, who
hath bleſſed him with proſperity! How beneficial to ſociety is ſuch benevolence! There is no claſs of men more
uſeful than ſchoolmaſters, when attentive to their duty,
and few worſe provided. Their ſalaries are ſmall, their
perquiſites in ſmall pariſhes, inconſiderable, and their payments, by the poor, not very punctual. The ſchoolmaſter
here, however, from having one of the ſmalleſt, will now
have as good a fixed income as moſt of his neighbours in
the country ſchools.

Mortification in behalf of the Poor.—George Gerard, Eſq.
of Midſtrath, late factor to Lord Banff, through attachment to the pariſh, in which he has long reſided, and
from pious motives, preſently pays the ſchool fees throughout the year of four of the preſent ſcholars, to enable
them to read the Bible, and to write their name; and in-
tends mortifying a ſum ſufficient to make the payment
perpetual.

Character and Manners of the People.—The people, excepting two or three of the Scottiſh Epiſcopal congregation at Turriff, are all of the Eſtabliſhed Church. There
is no Catholick nor Seceder in the pariſh. They are ſober and induſtrious, and diſcreet in their behaviour; reſpectful to their maſters and ſuperiors, and kind to their
miniſter; and give regular attendance to the ordinances.

The

The fuperftition of former times is now much worn out *.

This parifh, from its fituation, is dry, and the air pure and healthy. There are no epidemic difeafes ; fevers occafionally, but not fo mortal as in other corners. They now fee by experience the advantage of medical fkill, and more readily apply to the doctor than formerly in time of need ; and many are now reconciled to inoculation for the fmall pox. They find it as good to let the doctor prepare them, and do it, as to let the children inoculate themfelves at random. They live to a good old age. A good many are on the borders of fourfcore, healthy and vigorous ; and feverals of late have paft 90.

Drefs.—There is a great change as to this article of late. Hats are as common as bonnets now ; and the bar plaid is changed for a fcarlet one. On Sundays, there is no diftinguifhing the country clown from the town beau ; the farmer's goadman from the merchant's clerk ; and the laffes have their ribbands and muflins to match them. There is a great odds in their living too ; they are more

social

---

* There remains, however, ftill a little. Some charms are fecretly ufed to prevent evil ; and fome omens looked to by the older people. There are happy and unhappy days for beginning any undertaking. Thus, few would choofe to be married here on Friday, though it is the ordinary day in other quarters of the church. There are alfo happy and unhappy feet. Thus, they wifh bridegrooms and brides a happy foot ; and to prevent any bad effect, they falute thofe they meet on the road with a kifs It is hard, however, if any misfortune happens when you are paffing, that you fhould be blamed, when neither you nor your feet ever thought of the matter. The tongue too muft be guarded, even when it commends ; it had more need, one would think, when it difcommends. Thus, to prevent what is called forefpeaking, they fay of a perfon, God fave them ; of a beaft, Luck fair it.

focial in the way of vifiting; and flefh is more frequently ufed by all *.

How agreeable is it to fee people advancing and thriving. There is one drawback, however, upon them. Price of labour, and tradefmen's rates, are rather too much raifed againft the country man, and moft of all among the farm fervants.

Price of Labour.—The price of labour is much augmented of late. A farmer's fervant, though but an ordinary one, draws 7 l., and fome 8 l., inftead of 5 l., a few years back. Womens wages were long ftationary at 2 l., but are now up to 2 l. 10 s. † Day-labourers receive from 6 d. to 8 d. a-day, and victuals. Harveft wages are very high : women 1 l. Sterling, and men 1 l. 10 s., and above. In hurried times, fome have had the confcience to afk 2 l. ‡.

Rates of Provifions.—Butcher meat is raifed, in the fpace of a few years, from 2½ d. to 3½ d. and 4 d. the lb. ; butter from 6 d. to 8 d. the lb. ; cheefe from 3 s. 4 d. to 4 s.

* The farmer is defigned by the name of his farm, as the mafter is by his eftate. The goodwife is miftrefs ; and yet the hufband modeftly declines the compliment. When you afk for the goodwife, by the name of miftrefs, his return is, I thank you, my wife is well.

† Not, however, in proportion to the men. The men can more eafily remove to a diftance : and with them indeed now, all is a mercantile or rouping fpirit ; the higheft bidder, though a ftranger, is preferred to a good old mafter, who would willingly retain his fervant. But there is now little gratitude, or attachment with thefe perfons, and no room left for their mafter's generofity and compaffion, in cafe of ficknefs or fettlement.

‡ For fuch, one would almoft wifh a fcarcity to follow, that they might the fooner eat up their notes. Is it any wonder, when the farmer gets fuch in his power, that he fhould take his price for his meal ?

4s. 6d. the ftone; and fowls from 6d. to 8d. and 9d. *—
The moſt reaſonable article of all our proviſions is ſalmon,
which we have in the ſeaſon, if the fiſhing is tolerable, at
2d., and ſometimes even ſo low as 1½d. the lb, when
there is a good run. Eggs are ſcarcely to be had : they
are carried off to the Banff market, where they get 3d.,
4d., 5d., and 6d., in times of ſcarcity, the dozen.

Miſcellaneous Obſervations.—There are no natural curioſities. Two ſmall wells, one in the wood of Carnouſie,
and another on the N. ſide of the moſs of Whitefield, called the Red-gill Well, are medicinal, and uſed by the
neighbours. The one by the moſs is a pretty ſtrong
chalybeate, iron mineral ; if a little attention was paid to
it, it might be of uſe to the neighbourhood : the water is
ſaid to be as ſtrong as ſome of thoſe reſorted to. There
is a Druidical temple in the heart of the woods of Forglen, but ſhut up thereby from view, till the wood grows
up, and becomes penetrable. The tenants are in danger
of loſing their beaſts in them ſometimes. And the deer,
either chaſed from the herd in the Highland foreſts, or
pinched with hunger in ſevere winters, come ſome of
them down as far as this, and are ſeen to paſture with
the cattle on the ſide of the woods. Theſe woods abound
with foxes for ſport, for the ſupply of the Turriff hunts ;
but they frequently make ſad depredations among the
poultry around.

A loch, called *the Earl's Loch*, on the farm of Scotſ-
town, was probably named after one of the Earls of Buchan

---

* The fiſhers wives and daughters were in uſe formerly to ſupply us
with fiſh, and the farmers gave them a very adequate barter of meal for
them ; but now they are up at ſuch rates, that meal, in compariſon, is
of no value, and will not purchaſe them. From 6d. and 8d. they
are now up to 1s. and 1s. 6d. at times the dozen. Our own fiſh are
cheaper.

chan, who were proprietors here : it is now moftly drained up. There is a know, called *the Rounie Law*, where
formerly markets were held, on the fide of the wood of
Forglen, a little N. of the church ; but none are held now.
The privilege was probably transferred to Turriff, where
are now the beft cattle markets in the country.

The cattle on the water fide, by richnefs of the pafture,
are of a large fize ; one tenant in Eaftfide, had a plough
of 8 oxen, which would, in moft feafons, have been good
beef from the yoke, and would have weighed from 50 to
70 ftone, at an average ; and if full fed, from 70 to 90 ;
and fome feemed fize enough to carry 100. Now however, as more profitable, farmers change oftener, and difpofe of them when young. The fleeces of fheep, I am
informed, extend to 5 lb. Englifh weight. They fhear
the lambs, weighing 42 ounces.

We have marked weights for oats, at the medium of 14
ftone ; barley 18 ; but thefe are the loweft mediums. I
am informed, there have been oats as high as 16, and
have had from 19 to 20 ftone of barley, at the end of the
feed time, when the victual was clean and dry. This
parifh ufed formerly to be fupplied with lime, manufactured at Banff, at 9 d. the boll, of 2 firlots flacked. They
are now fupplied with fhells from Sunderland, at 3 s. the
boll, of 4 firlots ; both from Banffshire, diftant 10 Englifh
miles. This, when ufed as a manure, is laid on at the
quantity of from 80 to 160 firlots the acre. Some part
of it is brought from Streifa, Edingight's land, in the parifh of Grange ; and a fmall quantity is burnt in the parifh,
with peats. The ftones are brought from Whitehills quarry,
on Lord Findlater's eftate, in the parifh of Boyndie. But
this is very expenfive now, and little ufed, by reafon of
the fcarcity of peats. What is burnt with peats, muft be
                                                    mafhed

mafhed down with the hammer to the fize of an egg or fo.

Peat fuel is very expenfive, by reafon of the wafte of time and labour in cafting, winning, and efpecially carrying the peats. Country people, however, know not yet well how to make ufe of Mr. Dundas's bleffing, as they find the coal does not anfwer fo well on the hearth. They are at length beginning to get fmall grates for their chamber fires; and they will next fee it convenient to have grates for their kitchen fires alfo. The relieving of this quarter of the kingdom from the tax upon coals, is certainly a great benefit to the country at large, and a fpecial bleffing to the poor, of which the clergy know their people to be very fenfible : they feel the obligation ; they received the news with joy : and, if collected in a body, they would have been as forward to have borne publick teftimony to the effectual endeavours of the Honourable Secretary, Mr. Dundas, as any fociety. They, indeed, deferve of their governors whatever can be done for them; for they are fteady friends of Government. It does one's heart good to fee their loyalty ; while the clergy, in every corner of the church, have manifefted their fentiments in favour of Government. The people here, of every defcription, are in unifon with their teachers. There are no murmurers here : No evil men feeking only rebellion. " The King and the Conftitution," or, " The King, his Family, and Friends," are the toafts in the leffer, as well as in the greater circles. They pay the taxes without murmuring ; and when a juft and neceffary war impofes an addition, they do not grudge it. They bear the taxes, and they alfo go out readily, and in numbers, to fupply the fleets and armies, and fight the battles of their country

try. And this pariſh has afforded its due proportion at all times *.

***

* The gentlemen are all of the military profeſſion. One of them, Captain Hay, late of the Royals, has now indeed quitted the army. Colonel Duff of the Artillery, in the ſervice of the Honourable the Eaſt India Company, after long and honourable ſervice, and joining as a volunteer in proſecuting the war againſt Tippoo, returned from India upon the peace, and is now enjoying the *otium cum dignitate.* The Right Honourable Lord Banff, oldeſt Captain of the Inniſkillings, is in the actual ſervice of his country, under his Royal Highneſs the Duke of York. With his Lordſhip are two young men from this pariſh; and other two ſoldiers of the 53d, brothers, of the name of Gallant, who, both at the ſiege of Valenciennes, and defence of New-Port, behaved moſt gallantly.—The abſurd ſyſtem of France is univerſally deteſted. The cruelties practiſed to ſupport it ſhock the ſentiments and feelings of all, and diſgrace and degrade human nature to a level, indeed, with the moſt wild and ferocious beaſts of the brute creation. Say what the world will, the world, nor France neither, will never be governed by ſuch a ſyſtem. It has exhibited already, and will continually exhibit horrid ſcenes of butchery. It lays the foundation of conſtant jealouſies, plots, and maſſacres. There is no proper ſubordination of the governed, nor no confidence in the rulers. Such a government then, they know muſt be feeble and fluctuating, and can have no permanency. It gives every man an opportunity to gratify his private revenge. He has only to ſtir a little jealouſy againſt him, as an enemy to the Convention to-day, and to-morrow he will be guillotined without mercy or mediation.

PARISH OF GAMRIE.

By the Rev. Mr WILSON.

Origin of the Name.

IT has long been a general report, and the prevailing tradition in this country, that, some time before the year 1004, in which the church of Gamrie is said to have been built, (and there is at this day the date 1004 on the steeple), that the Thane of Buchan pursued the Danes to the precipice or brow of the hill above the church, and there defeated them with great slaughter. Several of their skulls (most likely of their chiefs who had fallen in battle) were built into the church wall, where they remain entire: From hence it came to be called by some the Kirk of Sculls. In the Gaelic language, the word *Kemri*, from which, probably, Gamrie is derived, signifies *running step*, or *running leap*. And this derivation seems a natural one; because, from the situation of the hill, which is one of the highest on this part of the coast, and very steep on one side, it must have been a running skirmish, and very fatal to the vanquished. In some old registers, the name of the parish is written Ghaemrie. On the said eminence, above the kirk of Gamrie, at the east end of one of the most level and extensive plains in Buchan, are a number of vestiges of encampments, which at this day are called by the name of *bloody pots*, or *bloody pits*.

Situation,

Situation, Extent, &c.—The church and manse of Gamrie are built in a very extraordinary and romantic situation, on a sloping piece of ground in the middle of a hill, and not a mile from the town and harbour of Gardenstown. By two headlands, called Gamrie and Troup head, which project a considerable way into the sea, a beautiful bay is formed, where there is fine anchoring ground, and vessels can ride in safety. At high water, a person could sling a stone into the sea from the church; and looking out of it, it has the appearance, to a stranger, as if the sea washed its foundations. The church is built, after the manner of some very old edifices, with unslacked lime, and with very thick walls; and, although it has already stood upwards of 700 years, it may, if the roof be kept in proper repair, last for hundreds of years to come. The north side of Gamrie parish is bounded by that part of the German Ocean called the Moray Firth; on the east by the parish of Aberdour; on the south by the parishes of Monwhitter and King Edward; and on the west by the river Dovern, which separates the parish of Gamrie from Banff. This parish stretches 9½ miles along the sea-coast, which is a very bold one. It is almost a continued chain of stupendous rocks, in many places perpendicular, and 200 yards above the sea. It is between 3 and 4 miles broad. Gamrie parish lies in the county of Banff, presbytery of Turriff, and synod of Aberdeen. The soil, in many places, is very fertile, and in others as barren; and, though much has been done of late years, there is still great scope for improvement. The hilly ground is in general covered with heath, and in some places with a coarse kind of grass, on which sheep and young cattle are fed. Sheep, indeed, are very much banished from the parish. When Mr Wilson first came to the parish, there was scarcely a farmer who had not a flock; but now there are only two or three that have any at all. This is in a great

measure

meafure owing to the introduction of fown grafs, and the difficulty there is in winter herding, unlefs the practice was general.

Sea Coaft, and Fifheries.—On this coaft a variety of different kinds of fifh are caught, viz. ling, cod, haddocks, whitings, turbot, fkate, &c. with which this country ufed to be remarkably well fupplied, and a confiderable quantity of them, when dried, were carried to the Firth of Forth, and fold there. From the beft information, it appears that the fifhermen in this parifh have fometimes received for their falt fifh L. 250 annually. Of late years, the fifhing has been fo remarkably poor, (to what caufe it is perhaps difficult to fay, but moft likely one principal reafon is, the immenfe quantities of fea-dogs, a kind of fhark, with which this coaft has been infefted), that there has hardly been fifh fufficient to fupply the markets at home. Of confequence, it is to be fuppofed they have rifen much in value. Long after the prefent minifter was fettled in the parifh, he could have purchafed haddocks at one penny and three half-pence a dozen, which now coft a fhilling to eighteen pence ; and in proportion for other kinds of fifh, and every other article of food. On this coaft, great quantities of fea weed, called ware, are thrown up on the fhore, which the farmers lay on the ground, and find very profitable in raifing crops of barley. In this parifh, it is laid on with a very fparing hand, owing to the fteepnefs of the coaft, and the bad accefs to the fhore. Confiderable quantities alfo of this fea-weed are cut off from the rocks, for the purpofe of making kelp. At an average, about 30 tons are made annually, which fell from L. 3 to L. 5 a ton. On the river Dovern, which fepaaates the parifhes of Banff and Gamrie, is an exceeding good falmon fifhery, the property of Lord Fife, which lets for

L. 1000

L. 1000 *per annum*. The ſalmon are all cured in the town
of Macduff. The pickled fiſh are all ſent to the London
market, and what are ſalted are generally exported to France
and Spain.

Mineral Springs, Quarries, &c.—Near the ſea-coaſt, and
in the neighbourhood of Macduff, is a pretty good mineral
ſpring, called the Well of Farlair, which has been uſeful in
gravelliſh complaints. Of late years it has come into conſiderable repute, and a number of people reſort to it annually.
In this pariſh, upon the eſtate of Meiroſe, now the property
of Lord Fife, is a very good ſlate-quarry. The quantity annually made has been various, depending on the demand, and
the number of hands employed. The ſlates are of a good
quality, of a beautiful blue colour, not inferior to the Eaſdale
ſlate, only thicker, larger, and make a heavier roof. Quarriers are commonly paid by the piece, which is cerrainly the
beſt way for themſelves and their employers. Common day-
labourers uſually receive from 7 d. to 9 d. a day in winter, and
from 9 d. to 1 s. in ſummer.

Natural Curioſities.—Near the eaſt end of the pariſh, and not
far from the houſe of Troup, are three great natural curioſities. 1. A perpendicular rock of very great extent, full of
ſhelves, and poſſeſſed by thouſands of birds called Kitty-
weaks. Theſe arrive in the beginning of ſpring, and leave it
again towards the end of Auguſt, after they have brought
forth their young. Some people are fond of eating the young
Kitty's ; but the ſhooting of them is a favourite diverſion e-
very year. The ſeaſon for this is commonly the laſt week
of July. Whither theſe birds go in winter is not known ;
moſt probably it is to ſome place upon the coaſt of Norway.
2dly, A cave, or rather den, about 50 feet deep, 60 long,
and

and 40 broad, from which there is a subterraneous passage to
the sea, about 80 yards long, through which the waves are
driven with great violence in a northerly storm, and occasion
a smoke to ascend from the den. Hence it has got the name
of Hell's Lumb, i. e. Hell's Chimney. 3. Another subterraneous passage, through a peninsula of about 150 yards
long from sea to sea, through which a man can with difficulty
creep. At the north end of this narrow passage is a cave a-
bout 20 feet high, 30 broad, and 150 long, containing not
less than 90,000 cubic feet. The whole is supported by immense columns of rock, is exceedingly grand, and has a won-
derfully fine effect, after a person has crept through the narrow passage. This place has got the name of the Needle's
Eye. There are in the parish several tumuli. Not many
years ago, one of them, in the neighbourhood of Macduff,
was opened ; and there was found in it an urn, containing a
considerable number of small human bones.

Population.—The population of the parish is nearly double
since the year 1732. At the above period the parish contained 1600 souls, and now nearly 3000. About the years
1704 and 1705, it appears by the Registers that the number
of births annually, at an average, were then 45 ; and, for several years past, they have not been under 60. The number
of deaths cannot be ascertained so far back. About 30 years
ago they were from 10 to 12, and for 7 years past nearly 20
annually. About 30 years ago there were from 12 to 14
marriages annually, and, for 7 years past, not less than 26.

In this parish, many instances of longevity might be mentioned. It is only a few years since a fisherman in Macduff
died at the age of 109 ; and there are living at present several
persons 90 years old and upwards. Mr Wilson is in his 97th
year ;

year; and laſt autumn, at the concluſion of the harveſt, the
age of him, and the two ſervants that aſſiſted in taking in his
crop, amounted in all to 257; and it is worthy remarking
that one of theſe has been his ſervant 50 years. Mr Wilſon
was the firſt that introduced turnips and potatoes into the pariſh. He had a few of them in his garden, which the people in coming to the church uſed to look at as a great curioſity; and it was thought, at that time, that none but a gardener could raiſe them. It was long before the method of
hoeing came to be thought of. Being ſown thick, and hand-
weeded, they came to no ſize. Another ſingularity deſerves
notice, viz. that, when he came to Gamrie, there was not a
watch in church except the laird's and the miniſter's.

Church.—The miniſter's living is, *communibus annis*, L. 100
Sterling; the crown patron. The preſent incumbent was ſettled in the year 1732. He has been a widower for ten years
paſt; has had 14 children; ten of whom (five ſons and five
daughters) he has lived to ſee well ſettled in the world.

Poor.—In ſuch a popular pariſh, it is to be ſuppoſed there
will be ſeveral poor, and accordingly between 50 and 60 receive charity out of the pariſh funds; and of theſe the year
1782 added ſeveral to the liſt. The weekly collection at
Gamrie and Macduff is at an average 14 s. L. 450, which
is at intereſt, belongs to the poor of this pariſh.

Rental.—The valued rent of the pariſh is L. 5489 : 6 : 8
Scots. The preſent real rent, excluſive of fiſheries, is nearly
L. 1680 Sterling.

Towns, Villages, and Miscellaneous Observations.—The principal cauſes of the increaſe of population are, the number of
fiſhing

fiſhing towns on the coaſt, the breaking of large farms into ſmaller ones, the encouragement given by the heritors to improve waſte ground, and their endeavouring to introduce a better mode of culture. The principal town in the pariſh is Macduff, the property of Lord Fife. In 1732 there were only a few fiſhermen's houſes in Macduff, but now there are ſeveral well laid out ſtreets, and 1000 ſouls in the town. The harbour, on which his Lordſhip has already laid out upwards of L. 5000, will, when finiſhed, be one of the beſt in the Moray Firth. There are ten veſſels from 60 to 120 tons burden, and 6 fiſhing boats, belonging to Macduff. Three of them are in the London trade, two in the eaſt country trade, and the others trade moſt commonly to the Firth of Forth.

Since the great increaſe of population in this part of the pariſh, his Lordſhip has erected a Chapel of Eaſe in Macduff, for the accommodation of the inhabitants, who are nearly ſix miles from their pariſh church, and gives a ſalary to a qualified clergyman to preach and diſpenſe the ordinances of religion among them.

On the eaſt end of this pariſh, there are very near to one another two other ſmall towns, Gardenſton and Crovie, both the property of Lord Gardenſton, and not far from his houſe at Troup. The town of Gardenſton contains nearly 300 ſouls, and Crovie 100. In theſe two places are the ſame number of veſſels and fiſhing-boats as in Macduff, only the veſſels are of a ſmaller ſize. Lords Fife and Gardenſton are the only heritors. Lord Fife does not reſide in the pariſh, but one of his principal ſeats (Duff-houſe) is very near it, being only about an Engliſh mile from Macduff. His Lordſhip has paid the greateſt attention to the improvement of his eſtates, and the good of the country, by encouraging,

incloſing,

inclosing, binding his tenants to have yearly a certain quantity of their ground in turnip, so much in fallow, and so much laid down in grass seeds. These regulations were highly proper and necessary some years ago, because people are led in chains by habit ; and it is by flow degrees, and well digested plans, they are made to depart from established customs : But, now that the propriety of these regulations are seen, it would be difficult to make the farmers have such small quantities of turnip, &c. as it was necessary at first to restrict them to. Lord Fife has also converted the whole customs and services (usually called bonnage) at a moderate rate. This is of the utmost importance to the tenants. Not many years ago, many of them paid nearly one-half of their rent in fowls, eggs, sheep, &c. delivered in kind, and the labour of themselves, their servants, horses, in seed-time and harvest, carriage of peats, and many other works in the different seasons throughout the year, when called for ; by which means they were often obliged to plough, dung, and harrow their landlord's ground, and lose the season for their own. Planting is a mode of improvement in which no person in this country has been more successful than the Earl of Fife. His Lordship has planted not less than from 7000 to 8000 acres on his different estates, which he continues yearly to increase ; and at this moment the whole is in a very thriving state. An account of the various kinds of trees, and the method taken to rear them, will be seen in Young's Annals of Agriculture, and the Minutes of the Society of Arts and Commerce. The most considerable plantation in this parish is what is called the Tore of Troup. There are upwards of 600 acres planted with trees of various kinds, in a thriving state. These were reared chiefly by the direction of the late Mr Garden of Troup, and begun by his grandfather. Mr Garden, who is now succeeded by his brother Lord Garden-

ston,

ſton, was unanimouſly elected member of parliament for the county of Aberdeen, during three ſucceeding ſeſſions of parliament; he conſtantly reſided at Troup, in this pariſh, excepting the time he attended parliamentary buſineſs, and paid great attention to the improvement of his eſtate, and the good of his country. He never gave a ſhorter leaſe than for a life; and to ſeveral of his tenants he gave very long leaſes, viz. a life, two nineteen years, and a life. He was not like many others, who, when they ſaw a tenant thriving, thought he had too good a bargain, and would demand a very high rent at the next letting. It was his joy to ſee his tenants carrying on their improvements, and proſpering by their honeſt induſtry. Nor, when any of his leaſes fell vacant, was it ever known that he did not prefer the tenant's own ſon, and continue him in the poſſeſſion, if he was diſpoſed to follow the ſame occupation with his father. And it may be ſafely ſaid, that, owing to the encouragement given by Lord Fife and Mr Garden, there are few tenants in the north of Scotland more thriving than in the pariſh of Gamrie. In the year 1782, when many others were not able to pay their rents, ſcarcity was not much felt except by the pooreſt claſs.

The language ſpoken in this pariſh is the Scottiſh, with an accent peculiar to the north country. There is no Erſe.

The fuel uſed in the pariſh is partly coals and partly peats. The latter has of late years become very ſcarce; and coals are every day much more commonly uſed; which, owing to a partial and oppreſſive tax, coſt very dear, and is a very great hindrance to improvement in this part of the country. It is certainly very unfair, and highly abſurd, that this neceſſary article, which at any rate muſt be conſiderably higher in price to conſumers in the North, from the expence of carriage,

riage, than it is to thoſe on the other ſide of the Redhead, ſhould alſo be loaded with a tax from which the ſouthern inhabitants are exempted : And it is to be hoped the wiſdom and juſtice of the legiſlature will ſoon provide a remedy, either by a total repeal, or by making the tax payable at the pit, which would thereby become general, and be much leſs partially felt.

PARISH OF GARTLY

(*County of Banff—Presbytery of Strathbogie—Synod of Moray.*)

By the Rev. Mr. JAMES SCOTT, Minister.

Form and Extent.

THE parish of Gartly is of an oval form, though not very regular. It is about 12 English miles in length, from E. to W.; and 6 in breadth, from S. to N., about the middle.

River and Fish.——It is divided nearly in the centre, by the rivulet *Bogie*; which, running in a serpentine form, also divides the counties of Banff and Aberdeen, as it falls to the N., and forms a very pleasant strath, from which this county derives its name, *Strathbogie*. Its banks are mostly covered with aller; and it abounds with excellent yellow trouts, and salmon in the spawning season.

Surface and Soil, &c.——The boundaries of this parish, both on the

the E. and W. fides, are hilly, and moftly covered with heath. In thefe hills there is plenty of mofs, which not only fupplies the inhabitants of the parifh, but alfo the town of Huntly, with fuel. From thefe hills feveral fmall brooks fall into the Bogie. The vallies, fupplied by thefe brooks, are very fertile, as well as the lands on the different fides of the Bogie, when properly cultivated, though in general rather late.

Cultivation and Produce.—The cultivation of the foil has been annually more and more attended to, fince the year 1770 At that time there were only two gentlemen farmers, (both of whom had been in the army), who had a field in turnips or fown grafs; whereas now there is not one, who has not more or lefs of his farm under thefe crops. One of thefe gentlemen, who firft fet the example, and who is ftill refident in the parifh, is now carrying his improvements ftill farther, by introducing horfe-hoeing; whereby he raifes moft luxuriant crops of cabbages and turnips. The crops are, bear, oats, peafe, and potatoes; and the returns from thefe do much more than fupply the wants of the parifh.

Cattle.—The lands are now moftly tilled with horfes, which are of different fizes, fitted for the different ways they are employed; and are in number above 340. The black cattle here are generally fmall, but of a very tight Highland breed, and about 1,500 in number. The fheep are alfo of a fmall kind, and in number betwixt 4,000 and 5,000.

Minerals.—There is a lime quarry in the parifh, but fo deep, and expenfive to work, that the farmers, rather than dig ftone from it, choofe to bring their lime from the diftance of 4 or 5 miles. There is alfo a very fine flate quarry in the parifh. The

The flates found in it are of a dark blue colour, and very durable and light.

Proprietor and Rent.—The Duke of Gordon is fole proprietor of the parifh. The yearly rent is about 1,600l. Sterling; and the valued rent 2,080l. Scotch.

Population.—The number of inhabitants, about 10 years ago, was greater than it is at prefent. This decreafe can only be imputed to the principal tenants extending their farms, and removing their cottagers. Within thefe 40 years, however, it has increafed confiderably, as appears from the following table:

POPULATION TABLE of the Parifh of GARTLY.

Number of fouls in 1783, -	2000	Annual average for the laft 10 years,	
Ditto in 1793, - -	1800	Of births, - - -	21
	———	— marriages, - - -	6
Decreafe in 10 years, -	200	— burials *, - - -	24
Number of fouls in 1755, -	1328		
	———	* Several of thefe are from other	
Increafe in 38 years, -	472	parifhes.	

Wages.—Day labourers, in winter, get 6d. per day; in fummer, 8d.; in autumn, 1s., with their victuals. Men fervants receive, per annum, from 6l. to 7l. Sterling: Women fervants, by the year, from 2l. 10s. to 3l., and herds in proportion. Country wrights, that go from houfe to houfe, get 6d. per day in winter, and 8d. in fummer, with their victuals. Tailors receive 6d., befides their maintenance.

Church and School.—The kirk was built in the year 1621, and was lately repaired very fubftantially. A new manfe was
built

built in the year 1756: Both it and the school-house are in
good repair. The ſtipend is not quite 60l. Sterling. The
Duke of Gordon is patron.

Poor.—The poor's funds are from about 150l. to 200l.
The number of poor on the roll is from 20 to 23; among
whom are divided from 24l. to 27l. annually, ariſing from
the collections, intereſt on the funds, mortcloth, &c.; beſides
occaſional ſupplies to ſome neceſſitous perſons not on the roll.

Diſeaſes and Character, &c.—It cannot be ſaid, there is any
diſeaſe peculiar to this pariſh; but ſeveral of its inhabitants
are affected with ſcrofulous and gravelliſh complaints *.—
They are, in general, induſtrious, orderly, and well affected
to government.—There are two licenſed diſtillers in the
pariſh.

---

* Inſtances of longevity are not uncommon. A farmer, named JOHN FER-
RIER, died at Kirkney, in this pariſh, in the year 1788, aged 102. The only
antiquity in the pariſh is an old ruin, called the *Place of Gartly*.

PARISH OF GLASS.

(Counties of Aberdeen and Banff.—Prefbytery of Strath-
bogie.—Synod of Aberdeen.)

By the Reverend Mr JOHN COOPER.

Name, Situation, Soil, &c.

THE ancient and modern name of the parifh is *Glafs*.
It is faid to be called fo from the greennefs of its hills,
on which there is very little heath ; and that the word *Glafs*,
in Irifh, fignifies *green*.—The river Dovern runs through the
parifh ; and the church is fituated on the north fide of faid
river, the courfe of which is from fouth-weft to north-eaft.
The extent of the parifh, from north-eaft to fouth-weft, is
full five computed miles ; and, from north-weft to fouth-eaft,
upwards of four computed miles. The country is variegated
by a number of green hills, which afford pafture for black
cattle and fheep, of each of which, numbers are produced and
bred in the parifh. The foil, in general, is a pretty deep
loam. What lies along the river fide is tolerably early ; but
thofe parts which lie at any diftance are rather cold and late,
and the harveft very precarious. The roads, in general, are
very bad ; for, though the ftatute labour is exacted, yet it is
very fuperficially performed ; and, by the fwampinefs of the
ground, the communication from place to place is little
mended. Befides this, Dovern is frequently impaffable, as
there

there is no boat or ftone-bridge over it : Hence many accidents happen. Not fewer than 7 perfons have loft their lives in the river within thefe 30 years paft.

Population.—According to Dr Webfter's report in 1755, the number of fouls was 1000. For thefe 34 years paft, the amount of examinable perfons, at an average, was about 900. Laft year, the number of fouls was 942. This prefent year, (April 1791), the number is 970, which is confiderably lefs than for years before 1782. There are about 12 or 14 Seceders, fome of whom have families, and thefe are not reckoned. When the prefent incumbent entered, there were about 45 Papifts, and 4 Nonjurors; but, at prefent, there are none. During 36 years, from 1756 to 1791 inclufive, the baptifms in this parifh were,—males, 345;—females, 350.

Effects of 1782.—The King's bounty in 1782, tranfmitted by the Barons of Exchequer, of 50 bolls meal, with what the funds of the parifh afforded, preferved the lives of the poor. The people, at that period, were meagre and ghaftly; but the difeafes that were apprehended did not follow, owing, as was fuppofed, to their feldom getting a full meal of fuch corrupted victual as the feafon produced. So little productive was the oats or barley, that many were known not to have a peck of meal from a boll of dried corn; and the colour fo black, that it refembled more the ordinary duft in the mills, than meal for the ufe of man. The tenants were greatly reduced; and many of their cottars were obliged to retire to the manufacturing towns for employment, by which the numbers are fewer than before.

Rent, Prices, Wages, and Crops.—The valued rent is 2250 l.
Scotch;

Scotch; the real rent about 1000 l. Sterling, converting the victual at 10 s. *per* boll. Rent of acres is from 6 s. 8 d. to 20 s. Sterling. Moſt of the farms have paſture graſs, on which they feed cattle. The young ſtore, the butter and cheeſe they make from their cows, and the linen yarn ſpun by the women to the manufacturers in Huntly, are the principal funds for paying their rents. Butter ſells from 5 d. to 7½ d. *per* pound; cheeſe at 4 s. and 5 s. *per* ſtone; and beef and mutton at from 3 d. to 4½ d. *per* pound. Men's ſervants wages run from 4 l. to 5 l. and ſome 6 l. *per* year; and women's wages, at an average, may be computed at 2 l. 5 s.— Oats, barley, and a few peaſe, are the ordinary crops the country produces; only, of late, ſome few have ſown turnip, and planted potatoes in the fields after the plough; and have, with next crop, laid down clover and rye-graſs, which have ſucceeded very well.

Church, Poor, and School.—The Duke of Gordon is patron. The ſtipend is 36 bolls oat-meal, 16 bolls bear, and 46 l. 6 s. 8 d. Sterling of money, with a glebe of about 15 acres of arable and graſs ground. The manſe and office-houſes were built in 1772. The church, which was quite ruinous, is this year very ſufficiently rebuilt. There are only two heritors, neither of whom reſide.—There are few begging poor in the pariſh, but ſeveral houſeholders that are in indigent circumſtances; and theſe, to the amount of between 30 and 40, get ſuch aſſiſtance as the funds will admit. The collections in the church do not exceed 7 l. or 8 l. at moſt in the year; but mortifications, to the extent of 150 l. Sterling, help in part.—The ſchoolmaſter's ſalary is 100 merks. There were, this winter, 32 ſcholars at the ſchool.

PARISH of GRANGE,

(COUNTY OF BANFF, SYNOD OF MORAY, PRESBYTERY OF STRATHBOGIE.)

By the Rev. Mr FRANCIS FORBES.

Name, Situation, Extent, Mountains, Rivers, Soil, &c.

THIS pariſh takes its name from *Grangia*, a middle age term for a farm, or country reſidence. This name was given to the lands called the Davoch of Grange by the Abbots of Kinloſs, who had here a caſtle, in which they frequently reſided, attracted by the beauty of the ſituation, the caſtle being built upon the top of a ſmall mount, partly natural, partly artificial, ſurrounded with a dry ditch, upon the ſouth ſide of a riſing ground, overlooking extenſive haughs, then covered with wood, and the ſmall river Iſla meandring through them for ſeveral miles. The church lies 16 meaſured miles S. W. from Banff, 12 S. of Portſoy, 10 N. of Huntly, and nearly 4 E. of Keith. The pariſh

rifh is almoft fquare, being, at a medium, 6 miles from
N. to S. by 5 miles from E. to W *. The parifh extends N. from the banks of Ifla, in 3 long but low ridges,
terminating in the mountains called the Knockhill, Lurg-
hill, and hill of Altmore, which divide it from the fertile
countries of Boyn and Enzie †. The Knockhill is a very
high conical hill, upon the N. É. corner of the parifh. It
is detached all round from the reft of the ridge, and is feen
at a great diftance every way, both by fea and land, as it
rifes confiderably above any of the adjacent hills, and has
very

* This parifh is part of the diftrict called Stryla, or Strath-ifla ; fo called from the fmall river Ifla, which runs along the fouth fide of it from
W. to E.; dividing a farm or two, on the north fide of the ridge of hills
called Ballach, from the reft of this parifh ; and empties itfelf into the
Deveron, about two miles eaft of the parifh, after a fhort courfe of 12
miles, in which it receives a number of rapid mountain-ftreams, which
caufe it frequently to overflow its banks, and damage the crops upon the
haughs ; which, for 5 miles of its courfe, in this and the neighbouring
parifh of Keith, are about half a mile broad. In the the years 1768,
1782, 1787, and 1789, the river did incredible damage to the crops upon
the haughs. In 1768, the greater part of the crop being cut, but not got
in, a flood fwept the whole away. In 1782, 1787. and 1789 the floods
came earlier in the feafon, and blafted the crop in fhooting ; in 1789, in
particular, the haughs were 11 times overflowed, from the time they
were fown, before the crop was got in.

† *Altmore* fignifies ' The great Burn,' and is the name of a large and
rapid ftream, which takes its rife in thefe mountains, and running from N.
to S. falls into Ifla, dividing the parifh of Keith from Grange, the whole
length of its courfe. Other 3 burns in this parifh take their rife in thefe
mountains, and running from N. to S. parallel to the burn of Altmore,
fall alfo into Ifla ; two of them, the burn of Pathnie and the Lime-burn,
run between the 3 ridges or divifions of the parifh above mentioned ; the
third, the burn of Millagyn, is the boundary of the parifh upon the E.
feparating it from Marnoch and Rothefnay. Thefe burns, together with
Ifla, abound with very fine trout of different kinds: which are the only fifh
found in them, except in autumn, when the falmon, with which the Deveron abounds come up Ifla to depofit their fpawn ; but no clean falmon
are ever caught in Ifla. Otters are fometimes found in Ifla, and in thefe
burns.

very much the appearance of a volcano at a diſtance, though it has no figns of one when more nearly examined; for it is covered with peat bank over the top, to the depth of 6 or 8 feet at leaſt. The average height of the Knockhill above the adjacent vallies may be about 400 yards. It is faid, that in a clear day, part of 12 counties can be diſtinctly difcerned from the top of it. There are only other two hills in the parifh. The hill of Silliearn makes part of the eaſtmoſt of the three ridges, into which the parifh is divided. It rifes about 100 yards above the reſt of the ridge, extending from N. to S. about two miles, and from E. to W. above a quarter of a mile. The Gallowhill is a fmall hill of about 200 acres area, making part of the Davoch of Grange, lying N. of the church, upon the fouth end of the middle ridge or divifion of the parifh, and is fo called, becaufe it was the place of execution for criminals, tried and condemned in the abbot's regality-court; for the Abbots of Kinlofs, as well as the great feudal barons, had an heritable right of judging in all civil and criminal matters in their own domeſtic court, by their bailie of regality, within a certain diſtrict, generally their own eſtates, and from this court there lay no appeal; nay, they could even reclaim a caufe out of the King's courts, if it belonged to their jurifdiction, and judge it in their own. This right, fo derogatory to the honour and power of the Crown, and to the adminiſtration of juſtice in the national courts, as well as to the liberty of the fubject, was abolifhed after the rebellion in 1745, and a compenfation in money given by Parliament to the heritable proprietors. The low part of the parifh is in general pretty generally cultivated, except fome low moſſes, and the cultivation has crept more than half up the furrounding hills. The land for a mile N. of the water of Ifla, lying upon the fide of a rifing ground, floping to the fouth, is a good foil, tolerably dry and early, and

very

very fertile in good feafons, and when well cultivated; but two-thirds of the cultivated ground in the parifh to the N. are cold, wet, and late, the foil confifting chiefly of a poor clay, upon a till bottom, or a fpungy moffy foil. The air of the parifh is moift, owing not only to the wetnefs of the foil, but alfo to the ridge of hills between it and the fea, which attracts the clouds as they pafs from the Moray Frith, and make them difcharge their contents in torrents upon Stryla, when there hardly falls a drop on the coaft fide. Stryla feldom fuffers by a dry feafon, but always by a wet one.

Antiquities, Heritors.—This parifh appears to have been anciently covered with wood, and to have been part of a vaft foreft, extending from the river Deveron to the Spey, through the parifhes of Rothemay, Grange, Keith, and Boharm, as appears from the roots and trunks of oaks, alder, birch, and fir, found in great quantities, in the many and extenfive moffes, fo frequent in that tract; but at prefent this parifh is quite deftitute of wood, except fome folitary trees, fcattered in a few farmers yards, a copfe of 200 or 300 trees at the houfe of Edingight, and two fmall patches of firs, which are not thriving. This gives the whole country a bare and naked appearance. It does not appear that the parifh was early inhabited; there are no traces of Druidical temples in it; although thefe are fre-quent in the neighbouring parifhes. The places that have names derived from the Gaelic, (which are not many,) muft have been firft inhabited; becaufe that language was univerfal in Scotland till after the Norman Conqueft of England, when the tyranny of the Conqueror, occafioned the flight of great numbers of Anglo-Saxons into Scotland, who, obtaining fettlements in the low country, along the eaft coaft of Scotland, introduced their language, which
gradually

gradually diffused itself through all the more civilized and
beft cultivated part of the country ; perhaps the clergy alfo contributed to diffuse the Englifh language where they
had property or eftablifhments. There is reafon to think,
that the Scotch dialect of the Englifh languages has been
the language of the natives of this parifh for at leaft 400
years *. The lands of Strath Ifla, (Strath-heyliff, as it is
fpelled in the charter), containing the whole parifh of
Grange, and a great part of the parifh of Keith, were beftowed by William the Lyon upon the abbacy of Kinlofs,
in the 12th century. The Popifh clergy very much promoted the cultivation and improvement of the country,
where they had eftablifhments, and large tracts of land
granted to them, formerly not very valuable, nor well cultivated, which foon became, under their poffeffion, well cultivated and well peopled. While the barbarous wars and
depredations carried on between neighbouring chieftains,
often

---

* The names of places in this parifh, derived from the Gaelic, are faid
to be defcriptive of the local fituation, or peculiar properties. of the
places to which they belong ; and it is probable, that they have been
firft occupied for the purpofe of pafturage, rather than for raifing corn.
The principal of them, together with what is faid to be their meaning,
are as follows: *Edingight*, ' The Place oppofite to the Wind.' *Fortrie*,
' The cold South-eaft Hillock.' *Crannach*, ' The Gufhet, or Triangle,'
alluding to the fhape of the ground. *Balamoon*, ' The Mofs town.'
Pathnic, ' The Cow-Hillock.' *Cantley*, ' The frofty Height.' *Auchin-
boove*, ' The Field of Groves,' &c. This laft feems to take its name
from one of the fields of battle; with which this parifh abounds, and
which are faid to have been fought between the Scots and Danes, when
the latter landed at Cullen, in the reign of Donald III. in the end of the
ninth century ; who, as appears from the ancient Scotch hiftorians, defeated the Danes near Cullen, and afterwards at Forres in Moray ;
when, as Guthrie conjectures, the famous obelifk at Forres was erected. The Danes, in advancing into the heart of the country, muft neceffarily pafs through the parifh of Grange, which is only 4 computed miles
diftant

often defolated and depopulated their eſtates, the poſſeſſions of the clergy flouriſhed ; the oppreſſed often fled to
the church for protection, and took refuge under the wings
of the clergy, whoſe ſpiritual and temporal power was
long very great. Strath Iſla was ſoon well cultivated, and
well peopled, under the Abbots of Kinloſs, who had great
eſtates, and were very rich and powerful. They frequently lived at their caſtle of Grange, in great ſplendour and
hoſpitality, and kept a certain number of monks there,
to manage their eſtates, and cultivate their domeſtic farm ;
they erected mills upon Iſla for grinding corn, and bound
their tenants to bring their whole crop to theſe mills ; becauſe they here levied the tithe of corn, which, ſince the
Reformation, has been exacted under the denomination of
that oppreſſive ſervitude called multures, afterward to be
taken notice of. Upon the firſt appearance of the Reformation in this kingdom, the then Abbot, whoſe name was
Robert Robiſon, foreſeeing the approaching troubles, began,

diſtant from Cullen ; and there are ſeveral trenches or encampments,
ſuppoſed to be made by the Scots, upon the haughs of Iſla, with the defenſive ſide thrown up towards the coaſt. Two of the fields of battle
are clearly to be ſeen, being covered with cairns of ſtones, under which
they uſed to bury the ſlain. One of theſe fields is on the N. ſide of the
Gallow-hill, not far from the encampments above mentioned ; and the
other is on the S. ſide of Knockhill, to which there leads a road, from
the encampments, over the hill of Silliearn, called to this day, ‘ The
Bowmens Road.’ Auchinhove, which lies near the banks of Iſla, has
been another field of battle ; and in a line with it, towards Cullen, upon
the head of the burn of Altmore, ſome pieces of armour were ſaid to
have been dug up ſeveral years ago, but were not preſerved ; and in the
ſame line, towards the coaſt, upon the top of the hill of Altmore, there
is a cairn, called The King’s Cairn, where probably the Daniſh King or
General was ſlain in the purſuit. There are no other antiquities in this
pariſh but The Abbot’s Caſtle, already mentioned ; of which there now
remains nothing but a heap of rubbiſh ; being entirely deſtroyed for the
ſake of the ſtones, which are very ſcarce in this corner, for building houſes.

gan, about the year 1535, to feu out his lands in Stryla, to the tenants that then poffeffed them, for fuch fums of money as he could obtain, and the payment of a fmall yearly feu-duty, referving to himfelf, however, the tithe of corn paid at the mills. His fucceffor, who was the laft ecclefiaftical abbot, completed what his predeceffor had begun, referving only the feu-duty ; which, upon the diffolution of the abbacy, came into the poffeffion of Edward Bruce, created commendator, or lay abbot of Kinlofs, and paffed from him to the family of Lethen in Moray, who at prefent draw about L. 42 of feu-duty from this parifh. Grange, being thus feued out among a great number of fmall proprietors at the Reformation, continued in that fituation, except fome few changes, till towards the end of the laft century, when Alexander Duff of Braco got poffeffion of the greateft part of thefe fmall feus. The Davoch of Grange, with the heritable jurifdiction belonging to it, was the laft property which the abbots had in Stryla ; which, after being poffeffed fucceffively by Aber nethy Lord Salton, Lord Ochiltree, and Macpherfon of Cluny, belonged to the family of Gordon for more than a century, till the prefent Duke excambed it with the Earl of Fife, for fome lands in Moray, in the year 1779. At prefent, the Earl of Fife, the reprefentative of Alexander Duff of Braco, poffeffes four fifths of the parifh ; Captain Innes of Edingight, whofe anceftors were original feuars from the abbots, poffeffes one-fixth ; and the Earl of Findlater the remainder. Edingight is the only refiding heritor.

Population.—According to Dr Webfter's report, the number of fouls then was 1797. That the population of this parifh was confiderably greater a century ago than it is at prefent, and has gradually decreafed during all that period,

period, will appear probable, from the table below, accurately extracted from the register of baptisms and marriages *.

No

* In the Year 1684, from 15th March, the Baptisms are 51 ; and in the

Year	Mal.	Fem.	Bapt.	Mar.	Year	Mal.	Fem.	Bapt.	Mar.
1685	–	–	80	–	1716	28	37	65	16
1686	torn.	–	–	–	1717	28	36	64	11
1687		–	–	–	1718	26	20	46	10
1688		–	46	–	1719	37	31	68	14
1689	–	–	54	–	1720	25	21	46	16
1690	defaced.	–	–	–	Av.	$30\frac{1}{10}$	$29\frac{3}{10}$	$59\frac{4}{10}$	$14\frac{1}{10}$
1691	–	–	40	–					
1692	–	–	70	–	1721	30	26	56	14
1693	–	–	57	–	1722	33	17	50	11
1694		–	–	–	1723	23	18	41	19
1695	Defaced and imperfect.	–	–	12	1724	29	19	48	16
1696		–	–	15	1725	33	25	58	14
1697		–	–	13	1726	25	24	49	14
1698		–	–	9	1727	22	28	50	12
1699		–	–	9	1728	23	14	37	16
1700		–	–	2	1729	29	19	48	9
					1730	23	22	45	16
Av.			$57\frac{5}{8}$	10	Av.	27	$21\frac{2}{10}$	$48\frac{2}{10}$	$14\frac{1}{10}$
1701	17	9	26	14					
1702	21	18	39	18	1731	14	20	34	17
1703	17	21	38	19	1732	24	20	44	15
1704	24	22	46	15	1733	24	14	38	25
1705	16	24	40	21	1734	33	17	50	24
1706	28	22	50	18	1735	22	24	46	21
1707	30	26	56	–	1736	22	31	53	11
1708	21	21	42	–	1737	20	18	38	21
1709	37	31	68	9	1738	28	30	58	15
1710	29	17	46	12	1739	26	28	54	10
					1740	15	17	32	26
Av.	24	$21\frac{1}{10}$	$45\frac{1}{10}$	$15\frac{6}{8}$	Av.	$22\frac{8}{10}$	$21\frac{9}{10}$	$44\frac{7}{10}$	$18\frac{1}{10}$
1711	31	31	62	14					
1712	30	36	66	16	1741	18	23	41	8
1713	33	27	60	14	1742	20	17	37	19
1714	36	28	64	20	1743	27	22	49	19
1715	27	26	53	12	1744	36	28	64	15

Year

No regifter of deaths or burials was ever kept here till, in 1783, an act of Parliament was paffed, impofing a duty upon the regiftration of baptifms, marriages, and burials; after which, a regifter of burials was attempted to be kept, but the tax was fo odious and unpopular, (being confidered by the majority of the people as a tax upon their misfortunes), that it could not be collected, but with great difficulty; at the fame time, that it afforded little information concerning the ftate of mortality in the parifh, as a great part

Year	Mal.	Fem.	Bapt.	Mar.
1745	24	14	38	10
1746	19	18	37	10
1747	20	18	38	13
1748	24	21	45	7
1749	29	21	50	8
1750	21	23	44	11
Av.	$23\frac{8}{10}$	$20\frac{5}{10}$	$44\frac{3}{10}$	12
1751	22	20	42	7
1752	20	27	47	17
1753	16	20	36	24
1754	33	25	58	15
1755	26	14	40	13
1756	19	26	45	15
1757	17	17	34	12
1758	25	20	45	7
1759	21	11	32	20
1760	21	18	39	15
Av.	22	$19\frac{8}{10}$	$41\frac{8}{10}$	$14\frac{5}{10}$
1761	19	24	43	13
1762	22	21	43	20
1763	21	19	40	14
1764	17	15	32	15
1765	24	13	37	17
1766	25	23	48	19
1767	14	12	26	12
1768	17	17	34	21
1769	21	19	40	8

Year	Mal.	Fem.	Bapt.	Mar.
1770	18	21	39	14
Av.	$19\frac{8}{10}$	$18\frac{4}{10}$	$38\frac{2}{10}$	$15\frac{1}{10}$
1771	22	15	37	9
1772	13	19	32	17
1773	15	12	27	14
1774	9	23	32	22
1775	14	9	23	12
1776	17	11	28	18
1777	12	14	26	16
1778	14	12	26	13
1779	14	15	29	18
1780	12	17	29	28
Av.	$14\frac{1}{10}$	$14\frac{7}{10}$	$28\frac{9}{10}$	$16\frac{7}{10}$
1781	21	19	40	22
1782	17	18	35	10
1783	16	12	28	11
1784	20	19	39	12
1785	18	21	39	8
1786	26	19	45	11
1787	16	12	28	11
1788	14	18	32	5
1789	13	14	27	10
1790	16	13	29	11
Av.	$17\frac{7}{10}$	$16\frac{5}{10}$	$34\frac{2}{10}$	$11\frac{1}{10}$
1791	11	16	27	11

part of the burials comes from other parifhes, and many perfons dying in this parifh are buried elfewhere; fo that from the moft attentive obfervation, for 4 years that the regifter was kept, it appeared that the burials did not correfpond at all with the deaths; for thefe reafons the regifter was given up. The regifter of marriages is rather a regifter of the contract and publication of banns of every individual in the parifh that is contracted, whether they marry or fettle in the parifh or not; but thofe females that are contracted to men in other parifhes, though their contract be recorded here, do not add to the number of married couples in the parifh, for they generally remove from it altogether. This will account, in fome meafure, for the great difproportion that fometimes appears between the marriages and baptifms in the table; and it is likewife to be obferved, that the diffenters regifter all their contracts, but few or none their baptifms. The baptifm-regifter appears to have been accurately kept, except during the period from 1771 to 1780, during which the church was vacant $2\frac{1}{4}$ years, and the people were frequently obliged to go to neighbouring clergymen to get their children baptized; and not having an immediate opportunity of recording their childrens names, many of them did entirely neglect it. If, therefore, the regifter had been regularly kept during that period, the average number of baptifms, would probably have been about 36, inftead of $28\frac{9}{10}$; certainly it would have been greater than it is. At any rate, the writer of this is fure, that the names of all the children of the members of the Eftablifhment are regularly recorded from the year 1780; and though the Seceders, and other diffenters, do not regifter the names of their children, there is every reafon to believe, that their numbers are not fo great now, as that of the Papifts and Epifcopals were at the beginning of this century, when the firft Prefbyterian minifter was fettled

here;

here ; ſo that the regular decreaſe of the average number of baptiſms in every 10 years, from the beginning of this century, (the firſt 10 years only excepted, which, it is to be obſerved, immediately ſucceeded the 7 years of famine, during K. William III.'s reign), affords a ſtrong preſumption, if not a poſitive proof, of a decreaſing population. That the population has decreaſed very conſiderably ſince the year 1780, is perfectly conſiſtent with the incumbent's knowledge ; for that year, the number of ſouls was 1980 ; in the year 1782, it was 1875 ; in 1784, only 1760 ; in 1789, diminiſhed to 1598 ; and in this year 1791, when an accurate liſt of them was taken up, for the purpoſe of this ſtatement, the number of ſouls is 1572, of which 697 are males, and 875 females ; of whom

333 are below 10 years,	2 conſiſt of 12, -	24
312 between 10 and 20,	1 —— — 13, -	13
563 —— 20 and 50,		——
249 —— 50 and 70,	403 families.	Souls 1572
88 —— 70 and 80,		
27 —— 80 and 90.		Houſeholders.

There are 403 fam. of which

62 conſiſt of 1 perſon,	62	Married pairs, -	216
71 —— — 2, -	142	Do. men, whoſe wives do not reſide with them, - -	2
70 —— — 3, -	210		
53 —— — 4, -	212	Do. women, whoſe huſbands do not reſide with them, -	6
52 —— — 5, -	260		
36 —— — 6, -	216	Single women,	51
34 —— — 7, -	238	Widows, - -	70
10 —— — 8, -	80	Widowers, -	29
7 —— — 9, -	63	Bachelors, -	29
3 —— — 10, -	30		——
2 —— — 11, -	22		403

Not

Not householders.

Married pairs,	-	2
Do. women, whose hus-		
bands do not reside		
with them,	-	5
Widows,	- -	18
Widowers,	- -	7
Male-servants.	-	112
Female-servants,		82
Weavers,	- -	26
Shoe and brogue-makers,		21
Tailors,	- -	11
Blacksmiths,	-	12
Square and cart-wrights,		10
Merchants,	-	8
Masons,	-	3
Millers,	- -	2
Gardeners,	- -	2
Basket-maker,	-	1
Butcher,	- -	1
Wheel-wright,	-	1
Heckler.	- -	1

Cooper,	- -	1
Chelsea pensioners,		2
Clergyman of the Esta-		
blishment,	-	1
Do. of the Secession,		1
Schoolmaster,	-	1
Students at college,		3
Dissenters from the E-		
stablishment,	-	163
Papists, 5 of whom are		
below 10 years,		42
Episcopals, 7 of whom		
are below 10 years,		31
Seceders, 25 of whom		
are below 10 years,		90
Of the above, there have		
come into the parish		
since last year, of Pa-		
pists, 3 of whom are		
below 10,	-	10
Episcopals, 4 of whom		
are below 10,	-	16

There are 5 houses that sell ale or spirits; there is one village, a mill-town, called Nether-mills of Stryla, which contains 92 souls *.

Agriculture,

---

* The causes of the depopulation, that have come to the knowledge
of the present incumbent, are chiefly the following: 1st, The uniting several possessions into one farm; which has affected the population for a
long time past. What was formerly two or more freeholds, each of
which not only maintained the frugal and industrious proprietors, with
their families, but also several cottagers, who had likewise numerous families, are now frequently united into one farm, on which there are few of

Agriculture, &c.—Agriculture is in a worfe ftate at prefent in this parifh than it was 10 years ago. Before the
year 1782, the improvements in farming, introduced by
the

no fubtenants. The lime-trade, which, for centuries back, h-- been the
principal employment of all the inhabitants, was incompatible with large
farms. The largeft farm formerly did not exceed 15 or 20 bolls fowing;
and every farm was fkirted with a number of fubtenants, who were
bound to affift their mafters, in fpring and harveft, with their fervices,
which was generally the greater part of the rent they paid for their poffeffions; and they were allowed to keep as many cattle and fheep upon
the common pafture as they pleafed; and each diftrict of the parifh had
a large tract of pafture in common Whenever the feed time was over,
all hands were employed till harveft, and even after harveft was over, in
providing fuel, and in burning and driving lime; and before lime was
brought by fea from England, and the frith of Forth, Stryla fupplied almoft all Aberdeenfhire, Banfffhire, and Moray, with lime; for which
they received, as long ago as can be remembered by the oldeft people, nearly
the fame price as they do now. They had alfo a kind of fhort flax, which
is now entirely banifhed out of the country, but of which they formerly
raifed great quantities; the drying, breaking, fcutching, beating, heckling,
fpinning, weaving, and bleaching of which, not only afforded employment to men and women, at certain times of the year, when they could
not work at the lime trade; but brought in a great deal of money in
thofe days, and Keith market was formerly reforted to from all parts of
Scotland for purchafing linen-cloth. This, together with the low rents
which they paid, the cheapnefs of victual, for which there was no market
but among themfelves, and the numbers of black cattle and fheep which
the then extenfive paftures enabled them to keep, (many of which they
fattened and killed for their own ufe, becaufe there was no demand for
them at that time from the fouth country or from England), enabled
them to live comfortably, and bring up numerous families; and young
people were not deterred from entering early in life into the married
ftate from fears of want. A very fmall ftock was fufficient to begin the
world, and that ftock was eafily acquired. But when fhipping and trade
became more common upon the coaft, and the exportation of corn commenced at Portfoy, then the farmers thought they could make more profit by the fale of corn, than by the lime-trade, or by fubtenants; they
therefore enlarged their farms, by removing their fubtenants. The he
ritors alfo extended the corn-land, by dividing the commons, and fetting
of

the late patriotic Lord Findlater into his adjoining eſtates
upon the coaſt ſide, had crept gradually into this pariſh.

Carts

off portions of them to the poor peeople to cultivate. Theſe were bad
ſubjects for bearing corn, being naturally of a poor, wet, ſour, ſtony, or
moſſy ſoil; and when once the ſward of them was broke, they ſoon ceaſed
to be good either for graſs or corn, and improvers were unable to cure
the natural barenneſs of the ſoil with plenty of rich manure. The loſs
of the paſture was an irreparable loſs to the farmers, the immenſe numbers of ſheep and black cattle, which were formerly kept upon the hills
to which there was eaſy acceſs, on the paſtures, and on the green moſſes,
now almoſt wholly caſt up for turff, or ploughed and burnt for corn,
produced a great deal of manure, which raiſed plenty both of graſs and
corn; but the paſture being curbed and deſtroyed by the new improvements, the cattle and ſheep dwindled away, and the fields of conſequence
did not produce as formerly. The farms were neceſſarily enlarged; this
increaſed the number of candidates for farms, and conſequently raiſed the
rents, by ſuggeſting the plan to heritors, which they have too ſteadily adhered to, of ſetting up farms to roup. The high prices given for cattle
within theſe 30 years, alſo tended greatly to advance the rents, and to diminiſh the number of ſubtenants, whoſe poſſeſſions were now become neceſſary for paſture. The new improvements ſoon became unfit, for the
reaſons already aſſigned, to maintain the improvers and their families,
even with all the advantages of moſs and lime; this occaſioned the uniting ſeveral improvements into one poſſeſſion. All theſe changes, tended
to leſſen the population. 2*d*, The decay of the lime-trade. Many places that were formerly ſupplied with lime from Stryla, can now be ſupplied with Engliſh ſhells, cheaper than it can be manufactured here with
peat, (always a precarious fuel, and obtained at much expenſe of time
and labour), and carried to a great diſtance, not leſs than 8 or 10 computed miles: whereas formerly people came from a great diſtance, and
bought it at the kilns and carried it themſelves. 3*d*, Emigrations, principally to the ſouth country, occaſioned partly by the riſe of wages, and
the demand for hands, for the purpoſes both of agriculture and manufactures there; but chiefly by the impolitic ſeverity of the landholders, afterward to be taken notice of 4*th*, and laſtly, A great mortality has prevailed in this pariſh for ſeveral years paſt. The pariſh was always e-
ſteemed healthy, till within the laſt 10 years. notwithſtanding the moiſture
of the climate; but the moiſture cannot ſtagnate, as it is expoſed to very
high winds from almoſt every quarter. As a proof of its healthineſs,

there

Carts for carrying dung, lime, and grain, were univerſally adopted in place of creels, currocks and ſacks on horſes backs. The levelling and ſtraighting of ridges, and culti-vating of green crops, ſuch as turnip, potato, and ſown graſs in ſmall quantities, were becoming pretty common a-mong the moſt conſiderable farmers, and were rapidly gain-ing ground, when the ſcarcity in 1783 put a ſtop to all im-provement by green crops, and made the farmers think of nothing but raiſing grain ; and the more ſo, as in theſe wet and late ſeaſons, the beſt cultivated lands often produced the worſt crops, becauſe they continued to grow till the froſts

there were about 200 of the inhabitants alive, upwards of 70 years of age, in the year 1780. Before that time conſumptions were not near ſo frequent as they have been ſince. This may be juſtly attributed, in a great meaſure, to the effects of the ſcarcity, and bad victual, in the year 1783; to the long and inclement harveſts in 1782 and 1787; in both which ſeaſons, the labourers were expoſed to much cold and wet, during three months that each of theſe harveſts continued ; but principally to the change that has of late years taken place, in the manner of living among the lower ranks. Formerly every houſeholder could command a draught of ſmall-beer, and killed a ſheep now and then out of his own little flock ; but now the caſe is very different ; few of the poorer ſort of houſe-houlders can keep any ſheep, for the reaſons already aſſigned, or even afford a little beer, or a bit of meat, upon the Chriſtmas holidays. A-mong the poor, the want of nouriſhing diet, nay, the frequent want even of the very neceſſaries of life, which their induſtry is often not ſufficient to procure for them, to which may be added, their wretched damp un-comfortable houſes, to which they enter through the dunghill, the putrid effluvia of which they breath continually ; and among the middling ranks, dejection of mind, conſequent upon a change of circumſtances from affluence and independence to ſtrugling with debt and want, ap-pear to be the principal cauſes of the prevailing diſtempers, and mortality in this pariſh. Young people are in general cut off by conſumptions, and thoſe more advanced in life by low nervous fevers and dropſies. There are no diſorders that ſeem to belong peculiarly to the climate, un-leſs that old people are generally diſtreſſed with rheumatiſms. Of late, neitherthe ſmall-pox nor any inflammatory diſorder has been very preva-lent or mortal. The complaints are principally nervous.

frosts came upon them before they were properly filled. The tenants in this parish were in general at that period in very good circumstances, the greater part of them having from L. 50 to L. 150 or upwards out at interest, besides the stocking of their farms; but the whole rent of the parish was more than doubled a few years before; and in 1783, not only between L. 3000 and L. 4000 Sterling, supposed to be brought into the parish, one year with another, for grain and lime, was wanting, but nearly as much was given out for victual and seed. This, together with a succession of bad seasons and crops, and the advance of servants wages, greatly reduced the tenants, and brought many of them in arrears, upon which they were summoned out of their possessions. This broke their spirit for industry and exertion, as they then laboured only for, and held their all at the discretion of the landholders, who from time to time seized and confiscated their whole effects for payment of their arrears, and left the poor families no resource, but to go to service, to begging, or to emigrate to the south country, or elsewhere, in quest of employment; and even some of those tenants that were able to weather the storm, are only now receiving new leases for 8 or 9 years, including two or three of their former leases not expired. But in general new leases are never granted till the former be entirely expired, which always exposes the farm to be overcropped, as nothing but its being quite worn out will give the possessing tenant a chance to renew upon reasonable terms, and that only for 19 years at farthest, without any encouragement to inclose, or build good houses; and no respect is paid to the best cultivator, nor even to the tenants in best circumstances; he that will promise most rent is always preferred. Considering these circumstances, and the heavy oppressive multures and mill-services to which they are subjected, amounting to

between

between an eighth and ninth part of the whole crop, it is
a wonder that the state of agriculture is even so good as
it is.—The surface of the parish may be estimated to contain about 16,000 acres; little more than 4000 of which
are under tillage; and only 2567 are in crop this year;
1873 in oats; 538 in barley; 76 in pease; 60 in turnip
and potato; about 20 in flax; and between 80 and 90 in
sown grass. There are 167 ploughs yoked; of which 42
consist of 8 or 10 oxen each. There are only 3 or 4 two-horse
ploughs, that go without a driver, and 1 two-oxen ploughs.
This is a great saving; and it is astonishing, that 2 horses, or
2 oxen in a plough, are not more generally adopted, considering the great scarcity and high wages of servants. The rest of
the ploughs consist of 4 or more horses each, or cattle and
horses yoked together, as those who have small possessions
can afford. Almost all the farmers, who yoke oxen
ploughs, yoke one or more horse ploughs. The plough
almost universally used is the plough with curved mould-
board. There are upwards of 400 carts of one kind or
other; of these only 12 are two-horse draughts, and 6 are
oxen wains.

There are in this parish 388 oxen, 521 cows, 944 young
cattle, 452 horses, and 2582 sheep, mostly of the black
faced kind, which, by a most unaccountable predilection for
size, (the only property of this breed,) has very generally
banished from the North of Scotland, the small white faced
native breed, which produced a very fine wool, and fine
flavoured mutton. Some farmers are improving their
breed, by crossing with English rams. The black cattle
are all of the Scotch breed, and generally of a small size,
being worked too young, which stints their growth, and
they are frequently sold off to the dealers before they arrive
at their full size. The average price of oxen may be stated
at

at L. 5, 5 s. Sterling; of cows, about L. 4 Sterling; of young cattle, about L. 2 Sterling each. The prices of horfes are from L. 3 to L. 30, but the average price of the ordinary fize of work horfes may be about L. 8 Sterling, and the average prices of fheep about 6 s. Sterling each. There are 40 farmers in the parifh, that pay from L. 15 to L. 50 rent; and one farmer pays L. 250 a-year. The parifh produces much more grain than is neceffary to maintain the inhabitants, unlefs in very bad feafons. The land yields very differently in different places, but, at an average, it may be eftimated to yield about five returns, including feed. The rent is as various as the foil; being from 2 s. 6 d. to L. 1, 1 s. Sterling the acre; at an average, it lets at about 10 s. Sterling the acre grofs rent. The whole rent of the parifh, including mill-multures, may be about L. 2000 Sterling a-year *. There are none of the farms in the parifh inclofed, except the farm of Knock, poffeffed by Lord Fife's factor, which is inclofed with ftones, with which that corner of the parifh is well fupplied; and the Mains of Edingight, which is inclofed with ftone fence and ditch. Hedges and ditches are, indeed, the only practicable mode of inclofing the greater part of the parifh, as there are few or no ftones to be had, except limeftone quarried at a confiderable expenfe, and which can hardly be obtained of any fize fit for building. But hedges and ditches are much more proper for inclofing the greater part of this parifh than ftone fences; as the ditches would tend to drain the wet foil, and hedges to fhelter a bleak and

open

---

* Peafe and oats are generally fown in March and April, and barley fometimes in the end of April, and till the end of May, and beginning of June. Turnips are fown from the middle of June to the middle of July. Hay is cut in the month of July. Harveft generally begins about the middle of September, though in early feafons it ufed fometimes to be finifhed by that time; but it is more frequently ended in November; and in 1782 and 1787, it was not all got in till the end of December.

open country ; but the heritors give no encouragement fot incloſing of any kind *.

Manufactures.

* Wages of all kinds have advanced greatly within the laſt 40 years. Here follows a comparative ſtatement of the wages then and now.

		1750			1791		
The beſt ploughmans wages in the year 1750 were yearly,		L. 1	13	4	in 1791, L. 6	0	0
The ſecond beſt ditto.	in 1750	1	6	8	5	0	0
A man in harveſt,	in do.	0	12	0	1	10	0
A woman ſervant,	in do.	0	16	0	2	2	0
Ditto in harveſt,	in do.	0	6	0	1	0	0
A common labourer for ordinary work, the day,	in do.	0	0	3	0	0	6
Ditto, caſting peat, cutting hay, or in harveſt,	in do.	0	0	5	0	0	10
Women when employed in the moſs, or in harveſt,	in do.	0	0	3	0	0	6
Ditto, at hay making, or lint pulling,	in do.	0	0	3	0	0	4
A maſon's wages,	in do.	0	0	6	0	0	10
A wright's wages,	in do.	0	0	4	0	0	8
A tailor's wages,	in do.	0	0	2	0	0	6

With the above wages they receive their victuals from their employers. Here follows alſo, a comparative ſtatement of the prices of proviſions for the ſame years.

A boll of barley in 1750, ſold at L. 0 10 0	in 1791, L. 0 16 0
A boll of oats,	0 6 0	0 10 6
A boll of oat-meal, at 9 ſtone, (157½ lb. aver.)	0 8 4	0 15 0
1 lb. of butter, (24 oz. aver.)	0 0 4	from 5 d. to 9 d.
1 lb of cheeſe, ditto, formerly ſold by the piece	from 2 1 d. to 4 d.
A gooſe,	0 1 6	from 2 s. to 2 s. 6 d.
A duck,	0 0 3	from 5 d. to 7 d.
A hen,	0 0 3	from 5 d. to 7 d.
A chicken for the brander,	0 0 1	from 2 d. to 3 d.
A dozen of eggs,	0 0 1	2 d.
Beef the pound, ⎫ formerly ſold by the leg.	0 0 1	from 2½ d. to 4 d.
Mutton, ⎬	0 0 1	from 2 d. to 3 d.
Pork, ⎭	0 0 1	from 2 d. to 3 d.
A pair of brogues to a man,	0 0 10	3 s. 4 d.
A pair ditto, to a woman,	0 0 7	2 s. 6 d,

Manufactures.—The only manufactures in the parish are lime, and linen yarn. There are inexhaustible quarries of the very finest limestone in almost every part of the parish, and nature had amply provided the means of manufacturing it, in the extensive mosses, with which a great part of the parish was formerly covered, and which are not by any means exhausted by the consumption of many centuries; though they are become more distant and inaccessible than they were, and will now wear out much faster, as the surface of them is generally dug up for turf, which puts an end to their growing. The quantity of lime burnt in this parish, about 40 years ago, was estimated at 60,000 bolls, of 64 Scotch pints to the boll, which was sold, at an average, at 6 d. the boll. The quantity at present manufactured, may be estimated, at between 20,000 and 30,000 bolls, which sells, after being carried from 6 to 10 computed miles, at an average, at 8 d. the boll. The heritors lay restraints upon the making of lime, both because it exhausts the mosses, and draws off the attention of the people from their farms. Indeed they seldom lay any of it on their own possessions, from an ill founded prejudice, that it would not be useful, but hurtful, to ground that stands on limestone, though frequent experiments, made by different farmers in the parish, prove that it is capable, when judiciously managed, of producing remarkable crops. The spinning of linen yarn, and making of coarse linen from Scotch flax, was long practised, (as already observed,) before the manufacturers began to import Dutch flax, and gave it out to spin, which they have done for many years. Since that time, there is but a small proportion of the Scotch flax spun for the market; as the quality of the flax is not so soft and fine as the Dutch flax, owing perhaps both to the nature of the soil, and to the management of the flax. There is, however, a good deal of it made into coarse linens,

nens, both for home confumption, and likewife for fale, and fome of it is fold in yarn ; but the manufacturers complain, that the fpinners draw it beyond the grift, that they may have the more out of their flax, which hurts the fale of the yarn at the market. But the fpinning of yarn from Dutch flax is the principal employment of the women, and is computed to bring in about L. 1500 Sterling annually.

Roads and Bridges.—There are 24 meafured miles of roads within this parifh, made and repaired by ftatute-labour.

	Miles.
The road from Banff to Keith, - -	7
The road from Cullen and Portfoy to Keith, -	4
The road from Aberdeen, Huntly and Rothemay, through Grange, by Newmill, to Fochabers, &c. -	4
The private road from Rothemay to Edingight, by Knock, - - - - -	3
The private road from Braco-houfe to Knock, -	4
The private road from Berryhillock to the houfe of Edingight, - - - . -	2

On the road from Aberdeen, Huntly and Rothemay, through Grange, there are 4 good bridges over the 4 ftreams that interfect the parifh ; two of thefe bridges were built laft year, out of the vacant ftipends of the neighbouring parifh of Rothemay, and are of great importance to the whole country, as they are upon a well frequented road, and acrofs two very rapid and dangerous ftreams. There is alfo a bridge over Ifla, near the church, which " was built in 1699, by Alexander Chriftie, tenant in " Cantley, for the glory of God, and the good of the " people of Grange," as the infcription bore, being built to render the church acceffible to the people of Cantley, which is the farm upon the fouth fide of Ifla. 100 merks
Scots

Scots were lodged in the hands of Edingight, by the said Alexander Chriftie, to be laid out by the direction of the kirk-feffion, for repairing and upholding faid bridge ; which appears from the records to have been all expended before the year 1740. As the bridge was too narrow to allow carts to pafs, being intended originally for foot-paffengers only, and as it was then the only bridge upon Ifla below Keith, Sir William Forbes, the patron of the parifh, gave a year and half's vacant ftipend for repairing and enlarging it, which was done in the year 1783, in a very fuperficial manner, fo that the new part of it threatens foon to go to ruin : And indeed the bridge is not even fo publicly ufeful as could be wifhed, as it is not on any of the public roads. The old bridge, which was fit for anfwering every necef-fary purpofe in the place where it was, could have been repaired at a very fmall expenfe, fo as to have ftood for many years, by a parifh contribution : it is to be regretted, therefore, that the vacant ftipend was not made part of a fund for the purpofe of building a new bridge over Ifla, in that part of the parifh where the roads from Banff, Cullen, Portfoy, Keith, &c. all meet, and crofs Ifla at the fame place. The roads are in wretched repair, the ftatute-labour being employed upon them principally in autumn, when the day is fhort, and the earth foaked with the autumnal rains. The difficult paffes are rendered ftill worfe, by ha-ving the loofe wet clay thrown into them ; for proper ma-terials are never fought for, nor brought from a diftance when they are not at hand, but the mire from the ditches is thrown into the middle of the road, fo that a piece of new made or mended road is generally impaffable. Add to this, that the ftatute-labour (which is a moft unequal and oppreffive tax upon the poor, in the way in which it is at prefent levied) is performed with the greateft reluctance. A poor labourer, who has neither horfe nor cart, and per-haps

haps little or no crop, and whoſe labour cannot maintain a numerous family of young children, who therefore muſt be ſupplied from the poors funds, is obliged to work on the roads ſix days in the year, while a farmer who pays L. 40 or L. 50 rent, works 4 carts, and needs only one ſervant and himſelf, except boys for herding, is liable only for twice as much as the poor labourer; and ſervants are entirely exempted from this heavy tax, though they are much better able to bear it than many houſeholders *.

Church, Stipend, School, Poor.—This pariſh, in times of Popery, belonged to the pariſh of Keith, and was erected into a ſeparate pariſh in the year 1618, (Preſbytery records). The preſent church was originally a chapel of eaſe, built by the abbot, and dedicated to the Virgin Mary; it is now in a ruinous condition, and never was fit to contain the congregation. The manſe, which was built about 40 years ago, was repaired in 1778 and in 1787, and is ſtill a bad houſe. The offices are tolerably good, but

* The ſtatute labour ought therefore to be converted into money by act of Parliament, and exacted in different proportions, according to the circumſtances of the perſons; for inſtance, a poor houſeholder, that has little or no crop, ought not to be aſſeſſed above 1 s. a year; a ſervant that has no family ought to be aſſeſſed 1 s. 6 d.; tenants ought to pay according to their rent, or the number and kind of carts they employ; and heritors (who are at preſent entirely exempted, and whoſe rent riſes in proportion to the eaſy communication by good roads) ought to be taxed in proportion to their rent: If ſuch a ſcheme was adopted, and the roads contracted for, they would ſoon be made, ſo as to ſave 50 *per cent.* of the expenſe of tranſporting commodities, and alſo of the tear and wear of carriages and harneſs: And after the roads were once effectually made or repaired, the tax could be reduced conſiderably, and yet the roads be kept in excellent repair. The act ought alſo to contain a clauſe, appointing a committee, of equal numbers of the moſt reſpectable tenants, as well as landholders, in each diſtrict, to carry the act into execution, that there might be no improper exemption.

but only thatched with heath, which is a bad roof. The stipend is 1000 merks Scots in money, and 25¼ bolls of meal, at 8 stone, including L. 4, 4 s. for communion elements; and a glebe of 5 acres, of tolerably good soil. Sir William Forbes of Cragievar, Bart. is patron. The schoolmaster's salary is 12 bolls of meal, collected in lippies and pecks, from every householder in the parish that possesses any land, in proportion to what they possess; 10 merks Scots of a mortification; L. 2 Sterling as precentor and session clerk; 2 s. for every proclamation of banns; and 4 d. for the registration of every baptism; about 30 scholars, at an average, attend the school; from whom he receives 1 s. 3 d. the quarter for reading English; 1 s. 6 d. for reading and writing; and 2 s. for arithmetic and Latin; which altogether may amount to about L. 18 Sterling yearly. The number of scholars might be many more; but the school-house is small, and at a corner of the parish; the schoolmasters are frequently changed, owing to the poor encouragement; and the people are, from habit, backward in sending their children to school; they allege, that by the time their children begin to make any progress with a schoolmaster, he is about to remove to a better place or business. The school is not accessible in winter to above one third of the parish; the minister, therefore, with concurrence of the heritors, made application to the Society for propagating Christian Knowledge, in the year 1782, and got a schoolmaster appointed to the most distant parts of the parish, upon condition, that the heritors would pay L. 4 yearly of his salary, and give him a house, garden, fuel, and a cow's grass *gratis;* which they would not agree to do, and the schoolmaster was removed; the consequence of which must be, that the rising generation will be bred up in ignorance. If the salaries of parochial schoolmasters are not made something better

worth

worth the while of a man of liberal education, that moſt
uſeful inſtitution will ſoon be abandoned altogether, (as
it would have been already, in many places, were it not
a kind of interim employment to poor young lads, while
at college, and during the time they are ſtudying divinity,) and then the country people will return to ignorance
and barbariſm : but the preſent faſhionable paradox is, that
ignorance is the mother of *induſtry ;* which is equally well
founded with the ancient aphoriſm, that *ignorance* is the
mother of *devotion*. As ignorance is the nurſe of ſuperſtition, ſo is it peculiarly favourable to a ſtate of ſlavery ;
and the ſavage ſtate, which is a ſtate of ignorance, is a ſtate
of *indolence,* not of *induſtry*.—The poor are ſupported by
the weekly collections, fines from delinquents, hire of two
mortcloths, and hand-bell at funerals, rent of the church
yard, rent of the ſeats of a gallery in the church, with the
intereſt of L. 240, previous to the year 1783. In the year
1782, the crop in this pariſh was ſo wretched, that if it
had been all made into meal, it would not have maintained the inhabitants for two months ; and the victual was ſo
bad, that its effects, together with the ſcarcity, proved fatal to the conſtitutions and lives of many, (as already obſerved) ; however, the inhabitants were ſupported, one
way or other, with what they had remaining of the former
crop, and what they could purchaſe at L. 1, 4 s. Sterling
the boll, of 9 ſtone, (157½ lb. Averdupoiſe,) from the
neighbouring countries of Enzie and Moray, (where the
crop was much leſs affected by the bad ſeaſon,) till they
were relieved, by the importation of white peaſe, and o-
ther grain, in April and May. The ſeſſion imported 200
quarters of white peaſe, with their funds, together with
L. 100 Sterling, lent to the ſeſſion, free of intereſt for nine
months, to purchaſe grain for the benefit of the poor, by a
manufacturer in the pariſh, who, by uncommon induſtry,

attention

attention and integrity, had, without any original ſtock, in
a few years, acquired ſome hundred pounds, and who, beſides the above generous and benevolent exertion in behalf of the poor, imported great quantities of all kinds of
grain, flour, biſcuit, &c. which he ſold out at little or no
profit. Lord Fife alſo bought excellent barley at the London market, and oats for ſeed ; but as they were ſold out
for ready money, many of the poor tenants, who were under the neceſſity of employing all their ready money for
purchaſing victual for their families, were obliged to ſow
their own ſeed, which did not grow ; and even the oats,
they bought from the coaſt ſide for ſeed, at L. 1, 1 s. and
upwards the boll, though it looked beautiful, and was well
filled, did not grow, but rotted in the ground ; and indeed,
in this country, the worſt filled corn, and the corn that
was laſt cut in harveſt 1782, was the only corn that did
vegetate tolerably next year. This ruined the next crop,
which, had the ſeed been good, would have been a plentiful one, as the ſummer and harveſt 1783 were the beſt
that have been ſince ; this made the ſcarcity and dearth
continue in this country, till crop 1784 relieved it.
The ſeſſion made the peaſe they bought into meal, and
ſold it out at or below prime coſt to poor families, and
great numbers were ſupplied *gratis*, beſides thoſe upon the
roll, whoſe numbers were alſo greatly increaſed ; ſo that
when the heritors and ſeſſion met upon the 1ſt of July
1783, to report to the Barons of Exchequer the ſtate of
the pariſh, in order to enable them to judge what proportion of the victual bought by them, with the L. 10,000
granted by Parliament for the relief of the poor, in the
northern counties of Scotland, they reported, " That the
number upon the poors roll amounted to 200, and that
L. 50 Sterling is already expended in a partial relief to
thoſe in greateſt diſtreſs ; that upwards of 1200 have been
ſupported,

supported by imported grain from the end of February; and that more than 800 souls will stand in need of assistance from the poors funds, (supposing they were sufficient for that purpose), before they can be supplied from the crop upon the ground, which cannot be expected sooner than three months hence." Upon this report, the Barons of Exchequer, sent in all, 79 bolls of meal, at different times, to be distributed *gratis*, and 102¼ bolls, to be sold at 8 s. 8 d. the boll. This was a great relief. Lord Fife also sold out the meal in his girnel, and what multure farm came in, at 16 s. Sterling the boll; and he deducted a fifth part of the tenants money-rent for 1783, upon condition, that they paid up the remainder, together with the arrears of the former rent, and the price of their deficient farm or victual rent, by the 1st of February 1784; but many of them were rendered unable to take the benefit of his Lordship's liberality *.

Advantages.

* Here follows a statement of the amount, and disposal of the poors funds, for three different periods, *viz.* for 4 years preceding 1783; during 1783 and 1784; and for 4 years immediately preceding the date of this report.

1st Period.

Average annual collections, fines, interest, legacies, loft-rents &c. from 1st December 1778 to 1st December 1782, - - - -	L. 31 19 4
Average annual distributions to the poor, for the above period, including about L. 5, 5 s. Sterling annually to the infirmary at Aberdeen, and for paying session-clerk and kirk officer's (beadle) fees, - -	L. 25 10 8½
Average number of the poor upon the roll for said period, 31.	

2d Period.

Collections, &c. during 1783 and 1784, - -	L. 47 19 0
Distributed in money in 1783 and 1784, including L. 10, 4 s. to the infirmary at Aberdeen, and to pay session-clerk, and kirk officer's fees. - - -	L. 48 2 2
Distributed to the poor upon the roll, in meal, during these two years, 125 bolls 2 firlots 1 peck, at 16 s. the boll,	L. 100 9 0

3d

Advantages and Disadvantages.—The advantages that this parish possesses are, that it is not far from a sea-port, where

3d Period.

Average annual collections, &c. from 1st December 1787 to 1st December 1791, - - - L. 35 16 9

Average annual distributions to the poor for said period, including about L. 5. 5s annually to the infirmary at Aberdeen, and to pay session-clerk and kirk officer's fees. - - - - L. 33 6 0

Average number of the poor upon the roll in said period, 35.

Besides the above mentioned sources of relief to the poor, there is a great deal given in private charity, not to travelling beggars only, but the people in general are uncommonly humane and benevolent; and when any poor person or family is afflicted with sickness, or any other unexpected calamity, the neighbours do not wait to be solicited but carry meal, or whatever else the situation requires, or their circumstances can afford, and they watch with the sick, &c. Many of the poor also have bags in the mills, into which every one puts as he can spare, or as charity disposes him. And on the Christmas holidays, the young men go out in parties through the parish a-begging for th greatest obj cts; nd several bolls of meal, and some pounds Sterling of money, are collected every year, and committed to the care of the members of session, for behoof of those for whom it is collected. This practice has an excellent effect upon the morals, both of young and old; it disposes the old to acts of liberality, and draws forth their sympathy towards the distressed, and it trains up the young to acts of benevolence and charity: This practice is also a great support to the funds, which are beginning again to recover, from their dilapidation in 1783 and 1784. The heritors also, being convinced by experience of the importance of having a fund in reserve against a time of scarcity, resolved to take the poors money and pay 5 *per cent.* yearly for it; (whereas before 1783 it was lent out at 4 *per cent.* a-year, payable only once in two years.) By this means, together with some legacies, and strict œconomy, the funds are again accumulated to L. 200 at interest. The session takes a disposition to the effects of those that are taken upon the roll, (unless in such years as 1783 and 1784), with the burden of taking care of them in sickness and in their last illness, and of defraying their funeral charges, which must not exceed L. 1 Sterling; allowing the relations of the deceased to redeem the effects, by repaying to the session a ea 's contribution, immediately preceding the death of the pauper, and defraying the funeral charges.

where there is generally a market for grain, victual, &c. when it is plenty ; and in the neighbourhood of the fertile countries of Boyn, Enzie and Moray, from whence, and by importation, a supply can be obtained in wet and late seafons, when the crop fails in Stryla ; and that it poffeffes the means of improvement by lime, fo near, and in fuch plenty. But the difadvantages are many ; a cold, wet, and late foil and climate, and confequently uncertain crops; fhort leafes ; no encouragement to tenants to improve their land, to inclofe or build good houfes ; heavy and op-preffive mill-multures, which take between an eighth and a ninth of all that the tenant carries to the mill, and even of what he buys, in times of fcarcity, if it be manufactured within the fucken. The tenant alfo is obliged to pay 10 d. for every boll of oats carried to the fhore, and fold fome-times as low as 7 s. and never above 12 s. the boll, and e-very farm pays a certain number of bolls of barley, for what barley is fold, and for keeping in the mill-water ; notwithftanding which, the tenants are compelled to per-fonal fervice, for keeping in the mill-water, and to per-form other mill-fervices, fuch as bringing home millftones, and upholding the mill, if required fo to do ; and to carry the mill farm-meal to Macduff, 17 miles diftant, which they are generally called to do in the fpring feafon. This fervitude amounts almoft to a prohibition to improve, as it is at leaft a tax of 12 *per cent.* upon the produce of im-provements ; befides, the tenants are liable to be called to give an account upon oath, before the baron-bailie, what they have bought or fold for three years back ; and if a man's memory, who cannot keep accounts, has failed him, and he confcientioufly refufes to take an oath, he is char-ged arbitrarily. Such a mode of proceeding is furely con-trary to the effential principles of juftice, and very hurtful to morals, as frequent oaths, (efpecially where the intereft

of

of the perfon taking the oath may be materially affected
thereby), muſt often be *. Bad roads is another diſadvantage, and the unequal and oppreſſive tax of ſtatute-labour, totally inadequate to the making or upholding ſuch
an extent of road ; beſides that it is often miſemployed, at
the will of the commiſſioners or directors of the diſtrict, on
private roads, while public ones are neglected.—The tax
upon coals alſo is a great grievance. A great and precious
part of the year, both to the farmer and limer, muſt be
employed in providing and driving fuel ; whereas, were it
not for the heavy tax upon coal, the farmer would gain
two months of the ſummer, which could be employed in
cultivating turnip, managing hay, working fallow, or preparing manure ; and, at the ſame time, be better ſerved
with fuel, by bringing coal from the ſhore, when he carried his grain thither ; and the limers would find it their
intereſt alſo, to burn their lime partly with coal, rather
than with peat alone ; becauſe, inſtead of driving it ſome
miles farther to get a penny more for the boll, that they
may make as much as poſſible of their fuel, they could
burn more, and ſell cheaper ; and when they went to the
ſhore for coal, they could always carry a draught of lime
with them. Some years ago, a very wet ſeaſon compelled ſome of them to try coal, and they found a mixture of
peat and coal anſwer ſo well, that they continue to uſe a
little coal now and then.—The people alſo complain much
of the unequal and oppreſſive nature of the exciſe and diſtillery laws. The laſt partakes ſo much of the nature of
a monopoly, that the diſtillers, unleſs in a time of ſcarcity,
when the grain is wanted for meal, combine and keep the
price

* Since writing the above, the multures in this pariſh have been converted by the baron-bailie at 2 s. 3 d. upon the pound groſs rent ; beſides
paying the miller largely for work and mill ſervices as before.

price of barley low ; and consequently the spirits, which
are generally of a bad quality, are sold at a low price,
which has a tendency to destroy both the constitutions and
the morals of the people, for punch and dram-drinking are
now too generally substituted in the public houses in place
of beer, which was a much more wholesome beverage ;
and the heavy excise on malt, which is also rigorously enforced by the distillers for obvious reasons, tends to produce the same effect, and also to prevent poor people from
having malt or beer in their own houses, the want of
which proves very hurtful to the health and constitutions
of the labouring poor ; and when a poor man has a boll of
barley to dispose of, he can hardly sell it at all, or only at
a very low price, generally what the distiller pleases to
give ; whereas, before the establishment of distilleries, and
the additional excise on malt, a poor man made his boll of
bear into malt, and paid the duty for it, and then distilled
from it an excellent spirit, which he sold at a high price
to the rich, and thus obtained a good price for his grain,
and the grains and offals helped to maintain, and often to
preserve the lives of his cattle when provender was scarce ;
now the whole advantages that were before enjoyed by
the poor, are, by the distillery law, thrown into the hands
of the rich distillers, (for none can be distillers upon the
present plan but the comparatively rich), while malt and
beer are in a manner entirely prohibited *.

* The impolicy as well as oppression of the distillery law will appear
from this circumstance, that a distiller takes out a licence for a 40 gallon
still, for which he pays a duty to Government of L. 40 a-year, and an
officer employed to attend that still receives a salary of L. 50 a-year.
The heavy excise on malt also, which in effect amounts to a total prohibition, necessarily promotes smuggling, which is always injurious to morals, as well as hurtful to the revenue ; and it is universally thought, that
Government does by no means draw so much from the northern counties

of Scotland of excise-duties. as even to pay the falaries of the officers employed to levy it, notwithstanding the oppressions that the people suffer on account of it. It seems to be the general opinion, that if the excise and distillery laws were repealed in the north of Scotland, and the revenue raised by them yearly, including officers falaries, were transmitted to the commissioners of supply of the counties, to proportion it among themselves and tenants, they could pay in the fame with the land tax, and by this means, the revenue would be improved by the whole amount of the officers falaries at least, and the country would think themselves infinitely better, as they would then be permitted to do with their grain what they pleased without molestation.

NOTE.

Miscellaneous Observations.—There are no objects of natural history peculiar to this parish. Limestone is the only mineral worth mentioning. The only wild beasts are the fox, the weasel or polecat, and the hare. The birds are few and common ; moorfowl, partridge. plover, wild duck, bittern, rook, jackdaw, magpie, lark, sparrow, yellow-hammer, robin, wren. watercock, linnet, and a few others. The parish is occasionally visited in winter by snow-birds, and in spring by flocks of sea-gulls. and now and then by hawks, kites, ravens, and herons. The migratory birds, are the lapwing. cuckoo, corn-rail, and swallow. There are no noted mineral springs in this parish, though some of them are considerably impregnated with iron ; but there are two confecrated wells, one at the foot of a small natural mount adjoining to the castle of Grange, which, with the mount, had been dedicated to the Virgin Mary, and are now called the Ladyhill and the Ladywell. The other spring is on the south bank of Isla, directly opposite to the church-door, and is called the Croikwell, probably from *Croix*, crofs. The greater part of the people are rather above the ordinary size, and it seems have always been so. There are at least as many men in the parish above 5 feet 8 inches as there are below it ; and several are 6 feet high : Accordingly such of them as go into the army, generally enlist either into the Guards or Train of Artillery. The ancestors of the greater part of the present inhabitants have lived in this parish for some centuries back, and many of them are defcendents of the ancient feuars in the parish. The most ancient names are, Innes, Adamson, Richardson, Riddoch, Longmoor, Carr, Kelman, Scot, Sim, Ballach, Beg, Craib, Gray, Howie, Allan, Wilson, Taylor, Reaper, Dyker, Neil, &c. &c. There are no persons of remarkable eminence, that have been born, lived, or died in this parish. It has indeed been

long

long famous for producing a great number of clergymen, and there are
five miniſters of the Eſtabliſhment, and one of the Church of England,
now alive, that were born in this pariſh. Beſides, there are many natives
of it in the Eaſt and Weſt Indies, in America, in London, and through
many parts of Great Britain, that are all doing well in different lines of
life. The people are in general regular in their attendance upon the
ordinances of religion, and they are, upon the whole, fenfible, fagacious,
focial, humane, obliging, fober. induſtrious, and well behaved : no in
ſtance having occurred of any native being executed or baniſhed within
the laſt 50 years ; two inſtances of fuicide, indeed, have happend within
that period, the one of a man about 25 years ago, the other of a woman
about 50 years ago.

PARISH of INVERAVEN,

(Counties of Banff and Elgin *, Synod of Moray, Presbytery of Aberlour.)

By the Rev. Mr James Grant.

Name, Extent, Rivulets, &c.

THE parish takes its name from the Gaelic word *In-ver*, " Entrance," and *Aven*, the name of a stream which has its source in Lochaven, which lies among the hills between Braemar and Strathspey, and after running about 20 or 22 miles, falls into the river Spey, near the house of Ballendalloch, and about an English mile above the church, which is scarce 150 yards from that river's side. The parish is computed about 12 miles long, and its breadth is in some places 3, in other parts 2, and in one part only one mile.—From the entrance of Aven into Spey, the parish extends southward on both sides of Aven, till it meets with the parish of Kirkmichael in Strathaven. About a mile below, where the two parishes meet, and about $3\frac{1}{2}$ miles from the parish-church, the water of Livet empties itself

felf into Aven, near the ruins of an old caftle called Drum-
min. From the confluence of Aven and Livet, the parifh
extends S. E. up both fides of Livet about 7 miles nearly *.

Population,

* All this part of the parifh is called Glenlivet. About a mile from
the confluence of Aven and Livet, Tervy, a rivulet, (which has its fource
in Belrinnas, a high mountain, intervening between the parifh of Aberlour, and a part of the parifh of Inveraven), after running thr·ugh the
Davoch of Morange, and a little way through the lower part of Glenlivet. falls into Livet. Morange lies eaftward from the lower part of
Glenlivet, and between it and a part of the hill of Belrinnas. From the
mouth of Tervy, up Livet about half a mile, lies Achbrake, where the
Proteftant meeting houfe is built, the itinerant minifter officiates and the
Proteftants in Glenlivet and Morange attend divine worfhip. At the diftance of half a mile eaftward from Achbrake, the burn or rivulet of Altachoynachan falls into Tervy; and about 1 ½ mile, almoft up this burn,
and S. E. from its mouth, the battle of Altachoynachan in October 1594
was fought, between Huntly and Argyle, in which the latter was defeated. About 2 miles from the Proteftant meeting-houfe, and up Livet,
Cromby a rivulet falls into it on the fouth fide. Cromby rifes between
two hills on the fouth fide of the head, or higher part of Glenlivet, and
after running a fhort way, paffes by the Scala, (or Scalan, as it is commonly called), a Popifh feminary or college, erected upwards of 80 years ago.
As Scala is the Latin word for a ladder, it perhaps got that name from a
fteep road, (called the ladder), leading from the head of Glenlivet, up a
fteep hill to Strathdon Be that as it may, there are 8, 10, and fometimes
12 children of Popifh gentlemen taught at the Scala; and there alfo (I
have been told) fome priefts were educated and put into orders. There
Mr George Hay, a Popifh bifhop, at prefent refides, and there is a mafter
befides, who teaches the youth. From the Scala Cromby runs northward
for 1 ½ mile, to the foot of the Bochle, (a little hill), on the S. E. fide of
which is Bedavochle, where is a fchool-houfe for one of the Society's
fchools, and in which the itinerant minifter alfo preaches one Sabbath
every fix weeks. From the part where Cromby firft wafhes the Bochle,
it runs northward with a little winding about 1 ½ mile, till it meets with
Livet. From the entrance of Cromby eaftward, and up Livet more than
a quarter of a mile, is Caanakyle, where the Popifh prieft refides, and
where on the bank of Livet, about near 20˜ yards from the prieft's houfe,
is lately built a new mafs-houfe, with ftone and lime, and flated. From the
mafs-houfe to the Sowie, a fmall farm not far from the head of Livet, are
long 3 miles.

Population, &c.—The following is a ſtate of marriages
and baptiſms, from the pariſh regiſter, from 1781 to 1790,
incluſive :

Years.	Marriages.	Baptiſms.
1781	22	28
1782	8	19
1783	10	18
1784	4	7
1785	6	22
1786	8	13
1787	7	15
1788	7	11
1789	10	16
1790	3	7
	85	156*

No regiſter of burials is kept in the pariſh, nor could it be
eaſily done ; becauſe, beſides the church-yard, there are two
other burying places, one upon the eaſt ſide of Livet, near 4
miles from the pariſh-church, near the walls of the old chapel of Dounan; and another, almoſt 5 miles higher up the
glen, on the weſt ſide of Cromby, and oppoſite to the Bochle.

* The Papiſts were never forward to enter the baptiſms of their children into the pariſh regiſter. Their marriages, unleſs when the prieſt married them clandeſtinely, were generally regiſtered, becauſe their marriage
banns were regularly proclaimed in the church. But ſince the repeal of
the penal ſtatutes in England, they publiſh their marriage banns at their
maſs-houſe, and not at the church ; and never inſert either their marriages
or baptiſms in the parochial regiſter; whereby the taxes, appointed by law,
are evaded, and the ſchoolmaſter, who is ſeſſion-clerk and keeper of the
parochial regiſter, loſes his dues, which are part of the emoluments of his
office. Some years ago, I was told by ſome Papiſts, that their prieſts for-
bade them to enter their childrens baptiſms in the pariſh regiſter, becauſe
they kept a liſt of the children they baptized. And it muſt be acknowledged, that many of the poorer ſort among the Proteſtants often omit to
enter their childrens baptiſms in the pariſh regiſter, on account of the tax,
and the dues of the clerk for inſerting them.

chle. It is called the Buitterlach, and was confecrated more
than 40 years ago, by two Popifh bifhops, to be a burying-
place for the Catholics, but few are yet buried in it*.—According to Dr Webfter's report, the number of fouls was then
2464.—About 28 years ago, when I took an exact lift of
all the people in the parifh, both old and young, they a-
mounted to 2200 ; and, in 1779, when another exact account of the people was taken, they only amounted to
2244 fouls. Of this number 850 are Roman Catholics.

Heritors, Stipend, School, Poor, &c.—Sir James Grant
of Grant is patron of the parifh. The Duke of Gordon,
and General James Grant of Ballendalloch, are the only heritors in it. Mrs Penuel Grant, of Kilmachlie, mother of
the late Major William Grant of Ballendalloch, and widow
of the late Captain Alexander Grant of Ballendalloch, who
was brother to the prefent General Grant, liferents a great
part of the lands of Kilmachlie, and the whole Davoch of
Morange. The church feems to have been built upwards
of 200 years ago, as appears from an infcription upon a ftone
above the door of an ifle, (which at firft was joined to the
church, and intended for a burying-place to the then family of Ballendalloch, but was many years ago disjoined from
the church, and is now in ruins), the date of which is

1586

---

* There was in old time alfo, a chapel and burying place on the eaft
fide of Livet, about half a mile above the Proteftant meeting-houfe, called
Chapel Chrift, but very little remains of the chapel are to be feen, and the
burying ground, with what was depofited in it, has been wafhed away by
a fmall rivulet, which runs between it and Nevie, and by the water of
Livet. There was alfo once a chapel, and burying ground on the weft
fide of Aven, in the eftate of Kilmachlie, almoft oppofite to the mouth of
Livet ; and the farm-town, in the midft of whofe land it is, is from it called Chapeltown. There are evident marks of graves, with ftones fet up at
the heads of fome of them ; and hard by is an excellent fpring, which emits
a large ftream of water. But none have been buried at this place for time
immemorial.

1586*. A new manſe was built in ſummer 1775, but the
walls drew water, till they were rough plaſtered (or, as it
is termed, harled) on the outſide. The offices were new
built in 1769, and have ſince been twice thatched with
heath, but ſtill let in rain water. The ſtipend was modified
in 1769 to be 800 merks Scots, and 60 merks Scots for
communion-elements, with 48 bolls of meal, at 8 ſtone
weight the boll. The glebe conſiſts of 4 Scotch acres and
28 falls ; but of theſe there are only about 3 acres 2 roods
and 17 falls that are arable. There is beſides graſs for two
ſmall cows, but no graſs for a horſe †.—There is a ſchool-
houſe built within the church-yard, and ſlated. The
ſchoolmaſter's ſalary is only 12 bolls of meal, at 9 ſtone
weight the boll. There may be in winter time between

30

* In 1711 the church got ſtrong new deals (or, as they called it, ſark-
ing) put upon the couples, but few new couples were put in And as the
lower part of the inner half of the back wall, in one place had ſunk down
from the half above it, and the other half on the outſide in that place
ſeemed to bend inwards, and ſome of the couples were rotten; the heritors,
in 1790, agreed with a maſon to repair and uphold the church for ſeven
years. He cauſed underfoot (as they term it) the inner part of the back
wall that had ſunk down, and took down the outſide half of the fore wall,
half the length of the houſe, and rebuilt it He alſo put in a few new
couples, rough plaſtered the walls on the outſide, and pointed the
ſlates.

† The preſbytery of Aberlour, therefore, in April 1791, decreed 3 roods and
36 falls of arable land neareſt to the kirk and glebe, with 23 falls of graſs,
alſo bordering upon the glebe, as graſs for a horſe. This decreet of the preſbytery, General Grant ſuſpended, and interdicted the miniſter to poſſeſs
the ground. Againſt the ſuſpenſion and interdict the miniſter entered a
proteſt ; but as he is an old man, and ſaw the proceſs would be expenſive,
he did not inſiſt to diſcuſs the ſuſpenſion and interdict. He therefore com-
promiſed the affair with General Grant, upon receiving a ſmall piece of arable land, and ſome paſture ground, (not ſo near to the glebe as what the
preſbytery had appointed for him), a part of which was over-run with broom,
and a part of it was a quagmire and overſpread with alder. This he is to
poſſeſs during his incumbency, and to pay for it a rent of 10 s. Sterling annually. But General Grant has ſince made a large road through it.

30 and 40 scholars, but in the summer season the number amounts only to 12, and rarely to 20. In Glenlivet, there is one of the Society's schools, which is ambulatory between Deskie and Badavochle, being stationed sometimes at the one place, and sometimes at the other. The former master of this Society school had L. 22 Sterling from the Society; but the present has only L. 15 Sterling, which is really too little in Glenlivet. In the winter season he may have sometimes 90 scholars, but in the summer time they often do not exceed 20.—The inrolled poor in the parish, are 38 Protestants and 29 Papists, in all 67 persons. The Roman Catholics, as they have their own collections made in the mass-house, get no part of the collections gathered up in the church and meeting-house; but they get a share of the interest of the mortified money. About 15 years ago, there was L. 100 Sterling, which the kirk-session lent out on interest; and as neither of the two heritors would accept of it, they were obliged to lend it to such persons as they thought good and sufficient, and would take it. Accordingly, they lent about L. 61 Sterling to one landed gentleman, and about L. 35 Sterling to another, who were both thought good and sufficient when they received the money; but, in a few years afterward, both of them became bankrupts; whereby not only several years interest was lost, but also half the principal. The collections in both church and meeting-house, amount annually only to about L. 6 or L. 7 Sterling: Therefore, as the collections amount to so small a sum, and no assessment is laid upon the parish for their support, the poor are often obliged to travel and seek their maintenance.

Soil, Agriculture, Plantations, Sheep, &c.—The soil is not all of the same kind. In the lower part of the parish, the land is, in some places, light and dry, and naturally produces

ces broom; in other places it is deeper and wet, and in
ſome places moſſy. In the higher part of the pariſh, as in
Morange, (a great part of which lies upon limeſtone,) it is
clayey and wet, and in ſome places moſſy; but when the
ſeaſon is neither over dry, nor over rainy, it produces excellent crops. In Glenlivet, the lower part of it is loamy, or
mixed with clay; in the higher parts of it, the land is in
ſome places mixed with clay, and in ſome places moſſy; but
when the ſeaſon is moderate, it yields excellent crops. There
is in the head of Glenlivet, an excellent marl-pit, and the
farm of Tomalinan, beſide whoſe land the marl-pit is, lies
moſtly on a rock of limeſtone. Some who have large farms,
when a part of them is ſown with barley, they ſow the ſame
alſo with graſs-ſeeds, which yield good crops of graſs. Oats,
barley, and peaſe, and, in ſome dry land, rye, are the grain
generally ſown. No wheat is ſown, except in the mains or
manor of Ballendalloch, and there, for the moſt part, it
thrives well, becauſe fallowed and well manured. The
rent of the whole pariſh was ſtated before the Court of
Teinds in 1768, to be L. 13,771 : 12 : 1 Scots; but ſince
that time has conſiderably increaſed.—The pariſh, except
where it is waſhed by the river Spey, is ſurrounded with
hills, which are covered with heath, unleſs in ſome very
wet places, where ſome rough graſs grows alſo. The ſides
of Spey, Aven, and Livet, abound, in many places, with
birch and alder. There grow alſo oaks on the banks of
Spey and Aven, in ſome parts belonging to General
Grant's eſtate. The General has alſo ſome plantations of
firs, which are thriving well, and beautify the country. As
the land of moſt farms, (except where it is clayey and wet,)
hath many ſmall ſtones in it, the old Scotch plough is made
uſe of; but at Ballendalloch, and two or three more places,
the Engliſh plough is uſed. Many have their ploughs

drawn

drawn by oxen, few by horfes only; but the poorer fort yoke fome cattle, and put two horfes before them.

Meal is fold juft now here at between 15 s. and 16 s. Sterling the boll, of 9 ftone weight; oats and fodder at L. 1 and a guinea the boll of victual, *i. e.* as much oats is given for the boll, as, by the eftimation of two judicious honeft men, will make 9 ftone weight of meal; barley, with fodder, is fold a little higher, efpecially, if weighty and good, and fit for malt and for the ftill.—It is faid, there may be about 2500 fheep in the parifh; fome of them are of the Linton breed, (bought when lambs,) with black faces and feet. Some are of the old Scotch breed, altogether white. The Linton breed are the largeft and biggeft, and their wool rougheft. The others are lefs than the Linton kind, and their wool fofter and finer. It is faid, that fheep houfed or cotted in the winter feafon, have finer and fofter wool than thofe that are allowed to run in fields, and are kept there all winter. The beft wool is fold fometimes at L. 1 Sterling the ftone weight. Laft fummer the foft wool fold at 1 s. Sterling the pound, of 24 ounces. Every the leaft farmer, if near the hills, keeps fheep, but none have farms for that purpofe alone, and fome of the richeft farmers keep no fheep, becaufe not lying near the hills.

Bridges and Roads.—In fummer 1792, General Grant caufed build a good ftone bridge of three arches over Aven, about half a mile above the houfe of Ballendalloch, and a good road was made to and from it, which will be of great fervice and benefit to thofe who travel from the low country to Strathfpey and Badenoch. There is alfo a ftone bridge of two fmall arches built over Livet, about two furlongs below the mouth of Tervy. It is faid to have been built many years ago at the expenfe of fome of the Dukes of Gordon, or Marquiffes of Huntly. About 16 years a-

go

go, General Grant, to render the intercourse between Inveraven and his estate of Morange more easy and expeditious, at his own expense caused a large road for carriages
and carts, to be made from Inveraven to Morange and
Glenlivet, over the hill of Carnocay, (a ridge of hill
extending from Belrinnas, south-west to Aven, as far as his
right extended;) and when the road reached to the Duke of
Gordon's property, it was carried on by the statute-work of
the country. Across this road runs the rivulet or burn of
Tommore in Inveraven, (which has its rise in the north-
west side of Belrinnas;) he, therefore, that it might be no
hindrance, at his own expense also, put a stone bridge of
two arches, 8 or 12 feet wide, over it; but, in a few years
afterward, (in 1782), the burn, when greatly swelled by
an impetuous torrent from the hills, undermined the foundation, and carried it away, together with the meal-mill
and all its implements, (which was a quarter of a mile below it on the same burn), into Aven. This was a great loss
to the parish and travellers, as the burn, when it is big,
cannot be passed but by a bridge. The Duke of Gordon also
caused a road for carriages to be made from Glenrinnas,
up through Glenlivet, to Tomantoul in Strathaven.

Fish.—There come plenty of salmon up Spey; but they
are taken here only by the angling rod and line. There
are also very good trouts in this river. The salmon is sold
in the first of the year, at 4 d the pound; in June, it is sold at
2¼ d. and 2 d. the pound; and in July last summer it was
sold for 1¼ d. the pound. A few small salmon go up Aven,
and there are large good trouts taken in it. There are
trouts also in Livet, Tervey, and Cromby.

Antiquities.—There were upon an eminence on the east
side of Aven, and a short way up from the house of Ballendalloch,

dalloch, a few long ftones incloſing a ſmall piece of ground, which was ſaid to be a Druidical temple. The moſt of the ftones have been taken away, except one very broad, thick and long ftone, which ftands ſtill there : And oppoſite to this, on the weſt ſide of Aven, upon a riſing ground amidft the corn land of Bellaviller, is ſuch another place, where ſeveral long, broad ftones, encompaſs about 72 ſquare yards of ground; ſome of the long ftones are broken, but ſeveral of them ſtill ftand whole. Such another temple there is in the lower end of Glenlivet, on the eaft ſide of Aven, upon a hillock, or ſmall riſing ground, a little below the mouth of Livet, called the Doun of Dilmore. I never heard that oaks grew around thoſe places; but there are oaks growing between the water of Aven and the temple, near Ballendalloch ; and there grow oaks on the weſt ſide of Aven, oppoſite to that at Delmore, but none grow near to that at Bellaville.

Miſcellaneous Obſervations.—There are only two houſes where the ferry-boats on Spey and Aven are kept, that ſometimes keep a dram of whiſky to accommodate paſſengers who may lodge with them, but ſeldom have ale. There are alſo two ftills for aquavitæ, or whiſky, in the pariſh. This ſpirit is no doubt hurtful to the conſtitution, and alſo to the morals of the people.—I know only four houſes or cottages which have been pulled down and left uninhabitable within the laſt ten years, and four that have been new built in that ſpace of time.—The fuel here uſed is peats, of which there is no ſcarcity in a dry year, becauſe in every corner of the pariſh there is plenty of moſs, or of that black, ſoft, oozy ground from which peats are digged ; but the peats are not in all parts equally good. Some are of an excellent quality, hard, when dried, make ſtrong fire, and

and are not ſoon waſted. Others are, when dry, light and ſpungy; and though they ſoon take fire and get into a blaze, they are ſoon conſumed into aſhes. The climate in Glenlivet is colder than in Inveraven; for in Glenlivet there will be a pretty deep ſnow, when there will not be much in Inveraven; and ſometimes the people of Inveraven will plough, ſow, and harrow, when they cannot do ſo in Glenlivet. The reaſon of this is, becauſe Glenlivet is higher and ſurrounded with hills more than Inveraven is.

PARISH OF INVERKEITHNY.

(County of Banff—Synod of Aberdeen—Presbytery of Turriff.)

By the Rev. Mr. John Milne, *Minister.*

Name, Situation, River, and Extent.

A VERY large burn, or rivulet, which comes through the parishes of Drumblade and Forgue, falls into the river Deveron, near the church, from which it is probable the parish derives the name of *Inverkeithny.* The parish is situated on the S. side of the river, and is in the commissariot of Moray. It is in length, along the river side, from 5 to 6 English miles, and between 4 and 5 in breadth.

Produce and Rent.—A considerable quantity of grain is annually raised in the parish. The rent is fully 900l. Sterling.

Fuel.—There is scarcely any thing in the parish, that can be
called

called *moſs* or *peats*. The inhabitants are ſupplied with peats from the moſſes of *Foudland*, in the pariſh of Forgue, and of *Auchintoul*, in the pariſh of Marnoch. They alſo burn a kind of turf, which they get upon the hills. Banff is the neareſt ſea-port where coals can be got, which is about 12 Engliſh miles diſtant from the church.

Eccleſiaſtical Matters.—The church and manſe are ſituated in a narrow valley, near the bank of the Deveron. The pariſh formerly belonged to the Synod of Moray and Preſbytery of Huntly. An exchange was made with the pariſh of Mortlich, which originally was in the Synod of Aberdeen and Preſbytery of Turriff, and the miniſter of Inverkeithny ſtill draws 6s. 8d. Sterling as the feu-duty of a houſe in Elgin, which has, probably, been one of the ſtalls in the cathedral at Elgin. There are no diſſenters from the Eſtabliſhed Church, except a few members of the Epiſcopal Church of Scotland.

Population.—The population of Inverkeithny has decreaſed conſiderably within theſe 20 years. This has been partly occaſioned by the ſcarcity of fuel, but chiefly by the farmers thinking, from the high prices obtained for cattle and grain, that they had more profit, by cultivating their farms themſelves, than by ſubſetting a conſiderable part of them, as was formerly done in all the northern parts of Scotland.

The return to Dr. Webſter, in the year 1755,
was - - - - - 571 ſouls.
The number of ſouls at preſent (in 1793) is   460

Decreaſe, - 111

Employments

Employments and Character.—There is no village in the parish; but there are tradesmen of different sorts, such as smiths, weavers, wrights, and tailors. All the rest are farmers. The inhabitants are in general an industrious people, in the middle rank of life, and are particularly distinguished, by their paying due respect and attention to the ordinances of religion.

PARISH of KEITH,

(COUNTY OF BANFF.)

By the Rev. Mr ALEXANDER HUMPHREY, *miniſter of Fordyce, and late aſſiſtant miniſter of Keith.*

Name, Situation, and Extent.

THE ancient and modern name of this pariſh, as far as
can be aſcertained, is the ſame. Like all other
old names in it, it is evidently of Gaelic origin, and derived
from the word *ghaith*, which, in that language, ſignifies
wind, and which, when pronounced by a native Highlander, is not very diſſimilar in ſound from the word *Keith*.
This etymology is countenanced by the local ſituation of the
kirk and old village, near which lies an eminence, peculiarly expoſed to violent guſts of wind, vulgarly calle *Ar-
keith*, an evident corruption of the Gaelic words Ard-
Ghaith, pronounced *Ard Gui*, and ſignifying high wind. It
is alſo ſupported by the ancient manner of ſpelling the
name: In ſome old charters it is written *Gith*, which
ſtill more reſembles the word *ghaoth*. It is an inland pariſh,
9 miles

247

9 miles from any shore. It is situated about the middle of the county of Banff, in the presbytery of Strathbogie and Synod of Murray. It is about 6 miles long, and as many broad, being nearly circular. Suppofing the church the centre, a radius of about 3 miles would almost describe it. It lies in the middle of a large strath, called Strath-Ifla, or *Stryla*, from the water of Ifla that runs through it; and contains a tract of as close, extensive, and fertile a field of arable ground, as is to be found in any strath in the north.

Soil, Produce, Minerals, &c.—The prevailing soil is loam and clay; the reft of it is light. It is in general fertile in its productions, though, on account of its depth and moifture, it is commonly late in bringing them to maturity. For, though the oat feed-time begins generally about the end of March, and the barley feed-time about the end of April; harveft feldom commences before the end of Auguft or beginning of September. At prefent, the parifh is entirely deftitute of trees, except a few afhes and elms in country gardens; nor are any of its furrounding hills planted, but the hill of Mildary, belonging to Lord Findlater, where the planting is in a thriving way. Its general produce in grain, is oats, barley and peafe. The firft is the prevailing crop; but what quantity may be raifed, or what proportions the different fpecies of grain bear to each other, cannot eafily be afcertained. Wheat has been feldom tried, though with one farmer, before 1782, (fince which the feafons have generally been wet, late and cold,) it profpered well, for he reaped 22 returns. Almoft every tenant has annually a plot of ground under flax, but feldom above an acre; except one gentleman, furveyor for the truftees, who has annually from 16 to 18 acres under flax, and feems to be perfectly mafter of its whole economy. In general, it is a thriving and profitable crop,

and

and feems well adapted to the foil of Keith. Could a ready market be found for it, as it comes rough from the mills, (of which there are 3 in the parifh), the quantity raifed would be inconceivably increafed. The manufacturers, wifhing, (as is fuppofed, by thofe who have confidered the fubject moft attentively), to monopolize the flax trade, difcourage the raifing flax at home, as much as poffible, by ufing none but Dutch flax. The parifh abounds in ftone, which, in moft places, may eafily be obtained, only by digging a few feet; though not of an excellent quality, it anfwers tolerably well for building and inclofures. It has alfo plenty of a coarfe gray flate, fit enough for flating houfes. Limeftone is to be had in abundance, on almoft every farm, with plenty of peats at a moderate diftance, for converting it to the purpofes of building or agriculture. Notwithftanding that great advantage, agriculture is here juft in its infancy; the long drawling team of 8 or 10 oxen in yokes, fometimes preceded by a couple of horfes, is yet often to be feen creeping along, dragging after them an immenfe log of a clumfy Scotch plough; when 2, or at moft 4 good horfes, or even good oxen in collars, with the modern light plough, (which has been found to anfwer well by thofe who have tried it), would perform the fame work, equally well, in a much fhorter time. This laft mode begins now to take place, particularly about the village. The farmers have at laft perceived the advantage of a proper rotation of crops, and of cultivating fuch as are green, though, for want of inclofures, they can only be cultivated in an imperfect manner. A confiderable quantity of the produce of the parifh is exported. Were not that the cafe, it is believed, that populous as it is, it could maintain its own inhabitants. It has feveral mineral fprings of the chalybeate kind, fending forth large ftreams of pleafant water, which, upon trial, has been

found

found to be equally light with the Peterhead water. Its ftrengthening influence on the ftomach, and power of increafing digeftion, many of the inhabitants have experienced, though it has not yet been diftinguifhed for any very powerful, or particular medicinal virtue.

Climate and Difeafes.—The climate, as may be expected, from the fituation and nature of the foil, is moift and cold. It is not, however, peculiarly unhealthy, though the inhabitants are by no means careful to guard againft the defects of their fituation ; for their houfes are generally low, and confequently very damp in the floors; nor is there, for the moft part, any accefs to the houfes of the lower ranks, but over a dunghill, which reaches to the very threfhold ; and whofe peftilential fteams, increafing the moifture of the air in their dwellings, muft concur, with the nature of the climate, to multiply difeafes, or to increafe their power. A regard to their health, independent of cleanlinefs, ought, therefore, to excite the moft indolent, to remove fuch nuifances to a greater diftance. The difeafes moft frequent are, fevers, rheumatifm, toothach, inflammation of the eyes; coughs, pulmonary confumptions ; and, in fome old people, humid afthma, efpecially in the winter and fpring. Acidities in the ftomach, flatulency in the bowels, and other fymptoms of dyfpepfia, are frequent complaints; more efpecially fince potatoes have become fuch a common article of food, and chiefly among the lower ranks, who ufe no pepper. Thefe two laft years, many more have been afflicted with jaundice than formerly, both in this parifh and neighbourhood, and even in the adjacent parts of Murray and Aberdeenfhire, but from what caufe is uncertain. Scrophulous habits are alfo unhappily too common, particularly among fuch as are employed in the linen manufacture. It is commonly obferved, that many more fevers of the low ner-

vous

vous kind, and greatly fewer of the inflammatory, have prevailed for the laſt 20 years ; and that patients do not now bear ſuch liberal evacuations by blood-letting, as before that period. Whether this be not owing to ſome particular alteration in the ſeaſons, may be a queſtion not eaſily ſolved.

Proprietors and Rent.—There are 6 proprietors in the pariſh, the Earls of Findlater and Fife, Stewart of Whitely and Achanacy, Stewart of Birkenburn, and Brodie of Lethen. The valued rent is L. 5332 : 18 : 4 Scotch. The real rent cannot exactly be aſcertained, as ſome of the heritors have declined giving any information on the ſubject. As nearly as can be conjectured, it is rather above, than under L. 3000 Sterling. Within the preſent century, there were 14 heritors in the pariſh, moſt of them reſident. Of the 6 exiſting heritors, only 1 is reſident, *viz.* Mr Stewart of Birkenburn.

Population.—By the return made to Dr Webſter, in 1755, it appears that the population of Keith was as follows:

Proteſtants, - - 2653 ⎫
Papiſts, - - 30 ⎭ In all 2683.

In 1783, according to a roll, laid before the heritors and gentlemen of the pariſh by the miniſter, the population was 3583 ſouls: At preſent, (1791) from a very accurate ſurvey it appears, that there are only 3057 ſouls.

Of theſe, the number who live in		Between 30 & 40, -	476
villages, is, -	1662	—— 40 & 50, -	422
In the country, -	1395	—— 50 & 60, -	347
Of males, -	1709	—— 60 & 70, -	187
Of females,	1348	—— 70 & 76, -	38
Of perſons under 11 years of age,	592	—— 80 & 90, -	3
Between 20 & 30, -	570	Aged 96 *,	1

Among

* This is a woman who ſays ſhe was 18 or 20 in 1716.

Among thefe, there are 312 Diffenters, including children, of whom there are of the Affociate Congregation,   131

Papifts *,   -   -   -   122

Scotch Epifcopalians,   -   -   59

If the parifh regifters be exact, the average of births for the following periods, are as under:

From January 1701, to ditto 1704, the average is, $38\frac{1}{3}$

From January 1743, to ditto 1746,   - $91\frac{2}{3}$

From January 1770, to ditto 1773,   - $65\frac{2}{3}$

From January 1787, to ditto 1790,   - $62\frac{1}{3}$

It is, however, to be obferved, that few of the Diffenters enter their childrens names in the parifh regifters. The average of marriages for the laft 3 years, is $14\frac{2}{3}$. From the above ftatement it appears, that fince 1755, population in Keith has increafed upon the whole 374, but fince 1783, it has decreafed 526. Since the writer of this had the charge of the parifh, or for three years back, it has decreafed 90. This may eafily be accounted for, from the ftate of the manufactures.

Manufactures.—The principal branches of manufacture carried on in Keith are flax-dreffing, fpinning, and weaving. The two firft of thefe, during the above mentioned period, have been in a very unprofperous condition; fo much fo, that many flax-dreffers have been difmiffed by their employers, and, with their families, have left the place. This decline

---

* It is obfervable, that the Papifts have increafed 92 fince the year 1755. This increafe is not owing to new converfions, of which very few occur, but to the migration of feveral Popifh families from the Enzie, where, when the family of Gordon, the fuperiors of that country, were Popifh, they greatly abounded, and where they are ftill very numerous. There are no inftances of longevity, except as above. It may, however be obferved, that there is a couple yet alive, whofe ages together make 171, and who have now eaten 64 Chriftmas dinners together, fince they were man and wife.

decline in the yarn trade arifes from three caufes, the prevailing demand for cotton cloths, which are now afforded at a very cheap rate; the advanced price of Dutch flax, the only flax ufed by our manufacturers of yarn, and a very large importation of linen yarn from Ireland to Glafgow, the principal mart for Keith yarn. It may alfo be added, from their neglecting to take care, that all the yarn manufactured by them was of good quality, owing to which it had fallen into difrepute; this laft caufe, however, will foon be removed, as the manufacturers have refolved to receive no yarn from their fpinners, but what is of the very beft quality. There are alfo in the parifh, a tannage, a diftillery, and, of late, a bleachfield, very complete in its apparatus, which has been erected at a very confiderable expence on the banks of the Ifla, and is allowed to equal in execution any bleachfield in the North.

Villages and Markets.—There are 4 villages in the parifh, one of old ftanding, the Kirk-town of Keith, partly feued by the predeceffors of the family of Findlater, and partly feued by the minifters, and ftanding on the glebe. This village is greatly on the decline, and almoft a ruin; it contains 192 inhabitants. About the year 1750, the late Lord Findlater divided a barren muir, and feued it out in fmall lots, according to a regular plan, ftill adhered to; on which there now ftands a large, regular, and tolerably thriving village, called *New Keith*, containing 1075 inhabitants. The feus contain 30 feet in front by 70, at a feu-duty of 10 s. *per annum*. This village is the refidence of all the manufacturers of note in the parifh: according to the fuccefs of their bufinefs, therefore, it muft either profper or decline. It enjoys the benefit of a well frequented, and plentifully fupplied weekly market; it has, therefore, provifions of all kinds in plenty, and at a moderate price. It has alfo 4 annual

nual fairs; one in September, of very old standing, and which, some 60 or 70 years ago, was the general mart for merchant goods from Aberdeen to Kirkwall; it is still the best frequented market in the north for black cattle and horses *. Soon after the commencement of the village of New Keith, the late Lord Fife began to erect a village on the north side of the parish, and then feued out a considerable tract of land, called the *New Town* of *New Mill*, to distinguish it from another town nigh it, called *New Mill*, which is also his Lordship's property, but was never feued. This New Town contains 330 inhabitants, of which there are a very few weavers, who are the only manufacturers; the rest, excepting 5 or 6 families, consist of very poor people, who have fixed their abode there, for the conveniency of the land and moss. The old town, called New Mill, contains 65 inhabitants.

Tenantry,

* The weekly market in Keith, (which, before the erection of the new village, was held in the old), is well supplied with provisions. These, of late years, have greatly increased in price. The average price of oat-meal 50 years ago, was 6 s. or 8 s. for the boll of 16 measured pecks, weighing upwards of 10 stone; beef, 1 d. *per* lb.; mutton, from 4 d. to 6 d. *per* quarter of 6 and 7 lb.; a fed goose, from 10 d. to 1 s.; a hen, 3 d.; a duck, 4 d.; a large chicken, 1 d.; butter, 3 d. *per* lb. of 22 Dutch ounces; cheese, from 9 d. to 1 s. *per* quarter, according to its age. It is, however, to be observed, that, at that time, fresh meat was only to be had at certain seasons, and such as used much meat, killed for their own consumption; now, however, well fed fresh meat is always to be had in the market, every week throughout the year, which, with other provisions, now sells at the following average prices: Meal, which is extremely variable, from 10 s. to 12 s. *per* boll, of 8 stone; beef, from 2½ d. to 4 d. *per* lb. according to the season; mutton, from 2 d. to 3⅓ d. *per* lb.; a goose, 2 s. 6 d.; a duck, 10 d.; a hen, 8 d.; butter, 8 d. *per* lb. of 22 Dutch ounces. Though an inland parish, fish is plentiful, and generally as cheap as at the shore. At the above mentioned period, men servants received of wages *per annum* from L. 1 : 6 : 8 to L. 1 : 13 : 4; maids, from 12 s. to

L. 1.

Tenantry, Servitudes, and Cattle.—The farms in general are fmall, renting from L. 20 to L. 40, which is paid partly in victual, and partly in money, but without any ftated proportion. There are a very few farms from about L. 60, to L. 100 ; only one farm is completely inclofed, and two partially. The villagers occupy many parks and acres, which are in a rapid ftate of improvement, and which are not yet rented, even when moft contiguous, above L. 20 Sterling *per* acre. The rent of the farms is very various, according to the quality of the foil, and ftate of improvement ; probably from 5 s. to 15 s. *per* acre. The farmers are exceedingly fober and induftrious, and yet they are far from being in a comfortable fituation. There is hardly fuch a thing as a farmer, with a family, betttering his circumftances ; but many inftances of farmers of fobriety and induftry, in fpite of all their care, fpending the capital with which they began. The expence of labour is now fo great, and the rent of land fo high, that the profits of a fmall farm are not fufficient, with the utmoft frugality, or even parfimony, to maintain a family ; the holders of fuch farms find it exceedingly difficult to fupport credit at all, and very often, particularly when the landholders or their factors are rigid in exacting their dues, fink to poverty. However hurtful it may be to the production of a numerous and healthy population, large farms are increafing, and muft increafe, in order to afford their holders a fubfiftence ; and the tenants of fmaller poffeffions will be under the neceffity of devoting themfelves to manufactures of

fome

L. 1, 2 s. befides board and lodging. Now, befides thefe, men fervants receive from L. 4 to L. 6, according to their ftrength and capacity ; maids, from L. 2 to L. 2, 5 s. It is difficult to afce tain the expence incurred by a day-labourer and his family. When fuch a family is not extremely numerous, and both the man and the wife are fober and induftrious, they generally enjoy the neceffaries of life in plenty.

some kind or other. To them, if they were better informed, that should not be a disagreeable necessity ; for, it is certain, that, in most places of this island, tradesmen, if sober and industrious, of almost every denomination, can live and bring up their families, much more comfortably than they can do. Here the tenants are subjected to very few services, and these few are seldom exacted. They are bound, however, to carry their farm victual to whatever port it is to be shipped at, and to perform kirk and mill services, as is usual in most parishes. The multures belong to the proprietors of the several lands, except in one instance ; the small estate of Edinteve being thirled to a mill of Lord Fife's. The heritors, however, think proper to oblige their respective tenants to grind at their own mills, the multures of which vary ; sometimes the 10th, sometimes the 16th part is exacted, which is accounted a great bar to improvement. Among these tenants, with the village feuers, there are 381 oxen, 523 horses, 645 cows, 990 young cattle, 39 young horses, and 2240 sheep.

Language.—In this parish, and in all the neighbourhood, the language spoken is the Scotch dialect of the English language. All the old names of places are evidently derived from the Gaelic, which language is generally spoken in a detached corner of the parish, by a colony from various districts of the Highlands ; who being indigent, and supported by begging, or their own alertness, are allured there by the abundance of moss, and the vicinity of a very populous and plentiful country. Many instances of the above mentioned derivations might be given : for example, *Aultmore,* signifying ' the great burn, or brook ;' *Altonbuy,* ' the yellow island ;' *Bog-bain,* ' the white moss ;' *Achanacy,* ' the field in the muir or desert,' &c ; all which

which derivations are evidently confirmed by the local ſituations, and natural appearances of the ſeveral places.

Church and Poor *.—The church is a capacious, though not very commodious building. At preſent it is in good repair, being lately put into that condition, at the expence of ſeveral hundred pounds. The manſe and offices are in a ſtate of rapid decay, though repaired ſince the preſent miniſter's incumbency. The living is L. 88 : 17 : 6 in money, 32 bolls of meal, and about L. 12 of feu-duty and rents from the old village. The poor within the pariſh, receiving alms, are extremely numerous, occaſioned principally by the great influx of highlanders above mentioned, moſt of whom are very indigent ; and during the ſummer months, they range this and the neighbouring pariſhes, and are a great encroachment on what is truly the property of the native poor. For the ſupport of theſe, there are no mortified or public funds, beſides the intereſt of the very ſmall ſum of L. 30 Sterling, and the weekly or occaſional collections, which may amount to about L. 32 annually ; which ſums are almoſt entirely devoted to the uſe of ſuch poor, as are unable to leave their beds or houſes, or make any exertion for their ſupport at all, which, at preſent, and generally, may be about 30 in number. This ſtatement evidently

---

* The oldeſt ſeſſion-records in Keith, bear date only 1686 ; at which time Sir James Strachan of Thornton, was miniſter of Keith. In the year 1690, he was deprived of his living for non-conformity to the new Government. After his deprivation, for ſome time the people of Keith were very ſeldom accommodated with preaching. On that account the pariſhioners and heritors agreed with a Mr Lachlan Roſe, to officiate as miniſter at Keith. In 1694, ſome complaints againſt this Roſe were lodged before the Committee of Aſſembly for the north, then ſitting at Elgin ; which Committee declared Roſe an intruder, and proclaimed the kirk vacant. This vacancy, however, was not ſupplied till Mr John Chriſtie's admiſſion in 1700.

dently fhews, that thefe fmall funds are by no means fufficient, for the maintenance of thofe to whom they are devoted. This deficiency, however, is, in general, amply
made up, either by the generofity of their relations, or by
the charity and liberality of their neighbours. For it
ought to be recorded, to the honour of the inhabitants of
Keith, that in liberality to the poor they are not exceeded,
it is believed, by any people of their circumftances and ftation in Scotland. Befides the above fum, there is annually collected from L. 5 to L. 6 Sterling, for the benefit of
the Infirmary of Aberdeen.

School.—The parifh of Keith has long enjoyed, with little interruption, the benefit of a good fchool, to which, before other able fchoolmafters were fo frequent, there was a
great refort of young lads for the benefit of education. At
prefent it is in a very profperous ftate, the office of fchoolmafter being filled by a gentleman fully capable, and of the
moft indefatigable application. Befides the ufual falary and
perquifites, he enjoys annually 300 merks Scotch from a
mortification, of which a brief account is fubjoined *.

Roads,

* In the year 1647, Alexander Ogilvie of Edindeach, clerk to the
Signet, mortified his lands and mill of Edindeach, " for building and up-
" holding a fchool-houfe, and maintaining a fchoolmafter in the parochin
" of Keith," appointing the minifter and elders truftees for the faid mortification. In the year 1687, the laird of Braco, anceftor to Lord Fife,
raifed a procefs as titular of teinds, for abftracted teinds, againft the perfon who was then fchoolmafter; obtained decreet before the Commiffary
of Murray, and got the lands adjudged to him for thefe teinds. In confequence of that adjudication, the laird of Braco, got poffeffion of the mortified lands, paying annually to the fchoolmafter only L. 68 Scotch. In
the year 1747, a fchoolmafter of fpirit fucceeded, who being affured by
good counfel, that he had a right to thefe mortified lands, raifed a procefs
of reduction of the deed of adjudication. This procefs he maintained for
ten years before the Court of Seffion. His little funds being then exhaufted,

Roads, Bridges, and Poſt-office.—The roads are, in general, in very bad repair ; partly owing to the wetneſs and depth of the ſoil ; partly to the injudicious and imperfect mode of repair, and partly to the ſtatute labour not being regularly exacted, by which the roads in this corner were originally made, and which is the only means of their ſupport. Within theſe few years, Lord Findlater's factor in that diſtrict, has exerted himſelf in a very laudable manner to remedy that defect ; has introduced a more judicious and perfect mode of repair, and is more regular and ſtrict in exacting the ſtatute labour ; for which, though the inhabitants in the mean time, murmur a little, he deſerves their beſt thanks ; and were his commendable zeal properly ſeconded, by the other heritors and factors, the complaint of bad roads in Keith would ſoon be no more heard of. The pariſh is tolerably ſupplied in bridges, moſtly new and in good repair. In the new village there is a Poſt-office, to which the letters are brought by runners from Fochabers thrice a week ;— an office, which, from its increaſing conſequence, ought to be more liberally ſupported and ſupplied with runners. It ought to have at leaſt 6 inſtead of 3. Without this increaſe of runners, it can never properly anſwer the purpoſe ; for when there is a neceſſity of anſwering any letter in courſe

of

---

ed, and finding no ſupport from ſeſſion, preſbytery, or public funds of the church, and perhaps a little ſoftened by the promiſe of a living in the church, from the laird of Braco, now become Lord Braco, he was induced to conſent to a compromiſe. By that compromiſe, the mortified lands were valued, and found to be worth 300 merks of rent annually. This ſum, Lord Braco engaged to pay to the ſchoolmaſter and his ſucceſſors in office, annually, in all time coming, upon condition of his being allowed to retain the lands. The compromiſe was afterwards ratified, by the preſbytery of Strathbogie, and the Synod of Murray.

of poft, there is no poffibility of doing it, but by an exprefs
to Fochabers, which is a great drawback on the increafing
trade of the place, and calls for the exertion of all who wifh
well to its profperity, to endeavour to procure its removal.
The additional expence ought not to be put in competition
with the additional advantages. This expence its revenue
may well bear, which, within thefe 30 years, has increafed
an hundred fold.

Remarkable Events.—Tradition has recorded only two
fkirmifhes, that have happened in the parifh: One in 1746,
when about 70 of the Campbells, and 30 of Kingfton's
horfe, were furprifed by the rebels in the old village, and
difperfed or taken after confiderable flaughter. The other
about a century before, when a Peter Roy Macgregor, the
head of a band of robbers, who infefted that country, was
taken, and his gang completely difperfed by Gordon of
Glengerack, then one of the heritors, after a defperate re-
fiftance. In July 1789, during a violent thunder ftorm, there
fell a very remarkable fhower of hail, which fortunately extended only to a few farms on the fouth fide of the parifh :
where it fell, it fo completely ruined the crop, that feveral
fields were plowed down, and thofe, that were fpared, produced nothing worth the expence of cutting. The hail-
ftones were fully the fize of piftol bullets, very irregular in
their fhape, moftly angular, bearing the appearance of two
or three large hail-ftones joined; though the weather was
exceedingly fultry, and the ground very wet, they were not
completely diffolved in three days. In the year 1782, there
was the greateft deficiency in the crop, that has happened,
at leaft fince the years of famine, at the beginning of the century. Had not the noblemen, gentlemen, and principal inhabitants exerted themfelves, (which they did in a very
laudable manner,) and procured a very large importation
of

of victual, thouſands might have periſhed for want. Very little of the grain was found fit for feed, and by a ſurvey, made under the inſpection of gentlemen of ſkill, to aſcertain the real ſtate of the crop, it was found, at an average, to be ſufficient to ſupply the inhabitants only five months, without reſerving any for feed. In ſome of the lateſt farms, the produce could not ſupply the farmer's family, above ſix weeks or three months. Ten bolls of oats frequently yielded no more than one boll of meal, and that too of a quality which, in other years, would not have been uſed, but deemed only fit for hogs. Notwithſtanding ſuch dreadful ſcarcity, not one ſingle individual periſhed for want, though many hundreds were on ſhort allowance.

Manners and Character.—As there are no perſons of independent fortune within the pariſh, the inhabitants are diſtinguiſhedly ſober and induſtrious. Several of them have thus raiſed themſelves to eaſy circumſtances, which enables them to enjoy the comforts of life and of ſociety, in the greateſt perfection. Unaccuſtomed to the elegancies and luxuries of life, or ignorant of them, they feel not their want; they are not diſquieted with their deſire; ſatisfied with their neat abundance, they enjoy it with ſatisfaction; they ſhew it with pleaſure among their equals, and extend it with liberality to ſuch as are in want. The taverns are now nearly deſerted; 20 years ago, there was more ſpent in alehouſes in one month, than is now ſpent in 12. All ranks are regular in their attendance on the ordinances of religion; maintain, in general, great decorum of behaviour, and value themſelves on reſpectability of character, which excites them, of conſequence, to ſupport it. Nor are they, in any gradation of ſociety, notorious for any particular vices. They have no paſtimes or holidays, except

dancing

dancing on Chriſtmas and New Year's day. They are generally ſenſible, ſhrewd, and intelligent. The tradeſmen and manufacturers appear more chearful, and ſeem happier, than the farmers and their tenants. This evident difference naturally ariſes, from the difficulty the latter now find, to procure a ſubſiſtence. For though the generality of the tradeſmen and manufacturers live more expenſively, than moſt of the farmers, ſeveral of them are, notwithſtanding, improving their circumſtances, while the farmers, with a very few exceptions indeed, are doing the reverſe.

Miſcellaneous Obſervations.—This pariſh cannot boaſt of having given birth to any eminently diſtinguiſhed characters, if we except the illuſtrious Mr JAMES FERGUSON, well known for his mechanical and philoſophical genius and publications.—There are no birds or quadrupeds, either ſtationary or migratory, but what are common in this corner of the country; nor are there any breeds of animals peculiarly valuable.—There are no curioſities, either natural or artificial, in the pariſh, worth recording. There are the remains of ſeveral Druidical circles, which are now moſtly demoliſhed, for the ſake of their ſtones. There is one yet very diſtinct on the top of a hill, vulgarly called the *Card's hill*, probably from the Gaelic word *carald*, which ſignifies a friend; the true name of the hill may therefore be the *hill of friends*, originating from the brotherly Druids, who worſhipped on its top. A little below this circle, there is a very fine fountain of excellent water, called *Taber-chalich*, an evident corruption of the Gaelic words, *Taber-chalaich*, ſignifying the *Old Wife's Well*, having been perhaps, of old, frequented by ſuch perſons, for ſome ſuppoſed ſanative power, though now fallen into diſrepute. Near another of theſe circles, there is another well of the ſame kind, to which ſome per

ſons

ſons reſorted, even in the memory of perſons ſtill alive, always leaving ſome offering behind them; but it alſo has
loſt its fame. A little below the old village, there is a beautiful fall of water, called the *Lin of Keith*, where the Iſla
precipitates itſelf over a pretty high rock, forming a very
pleaſant caſcade. On the top of the rock, which overhangs
this caſcade, ſtand the ſcanty remains of a once large ruin,
ſaid to have formerly belonged to a gentleman of the
name of Oliphant, who had been one of the Senators of the
College of Juſtice.   Tradition gives no particular account
of this ruin ; it does not, however, ſeem to have been of
any very great antiquity.

PARISH of KIRKMICHAEL.

(COUNTY OF BANFF, SYNOD OF MORAY, PRESBYTERY OF
ABERNETHY.)

By the Rev. Mr. JOHN GRANT.

Name, Extent, Surface, &c.

IN Monkish history, this parish derives its ecclesiastic name
from St. Michael, to whom the chapel, where now the
kirk stands, was anciently dedicated. If this account be
true, it may be observed, that the tutelary patron, ever since
the period of his election, has paid little regard to the morality of his clients. In the Gaelic, the vernacular idiom,
it is called Strath-āth-fhin, from " Strath," a dale, " āth,"
a ford, and " Fin," the hero Fingal, so highly celebrated in
the Poems of Ossian. It is generally written Strath-avan,
avan being the appellative for a river ; but the former etymon approaches much nearer to the provincial pronunciation.

tion. It is further confirmed by a ſtanza, which is ſtill recited by the old people of the country.

Chaidh mo bheans bhatha',
Ain uiſg āth-fhin, nan clachan ſleamhuin ;
'S bho chaidh mo bheans' bhatha',
Bheirmeid āth-fhin, ainm an amhuin.

" On the limpid water of the ſlippery ſtones, has my wife
been drowned, and ſince my wife has there been drowned,
henceforth its name ſhall be the water of Fingal." It is the
tradition of the country, that in one of Fingal's excurſions,
in purſuit of the deer of the mountains, after having croſſed
the river, he was followed by his wife, who being carried
down by the violence of the ſtream, ſunk, and was drowned.
To commemorate this melancholy event, in which the hero
was tenderly intereſted, he uttered the above ſtanza. Since
that period, the water, which was formerly called An-uiſge-
geal, or the White Water, in alluſion to its tranſparency, aſſumed by an eaſy tranſition, the name of the ford or river of
Fingal.

The pariſh of Kirkmichael* is divided into 10 little diſtricts,

* It is preſumable, from its deſolated ſituation, the natural barriers by which
it is ſeparated from the circumjacent countries, the detached hills, and numerous ſtreams, by which it is interſected, that the pariſh of Kirkmichael has not
been inhabited till of a late period. Several old people, now alive, remember
the firſt culture of a ſpace of ground within its precincts, that may contain, at
preſent, a tenth part of the whole population. To this circumſtance, and the
coldneſs of the climate, it has been owing, that the poſſeſſion of the property
has undergone ſo few changes. The firſt proprietor, as far as can be traced
back by the light of authentic records, ſeems to have been Macduff, Thane of
Fife. In a charter, where he makes a gift of the contiguous pariſh of Inveraven, it is ſaid, " Malcolmus de Fife, ſalutem. Sciant præſentes, me dediſſe,
et hac carta confirmaſſe, Deo et Epiſcopo Moravienſi, eccleſiam beati Peteri de
Inveraven,

tricts, called Davochs *. Several antiquaries have miftaken the etymon of Davoch ; but the word is evidently derived from Daimh, oxen, and Ach, field. In its original acceptation, it imports as much land as can be ploughed by 8 oxen. In the Regiam Majeftatem, it is clearly defined †.

This

Inveraven, quam Bricius tenuit, et cum omni parochia totius Strathaven, cum decimis et oblationibus, in perpetuam Eleemofynam." This gift was made in the 13th century ; and, upon the decline of the ancient family of Macduff, the property was transferred to Alexander Stewart, Earl of Buchan, of the Royal Family. In 1482, Sir Walter Stewart, grandfon of the Earl of Buchan, in the illegitimate line, refigned it to King James the III. By King James the III., it was given to the Earl of Huntly. In 1492, this gift is confirmed by King James the IV., in favour of Alexander, Lord Gordon, Mafter of Huntly. This noble family have continued the proprietors of the parifh of Kirkmichael ever fince. So that during a period of near 500 years, the obfervation of a Greek poet, juftified by general experience, upon the fluctuations of property, can fcarcely be applied to this diftrict.

Αγρος Αχαιμεινιδυ γενομην ποτε, νυν δι Μενιππα
Και παλιν εξ ετερυ, βηϲομαι εις ετερον,

* One of thefe belongs to that refpectable character, Sir James Grant ; the other 9 are the property of his Grace the Duke of Gordon, a nobleman not more diftinguifhed by his great and opulent fortune, than for the antiquity of his family, his fplendid hofpitality, his patriotifm and humanity. What the poet Buchanan applied to one of his anceftors, may, with equal propriety, fubftituting the paft for the prefent, be applied to his Grace :

Dives opum, luxuque carens, domus hofpita cunctis.
Pacis amans pectus, fortis ad arma manus.

It is obferved by an eminent hiftorian, that Charles V., was not more confpicuous for his own good fenfe, than for that proof which he exhibited of it, in the choice of his miniftry. This obfervation will apply to his Grace, in its full latitude ; as the gentlemen, to whom his Grace has intrufted the management of his bufinefs, have acquired an efteem, to which candour, integrity, and affability have juftly entitled them. In this character Mr. Tod is too well known to require the feeble panegyric of the writer of this Statiftical Account.

† " Davata," fays that writer, " apud prifcos Scotos, quod continet quatuor aratra terræ, quorum unumquodque trahitur octo bobus. Alii quatuor aratra duplicia

This parish lies at the western extremity of the county of Banff, from which it is distant between 30 and 40 computed miles. On every side, there are natural barriers which separate it from the surrounding countries; from the parish of Strath-don, toward the S., by Leach'-mhic-ghothin, the declivity of the smith's son; from the parish of Cromdale toward the N. by Beinn Chromdal, the hill of the winding dale. These are two long branches of hills, that, running in an easterly direction, project from the northern trunk of the Grampian mountains *. From the parish of Abernethy toward the W., it is separated by moors and hills, that connect Cromdale hill with Glenavon; from the parish of Inveravan, by moors, and hills, and narrow defiles. The length between the extreme points that are habitable, may be about 10 computed miles. The breadth is unequal. Where it tapers at the extremities, in some places, it is less than a mile; between the verges that bound the middle, it may be about

plicia intelligunt, quæ sunt octo simplicia: sed servari debet usus, et consuetudo locorum. In nonnullis libris hoc legitur bavata terræ contra fidem veterum codicum authenticorum. Bavata autem terræ continet tredecem acras, cujus octava pars comprehendit unam acram, dimidium acræ, et octavam partem acræ." This passage shows, that in ancient times, in the Highlands, a small portion of land was cultivated, in comparison of the present. A davoch of the ordinary extent of these districts, would now require, at least, three times as many cattle to labour it, as were formerly employed according to the above passage from the Regiam Majestatem. Hence, it may be inferred, that the population has increased in proportion.

* Grampian, from Grànt and Beinn. Grànt, like the ἀγος of the Greeks, has two opposite meanings. In some fragments ascribed to Ossian, it signifies beautiful. This meaning, now, is obsolete, and it signifies deformed, ugly, &c. The old Caledonians, as these mountains abounded in game, and connecting beauty with utility, might have given the name in the former sense. Mr. Henry Saville, and Mr. Lhuyd, two eminent antiquaries, call them Grànt Beinn, from which comes the soft inflected Grampian of the Romans.

about 3 computed miles. In its shape, it resembles an irregular oblong oval.

Cairn-gorm, or the Blue Mountain, one of the high, though perhaps not the highest of those lofty mountains that stud the Grampian desert, rises 4050 feet above the level of the sea; and Loch-avon not more than a mile from the foot of the Cairn-gorm *, 1750 feet. At the southern extremity of the parish, there is a cataract falling from a height of 18 feet. From this cataract to Lochavon, the source of the river, there are 8 computed miles; between the manse of Kirkmichael, which lies within 2 miles of the northern extremity of the parish, and the above cataract, there are 7 computed miles. As the source of the river there, is situated so near the cultivated part of the country, it may be inferred, that the situation of the whole ground is very considerably elevated above the surface of the sea †. The face of the country,

* For the height of this mountain and Lochavon, the writer is obliged to James Hay, Esq. of Gordon Castle, a gentleman of much knowledge, whose skill in observing, and whose accuracy in describing natural appearances, are well known to the Linnæan Society in London.

† Close by Lochavon, there is a large stone called Clach-dhian, from clach, a stone, and dhian, protection, or refuge. It has been a cavity within, capable of containing 18 armed men, according to the figure made use of in describing it. One corner of it rises 6 feet 4 inches in height. The breadth of it may be about 12 feet. Plain within, it rises on the outside from the several verges of the roof, into a kind of irregular protuberance of an oblong form. In times of licence and depredation, it afforded a retreat to freebooters.

Clach-bhan, from clach, a stone, and bean, a woman, is another stone situated upon the summit of a hill, called Meal-a-ghaneimh, from meal, a knoll or mound, and ganeimh, sand. On one side, it measures 20 feet in height. On the other side, it is lower and of a sloping form. In the face of it, 2 seats have been excavated, resembling that of an armed chair. Till of late, this stone used to be visited by pregnant women, not only of this, but from distant countries, impressed with the superstitious idea, that by sitting in these seats, the pains of travail would become easy to them, and other obstetrical assistance rendered unnecessary.

try, in general, exhibits a bleak and gloomy appearance. In
croſſing the centre of it, few cheering objects attract the eye
of the traveller. From detached hills covered with heath,
and deſtitute of verdure, where here and there a lonely tree
marks the depredations of time, he naturally turns with a-
verſion. But, ſhould he happen to paſs after a heavy fall of
rain, when the numerous brooks that interſect the country
pour their troubled ſtreams into the roaring Avon, he muſt
commiſerate the condition of the inhabitants, at ſuch a ſeaſon, precluded from the reſt of the world, and even from enjoying the ſociety of each other. Frequently in winter, the
ſnow lies ſo deep, that the communication between it and
other countries, becomes almoſt impracticable. The banks
of the Avon, however, are pleaſant enough, and in different
places tufted with groves of birch, mixed with ſome alder.
This being the largeſt ſtream that waters the country, from
its ſource to where it falls into the Spey (the Tueſſis * of An-
toninus's Itinerary), it flows over a ſpace of 24 or 25 miles,
including its windings. In the pariſh, there are 2 other leſſer
ſtreams, beſides a variety of brooks ; the one called Conlas,
from cuthin, narrow, and glas, green, and the other, ailnac,
from eil, a rock, and nidh, to waſh.

Climate.—From its elevated ſituation, the numerous brooks
by which it is interſected, and its vicinity to the Grampian
mountains, it might naturally be expected, that the atmoſphere of this country has little to recommend it. Of this,
the inhabitants have ſufficient experience. Their winters are
always cold and ſevere, while their ſummers are ſeldom warm
and

---

* Tueſſis, from Tuath, north, and uiſg, water, by way of eminence, being
the largeſt river in the N. of Scotland, it was afterward called Spey, from
Spadha, a long ſtride, in alluſion to the length of its courſe.

and genial. The diforders confequently to which they are fubject, may, in a great meafure, be attributed to their climate. Thefe, for the moft part, are coughs, confumptions, and affections of the lungs, by which many of thofe advanced in life are cut off, and frequently feverals of thofe who die at an earlier period. In fummer and autumn, what the Medical Faculty call nervous fevers, chiefly prevail, and frequently prove fatal. Thefe are the common diforders.

Soil, Springs, Natural Hiftory, &c.—As the face of this country rifes into hills, or finks into valleys, as it flopes into declivities, or extends into plains, the foil accordingly varies. Along the banks of the Avon, and the brooks, it generally confifts of a mixture of fand and black earth ; in the more elevated plains, of a pretty fertile black mould, on the floping declivities, of a kind of reddifh earth and gravel ; the nearer it approaches the fummits of the hills, it is mixed with mofs and gravel. In fome few places, it is deep and clayey. In the parifh, there are feveral fprings of mineral waters : One in particular, is much frequented by people troubled with the ftone, or labouring under ftomachic complaints. Some medical gentlemen, who have made the experiment, affert that it is fuperior to the celebrated wells of Pananich on Deefide. It has been obferved, that the hills of this country are covered with heath, and deftitute of wood ; yet, in the interftices of the heath, there grows a rank grafs, and a plant called Canach an Shleibh, or the mountain down, on which cattle and fheep feed in fummer, and grow tolerably fat. The foreft of Glenavon which is 11 miles in length, and between 3 and 4 in breadth, contains many green fpots, and during 4 months of the fummer and autumn feafons, affords pafture for a 1000 head of cattle. This foreft is the property of his Grace the Duke of Gordon. Further, toward the

the S., and forming a diviſion of the foreſt of Glenavon, lies Glenbuilg, alſo the property of the Duke of Gordon. Glenbuilg will be about 5 miles in length, and between 2 and 3 in breadth. If no part of it were laid under ſheep, it might afford paſturage for 500 or 600 head of cattle.

The long and narrow defile that bounds the ſouthern extremity of the pariſh, and contiguous to the Avon, exhibits a beautiful and pichureſque appearance. It is every where covered with graſs, the ever-green juniper, and the fragrant birch. From the beginning of April, till the middle of November, ſheep and goats, in numerous flocks, are conſtantly ſeen feeding on its pendent ſides. In many of the Grampian mountains are found, precious ſtones of a variety of colours. But whatever may be their ſpecific difference, they are all denominated by the well known name of Cairn-gorm ſtones, that being the mountain in which they have been found in the greateſt abundance. Some of them are beautifully poliſhed by the hand of nature, while others are rude and ſhapeleſs. They are ranked by naturaliſts in the claſs of topazes *.

Population,

---

* Limeſtone is ſo plenty, that there is ſcarcely a farm in the whole pariſh above a mile and a half's diſtance from a quarry of it. Freeſtone is alſo found, but of a ſoft and friable quality. A flate quarry has been opened many years ago, and occaſionally wrought; the ſtone is of a greyiſh colour. It is hard and durable, and ſupplies the neighbouring countries in that article, particularly Strathſpey. So little tenacious is his Grace the Duke of Gordon of his right of property, that he allows every perſon to uſe theſe quarries at pleaſure, free from all reſtraint. Two marl pits have been diſcovered, but lying on the diſtant ſkirts of the pariſh. Farmers have not availed themſelves of the marl as a manure; there are few, however, who uſe not lime for this purpoſe. In the year 1736, an iron mine was opened in the hill Leach-mhic-ghothin, which ſeparates this pariſh from Strathdon, by a branch of the York-Building Company, then reſiding in Strathſpey. It was continued to be wrought till 1739, when, by a derangement in their affairs, they left that country. Since that period, it has been totally abandoned. This mine alſo, is the property of the Duke of Gordon.

Population, &c.—According to Dr. Webſter's report, the population in 1755, was 1288. No ſeſſional records are now in exiſtence belonging to this pariſh, previous to the 1725, when the incumbent before the laſt was admitted. Ever ſince, it has not been poſſible to keep them with accuracy. Diſſenters, of whatever denomination, watch the opportunity of encroaching upon the prerogative of the Eſtabliſhed Church. As the third, then, of the people of this pariſh are Roman Catholics, the prieſt generally takes the liberty of ſharing in the functions that belong to the Proteſtant clergyman *.

By the moſt accurate inquiry, it has been found that this pariſh contains 1276 inhabitants, young and old, and of both ſexes. Of theſe, 384 are Roman Catholics : all the individuals of each profeſſion are included, in 253 families, containing, at an average, 5 perſons to a family, with 265 children

* From this circumſtance, it muſt happen, that there will be ſeveral marriages and baptiſms unknown to the ſeſſion, and conſequently cannot have place in its records. Hitherto, the preſent incumbent has not checked this encroachment, from his averſion to every kind of illiberal intolerance ; but, on the contrary, allowed the Roman Catholic prieſt to uſe every liberty, as if toleration had extended to this country. He allows him to marry and baptize, impoſe penalties, and exact them among his own people, in the ſame manner as if he were of the Eſtabliſhed Church. The writer of this ſtatiſtical article mentions this circumſtance, as he thinks it ought to be an invariable rule of conduct to practiſe that divine precept, in doing to others, as we would wiſh others do unto us. Some years ago, too, the taxes impoſed upon deaths, marriages, and baptiſms, made them be conſidered as a kind of contraband goods, and for that reaſon, many of them were as much as poſſible concealed from publick view, that they might elude an impoſition, which they called tyrannical and oppreſſive. Though in a different language, this novelty, to their experience, incited the people frequently to utter the indignant ſentiment of Bajaculus, general of the Anſibarii, as mentioned by Tacitus, " Deeſſe," ſays he, " terra in qua vivamus, in qua moriamur, non poteſt." To the operations of theſe cauſes, it muſt be imputed, that ſo little ſatisfactory light, reſpecting the population, can be derived from the mutilated records of the ſeſſion of Kirkmichael.

dren under 8 years of age *. During the 4 laſt years, accord‑
ing to a late ſurvey, there have been born, at an average, an‑
nually, 32 children, in the proportion of 21 males to 19 fe‑
males. Old women are found to be more numerous than old
men, in the proportion of 3 to 2. In this period, 10 have
died of each; two men at the age of 95 and 86 years; and
two women at the age of 93 and 95 years. During the
ſame period, 14, at an average, have died annually. There
is juſt now living, two men 88 years each, and three women,
87, 89, and 91, each. The average of marriages for the laſt
4 years, has been 6 annually.—By a pretty accurate calcula‑
tion, the total of black cattle in the pariſh, amounts to 1400,
with 7050 ſheep, 310 goats, and 303 horſes. No other do‑
meſticated animals are reared, except ſome poultry, and a
few geeſe.

Acres, Rent, &c.—The whole pariſh, excluſive of the
foreſt of Glenavon, Glenbuilg, and the hill paſture belong‑
ing to the davoch of Delnabo, the property of Sir James
Grant, contains 29,500 acres, of which little more than 1550
are arable. The whole rent may be about 1100 l. Sterling;
but to a certain extent of graſs following each farm, no rent
is affixed.

Eccleſiaſtical State, Schools, Poor, &c.—The glebe, manſe,
and garden, occupy a ſpace of between 9 and 10 acres, ſitu‑
ated on an eminence, and hanging upon the ſloping ſides. A
part of the ſoil is poor, and a part tolerably fertile. The
value

* By conſulting the ſeſſion records for the years 1749, 1750, and 1751, when
the records appear to have been kept with more than uſual accuracy, in the
firſt of theſe periods, there were born 14 males, and 14 females; in the ſecond,
23 males, and 20 females; and, in the third, 16 males, and 16 females.

value of it may be about 61 *. The church was built in
1747, and has been never fince repaired. As a houfe of
worfhip, it would appear to a ftranger to be totally deferted.
A few broken windows mark the fable walls: the glafs is
broken, and gives free accefs to the winds from all the car-
dinal points. Were the people enthufiafts, a little current of
air might be neceffary to cool them; but in their prefent difpofition, they frequently complain of the inroads of the cold,
to difturb them in their fober meditations; yet they never
exprefs a wifh to remove the inconvenience. Their apathy
is the more extraordinary, as his Grace the Duke of Gordon,
is ever ready to liften to the reprefentations of his people,
and never refufes to grant them a juft and equitable requeft.
Sir James Grant is patron of the parifh. From 1717, till
1786, the ftipend of this parifh was no more than 47 l. 4 s.
5⅓d. Sterling. During the latter of thefe years, his Grace the
Duke of Gordon, informed of the fmallnefs of the living,
was pleafed to beftow upon the prefent incumbent, without
the painful feeling of folicitation, a gratuitous augmentation;
and this at a time when the Court of Seffion were inimical
to fuch claims. The ftipend, at prefent, is 68 l. 6 s. 8 d.
Sterling, with 10 l. Sterling, allowed by his Grace for a houfe.
It will not be deemed a digreffion, to mention that his Grace
gave a farm to the prefent incumbent, at a moderate rent,
when an advanced one, and a fine of 20 guineas were offered
by others.—There are 2 fchools; a Society one at Tammtoul,
with

---

* No grafs is annexed, except a fhare of the common hill pafturage. It lies
at the diftance of 3 computed miles from the mofs, to which there is a bad road,
rifing into afcents, and falling into declivities. In rainy weather, a kind of
gully contiguous to it, becomes impaffable, which frequently prevents the minifter from getting home his fuel in the proper feafon. Owing to this circumftance, he is generally ill fupplied, and obliged to accommodate himfelf at fome
diftance in the neighbourhood, at a confiderable expenfe.

with a ſalary of 13 l. 10 s., and a parochial one at Tamch-
laggan, with a ſalary of 8 l. 6 s. 8 d.—No funds appropriated
for the relief of the poor, have been hitherto eſtabliſhed in
this pariſh. Three years ago, the trifling ſum of 5 l. Sterling, was bequeathed by an old woman ; and, without exaggeration, few pariſhes ſtand more in need of the charitable
contributions of the well diſpoſed. The number of the old
and infirm at preſent on the liſt, amounts to 32 perſons ;
while the annual collection, diſtributed laſt week, came to no
more than 42 s. 6¼ d. Sterling. In this large treaſure, deſign-
ed to be incorruptible, beyond the power of moths and ruſt,
there were 1 s., 5 ſixpences, 443 d., and 50 farthings *.

The price of proviſions in this country has been different,
at different times. In the reign of King William, it is well
known

* In the years 1782 and 1783, the incumbent felt experimentally, the wretched condition of the poor here, and from the neighbouring countries. Though
his own income was only, at that time, 47 l. 4 s. 5⅓ d. ; yet, of this pittance, he
expended, at a moderate calculation, 7 l. Sterling, each of theſe years, in charity. Preaching that virtue to others, the forlorn urged their claims to him for
the practice of his doctrine ; nor were their claims, proportionate to his abilities, refuſed. During the above years, his Grace the Duke of Gordon extended a humane concern to the diſtreſſes of the inhabitants, by ſupplying them in
meal and feed-corn, at a moderate price. No perſon, as far as the writer of
this ſtatiſtical article knows, died of want, though, it may be preſumed, that
a portion of aliment unuſually ſcanty, might prove the ultimate cauſe of the
death of ſeveral. As the poor are peculiarly under the protection of providence, and left as a tax upon the affluence and luxury of their more fortunate
brethren of mankind, it were to be wiſhed, that in pariſhes where there are
no funds, where the contributions are ſmall, proprietors would be pleaſed to
beſtow ſome little annual ſum, under proper reſtrictions, to afford them relief.
Such charity might contribute to ſecure themſelves a property in a more permanent country, and better climate than the preſent, where, even according to
Homer,

Ου νιφετος, ετ αρ χειμων πολυς ετε ποτ ομβρος
Αλλ αει Ζεφυροιο λιγυπνειοντος αητας
Ωκιανος ανιησιν αναψυχειν ανθρωπες.

known that a famine prevailed over the whole kingdom, and continued during feveral years. Either agriculture, at that time, muft have been imperfectly underftood, or the calamity muft have been fevere, when a boll of meal coft 1 l 6 s. 8 d. Sterling. The year 1709, is alfo noted for a dearth, and winter, uncommonly rigorous over every part of Europe *.

Among

* In France, it is defcribed by a Poet of the time, as blafting trees, and af-ecting even the vine.

" ———— hinc," fays he, " noftros et nux et oliva per agros
Interiit, brumæque truci vix reftitit ilex."

The effects were felt in this country, and victual rofe in proportion; the boll of meal coft 1 l. 3 s. Sterling. There are many ftill alive, who remember the year 1740. The frofts came in September, and the fnow fell fo deep in October, that the corn continued buried under it, till January and February following. At that period, the boll of meal rofe to the exorbitant price of 30 s. the boll: and to increafe the mifery of the people, thofe who fold it, frequently mixed it with lime, which to many proved fatal. To fupport life, the people over the Highlands, in general, were obliged frequently to let blood from their cattle, a practice now that is never ufed in this country. About 30 years ago, the feafons being favourable, the boll of meal fold at the low price of 6 s. 8 d. During the laft 20 years, the average price, exclufive of 1782 and 1783, has been about 16 s. Sterling. The price of black cattle and fheep, for 8 years backward, has been, upon the whole, high; cows and calves have fold for 5 l., 6 l., and 7 l. each; fheep and lambs for 10 s. and 12 s. each; oxen for 5 l. and 7 l. each, fometimes 8 l. For the 3 laft years, the prices have abated near a third. Poultry fell for 6 d. and 7 d. each, and pullets for 2 d. and 3 d. each; eggs fell at 2 d. and 3½ d. the dozen. The difference between the prices of thefe articles at prefent, and in ancient times, cannot be accurately afcertained; but before the year 1745, which forms a remarkable æra in the Highlands, oxen fold for 2 l. and 50 s.; cows, with their calves, for 25 s., and 20 s., and 30 s.; and fheep, with their lambs, 2 s. 6 d., and 3 s. 6 d.; and other articles in proportion.

From a confideration of the circumftances of the Highlands, which, previous to the 1745, were in fome meafure ftationary, it may be prefumed, that during a confiderable time, thefe were the ftandard prices; but the fpirit of commerce introduced into the S. of Scotland, operates with extended influence,

and

Among other grievances, it muſt not be omitted, that the inhabitants in this, and the contiguous diſtricts, deſcant with melancholy declamation, on the heavy and increaſing taxation impoſed by Government.   Salt, leather, and iron, whether it be, in order to increaſe the revenue, they are, as it were, farmed out, and have become a kind of monopoly, or that an additional tax is laid upon them ; whatever be the cauſe, they bitterly complain of the unuſual and exorbitant prices of theſe articles.   It is pleaſant to hear them obſerve, that from the tax upon leather, in particular, they will derive one advantage : it will diminiſh the number of beggars, by confining them in winter to their booths to die at leiſure, without the trouble of expoſing them, as the Scythian Alani did their in-

                                                                        firm,

and makes the prices vary here, according to the changes and fluctuations which it produces.

Male ſervants receive 3 l. Sterling, in the half year, the period for which they uſually engage ; boys, 20 s. and 30 s. ; and maids, 20 s. and 25 s. Sterling, in the half year.   The price of day's labour, to men, is 8 d., 10 d., and 1 s. ; and to women 6 d., and ſometimes 8 d.   In theſe, their meat is ſometimes included, but in harveſt, theſe wages are given, excluſive of their victuals.   The advanced price of labour, is one of the grievances of which farmers chiefly complain.   They feel, from experience, that, in point of eaſe, comfort, and independence, the condition of ſervants, is more eligible than that of their maſters. The ſhort term of engagement, wages immoderately high, inſpire them with a pride, inſolence, and indifference, that would frequently require a meek and patient ſpirit to brook.   Nice in the choice of their food to ſqueamiſhneſs, it muſt neither fall ſhort, nor exceed that exact proportion of cookery, which their appetites can reliſh.   Care too muſt be taken, that no offence ſhall be offered them.   They muſt ſleep in the morning as long, and go to bed at night as ſoon, as their pleaſure dictates.   Expoſtulations are oppoſed by rudeneſs.   If their behaviour is diſagreeable, their maſters are at liberty to provide themſelves with others, againſt the firſt term.   And ſeldom do they fail to give ſcope for this liberty.   When the term arrives, then, like birds of paſſage, they change their reſidence, or migrate to diſtant countries.   In the preſent period of their hiſtory, in this and the neighbouring countries, they ſeem to be the only claſs of ſubjects who enjoy the moſt, and abuſe the freedom of the Engliſh Conſtitution.

firm, to the frozen blafts of their bleak mountains. Of every
tax impofed, as felt from experience, the feller is ever fure
to avail himfelf, by exacting double in the price paid by the
purchafer. May not then the queftion be put, whether Poli-
ticians, and the fharp-eyed Argufles of the ftate, fhould not
make provifion againft this fpecies of fraud. The rent of
land is no doubt confiderably augmented, but ftill not beyond
a juft proportion to its productions. But when all the burdens under which the farmer labours are put together, the
exactions of Government, advanced price of labour, augmented rents, fhort leafes, and confiderable fines, it muft be
acknowledged, that the condition of the farmer is far from
being eligible ; and that what Virgil faid of that profeffion,
in his own time, cannot be afferted at prefent.

O fortunatos nimium fua fi bona norint *.

Village, &c.—Tammtoul is the only village within the pre-
cincts of this parifh. It is inhabited by 37 families, without
a fingle

* It is the lot, however, of the generality of this clafs of men, in moft parts
of the Highlands of Scotland, to be better acquainted with the reverfe of the
defcription. To go into their houfes, and take a view of their contents, feats
covered with duft, children pale and emaciated, parents ill clothed with care-
furrowed countenances, exhibits a ftriking picture of Bythinian Phineus, as
defcribed by Apollonius Rhodius, whofe victuals the harpies continually de-
voured, and left the miferable owner to hunger and defpair.

Αρπυιαι στοματος χειρων τ᾽ απο γαμφηλησι
Συνεχεως ηρπαζον.

But in equity, moderation, and humanity, his Grace the Duke of Gordon, is
as much diftinguifhed from many of the other proprietors in the Highlands, as
by his great and opulent fortune. From that rage which now prevails for co-
lonizing the country with fheep, his Grace is happily exempted, and is determined at the expiration of the prefent leafes, to difcourage a practice, that, by
an unreftrained licenfe, would foon depopulate the country of its ancient inhabitants.

a ſingle manufacture, by which ſuch a number of people
might be ſuppoſed to be able to acquire a ſubſiſtence. The
Duke of Gordon leaves them at full liberty, each to purſue
the occupation moſt agreeable to them. No monopolies are
eſtabliſhed here ; no reſtraints upon the induſtry of the community. All of them ſell whiſky, and all of them drink it.
When diſengaged from this buſineſs, the women ſpin yarn,
kiſs their inamoratos, or dance to the diſcordant ſounds of an
old fiddle. The men, when not participating in the amuſe-
ments of the women, ſell ſmall articles of merchandiſe, or
let themſelves occaſionally for days labour, and by theſe means
earn a ſcanty ſubſiſtence for themſelves and families. In
moulding human nature, the effects of habit are wonderful.
This village, to them, has more than the charms of a Theſſa-
lian Tempe. Abſent from it, they are ſeized with the mal
de pais ; and never did a Laplander long more ardently for his
ſnow-clad mountains, than they ſicken to reviſit the barren
moor of their turf-thatched hovels. Here the Roman Catholic prieſt has got an elegant meeting-houſe, and the Proteſtant clergyman, the reverſe of it ; yet, to an expiring mode
of worſhip, it would be illiberal to envy this tranſient ſuperiority, in a country where a ſucceſſion of ages has witneſſed
its abſurdities. A ſchool is ſtationed at this village, attended
by 40 or 50 little recreants, all promiſing to be very like their
parents *.

Antiquities,

* In perſonal reſpect and fortune, at the head of the inhabitants, muſt be
ranked, Mrs. M'Kenzie, of the beſt inn, at the ſign of the horns. This heroine began her career of celebrity, in the accommodating diſpoſition of an eaſy
virtue, at the age of 14, in the year 1745. That year ſaw her in a regiment
in Flanders, careſſing and careſſed. Superior to the little prejudices of her ſex,
ſhe relinquiſhed the firſt object of her affection, and attached herſelf to a noble perſonage high in the military department. After a campaign or two ſpent
in acquiring a knowledge of man, and the world, Scotland ſaw her again ; but
wearied

Antiquities, Eminent Men, &c.—No croſſes, no obeliſks, no remains of antiquity have been hitherto diſeovered in this pariſh. That it was ever viſited by the Romans, is not probable. In that expedition, in which Severus loſt 50,000 men, as recorded by the abbreviator of Dio Caſſius, no veſtige exiſts that any part of his army purſued their rout through the mountains and defiles of Strath-ath-fhin : no marks of encampments are to be ſeen ; there is no tradition, that either Roman urns, or Roman coins have been ever diſcovered. In the year 1715, a ſmall fort was erected in the ſouthern extremity, but ſoon after, it was abandoned, and now lies in ruins *.

As

wearied of the inactivity of rural retirement, ſhe then married, and made her huſband enliſt in the Royal Highlanders, at the commencement of the war in 1756. With him ſhe navigated the Atlantic, and ſallied forth on American ground in queſt of adventures, equally prepared to meet her friends, or encounter her enemies, in the fields of Venus or Mars, as occaſion offered. At the concluſion of that war, ſhe reviſited her native country. After a variety of viciſſitudes in Germany, France, Holland, England, Ireland, Scotland, America, and the Weſt Indies, her anchor is now moored on dry land in the village of Tammtoul. It might be imagined, that ſuch extremes of climate, ſuch diſcordant modes of living, ſuch aſcents and declivities, ſo many rugged paths, ſo many ſevere bruſhes, as ſhe muſt have experienced in her progreſs through life, would have impaired her health, eſpecially when it is conſidered, that ſhe added 24 children to the aggregate of general births, beſides ſome homunculi that ſtopped ſhort in their paſſage. Wonderful, however, as it may appear, at this moment ſhe is as fit for her uſual active life as ever; and except 2 or 3 grey hairs vegetating from a mole upon one of her cheeks, that formerly ſet off a high ruddy complexion, ſhe ſtill retains all the apparent freſhneſs and vigour of youth.

* The great road that paſſes through the country, to facilitate the march of the troops between Perth and Fort-George, was not made till the year 1754 : and now the ſtages are ſo bad, that few travel it. The roads here, in general, are wretched beyond deſcription ; and yet the people, in terms of the ſtatute, are annually called out to work at them. This only can be imputed to their indolence, their want of the neceſſary implements, and the ignorance, or indifference

As far as tradition can be depended upon, no battle, nor
ſkirmiſh of conſequence, ever happened in this country. The
only one mentioned, was fought between Macdonald of the
Iſles, and an Alexander Stewart, chief of that name. The
former, with the greateſt part of his men, was killed, and
from the carnage of that day, the place is ſtill called Blar
nan Mairbh, the moſs or field of the dead *.

If any perſons of eminence were ever born in this diſtrict,
time has ſwept them from its annals. But, if ſuch there have
been, Mr. George Gordon of Foddaletter, is juſtly entitled
to be ranked in the number. This gentleman's abilities roſe
beyond that mediocrity, which ſometimes acquires celebrity
without the poſſeſſion of merit. As a chymiſt and botaniſt,
his knowledge was conſiderable ; and this knowledge he applied to the extenſion of the uſeful arts. At an early period
of life, he diſcovered, that by a certain preparation, the ex-
creſcence of the ſtones and rocks of the mountains, forms a
beautiful

difference of the perſons appointed to ſuperintend them. No good roads can
be expected according to the preſent mode of management. To effect this, a
commutation is abſolutely neceſſary. On the river Ath-fhin, there is a bridge,
where it is croſſed by the great road. Two other bridges, one at Delvoran, and
one at Delnacairn, a little E. of the kirk, would prove eſſentially uſeful, as
they would facilitate the water-courſe, which at preſent is frequently inter-
rupted, and render the communication ſafe and commodious. Another upon
Ailnac at Delnabo, and one upon Conlaſs at Ruthven, would alſo be very neceſſary.

* Caſual rencounters have frequently happened. Manſlaughter, murder, and
robbery, at a period not very remote, form a diſtinguiſhing feature in the character of the Highlanders. But from the detail of ſuch ſcenes of barbarity, the
human mind turns away with horror. One inſtance, however, it may not be
improper to mention: In the year 1575, ſoon after the eſtabliſhment of the Reformation in Scotland, a prieſt who had refuſed to marry the uncle to the niece,
was ſeized by the ruffian and his party, laid upon a faggot, bound to a ſtone,
and in this manner burnt to death. The remembrance of this attrocious deed
is ſtill preſerved in the name of the ſtone, which to this day, is called Clach-ant-
ſhagairt, or the Prieſt's ſtone.

beautiful purple dye. It is called in the Gaelic, crottal, from
crot, a bunch, and eil, a rock. He erected a manufacture of
it at Leith. At that place, in 1765, the inventor died, much
regretted ; while his mind was teeming with various and original projects for the improvement of his country *.

Stature,

---

* As a contrast to the above gentleman, may be mentioned James an Tuim,
or James of the Hill. His real name was Grant, and the nephew of Grant of
Carron, a gentleman of property. While a very young man, he committed
manslaughter at Elgin. Being rigorously profecuted, he betook himself to the
hills and woods of this country for shelter. From that wandering kind of life
to which neceffity had reduced him, he foon became noted for addrefs, ftratagem, activity, and thofe talents that are the refult of the fchool of adverfity.
In confequence of the fucceff attending fome of his folitary adventures, a band
of defperadoes belonging to this parifh, attached themfelves to his fortunes; under his conduct, they became the terror of the furrounding countries, till at
length embracing a wider range, their lawlefs depredations drew the attention
of the parliament of Scotland. A confiderable reward was offered for apprehending him. A gentleman of the name of Macintofh undertook the atchieve-
ment. By corrupting the landlord of an inn, which James an Tuim frequented, he expected to accomplifh his purpofe ; but an hour or two before the
time concerted for the perfidy, fuch was the intelligence of the freebooter, that
he came with his party to the houfe, forced away the landlord, and hung him
to an apple-tree, that marked the march of the contiguous parifh. There is a
letter ftill extant at Caftle-Grant, written by the Privy Council, thanking the
laird of that name for having apprehended him. Imprifoned in the caftle of
Edinburgh, his wonted prefence of mind did not defert him.. His wife came
to vifit him in his confinement, and brought a kit full of ropes with her, covering the furface with butter. By the aid of this machinery, James an Tuim made
his efcape. He went over to Ireland, where having killed one of the moft formidable freebooters of that country, Lord Antrim, as a reward, procured him
a pardon from the Crown ; and having returned to this country, he died a natural death. Such frequently is the exit of the profligate, as well as the virtuous, with refpect to this world. A ftanza is ftill recited in this country, defcriptive of his character, according to the ftandard of excellence that prevailed at the time.

'Ta mo ghradh 's thar gach duinne
   Air Sheimas an Tuim',

Ruidh

Stature, &c.—Many have afferted, that in fize and ftature, the people of modern times, have decreafed confiderably from that of their anceftors. The calculations of a Mr. Hennan of the French Academy, upon this fubject, are curious and eccentric. This gentleman afferts, that Adam meafured 123 feet, and Eve 118. To what diminutive dwarfs is the prefent generation dwindled down, in comparifon of thefe venerable prototypes of the human race. If this account were true, the fable of Tithonus fhould have been realized long ago; and before this period, we muft have been reduced to a fize lefs than that of the grafs-hopper. But laying afide the chimeras of conjecture, every old man in this diftrict can recollect the time when many of the inhabitants were ftronger, bigger, and more robuft than at prefent *. In this and the furrounding countries, the mean fize may be about 5 feet 7 inches.

> Ruidh tu, leumè thu, 's dhanfadh tu cruinn,
> 'S chuireadh tu treun-fhir, a bhar am buinn,
> 'S cha d' fhailnich riamh d mhifnach, do
> Thappa', na d' luim.

" Above all others, James of the Hill is the object of my affection, expert in running, in leaping, and dancing, and in overcoming the brave in wreftling. Thou art the object of my fecret affection." Such accomplifhments, under the direction of an enlightened reafon, might have converted the freebooter into a hero.

* Some little difference may be accounted for, from the operation of natural caufes. When the feafons were more favourable, the population lefs crowded, when neither a heavy taxation, augmented rents, nor conftant labour crufhed the body, nor enfeebled the mind; there is no abfurdity in fuppofing, that in fuch circumftances, men might have attained to a fuller growth and developement of ftature. The tree planted in a kindly foil, ftrikes a ftronger root, and fpreads more verdant branches, than that of the defert, ftinted in its vegetable nutriment, and affailed by the blafts from the N. And it is remarkable, that in that rank of fociety, that is, neither on the one hand, oppreffed by poverty, nor on the other, pampered with luxury, the fymmetry of the human form, is the moft beautiful and perfect.

inches. There are 3 individuals in this pariſh above 6 feet; 13, 5 feet 10 inches; and ſome of them 5 feet 11 inches; there are many who meaſure 5 feet 8 inches in height.

Means of Improvement.—From the geographical view of this country, it will occur to the attentive obſerver, that the condition of the inhabitants appears to admit of little melioration. For the improvements of agriculture and manufactures, the country is ill calculated. Till the country be encloſed, artificial graſs cannot be raiſed; and encloſures would be attended with an expenſe diſproportionate to their circumſtances, as the farms are broken and diſcontiguous; beſides, that to ſucceed in this branch of huſbandry, they would be obliged to diſpenſe with ſheep, at preſent their ſtaple commodity. Upon the ſuppoſition that ſuch a change ſhould happen, as the people are far from the market, graſs would become a drug upon their hands; and to ſubſtitute it in place of ſtraw for provender, would not indemnify them for the expenſe. Such reaſoning may be fallacious, but it is their own, and hitherto has determined them to follow the practice of their anceſtors, to which they have invariably adhered, except in the articles of turnips and potatoes. Of theſe, they raiſe a conſiderable quantity, what may be equal to two months of the annual conſumption of the whole inhabitants.

Manufactures.—In this pariſh, there are 4 mills; the multures of theſe together, will ſcarce amount to 80 bolls of meal, and this quantity multiplied by 32, the proportion paid to each, will make the whole quantity of victual raiſed in the country 2560 bolls. When this number is divided by 1276 individuals, it will be found, that each will have little more to live upon, during the year, than 2 bolls of meal; beſides,

ſides, that from the whole quantity of victual, as mentioned
above, foreign beggars ſubtract, at a moderate calculation,
60 bolls. No manufactures of any kind have as yet been
eſtabliſhed in this country; and the preſumption is, that a conſiderable time muſt elapſe before ſuch an event can happen *.

Learned Profeſſions.—All retainers to the law, except one
ſheriff-officer and three conſtables, if they can be claſſed a-
mong that ſpecies of men, feel this country rather cold for
their reſidence. Never was the ſolemn brow of a Juſtice of
Peace ſeen in the pariſh of Kirkmichael, before laſt autumn.
At that time, two gentlemen, natives, were inſtalled in the
office. Nor is there any danger like the poor ſhoemaker and
tailor, that they will not find ſufficient employment. A ſpirit of litigation, during many years ago, has prevailed among
the people. Unfortunately for them, this ſpirit was originally imported by ſtrangers, perſons whom the courteſy of the
country dignified with the name of gentlemen, but as much
entitled

* Precluded from an eaſy communication with the countries around, living
in the midſt of hills and ſcattered defiles, at the diſtance of 40 meaſured miles
from the neareſt ſea-port, the ſituation of the people is very unfavourable for
ſuch an attempt ; beſides that, they have few materials to work upon. Their
cattle and ſheep, the ſtaple commodities, are driven to the S., and ſold there,
and their wool raw and unwrought, to the low countries of Banff and Moray-
ſhires. Even ſhould that ſpirit of enterpriſe rouſe them, it could not be of
long duration. The difficulty of getting fuel where the centre of the country
lies far from moſſes, the dearneſs of proviſions where the land ſeldom produces
a ſufficiency to ſupport its inhabitants, would dampen their efforts, as they
would ſoon experience the manifeſt advantage of others over them, in the competition of the diſtant market. Before the year 1745, that æra of innovation
in the Highlands, every one almoſt in this country, like the famous Cruſoe, was
his own artiſan. No later than laſt ſummer, a ſhoemaker from Edinburgh, and
a tailor from Dundee, were obliged to deſert the country for want of employment. Where there are almoſt no handicraftſmen, there can be no apprentices.
In a country ſo remote from that element, there can be no ſeamen.

entitled to that character as a Ruffian bear. Now, at 2 annual fairs held at the village of Tammtoul, one may fee the
law-fed vampers walking in confequential ftate, attended by
their clients, while words fweet as honey from their lips
diftil. But this honey, in the iffue, never fails to change into
gall, to fome one or other of the contending parties *. Medical gentlemen are feldom called to this country. Mountain
air, and conftant exercife, render their aid, for the moft part,
unneceffary; befides that, the people can ill afford to pay doctors and retainers of the law at the fame time.

Animals.—The domefticated animals here, have no peculiarity to diftinguifh them from fuch as may be met with almoft in every other part of the Highlands. Thefe have been
defcribed already. The wild ones are deer, foxes, badgers,
polecats, otters, and hares. In former times the ravenous
wolf †, and the bounding chamois, were numerous in the
Grampian mountains ‡. As a proof of this, it may not be
unacceptable

* The gentlemen of the law may be offended at the fuggeftion, but it is
much to be defired, that proprietors would interpofe their authority, by appointing fenfible and impartial men to decide upon the differences arifing a-
mong their people. Such, or the like expedient, might preferve induftrious families from ruin, and the unwary parents, from the dangerous impofition of
pettyfoggers.

† The laft faid to be killed in this country, was about 150 years ago; yet it
is probable that wolves were in Scotland for fome time after that period, as the
laft killed in Ireland was in 1709.

‡ It has been already mentioned, that the Grampian mountains bound this
parifh toward the W. From this country they ftretch in a continued range, almoft without interruption to the Corran of Ard-gothar, where Invernefsfhire
is divided from Argyllfhire, by an arm of the Diu-caledonian fea. Diu-caledonian is derived from Tail, a body of water, and Cael-doine, the Celtic men.
This word the Romans inflected into Caledonia. Mr. Whitaker of Manchefter,
fays, that diu fignifies water. In the Caledonian dialect of the Celtic, at prefent, fuch a word fignifying water, is not known; yet, fuch a word may be fuppofed

unacceptable to the curious reader, to ſubjoin a paſſage from
" Barclay de Regno, et Regáli poteſtate," deſcribing a ſingular
kind of hunting feaſt, with which the Earl of Atholl entertained Mary Queen of Scots *.

In

poſed to have exiſted formerly, as it may ſtill be traced in the name of ſome
rivers. The Caledonian ſea, according to the Alexandrian geographer, extended from the Mull of Galloway to Faro Head. Αρκτικης, ſays he, πλευρας περι-
γραφης υπερκειται Ωκεανος καλεμενος Δεκαλιδονιος.

* " Anno," ſays he, " 1563, Comes Atholiæ ex regio ſanguine princeps,
venationem ingenti apparatu et magnis ſumptibus, optimæ atque illuſtriſſimæ
reginæ Scotiæ exhibuit, cui ego tunc adoleſcens intereci. Cujuſmodi venationem
regiam noſtrales appellare ſolent. Habebat autem comes ad duo millia Scotorum
montanorum, quos vos hic Scotos ſylveſtres appellatis, quibus negotium dedit
et cervos cogerent ex ſylvis et montibus Atholiæ, Badenachæ, Marriæ, Mora-
viæ, aliiſque vicinis regionibus ; atque ad locum agerent venationi deſtinatum.
Illi vero, ut ſunt valde pernices et expediti, ita dies noctesque concurſarunt, ut
intra bimenſis tempus amplius 2000 cervorum, cum damis et capreis unum in
locum compulerint : quos reginæ, principibuſque in valle confidentibus, et cæ-
teris qui una aderant omnibus viſendos venandoſque propoſuerint. Sed ita
mihi crede, omnes illi cervi, velut agmine compoſito incedebant. Hæret enim,
hærebitque ſemper id animo ſpectaculum meo, ut ducem unum et recto-
rem cerneres præeuntem, quem alii quoquo iret ſubſequebantur. Is autem,
cervus erat forma præſtanti et cornibus, ingens qua ex re non mediocrem
animo cepit voluptatem ; cepit mox et timorem, ubi ad eam Atholius, qui ta-
libus a pueritia venationibus aſſueverat, vides inquit ducem illum cornigerum,
qui turmam præit ? periculum nobis ab illo eſt. Si enim aliquis eum furor, ti-
morve ab iſto montis dorſo in hanc planitiem compulerit noſtrum ſibi quiſque
proſpiciat : nemo certe ab injuria tutus erit : quandoquidem cæteri eum ſequen-
tur confertim, et viam, ſibi ad hunc, qui a tergo eſt montem nobis proculcatis
ſtatim aperient. Cujus ſententiæ veritatem alius illico eventus patefecit. Laxa-
tus enim reginæ juſſu atque immiſſus in lupum inſignis admodum atque ferox
canis fugientem inſequitur, ita cervum illum ductorem exterruit, ut retro unde
venerat fugam capeſſeret : cunctique cum eo regreſſi eruperunt ea parte, qua
montanorum corona arctiſſimè cingebantur, ipſis vero montanis nihil ſpei, nihil
perfugii reliquum fuit, niſi ut ſtrati in erica pronos ſe proculcari, aut præteriri
paterentur ; quorum nonnullos cervi tranſiliendo vulnerarunt, alterum quoque
aut tertium peremerunt, ut ſtatim reginæ nunciatum fuit. Et vero ita glome-
rati evaſiſſent omnes, ni homines illi venatus peritiſſimi ipſos è veſtigio ſecuti

arte

In thefe mountains, it is afferted by the country people, that there is a fmall quadruped which they call famh. In fummer mornings it iffues from its lurking places, 'emitting a kind of glutinous matter fatal to horfes, if they happen to eat of the grafs upon which it has been depofited. It is fome-what larger than a mole, of a brownifh colour, with a large head difproportionate to its body. From this deformed ap-pearance, and its noxious quality, the word feems to have been transferred to denote a monfter, a cruel mifchievous per-fon, who, in the Gaelic language, is ufually called a famh-fhear. Other quadrupeds once indigenous to the Grampian mountains are now extinct, and now known only by name; fuch as the Torc-neimh, or wild boar *, an Ion, or the bifon. Lizards, and ferpents, may be frequently met with, and, of the latter, different fpeciefes, fome of them ftriped and variegated, others black and hairy. It is a curious fact, that goats eat ferpents, without any prejudice from their bite. Hence, it has paffed into a proverb, cleas na gaoithr githeadh na nathrach, "like the goat eating the ferpent," importing a querulous temper in the midft of plenty. Incredible as this fact may appear, it may not be improbable. Goats are ani-mals that feed much upon plants and herbs; and upon the fuppofition that the bite of ferpents were more poifonous than what they are known to be in our northern latitudes; yet, by an inftinct of nature, goats might be led to have re-courfe

---

arte quadam extremos ab ipfo agmine diftraxiffent, qui mox reginæ et nobilium canibus in prædam ceffere. Confecti autem eo die fuerunt circiter 360 cum 5 lupis et capreis aliquot."

* It has been afferted by fome antiquaries, that the bear was never a na-tive of Scotland. It is a fact, however, well vouched, that during the refi-dence of the Romans in Britain, bears were fent from it to Rome and baited there. In an ancient Gaelic Poem afcribed to Offian, the hero Dermid is faid to have been killed by a bear on Beinn Ghielleinn in Perthfhire.

courſe to ſuch plants and herbs as are an antidote againſt their bite *.

Wood,

* In confirmation of this ſuppoſition, there is a pleaſant little ſtory told in elegant Latinity, by Vanier the Jeſuit. It will not perhaps be altogether a di-greſſion to cite the verſes.

> Muſtela didicit quondam monſtrante colonus
> Tabificos, quid ruta valet ſerpentis ad ictus,
> Illa reluctantem cum forte laceſſeret anguem ;
> Infectis quoties membris lethale venenum
> Hauſerat, ad rutam fugiens, tactuque ſalubri
> Occulte medicans, non ſegnior ibat in hoſtem,
> Ruſticus excelſo rem demiratus ab agro,
> Avulſis, quæ ſola fuit, radicibus herbam
> Abſtulit ; exanimis cadit heu ! muſtela veneno
> Turgida nam toto rutam dum quæritat agro,
> Intima corda ſubit, jam non medicabile virus.

After this caſual manner, many of the medicaments of modern pharmacy, have been originally diſcovered.

There is alſo a ſmall kind of reptile called bratag, covered with a downy hair, alternately ſpotted into black and white ; if cattle happen to eat it, they generally ſwell, and ſometimes die. It has the ſame effect upon ſheep. The birds in this pariſh are of the ſame genus and ſpecies with thoſe of the neigh-bouring countries ; ſuch as moorfowl, partridges, wild duck, crows, magpies wood pigeons, hawks, kites, owls, herons, ſnipes, king's fiſher, ſwallows, ſpar-rows, blackbird, and thruſh. In the higher hills, are ptarmagans. In the ſteep and abrupt rocks of Glenavon, the eagle builds its eyry ; and during the latter end of ſpring, and beginning of ſummer, is very deſtructive to kids, lambs, and fawns. Some of the more adventurous ſhepherds, watching them at this ſeaſon of depredation, frequently ſcale the rugged rocks, where they neſtle, and ſhare with their young in the ſpoil. Till of late years that his ſe-queſtered haunts have been diſturbed by the intruſion of more numerous flocks of ſheep, the black cock, or gallus Scoticanus, was wont to hail the dawn of the vernal morning amidſt the heaths of this country. If, like the feathered tribe in Æſop, this fine bird could articulate, he might complain with the Poet, " Nos patriam fugimus, et dulcia linquimus arva." Now he has fled to Strath-ſpey, where the numerous and extenſive woods afford him a ſecure retreat. The black cock is well deſcribed by Leſlie, in his Hiſtory of Scotland. " Alia avis," ſays he, " eſt etiam in his regionibus numeroſa, ſuperiore minor [the caper-coille]

Wood, Shrubs, Herbs, &c.—At a period perhaps not very remote, this country was covered with wood. In the hills and moffes by which it is bordered, fir-root is found in fuch abundance, that it fupplies the inhabitants with a warm and luminous light during the tedious nights of winter. Frequently large trunks of the fir are found at a confiderable depth below the furface. Occupied in this employment, many of the poorer people drive the root to the low country, from which they bring meal, iron, falt, and other articles in exchange ; and by this mode of induftry, earn a precarious fubfiftence for themfelves and families during the fummer feafons. No fir-wood, however, at prefent exifts, except a few fcattered trees in the fouthern extremity, upon the banks of the Avon. The only woods to be feen, are birch and alder, and thefe covering but a fmall extent of ground. Till of late, groves of alder, in which were trees of pretty large dimenfions, grew, in feveral places along the banks of the river, but now they are almoft cut down, and will foon be totally confumed. Thefe, with a little hazel, thorns, haw-thorns, holly, willows, and mountain-afh, are the only fpecies of wood that ftill remain. Indigenous fhrubs of different kinds grow wild in the hills, that carry fruit, fuch as wild ftrawberries,

coille] hirfutis pedibus, palpebris rubricantibus; noftri gallum nigrum tefqucrum appellitant." The caper-coille, once a native here, is now totally extinct, and known only by name. He continued in Strathfpey till the year 1745. The laft feen in Scotland, was in the woods of Strathglas, about 32 years ago.

If the fwallow may be excepted, the cuckoo and lapwing, " tiring its echoes with unvaried cries," are the only migratory birds that pay their annual vifits to this country; and after a fhort ftay, wing their flight to more genial climates. The former feldom appears before the beginning of May, and often its arrival is announced by cold blafts from the N., and fhowers of fnow, which are confidered as an aufpicious omen of the approaching fummer. This temporary rigour of the weather is called by the people, glas-fhiontachd na cuach, or the heavy ftorm of the cuckoo.

berries, two kinds of black berries, and two of red berries. In the beginning of harvest, when these fruits are ripe, they are sought for with avidity by the poorer children, to whom, during the season of their maturity, they supply a portion of food. It is probable, that formerly, if at any time the labours of the chase proved unsuccessful, even the men and women of ancient Caledonia allayed their hunger by these spontaneous productions of nature. Dio Cassius expressly asserts, that our ancestors made use of a vegetable preparation, by which they repressed, for a time, that importunate appetite. Cæsar seems to allude to it in his description of the Chara. The soft inflected Chara of the Roman, evidently points to the Còr of the Caledonians. Cor signifies excellent, supereminent, a very expressive and appropriate name, if it supplied the place of food. It grows a little below the surface of the ground, and spreads laterally into several ramifications, carrying larger or smaller knobs according to the soil, and at irregular distances. In spring it protrudes a small greenish stalk, and in summer bears a beautiful flower, which changing into pods, contains seed, when the root becomes insipid and loses its virtue. The country people, even at present, are wont to steep it among water, where having continued for some days, it becomes a pleasant and nutritive drink. Till of late that the little wood of the kind has been better preserved, the inhabitants used in the month of March to extract a liquid from the birch, called * fion-na-uifg, a bheatha, which they considered as very salubrious and conducive to longevity. By an easy metaphor, the name has been transferred to denominate that well known spirit distilled from malt; but a spirit of different effects in its consequence.

It

---

* The wine or water of the birch, or the water of life, in allusion to its salubrity.

It may not perhaps be improper to obferve, that a tradition prevails among the Highlanders, that together with thefe, the Picts were acquainted with the art of extracting a delicious beverage from heath, and of an intoxicating quality. Except to make a yellow dye, the ufes of this fhrub at prefent, are unknown. But there is a probability, that in Auguft, when it carries a beautiful purple bloom, if it were cropped in fufficient quantities, what is now confidered as a fiction, might, by proper fkill, be realized ; for, at that feafon, it emits fragrant and honied effluvia *.

Language.

* The writer of this ftatiftical article is not fo well acquainted with the fcience of botany, as to be able to enumerate the various plants and herbs that grow in this diftrict. He believes few uncommon ones are to be met with, unlefs among the Grampian mountains, which might afford a rich field of obfervation to the naturalift. The plant called an dubh-chofach, black footed, or maiden hair, is frequently gathered among the woods and rocks, and ufed as a tea in afthmatic complaints. Another plant grows in feveral parts of the parifh, and rifes on a ftalk near 2 feet in height. It fpreads into fmall branches, with fharp-pointed leaves of a pale green, and bears a pretty large berry, red at firft, but changing into a livid hue as it ripens. Perhaps it may be the folanum fomniferum of the hiftorian Buchanan, by the aid of which, infufed in the drink, and mixed with the meat prefented by King Duncan to the Danes, he and his generals gained a decifive victory over that barbarous people. This berry is ftill confidered as poifonous by the country people, and they cautiously abftain from it.

Modern fcepticifm rejects the above paffage of the hiftory, and confiders it as fictitious ; but in ancient times when the wants of the inhabitants were few, gratified from the fpontaneous productions of the field, or the beafts of the foreft ; as they lived almoft conftantly in the open air, climbing rugged mountains, or plunging into woody dales ; they muft neceffarily acquire a confiderable knowledge of plants and herbs, together with their various and fpecific qualities : befides that agriculture being in a rude ftate, and many of the prefent domefticated animals unknown, owing to thefe caufes, the vegetable race would arrive at a higher degree of perfection, and their virtues would confequently operate with more energy and effect. In the lift of plants, muft be reckoned the feamrog, or the wild trefoil, in great eftimation of old with the Druids. It is ftill confidered as an anodyne in the difeafes of cattle : from this

circumftance

Language.—The common idiom of this country, is a dia‑
lect of the ancient Celtic, which in remote ages pervaded the
ſouthern and weſtern regions of Europe ; and together with
the Gothic, divided this quarter of the globe into two radi‑
cal and diſtinct languages. Though the latter, owing to the
better fortune of the people who ſpoke it, has prevailed over
the former, yet may a conſiderable portion of the roots of
ſeveral modern languages be traced to a Celtic original. This,
however, is not the place for ſuch difcuſſions. The dialect
ſpoken in this country is growing daily more corrupted, by
the admiſſion of Angliciſms, and a number of terms unknown
to the ſimple arts of the ancient Highlanders. Such is the
folly or bad taſte of the people, that they gratify a prepoſter‑
ous vanity from this kind of innovation. It may therefore
be well ſuppoſed, that the language is upon the decline ; that
the harmony of its cadence is gradually changing, and the
purity of its ſtructure mixing with foreign idioms. The
young people ſpeak Gaelic and Engliſh indifferently, and
with equal impropriety. Their uncouth articulation of dif‑
cordant words and jarring ſounds, reſembles the muſick of
frogs in a Dutch canal, harſh and difguſting to the Attic ear
of a genuine Highlander. Some of the old people ſpeak the
Gaelic, and confequently with a degree of propriety. On
ſubjects of common occurrence, they are at no loſs for ex‑
preſſion in well choſen and natural language. Hence, it may
be inferred, that the pariſh of Kirkmichael ſpoke the ſame
dialect of the Celtic that is now ſpoken in Badenoch, making
allowance for ſome little difference, in point of pronunciation.

In

circumſtance it has derived its name. Seimh, in the Gaelic, fignifying paci‑
fick and ſoothing. When gathered, it is plucked by the left hand. The per‑
fon thus employed, muſt be ſilent, and never look back till the buſineſs be fi‑
niſhed.

In terms defcriptive of the objects of nature and local fituations ; in the names of the feafons of the year, of mountains,
lakes, brooks, and rivers, their language is as juft and appropriate as any in the Highlands of Scotland. There are a
few words, however, that would feem peculiar to themfelves,
but which may be traced to the parent Celtic ; fome words
are ufed by them metaphorically and not unappofitely applied ;
of the latter are brath, fignifying in the Druidical mythology,
fire, particularly the fire of the univerfal conflagration.
Brath is ufed in this country to denote a high degree of vehemence and paffion. Thanig-brath-air—he was feized with
rage. When they would exprefs the impoffibility of per-
forming any thing ; they fay, cha neille linn domh a dheaun-
eamh—no age of mine can perform it. Line in its primitive acceptation, fignifies a generation, but figuratively that
period of time in which a generation becomes extinct. Màné
too, in this country, is ufed to denote good fortune. Ata
manè an èifg air—he has the luck of fifh. From this word,
the manes of the Romans have been originally derived. According to Varro, Manus Deus was a propitious deity with
the ancient inhabitants of Latium. Armun is another word
in ufe among the people here, efpecially in their fongs. They
borrowed it from the Hebrid Ifles. It is of Norwegian extraction, and ufed as the appellative for a hero, derived from
Arminius the celebrated hero of Germany, mentioned by Tacitus. Præliis, fays that admirable writer, ambiguus, bello
non victus.—caniturque, adhuc barbaras apud gentes. In
this country they have ftill many proverbs, and many of them
beautiful, both with refpect to language and fentiment. The
infertion, however, of one of thefe, at prefent, may be fufficient. Eifd, fay they, ri gaoth non gleann, gus an traogh
na 'huifgachaibh—Liften to the winds of the hills till the

waters

waters affuage; importing that paffion fhould be reftrained till the voice of reafon be heard *.

Superftitions,

* The feveral branches of the Celtic now exifting in Europe, are a venerable monument of antiquity. Independent of the intrinfic excellence, were all the words contained in them digefted and formed into a dictionary, it might throw confiderable light upon the hiftory of a people, whofe manners, cuftoms, arts, and fciences, the revolution of ages has fnatched from authentic records. Mr. Gibbon in his Decline and Fall of the Roman Empire, obferves, that there is room for a very interefting work, to lay open the connexion between the language and the manners of a people. Few languages are better calculated for this purpofe than the Celtic. Every one acquainted with it, and endued with a tafte to relifh its beauties, muft acknowledge its energy and defcriptive powers. Equally adapted to melt, or to roufe, it has a ftyle appropriated to the various paffions. Inftead of conveying feeble ideas, it exhibits lively pictures. Sonorous and impreffive, when the occafion requires, it penetrates the inmoft receffes of the foul. When the Greek and Roman languages were in their infancy, the Celtic lent them its aid ; for, many words of the two former are obvioufly derived from the latter. In a period then of fuch enterprife and improvement as the prefent, when philofophic curiofity explores the remoteft corners of the globe, to enlarge the circle of human knowledge, it is fomewhat extraordinary, that a language fo ancient, and once fo widely diffufed, fhould be configned to its fate, without one public effort to preferve its relicks and tranfmit them to pofterity. To accomplifh fuch a defirable object, would not be unworthy of the patronage of the Highland Society of London. As that refpectable body confifts of noblemen and gentlemen of independent fortunes, a fmall fhare of the fuperfluity of their affluence, might be fuccefsfully employed to arreft what ftill remains of the Celtic, and retrieve it from oblivion. Several attempts of this kind have been made, but they have been partial and imperfect. There is ftill wanting a work to embrace the whole, and which cannot be accomplifhed without the patronage and munificence of the great. If the Emprefs of Ruffia has fent learned men to collect and explain the jargons fpoken by the various tribes of barbarians inhabiting the inhofpitable Caucafus, fhould not fuch a liberal example engage the attention, and excite the imitation of a more refined and civilized people ? A dictionary of the Gaelic is now in contemplation in Argyllfhire, and the letters of its alphabet are divided among an equal number of clergymen ; but as thefe gentlemen are confined to a particular county, and confider their own as the ftandard dialect of the Highlands, they make little inquiry concerning the modes of fpeech that prevail in other countries; confequently many pure and genuine Celtic words

muft

Superſtitions, Ghoſts, Fairies, Genii, &c.—In a ſtatiſtical account, even the weakneſſes of the human mind may afford ſome little entertainment. That fear and ignorance incident to a rude ſtate, have always been productive of opinions, rites, and obſervances which enlightened reaſon diſclaims. But among the vulgar, who have not an opportunity of culti-vating this faculty, old prejudices endeared to them by the creed of their anceſtors, will long continue to maintain their influence. It may therefore be eaſily imagined, that this country has its due proportion of that ſuperſtition which ge-nerally prevails over the Highlands. Unable to account for the cauſe, they conſider the effects of times and ſeaſons, as certain and infallible. The moon in her increaſe, full growth, and in her wane, are with them the emblems of a riſing, flouriſhing, and declining fortune. At the laſt period of her revolution, they carefully avoid to engage in any buſineſs of importance; but the firſt and the middle they ſeize with a-vidity, preſaging the moſt auſpicious iſſue to their undertak-ings. Poor Martinus Scriblerus never more anxiouſly watch-ed the blowing of the weſt wind to ſecure an heir to his ge-nius, than the love-ſick ſwain and his nymph for the coming of the new moon to be nooſed together in matrimony. Should the planet happen to be at the height of her ſplendour when the ceremony is performed, their future life will be a ſcene of feſtivity, and all its paths ſtrewed over with roſe-buds of delight. But when her tapering horns are turned towards the N., paſſion becomes froſt-bound, and ſeldom thaws till the genial ſeaſon again approaches. From the moon, they

not

muſt eſcape their reſearches, and be loſt to the language; for this reaſon it would be neceſſary that every corner of the Highlands ſhould be ranſacked, and the words peculiar to each, collected and explained. It may further be obſerved, that the Celtic philologiſt ſhould be well ſkilled in the Latin and Greek lan-guages, and perhaps in thoſe of France and Italy.

not only draw prognoſtications of the weather, but according to their creed, alſo diſcover future events. There they are dimly pourtrayed, and ingenious illuſion never fails in the explanation. The veneration paid to this planet, and the opinion of its influences, are obvious from the meaning ſtill affixed to ſome words of the Gaelic language. In Druidic mythology, when the circle of the moon was complete, fortune then promiſed to be the moſt propitious. Agreeably to this idea, rath, which ſignifies in Gaelic, a wheel or circle, is transferred to ſignify fortune. They ſay, " ata rath air," he is fortunate. The wane, when the circle is diminiſhing, and conſequently unlucky, they call mi-rath. Of one that is unfortunate, they ſay, " ata mi-rath air." Deas uil, and Tuath uil, are ſynonimous expreſſions, alluſive to a circular movement obſerved in the Druidic worſhip.

Nor is it to the moon alone that they direct their regards ; almoſt every ſeaſon of the year claims a ſhare of their ſuperſtition: Saimh-theine, or Hallow Eve ; Beil-teine, or the firſt day of May ; and Oidhch' Choille, or the firſt night of January. The rites obſerved at Saimh-theine, and Beil-teine, are well known, and need not be deſcribed. But on the firſt night of January, they obſerve, with anxious attention, the diſpoſition of the atmoſphere. As it is calm or boiſterous; as the wind blows from the S. or the N.; from the E. or the W., they prognoſticate the nature of the weather, till the concluſion of the year. The firſt night of the New Year, when the wind blows from the W., they call dàr-na coille, the night of the fecundation of the trees ; and from this circumſtance has been derived the name of that night in the Gaelic * language.

* The opinion of the genial and fertilizing nature of the weſt wind, ſo prevalent in many countries of the Highlands, is one of thoſe opinions that ſeem to have deſcended to them from the Druids. Virgil who was born in the Ciſalpine

guage. Their faith in the above figns, is couched in the following verfes:

> Gaoth a deas, teas is torradh,
> Gaoth a niar, iafg is bainne,
> Gaoth a tuath, fuachd is gailinn,
> Gaoth a near, meas air chrannaibh.

" The wind of the S. will be productive of heat and fertility; the wind of the W. of milk and fifh; the wind from the N. of cold and ftorm; the wind from the E. of fruit on the trees."

The appearance of the firft three days of winter is alfo obferved:

> Dorach doirauta' dubh,
> Chead tri la do'n gheamthra;
> Ge be bheire geil dhe'n chroi,
> Cha tugainn 's e gu famthra.

" Dark,

alpine Gaul, and from his fituation had an opportunity of being well acquainted with the doctrines of that order, has adorned his poetry with feveral beautiful allufions borrowed from their philofophic fyftem. It was the impreffion of the fame belief with them, of the impregnating power of the air, that influenced his fancy in that fine paffage in the Georgicks.

> Tum Pater Omnipotens fæcundis imbribus Æther
> Conjugis in græmium lætæ defcendit, et omnes
> Magnus alit, magno commixtus corpore fœtus.

In a fimilar ftrain of belief, he wrote that paffage in the Third Georgick, where he defcribes the effects of the weft wind in a latitude bordering upon the marvellous.

> ——————————————————— illæ
> Ore omnes verfæ in zephyrum, ftant rupibus altis,
> Exceptantque leves auras: et fæpe fine ullis
> Conjugiis, vento gravidæ———————

" Dark, lurid, and ſtormy, the firſt three days of winter ; whoever would deſpair of the cattle, I would not till ſummer."

The ſuperſtitious regard paid to particular times and ſeaſons, is not more prevalent in this country, than the belief in the exiſtence of ghoſts. On the ſequeſtered hill, and in the darkſome valley, frequently does the benighted traveller behold the viſionary ſemblance of his departed friend, perhaps of his enemy. The former addreſſes him in the language of affeﬅion ; if danger is approaching, he is warned to prepare againſt it, or the means of avoiding it diſcloſed. By the latter, he is attacked with the vehemence of reſentment. The inhabitants of this, and the viſitant from the other world, engage in furious combat. For a while, the viﬅory is in ſuſpenſe. At length the ghoſt is overthrown, and his violence appeaſed : a few traits of his life upon earth are deſcribed. If he ſtole a ploughſhare from his neighbour, the place where it lies concealed is pointed out. His antagoniſt is requeſted to reſtore it to the owner ; and if he fails, puniſhment is threatened to follow the breach of promiſe ; for, till reſtitution be made, ſo long muſt the miſerable culprit be excluded from the regions of the happy *.

Not

* Theſe illuſions of fancy operate ſometimes with ſuch force, that ſeverals have died in conſequence of them ; and ſome have been deprived of their reaſon. Fragments of the ſpeeches of ghoſts are frequently recited ; and, like the reſponſes of the Grecian oracles, are generally couched in verſe, eſpecially the more ancient fragments. Two of theſe it may not perhaps be improper to cite in the original. The one is an apoſtrophe from a beloved wife, to ſoothe the melancholy of a deſponding huſband.

Na bidhea' (ſays ſhe) ro ghaol, 's na bidhea' fuath,
Agad air ſluagh innis thrèud ;
Na ſmuanaigh air na chaidhe bhuait,
'S chuid nach teachaidh bhuait, gun deid.

" Indulge

Not more firmly eſtabliſhed in this country, is the belief
in ghoſts, than that in fairies. The legendary records of
fancy, tranſmitted from age to age, have aſſigned their man-
ſions to that claſs of genii, in detached hillocks covered with
verdure, ſituated on the banks of purling brooks, or ſurrounded by thickets of wood. Theſe hillocks are called ſioth-
dhunan, abbreviated ſioth-anan, from ſioth, peace, and dun,
a mound. They derive this name from the practice of the
Druids, who were wont occaſionally to retire to green eminences to adminiſter juſtice, eſtabliſh peace, and compoſe
differences between contending parties. As that venerable
order taught a Saoghl hal, or world beyond the preſent, their
followers, when they were no more, fondly imagined, that
ſeats, where they exerciſed a virtue ſo beneficial to mankind,
were ſtill inhabited by them in their diſembodied ſtate. In
the autumnal ſeaſon, when the moon ſhines from a ſerene
ſky, often is the wayfaring traveller arreſted by the muſick
of the hills, more melodious than the ſtrains of Orpheus,
charming the ſhades, and reſtoring his beloved Eurydice to
the regions of light.

> Cantu commotæ Erebi, de ſedibus imis,
> Umbræ ibant tenues.

Often

" Indulge exceſs neither of joy nor grief toward frail mortals; dwell not on
the remembrance of the dead ; for theſe that now are, muſt ſoon depart."

The other is a ſtanza deſcriptive of the unembodied ſtate, and ſuppoſed to be
uttered by a ghoſt, not unlike that of Patroculus in Homer.

Ψυχη και ειδωλον αταρ φρενες εκ ενι παμπαν

Bha mi (ſays he) fad an cein an roir,
B' eatrom 's bu luainach mo chèim ;
'N duradan 'n gath na grèine,
Cha neille connam fein do neart.

" Far diſtant laſt night, was my journey ; light and bounding were my ſteps;
unſubſtantial as the atom in the beam of the ſun, is the ſtrength of my form."

Often ſtruck with a more ſolemn ſcene, he beholds the viſionary hunters engaged in the chaſe, and purſuing the deer
of the clouds, while the hollow rocks in long-ſounding echoes
reverberate their cries.

Chorus æqualis Dryadum *, clamore ſupremos,
Implerunt montes †.

The

* If one were allowed to indulge in conjecture, and reaſon from analogy, it
might be aſſerted with an appearance of probability, that the dryads and ha-
madryads of the Romans, were the ſame with the druids and druideſſes of the
Celtæ. It is univerſally acknowledged, that the dryads of the Greeks and Romans derive their name from the Greek word δρυς, ſignifying an oak, and druid,
in the Celtic, from darach, or deni, to which the ſame meaning is affixed. Ha-
madryad, is evidently derived, from oi', or oigh, a virgin, always aſperated after the prefix article of the oblique caſe in the Celtic. Notwithſtanding the
progreſſive increaſe of knowledge and proportional decay of ſuperſtition in the
Highlands, theſe genii are ſtill ſuppoſed by many of the people to exiſt in the
woods and ſequeſtered valleys of the mountains, where they frequently appear
to the lonely traveller, clothed in green, with diſhevelled hair floating over their
ſkoulders, and with faces more blooming than the vermil bluſh of a ſummer
morning. At night in particular, when fancy aſſimilates to its own precon-
ceived ideas, every appearance, and every ſound, the wandering enthuſiaſt is
frequently entertained by their muſick, more melodious than he ever before
heard. It is curious to obſerve, how much this agreeable deiuſion correſponds
with the ſuperſtitious opinion of the Romans, concerning the ſame claſs of genii,
repreſented under different names. The Epicurean Lucretius deſcribes the credulity in the following beautiful verſes:

Hæc loca capripedes ſatyros, nymphaſque tenere
Finitimi pingunt, et faunos eſſe loquuntur;
Quorum noctivago ſtrepitu, ludoque jocanti
Adfirmant volgo taciturna ſilentia rumpi
Chordarumque ſonos fieri, dulceiſque querelas
Tibia quas fundit digitis pulſata canentum :

The fauni are derived from the eubates, or faidhin of the Celtæ. Faidh is a
prophet; hence is derived the Roman word fari, to prophecy.

† There are ſeveral now living, who aſſert that they have ſeen and heard
this aerial hunting; and that they have been ſuddenly ſurrounded by viſionary
forms, more numerous than leaves ſtrewed on the ſtreams of Vallumbroſa in
November

The fame credulity that gives air-formed inhabitants to green hillocks and folitary groves, has given their portion of genii to rivers and fountains. The prefiding fpirit of that element, in Celtic mythology, was called Neithe. The primitive of this word, fignifies to wafh, or purify with water. In the name of fome rivers, it is ftill retained, as in the river Neithe of Abernethy in Strathfpey. To this day, fountains are regarded with particular veneration over every part of the Highlands. The fick who refort to them for health, addrefs their vows to the prefiding powers, and offer prefents to conciliate their favour. Thefe prefents generally confift of a fmall piece of money, or a few fragrant flowers. The fame reverence, in ancient times, feems to have been entertained for fountains by every people in Europe. The Romans who extended their worfhip to almoft every object in nature, did not forget in their ritual, the homage due to fountains. It is to this, Horace alludes in his addrefs to his limpid fountain of Blandufia.

O fons Blandufiæ fplendidior vitro,
Dulci digne mero, non fine floribus,
Cras donaberis hædo *.

Near

November blafts, and affailed by a multitude of voices, louder than the noife of rufhing waters.

About 50 years ago, a clergyman in the neighbourhood, whofe faith was more regulated by the fcepticifm of philofophy, than the credulity of fuperftition, could not be prevailed upon to yield his affent to the opinion of the times. At length, however, he felt from experience, that he doubted what he ought to have believed. One night as he was returning home, at a late hour, from a prefbytery, he was feized by the fairies, and carried aloft into the air. Through fields of æther and fleecy clouds he journied many a mile, defcrying, like Sancho Panza on his Clavileno, the earth far diftant below him, and no bigger than a nut-fhell. Being thus fufficiently convinced of the reality of their exiftence, they let him down at the door of his own houfe, where he afterward often recited to the wondering circle, the marvellous tale of his adventure.

* Some modern antiquaries have afferted, that the Celtic nations never worfhipped

Near the kirk of this pariſh, there is a fountain once high-ly celebrated, and anciently dedicated to St. Michael. Many a patient have its waters reſtored to health, and many more have atteſted the efficacy of their virtues. But, as the pre-ſiding power is ſometimes capricious, and apt to deſert his charge, it now lies neglected, choked with weeds, unho-noured, and unfrequented. In better days it was not ſo ; for the winged guardian under the ſemblance of a fly, was never abſent from his duty. If the ſober matron wiſhed to know the

ſhipped rivers, and had no divinities appropriated to them. Several ancient au-thorities, however, might be adduced to evince the contrary. Gildas expreſsly ſays, " Ut omittam," talking of the Britons, " montes ipſos, aut colles, aut flu-vios, quibus divinus honor a cæco tunc populo cumulabatur." The vulgar in many parts of the Highlands, even at preſent, not only pay a ſacred regard to particular fountains, but are firmly perſuaded that certain lakes are inhabited by ſpirits. In Strathſpey, there is a lake ſtill called Loch-nan Spioradan ; the lake of ſpirits. Two of theſe are ſuppoſed frequently to make their appearance, the one under the form of a horſe beautifully capariſoned, with golden trap-pings. With the bit of his bridle, the anti-conjurer of this pariſh expels jea-louſy, and cures other maladies of the mind. The other under that of a bull, docile as Jupiter wafting Europa over the Helleſpont. The former is called, an each uiſg, the horſe of the water ; the latter, an taru uiſg, the bull of the water. The mhaidan mhare, or mermaid, is another ſpirit ſuppoſed to re-ſide in the waters. Before the rivers are ſwelled by heavy rains, ſhe is fre-quently ſeen, and all the attributes of a beautiful virgin aſcribed to that part of her perſon that is viſible. Her figure is enchanting, and her voice melodious as that of the Syrens. But fair as ſhe is, her appearance never fails to announce ſome melancholy accident on her native element. It is always conſidered as a ſure prognoſtication of drowning.

In Celtic mythology to the above named, is added a fourth ſpirit. When the waters are agitated by a violent current of wind, and ſtreams are ſwept from their ſurface and driven before the blaſt, or whirled in circling eddies aloft in the air, the vulgar, to this day, conſider this phenomenon as the effect of the angry ſpirit operating upon that element. They call it by a very expreſſive name, the mariach ſhine, or the rider of the ſtorm. Anvona is alſo reckoned as a divinity of the waters, derived from anfadh, a ſtorm or hurricane, a com-pound from an, a particle of privation, and feadh, ſerenity, tranquillity.

the iffue of her hufband's ailment, or the love-fick nymph, that of her languifhing fwain, they vifited the well of St. Michael. Every movement of the fympathetic fly was regarded in filent awe ; and as he appeared cheerful or dejected, the anxious votaries drew their prefages ; their breafts vibriated with correfpondent emotions. Like the Delai Lama of Thibet, or the King of Great Britain, whom a fiction of the Englifh law fuppofes never to die, the guardian fly of the well of St. Michael, was believed to be exempted from the laws of mortality. To the eye of ignorance he might fometimes appear dead, but, agreeably to the Druidic fyftem, it was only a tranfmigration into a fimilar form, which made little alteration on the real identity *.

Among the branches into which the mofs-grown trunk of fuperftition divides itfelf, may be reckoned witchcraft and magic. Thefe, though decayed and withered by time, ftill retain fome faint traces of their ancient verdure. Even at prefent, witches are fuppofed, as of old, to ride on broomfticks through the air. In this country, the 12th of May is one of their feftivals. On the morning of that day, they are frequently feen dancing on the furface of the water of Avon, brufhing the dews of the lawn, and milking cows in their fold. Any uncommon ficknefs is generally attributed to their demoniacal practices. They make fields barren or fertile,

---

* Not later than a fortnight ago, the writer of this account was much entertained, to hear an old man lamenting with regret, the degeneracy of the times ; particularly the contempt in which objects of former veneration were held by the unthinking crowd. If the infirmities of years, and the diftance of his refidence did not prevent him, he would ftill pay his devotional vifits to the well of St. Michael. He would clear the bed of its ooze, open a paffage for the ftreamlet, plant the borders with flagrant flowers ; and once more, as in the days of youth, enjoy the pleafure of feeing the guardian fly fkim in fportive circles over the bubbling wave, and with its little probofcis, imbibe the Panacean dews.

tile, raife or ftill whirlwinds, give or take away milk at pleafure. The force of their incantations is not to be re-fifted, and extends even to the moon in the midft of her aerial career. It is the good fortune, however, of this coun-try to be provided with an anti-conjurer that defeats both them and their fable patron in their combined efforts. His fame is widely diffufed, and wherever he goes, *crefcit eundo*. If the fpoufe is jealous of her hufband, the anti-conjurer is confulted to reftore the affections of his bewitched heart. If a near connexion lies confined to the bed of ficknefs, it is in vain to expect relief without the balfamick medicine of the anti-conjurer. If a perfon happens to be deprived of his fenfes, the deranged cells of the brain muft be adjufted by the magic charms of the anti-conjurer. If a farmer lofes his cattle, the houfes muft be purified with water fprinkled by him. In fearching for the latent mifchief, this gentleman never fails to find little parcels of hetrogeneous ingredients lurking in the walls, confifting of the legs of mice, and the wings of bats ; all the work of the witches. Few things feem too arduous for his abilities ; and though, like Paracelfus, he has not as yet boafted of having dif-covered the Philofopher's ftone; yet, by the power of his occult fcience, he ftill attracts a little of their gold from the pockets where it lodges ; and in this way makes a fhift to acquire a fubfiftence for himfelf and family. What Dry-den faid of Shakefpear, may, with propriety, be applied to him :

"Shakefpear's magic could not copied be ;
"Within that circle none durft move but he."

If the fhort limits of a ftatiftical effay permitted, more juftice might be done to this fingular character, but, *ex pede Herculem ;*

Herculem ; the outlines already given, will enable fancy to draw the portrait.

Dreſs.—Since the year 1745, there is a conſiderable change on the dreſs of the people of this diſtrict. By a ſingular kind of policy, as if rebellion lurked in the ſhape and colour of a coat, at the above period, the ancient dreſs was proſcribed and none durſt wear it without running the riſk of a rigorous proſecution. It was conſequently ſuperſeded by the Low Country dreſs. To the ancient braccæ, or truiſh * and belted plaid, ſucceeded ſtrait breeches, and an awkward coat of a uniform colour ; ſometimes a long ſurtout dangling down to the heels, encumbring the freedom of motion. The barbarous policy of Edward the Firſt, did not more effectually deſtroy the ſpirit of the indignant Welſh, by the murder of their bards, than the prohibition of their ancient garb, that of the poor Highlanders. In the enthuſiaſm of patriotiſm, Mr. Fraſer of Lovat got the prohibitory act repealed, in order, according to his own emphatic words, " to divert the minds of the people from Tranſatlantic notions." Let metaphyſicians, if they chooſe, trace the connexion. But, though this reſpectable gentleman, with the view of making them good ſubjects, procured liberty to the Highlanders of expoſing their naked poſteriors to the north wind, on their bleak mountains, few have availed themſelves of the privilege. Habit reconciles them to the preſent, and they ſeem to have no deſire of reſuming their ancient garb. The blue bonnet, however, with the exception of ſome round hats, ſtill maintains its ground. Since the year 1745, the women too, like the men, have altered conſiderably in their apparel. Before that period, they wore ſometimes white blankets covering

their

* Truiſh, from trusà, or dreſs.

their heads, fomctimes their fhoulders, drawn forward by
their hands, furrounded on each fide by a fold. Thefe, as
fafhion varied, were fucceeded by barred plaids. or blankets,
where different colours blended, croffing each other at right
angles, fomewhat diftant, and bearing a fquare fpace in the
middle. Wearied of barred plaids, they betook themfelves
to Stirling ones, and now duffle cardinals begin to have the
afcendant. Formerly their hair flowed in eafy ringlets over
their fhoulders; not many years ago, it was bound behind into a cue, now it fpreads into a protuberance on the forehead,
fupported by cufhions ; fometimes, it is plain, and fplit in
the middle. But who can defcribe the caprice of female ornament more various than the changes of the moon !

Manner of Living.—Not more than 50 years ago, their
mode of living in this country was different from what it is
at prefent. Places that were at that time wafte, are now planted with inhabitants. And though fheep, upon the whole, be
more numerous than formerly; yet they are chiefly the property of thofe who occupy the out-fkirts, and to whom the
hills and glens lie more convenient. In the centrical places,
the farms are enlarged, at leaft as much as the nature of the
ground can admit; confequently the fmaller tenants are fewer,
and live lefs at their eafe : but previous to the above period,
even cottagers kept a few fheep, becaufe the hill pafture was
a common, and there were few of any defcription who did
not occafionally feed upon flefh. But at prefent, unlefs it be
at Chriftmas, or when any little feftivals are celebrated, the
fold is kept facred for the market, in order to make money
to fupply the exigencies of the family, and fatisfy the many
demands to which it is expofed, from bad feafons, precarious
crops, and increafing taxes : befides that, the luxury of the

times

times has imported into this country, inacceffible as it is to other improvements, a portion of factitious wants, which muft be gratified. Fifty years ago, they ufed burnt plates of whifky, inftead of that fpirit, which muft now be diluted with warm water, and fweetened with fugar. It muft, however, be acknowledged, that it is feldom they indulge in this beverage; they oftener drink it raw and unmixed. It may eafily be fuppofed that a plant of fuch univerfal confumption as tea, fhould not be unknown to the people of this country. Few of the better families are without it, though fparingly ufed; and fome of the old women, even when they cannot afford fugar, infufe it in boiling water, and drink it for their headachs. Thefe headachs frequently return, but fortunately by the aid of the grand elixir, they are feldom of long duration.

Character, &c.—The character of a people never fails to change with their changing condition. In contemplating them at the extreme points of a period of 70 or 80 years, it would be as difficult to recognife their identity, as that of Sir John Cutler's worfted ftockings, when fcarcely an atom of the original texture remained. Not further removed than the more diftant of thefe extremes, the people of this country were generous and hofpitable. If they were occafionally fubject to the foibles, they poffeffed the virtues of genuine Highlanders. If they refented injuries with vehemence and paffion, their breafts felt the glow of affection and friendfhip. Attached to their chieftain, they followed his ftandard whereever it led; and never fhrunk from danger in the defence of his caufe: Connected with the freebooters of Lochaber, they imbibed no inconfiderable portion of their fpirit and manners: Addrefs and ftratagem marked their enterprifes: Active abroad

broad, they were indolent at home : Addicted to depredation, they neglected the arts of industry and agriculture : Disengaged from those pursuits that require vigour and exertion, they passed the vacant hour in social enjoyment, in song and festivity, and in listening to the tale of other years : Rude in their manners, their bosoms frequently opened to the warm impressions of a disinterested benevolence. The indigent and the stranger found them always ready to sympathize with their distress. What Paul the Deacon, in his barbarous Latin, said of the Lombards of Italy, might be applied to them :

> Terribilis facies, hirsutaque barba,
> Sed corda benigna fuerunt *.

But, in contemplating the nearer extreme of the above period, a different picture appears. The spirit of commerce which, in a certain degree has pervaded every corner of the Highlands, with its natural concomitants, avarice and selfishness, has penetrated hither. In the private views of the individual, the interests of the community are disregarded. Cunning has supplanted sincerity, and dissimulation candour : Profession supplies the place of reality, and flattery is used as a lure to betray the unwary. Obligations are rewarded by ingratitude ; and when the favour is past, the benefit is no longer remembered. Opposed to interest, promises cease to be binding ; and the most successful in the arts of deception acquires the esteem of uncommon merit and abilities. It may therefore be supposed, that, in a field where the prize is so attractive,

* A dreadful countenance, with rough beards, but with hearts benevolent.

tractive, there will be many candidates. To aid them in this career of ambition, it muſt be acknowledged, in alleviation of their bias, that they have had models of imitation not unworthy of the doctrines of a Machiavel. Unfortunately for them, theſe models have been ſtrangers, and of that rank in life who have always the moſt powerful influence in making proſelytes among the vulgar.

Such are the cauſes to which it muſt be imputed, that there is ſo little diſcrimination to be obſerved in the character of the people of this country; for, where one object is purſued, the means of attainment will be generally uniform. Suſpended between barbariſm and civilization, the mind is never ſo ſtrongly influenced by virtue, as it is attracted by the magnetiſm of vice. In this view, however, they are not ſingular from their neighbours. From a combination of cauſes, particularly high taxation, and increaſing commerce, avarice and ſelfiſhneſs muſt neceſſarily conſtitute a prominent feature in the character of many. At the ſame time, there may ſtill be found the uſual proportion of perſons of a different character, conſpicuous for honour and integrity, humane and benevolent, juſt and upright in their tranſactions.

Miſcellaneous Obſervations.—It has been obſerved, that the centrical parts of this country lie at a conſiderable diſtance from moſs, which is yearly diminiſhing in proportion to the conſumption. From the increaſe of population, and as the natural woods are every where decaying, the period is approaching, when the Highlands muſt ſenſibly feel the difficulty of procuring the neceſſary accommodation of fuel. To anticipate ſuch an event, is an object that peculiarly calls for the attention of proprietors. There are few of this deſcription in the Highlands, who are not poſſeſſed of conſiderable

tracks

tracks of moor and hill. In this diſtrict, there are at leaſt 18,000 acres that lie barren, and at preſent of little value. This ſpace of ground laid under fir, would contain, at a moderate calculation, 80,000,000 plants, excluſive of the foreſt of Glenavon, and without much injury to the paſture. By converting the waſte ground to this purpoſe, the rent of the proprietors would increaſe, while the farmer would be ſupplied in fuel, and materials for building. Plantations of fir ſo extenſive, may appear an arduous undertaking ; but by giving farmers long leaſes, indemnifying them at removal, appropriating a portion of the rent for the purpoſe, and various methods that might be deviſed, it might be ſucceſsfully carried into execution ; and when accompliſhed, would be worthy of a great and patriotic proprietor. It has been aſſerted, that moſs grows ; but this is a fallacy too obvious to be credited. Being the production of wood and moiſture, it is well known from experience, that when the component ingredients are once exhauſted, the ſubſtance itſelf cannot be reproduced. Upon the formation of moſs, there is a curious fact mentioned by Lord Cromarty, and recorded in the 5th volume of the Abridgement of the Philoſophical Tranſactions *.

No

* In the year 1651, his lordſhip being then 19 years of age, he ſaw a plain in the pariſh of Lochbroom, covered over with a firm ſtanding wood, which was ſo old, that not only the trees had no green leaves, but the bark was totally thrown off, which he was there informed, by the old people, was the univerſal manner in which fir wood terminated ; and that in 20 or 30 years the trees would caſt themſelves up by the roots. About 15 years afterwards, he had occaſion to travel that way, and obſerved that there was not a tree, nor the appearance of a root, of any of them ; but that, in their place, the whole plain where the wood ſtood, was covered with a flat green moſs, or morafs : and, on aſking the country people what was become of the wood, he was anſwered, that no one had been at the trouble of carrying it away, but that it had been overturned by the wind ; that the trees lay thick over one another ; and that the

No complaint feems to be more univerfal over the Highlands, nor in this country in particular, than the increafing inclemency of the feafons. Modern philofophers attribute this phenomenon to the vaft fhoals of ice accumulating in the northern feas. But whatever be the caufe, the opinion of the effect prevails among the people. Since the year 1768, they obferve, that the fummers are colder, and productive of greater quantities of rain, than was remembered in the fame fpace of time, during any preceding period. The affertion, though conjectural, appears to be founded upon probability. Even within thefe 20 laft years, the beds of brooks and rivers are confiderably enlarged, and much of the contiguous grounds deftroyed by the floods. The trouts, that formerly fwarmed in lakes and rivers, are exceedingly decreafed. The few migratory birds that vifit the country, are later in their arrival, and fooner take their departure: The hum of the mountain bee is not fo frequently heard: even the infect tribes that fluttered in the air of a warm fummer, are lefs prolifick than ufual. In Glenavon, of this parifh, are moffes, near 3000 feet above the level of the fea, full of the fir root; where no wood at prefent, owing to the cold, could grow. Some of the higheft hills in the Grampian defert, are denominated from the wood which formerly grew upon them, fuch as beinn a chaorin, the mountain of the fervice tree. Are thefe then appearances the refult of a temporary ceffation, or has nature become more languid in her energies? Such, however, are the affertions of the old people, the never-failing

the mofs or bog had overgrown the whole timber, which they added, was occafioned by the moifture which came down from the high hills, and ftagnated upon the plain; and that nobody could yet pafs over it, which, however, his lordfhip was fo incautious as to attempt, and flipt up to the arm-pit. Before the year 1699, that whole piece of ground was become a folid mofs, where the peafants dug turf or peat, which, however, was not yet of the beft fort.

failing panegyrists of the times that are elapsed. Mr. Hume, and the Abbè du Bois, are of a different opinion, and assert, that in ancient times, the seasons were colder than at present, but the facts adduced by these respectable writers are too vague and remote to overthrow the experience of feeling *.

* William the Norman, after the conquest of England, surveyed that country, and committed the admeasurement to Doomsday Book, designed to be a permanent record of the nature and value of the soil; that gradation of offices, and those institutions which he embraced in his political scheme. The imitation of a model that might be so conducive to promote the welfare of the great body of the people employed in agriculture, should perhaps, with that variation required by circumstances, be in some measure adopted by all the proprietors in Scotland. It is well known that the value of land must rise or fall, according to the flourishing or declining condition of the state. Reason dictates that it is by this criterion the rents of a landlord ought to be regulated. When at a certain term lands are to be let, and exposed, as it were to a public sale, the highest biddder to have the preference, it must occur, that in such a collision of passions, and jarring interests, as must necessarily arise upon those occasions, the desperate and unprincipled will frequently be preferred to the honest and industrious; besides that, the rents of some farms will be low and moderate, while that of others will be high and exorbitant. To prevent, therefore, this inequality, and to extend distributive justice to every individual, proprietors should not only survey their properties, but also affix a value to the farms, according to the value of the productions at the time, and the probable continuance of that value. Every circumstance of convenience and inconvenience, whether with regard to fuel, the nature of the soil, and the condition of the farm, should likewise be taken under consideration, and a rent proportionate affixed. Judicious men acquainted with the place, and obliged, by proper sanctions, to observe a strict impartiality, would perhaps be the most proper to accomplish such a desirable object. These hints may appear chimeral, but there would be no harm in the experiment; and, if practicable, might prove highly advantageous, both to the proprietor and tenant, by promoting their reciprocal interests. Such a plan, without having recourse to the levelling principle of modern innovations, might have a happy tendency in diffusing the comforts of life more equally, and at the same time, maintain that distinction of ranks so necessary to the existence of society.

Referring to p. 312

Iᴛ is curious to obſerve the oppoſition between the opinion of the Highlanders, founded upon experience, and the reaſoning of philoſophers derived from ſpeculation, with reſpect to the varying degrees of the heat and cold of the ſeaſons in ancient and modern times. Thoſe who aſſert that the ſeaſons have become more mild and genial, maintain this opinion upon the authority of the claſſick writers, without conſidering, that in eſtimating, the cold and heat of other countries, a Greek or Roman, would naturally make their own warm latitudes the ſtandard of their feelings. In forming a ſyſtem, few facts ſerve as a foundation for rearing a ſpecious ſuperſtructure. That the quantity of water upon the face of the globe is decreaſing, has been attempted to be proved from the induction of experiment. The philoſophers of Sweden, by meaſuring the waters upon the ſhores of the Baltick, have found that they ſink in the proportion of half an inch annually. But are there no inſtances in other countries, where they riſe in a ſimilar proportion. During the ninth century, the Danes in their predatory excurſions, built a fort upon the Moray Frith, which is now covered by water, but ſtill viſible in its ruins when the ſea is tranquil on a ſerene ſummer day. It muſt, however, be acknowledged, that the above opinion of the gradual decreaſe of the waters, is not a novelty in ſpeculation. It was embraced, in part, by the ancient ſect of the Druids, who held the deſtruction and renovation of the world by fire and water alternately. The Stoicks alſo taught the ſame doctrine, as may be ſeen, by conſulting the ſecond book of Cicero's beautiful Treatiſe, " De Natura Deorum."

PARISH OF MARNOCH,

(*County of Banff.*)

By the Rev. *Mr* JAMES INNES.

———————

Name, Situation, Soil, and Productions.

ABERCHERDER was the old name of this country and pariſh, which is now called *Marnoch*, the church being dedicated to St Marnoch. This pariſh lies in the county of Banff, preſbytery of Strathbogie, and ſynod of Moray. It is from nine to ten meaſured miles in length, and from four to five in breadth. In general it is rather flat, low-lying land, being moſtly ſurrounded with hills upon the weſt, north, and eaſt, which are covered with heath. The river Doveron, which is not navigable, runs from five to ſix miles along the ſouth ſide of the pariſh. The ſoil near the banks of the river, is a rich loam, and produces good crops. Toward the upper part of the country, it is wet, ſtoney, and ſtiff. The crop conſiſts of barley, oats, peaſe, potatoes, and turnips. A very large quantity is annually exported from Banff, Port-ſoy, or M'Duff. The beſt arable and meadow ground rents *per* acre from 15 s. to 20 s.; the rent of inferior from 6 s. 8 d. to 2 s. 6 d. The pariſh is fully provided with good peats. Conſiderable numbers of cattle are reared yearly and ſold, and likewiſe a large quantity of butter and cheeſe. There are ſeveral extenſive plantations of various kinds of

wood,

wood, viz. common fir, fpruce, larix, and pine, beech, oak, elm, afh, birch, and alder, moft of them in a very thriving condition, and fome of them well advanced in fize. There being no meafurement of the parifh, the extent of the farms cannot be precifely afcertained. There are farms that pay rent from L 40 to L. 70 Sterling, and many leffer ones from L. 10 to L 8 Sterling, and a very great number of fmall crofts from L. 5 and L. 6 down to L. 1 of rent.

Difeafes.—The air is wholefome, and the people in general healthy. Except a few tradefmen, they are not employed in a fedentary life; being either country gentlemen, farmers, or crofters, their bufinefs occafions them to be much in the open air. No local diftempers take place in this parifh, confumptions and fevers are the moft prevalent.

Rent, &e.—The rent of the parifh is L. 2300 Sterling yearly. The only language fpoken in it is Englifh.

Church.—The church is very old, and in a very ruinous condition. James Donaldfon, Efq; of Kinnairdie, is the patron. About twenty years ago, the church was repaired, and galleries were erected fufficient to accommodate 300 people. A new and much larger church is to be built next year, which clearly fhows the increafe of population here, occafioned partly by a good many extenfive farms being parcelled out and let in crofts, which alfo made a confiderable increafe of rent to the heritors.

The living was augmented in 1789; and is now L. 45 in money, 90 bolls of meal, and 22 bolls of bear. There are ten heritors in this parifh, four of whom refide in it,

whofe

whose farms are mostly inclosed ; but the rest of the country, in general, is not.

Poor.—There are seven upon the poor's roll. The sum of L. 40 Sterling is yearly expended for their relief, which arises from the collections of the church, penalties, a small payment for the mort-cloth, and hand-bell, at burials, with the annualrent of L. 100 settled for their relief.

Prices of Labour,—A ploughman's wages are from L. 5 to six guineas a-year, other men servants about L. 5 Sterling. A woman servant from L. 2 to L. 3 a-year.

Eminent Men.—Marnoch has produced no man eminent in learning or science, except Alexander Gordon, Esq; late of Achentoule, who entered into the army of Czar Peter the Great, and by his personal valour and good conduct in the war carried on against Charles XII. King of Sweden, was raised to the rank of Major-General, and wrote his history.

Character of the People.—The people are industrious. Few of them inlist in the army. They enjoy in a reasonable degree, the comforts and advantages of society, and are contented with their situation. They are decent, active, and humane. It is very remarkable, that during the time of the present incumbent, which is now almost 36 years, none have emigrated, neither has any single person been condemned or even tried for a capital crime.

Population, &c—The births, deaths, and marriages, as entered in the parish register, for the last seven years, stand thus :

Years.

Years.	Births.	Deaths.	Marriages.
1784	28	20	13
1785	24	20	15
1786	37	21	8
1787	28	12	7
1788	36	17	8
1789	37	16	14
1790	37	9	7

By an enumeration made this year, the whole population amounts to 1960, 84 of which are Roman Catholics, 60 Episcopals, and eight or ten Seceders. In Dr Webster's report the number was 1894.

The bridges were built, and are held in repair by the county, and the roads by the statute labour. There are about 500 work horses, and about 3000 cattle, in the parish. There are about 500 different families, which, at an average, will make near four persons in each. There are no houses uninhabited, and many more have been lately built than pulled down.

School.—The schoolmaster has only 100 merks salary, two guineas as session-clerk, 1 s. *per* quarter for teaching English, 1 s. 6 d. for writing and reading, and 2 s. for Latin and arithmetic; 3½ d. for each certificate, 6½ d. for each baptism, and 1 s. 7 d. for each marriage. At the parochial school there are from 12 to 20 or 30 scholars; at the charity school in Foggicloan from 40 to 60.

There are six alehouses in the parish.

PARISH OF MORTLACH.

(COUNTY OF BANFF.—PRESBYTERY OF STRATHBOGIE.
SYNOD OF MORAY.)

By the Rev. Mr GEORGE GORDON, *lately Minister there, and now one of the Ministers of Aberdeen.*

Name.

THE name is very ancient. About 800 years ago, in the charter given by Malcolm the Second to the first Bishop of this early See,—and how long before, no body can say, it was called Murthelack or Murthlac, much the same as at present.

Etymology.—The word is most probably of Gaelic origin, derived from something local. Because the church is in a deep though narrow valley, some naturally enough think it a corruption of Morlay, Great Hollow. Others again chuse to bring it from mortis lacus, the lake of death ; alluding to a battle which was fought here, and which shall afterwards be taken notice of. But this seems only a fancy of Buchanan, and is far fetched : More conjectures have been made, and on the whole the etymology is doubtful : Luckily however, like many an obscurity of the kind, it is of very little importance.

Situation.—Mortlach is encircled by six other parishes, having Glass on the east, Cabrach and Inveraven to the south, Aberlour on the west, with Boharm and Botriphny towards

the

the north ; and several of these, it is not unlikely, are the offspring of the mother church. It is in the county of Banff, in the Commissariot of Aberdeen, and in the province of Moray ; lying nearly 50 miles to the westward, but a little to the north, from the city of Aberdeen, and about 30 south west from the town of Banff, the capital of the shire. Since the 1706, it has been, by an act of the General Assembly, in the presbytery of Strathbogie and synod of Moray : Before that time, it was in the presbytery of Fordyce and synod of Aberdeen : And in a connection with Fordyce, the minister of Mortlach, it is said, has still a vote for delegates, from that presbytery, to elect the professors of Divinity of King's College of Aberdeen, and has also some trust and management in certain lands or sums of money bequeathed to that university.

Extent, &c.—The form of the parish is irregular, and not easily described, so as to be understood. The best idea of it would be obtained by a map from actual survey. Its greatest length from the head of Glenrinnes to the opposite end near the Spey, that is from south to north, is eleven or twelve English miles ; and its greatest breadth from the banks of Doveron to the foot of Belrinnes, that is from east to west, may be about as much. It consists of the lands of Edinglassie and Glenmarky, which are Lord Fife's,—of the Lordship of Auchindown, Glenfiddich, and the greater part of Glenrinnes, the Duke of Gordon's,—of Dullanside and a part of the Lordship of Balveny, Lord Fife's again,—and of the barony of Kinninvie, which is, and for centuries has been, in the possession of a branch of the old family of Balquhan, and of which James Leslie, Esq; the only residing heritor, is the present laird, and makes a very good one, being kind to his tenants, an honest hospitable gentleman, and an excellent farmer.

farmer. Mr Duff of Drumuir is likewife a proprietor in Mortlach, having a fmall piece of ground in it, called Lochend, near the kirk of Botriphny.

The arable fields. which, by a rough guefs, may be from 4 to 5 thoufand acres, lie chiefly pretty high along the Fiddich and Dullan, two beautiful rivulets ; or on the fides of rills falling into thefe ; or on the more gentle declivities of the mountains. The lands of Glenmarky and Edinglaffie are remote and disjoined from the reft of the parifh. A fmall ftream called Marky, running with rapidity down the glen, meets with the Doveron near the houfe of Edinglaffie, where that river takes a pleafant winding towards Huntly on the eaft. There are fome low or haugh grounds, but not very confiderable. The extent of meadow grafs, coarfer greens, moor, and hills,—which laft are in general covered with heath, and but little improveable except by planting, may amount to about twenty times as much as the cultivated field.

Landfcape.—The appearance of the country is very fine. Variegated with hill and dale, wood and water, growing corns and pafture covered with flocks, it looks both beautiful and rich : And even in winter, the trees fkirting the river banks with their fnowy foliage, and the lofty mountains all in white, exhibit a diverfity of view abundantly pleafing and grotefque. Fiddich-fide is one of the lovelieft ftraths to be feen in any country. There are fome landfcapes, efpecially in Glenfiddich, and about Pittyvaich, Tininver, and Kinninvie, which any one, who has a tafte for fuch things, will not grudge a day's ride or two to come and fee. They are a mixture of the fweet and the wild ; and furnifh a great deal of picturefque and very rural fcenery : If a Thomfon or an Allan Ramfay had lived here, they would have been famous in fong. One of the moft remarkable is the Craig of Balveny, with the

old

old caſtle there, and the objects which accompany them:
What goes by the name of the Giant's Chair, formed by the
wearing of the water of Dullan many an age ago, with a pretty little caſcade, called the linen apron, and their ſurrounding
drapery, is another.

Soil and Air.—The ſoil is almoſt intirely of the loamy kind,
deep enough and fertile: Any exception of its inclining
either to ſand or clay is ſcarce worth the mentioning. The
air is pure and wholeſome, though it is rather moiſt than
dry; and fair weather is ſometimes enjoyed on the farms below, when there are fogs or rain, or perhaps ſnow, on the
heights around: But this is no doubt more or leſs the caſe
in every highland ſituation; though many a remark muſt
one make in an account of this nature, equally applicable to
a ſhire or even a larger diſtrict, as to a pariſh.

Health, Spirits, Ages, &c.—The writer of this knows of
no diſtemper peculiar to the pariſhioners of Mortlach; nor
of any, which can be ſaid, above all others, to be prevailing;
and on the authority of a Phyſician, who has long known the
country and the people well, he can with the greater confidence ſay, that there are none. Here, as in other places, while
many of the ailments of the more affluent proceed from
their living in luxury and too freely, to colds and too ſcanty a
fare, may thoſe of the lower claſs be frequently traced. There
are no inſtances of very extraordinary longevity: But many
arrive at the age of 70, ſome to 80, and one now and then,
though rarely, to 90 or upwards. The inhabitants may be
ſaid, on the whole, to be lively, active, and vigorous; though
from the backwardneſs of the ſeaſons for ſeveral years, and
other difficulties in the way of their getting a comfortable
ſubſiſtence, both the ſpirits and ſtrength of the ordinary farmer

mer and the labouring man are weaker and worſe than they were, it muſt be owned,—and owned with particular regret ; for ſuch men, engaged with heart's eaſe in the healthful pur- ſuit of agricultural employments, are the very nerves and per- manent riches of a country.

Springs.—Here are ſeveral ſteel or chalybeate ſprings ; and ſome of them pretty powerful. One, in particular, near the old caſtle of Auchindown, has been found, on chymical exa- mination, very much to reſemble the Peterhead water, and to be as light as it. They are of uſe in graveliſh complaints and diſorders of the ſtomach. There is likewiſe, below the houſe of Kinninvie, a ſpring of a petrifying quality, on the li- mits between Mortlach and Boharm.

Rivers.—Fiddich and Dullan, the two little rivers of this pariſh, have been already mentioned. Dovern is much larger than either of them. But Mortlach can ſcarce claim any property in it ; as it only borders, for a few hundred yards, upon one of its extremities. Fiddich riſes in Glen- fiddich, towards Strathdon ; and Dullan, in Glenrinnes, on the boundaries of Glenlivet. They join a little below the kirk, near the houſe of Tininver, and fall into the Spey a- bout 4 miles below. After their confluence, Fiddich is the name. Their whole run may be about a dozen or fourteen miles each ; and there is good angling for ſmall trout, in plen- ty, on them both.

Lake.—From the public road, leading from this to Botriph- ny, may be ſeen, on the left, in a den confined by two al- moſt perpendicular hills, a ſmall but deep lake, called Loch- park, the ſource of the Iſla, which flows into Doveron in the pariſh of Rothiemay. It is frequented by wild ducks, and is

ſaid

ſaid to have pikes in it. It belongs to Drummuir. Among the mountains, which enconipaſs the pariſh except an openning to the north, Bellrennis towers conſpicuous. It height above the ſea, from which it makes a good land mark in ſailing into the Moray-frith, is above 2650 feet; and from its baſe, about 1680.

Quadrupeds.—Beſides the tame and domeſtic quadrupeds, which are every where, here are foxes, weaſels, hares, ſome badgers and otters. In the foreſt of Glenfiddich, there is abundance of red deers—a thouſand and more with a few roes. The farmers round it think them by far too numerous: And yet 40 or 50 of them ſometimes in one flock, with their ſtately carriage and branching horns, on the tops of thoſe ſylvan and romantic hills, make a noble view. The Duke of Gordon has a ſummer reſidence in this glen, as a convenience for fowling, and taking a ſhot at the deer.

Birds.—The ſhelter and accommodation of the woods bring together a great variety of ſinging birds, making an aviary of nature, the moſt innocent and melodious of all, happy and unconfined. The black bird and thruſh, gold-finch, bull-finch, linnet, and robin, blend their notes, and compoſe a delightful concert. Many other birds there are, but none of them uncommon. The migratory cuckoo, green-plover or lapwing, and the ſwallow, pay their annual viſit, and are always welcome. For the ſportſman, there are moorfowls or grouſe, patridges, and a few ſnipe: The black-cock alſo is to be met with in Glenfiddich, and ſome ptarmagans have been ſeen on Belrennis.

Minerals.—There is a ſufficiency of moorſtone for the purpoſe of building, with ſome ſlate quarries of a dark grey colour

lour and pretty good : And the vaſt quantities of limeſtone here would be an exhauſtleſs treaſure to the huſbandman, if the expence of fuel were not ſo high, as nearly to prohibit the uſe of it. There is the appearance of allum and vitriol, and likewiſe of a lead mine, on the burn of Tullich, which belongs to Kinninvie. In one or two places, there is a laminated rock, which ſome think of the nature of whetſtone or hones: A kind of marble alſo there is both on Dullan and Fiddich ſide : And, in ſeveral parts, the ſurface of the ground would ſeem to indicate, that there are coals below, any diſcovery of which kind judiciouſly proſecuted would be of the greateſt conſeqence both to the comfort of the people, and the improvement of the lands ; for they are rather far from the ſea, and many of them too poor, to reap any general benefit from the late repeal of the coal tax, the neareſt port, at the mouth of the Spey, being about 16 miles diſtant from the centre of the pariſh.

Population.—From the liſt of baptiſms, and the recollection of the oldeſt reſidenters, it would appear that Mortlach was more populous 50 or 60 years ago, than it is at this day. In the 1782, on an accurate ſurvey for the information of the Barons of Exchequer, in the view of an approaching ſcarcity of grain, the inhabitants of every age amounted to 2169 ; of whom there were about 560 under twelve. Ten years afterwards, in the 1792, when again, in like manner, exactly taken by the ſame incumbent for this ſtatiſtical account, the number was found to be 25 fewer than in the 1782, being in whole but 918—of whom 901 were males and 1017 females, and of whom alſo there were,

Under

Under 10 years of age	—		412
From 10 to 20	—	—	398
—— 20 to 30	—	—	304
—— 30 to 40	—	—	251
—— 40 to 50	—	—	230
—— 50 to 60	—	—	145
—— 60 to 70	—	—	113
—— 70 to 80	—	—	53
—— 80 to 90	—	—	11
—— 90 to 100	—	—	1

In all   1918

Theſe occupied 415 houſes, for every family had its own ſeparate dwelling, making between 4 and 5 at a medium in each, though very unequally divided, ſome as large as 18 or 20, including huſband, wife, chidren, land ſervants, and ſome as ſmall as one. Such ſolitary houſeholders, however, and ſuch numerous families were both but few.

Of the above 415 houſes, farmers might be ſaid to poſſeſs 176; and crofters, or cottagers, the remaining 239: And on the lands of the ſeveral proprietors, the proportions of the people and their habitations were as follows:

On the Duke of Gordon's	927	in	193 houſes.
—— Lord Fife's	— 761	in	176 ditto
—— Kinninvie's	— 226	in	45 ditto
And on Drummuir's	— 4	in	1 houſe.

As before   1918 in 415 houſes.

The ſubjoined ſtatement of births, for 30 years, from the 1ſt of January 1763 to the 31ſt of December 1792 incluſive, arranged in 3 equal periods, is taken from the pariſh regiſter, and is thought tolerably correct. An allowance may be made perhaps for 2 or 3 being omitted every year.

In

In 1763	28	In 1773	39	In 1783	48
1764	29	1774	41	1784	46
1765	46	1775	39	1785	33
1766	46	1776	61	1786	32
1767	45	1777	55	1787	35
1768	39	1778	50	1788	19
1769	55	1779	47	1789	39
1770	47	1780	42	1790	27
1771	38	1781	43	1791	31
1772	48	1782	56	1792	33
Total	421	Total	473	Total	343

So the average for the firſt 10 years, is $42\frac{1}{10}$, for the ſecond, $47\frac{3}{10}$. Here it may be remarked, that the rule for finding the population, by multiplying the births by 26, ſeems from this inſtance to be exceedingly erroneous, for the product of ſuch multiplication would not in the preſent caſe be the half of the reality. The decreaſe in the laſt 10 years is very obſervable, and is probably to be aſcribed to the calamitous eighty two. The difference betwixt the 1766 and the 1788 in the foregoing table, the baptiſms in the one being more than three times as many as thoſe in the other, will alſo ſtrike one : And for this difference no ſatisfactory reaſon can be aſſigned. It is likely, that, in the latter of thoſe two years, the effects of the 1782, which reduced the country in general to much want and a train of conſequent diſtreſſes, were at their height ; that the greateſt number of emigrants had then left the pariſh, in ſearch of employment and maintenance, among the farmers towards the ſouth or in the manufacturing towns ; and that, after that period, they began to return, to find home more comfortable, and to increaſe. Such is the attachment to one's native ſoil, that it is ſeldom deſerted but either from neceſſity or the gratification of an ambitious deſire ; and as ſoon as circumſtances will permit, or the paſſion is cured, it is commonly reſorted to again. Of

an

an old acquaintance, whether an agreeable friend or a favourite scene, it is natural to be fond. Early or established prepossessions are with difficulty removed, and it is hard to be put to the trial of eradicating in a distant land, the sweet remembrance of happier days.

In the register of marriages, there is, through some negligence or other, a chasm, which prevents from going farther back, with any precision, than the last 20 years; viz. from the 1st of January 1773 to the 31st of December 1792. But this shall be done, as under, in two equal periods.

For the *first* 10 Years.			For the *second* 10 years.	
In 1773	—	12	In 1783	—	11
1774	—	15	1784	—	7
1775	—	16	1785	—	8
1776	—	14	1786	—	17
1777	—	13	1787	—	6
1778	—	21	1788	—	14
1779	—	17	1789	—	17
1780	—	16	1790	—	14
1781	—	24	1791	—	17
1782	—	16	1792	—	15
		164			126

Or $16\frac{4}{5}$ marriages annually.   Or $12\frac{3}{5}$ marriages annually.

Each marriage, at a medium, may produce 4 or 5 children. There is no register of deaths or burials kept.

The number of men servants is 135, and of women servants 102 or thereabout; all for the purposes of husbandry or the care of children. This number may seem small. But many of the farmers have their sons and daughters to assist them; and servants wages have risen to such a height, that they must do with as few as possible.

The

The handicraftfmen are,

22 Weavers,	4 Coopers,
11 Mafons,	2 Dyers,
10 Shoemakers,	2 Slaters,
6 Houfe carpenters,	2 Wheel-wrights,
5 Smiths,	1 Plough and cart
5 Tailors,	wright,
	1 Harnefs maker,

in whole 71 : And they have almoft all of them a few acres along with their houfes. The number of apprentices is about 20. There are likewife 4 fhop keepers, 2 innkeepers, 3 diftillers of whifky, 3 gardeners, 3 meal-millers, 1 lint-miller, and 1 faw-miller.

Agriculture.—Agriculture is on the improving hand : But fhort leafes are the bane of every improvement. Who in his fenfes would make a farm more valuable, at his own dear expence, only to induce another to covet and to bid for it ? or if no fuch offerer fhould interfere, to tempt the proprietor, who in general is fufficiently apt to yield to thofe temptations, to take the advantage and fqueeze too high a rent from his tenant, grown fond of the poffeffion, and thus incautioufly ftanding on very unequal ground ? Some of the farmers are giving very good example, by dreffing their fields with green crops, often in drill, or by a fallow ; laying them down with grafs feeds, and introducing a proper rotation : But winter herding is not yet much relifhed ; and till it be the practice, a man's fields, when in turnips or clover, are but half his own. There are very few complete inclofures, though on feveral farms, and particularly Pittyvaich, a good deal is done in the way of dikes and hedges too. The ploughs may be reckoned about 170, fome of them of 8 or 10 good oxen, others of good horfes, generally 4, but the greater part made up of horfes

horfes and oxen mixed together, both of a very indifferent
kind. There are 3 or 4 wains or waggons drawn by oxen,
and ploughing with a pair of horfes is introduced. The grain
raifed here is oats, bear, or barley and peafe : A very fmall
quantity of either rye or wheat, though for the latter, both
foil and climate, in various parts of the lands of Balveny
and Kinninvie, are well adapted. It is reckoned good and fufficient bear, which weighs about 18 ftones the boll Banffſhire,
which is nearly the Linlithgow meafure or ftandard for Scotland : And 16 pecks or a boll of oats, in a favourable feafon, will yield about 8 ftones of meal. Potatoes alfo are raifed, and found very ufeful. And there is fome flax ; the experiments of which fhow, that it might turn out a profitable
article, if the management of it, after being pulled, were better underftood, and if there were a ready market. It is at
prefent but a bye kind of a crop, and therefore neglected.
For want of fkill and attention in the grafing, watering, and
milling, it is often much injured. Failing in fuccefs through
bad ufage, it unjuftly receives the blame ; and the farmer is
difcouraged from extending his attempts.

This parifh, which is a plentiful one, after fupplying itfelf,
can, in the opinion of fome of the moft intelligent on this fubject, fpare, in ordinary years, about a thoufand bolls of bear,
and five or fix hundred of oats and oat meal. The oat feed
feafon is from the beginning of March, or fooner, if the weather will allow, till towards the end of April. And bear is
fown from the middle of April, to near the end of May. Ba-
ley harveft, generally fpeaking, begins about the firft or fecond week of September; and the oats may be faid to be
reaped in the month of October, though fometimes earlier
and often later. Early oats, which have been much and be-
neficially ufed fince the 1782, ripen almoft in the fame time
as the bear. After the winter fnows, however, or heavy rains,

there

there muſt be the difference of 8 or 10 days, at leaſt, in the time of ſowing, in the different parts of this extenſive country ; and even the ſame kind of grain, ſown in the ſame day, will be ready for the hook ſeveral weeks ſooner in Balveny and Kinninvie, than in Glenrinnes and Glenmarky. In this view, Auchindown and Edinglaſſie have an intermediate place, being neither ſo early as the two firſt of thoſe diſtricts, nor ſo late as the other two *.

Cattle and Paſturage.—As to the live ſtock here, there will be about 2000 black cattle, from 300 to 400 horſes for plough, cart, and harrow, 4000 or 5000 ſheep, ſome goats, and a few ſwine about the mills and diſtilleries. The black cattle are of the middle ſized and handſome highland breed ; the ox from 5 to 8 guineas, and the cow worth 4 or 5, as the prices happen to go. Many of the farms, having plenty of ſummer graſs, are well ſuited for cattle and corn too. There are alſo ſome very good ſheep-walks, one of the beſt of which is in Glenmarky. The ewes and lambs, which are moſtly now of the black-faced Linton ſort, ſell from 5 l, to 7 l. the ſcore ; and wedders much about the ſame : But all ſuch calculations muſt be underſtood with a little latitude, and as only there and thereabout. It is impoſſible to make them otherwiſe. The white-faced ſheep, who may be ſtiled the *aborigines* of the country, are wearing out ; and yet, tho' ſmaller, they are allowed by many to yield both the ſweeter mutton and the finer wool. Wool ſells from 10 s. to 16 s. per ſtone, according to the quality and demand ; but the ſtone conſiſts, it ſeems, of 22 lib. Dutch ; one inſtance, among a thouſand, of the great propriety of ſimplifying our weights

* The average rate of an acre is about 10 s. ; and the farms are of many a different ſize, from a 5 l. rent, and even leſs, to 70 l. or 80 l.

weights and meafures, and making them every where alike, by the fame general ftandard. The breeding of horfes is but little practifed here, though it would probably anfwer very well. As a fpecimen, fome have lately been reared to the value of 15 l. and 20 l. Sterling.

Woods.—There are feveral plantations of firs in Mortlach, and fome of them full grown, the property of Lord Fife and Kinninvie; in whole from 300 to 400 acres; and about the like quantity of natural wood, chiefly aller and birch. The oldeft fir wood is on a piece of rifing ground, planted about 60 or 70 years ago, then arable, and fo fertile as to be called the *meal-girnel* of Tininver, of which farm it was a part, and ftill is. It feems it has then been the opinion, that a rich mould, if not neceffary, was at leaft very favourable for fuch a purpofe; though it is fince known, that firs will profper in waftes fit for nothing elfe. Some elms, planes, and oaks, have thriven pretty well. One old oak, in particular, in the Craig of Balveny, though not a very large tree, has a refpectable appearance. The afh, too, appears very congenial to the foil, and fhoots up luxuriantly ; and, amidft the trees of native growth, there is a great variety of fhrubs, many of them flowering. There is, however, an ample fcope for planting here ; and, when it is fet about, attention will no doubt be paid to the ufeful and beautiful larix. If coal be not difcovered, timber, as a fuel, will, ere long, in many parts of the parifh, be a much wanted *fuccedaneum* for the exhaufted moffes.

Language.—The language is a dialect of the Scottifh and Englifh blended together. There is hardly a word of Earfe now fpoken in any part of the parifh: If any where, it is in Glenrinnes, where the inhabitants do alfo moft retain the

look,

look, manners, and genius of the Highland Caledonian, as appears from their dreſs, their vivacity, their ſocial and merry meetings, their warm attachments, their keen reſentments, their activity on occaſions, and indolence on the whole, their intelligence, and their love of their country.

Names of Places—The names of places, except ſuch as are of late cultivation, are all Gaelic, and commonly deſcriptive either of the ſituation or of ſome noticeable circumſtance. Of his, examples would be needleſs. Let the two rivulets ſuffice. *Fiddich* or *Fiodhidh*, means woody; and its banks are almoſt covered with trees. *Dullan*, or *Tuilan*, ſignifies rapid; and it tumbles from pebble to pebble almoſt all its courſe.

Rent.—The real rent of this pariſh, which ariſes entirely from lands, is 2000 l. Sterling and upwards. Some neceſſary information on this head having been with-held, from a jealouſy of an improper uſe being made of it, it cannot be exactly ſtated: But the valued rent, as taken in the year 1690, is 3900 l. Scotch.

Farm-houſes—There is neither town nor village in all the pariſh: The whole is country. The Kirktown of Mortlach is only 2 or 3 houſes on the glebe, or about the church. The farm-houſes are getting a more decent look than they had; and it is to be hoped they will yet mend in this reſpect. They are built for the moſt part of granite ſtone, and thatched with ſtraw. A few, however, are ſlated; and ſeveral gentlemen farmers, ſome of whom have retired from the army, beating their ſwords into plough ſhares, have both their dwelling houſes and offices very ſubſtantial and commodious. It were to be wiſhed that heritors would be ſome-

what

what more liberal in granting an allowance for meliorations of this ſort. Under proper limitations, much advantage would accrue from it, both to their tenants and themſelves too.

Religion.—The pariſhioners are all of the Eſtabliſhed Church, except about 30 or 40 Roman Catholics, perhaps as many Seceders, and 1 Epiſcopalian. Any ill-will or violence of temper, ariſing from a difference in religious ſentiment, is rare.

General Character.—As to the character of the people at large, much may juſtly be ſaid ro their praiſe. Like the people of other diſtricts, they are not without their faults; and there are ſome inſtances of great worthleſſneſs. almoſt in every pariſh, to be regretted. It here obviouſly occurs, that a miniſter may be induced, from various motives. to go to the extreme of truth, on the favourable ſide for his flock. His regard for them may blind and miſlead him; or, by condemning them, he may think that he obliquely condemns himſelf; at leaſt, if another did it, he might perhaps be led too readily to think ſo. Few chuſe to depreciate their own importance; few to diminiſh the happy effects of their paſtoral care; and fewer ſtill are inclined to render themſelves ungracious. Thus it may often place a clergyman in a delicate ſituation to be obliged to characterize his pariſhioners; and, though a man of honeſty and reſolution would, in any neceſſary caſe of the kind, immediately determine that he is to ſpeak or write the truth, yet ſuch characters, which in general will be found to be only an indiſcriminate repetition of the ſame and the ſame good qualities, are ſurely to be received as probably partial. But, unleſs there be an egregious deluſion indeed, it can be told with pleaſure and with the ſtricteſt impartiality, of the people of Mortlach, that,

with

with few exceptions, they are, and long have been, induſtrious, honeſt, neighbourly, ſober, and humane; peaceable, orderly, and affectionately attached to the free and glorious
conſtitution of Britain; decent in obſerving the ordinances
of religion, and rationally impreſſed with the great end of
them all, as aiding and ſubſervient to piety of heart, upright-
neſs of conduct, and purity of life. If ſome of them be ſtill
too much given to *frets*, or ſuperſtitious remarks, they are
commonly of the harmleſs kind.

Inoculation.—One thing, however, truly to be lamented, is
their yet too great diſlike to inoculation for the ſmall-pox,
the neglect of which, though it is in uſe rather more than it
was, makes this very infectious and virulent diſeaſe frequently mortal; and it is the more difficult to overcome ſo unfortunate a prejudice, as, in a great degree, it has its origin in
conſcience, however erroneous and miſinformed. But, it is
to be hoped, both for the ſake of their children, and as an
expreſſion of their thankfulneſs to God for ſo gracious a diſcovery, that they and others around them, for they are not
ſingular, will ſoon ſee this matter in another and juſter light,
and chearfully, with a dependence on ſucceſs from Heaven,
embrace the benefit of ſo kind a mean afforded by Providence.
They are, in general, much diſpoſed to chearfulneſs and contentment, but keenly alive to a ſenſe of injuſtice, rigorous
exactions, or any ſpecies of oppreſſion whatever. That they
have a martial genius, there is little doubt; but our ordinary
wars, it appears, do not call it forth; for they are not fond of
a military life: Indeed, the buſineſs of a ſoldier is held rather
in low eſtimation among them. They ſeem to conſider it as
poor, diſſipated, and ſlaviſh. As to ſize, ſtrength, complexion, abilities, or any other perſonal or mental qualifica-
tion, there is here nothing remarkable.

Miniſters.

Miniſters —The writer of this was miniſter of Mortlach, being the fourth ſince the revolution from Auguſt 1781 to December 1793; when he was tranſlated to Aberdeen or Sr Nicholas; he is married, and has four ſons. Mr George Grant, who was one of the miniſt rs of old Macher, has ſucceeded him, a batchelor. As to his predeceſſors, Mr Shaw's Hiſtory of the Province of Moray will inform thoſe who have the curioſity to know.

Patron and Stipend.—The Crown is patron. The ſtipend is 63 l. 2s. Sterling, including in that ſum communion element money, one chalder of bear and two chalders of oat meal at 8 ſtones per boll.

Glebe —There are five or ſix acres of a glebe, with a pretty good orchard and kitchen garden, pleaſantly ſituated on the bank of the Duilan.

Manſe and Church.—The manſe has been a ſpacious one in its day, but is now going to wreck, and muſt ſoon be either rebuilt, or have a thorough repair. The church is indeed venerable, but it is only becauſe it is old; having none of that magnificence, nice architecture or elegant decorations, which we ſo juſtly admire in the more modern cathedrals of after times. Tradition reports that its walls are the very ſame as in the beginning of the eleventh century; and they are ſo ſtrong that it is thought they might ſtand for hundreds of years to come: But the roof, which it got about 80 years ago, is ruinous. The doors and windows, and the ſimplicity of the whole edifice bear witneſs to its age. The windows are long narrow ſlits of ſix feet high, and only 10 or 11 inches wide on the outſide, but ſo much ſloped away as to meaſure at their utmoſt projection ten or twelve feet within. And as

its

its fhape, that of an oblong fquare of about 90 feet by 28, is a very incommodious one, as a place of public worfhip, both for the fpeaker and hearers, it will probably be found advifeable to get over the veneration for its antiquity, and new model it into a more convenient form The choir on the eaft end, where the mufic was, and where the altar alfo would be. is 27 feet long, and a few feet higher than the reft of the building Here the door to the organ loft is ftill to be feen ; and on the ridge of the choir, is what they call the Three Bifhops, a pyramid like ftone of little fhow, with the femblance of a face on each of its fides, right rudely cut. It has been faid that the effigy of Bifhop Beyn is to be feen in the wall near the *poftern* door ; whereabout it is imagined the tomb of the three firft bifhops might be found under a vault : But this, as to the effigy, is not the cafe. And for the tomb, there has been no fearch ; nor are there any effigies in the church, except one at full length, over the door which leads from the choir to the Leflies Aifle or burying ground, with no infcription, but called a predeceffor of the Kinninvie family, and celebrated as a man of marvellous gallantry ; and two half lengths, Alexander Duff of Keithmore and Helen Grant of Allachie his fpoufe,* on the fouth fide of the choir, with a Latin infcription ; all in freeftone and baffo relievo. There is another infcription in marble†, on a monument of Mr Hugh

Innes

* Great grandfather and great grandmother of the prefent Earl of Fife.

† *Copies of the two Infcriptions.*

Hoc conduntur tumulo, reliquiæ Alexandri Duff de Keithmore et Helenae Grant uxoris fuæ chariffimæ. Qui quadringinta annos et ultra, felici et tæundo connubio juncti, vixerunt. Uterque quidem ingenue natus, ille ex nobiliffimis Fifæ Thanis

per

Innes firſt preſbyterian parſon of Mortlach after the Revóluꞏ
tion. It is in the wall, beſide the miniſter's ſeat, under which
he was buried *. There are likewiſe ſome very ancient lookꞏ
ing grave ſtones with Saxon charaɛters, below the ſeats and in
the paſſages ; but it would take a great deal of trouble to make
out what is upon them, and, except to a patient and inquiſiꞏ
tive antiquary, the labour would perhaps be very ill repaid †.

School.—The ſchool is very uſeful ; but the ſchoolmaſter,
as

per vetuſtam familiam de Craighead, paulo abhinc ſuperſtitem
proxime et legitime oriundus ; illa ex ſplendida et potenti Granꞏ
teorum familia, eodem quaque modo originem trahens ortu non
obſcuri, ſuis tamen virtutibus illuſtriores ; opibus afflaxerunt,
et liberis ingenue educatis, floruere pie, juſte et ſobrie vixerunt,
et ſic in Domino mortem obiere. Illa anno Domini 1694,
aetatis ſuæ ſexageſimo.

M. S.

Mri. Hugonis Innes, filii honorabilis viri Johannis Innes de
Leichnet, qui, cum, annos triginta quatuor, ſacra in hoc temꞏ
plo peregiſſet, obiit anno Chriſti 1733, natus annos LXVIII.
Poſuit hoc monumentum pia ac dileɛtiſſima conjux Eliz. Aberꞏ
nethie filia Domini de Mayen.

* This gentleman, it is ſaid, was poſſeſſed of a conſiderable
ſhare both of bodily ſtrength and perſonal courage ; and, in
thoſe days, if various anecdotes which are told of him be true,
it ſeems he had occaſion for the exerciſe of theſe qualities, in
the diſcharge of his clerical funɛtions.

† On the banks of the Dullan, a little below the preſent church
or ancient cathedral, appears the foundation of a houſe, overꞏ
grown with graſs, which would be walked over with little noꞏ
tice, if one were not told, that here was the biſhop's palace :
And not far from thence is a part of the public road, on the
oppoſite ſide of the ſame rivulet, leading to the eaſt, called Gorꞏ
don's croſs ; the firſt deſign or uſe of which cannot now with
certainty be diſcovered ; and ſuppoſitions are endleſs. It might
be for ſome religious purpoſe, or it may have been a market
place. A round ſtone, which is thought to have been the pedeſꞏ
tal of the croſs, remains to be ſeen.

as in moft other places, is poorly rewarded for his trouble : Mr Alexander Thomfon, the prefent one, has been
long much efteemed as a teacher, and is a very deferving man. The whole emoluments, including falary, fees,
a donation by Duff of Dipple, with perquifites as feffion
clerk and keeper of the regifter, amount to but about twenty guineas, for which, befides the other duties of office, a
moft faithful charge is taken of 30 or 40 fcholars, at leaft,
through all the year.

Moir's Burfaries.—There are four burfaries at the King's
College of Aberdeen for boys educated here, an endowment
which is a great encouragement, and has been of important
fervice to many young men in the parifh, and merits particular notice. It is a privilege indeed, which, for the fake
of the parifhioners, will no doubt be always moft facredly
preferved. They arife from 600 l. Sterling, bequeathed to
the above univerfity, between 30 and 40 years ago, by Dr Alexander Moir, an Auchindown man, and for fome time the parifh
fchoolmafter, for the education of four boys annually at the
College, from this fchool, to be recommended by the minifter.
If two or more boys fhould happen to be fent at the fame
time, the beft fcholar, other things equal, is preferred : But if
only one goes, he is entitled by ufe and wont, and writings
explanatory of the will, without any competition, to the benefit of this legacy ; if found *habile* or fit for being received
at a college at all, and if attefted by the parfon of Mortlach
as a proper boy and from this fchool, for there muft be one
burfary to be given away every year. Dr Moir died in St
Croix, where he had made his fortune, which was handfome,
as a phyfician.

It is faid that Dr Lorimer of London, a native of this parifh and extremely fond of it, means to give a fum of money
for

for another burfe to the boys of this fchool : And if at the fame time he could think of the fchoolmafter, and leave any thing for him, it might be of much utility, as an inducement to a proper man either to come or to continue in the place.

The Poor.—The number on the poors roll, at an average, is from 50 to 60, and the funds for their relief, being the produce of all the collections in church, except the yearly one for the infirmary of Aberdeen, and the intereft of 1000 l. Scots, a bequeft of the fame Duff of Dipple who left a thoufand merks for the fchool, do not exceed twenty pounds per annum : So it is only a fmall affiftance, and not a fupport which can be derived from them. But even in the 1782 no body perifhed for want ; though many were on fhort allowance : With fome favings of former years, laid out in purchafing white peafe, almoft the only grain then to be got, and the help of fome meal from government, a fhift was made to meet the fucceeding crop. And, moft luckily for the poor, the prices for fpinning linen yarn, the chief employment of the women in this part of the country, were then very high.

Price of Provifions and Rate of Wages.—Provifions of all kinds are confiderably dearer than they were about 20 or 30 years ago, fome articles a third, and others a half, and they are ftill rifing in their value. The prices at prefent are fo much fimilar to thofe which will be mentioned in the neighbouring parifhes that it is needlefs to be particular : And the fame may be faid of the rate of wages, whether for artificers, fervants, or day labourers. Of the three, however, farm fervants have come to the moft extravagant pitch. Indeed as to the labouring man at fixpence a day with his victuals, when married and with a few young children, it is rather furprifing

prifing how he makes out at all, confidering that he cannot
get work all the year round, unlefs the winter feafon be uncommonly mild : Much, efpecially for clothing, muft depend
on the induftry and economy of the wife ; and after all, on
their fmall and honeft earnings, one would imagine there is a
portion of fuch a bleffing, as, in the days of old, there was
in the widow's barrel of meal and cruife of oil.

Advantages and Difadvantages.—It may be remarked as a
peculiar advantage to this parifh, that it is plentifully fupplied with timber, both for the purpofe of building and for all
farming utenfils chiefly within itfelf and partly from its vicinity to the Spey, which floats down conveniently and at an
eafy expence, the trees of Glenmore and other highland forefts, on the banks of that ftately river; And, as to its natural difadvantages, it has few or none, but fuch as are almoft
infeparable from an inland and mountainous fituation.

Meliorations.—But, undoubtedly, the condition of the people might in many refpects be made better.

Services.—Services or bondage, as a part of the value of
their lands, do ftill difgrace the rentals of fome of the heritors : And though they are required with great indulgence,
and not nearly to the extent of the obligation in their tacks,
yet they hang over the heads of the tenants like a depreffing
weight, and ought moft certainly to be abolifhed.

Multures.—Multures, or aftrictions in the way of thirlage
to any particular mill, fhould alfo be reafonably converted,
and done away. The farmer would then go with his victual, wherever he pleafed, and have nothing to pay but to the
operative miller for his trouble and expence Thus it would
become the intereft of the workman, and it is always fafeft
to make intereft and duty go together, to grind the corns well,

give

give ready fervice, and not to overcharge ; and it would alfo
be the intereft of the farmer to go to the neareft mill, if properly conducted.

Leafes.—Leafes ought to be longer than they are : The
longeft juft now is nineteen years.

Roads.—Our bad roads are a great inconvenience and a
great lofs ; and very bad they are in general, except where it
is almoft impoffible to make them fo. They are much neglected, and never will be tolerable, it is to be feared, till
either the ftatute labour be commuted, or turnpikes eftablifhed. The people turn out to this work with reluctance,
becaufe they do not experience the benefit of it ; for, by
unfkilful management, the roads are often worfe rather than
better of all they do : And the overfeer, loth to impofe a
hardfhip on thofe who are generally his neighbours, or to
offend them, is too eafy in his duty ; and, on the whole, their
work is a mere farce. The difficulty of providing fuel is ano-
the evil. Cutting, fetting up, and leading home the peats
and turfs occupy the greater part of the fummer, from the
end of the bear feed to the beginning of harveft.

Fuel.—Coals muft be the remedy for this. Even with our
prefent roads, it is allowed, by thofe who have made the trial,
that they are the cheapeft firing : And if the roads were
good, or, which would be better ftill, if one might indulge
the idea of a canal, there would be a moft comfortable relief in this requifite article.

Game Laws.—The game laws, though not immediately connected with agriculture or the neceffaries of life, are loudly
complained of, by numbers in this part of the country, as a
heavy grievance. It is thought exceeding hard, that a man
                                                      dare

dare not fhoot a hare or a patridge, on his own farm or in his own garden, but like a poacher or a thief; and that others may come and do fo at his very door, to his great mortification, and perhaps to the injury of his crop.

Surely the tax on licences of this kind can be no mighty object for the revenue; and it aids in fupporting and rivetting this purfe proud and unjuft procedure. In truth, thofe arbitrary acts are the vileft veftige of feudalifm and ariftocracy now remaining in our free and happy land; and it is to be fufpected that Britain may one day fadly mourn their effects: For nothing can have a ftronger tendency to enervate and enflave the inhabitants of any country, than a prohibition of the ufe of arms, to which thefe laws eventually do amount. In the time of need, they will neither know how to load nor fire. And, if ever an invafion fhould come upon us, we will be able to do but little in our own defence. Inftead of lounging over the coals in an idle morning, inactive and fpiritlefs as he now muft do, when the operations of hufbandry are arrefted, by the froft and fnow, the peafant, fportfman, and there is no inconfiftency, efpecially in the highlands, in one's being both, was wont to rauge over the fields and hills, with his dog and his gun, in manly exercife, which gave health to his body and vigour to his mind. On this fubject, it is frequently obferved, and the obfervation feems juft, that there was greater plenty of all forts of game before thefe confinements than fince. And the reafon is pretty plain. Every body almoft then had an intereft in deftroying hawks and other ravenous animals, and likewife in taking care of the eggs and young in the fpring; whereas now, as they are to have no fhare either of the pleafure or profit afterwards, to ufe no ftronger language, they are entirely carelefs and indifferent about the matter.

Mifcellaneous.—There was an uncommon mortality in this parifh parish in 1763, occasioned by a putrid fever; and, during the rage of the disease, the frost was so very intense, that it was necessary to kindle fires in the church-yard to soften the ground for digging the graves : In the month of January Mr Walter Sime the minister was one of thirteen corps unburied at the same time.

Balveny house may be admitted here, a large and modern mansion, one of the seats of Lord Fife, and built by his father, about a quarter of a mile below the old castle, which will be mentioned soon. It has a flat roof, and is covered with lead.

It is a pity that this house is so ill set down, and that it has no inhabitants. Lying naturally too low, the architect has contrived to sink it lower still : And yet, with the association of life and plenty and chearfulness within, it would communicate the sensation of a very shewy and pleasant dwelling, but, as it is, it looks solitary and forlorn.

Within this century, the mode of living is much altered here, and not to the better : On the whole it is not so strengthening. The drinking of whisky instead of good ale is a miserable change, and so likewise is the very general use of tea. These put together have been exceedingly hurtful both to health and morals. Hence too many become *tipplers*, neglect their business, and go to ruin : And hence it is thought that consumptions, stomach complaints, and a multiplicity of disorders, which go under the name of nervous, are more frequent than they were. It will probably be considered as a pretty curious fact, that instead of two or three tea kettles, about 60 or 70 years ago, perhaps one for the laird, another for the parson, and a third for the factor, there are here now two hundred at least. But while these remarks must be made, as impartiality requires, it is agreeable, on the other hand, to observe a circumstance of a very different aspect. Some time ago, the country hereabout was too much given to the indulgence

gence of a litigious fpirit, a fpirit, which, wherever it prevails, will not fail to four the temper, wafte the fubftance, and corrupt the principles of honefty : But now a law fuit is fcarcely heard of among them ; and when any little difference arifes, they refer it to a friend or two in the way of amicable decifion. This happy alteration is owing partly to dear bought experience; and partly to the removal of a judicatory at Keith, a village within a few miles of them, where a fubftitute of the fheriff of Banfffhire was wont to hold his meetings and difpenfe the law, and where fome pettifogger or other was never wanting to fofter, if not to inftil, an inclination to a procefs, as often as he could. A bleffing when abufed is converted into a curfe, and now the people find, that though they are farther from the court, they are nearer to juftice. To Keith, they had frequent occafions for the poft office, or the fhop or the market, and if the fmalleft difputable trifle happened to be rankling them at the time, the coal was blown ; and they came home, buoyed up by their counfel, with the affurance of ample fatisfaction and all their expence, though the affair generally ended in their pockets being picked, and their peace and good neighbourhood deftroyed. A caufe not worth a groat, on either fide, has been known to be contefted for years, through all the rounds of the moft quibbling and tedious forms, and to coft each of the contending parties pounds inftead of the original pence.

Mortlach, though it has not much to fhow that it is a favourite of the mufes, claims a relation to two Scotch fongs of no little vogue, Roy's wife in Aldevallach, and Tibby Fowler in the Braes. There are fome old men yet alive who remember to have feen the heroine of the latter. She lived in the braes of Auchindown, and was a plain looking lafs

with

with a ſwinging tocher. The Glacks of Ballach, mentioned as the ſcene of the former, is a narrow and remarkable paſs, near the old caſtle of Auchindown, between this pariſh and the Cabrach. Both ballads are ſaid to have been compoſed by diſappointed woers.

Antiquities and Families of Note.—There are two old caſtles, in this pariſh, well worthy of notice. Auchindown, or Auchindune, and Balveny: And when a ſtranger is travelling through this part of Scotland, for curioſity or pleaſure, they deſerve his attention, and willcontribute to his amuſement. Leſs than an hundred years ago, both were inhabited. When they were firſt built, it is not known, or by whom. The caſtle of Auchindune ſtands on a green mount of conical ſhape, over the Fiddich: Its ſituation is bold and commanding. In the central apartment of the building, there is a piece of admirable workmanſhip, in grand and gothic ſtile. It has been in the poſſeſſion of the family of Gordon ſince 1535; and of that name, there have been both Knights and Lords of Auchindune. Before that period, it belonged to the Ogilvies; and, with all its barony, was a part of the Lordſhip of Deſkford. Balveny caſtle is another very magnificent ſtructure. It is placed on a beautiful eminence, on the banks of Fiddich likewiſe, a little below its confluence with the Dullan, and has a variety of charming ſcenery in its view. Tradition calls the oldeſt part of it, for it has evidently been built at different times, a Pictiſh tower. In days of old, it ſucceſſively owned as its maſters the Cummings, the Douglaſſes, and the Stewarts; and, after them, paſſing through ſeveral other families in the 16th and 17th centuries, it became the property of Duff of Bracco about the year 1687, and is now the Earl of Fife's. In the 1446, there was a Lord Balveny of

the

the name of Douglas. In the front, and high over its iron and maffy gate, which ftill remains, is a motto of the Stewarts, Earls of Athol, defcriptive of the favage valour and unhappy circumftances of the times. FVR TH. FORTVIN. AND. FIL. THI. FATTRIS. The fituations of both thefe ancient fortalices are well chofen for defence. They have alfo had their walls, their ditches, and their ramparts, and have been ftrongly fortified by art. For prints of them, and more minute obfervations, fee Cordiner's Remarkable Ruins, No. 11. and 12. Such objects, prefenting themfelves to the eye, lead the mind to reflect on the tranfitory nature of human things, and infpire a contemplative and melancholy pleafure. Although now they are ruins, they were once the fcenes of feftivity and triumph. Many of diftinguifhed fame, though chiefly as warriors, have dwelt within them, for warlike feats were almoft the only accomplifhments, which, in the days of their glory, conferred renown.

There was another old building here, though of inferior note, at Edinglaffie : One occurrence about it, however, is very memorable. In 1690, the year of the engagement on the haughs of Cromdale, fome of the highland clans, on their march from Strathfpey, through Mortlach to Strathbogie, and in a connection with the public diffentions of the day, burnt this houfe: For which, the laird, whofe name was Gordon, took his opportunity of revenge, in their return a few weeks after, by feizing eighteen of them at random, and hanging them all on the trees of his garden *: A fhocking inftance of the miferies of a civil war, and alfo perhaps of the tyrannical and deteftable power then too often exerci-
 fed

---

* There is a piece of moor-land on the eftate of Edinglaffie, called the Highlandmen's *moffie*, where it is currently faid they were all buried.

sed by chieftains or haughty landholders, over the property, liberty, and lives of their fellow men, for either without any trial at all, or with a mere shadow of one, they condemned even to death, by *pot* or gallows. It is well known, that the abuses of these hereditary jurisdictions became so intolerable, that they were put an end to, by an act of Parliament, in the reign of George II. and a great and happy reform it was.

On the declining side of a hill, bordering upon this parish, betwixt Glenrinnes and Glenlivet, the battle of Glenlivet was fought, on the 3d of October 1594. The Earls of Huntley and Argyle were the leaders of the two armies, of whom the latter, according to some accounts, brought 10,000 men to the field. Huntly was victorious, though his numbers were, it is said, but as 1 to 10. Many a gallant man was killed. Adam Gordon's cairn, on the side of the burn of Altonlachan, is a testimony of the place on which he fell. He was Sir Adam of Auchindune, and Huntly's uncle. Argyle was only 19 years of age, of a resolute and noble spirit, and felt severely on the defeat. For the cause of this battle, and its more particular circumstances, see the History of the Family of Gordon, &c.

Battle of Mortlach.—In the year 1010, Malcolm II. obtained, in this parish, that signal victory over the Danes, which has ever since given the place a superior degree of fame, and makes it respected as classic ground. Human nature is inclined to regard, with a peculiar reverence, the very spot of earth on which was of old transacted any remarkable event. Malcolm had been beat the year before by the Danes, and was obliged to leave them in possession of the lands of Moray. Anxious, however, to expel such intruders, he now returns upon them from the south, with a powerful force; and the Danes, having intelligence of his motions, came forward

ward to give him battle. The armies get their first fight of one another not far from the church of Mortlach; and a very little to the northward of it they engage. In the beginning of the attack, while pushing on with too ardent an impetuosity, Kenneth, Thane of the Isles; Dunbar, Thane of Laudian; and Graeme, Thane of Strathern, are unfortunately slain. On the loss of three of their generals, the Scotch are struck with a panic, and go into confusion. Every thing was now in a most doubtful suspense, and too likely to be decisive. The King, who has the character of a brave, sensible, and pious man, is most reluctantly borne along with the retreating croud, till he was opposite to the church, then a chapel dedicated to Molocus. The narrowness of the passage here abated a little the career of the pursuing Danes; the flying army got a minute to breathe; and, from the very situation of the ground, were again almost necessarily collected. On a mere incident, a presence of mind, or a happy thought, under providence, often depends the fate of war. The monarch was seized, perhaps from the very appearance of the consecrated walls in that aera of superstition, with a devotional impulse. He prays, pays his homage to the Virgin Mary, and the tutelary saint, according to the manners of the times, makes a vow, is inspired with a confidence of the aid of Heaven, and addresses himself, in an animating speech, to his countrymen and fellow soldiers. It was the critical moment—his crown, his all was at stake, and the Danes were a cruel enemy. He immediately takes the lead; presses on the foe; throws Enetus, one of the Danish generals, from his horse, and kills him with his own hand. Without a certain degree of enthusiasm, there is nothing great to be done. The charge, without delay, is generally and vigorously renewed; and, under the mingled influence of patriotism and religion, the Scotch carry every thing before them,

and

and win the day ; And a bloody day it is reported to have been, though a glorious one, for Malcolm and his victorious troops. Some think that, for conveying its celebrity to future ages, was erected the ftately obelifk ftill ftanding at Forres. Certain it is, that foon after the Danes finally left the kingdom. There is an appearance, that the fecond and finifhing conflict, after rallying, happened a few hundred yards to the fouth weft of the Caftle of Balveny ; and probably the more ancient part of that building was then in exiftence ; for a fort is mentioned as near the field of battle. Perhaps it will be expected, that the ftratagem of ftopping the courfe of Dullan for a night fhould be taken notice of here, and the letting it down in a prodigious torrent on the furprifed Danes, thought to have been drawn up on each fide of this little river, by which their army is faid to have been divided, and to have become an eafier conqueft. Such a thing may have been, and, from the prefent face of the ground, is not incredible ; for the rivulet runs, about an Englifh mile above the church, in a very contracted channel, between high rocks ; and beyond that there is a moft capacious bafon, for the water to flow quietly back for a long time indeed. But if fuch a manoeuvre was practifed at all, it is more likely that it had been on fome other occafion than that of the engagement juft now related. See Fordun, Boece, &c.

As traditional and pretty fure memorials of this famous battle, are pointed out ;

1. The veftiges of an intrenchment, very diftinct at this day, on the fummit of the little Conval-hill, called by the neighbourhood the Danifh Camp.

2. A number of tumuli, or cairns, fuppofed to have been collected over the bodies of the fallen.

3. A huge and irregularly roundifh ftone, formerly, it is faid, on the grave of Enetus, but now rolled a few ells from

its

its ftation over the corpfe, and made a part of a fence about a field of corn ; where it is denominated the Aquavitae Stone. To account for this appellation, and to prevent antiquarians from puzzling their brains with dark and learned hypothefes in time to come, it may not be improper to tell, that the men, whofe brawny ftrength removed this venerable tenant, finding it rather a hard piece of work, got, as a folace for their toil, a pint of whifky, out of which, immediately, around the ftone, they took a hearty dram. Every body knows, that, in Scotland, whifky and aquavitae are the fame.

4. A fquare bit of ground, almoft covered with whins, into which multitudes of the dead were tumbled. This is very near the north-weft corner of the fir-park of Tomna-muid, and about 120 yards or fo from the above ftone, almoft directly fouth.

5. The length of Malcolm's fpear added to the church, at the weft end, in performance of a part of his vow. It has been the fpear of a Goliah, 23 or 24 feet long.

6. Three holes, exactly of the fhape of fkulls, in this ad-ditional and votive part of the houfe, yet to be feen ; where the heads of three Danes of diftinction had, with too barba-rous a triumph, been originally built in the wall. At what-ever time, or in whatever way, three fkulls may have firft been put there, there they furely were ; and, not longer than about 30 years ago, was the laft of them picked out, and toffed about by the fchool boys.

7. A ftanding ftone on the glebe, having on two of its oppofite fides fome rude and unintelligible fculpture.

Human bones, broken fabres, and other military armour, have been at different times accidentally difcovered in this part of the country : And in plowing the glebe, about 40 or 50 years ago, there was a chain of gold turned up, which looked like an ornament for the neck of one of the chiefs.

Bifhopric

Bishopric of Mortlach.—It is clear, from the evidence of history, that on this occasion, by the pious gratitude of Malcolm, and in fulfilment of a sacred engagement, Mortlach was exalted to Episcopal honours. One Beyn, or Bean, was, by Pope Benedict, made its first bishop, who, about 30 years after, died, and was buried here. Donortius was the second, and next to him came Cormac. These two, between them, enjoyed their preferment more than 80 years, and, on the death of the latter, succeeded Bishop Nectan, the fourth and last of Mortlach; for in his fourteenth year, he was translated by King David I. to Aberdeen, which soon got the name, and became the seat of the diocese. And thus Mortlach, from a dignified bishopric, sunk into an humble parsonage. The see was at Mortlach 129 years, from 1010 to 1139 [*]. Bishop Ramsay of Aberdeen, in the year 1246, appointed 13 prebendaries, of whom the 7th in order was the parson of Mortlach.

[*] Its jurisdiction and revenues were but small, comprehending no more than the church of Mortlach, the church of Cloveth, and the church of Dulmeth with all their lands: But, in regard to precedence, it was the second in Scotland, that of St Andrews being the only one before it, which extended over all the kingdom, and whose bishop was then designed *Episcopus Scotiae*, or *Episcopus Scotorum*.

Parish of Mortlach.

Additions and Corrections, by the Rev. George Gordon.

Mission.——There has long been a mission or itinerancy in Glenrinnes, supported by the committee for managing the royal bounty, which greatly accommodates five or six hundred people; of whom two thirds are reckoned in the parish of Mortlach, and one third in the parish of Aberdour. It has been a very useful appointment; and was, most probably from a strong sense of the propriety of it, one of the earliest of the kind. The people are so much convinced of its benefit, that they are just now rebuilding the meeting-house, and giving it a slate roof, at their own expence. It is between 4 or 5 miles from any church.

Society School.——There was a society school too in the same glen, which was very serviceable; and yet it was taken away lately: But, it is hoped, it will soon be restored; and it should be ambulatory betwixt Glenrinnes and Glenmarky, a year or two in the one place, and then as long in the other. For education and the interests of religion among the young in this corner, such a school may be said to be almost necessary.

The above two paragraphs should have come in immediately before the account of the poor.

Page.	Line.	Errata.
319.	4.	For ‘ Murthelack,’ read ‘ Murthelach.’
do.	9.	For ‘ Morlay,’ read ‘ Morlag.’
324.	5.	Dele ‘ above.’
do.	10.	For ‘ deers,’ read ‘ deer.’

.43⦁.

326 . 15.   For ' land,' read ' and.'

327 . 19.   For ' 1766,' read ' 1776.'

do.   13.   After ' 47$\frac{3}{10}$,' add, ' and for the third, 34$\frac{3}{10}$.'

333 .   9.   For ' needlefs,' read ' endlefs.'

335 .   —   The laft ten lines are mifplaced.

337 .   3. from the bottom.   For ' *quadringinta*,' read ' *qua-draginta.*'

338 . 11.   For ' *quaque*,' read ' *quoque*.'

344 .   5.   For ' corps,' read ' corpfes.'

346 .   5.   For ' woers,' read ' wooers.'

Befides the above, there are fome fmaller errors in fpelling and pointing, and feveral mifplacings of words and whole fentences, which the reader will eafily difcover and correct himfelf.

PARISH OF ORDIQUHILL.

(PRESBYTERY OF FORDYCE, SYNOD OF ABERDEEN,
COUNTY OF BANFF.)

By the Rev. MR. ROBERT OGILVIE.

Name, Extent, and Stipend.

ORDIQUHILL is of Gaelic original, and ſignifies, the " hollow beſide the height." The Earl of Findlater is patron; and, though he has not a foot of ground in the pariſh, pays moſt of the ſtipend. The pariſh is of an oblong form, being near 4 miles in length, from N. to S. and about 3 in breadth. It was formerly a chapelry in the pariſh of Fordyce, where public worſhip was performed once a month; and ſeems to have been erected into a ſeparate pariſh, about the year 1622. The church, which was built about the ſame time, on the ſpot where then ſtood St. Mary's chapel, is, at preſent, in bad repair; as is alſo the mance and office houſes. The ſtipend, including the glebe, which here is not worth much, is about L. 70 ſterling yearly——Previous to the augmentation, which took place in 1766, it was one of the ſmalleſt ſtipends in Scotland, being in all not above L. 30 ſterling *per annum.*—The ſchoolmaſter's

mafter's falary is 8 bolls of meal, L. 1 : 5 as feffion clerk ; and, the profits arifing from baptifms and marriages, and from about 40 fcholars.

Names of Places, Mineral Springs, &c.—The names of places in this parifh feem moftly of Gaelic original.——There are feveral excellent mineral wells in the parifh ; which were formerly much frequented. They are of a medicinal quality, and are known to be ufeful in many complaints, particularly thofe of a fcorbutio nature. One of them, being dedicated to the Virgin Mary, was formerly at certain feafons much reforted to by the fuperftitions as well as the fick. The air here is falubrious, and the people healthy, hofpitable and induftrious. —The face the country is wildly beautiful, and correfponds exactly with the fignification of the name given to it.

Produce and Rent.—About two thirds of the parifh are arable ; the other is ftill in a ftate of nature, and partly covered with heath. The foil is, in general, deep ; but cold and wet at the bottom. A confiderable quantity of lint, turnips and potatoes are raifed here ; but hemp, cabbages, and the like, however, are feldom produced in the fields. Though there are 3 or 4 farms of about 100 acres arable, befides a confiderable extent of pafture, the higheft rent, every thing included, does not exceed L 40 fterling yearly. The valued rent of the parifh is L. 1700 Scots ; the real rent at prefent, including fervitudes, amounts to about L. 700 fterling.

Proprietor and Improvements.—Sir Erneft Gordon of Park, who generally refides in the parifh, is fole proprietor ; and his houfe, which is lately fitted up in the modern tafte, is commodious and elegant ; and furrounded by a number of venerable afh, and other trees, in a thriving way. He is fpread-

ing

ing improvements rapidly around him; and there is now a probability, that agriculture will advance apace; though, in this part of the country, it muſt be confeſſed ſhe is but in her infancy. There is moſs enough here for generations to come, and ſtones ſufficient for the purpoſe of incloſing; and, though the pariſh cannot boaſt of woods, and groves, of foreſts, and water-falls, yet it can be ſaid that it has winding rills, and purling ſtreams, in abundance; and that there is ſcarcely a farm, or cot-houſe, in this diſtrict, but has ſome ſpreading trees to ſcreen and adorn it. Aſh and other hard woods thrive tolerably well; however, the ſoil, in general, ſeems better adapted for aller and other aquatics; and there is the pleaſing proſpect, that the oaklings, and various ſeedlings, that have lately been planted, will give an agreeable variety to this part of the country, and prove a laſting ſource of wealth and amuſement to the induſtrious proprietor.

Hills.—The Knock hill, part of which belongs to this pariſh, is about 2500 feet above the level of the ſea; and, as its towering head in ſeen from afar, it becomes an excellent landmark to thoſe who trade in the Murray Firth. It is ſituated, as it were, in a large capacious plain; and, while it produces a variety of excellent game for the amuſement and health of the ſportſman, and ſuggeſts to the contemplative mind an idea of the grand, the ſublime, and the beautiful, it affords a delicious repaſt for the flocks and herds of thoſe that live near. The pariſhes of Grange, Fordyce, and Ordiquhill meet on the top of this hill; and, on the very ſpot where they meet, is a terminus, or mark, from which is ſeen the greater part of Caithneſs, Roſs, Banff, Murray, &c. the windings of the Devern, part of Spey, the Murray Firth, the German ocean, &c. &c. as far as the eye can reach. In ſhort, this hill affords one of

the

the moſt grand, beautiful, and variegated proſpects ſouth of the Tweed *.

Population.—There are, at preſent, 517 ſouls in the pariſh, and, of theſe, 130 below ten years of age.—Several old people died lately, upwards of 90. The oldeſt perſon juſt now, is about 86, there are three men above 80, and as many women; one of them was never married. The number of males and females, is nearly equal. There 452 examinable perſons in it, 6 Seceders, about as many Methodiſts, two Roman Catholics, and one Epiſcopalian.

There is only one village in the pariſh. It contains, at preſent but 12 families. It is called Cornhill: and near it, during the ſummer ſeaſon, there are annually held ſome well frequented markets. There are but few handycraftſmen; and, at preſent, only 3 apprentices.——The farms are, in general, uncloſed, and but ſmall; being commonly from L. 5 to L. 20 ſterling yearly rent.—Till of late, however, few leaſes were given without a graſſum.—The people are, in general, modeſt, ſober, and of a religious deportment; and, though few of them may be ſaid to be rich, yet there has not been any begging poor, belonging to the pariſh, in the memory of man.—The contributions, ſeat rents, &c. &c. for the behoof of the poor, amount to about L. 6 : 10 *per annum.*—There are, at an average, in the pariſh, 5 marriages, 18 births, and 10 deaths annually.

* The ſeed time here is commonly finiſhed ſoon after Whitſunday, and, by the middle of October, the farmer, in general, ſees his corn beyond the power of the ſtorm.

Among the many improvements that might be introduced into this part of the country, a bridge, on the great road between Huntly and Portſoy, over the Boyn, which partly runs through the pariſh, is much needed. For want of ſuch an accommodation, ſeveral uſeful members of ſociety have loſt their lives; and a woman, in attempting to croſs it, was with her horſe hurried down the ſtream, wh ere they periſhed.

annually.——The number of inhabitants has continued for theſe hundred years paſt, nearly what it is at preſent. The return to Dr. Webſter, however, was 666 ſouls *.

Miſcellaneous Obſervations.—The people here are, in general, of a contented mind, not given to any peculiar vice, and regular attendants on public worſhip; and, though few of them are gaudily dreſſed, yet moſt of them appear at the church in clean and decent apparel.—About 30 years ago, there were only 3 hats, and 3 watches in the pariſh, being thoſe the proprietor, the miniſter, and the ſchoolmaſter; but now almoſt every labouring ſervant has his hat, and watch, his Engliſh cloth coat, his white thread ſtockings, &c. The ordinary fuel is peat, and turf; and the making of tether bindings, and ropes from moſs-fir, is common all round this part of the country †.

Mr. Walter Goodall, a native of this pariſh, aſſiſted Mr. Thomas Ruddiman, in ſeveral of his productions; and, about the year 1750 publiſhed 2 vols. 8vo. in defence of Mary Queen of Scots.

There

---

* The price of labour here is much increaſed of late; as is alſo that of every thing. About 30 years ago a labouring ſervant would have been got for L. 2 : 10, and now he cannot be had under L. 6 ſterling a year. Female ſervants earn from L. 2 to L. 3 ſterling yearly.—The ſurplus grain, which annually amounts to ſome hundred bolls, is generally carried to Portſoy, or Banff, the neareſt ſea port towns; to which places, alſo, and Cullen, moſt of the other ſurplus products are carried for ſale.

† There is a woman in this pariſh, that has the perfect uſe of all her faculties, though ſhe has not been above half an hour *at once* out of bed theſe 30 years. A diſappointment in love is thought to have been the cauſe; for, about 33 years ago, upon her father's diſcouraging a young man's paying his addreſſes to her, ſhe went to bed, and has never left it ſince. The ſtruggle, it ſeems, between love and filial affection, ran ſo high, as materially to affect her active powers.

There is but one inn in the parifh.—Several hundreds of cattle, fheep, &c. are carried annually from hence to the fouthward. Land is commonly ploughed by oxen; oxen and horfes, however, are joined to the fame plough.—But to conclude this fhort imperfeét account; at a diftance from the abodes of luxury and vice, the wants of the people of this parifh are but few; and nothing feems more calculated for bettering their external circumftances, and making their days glide on comfortably, than extending leafes to a greater length, and encourageing them to inclofe, drain, and improve their farms. Such a meafure would alfo be highly beneficial to the proprietor *.

* Meal generally fells at about 9d halfpenny per peck;—beef and mutton at 3d halfpenny;—a good hen at 8d.—and a fat lamb at 3s.—A labourer earns about 10d. a day;—a mafon 16d.—a carpenter 14d.—and a taylor 6d. and his maintenance.

PARISH of RATHVEN,

(County of Banff, Synod of Aberdeen, Presbytery of Fordyce),

By the Rev. Mr George Donaldson.

Name, Situation, Extent, &c.

RATHVEN is ſaid, by thoſe converſant in the Gaelic
language, to be derived from two original words, the
one ſignifying brake, or fern, and the other, rock, eminence,
or hillock. In ſupport of this derivation, it may be obſerved, that there is a ſpot in the neighbourhood of the church,
called Brakenhaugh ; and a farm named Rannachie, *i. e.* the
Brakenfield. This pariſh is ſituated in that diſtrict of
Banffſhire, named Enzie. It is 10 miles long from E. to
W.; and from 3 to 5 miles broad from N. to S. On the N.
it is bounded by the Moray Frith. Cullen is the neareſt poſt-
town to the eaſtern end of the pariſh ; and Fochabers to the
weſtern, from which it is ſcarce 4 miles diſtant. The church
and manſe are on the N. ſide of the poſt-road, and at the
diſtance

diftance of 3¼ miles from Cullen. The whole of the parifh has never been furveyed ; and therefore the number of acres cannot be precifely afcertained. Partly, however, from plans, and partly from computation, it may be ftated at 27,000 acres Scotch meafure, and in the following proportions nearly :

Arable, - - - - 4700
Meadow and pafture, - - 1600
Hills, moors, and moffes, - - 16,200
Plantations, - - - 4500

Soil, Surface, and Climate.—In a parifh of fuch extent there is generally a great variety of foil ; and this parifh affords no exception to the general rule. In one corner the foil is a light loam, extremely rich, on a bottom of clay ; in another it is thin, but abundantly fertile, on a red mud. Some places are very fandy, and others clayey ; and, in general, with the exception of what is fandy, an amazing number of fmall roundifh ftones cover the ground. The furface is variegated with hills and eminences, ftreams of water, and fertile plains. The Binhill, in the S. E. end of the parifh, is moftly planted with trees. It is covered with heath, and of fo confiderable an altitude as to ferve as a landmark to the fifhers, being perceived by them, according to their way of reckoning, at full 15 leagues diftance. The hills of Maud and Adie, alfo covered with heath to the top, are contiguous to it, but of lefs elevation, and proceed in a wefterly direction to the confines of the parifh. The greateft part of the parifh has a N. W. expofure, and fuffers from the ftorms which blow from that point ; but this inconvenience is greatly over-balanced by a fea-coaft, including its windings, of 12 miles. The vicinity of the fea, independent of all its other advantages, ferves in fome meafure to mitigate the heats in fummer, and to leffen, both in point

of

of ſeverity and duration, the cold in winter. The pariſhioners, being ſubject to no epidemical diſeaſes, are in
general healthy, and many attain to old age. In proof of
the ſalubrity of the air, and goodneſs of their conſtitutions,
it may be remarked, that notwithſtanding the populouſneſs
of the pariſh, no man bred to phyſic or ſurgery has ever
thought it worth his while to ſettle in it.

Number of Proprietors.—Theſe are 8 : The Duke of Gordon, the Earl of Findlater, Mr Baron Gordon, Mr Gordon
of Letteſcourie, Mr Gordon of Cairnfield, Mr Dunbar of
Nether Buckie, Mr Stuart of Tanachy, and Mr Stuart of
Oxhill. Only 2 of them, the proprietors of Letteſcourie
and Cairnfield, reſide in the pariſh. The former of theſe
gentlemen has laid out a part of his fortune in embelliſh-
ing his paternal property, and in building elegant houſes on
his different eſtates ; and the latter directs his attention to
the improvement of his eſtate, and the cultivation of his
farm.

Mode of Cultivation.—The climate is early, and the ſoil
in general good, and ſuſceptible of the higheſt cultivation.
Some of the heritors have availed themſelves of all the
modern improvements in agriculture ; and of late the tenants have begun to improve their ſyſtem of farming. In
their ſeaſons, one ſees fields properly cleaned, ridges
ſtraighted, ſmall ſtones removed, and luxuriant crops of
grain and of graſs growing. By means of planting, nui-
ſances are converting into beauties, and the country is gradually aſſuming a pleaſanter appearance. In ſhort, as a ſpirit of induſtry and of imitation is becoming prevalent a-
mong the tenants, with a proper degree of encouragement,
the face of the country would, in a ſhort time, be mightily
improved. Wheat, barley, oats, and peaſe are the grains
usually

ufually cultivated. A fummer fallow is the ordinary preparation for wheat ; and after the field is thoroughly cleaned, and well manured with dung from the fifher-towns, if it
can be procured, the crop is laid down in October. Barley
is fown without manure, after oats from a ley-furrow, and
with manure after peafe or turnip. The turnip field is generally ploughed once, and the peafe twice, before laying
on the dung for the feed-furrow. Oats are fown on ley
ploughed in February, and frequently after barley. When
the oats after barley are reaped, the field gets a ploughing
in autumn, and remains in that ftate till fpring, when it receives the feed furrow, and is fown with peafe. On the S.
fide of the poft-road, towards the hills, the acre fows from
from 12 to 14 pecks ; on the N. fide, towards the coaft,
from 16 to 18 ; of gray peafe the fame quantity is allowed ;
but of the late kind, which is feldom ufed, as they do not
ripen in feafon, and fo prove unproductive, 13 or 14 fuffice.
About a peck lefs of barley, than of the above kinds of
grain, is allowed to the acre, and of wheat the ufual allowance is a boll. Of wheat the average produce is 10 returns ;
barley 7 ; oats 4 ; and peafe 3. On many places peafe do
not thrive ; and oats, on a field that has been manured with
dung from the fifher-towns, generally fails, and on that account they are feldom a lucrative crop, except after ley.
As a common tenant does not often lay down his beft
ground with grafs-feeds, many excellent fields have been
under a regular courfe of cropping time immemorial. A
fmall fpot of about ¼ of an acre, in Mr Baron Gordon's eftate,
has produced barley-crops for 47 years, without any lofs
of fertility. It is fituated near the beach at Buckie ; has
been uniformly twice ploughed, and gotten fome loads of
fea-weed, or other manure annually. It fows 12 pecks,
and has produced from 4 to 5 bolls. Turnips and potatoes
are cultivated for home-confumption ; and flax is pretty
fuccefsfully

successfully raised for family purposes only. The distinction between infield and outfield is scarcely known here. Ground lately improved out of moors, or such like, which will not bear the same rotation of crops as the farm, is called outfield. Land near the hills gives from 8 s. to 15 s. and on the coast from 15 s. to L. 1, 10 s. an acre. In general the farms are small, and cottagers almost unknown. Two tenants pay from L. 80 to L. 100; a few from L. 40 to L. 60; and all the rest from L. 10, or even lower, to L. 40 *.

Manures.—Different tenants employ different manures. Some are satisfied with what their cattle produce. Those on the coast are exceedingly attentive to procure sea-weed. In summer they spread it on ley to the extent of 300 single cart-loads an acre; of 160 after the crop is cut down, and during winter; and of 100 in April and May, when it is strongest. This process is renewed every second year. The weed is loosed from the rocks by a north-easterly storm, and driven ashore in great quantities. In a small bay, called the holl of Gollachie, 10,000 cart-loads have been accumulated by the tide in the course of a week. Sea shells purchased at any of the fisher-towns for 2 d. the cart-load, are spread on the fields as a manure, and like sea-weed left to the influence of the weather. It would be a better plan to burn them, as it is done at a small expense, and they produce

---

* *Implements of Husbandry.*—The ploughs are well adapted to the state of the country; as the soil is light, they are of a slender but neat make. A few of them are drawn by 2 horses, many by 4, and still more by 2 small horses and 4 black cattle, either oxen or cows. Carts are in universal use; some of them are neatly and substantially made; but far the greater number are of so bad materials, so unartificially put together, and of so diminutive a size, as hardly to deserve the name.

produce a moderate quantity of excellent lime. A fpecies of limeftone, called by fome ftone-marl, is dug out of a quarry at Cuttlebrae, in the Duke of Gordon's lands, fpread on the field, and left to the operation of the feafons to pulverize it. This is reckoned an expenfive, but valuable manure. As moft people have accefs to one or other of the above manures, recourfe is feldom had to lime, though it can be procured in fufficient quantity for the purpofes of agriculture.

Seed Time and Harveft.—As the foil is early, feed time for peafe feldom commences before the middle of March ; for oats it begins about the 26th, and continues to the end of April or middle of May ; and for barley thence to the middle or end of June. Harveft begins about the middle or end of Auguft, and is finifhed in October *.

Crops, Produce, and Rent.—It is no eafy matter to ftate with any kind of precifion, what proportion of the farm is allotted to each kind of grain. Here no uniformity can be expected, becaufe the leaft alteration in circumftances may introduce deviations from eftablifhed rules. The following however, is the moft fatisfactory ftate of the general practice that I have been able to obtain. One fourth of the farm is laid down with peafe and barley ; fcarce one fourth in grafs ; and the other two fourths in oats, fallow, flax, turnips, and potatoes. Wheat is feldom fown by the tenants,

as

* In 1782, recorded in Scotland for the failure of the crop, this parifh had the good fortune to efcape the general calamity. Scarcely had they ever a better crop, or more to fpare. The great demand for meal and feed, and the high prices which they brought, bettered their circumftances. Seed-oats and meal fold at L. 1, and barley at L. 1, 5 s. the boll.

as they do not reckon it a lucrative crop; and beſides the want of winter-herding diſcourages them from any attempts to raiſe it. Some of them begin to make hay, as there is a ready market for it at 6 d. the ſtone. 200 ſtone, at 20 lb. Amſterdam, is accounted a good crop, and 160 a medium one, the acre. Of the different kinds of grain the produce has already been ſtated. The pariſh ſerves itſelf with grain, and exports 2000 bolls yearly. The valued rent is L. 6395 Scots, and the real rent may be from L. 4000 to L. 5000 Sterling; but, like moſt pariſhes in Scotland, where the rent is paid in money and victual, it muſt vary with the price of grain *.

Commerce.

* *Prices of Grain and Proviſions.*—The grain of crop 1792, during the winter ſeaſon was very moderate. Since April meal has riſen to 15 s. and barley to 18 s. the boll. Beef and mutton 3¼ d. the lb. a duck 10 d. a hen 8 d. a chicken 3 d. eggs 2½ d. the dozen, butter 8 d. the lb. at 24 oz. Engliſh; cheeſe 5 s. the ſtone, at 24 lb. Engliſh.

Wages and Price of Labour.—Men ſervants employed in huſbandry get from L. 6 to L. 8: women from L. 2 to L. 3; herds from L. 1 to L. 2; a tailor 8 d. and his meat; a day-labourer from 10 d. to 1 s.; carpenters 1 s. 4 d. to 1 s. 6 d.; and ſlaters 2 s. without meat.

Services and Cuſtoms.—The ſervices, though not in general aboliſhed, are, according to my intormation, exacted with ſuch moderation, as not to be eſteemed a grievance by the tenants. Cuſtom fowls to a certain extent are payable when required. Reſtriction to mills prevails. Leet-peats, as they are called, (meaſuring 8 feet in length, 12 broad, and 12 high), muſt be paid in kind when demanded. Long carriages, as they are termed, that is, carriages to a ſpecified diſtance from the proprietor's houſe, are ſometimes exacted: And in ſeed-time and harveſt, as well as at hay-making, certain ſervices are required. For all theſe the tenants are liable, and they are paid without murmuring, becauſe never exacted to the extent mentioned in their leaſe. Still, however, the very name implies bondage, becauſe ſervices, being in ſome meaſure arbitrary, muſt ever be reckoned grievous.

Commerce.—Five and forty years ago there was not a single shop, nor any imported article for sale in the parish. About the year 1750, the first shop was opened in Buckie, at that time known as a fishing station only; at present there are 8 merchants or shop-keepers in it who trade to the extent of L. 5000, exclusive of grain, annually. Originally unbred to business, and possessed of a small stock, they began their merchandise on a very narrow scale; as their stock increased, they extended their views, and launched out into new branches. They import coals, salt, iron, and other necessaries; and export fish and grain. About 500 bolls of salt are imported annually; and this summer (1793) 2500 bolls of wheat, barley, oats, and meal have been exported from Buckie.

Manufactures.—Two or three weavers manufacture linen to the amount of L. 200 yearly; and some months ago a small manufacture in hemp was established at Buckie. A man from Dundee is employed to dress the hemp, and it is afterward converted into lines, canvas, and nets. We have no flax-dresser in the parish, and yet the spinning of flax into yarn is an important article. In 1750, a manufacturer * in Cullen introduced this branch here; and in 1759, a weaver, still alive, was the first residing agent employed in this new line; since the above period, considerable progress has been made in it. The flax, mostly Dutch, is sent dressed from Aberdeen, Fraserburgh, Banff, Portsoy, Cullen, Huntley, Keith, and Fochabers, to different agents,

to

grievous. Sound policy requires their total abolition; and it is to be hoped. that the time is fast approaching. when every vestige of the pristine servitude will disappear for ever; and mutual stipulations, on equal terms, properly defined and clearly expressed, will ascertain what man has a right to exact from man.

* Mr Mungo Rannie.

to the amount of 38,900 cwt. which is given out to the ſpinners at the average price of 1 s. the lb. and brings in annually L. 1945. A few tons of kelp are manufactured on that part of the coaſt belonging to the proprietor of Buckie.

Fiſher-towns and Fiſheries.—There are 4 fiſher-towns in the pariſh: Buckie, Port-eaſy, Findochtie, and Port-nockie. The firſt belongs to two proprietors, and the 3 laſt to Lord Findlater.

1. Buckie, the moſt weſterly of the fiſher-towns, is ſituated at the mouth of the rivulet or burn of Buckie. Mr Baron Gordon is proprietor of the lands and houſes on the E. ſide of the burn, and Mr Dunbar on the W. On the W. ſide there are 102 houſes, and 400 inhabitants; of whom 175 are males, and 225 females: And on the E. ſide, 63 houſes, and 303 inhabitants; of whom 136 are males, and 167 females. The W. ſide has been a fiſhing ſtation for 150 years, and is, according to my information, the oldeſt in the pariſh. The date of the other ſide as a fiſhing ſtation, I have not been able to aſcertain. In 1723, a fiſhing-boat and crew belonging to the Duke of Gordon, removed from Gollachie, which lies a mile weſtward, to Buckie, as being a ſafer and more commodious ſtation. At that period the proprietor of Nether Buckie, who held his lands in feu from the Duke, had only one boat; and as he was out of the kingdom, and in arrear to his Grace, the deſired accommodation was the more eaſily obtained. At preſent, there are 14 boats and 1 yawl * employed in the fiſheries. The boats are about 9 tons, and the yawl 4. Of theſe, 3 boats and 1 yawl belong to his Grace, 3 to Mr Dunbar, and 8 to Mr Baron Gordon. The merchants, and others of Buckie, are proprietors

---

* The yawl's crews are old men, who fiſh near the ſhore, if poſſible.

prietors of 4 floops of 18, 25, 30 and 36 tons, and 2 of 60 tons burden, navigated by 24 feamen.

2. Porteafy is fituated at the diftance of fcarce 2 miles from Buckie. It became a fifhing ftation in 1727, when 5 houfes were built by the proprietor of Rannes for the accommodation of the original fifhers from Findhorn. This information was obtained from a man aged 90, ftill alive, and a native of this parifh, who helped to man the firft boat. At prefent this fifher town contains 44 houfes, and 178 inhabitants; and of thefe 84 are males, and 94 females: They have 5 large and 7 fmall boats. At the commencement of this ftation, Buckie had 5 boats, Findochtie 3, and Portnockie 5.

3. Findochtie lies at the diftance of 2 miles from the former ftation, and has 45 houfes, and 162 inhabitants; 74 males and 88 females. It was fettled in 1716 by fifhers from Fraferfburgh, according to the information of a woman aged 91, who was married to one of the original fifhers in 1721. Portnockie, of which fhe is a native, at the time of her removal, had 3 boats. There are at prefent 4 large, and 6 fmall boats in Findochtie.

4. Portnockie is at the diftance of 2 miles from Findochtie. The following anecdote afcertains its origin as a fifhing ftation: About 20 years ago died Kattie Slater, aged 96. Like many old people fhe was unable to tell her age precifely; but fhe recollected that fhe was as old as the houfe of Farfkane, as her father had often told her that he built the firft houfe in Portnockie the fame year in which the houfe of Farfkane was built, and that fhe was brought from Cullen to it, and rocked in a fifher's fcull inftead of a cradle. Now by the date on the houfe of Farfkane, it appears to have been built in 1677. Thus the origin of Portnockie is fixed with fufficient accuracy. At prefent

it

it confifts of 80 houfes, and 243 inhabitants; and there are 7 large, and 9 fmall boats in it *.

Herring

* The large boats in the three towns laft mentioned are about 10 tons, and the fmall ones 4. The original coft of one of the former. including fail, maft, oars, and lines, is about L. 24; and of the latter, half that fum. In confideration of receiving a fpecified rent annually, the proprietor allows L. 11 to every crew to purchafe a new boat, which is underftood to laft 7 years, called here the long run. Then a mutual contract is entered into between the proprietor and the crew, wherein he engages to fecure them in the property of the boat; and they bind themfelves to ferve in it, and pay their rent during the term of 7 years. If the boat is judged unfit for fea before the end of the leafe, and application is made for a new one, a deduction is made for every deficient year of the boat's run to the extent of L. 1, 15 s. which goes in part of the L. 11 for another boat. In the different towns the rent is different. The average rent of each boat is L. 5 : 3 : 3, and 6 dried cod or ling. The fmall boats are the property of the fifhers, and pay no rent. As they have no fmall boats at Buckie, the large ones are ufed at all feafons. In the other towns, the large ones are ufed from the end of February to the end of July; and the fmall ones at all other times.

Every large boat has a crew of 6 men and a boy. Each man has a line containing from 100 to 120 hooks, at the diftance of 7 fathoms from one another. The boy's line is half the length of a man's. From the end of February, when the feafon for great fifh begins, till the end of April, they feldom go above 16 leagues from the fhore in queft of cod and ling. From the beginning of May they launch out to the diftance of 23 leagues in fearch of fkate. They are found in greateft number in a particular place of Caithnefs, called the Skate-hole. Cod, ling, fkate halibut, and a few tufk, are the only great fifh caught in the Moray frith. Cod, ling, and tufk are falted in pits on the beach, as they are caught and dried on the rocks for fale. Skate is dried without falt, and the halibut is ufed frefh. Of thefe, ling and fkate are the moft valuable to the fifhers, becaufe their livers yield much oil. Cod, ling, and tufk are in feafon from May to February; fkate is good through the whole year, and halibut in higheft ftate of perfection about July. About the end of June, the dry fifh is ftowed in boats. navigated by 4 or 5 men, and carried to market in the towns along the coaft of Fife and the frith of Forth. The large boat will

carry

Herring-Fishery.—The boat's crew, after difposing of their great fish, generally engage in the herring-fishery on the Caithnefs coaft for 6 weeks, from the 24th July. The fmall boats, having 4 men a-piece, are ufed. Every man has at leaft 2 nets, which coft him L. 4. The boats either enter on the bounty, or engage for 10 s. the barrel, and a bottle of whifky a-day, in lieu of all demands. It is cuftomary to give the crew 2 s. at the time of engaging, and as much at the end of the fifhery. Thofe, again, who prefer the-bounty, receive L. 8 certain, with the ufual quantity of whifky, 5 s. arrival money, as they call it, 2 s. weekly for their Saturday's pint, and 5 s. at the time of their departure. When the fifhery fails, this is the preferable plan, but when it anfwers tolerably well, the former is moft lucrative. In a good feafon, a boat may take 40 barrels in a night ; however, from 50 to 100 barrels is the ufual rate of fifhing in favourable feafons. The general

ral

carry from L. 60 to L. 70 worth. The great fifh generally bring from L. 8 to L. 12 a man, and half that fum for the boy.

The crew of a fmall boat confifts of 5 men and a boy. In the fame fifhing ftation, every man's line is of equal length ; but in the different ftations they are of different lengths. It contains from 600 to 900 hooks, at the diftance of one fathom from one another; and a boy's half as many. The fmall boats are ufed for catching haddocks, whitings, flounders, &c. Befides thefe, a good many great fifh are caught with the fmall lines, and pickled for the London market. Haddocks are in prime from Auguft to February; whitings are worft in Auguft; the gray flounder is beft in harveft ; and the fpotted, which is inferior to the gray, is beft in fpring. Mackerels are caught from the beginning of July to the end of Auguft, by a line funk with lead. Herrings are fometimes plentiful on the coaft, and their feafon is the fame with that of mackerel. Haddocks, 10 years ago, were caught within half a mile of the fhore ; for feveral years none have been found nearer than from 7 to 10 leagues off land, till of late, that they have again made their appearance hard by the fhore. The income of the fmall fifh is eftimated by the fifhers to be at leaft equal to that of the great.

ral courſe of their fiſhing has been at Staxigo, and in the head of the Moray frith; and their engagements with the owners of veſſels cleared out on the bounty. The herrings on this coaſt are generally better than thoſe caught farther ſouth, and bring a higher price by 2 s. the barrel at leaſt for home uſe. Montroſe, Dundee, the towns on the frith of Forth, and Newcaſtle, are the beſt markets for large herrings; and Jamaica, and the Weſt India iſlands, for the middle ſized and ſmall herrings. They are exported from London, Newcaſtle, Greenock, and a few from Leith. The herring-fiſhery is fluctuating and precarious. When the fiſhing is ſmall, the adventurer loſes; when a full cargo is caught, or nearly ſo, the profit may amount to about 4 s. the barrel *.

Cod-Fiſhery.—This is ſuſceptible of conſiderable improvement. From 1ſt October to the middle of February, a great many cod are caught on the ſmall lines, which, if they are not loſt, are ſold for a trifle, as they cannot be dried. From 300 to 400 barrels of cod, and from 100 to 200 of codlings, a ſmaller cod, might be cured annually, during the period ſpecified above, in the 4 fiſher-towns belonging to the pariſh. Two attempts have been made in this

---

* In July 1786 a number of very large herrings was diſcovered, chiefly by ſome country people, in the Bay of Buckie, and along the coaſt. In 1787, Meſſrs Falls employed ſeveral boats on the coaſt with great ſuccefs. Some of the boats caught in a night 27 ſalmon crans, *i. e.* 27,000 herrings. Theſe gentlemen dropped this fiſhery after one trial; and it remained neglected, except by the country people, who, in fine nights, were very ſuccefsful, till 1791 and 1792, when ſome boats were employed by Mr J. Geddes and ſon; and they ſometimes caught from 12 to 19 crans the boat in a night. But it was ſoon diſcovered, that the want of a harbour rendered Buckie unfit for a herring-fiſhing ſtation, as no veſſel could repair to it with materials.

this line; but the want of a harbour to ſhip the fiſh regularly to market, and the high price of ſalt, rendered them unſucceſsful. Were a proper quay built, and ſalt free from duty allowed for curing cod, the above being the beſt ſeaſon, a large ſupply of excellent cod might be ſent regularly to market. The cod caught at this ſeaſon, after lying as long as neceſſary in the ſalt, are generally dried for a few days, and even the winter ſeaſon, after ſalting, will dry them ſufficiently. The beſt markets in Scotland for ſalt cod, are Edinburgh, Glaſgow, Leith, Borrowſtounneſs, and all the coaſt-towns on the frith of Forth. The principal market for pickled or barrelled cod is London.

Lobſter-Fiſhery.—In 1792, all the fiſhers on the coaſt entered into a contract for 5 years with Meſſrs. Selby and Company of London, or with the Northumberland Fiſhery Society, to fiſh for lobſters, when they did not find it prudent to go in ſearch of other fiſh. The ſkiff and tackling for this fiſhery coſt about L. 5, 5 s. The Companies furniſh the ſkiffs, and are reimburſed by inſtalments. They take all their lobſters at $2\frac{1}{2}$ d. a-piece, provided they meaſure 6 inches from the point of the noſe to the end of the boſs, and when under that ſize, two are eſteemed equivalent to one. Lobſters are in ſeaſon from 1ſt February to the end of June, and from 1ſt November to Chriſtmas. Laſt year lobſters to a conſiderable value were caught on this coaſt; but leſs attention has been paid to them this year, owing partly to the great ſucceſs of the white fiſhery, and partly to the amazing quantity of lobſters caught on the coaſt of Caithneſs, which the Companies have at a cheaper rate, *viz.* at $1\frac{1}{2}$ d. for the largeſt ſize. I am unable to ſtate the product of this fiſhery for the laſt year in all the 4 towns, by reaſon of the removal of ſome of the Companies agents.

The

The agent at Portnockie has furniſhed me with the following note :

To 7913 lobſters received at Portnockie, for the Northumberland Fiſhery Society, at 2½ d.   -   L. 82 8 6½

To caſh paid for cork, cords, twine, crill bottoms, iron rims, and other neceſſary expenſes for behoof of the Society,   -   125 1 1½

Now, allowing the other 3 towns in this pariſh to have had ſimilar activity and ſucceſs in this fiſhery in 1792, the total product is,   -   -   -   -   -   -   365 9 6

And the total caſh paid out by the Company's agents for cork, &c.   -   -   -   554 1 5

To the above let us add an average ſtate of the 31 boats, excluſive of the herring fiſhery, reckoning every man's annual income from the great and ſmall fiſh at L..20, and the boys at L. 10, and every boat to have 6 men and a boy, the total product is   L. 4030 0 0

N. B. The average product of the herring-fiſhery is not ſtated, as it was begun only 5 years ago, and all the fiſhers do not engage in it.

I have only farther to obſerve on the ſubject of the fiſheries, that a few ſalmon are caught in the pariſh at the mouths of the rivulets or burns of Gollachie and Tynet. They are commonly called ſtall fiſheries. Of theſe there are 2 at Tynet, belonging to Mr Stuart at Tanachie, and 2 at Gollachy, belonging to Mr Baron Gordon and Mr Dunbar. The 4 might produce about L. 24 annually to the proprietors.

Roads.—The roads in the pariſh were originally made, and are kept in repair by the ſtatute-labour. The poſt-
road

road paffes through the parifh in a wefterly direction for
upwards of 8 miles. The firft 5 from Cullen to the burn
of Buckie, are almoft equally good in all feafons, and eafily
kept in excellent repair. The other 3 miles not having
fo good a bottom, are apt to become deep in rainy weather; it is in contemplation to change the direction of this
road in part; and it will require great attention to prevent the public from fuffering by the alteration, when carried to the intended extent. On entering the parifh, the
beautiful arch of the bridge over the rivulet at Cullen
houfe, ftrikes the eye of the beholder on the left hand.
After paffing the bridge in the line of the public road,
which is too narrow and wants parapets, fine fields, and
thriving plantations adorn the fcenery for the firft 3 miles,
and cheer the weary traveller, in fpite of a mofs on the
left, which forces itfelf on his obfervation, and accompa-
nies him for more than 2 miles. A bleak and dreary profpect fucceeds for 2 miles through the moor of Ranna-
chy *.

Harbours.—Nature has formed the only harbours at the
fifhing ftations. But to render them fafe and commodious,

quays

* To the right, on this moor, at the diftance of 100 paces from the
road, is an eminence evidently artificial, called Tarrieclerack, and fuppofed by fome to be a burial-place. The view is confined, as before, by
hills and moors, covered with heath. Hardly does any pleafant object
appear to break the barren uniformity, and relieve the mind. At length
a peep of the Moray frith, and of the Caithnefs hills, at the diftance of
90 miles, diffolves the gloom, and awakens the attention to a fertile
country, finely variegated with little hills and fertile plains, in a high
ftate of cultivation. The burn of Tynet, which feparates this parifh
from Belly, ftands in need of a bridge. Though its courfe be but fhort,
and quantity of water trifling in dry weather; yet in rainy feafons, it is
frequently fwelled into a torrent, which the traveller cannot pafs without fear and danger.

quays would be neceſſary. In their preſent ſtate, the united exertions of the men and women are employed in
dragging the boats up the beach, to ſecure them from being broken by the waves, and ſimilar efforts muſt be made
in launching. Theſe daily operations are very hurtful to
the boats, and ſometimes fatal to the men. At Buckie and
Findochtie only can piers, or quays, be conſtructed. Their
advantages are many and important, and the want of them
is ſeverely felt by people of all deſcriptions. The land-
carriage of heavy goods from Aberdeen, Banff or Portſoy,
adds conſiderably to their price, and operates as a tax on
the conſumer. Coals, ſalt and iron are ſometimes unload-
ed in the ſummer ſeaſon at Buckie, but at the riſk of loſing the veſſel. With the laudable view of obviating theſe
inconveniencies, the proprietor of Buckie, not many years
ago, cauſed a ſurvey of the harbour, and plan of a pier to
be made on the eaſt ſide of the burn ; and ſanguine hopes
were entertained by the public, of the advantages that
would accrue from the execution of a plan which promiſed
ſafety, and 14 feet of water at neap tides. But this uſeful
and meritorious undertaking has not hitherto been executed. It is, however, I would fain hope, only ſuſpended,
not abandoned. A pier at Buckie would be a ſtanding
monument of the Baron's generoſity, and ſerve to hand
him down to future ages as the father of his people, and
friend of mariners *. Findochtie, though at preſent neglected,

* In the mean time, another plan has been adopted on a ſmaller
ſcale, and leſs eligible ſituation, at the mouth of the burn, on the weſt
ſide, belonging to Mr Dunbar. Active ſteps have been taken by the
Buckie merchants and fiſhers to effectuate it. To render this undertaking ſafer and more extenſively uſeful, it was judged proper to have a
ſmall pier or bulwark on the eaſt ſide of the burn, which could not be
done without permiſſion from Mr Baron Gordon. A petition was therefore
made out, and preſented in 1792, craving leave to build, at their own
expenſe,

glected, claims the public attention in an eminent degree. It is fusceptible of being improved into one of the beft and fafeft harbours in Scotland, equal, in every refpect, to Cromarty, except in extent. It feems to have been moulded by the hand of nature, for a fafe and eafy retreat in tempeftuous weather to veffels in the Moray frith, that are unable to make Cromarty on the oppofite fhore. The diftance between them is 60 miles due eaft and weft. It is faid that Government once ordered a furvey of Findochtie to be made, but from what motive I never heard. I employed one of the fifhers to take the breadth of the entrance into this beautiful bafon, at a rock called the Beacon, on the weft, and low-water foundings at a neap tide, in the central point, where the water is moft fhallow ; and from an exact menfuration, the entrance was found to be 90 yards wide, and the water 21 feet deep. Hence, it is capable of receiving a fhip of the line, and capacious enough to contain all the veffels belonging to the Moray frith. Language can hardly paint it in a more advantageous light than it deferves. It attracts the obfervation, and arrefts the attention of every beholder. I am well affured that it might be made a moft complete harbour, for the

expenfe, on a rock, part of his property, a bulwark, which they conceived could not hurt his intereft. This petition was unfortunately prefented at a time, when the Baron, by reafon of a circumftance in which he was deeply interefted, took little or no concern in bufinefs of any kind. It has therefore, in all probability, efcaped his notice, or it is moft likely, that he would have granted a requeft that could not poffibly be hurtful to him, and might be beneficial to his own people. It is imagined, that L 300 would build a tolerably commodious harbour at the burn mouth ; L. 200 would make it a good creek at all feafons ; and even L. 100 would make it fafe for fmall craft in fummer only. Buckie is advantageoufly fituated on a central part of the coaft, near Keith and Fochabers, and has frequent communication with the parifhes of Mortlach, Boharm, Botriphnie, Glafs, Glenlivet and Cabrach.

the moderate ſum of L. 3000 *. A more induſtrious, in-
trepid, adventurous race of mariners than thoſe in this pariſh, is nowhere to be found in his Majeſty's dominions.
They are expoſed to continual danger in open boats from
an inconſtant climate and a ſtormy ſea. In clear nights, by
the aid of a compaſs, the obſervation of certain ſtars, and
a few land-marks, they reckon their lives in perfect ſafety.
But when the clouds begin to gather, the winds to riſe, the
waves to heave, and all nature to wear a lowering countenance, they are perplexed whither to direct their courſe ;
to attempt the ſhore is certain death ; and to live at ſea
ſcarcely poſſible. In ſuch dreadful alternatives, the love of
life moſt frequently ſuggeſts the propriety of ſteering a
middle courſe ; yet this dangerous navigation often terminates in death. Such dire diſaſters have given riſe to rei-
terated propoſals for building a ſmack of about 30 tons,
and with proper accommodations, to be employed in the
white fiſhery. It is the opinion of the moſt ſkilful and experienced fiſhers, that in ſuch a veſſel the fiſhery might be
carried on with greater ſafety, and more benefit to the un-
dertakers, and with advantage to the country. But the
want of a ſafe harbour has always occaſioned ſchemes of
this nature to prove abortive. A regard therefore for the
preſervation of men's lives and the good of ſociety ſhould
induce all ranks to join in forwarding ſuch plans of public
utility.

The

---

* Lord Findlater could not beſtow a part of his princely fortune to
better purpoſe, than in conſtructing a harbour that would promote his
own intereſt, prove a benefit to thouſands, and tranſmit his name with
honour to poſterity But as his Lordſhip's views are at preſent directed
to other uſeful objects, there is no immediate proſpect of his executing
ſuch an undertaking. Still, however, a harbour is much wanted at Findochtie, and would be attended with many advantages to the country ;
and conſequently is one of thoſe public works which merits the attention
of Government.

The following state of the loss sustained by the fisher-towns in this parish, will show this matter in a stronger light.

1. In Buckie, since 1723, 8 boats, with their crews and passengers, have perished, amounting in all to   -   60 men and boys.

Of that number, 50 have been lost within these 40 years; and it is well attested that so many have not died a natural death in the same period.

2. Porteasy has lost since it became a fishing station,   -   4 men.

3. Findochtie, about 38 years ago, lost 1 boat, and   -   -   7 men.

4. Portknockie, within these 26 years, has lost 5 boats and their crews, with a yawl and 6 boys, in all,   -   41 men and boys.

Total,   112 men and boys.
And   14 boats, 1 yawl*.

State of the Church.—As the heritors have entered into a contract with an undertaker to build a new church, on an approved plan, to contain 1000 persons, it is not necessary to say much respecting the present one. It may, however, be mentioned, that part of it, according to the tradition

* The above contains a powerful claim on the feelings of humanity, and on the aid of Government for the protection and preservation of human lives. In the estimation of those who are best acquainted with the Moray frith, and most skilful in naval affairs, a harbour at Findochtie would save the lives of mariners, and prove extremely beneficial to the country. In its present state, it is of easy access, and the boats when overtaken by a north westerly storm, generally direct their course to it, as to a place of safety.

tradition of the pariſh, is as old as the caſtle of Edinburgh; and that the couples, which are of oak, grew on the eſtate of R..nnes. It is of conſiderable length, and has a roof of different altitudes. Viewed from the public road, or at a diſtance, it has a venerable appearance. Next year it is to be taken down, and the materials employed in building the new church.

Bede-Houſe.—Its origin is mentioned by Spottiſwood, in his account of religious houſes in Scotland, and is as follows: " Rothſan, John Biſſet gives to God, and the church " of St Peter's of Rothſan, for ſuſtaining ſeven leprous per- " ſons; the patronage of the kirk of Kyltalargy, to pray for " the ſouls of William and Alexander, kings of Scotland, " and the ſouls of his anceſtors and ſucceſſors, about the " year 1226; Chartulary of Moray, ſ. v. 27. He grants " another donation to the ſame purpoſe, in the ſaid year, " f. 126." There is a bede-houſe ſtill in being, though in bad repair; and ſix bede-men on the eſtabliſhment, but none of them live in the houſe. The nomination to a vacancy is in the gift of Lord Findlater, as proprietor of Rannes; and their yearly income is as follows: From the lands of Rannes, every bede-man has half an acre of land during life, and 1 boll of oat meal annually; from the lands of Findochtie, 8 s. 1¼ d.; and from Mr Baron Gordon, as proprietor of Freuchnie, formerly a part of the lands of Rannes, 1 s. 4¾ d. making in all 9 s. 6 d. yearly; one of the bede-men lately dead, let his half acre, during his life, at L. 1, 1 s. of yearly rent.

Stipend, Manſe, Glebe, Patron, &c.—The ſtipend is 9 chalders of victual, half meal, half bear; L. 16 : 13 : 4 of
money,

money, and L. 5 : 11 : 1¼ for communion-elements *. The manse and kitchen received a substantial repair in 1792 ; and additional offices were built, to render the accommodation more comfortable and commodious. The glebe, including garden and grass, is about 7 acres. Colonel Hay of Rannes is patron †.

State

* The following curious paper, with several other articles of intelligence, was furnished by B——p Geddes, at the intercession of Mr Matthison, who has been very friendly in procuring me information. " The rental of ye parsonage of Rathwen, wt. ye annexis yrof, wt. in " ye diocefis of Aberdein and Murray respective, shirefdoms of Banff " and Murray respective."

In the first; ye tiend silver of ye parochin of Rathwen, seven score and six pounds.

Ye malles of ye baronie of Rathwen, thirty-one merks.

Ye fermes of ye Loynhead, akkers and mill-multures, extendis to five score bolls of beir.

Item, ye kirke of Dundurcus, sett for forty pounds.

Item, ye kirke of Kintallertie, twenty-four pounds.

Item, ye landis of Mulben, lying in the parochen of Dundurcus, sixteen merks.

Hereof deductit of ordinar charges to six bed-men, 42 merks.

Item, to their habits, 7 pounds four shillings.

Item, to the staller in Aberdein.

Item, given forth of Dundurcus to the abbey of Kinlofs, six pounds.

Sic subscribitur.

G. Hay ✕, my hand.

The above rental is copied from an original book of assumptions of the year 1563, which belonged to the late Mr James Cummyng, secretary to the Society of Scotch Antiquaries, and which is now probably in the Register Office at Edinburgh. This is attested by me,

(Signed)　　　John Geddes.

† There is an itinerancy, called Enzie Chapel, situated in the west end of the parish, at the distance of 4 miles from the church, for the accommodation of that corner, and part of the parish of Belly. The missionary is subsisted partly from the Royal Bounty, and partly from a fund belonging to the mission. This fund arose from two collections

through

State of the Schools.—The parochial ſchool-houſe is at preſent a bad one. But after the church is finiſhed, there is little doubt of its being rebuilt on a plan equally comfortable and convenient for maſter and ſcholars. The ſchoolmaſter's ſalary is inadequate to the importance of his ſtation. It is bolls 9 ; 3 : 3 : 2¼ lippies of meal, and L. 2, 1 s. 9⅔ d. of money. His other emoluments are L. 2, for officiating as precentor and ſeſſion-clerk ; for publiſhing banns of marriage, 1 s. ; for regiſtering a baptiſm, 6 d. ; writing a certificate, 6 d. ; teaching Latin, 2 s. ; arithmetic, 2 s. ; and Engliſh and writing, 1 s. 6 d. quarterly. As the number of ſcholars of late has not been great, his income may be from L. 15 to L. 20 *.

Poor,

through the church, with a view to build a chapel, and procure accommodations to the miſſionary With part of it, a chapel has been built, and ſome acres of ground purchaſed for a glebe. And it is to be hoped, that the Royal Bounty will be continued, till the fund, which is under the management of a committee appointed by the General Aſſembly, accumulate to a ſum fully adequate to the comfortable ſupport of a clergyman, who has, in the diſtrict of the pariſh moſt contiguous to the chapel, excluſive of the moſt adjacent part of Belly, 300 Preſbyterians, 72 Epiſcopalians, and 630 Roman Catholics.

There are other two clergymen in the pariſh, Mr Reid and Mr Shand. Mr Reid reſides at Preſshome, where he has lately built a neat and well finiſhed chapel, for the accommodation of the Roman Catholics in the pariſh. Mr Shand lives at Arradoul, and has one chapel in his neighbourhood for the Epiſcopalians of this pariſh, and another at Fochabers, where he officiates once a fortnight in ſummer, and once in 3 weeks during the winter ſeaſon. Both theſe gentlemen conduct themſelves with the greateſt propriety. As they are much reſpected by their hearers and acquaintance, they are comfortably lodged, and decently ſupported. Each of them has a ſmall farm, which, by ſkillful management, yields pleaſure and convenience.

* The preſent ſchoolmaſter has been upwards of 40 years a teacher; and from age and infirmities, muſt ſoon be reduced to a ſtate that will incapacitate him for teaching. It is a pity tnat no ſcheme has hitherto been

Poor, and State of their Funds.—The poor subsist by begging, and occasional supplies from the parochial fund. Notwithstanding the extent of the parish, it does not at present amount to above L. 50, of which L. 40 is out at interest. The above has been saved from the weekly collections, the use of a pall or mortcloth, and fines from delinquents. The weekly collections, and other contingencies for the year 1792, amounted in whole to L. 14, 12 s. The management of it, and of the whole funds, is, as in most parts of Scotland, intrusted to the church session. After paying L. 2 to the session clerk, and L. 1, 1 s. to the officer, the remainder is divided quarterly among the most necessitous of all descriptions. Last year, 30 poor persons received benefit from this small fund. In addition to the above, Lord Findlater orders an annual distribution of meal

been devised, nor any measures adopted to prevent men, who have had an University education, and spent their time and talents in teaching our children the elements of literature, and principles of religion, from feeling the accumulated evils of frailty and poverty in their old age.

The Society for propagating Christian Knowledge, has 2 schools in the parish; one at Buckie, with a salary of L. 14 to the master; and one at Couffurrach, near the Enzie Chapel, with a salary of L. 10 to the master, and L. 5 to his wife. In the course of the year, there are about 100 scholars at each of these schools. Their numbers show the propriety of planting and continuing schools in these stations, and their importance to the public. The latter school is only of 2 years standing; and the master is in possession of the accommodations required by the Society's regulations. He owes his present comfortable situation to the bounty of his Grace the Duke of Gordon. And I am proud to add, that above L. 300 of the Society's money are annually paid to their schoolmasters on the Duke's different estates, all accommodated by his munificence. Such disinterested liberality does honour to his feelings as a man, and is a substantial proof of the interest he takes in promoting the good of society, and the cause of religion.

It is believed, that the Society has not, in Scotland, a more important station than Buckie. It contains upwards of 700 inhabitants, who have

meal and money among the poor on his own lands ; and
that the ſame beneficent cuſtom may obtain in other corners of the pariſh, I have no reaſon to doubt.

Population.—According to the return made to Dr Webſter, the number of ſouls, in 1755, was 2898. By a minute of a viſitation in the preſbytery records, dated at the
kirk of Rathven, 30th Auguſt 1720, the population is
ſtated at 1700 catechiſable perſons ; and 600 Papiſts, by a
modeſt computation of thoſe above 10 years of age, by
Mr Robert Gordon, the miniſter, in preſence of the heritors, and in anſwer to the queries, How many catechiſable perſons in the pariſh ? Whereof, How many Papiſts ?
Before ſtating the population, it may be obſerved that part
of the eaſt end of the pariſh is annexed to Cullen *quoad ſa-*
cra. The date of the annexation I have enquired after in
vain.

130 children under 10 years of age. And by including a mile round
the town, their number is increaſed to 190. The Society's ſchool was
removed from another ſtation in the pariſh to Buckie in 1750 ; and has
ever been on a bad footing, the ſchoolmaſter having never been poſſeſſed
of accommodation to the ſame extent with his brethren on that eſtabliſhment. And this inconveniency has occaſioned loſs to the maſter, and a
conſiderable advance out of the poor's fund. At preſent the ſchool is
held on ſo precarious a tenure, as to endanger its being entirely loſt, to
the great prejudice of the place. It is true, that Dr Kemp, whoſe ſpirited exertions, as ſecretary to the Honourable Society have done ſo
much credit to himſelf, and good to the cauſe of virtue and religion, has
explaihed the ſituation of this ſchool to a gentleman of fortune, and of
polite literature, in an eminent ſtation, who has a natural intereſt in the
place. And, as it is pretty generally underſtood, that a promiſe of accommodation had been granted ; thoſe who patroniſed the former ſchool,
have withdrawn their ſupport, and ſeem reſolved not to renew it Hence,
the cauſe of its preſent precarious ſtate. At Findochtie, a ſchoolmiſtreſs
receives a guinea annually from Lord Findlater, as an encouragement
to teach the reading of Engliſh, knitting and ſewing. She is a ecent
woman, beſtows her time on her ſcholars, and gives ſatisfaction to the
town and neighbourhood.

vain. Exclufive of the annexed part, there were found, on an accurate inveftigation, finifhed about 3 months ago,

	Perfons.	Males.	Fem.	Prefb.	Epifc.	R. Cath.	Fam.
In the Parifh,	3019	1408	1611	1766	303	95	720
Annexed Part,	505	271	234	498	2	5	
Total,	3514	1679	1845	2264	305	955	720

Of whom there are in the Parifh,

	Males.	Fem.	Total.	
Under 10 years of age,	333	345	678	
Between 10 & 20,	322	291	613	
——— 20 & 50,	470	672	1142	
——— 50 & 70,	227	248	475	
——— 70 & 80,	43	39	82	
——— 80 & 90,	12	13	25	
——— 90 & 100,	1	3	4	
Total,	1408	1611	3019	720
In the annexation to Cullen, under 7 years,	57	45	102	

The different ages in the whole annexed part could not be conveniently obtained. To account fatisfactorily for fo great a difproportion between the males and females is not an eafy matter. Owing to the difference in our religious tenets, no regular regifter of baptifms can be kept. Confequently there is no means of afcertaining the proportion between the males and females born in the parifh. The great difproportion obfervable from the above ftate, may be attributed to loffes fuftained at fea, no numbers engaging in our fleets and armies ; and to an influx of poor women from the Highlands, for the convenience of living more comfortably.

Among the inhabitants enumerated above, there are 14 merchants or fhopkeepers, 6 millers, 12 mafons, 19 tailors,

19

19 fhoemakers, 70 weavers, 12 fmiths, 21 carpenters, 6 fhipmafters, 2 tidefmen, 1 dyer, 1 tobacconift, 2 butchers, 1 baker, 4 gardeners, 6 male domeftick fervants. Female domeftick fervants, as well as the farm fervants of both fexes, are extremely fluctuating, except in gentlemen's families. The common farmers are not opulent enough to afford wages to annual fervants, whofe termly demands are in a ftate of progreffion beyond all precedent. They muft make their children, to the great prejudice of their education, and at too early a period in life, anfwer inftead of fervants.

S T O C K.

	Horfes.	Bl. Cattle.	Sheep.	Ploughs.	Carts.	Wains.	Chaife.
In the Parifh,	550	1706	2500	187	215	3	1
Annexed Part,	76	166	200	16	47	1	0
Total,	626	1872	2700	203	262	4	1

The cattle are remarkable neither for beauty nor fize ; and therefore, at prefent, horfes might give from L. 3 to to L. 12 or L. 15 ; cows and oxen, from L. 2 to L. 5 or L 6 ; wethers, and ewes and lambs, from 3 s. to 6 s. As the foil is good, and anfwers well with fown graffes, a larger and handfomer breed of cattle might be introduced. No attention is paid to raifing fwine, except at the 5 meal mills in the parifh, where from 30 to 40 may be fold annually, at from L. 1 to L. 3.

Pigeon-Houfes.—Of thefe, there are 8 in the parifh, ftocked, at an average, with 150 pairs each. As they live on the crop, in fpring and harveft, not under 6 months yearly, we may fairly calculate their annual confumption of grain, from 24 to 30 bolls at leaft, for every pigeonhoufe.

houfe. In ftormy weather, during the winter-feafon, they muft have befides, at the loweft calculation, one peck of grain a-day, to preferve their lives, and keep them at home. They begin, and continue to lay and hatch from the middle of March to the middle or end of June; and from Lammas to the 1ft of November. The annual produce of each may be reckoned at 150 pairs, at 2 d. a-pair, and 16 s. for the dung. There is a well attefted inftance of 160 pairs being taken from the pigeon-houfe of Nether Buckie, at one harrying; the ufual run is about 30 pairs. Numbers of pigeons come from the inland country in the beginning of Auguft to the dovecots in this parifh, and remain in them till November, when they retire to their original place of refidence. Jays are the greateft enemies to the pigeon-houfes. In times of fcarcity, they enter them and deftroy the young; the old ones are not unfrequently a prey to hawks, and other ravenous birds.

Plantations.—Thefe have been already mentioned, as lying chiefly in the eaft end of the parifh. Lord Findlater has paid great attention to planting. His plantations are of confiderable extent, and in a thriving ftate. At firft they were moftly planted with Scotch firs; but have fince been filled up with oaks, elms, afhes, beeches, birches, larches, &c. They beautify and enliven the landfcape; and the annual thinnings foon reimburfe his Lordfhip, and are ferviceable in building cottages, and for fuel. His different plantations amount to   -   4300 acres.
Mr Gordon's of Letterfourie,   -   100
Mr Gordon of Cairnfield, and Mr Stuart of Tanachy, 50 each,   -   -   100
                                                        ——
                                        Total,   4500

Minerals

Minerals and Mineral Springs.—There are quarries of limeſtone at Cuttiebrae and Upper Clochin ; of ſtones for building at Tarwathie ; of ſlate at Tarriemout and Upper Aldyloth, belonging to the Duke of Gordon ; and of ſlate on the eſtate of Letteriourie. Near Litchieſton, there is a beautiful whitiſh ſand in great quantity, and, in point of fineneſs, almoſt equal to any Dutch ſand *.

Fuel.—Peat or turf from the hill of Oldmore, and the other moſſes, is the fuel in common uſe. As the moſſes are at a conſiderable diſtance, fuel is extremely dear, and in winter often very ſcarce. The ſmall cart-load of peats and turfs, ſold laſt winter in Buckie at 1 s. 2 d. and ſometimes higher. To give a clearer idea of the expenſe of fuel, it may be obſerved, that when the load is ſold at 1 s. the conſumer pays at the rate of a halfpenny for 4 peats and 1 turf. Under ſuch circumſtances, as the few only are able to afford this heavy expenſe, it is evident, that Mr Dundas has done an eſſential ſervice to the many, in procuring a repeal of the duty on coals, and merits well of his country, in general, for contributing to the comfort and happineſs of a numerous and an uſeful claſs of people, by redreſſing a real grievance.

Salt.—This neceſſary article, according to my information, which I have reaſon to believe authentic, is purchaſed

---

* A well at Burn of Oxhill is much frequented by the country people with their children in the chincough; but as nothing is ſaid of the benefit reaped from it, it is preſumed, that its vogue is owing more to cuſtom than to its medicinal qualities. There are two chalybeate ſprings on Mr Baron Gordon's lands ; one at Gollachie, and another at New Buckie, frequented occaſionally in the ſummer-ſeaſon. At Findochtie, a ſpring of a purgative nature, iſſuing out of a rock, far within flood-mark, is occaſionally applied to by the neighbourhood.

chafed from the merchants at the pit, at 6 s. 4 d. the boll, containing 4 Englifh bufhels, and weighing 200 lb. Englifh. The duty the boll is 5 s. 6 d.; the freight, and other dues, about 1 s. 1 d.; falt therefore ftands the importer at the rate of 12 s. 11 d. the boll. To the confumer it is fold out by the merchants at 1 s. the peck, of 14 lb. Englifh, which is the loweft price, and frequently at 1 d. the pound. This high price of falt is extremely hurtful to the fifheries, and felt as a ferious grievance by the poor. If therefore Mr Dundas, Sir John Sinclair, or any other gentleman diftinguifhed for Patriotifm and Parliamentary intereft, would procure a revifion of the falt-laws, the abolition of the duty on falt, and the extenfion of an adequate duty to boats, as well as buffes; he would endear himfelf to the prefent generation, and tranfmit his name to the future, as the friend and benefactor of his country. And were an act of Parliament procured, to enable proprietors in general, and others, who expend their money in making commodious harbours, to impofe a wharfage or tax on the trade, proportioned to the fum expended or the advantages fecured; and the foftering hand of Government ftretched out to aid the public to conftruct harbours, build piers, and form quays or wharfs, for lading and unlading veffels, little more would remain to be done in favour of the manufactures and fifheries.

Antiquities—Druidical temples are common. On the heights of Corridown, there was a remarkable one called the Core Stanes; the ftones of which were employed in building the new houfe of Letterfourie. Mr Gordon has fearched 3 of them to the bottom, and found only charcoal, and a whitifh foft fubftance, refembling the afhes of wood or of bones. The low grounds in the vicinity of his houfe, he imagines, muft have formerly abounded in wood,

wood, as he has dug out of the hollows, now under culture, and producing cabbages, and other articles for kitchen uſe, large pieces of oak and fir *.

Character of the People.—To delineate, in few words, the leading feature in the character of a people, different in their religious tenets, and conſiſting of natives and ſtrangers, landmen and ſeamen, is no eaſy matter. In general, however, as far as my obſervation and experience go, they are ſober, frugal and induſtrious ; peaceable and friendly to neighbours and acquaintances ; decent and exemplary in their attendance on the ordinances of religion. A taſte for comfortable houſes, both in the fiſher-towns and in the country, is become prevalent ; and a more faſhionable manner of dreſs is making rapid progreſs. On the whole then, being well clothed, well fed, and decently lodged, they have, in a comparative degree, a reaſonable ſhare of the comforts

* There is a large heap of ſtones on an eminence in one of Lord Findlater's encloſures, near Woodſide, ſouthward of the public road, commonly called the King's Cairn. And tradition ſays, that it is the grave of Indulphus, the 77th King of Scotland, who, after obtaining a complete victory over the Danes, was unfortunately killed near this ſpot. According to Abercromby, this victory was gained A. D. 961: according to Buchanan, in 967. In this pariſh, the above event is diſtinguiſhed by the name of the Battle of the Bauds, then an extenſive moor, now a plantation belonging to Lord Findlater : and it is believed, erroneouſly indeed, that by it the Danes were finally expelled from Scotland. Buchanan places their final expulſion in the reign of Duncan I. and 84th King of Scotland A. D. 1043; when, after receiving a great overthrow in Fife, and reflecting on their many unfortunate expeditions to Scotland, they bound themſelves by a ſolemn oath to return to it no more as enemies On the moor between Findochtie and the plantation of the Bauds, a great number of ſmall cairns are diſtinguiſhable, and ſuppoſed to be the burial places of the Danes, who were ſlain in the engagement with Indulphus. About 30 years ago, a country man diſcovered, in a tumulus or cairn, on the lands of Rannes, which he was removing, a ſtone coffin,
containing

comforts and conveniencies of life. Examples of natural
fagacity, and a talent for information and enterprize, is by
no means uncommon among thofe of every defcription.
They have penetration enough to difcover the road which
bids faireft to lead to the accomplifhment of their views,
and fteadinefs to purfue it. The intercourfe of the fifher-
towns with the country is frequent and eafy; neverthelefs
the difference in language and in manners is ftriking.
Here we fee men judging and acting for themfelves. E-
very one adopts thofe plans which beft fuit his circumftances and fituation in life. The fifhers indeed, as individuals, are placed more on a footing of equality; and
their purfuits are uniformly fimilar. Of courfe their language and tranfactions, are the language and tranfactions
of the community, rather than of individuals. All adopt
the fame meafures, and purfue fimilar plans in executing
them. The voice of one almoft always puts all in motion;
and

containing human bones of a large fize. Having obtained permiffion to
ranfack this grave, I found it covered with a large ftone, 4 feet long
3 broad, and about 14 inches in depth. On removing this, we found
4 other ftones, fet on their edges, which ferved as a coffin to part of a
fcull, and jaw-bone, with feveral teeth, and fome fragments of a thigh
bone. The dimenfions of this coffin were 3 feet 1 inch in length, 2 feet
wide, and 22 inches deep. There was no ftone in the bottom. The
bones were removed into a fimilar cheft, a few feet northward of this
one, in the fame tumulus; this laft one was difcovered 4 or 5 years ago,
by a man in the neighbourhood, who was removing a few more of the
ftones for building a houfe. It is of fmaller dimenfions than the other
one, and was originally covered with two ftones, one of which was carried off. No bones were found in it. There are many other cairns near
this one, but none of them have been fearched. They are at no great diftance from the houfe of Rannes, on a farm, lately improved out of moor,
called Wefter-fide. The ruins of an old chapel, near the houfe of Farfkane, of the houfe of Findocatie, and of fome buildings on the tops of
two hills, on the eaft and weft fide of the harbour of Portnockie, the former called the Green caftle, and the latter the Tronach caftle, are ftill
to be feen.

and the example of one is frequently followed by all; and yet, what is singular, no one seems to possess a character decisive enough to take the lead, and to rise to superiority by the strength of genius, or the arts of address. No moral duty is seldomer violated by them than chastity. They go to sea as boys, at 14 years of age, become men at 18, and marry soon after; for it is a maxim with them, apparently founded in truth, that no man can be a fisher, and want a wife. They generally marry before 24 years at farthest; and always the daughters of fishers from 18 to 22 at most. The fisher-wives lead a most laborious life. They assist in dragging the boats on the beach, and in launching them. They sometimes, in frosty weather, and at unseasonable hours, carry their husbands on board, and ashore again, to keep them dry. They receive the fish from the boats, carry them fresh, or, after salting, to their customers, and to market, at the distance, sometimes, of many miles, through bad roads, and in a stormy season. When northerly winds, or a high sea, prevent the boats from going a-fishing, the men are employed in repairing their sails, mending their lines, or making new ones. It is the province of the women to bait the lines; collect furze, heath, or the gleanings of the mosses, which, in surprising quantity, they carry home in their creels for fuel, to make the scanty stock of peats and turfs prepared in summer, last till the returning season. The men and women are in general remarkably stout and well shaped. Many of the former are above the common stature; and of the latter, many are pretty, and dress to advantage on holidays. The fishers of Findochtie are distinguished for decency and decorum, and for curing their fish, great and small, superlatively well. In the other towns, the greater number are decent and irreproachable; and according to the testimony of those who have known them long, a sen-
fible

fible improvement in manners and in morals, begins to take place among them.

Advantages and Difadvantages.—The parifh poffeffes all the advantages that local fituation can give. And its greateft difadvantages have already in part been mentioned. Many melancholy examples of the fatal confequences arifing from the want of harbours have been produced; and extreme inconveniency and frequent dangers are experienced, from having no cuftom-houfe nearer than Invernefs, which is 50 miles diftant. The failure of the plan in agitation, for obtaining a cuftom-houfe at Banff, muft prove a great lofs to the fifheries and manufactures in this corner. Short leafes, and what is here termed run rigging, are hurtful to the farmer. It has already been obferved, that a great part of the parifh is expofed to the north wefterly winds, which are often hurtful to the crop. And even this inconveniency is fufceptible, in fome meafure, of being remedied. For proper encouragement, to enclofe, and plant hedges, on a judicious plan, would contribute to counteract the ill effects of thefe winds, by fheltering the fields from their influence.

Mifcellaneous Obfervations.—There is a lint-mill at Gollachie, built by a manufacturer in Fochabers, for beating flax; which is fufficient to beat 6 mats a day. He imports 300 mats yearly from Rotterdam, of which the prime coft is about   -   -   -   L. 1000   0   0
To converting the above into yarn,   -   1000   0   0
To making part of the yarn into cloth,   400   0   0

The remainder of the yarn is fent to market at Glafgow. A mat, on an average, yields 50 lb. of dreffed flax, fit for fpinning into 4 hanks of yarn the lb. A hank of

yarn

yarn is in general the daily labour of the ſpinner, for which ſhe receives only 3 d.—*Tarwathie* was, in former times, the watch-word for convening the Enzie-men in times of danger; or at markets, and other places of public reſort, when any of them happened to be engaged in a fray. There are 2 annual fairs in the pariſh, the one in July for cattle, ſheep, and merchant goods, and the other in September, for butter and cheeſe. Both are named Peter-Fair; only the latter has the epithet *little* prefixed by way of diſtinction.

The houſe of Buckie was burnt in the civil wars. Since the beginning of this century, the fluctuation of property in land has been very conſiderable. Lord Findlater has purchaſed, at different times, Caſtlefield from the Dunbars; Farſkane from the Gordons; Findochtie from the Ords; Muldavat and Rannes from the Hays. Mr Baron Gordon is proprietor of Freuchnie, Buckie and Gollachie; the firſt purchaſed from the Hays; the ſecond from the Gordons; and the laſt obtained from the Duke of Gordon, in exchange for other lands. Mr Gordon of Letterfourie has bought Corrydown from the Roſſes; and Walkerdales from the Gordons of Aberlour. Mr Dunbar's eſtate of Nether Buckie was lately the property of the Gordons. Mr Gordon of Cairnfield has acquired Thornybank from the Hays; Arradoul from the Anderſons; Eaſter-Bogs from the Stuarts; and Birkenbuſh from the Gordons. The Duke of Gordon has purchaſed Couffurrach; Reſton hillock, Litchieſtown and Glaſtirum from the Gordons; Homie from the Paterſons; and Middle Bogs from the Reids. Oxhill is, of late, in poſſeſſion of the ſon-in-law of the former proprietor *.

* It is evident, from what has already been obſerved, that the parſons of Rathven were patrons of Dundurcus and Kintallertie, in the preſbytery

tery of Invernefs; but I have been able to difcover neither the time nor the manner in which thefe patronages were loft. At prefent they are both in the gift of the Crown.

I ought in juftice to acknowledge the obligations I am under to the gentlemen, and others who furnifhed me with information for this paper. Since writing the above, I have difcovered, that there are many caves on that part of the coaft, belonging to Lord Findlater. The moft noted are, 1ft, Farfkane's Cave, fo called, from the proprietor of Farfkane having, in 1715, retired into it along with two other gentlemen, to avoid trouble during the Earl of Mar's rebellion. In it they lived very fnugly and comfortably for 5 or 6 weeks; and returned to their own houfes, when all apprehenfion of danger was over. 2. Janet Corftair's cave, fo named, from a mad woman who took up her refidence in it. And 3. The Crofs Cave, fo denominated, from its taking a direction to the eaft and weft, at fome diftance from its entrance. The extent of none of them is known.

There is a well of frefh water on the north fide of a green hill, furrounded by the tide, called Prieft's Crag-well, between Findochtie and Portknockie.

The fifhers employ all kinds of fmall fifh as bait for catching the great fifh. And mufcles are purchafed at Tain for 15 s. 4 d.; Little Ferry, at 23 s.; and at Findhorn, from 10 s. to 25 s. the boat load, as bait for the fmall fifh, in the winter-feafon, and limpets, crabs, and other fhell fifh, worms dug out of the fand, called by the fifhers lugs; and fandals, a fpecies of fifh found in the fand, are employed in June, July and Auguft.

Refpecting the birds, migratory and indigenous, it may be proper juft to add, that of the former kind, we have plovers, cuckoos, rails, fnipes, &c. and of the latter, fuch as are common over all the north of Scotland.

PARISH OF ROTHIEMAY,

(County of Banff, Synod of Moray, Presbytery
of Strathbogie).

By the Rev. Mr James Simmie.

Situation, &c.

THE parish of Rothiemay is bounded, on the E. and
N. E. by the parish of Marnoch ; on the S. and S. E.
by Inverkeithnie, Forgue, and Huntly; on the W. and
S. W. by Cairny ; on the N. and N. W. by Grange. Its
greatest length is from 7 to 8 miles ; its greatest breadth
from 5 to 6.

The northern part of this parish is inferior to the rest,
both in fertility and beauty. Beside some hilly ground,
and some plantations of fir, it consists of a large plain, containing partly arable, partly pasture-ground, and an extensive moss that supplies with fuel, not only the parishioners,
but

but, in a great meaſure, the town of Huntly *, which is diſtant about 6 miles. From this plain is a gentle declivity of more than half a mile, on the W. and S. W. to the Iſla, and, on the S. to the Devoran ; a river adorned with plantations and natural woods on its banks, and abounding with common trout, eel, and ſalmon. About a mile below its confluence with the Iſla, the Devoran, running eaſtward, divides the pariſh into two parts, of which the northern follows the courſe of the river more than two miles, the ſouthern near two miles farther. At this point, where the Devoran begins to divide the pariſh, and on its northern bank, are the Milltown, a ſmall village containing about an hundred ſouls; the houſe of Rothiemay †; the church and manſe; and a happy mixture of well-incloſed fields

---

* When the pariſhioners carry peats out of the pariſh, they do ſo clandeſtinely, or merely by indulgence of their landlords,—not by ſtipulation and right. It is much to be wiſhed, that both they, and others whom they ſupply with peats, would uſe fewer peats, and more coal and wood, not only becauſe, in wet ſeaſons, peats are a very uncertain fuel, but becauſe the preparation of them conſumes much of their time, which might be more profitably devoted to various agricultural improvements.

† There is a tradition here, that the unfortunate Mary, Queen of Scots, paſſed a night in this houſe, and her bed-room is ſtill pointed out. This tradition is confirmed by the authority of Buchanan, who, deſcribing Mary's journey to Inverneſs, ſays, " *Proxima nox ad Rothimaium, Abre-* " *nethiorum villam, ſatis tranquillè tranſacta eſt :*" Hiſt. Rer. Scot. Lib. 17. cap. 36. The Abernethies here mentioned were Lords Abernethies, afterwards of Salton. The tragical fate of one of them is celebrated in a popular ballad, called Frennet-hall. Next to the Abernethies, a family of Gordons were proprietors of Rothiemay till the end of laſt or the beginning of this century, when it was purchaſed by Ogilvie, whoſe ſon (afterwards of Inchmartin in Perthſhire) ſold it to William Lord Braco, father of the preſent Earl of Fife. The moſt ancient part of the houſe, which was going faſt to ruin, his Lordſhip has lately taken down, and has repaired and furniſhed the reſt in a manner which does honour to his taſte.

fields and woods; which, with woods and corn-fields on the oppofite fide of the river, rifing, by a gradual afcent, to a great height, form a beautiful rural fcenery, equalled by few, and perhaps excelled by none, of equal extent, in the kingdom.

Soil, Produce, Rent.—Plantations and natural woods occupy a confiderable part of this parifh. They confift chiefly of fir, birch, afh, elm, and aller *, which, in confequence of the fcarcity of thefe in moft of the neighbouring parifhes, are fold at high prices, and bring the proprietors from L. 100 to L. 200 a-year. And it may be prefumed, that, fome years hence, they will bring much more, as many of them, efpecially firs, now young and thriving, will then be ready for fale ; and as the proprietors not only fupply from their nurferies the places of thofe they fell, but are carrying this kind of improvement ftill farther, by planting fuch parts of their eftates as are lefs fit for cultivation or pafture.

The pafture bears only a fmall proportion to the arable land of the parifh. It is fuch, however, as renders it profitable for fome farmers to rear a few fheep, and all a few black cattle, for the market.

The foil, in general, is rich and fertile. It produces excellent oats, bear, peafe, and lint, the common crops of the parifh ; and in fuch abundance, that large quantities, particularly of oats, oatmeal, and bear, are exported annually. A great part of the bear finds a good market at diftilleries in the neighbouring parifhes. Part of it, as well as oats

and

---

* Befide thefe, is a great variety of excellent larch, oak, beech, &c. particularly on the property of the Earl of Fife, whofe example in planting, and other improvements, is well entitled to the imitation of other proprietors. Some old afh, belonging to his Lordfhip, are of an uncommon fize meafuring, in diameter, four feet.

and oatmeal, is purchased, by commiſſion, for merchants in
other parts of the kingdom, and ſhipped at Portſoy, which
is 12, Banff, which is 15, or Macduff, which is 16 miles
diſtant.

Moſt farms are ſmall, only five or ſix being rented above
L. 40, of which one is rented at L. 110, another at L. 140.
Few leaſes exceed 19 years. *Graſſums* are in uſe. Perſonal ſervice * and harveſt-labour are no longer exacted.
Of late, a great part of victual-rents were converted into
money at the rate of 12 s. 6 d. a boll; and multure-rent,
formerly every thirteenth peck, is now 3 s. 6 d. for every
pound of farm-rent, Converſions not leſs favourable in
their conſequences to the progreſs of agriculture, than to
the immediate intereſt of the farmer. The miller's fee
(which remains to be converted into money) is every eighteenth peck. Aſtrictions to particular mills prevail here,
as in other parts of Scotland ; and the grain of one of the
beſt diſtricts of the pariſh is aſtricted to a mill in a neighbouring pariſh, and belonging to a different proprietor.
Would it be any diſadvantage to ſociety, if mill-aſtrictions
of every kind being aboliſhed by a juſt compenſation, every
one were at liberty to chooſe his miller, as well as his
ſmith, his carpenter, or any other mechanic ?

The valued rent of the pariſh is L. 3170 Scotch. The
whole pariſh is the Earl of Fife's, except about a tenth
part, the property of Major Alexander Duff of Mayen.
His Lordſhip occaſionally viſits his property here. Major
Duff † conſtantly reſides in the pariſh.

Advantages,

* By *perſonal ſervice*, as different from harveſt-labour, is meant, going
on errands, and the like. The ſervice of carrying the landlord's meal to
the ſhore is ſtill retained; nor, indeed, could it be conveniently diſpenſed
with, where victual-rents are paid, and eſpecially where the landlord does
not reſide.

† The Major, beſide ſome very laudable improvements of his eſtate by
planting and incloſing, has lately built an elegant and commodious houſe.

Advantages, &c.—Our chief advantage, refpecting agriculture, is the nearnefs of lime. In the neighbouring parifh of Grange, it is bought at the quarry for 1½ d.; at the kiln for 8 d. and fometimes 7 d. a boll *. The abundance of peat here induces moft farmers to buy it at the quarry, and enables fome of them, befide fupplying themfelves, to bring a profit by retail. There are about 50 lime-kilns in the parifh.

To this advantage I wifh I could add good roads; but the proper method of making and repairing thefe is not even underftood here. Inftead of ufing for this purpofe that abundance of metal and gravel which nature has fupplied, the ftatute-labour is employed in throwing on the middle of the roads the contents of the ditches on their fides, which, being clay or foft earth, fo far from improving them, (unlefs, perhaps, during the heat of fummer), generally makes them worfe than before. Though inclofing is far advanced in this, compared with neighbouring parifhes, ftill there is much room for this kind of improvement : A proof, among others, that a great part of our land has not yet reached half its value. Nor has draining by any means obtained that degree of attention, which a great part of our land evidently requires, though to this kind of improvement its natural fituation is, in general, very favourable †.

Population, &c.—The number of inhabitants is 1125; of whom, 481 are males, 644 females. In 1755 it was 1190. The average of marriages for the laft 10 years is 10; that of births, for the fame period, 19; of deaths there is no regifter.

Of

* The boll of lime here confifts of 2 firlots only.

† The mode of farming, and the prices of the various kinds of provifions, are the fame here as in the neighbouring parifhes.

Of the inhabitants 1067 are of the Established Church; 25 are Episcopalians; 27 Seceders; and 6 Roman Catholics. The occupations of part of them, with other particulars which shew the state of the parish, will appear from the following table:

Clergyman,	-	1	Tailors, - -	6
Schoolmaster,	-	1	Shopkeepers, -	7
Masons, -	-	6	Innkeepers, -	3
Dikers,	-	4	Butchers, - -	2
Wrights,	-	10	Meal-mills, -	2
Turners,	-	4	Meal-millers, -	3
Coopers,	-	3	Lint-mill, - -	1
Smiths, -	-	4	Lint-millers, -	3
Slaters, -	-	2	Wauk-mills, -	2
Flax-dressers,	-	3	Ferry-boats, -	2
Weavers,	-	27	Horses, - -	260
Dyers, -	-	3	Sheep, -	500
Shoemakers,	-	13	Black-cattle,	1208

All the men who are not tradesmen and mechanics, are employed in agriculture; and tradesmen and mechanics, who are housekeepers, likewise cultivate a few acres for the accommodation of their families. The women, when they are not employed in the moss in summer, or the field in harvest, sometimes knit stockings, but commonly spin linen-yarn for the merchant, who buys it, by commission, for the manufacturer in Glasgow, Paisley, or some other distant part of the kingdom. Beside maintenance, a farm-servant's yearly wages are from L. 7 to L. 9; a maid-servant's L. 2, 10 s. or L. 3. A day-labourer's wages vary with the kind of his labour; *viz.* for moss-labour, a man's 8 d. a woman's 6 d. with victuals; for harvest-labour, a man's 10 d. a woman's 6 d. with victuals; for hay-cutting, 1 s.;

1 s.; and for common labour, such as delving, 9 d. without victuals. A mason's day's wages are 1 s. 6 d; a wright's, 1 s. both without victuals; a tailor's, 8 d. with victuals; a diker's work is hired by the piece. By spinning linen-yarn, a woman earns 3½ d. at most 4 d. a-day! A poor pittance, indeed! and till manufactures be established here, (a thing more to be desired than expected), there is little reason to hope that female labour will find a better, at least an adequate reward.

Church, School, &c.—The parish-church, built about 40 years ago, is commodious and well lighted. The Earl of Fife is patron. By a late decree of the Court of Teinds, the minister's stipend is " 106 bolls 3 firlots of victual, half " meal half bear, and L. 533 : 6 : 8 Scotch, with L. 60 " money foresaid for furnishing the communion-elements." The schoolmaster's salary, which is 200 merks Scotch *, and the school-fees, with precenter's and session-clerk's fees and perquisites, do not exceed L. 20 or L. 21 a-year. The

parochial

---

* Till within these two years, it was only 100 merks Scotch. The late Rev. Mr Bruce of Dunbar, who received the principles of his education at this school, generously proposed to augment it by a donation of L. 100 Sterling. on the following terms: 1*st*, That the heritors should become trustees of his donation, paying to the schoolmaster the legal interest of it; and, 2*dly*, That they should augment the salary to the *maximum*, or 200 merks Scotch; Though the heritors complied with these terms as soon as proposed, and though afterwards Mr Bruce, informed of this, promised that his donation should *be forthcoming* at a time mentioned, yet, not long after, he died, without having fulfilled his benevolent purpose, and (so far as I have yet been able to discover) without leaving the fulfilment of it in trust to his heirs or testamentary executors. It is hoped, however, that sufficient vouchers of his purpose and promise being produced, his heirs (who are happily in sufficient circumstances) will, from due respect to his memory, esteem his will, respecting this matter, as sacred as if it had been expressed with all the circumstances of legal formality.

parochial poor (24 * at an average of the laſt twelve years)
are aſſiſted from the intereſt of L. 160, the rents of one of
the church-galleries, the weekly collections, fines for miſ-
demeanors, &c. ; the whole forming a yearly fund of L. 25
or L. 26 Sterling.

Antiquity, an Eminent Character.—About a furlong
north from the houſe of Rothiemay is a Druidical temple,
which, though ſituated in the middle of a beautiful and fertile field, a veneration for antiquity has hitherto preſerved
entire. Mr James Ferguſſon, well known, among men of
ſcience, for his publications on aſtronomy, was a native of
this pariſh †.

Character.—The inhabitants are, in perſon, ſlender rather than robuſt ; in mind, acute and ſenſible. They excel their forefathers leſs in the luxuries of the table than
elegance of dreſs ; are generally very healthy ; and live
                                                           many

---

* In 1783 and 1784, the number of poor was 45. In 1783, the kirk-
ſeſſion expended L. 70 of the poor's fund in purchaſing foreign grain.

† To certify this, it may be proper to ſubjoin, that my information of
Mr Ferguſſon's being a native of this pariſh I received from his brother,
John Ferguſſon, who was an elder of this pariſh, and died very lately. He
told me, that his father's name was John Ferguſſon, his mother's Elſpet
Lobban; that they dwelt at the Core of Mayen; that both he and his brother James were born there; that he himſelf was born in 1708 ; and that
his brother James was two years younger. Accordingly the ſeſſion-record,
which is now before me, confirms this information in every particular.
James Ferguſſon was born April 25. 1710.
     I do not recollect every particular related in the Memoirs of Mr Ferguſ-
ſon, prefixed to his works, not having ſeen them for ſeveral years; but
John, his brother, who had read theſe Memoirs, ſaid, that, though generally
agreeable to fact, they were not equally correct in every particular.

many of them 80, and fome 90, years. Devoted to agriculture and the mechanical arts, they are very little inclined either to a military or a fea-faring life. They are fober and induftrious, refpectful to fuperiors, obedient to the laws, charitable to the poor, and practife, among themfelves, the virtues of integrity and friendfhip. Of the form of godlinefs they are ftrictly obfervant ; and juftice, as well as candour, forbids me to believe that they are deftitute of its power.

PARISH of St. FERGUS,

(County of Banff, Synod of Aberdeen, and Presbytery of Deer.)

By the Rev. Mr John Craigie, *Miniſter.*

Name, Situation, and Extent.

THIS pariſh was anciently named *Inverugie*, and often *Longley*, the church being ſituated not far from the old place of Inverugie, on thoſe pleaſant and extenſive downs called *the Link of St-Fergus.* The church was removed from this ſite *anno* 1616, when the church and pariſh aſſumed the name of its patron ſaint, to whom the 17th of November, according to the Scotch calendar, was ſacred. This pariſh, though it belongs to the county of *Banff*, is ſituated in that diſtrict of *Aberdeen*, called *Buchan.* * The coaſt is waſhed
on

* The male line of the old Earls of Buchan, to whom this country originally belonged, failing in the perſon of Fergus, the laſt Earl of the ancient race, his only daughter married William Cumine of the family of Badenoch,

on the East by the German Ocean, and on the South, by the small river of *Ugie,* which separates it from the parish of Peterhead : The extent is as under :

Acres.

noch, who in her right became Earl of Buchan, about the beginning of the 13th Century. The parish of St Fergus, and some other small estates, seem to have been given off by the ancient Earls, but there still remained an immense estate, situated in Banff and Aberdeen shires, to which William Cumine succeeded by his marriage.

The Cumines continued to enjoy their vast fortune until the year 1308. This name, then one of the most powerful in Scotland, violently opposed the succession of King ROBERT BRUCE to the Crown, but were completely over. thrown by him at Inverury. The king, according to FORDUN, pursued the Cumines as far as Fyvie, where, having dispersed them, he encamped for for some time, until the parties which he sent out had burnt the Earl of Buchan's estate. In the Parliament holden at Perth, *anno* 1320, the King divided the Earl's lands among his own friends. To the family of DOUGLAS he gave the greatest part of the parishes of Crimond and Longmay, and a part of the parishes of Tyrie and Aberdour. This appears from a charter, which ARCHIBALD the 10th Lord DOUGLAS obtained from King Robert, " *Dilecto et fideli nostro,* ARCHIBALDO DE DOUGLAS, *pro homagio et servitio* " *sua"* of the lands of Rothsay, Crimond and Cairnglass, &c. in Buchan. Upon the family of CRAWFORD he bestowed the barony of Kelly, comprehending part of the parishes of Tarves, New-Deer, Old-Deer and Longside. These lands reverted to the Crown by the forfeiture of ALEXANDER Earl of CRAWFORD, and a considerable part of them was bestowed by King JAMES II. on JAMES GORDON of Methlic, Ancestor of the Earl of Aberdeen, (*Charta in pub. archiv.*) King ROBERT gave to the family of ERROL the parishes of Cruden, Slains, and part of the parishes of Logie, Ellon, and Udney. To the MARISCHAL family he gave the parish of Peterhead, part of Longside and Old-Deer, the lands of Auchines in the parish of Rathen, Pittendrum in Pitsligo parish, and Troup, in the parish of Gamrie. JOHN CUMINE, the fourth Earl of Buchan of that name, had, before his forfeiture and out-lawry by King Robert, given the barony of Philorth in portion with his daughter MARGARET, who was married to Sir JOHN ROSS, second son of the Earl of Ross, who disponed these lands to Hugh Earl of Ross, his brother, by a charter, dated at Inverness 1316. This barony was then of great extent, comprehending the parish of Frasersburgh, most part of Tyrie, Aberdour,

Acres.

Arable ground - - -	4439	3¹
Links, arable, but not allowed to be plowed,	435	50
Mofs - - -	795	5²

Soil and Surface.—The foil in general is a rich clay, and when properly cultivated is abundantly fertile. The appearance of the parifh is an alternate fucceffion of little rifing grounds and valleys, but no moor or barren ground. The piece of ground called *the Links of St. Fergus*, is perhaps one of the moft pleafant plains in Scotland, extending along the

dour, Pitfligo, and Rathen, (which laft comprehends the greateft part of Strichen parifh,) together with feveral lands in the parifhes of Turriff and King-Edward. This, together with the whole eftate of Rofs, was entailed by WILLIAM Earl of Ross, on his eldeft daughter Eupham, who was married to Sir WALTER LESLIE, and the heirs of her body; whom failing, to Janet his fecond daughter, who was married to Sir ALEXANDER FRASER of Cowie, anceftor of Lord SALTON. By this marriage Sir ALEXANDER FRASER got this barony, a confiderable part of which continueá to be the property of Lord Salton.

A part of the ancient Earldom of Buchan was fituated in the Thanedom of Formartine, which is that diftrict of Aberdeenfhire, that is bounded by the river Don on the South, and the Ythan on the North. This part of the Earl of Buchan's property remained with the Crown, until DAVID II. gave it to his brother in law WILLIAM, the 5th Earl of Sutherland, as appears by a charter of that King, dated at Dundee, 30th July, 1366. *Totam illam* ———— *thanagii noftri de Formartine, cum pertinentibus, jacen. in vice-comitatu de Aberdeen, &c.* Thereafter the Earl difpofed of thefe lands to William, eldeft fon of William, the 4th Earl of Orkney, as appears by an infeftment produced in Parliament, given by James II. *Dilecto confanguineo fuo, Gulielmo de Sancto-Claro, filio & hæredi apparenti comitis Orcadæ & Cathaniæ,* of the land and barony of Newburgh, and feveral others in Aberdeenfhire, together with the falmon fifhing on Ythan, 16th March 1459, (*Records of Parliament*) This WILLIAM was progenitor of LORD SINCLAIR, whofe family enjoyed thefe lands for 200 years, and then difpofed of them to Udny of that ilk, Turin-of Foveran, and others.

the coaft feveral miles, but of unequal breadth. It produces abundance of fhort fweet grafs, white clover, wild thyme, and other herbs, which are thought to contribute much to that delicacy and fine flavour, for which the mutton fed upon them is remarkable. Between the links and the fea there is a range of little hills, moftly clay, all covered with bent, which, as it is carefully preferved, is ftill encreafing, and proves an excellent defence againft the blowing of the fand, which, on a low fhore, without fuch a barrier, would do very material damage to the pafture ground of the links, and alfo to the adjacent fields.

Sea Coaft, Minerals, &c.—The fhore in the parifh of St. Fergus forms two fegments of a circle ; the one, beginning at the mouth of the Ugie, terminates at the Scotftown Craig, and the other reaches from this Craig to Rattray-head, the property of Mr Harvey of Broadland. The rocks both at Rattray and Scotftown afford plenty of lime-ftone, which at low water is eafily quarried. At Scotftown as well as at Craig-Ewan, hard by the mouth of the Ugie, there is abundance of excellent granite ; and, all along the coaft, an inexhauftible quantity of fhells, which are now ufed as manure with great advantage. From thefe two rocks of Craig-Ewan and Scotftown, a very trifling quantity of kelp is made every fecond year.

Fifhery, Proprietor, ‡ *&c.*—All kinds of fifh, found on the E. coaft of Scotland, are caught here in great abundance, fuch

as

‡ The proprietor, upwards of 20 years ago, attempted to eftablifh a fifhing town in this parifh ; and if there were a proper landing place for the boats, it would be an excellent ftation for fifhers, being fo near to Rattray-head, which has long been efteemed the very beft fifhing ground for cod and ling.

as ling, ſkate, flounders, cod, haddocks, crabs, lobſters, &c.
Mr FERGUSON of Pitfour, the ſole proprietor of this pariſh,
has the ſalmon fiſhing in the Ugie, for which he receives
100. Sterling yearly rent from Meſſrs Arbuthnot in Peterhead.
The quantity of ſalmon taken here in a ſeaſon, has ſometimes exceeded 1200 barrels ; but in one ſeaſon, they only a-
mounted to 14 barrels and a half. It very often happens, that
the mouth of the river is almoſt ſhut up, by large quantities
of ſea weeds, ſo that the ſalmon cannot enter it ; and this ob-
ſtacle generally remains until the ſea weeds are carried off by
a land flood.

Light-Houſe and Canal propoſed.—It is the opinion of ſhip-
maſters, who ſail along this coaſt, that a light-houſe on Rattray-head is highly neceſſary. Within the laſt twenty years,
ſeveral veſſels with their cargoes have been daſhed to pieces
on the rocks of Rattray and Scot-ſtown, which would have
been ſaved, had there been a light-houſe at Rattray-head. A
canal might alſo be made at a ſmall expence, from the mouth
of the Ugie, along the ſouth ſide of this pariſh, and might
be extended to the diſtance of ſeveral miles through the
country weſtward.

Agriculture. †—No ſown graſs or green crops were produced here, until the proprietor, and ſome other gentlemen,
formed

---

† About 25 years ago, a moſt execrable mode of farming was practiſed
in this pariſh. Four, and often ſix horſes dragged after them the old Scotch
ploughs. As there were at that time but few black cattle or ſheep, the only
manure was the dung of the horſes, excepting that a few farmers in the S. E.
part of the pariſh, laid ſea-weed on their grounds; the firſt crop after the
dung, or ſea-weed, was bear, which was ſucceeded by two crops of oats, and
a crop of beans or peaſe, and this was followed by a crop of bear, ſometimes
without ſea-weed or dung. This was the manner of treating the in-field.
The *out-field*, that is the ground which had never any manure laid upon it,
carried

formed a fociety for encouraging agriculture, and gave premiums for fallow, fown grafs, and turnips. By this encouragement, and by obferving the great advantage that accrued from early grafs, hay, and green crops, the farmers were induced to fallow, fow turnips, and lay down their fields in grafs; and at prefent, fome of them have generally one third of their farm in grafs, and a very confiderable number of cattle are every year fed on turnips. Although improvements in agriculture have made but little progrefs, as yet, in this parifh, it is a curious fact, that until the greateft part of the leafes were expired, there was nothing done in that way. This is chiefly owing to a well-placed confidence in the proprietor, who has never yet ejected a tenant, although many of them have had no leafes for upwards of 20 years. Many offers of an increafe of rent have been made for every farm, as foon as the leafe expired; but the poffeffors, or their heirs, if they inclined to remain, have been allowed to continue in their farms, and no rife of rent has been exacted. The proprietor, wifely judging that improvement fhould precede a rife of rent, has been at great pains to lead them to better management; and although the encouragement given has not had all the effect that

carried oats for three or four years. The fourth year, the return feldom doubled the quantity of feed that had been fown. The fifth year, they fallowed the out-field, but gave no manure of any kind; and the fixth year they had a tolerable crop of oats. The ground was then allowed to reft for fome years, and it was feldom before the 4th year, that it got a green furface. It no fooner had this appearance, than it got one plowing in winter, and was fuffered to remain in that ftate for a year, and then had a fecond plowing, and was fown with oats. If there was any part of the field, that had not undergone the firft plowing, the furface was dug up with the fpade, and therewith dykes were made of 2 or 3 feet in height, which having been expofed to the winter froft and rain, were in fpring pulled down and fpread upon the ground, from which the furface had been taken. This ground was then plowed, and feldom failed to produce one good crop of oats.

that might have been expected, the mode of farming is much changed. Instead of 6 horses in a plough, they never use more than 4, and many use only 2, without a driver. Some plow with 6 oxen, some with 4, and some with 2; but the horses and oxen are of a much larger size than formerly, and the Berwick-fhire plough is now generally used.

Produce, Seafons, &c.—The crops now raifed are oats, weighing from 14 to 16 ftone, Amfterdam weight ; bear from 17 to 19 ftone ; beans, peafe, turnips, potatoes, and a little flax. The feafon of fowing is from the latter end of March to the beginning of June ; and the harveft commonly begins after the middle of September, and is finifhed about the end of October. The rotation of crops, followed by the beft farmers, is turnips or fallow, bear laid down with grafs feeds, and after 3 or 4 years in grafs, two crops of oats are taken. If, after this, the ground is clean, beans are fown, but if otherwife, turnips or potatoes, and then bear and grafs feeds. Wheat has been neglected, although it is well adapted to the foil ; but as the heritor has kept fome good farms in his own hand, (when the tenants have died, or removed of their own accord,) to accommodate farmers from thofe countries where wheat is cultivated, it is to be hoped, that this grain will in a few years make a principal part of the crop of this parifh. The greateft part of the foil here being a ftrong clay, and all of it on a rich clay bottom, it is clear, that the carfe mode of plowing and cropping would fucceed well here. When this mode is introduced, the true value of this foil will be known.

Farm Rents and Improvements.—The tenants being numerous, the rents are various. Some pay 90 l. in money and grain ; and fome 2l. or perhaps even lefs. Every man who has

a

a horfe has alfo a cait. Some ufe no horfes, but do all kinds of farm work with oxen. One farmer, JAMES CLARKE in Nether-hill, ufes oxen for his threfhing machine, which is the only thing of the kind, that has as yet been introduced in this part of the country. It is to this induftrious honeft man, that we are indebted for introducing the fhell fand as a manure, which now turns out to fo great account, that many acres, which would not formerly have produced double the quantity of the feed, now produce weighty crops both of grain and hay.

Exports.—This parifh always produces more grain than is fufficient for the fupport of its inhabitants ; and even in the year 1782, had the produce been kept within the parifh, there would have been no need of any foreign fupply. About 1600 bolls of grain are exported annually ; butter and cheefe to the value of 600 l. Sterling ; fat cattle, horfes, and fheep, to a confiderable amount ; and a fmall quantity of hay and potatoes.

Population.—The population of this parifh is fomewhat lefs than it was 40 years ago. The following table fhows the decreafe, as well as the ages, profeffions, &c. of the inhabitants.

STATISTICAL TABLE OF THE PARISH OF ST FERGUS.

No. of fouls in 1755, as returned to Dr
Webfter,   1271

Ditto in 1775,	- -	1254 Decreafe,	17
Ditto in 1793,	- -	1240 Ditto	14

Total decreafe within 40 years,   31

AGES, SEXES, BIRTHS, &c.		No. of perfons between 50 and 70,	272
No of perfons under 10 years of		———Aged 70 and upwards,	221
age, - -	108	No. of males, -	559
——— Between 10 and 20	230	Females, -	681
———————— 20 and 50	409		
		Majority of females,	122
			No.

Annual average of births †, for 7 years preceding October 1792, 28

Ditto of marriages, 8

Ditto of deaths, - 22

CONDITIONS, PROFESSIONS, &c.

No. of proprietors, - 1

———— Miniſters, - 1

———— School-maſters, 1

———— Farmers, - 181

———— Shop-keepers, - 2

———— Weavers, - 43

———— Smiths, - 7

———— Wrights and Coopers, 12

———— Shoe-makers, 5

———— Tailors, - 5

———— Mafons, - 3

———— Inn-keepers, - 2

———— Millers, - 6

STOCK, RENTS, &c.

No. of Horfes, - 265

——— Black Cattle, 785

—— Sheep, - 908

—— Mills, - 3

——— Ploughs, - 70

Valued rent in Scotch money, - L. 3000 0 0

WAGES §.

A man fervant, per annum, when maintained‡, from L. 6 to L. 8 0 0

A woman ditto from L 3, to 4 0 0

A reaper in harveſt, with maintainance - 1 5 0

Ditto when hired per day, 10d or 1 0

A female ditto, per feafon, 1 0 0

Ditto per day, from 6d to 0 0 8

A wright per day, maintained, from 8d to 0 1 0

A tailor, ditto 0 0 6

A mafon, without maintainance, from 1s. 8d. to 0 1 10

A day labourer with meat 0 0 6

Ditto without it, 9d or 0 0 10

RELIGIOUS PERSUASIONS.

Members of the Eſtabliſhed Church, - 1145

Antiburgher Seceders, 25

Scotch Epifcopalians, - 70

Manufaɛturers.—The bleach-field at Inverugie, belonging to Meſſrs Forbes, Scott, and Co. employs a good many hands. There is every apparatus for bleaching thread ; and the

† ALEXANDER ANDERSON, miller at Inverugie, aged 70, has 40 grandchildren, all under 20 years of age.

§ The prices of proviſions are the fame here as at Peterhead.

‡ When the man fervant lives out of the family, he has, befides the above wages, 6 bolls and a half of meal, at 8 ſtone *per* boll Amſterdam weight, and 1 boll ten pecks of malt, Aberdeen-ſhire meafure with vegetables.

the value of the thread whitened here annually, is about 5000 l. Sterling.—A confiderable quantity of linen yarn is fpun in this parifh, by which a woman can earn about 4d. *per* day.—The weavers here are kept in employment by working for Meffrs Kilgours, woollen-manufacturers at Kinmundy, in the parifh of Longfide, and Alexander Dalgarno and Co. Peterhead. The beer and porter brewery at Inverugie is carried on by Mr Seller with fuccefs ; and a diftillery of whifky, by William Lillie, and Co. at the fame place, turns to good acount.

Difeafes.—The fmall-pox carried off great numbers formerly ; but as inoculation is now become general, this difeafe is lefs fatal. The fcurvy, with which many people here were affected, is not fo general, owing perhaps to the more liberal ufe of vegetables. Fevers, and often confumptions, prove fatal in this and the neighbouring parifhes ; but the moft terrible difeafe, that has been known in this part of the country for a century, is the putrid fore throat, which was not known here before December 1790. The number of deaths were more than double that year, owing to ravages made by this difeafe.

Language and Etymologies.—The dialect called broad Buchans is fpoken here. It is thought to approach nearer to the ancient *Gothic*, than the language of any other diftrict in Scotland. As the Picts were the antient inhabitants of the Eaft coaft of Scotland, they impofed names on the different places, expreffive, (in their language,) of their fituation or fome particular property. It is not eafy to affign any good reafon, for attempting to derive the names of places in this country from the *Celtic*, as there is no evidence, that it was inhabited by the Celts. The names of all the places in this

parifh

parifh, and the adjacent country, plainly appear to be Gothic, Saxon, or Danifh. For example, *South-effie, Middle-effie,* and *North-effie,* fignify the South, Middle, and North pafture, or feeding place, from the Teutonic *Effen,* to feed. *Pittinheath,* compounded of the Saxon *Pit,* and *Heath,* the name of a well known fhrub. *Pitfour,* the hollow trench; *Pitfligo,* anciently *Pitfligach,* the flaughter hollow. *Cruden,* was certainly a part of the ancient *Cruthenica,* or Pictifh kingdom, fo called ftom *Cruthen* the firft king of the Picts. *Deer,* the name of a neighbouring parifh, fignifies *a valley,* and is very expreffive of the fituation of that place. *Broadland,* the land of bread. *Crimond,* anciently *Creichmont,* the low or little mount. *Lonmay,* anciently *Longmay,* the long green, &c.

Woods.—At prefent there is no wood in the parifh, except a few old planes at Inverugie. ‡ The proprietor has paid much attention to the raifing of wood on his other eftates, particularly in the parifhes of Deer and Longfide, where he has planted 940 Englifh acres. They were all planted with Scotch firs, which fucceeded in about one fourth of the whole, and that part has been filled up with barren timber of different kinds. Where the Scotch firs have failed, the larch and fpruce have come forward; and it feems probable, that by

‡ There is clear evidence, that, at fome former period, a great part of this parifh has been covered with wood, chiefly oak, aller, birch, hazel, and willow, the remains of all which are found in the moffes. No roots or trees, however, of the Scotch fir have been found, which fhows that this kind of wood is not proper for this part of the country. It would appear that the woods in this country had, at one time or other, been deftroyed by fire, as the marks of that element are vifible on many of the roots and trees that are dug up in the moffes. It may not be an improbable conjecture, that this happened *anno* 1308, when King KOBERT BRUCE defeated CUMINE Earl of Buchan, near Inverury. Fordun, ¶ after narrating this defeat, adds, " *comitatum de Buchan igne confumfit.*

¶ *Fordun, vol.* II. *p.* 241.

by draining, and planting larch and fpruce firs for nurferies, other trees may be brought up. Many drains have already been made, and feveral thoufands of larches and fpruces have been planted, and the fame improvements are carrying on through the whole.

Roads and Bridge.—The principal roads, through this pa-rifh, are thofe leading from Peterhead to Fraferburgh and Banff, and from Peterhead to Old Deer. They are kept in tolerable repair by the ftatute labour, but will never be good roads until turnpikes are eftablifhed. It is not to be imagined that any man will work a day on the roads, when he may redeem his labour for 3d. If ever a mail coach be eftablifhed, for the accommodation of the country north of Aberdeen, the courfe muft be by the coaft fide, at leaft in winter, as the other road by Fyvie is often impaffable, on ac-count of the depth of the fnow; and the certainty of paf-fengers, from the towns on the coaft, efpecially at Peterhead, where there is always a great refort of company for the benefit of the mineral well, will make the road by the coaft fide eligible in fummer. The only bridge in this parifh is that over the Ugie, on the road from Peterhead to Fraferburgh and Banff. It confifts of two arches. This bridge was built, in confequence of an act of Parliament for that effect, in the reign of James the VII. of Scotland, and II. of England. *

Ecclefiaftical State.—This parifh is one of the 32 the tithes and patronage whereof belonged to the Abbey of Arbroath. §

The

---

* *Reprinted Acts of Parl.* JAMES VII. *Par.* I.

§ The minifter of St. Fergus formerly fupplied the charge at Fetterangus, by preaching there every third fabbath, until 1618, when Fetterangus was annexed to Deer. Fetterangus, as well as St. Fergus, is in Banff fhire; and the reafon

The family of Panmure acquired a right to thofe tithes and patronage ; but, by the attainder of the Earl of PANMURE, who unfortunately engaged in the rebellion in 1715, the patronage fell to the Crown. The ftipend is 90 l, including one chalder of bear, and three of meal, valued at 8 l. 6 s. 8d. *per* chalder. The glebe is about 8 acres of good land. The church was built in 1763, and the manfe in 1766 ; and both are in good repair. There is no diffenting meeting-houfe in the parifh.

Schools.—The fchool-houfe was built *anno* 1786. The falary of the fchool-mafter confifts of 10 bolls of meal paid by the parifhioners, and 3 l. 9 s. paid by heritors. He draws 2 l. from the kirk-feffion as their clerk, befides what he receives at baptifms and marriages. As there are generally fome private fchools in the parifh, the number of fcholars attending the parochial fchool feldom exceeds 30. Such as are taught Latin pay 2s. 6d, arithmetic, 2 s, reading and writing, 1 s. 6d, and reading Englifh, 1 s. *per* qaarter.

Poor —The number on the poor's roll in the parifh is 30 ; and the funds, from which they are fupplied, arife from 120 l. at intereft, the profits of a herfe for burials, which, at an average, produces 3 l. *per annum ;* feat-rents, 2l. 14s. 4d ; &c. the weekly collections 24 l. *per annum* ; amounting in all to 35 l. 14s. 4d. JAMES FERGUSON, Efq; of PITFOUR, the fole proprietor of the parifh, gives annually a liberal donation to the poor, by which, and the above funds, they are fo well fupplied, that there are no beggars in the parifh.

Eminent

reafon is faid to be, that the CHEYNES of Inverugie, the ancient proprietors, who were heritable Sheriffs of Banff, obtained an act of the Legiflature, declaring their own lands to be within their own jurifdiction. St. Fergus, Fetterangus, and Strolach, in New-Machar parifh, which alfo belonged to the Cheynes, pay the land tax and window tax, as parts of Banff-fhire, but in every other refpect are fubject to the jurifdiction of the Sheriff of Aberdeen.

Eminent Men.—It might be proper, under this article, to give a fhort account of the moft eminent family in Scotland, the CUMINES, who were Earls of BUCHAN, * and either proprietors

¶ The chief of this family was CUMINE Lord BADENOCH, of whom were defcended the Earls of Buchan and Monteith, and 32 knights §. This faction, with the Earls of MARR and ATHOLL, with whom they were connected by marriages, ruled the kingdom as they pleafed, during fome years in the latter part of the reign of ALEXANDER the II. and during the firft part of the reign of ALEXANDER III.

The male line of the antient Earls of Buchan failing in the perfon of FERGUS ¶, the laft Earl of the ancient race, his daughter MARJORY married WILLIAM CUMINE of the houfe of Badenoch, who in his right became Earl of Buchan about the beginning of the 13th century. His pofterity continued to enjoy this great eftate for 100 years, and were the moft powerful fubjects in the kingdom. This Earl founded the abbey of Deer, and endowed it with a confiderable revenue in lands fituated in the county of Aberdeen, *Anno* 1218. He was conftituted great jufticiary of Scotland by ALEXANDER II. in 1220; and his brother WALTER was by the fame King created Earl of MONTEITH, he having married the heirefs of that family, by whom he got a large eftate. The CUMINES being now fo rich and powerful, they became formidable, not only to the nobles, but even to the King. They were called to anfwer before the King and Eftates, anno 1255, for their various acts of *tyranny, oppreffion, murder, and facrilege,* and not appearing, a fentence of outlawry and forfeiture was pronounced againft them; but Government was too weak to put this fentence in execution. The faction, greatly irritated by this fentence, refolved to take the firft opportunity of getting the king's perfon into their power ‡. WALTER, Earl of Monteith, was the principal actor in this plot; and having along with him WILLIAM, the 2d Earl of Buchan of the

§ FORDUN *and* MAJOR.

¶ *A charter granted by* FERGUS *Earl of* BUCHAN *to* JOHN *the fon of* UCHTRED, *is to be feen in the Advocates library. From the charter it appears that Fergus had exchanged the lands, fituated betwixt Gicht and the Bank of Bebilch, with John for the lands of Slains ; and John was obliged to give attendance at the courts held by the Earl his fuperior at Ellon.*

‡ FORDUN.

prietors or ſuperiors of all that Earldom, beſides many conſiderable eſtates in other parts of the kingdom. But as it
would

the name of Cumine, the Earl of ATHOL, Lord BADENOCH, the Earl of
MARR, and others of their adherents, they entered the royal apartments
at Kinroſs, early in the morning of the 28th of October 1255, and made the
king a priſoner before he was awake, and carried him to Stirling. They
then diſmiſſed his Majeſty's ſervants, and filled all places of truſt with their
own adherents. So great was their power, that the king, after he had recovered his liberty, thought it prudent to give them a full pardon.

ALEXANDER, the 3d Earl of Buchan, of the name of Cumine, was
Juſticiary and Lord high Conſtable of Scotland, and was appointed one of the
ſix governors of the kingdom, after the death of King ALEXANDER III. He
founded an hoſpital at Turriff, *anno* 1272, for twelve poor huſbandmen, and
another at Newburgh, both in Aberdeenſhire. JOHN, the 4th Earl of Buchan,
conſtable of Scotland, was one of the arbiters choſen on the part of JOHN
BALIOL, in the competition for the Crown between him and ROBERT BRUCE.
At this time, JOHN CUMINE, Lord BADENOCH, commonly called the *Black
Cumine*, claimed the Crown of Scotland, as being deſcended of HEXASILDA,
daughter and heireſs of GOTHERIC, ſon and heir of DONALD king of Scotland.
It is well known how this affair was determined by EDWARD I. of England.
To the Black Cumine ſucceeded his ſon JOHN CUMINE, Lord of Badenoch,
commonly called the *Red Cumine*. Scotland had now for a conſiderable time
groaned under the yoke of Engliſh ſervitude : Baliol had meanly given up
his pretended right to the Crown to Edward ; and Bruce had ſecretly inti-
mated to his friends his intention of aſſerting his title to the royal dignity.
CUMINE, ever mindful of his own intereſt, made a ſolemn engagement with
ROBERT, to aid him with all his power in mounting the throne, provided he
ſhould be reſtored to the large poſſeſſions which his family had formerly enjoyed ; but, after deliberating upon the affair, he began to doubt the event : If
the attempt failed he was undone ; and he did not know how to retract : His
own black heart ſuggeſted the deteſtable remedy : His hopes of great rewards
from England induced him to divulge the whole ſcheme of the Scottiſh
patriots to EDWARD ; and BRUCE, finding that he was betrayed, with difficulty
eſcaped to Scotland, where, diſcovering clear proof of the villany of CUMINE,
he purſued him to the church of Dumfries, whither, from conſcious guilt, he
had fled for refuge, and puniſhed him as his crime deſerved, on the tenth
of February 1306. Having no iſſue, he was the laſt Lord Badenoch, of
the name of CUMINE. The ſlaughter of the *Red Cumine* by BRUCE inſpir-
ed

would greatly exceed the limits of a ſtatiſtical account to notice, even briefly, the many illuſtrious characters in this great

ed the whole clan with a deſire to revenge his death. They continued violently to oppoſe Bruce ; but, by defeating the Earl of Buchan at Inverurie, *anno* 1308, he put an end to the greatneſs of this too powerful family. Bruce purſued the Cumines to Fyvie, where they were entirely diſperſed. He encamped there, until the return of the parties which he had ſent out to burn the Earl of Buchan's eſtate : The Earl was then forfeited and out-lawed.¶.

At what particular period the Cheynes became proprietors of this pariſh, is not certainly known ; but it would appear, that they were in poſſeſſion of this eſtate before the Cumines ſucceeded to the Earldom of Buchan. Sir Reginold Cheyne of Inverugie was the founder of the Carmelites houſe in Aberdeen; and, beſides other revenues, beſtowed upon it 40s. † yearly out of his lands of Blackwater, in this pariſh. He had, by his wife, a daughter of Cumine, Lord Badenoch, two ſons ; Sir Reginald, who, in 1267, was promoted to the office of Lord Chamberlain of Scotland‡ ; Henry Cheyne, the Chamberlain's brother, was elected Biſhop of Aberdeen, *anno* 1281. He was one of thoſe who ſwore fealty to Edward, *anno* 1296. As he was nearly related to the Cumines, he adhered to that party, and was obliged to leave this country, and take refuge in England, where he remained in exile until King Robert was pleaſed to recal him. He was ſo happy in being allowed to reſume his functions, that he applied all the revenues of the ſee, which, during his abſence, had increaſed to a very conſiderable ſum, in building the bridge over the Don at Aberdeen. This bridge conſiſts of one Gothic arch, 72 feet wide at the water, and the height, from the water to the top of the arch, is 60 feet. He died *anno* 1329, having been biſhop of Aberdeen 48 years.

¶ *A ſilver ſeal, uſed by this Earl in his father's lifetime, was lately found at the monaſtery of Tungland in Galloway. It bears a ſhield embattled at top, and containing three garbs or wheat ſheaves : The Legend, S.* Jouis Comin, *Fel. Com. de Buchan. An impreſſion of this ſeal was ſent to that moſt ingenious antiquary Captain* Henry Hutton *of the Royal Regiment of Artillery, who it is hoped will ſoon favour the Public with his valuable collection of Antiquities.*

† *Writes of King's College.*

‡ *Fordun, vol.* 2 *p.* 106. *and Lives of Officers of State.*

great family ; and, as, indeed, ſuch diſquiſitions belong more properly to the department of the *hiſtorian* or *biographer*, than to

years. The direct male line of the CHEYNES ¶ of Inverugie failed in the reign of DAVID, II. and the pariſh of St Fergus, with the other eſtates belonging to the family, fell to two heireſſes, ‡ the eldeſt of whom, MARIOTHA CHEYNE, married John Keith of Ravenſcraig, ſecond ſon of Sir EDWARD KEITH, great Mariſchal of Scotland, who in her right became proprietor of this pariſh about the year 1360. The direct male line of JOHN KEITH failed in the perſon of Sir WILLIAM KEITH of Inverugie, who fell in the battle of Flowden. He left two daughters, the eldeſt of whom was married to William the 4th Earl Mariſchal, ſometime before 1538. By this marriage Earl MARISCHAL became proprietor of St Fergus. He was poſſeſſed of one of the greateſt land eſtates at that time in Scotland. In the years 1530, and

1540,

¶ *The pariſh of St Fergus made but a ſmall part of the property of this ancient family. Niſbet ſays, (Heraldry, vol. I. p. 130) that he ſaw a charter granted by Reynold Cheyne, ſon of Reynold who was the ſon of Reynold, of the lands of Dury. King* ROBERT BRUCE *gives the lands of Dalmeny, which formerly belonged to* ROGER MOUBRAY, *to* REGINALD CHEYNE, *as that king's charter bears in the Earl of Haddington's collections.* REGINALD CHEYNE *gives the lands of Ardlogie, in the pariſh of Fyvie, for ſupporting a chaplain in the priory of Fyvie, which was ſubordinate to the abbey of* ARBROATH. *(Chart. of Arbroath.)*

From CHEYNE *of Inverugie, were deſcended the Cheynes of Eſſelmont, Arnage, Pitfichie, and Straloch, all which are now extinct.*

CHRISITAN CHEYNE, *a daughter of Straloch, was married to Sir* ALEXANDER SETON *of that ilk, who bravely defended the town of Berwick againſt King Edward and the whole Engliſh army, anno* 1333. *Edward having ſummoned the town to ſurrender, threatened, in caſe of refuſal, to put to death Sir* ALEXANDER'S *two ſons, then in his hands, the one as an hoſtage, and the other as a priſoner; but nothing could prevail with the brave Sir Alexander to give up the town as long as it was poſſible to defend it. The perfidious Edward, thereupon, moſt barbarouſly executed the two young men,* WILLIAM *and* THOMAS SETONS, *in view of their father and mother; which ſhocking ſpectacle they bore with a moſt uncommon degree of fortitude.*

‡ *The youngeſt of the co-heireſſes of Cheyne of Inverugie was married to* NICOL SUTHERLAND *of Forbat, and brought with her the lands of* DUFFUS *in Moray. This* NICOL *was anceſtor of the Lords* DUFFUS.

to that of the *ſtatiſtical philoſopher*, we ſhall content ourſelves
with giving in this place only a brief ſketch of the character of
the great Field Marſhal KEITH, brother to GEORGE, laſt Earl
of Mariſchal ; and with throwing a few anecdotes of his moſt
illuſtrious

1540, he got charters ‖ on many lands lying in the counties, Caithneſs, Inverneſs, Moray, Banff, Aberdeen, Kincardine, Angus, Fife, Linlithgow, &c.
It is ſaid, that after Queen MARY's captivity, he took no concern in public
affairs, and by living a retired life in his caſtle of Dunottar, he got the name
of WILLIAM IN THE TOWER. He ſo much improved his eſtate, that at his
death it was reckoned worth 270,000 merks Scots, or 14,208l. 6s. 8d. Sterling.
This eſtate was ſo ſituated, that in travelling from the north point of Caithneſs, to the borders of England, he could ſleep every night on his own
ground. †

   This noble Lord died in an advanced age in 1581, and was ſucceeded by
his grandſon GEORGE, the 5th Earl Mariſchal, one of the moſt eminent men
of his time. After having ſtudied at Geneva, under the famous THEODORE
BEZA, he travelled through Italy and Germany, where he viſited the Land-
grave of HESSE, Prince of the CATTI, who, underſtanding who he was, received him kindly, and treated him with great magnificence, as a Scotch
deſcendant of the ancient CATTI. In 1589 he was ſent ambaſſador extraordinary to the court of Denmark, to eſpouſe the Princeſs ANNE in name of
James VI. of Scotland, and I. of England. Being poſſeſſed of a great eſtate,
he appeared with all the luſtre and magnificence with which the wealth of
Scotland could adorn him, and that chiefly on his own expences. In 1593,
he made a noble foundation of a college at Aberdeen, and obtained from the
Crown, for the ſupport of it, the lands and houſes belonging to ſome of the
religious at Aberdeen, which had not been ſued off before the Reformation.

‖ *Pub. Records, and Haddington's Collections, page 92, 93, &c.*

† *This Earl was a zealous promoter of the Reformation, but oppoſed all violent
proceedings in that affair. When the Confeſſion of Faith was preſented to Parliament,
in 1560, the Earl of Mariſchal ſtood up, and ſaid,* " It is long ſince I carried ſome
" favour to the truth, and was ſomewhat zealous for the Roman religion; but this
" day hath fully reſolved me of the truth of the one, and the falſehood of the other ;
" for, ſeeing (my Lords) the biſhops, who, by their learning, can, and for the zeal
" they ſhould have for the truth, would, as I ſuppoſe, gainſay any thing repugnant to
" it, ſay nothing againſt the Confeſſion we have heard, I cannot think but it is the
" TRUTH OF GOD, and the contrary of it is falſe deteſtable doctrine".

illuſtrious anceſtors into the notes. This great man was born at INVERUGIE, in this pariſh, and was baptized 16th June 1696, by the names of JAMES FRANCIS EDWARD. * He early entered into the military ſervice abroad, roſe to the higheſt rank in the army, and was inferior to no general of his time in military ·capacity. He accompanied his brother Earl Mariſchal to the battle of *Dunblane*, and afterwards went abroad to ſeek preferment at the Spaniſh Court ; but not finding a quick promotion there, he entered into the Ruſſian ſervice, and was by PETER the Great promoted to the rank of a general officer. He afterwards entered into the ſervice of FREDERIC III. King of Pruſſia, who raiſed him to the rank of Field Mariſhal. He commanded that king's armies ſometimes alone, and at other times along with his Majeſty, until the fatal battle of Hochkirchen, on the 14th October 1758. The Field Marſhal, returning from a ſeparate command, found that the King had encamped in a very improper place, and inſtantly told his Majeſty that DAUN would ſurprize them that night. His prediction proved too true ; and the Field Marſhal, making a glorious defence, was unfortunately killed. He was buried in the church-yard of Hochkirchen, but the King of Pruſſia had his corpſe taken up, and ſent to Berlin, where he was again interred with the greateſt military honours. ‡

Antiquities.

* *Baptiſmal Regiſter of pariſh of St. Fergus.*

‡ The Field Mariſhal, with all his great qualities was a very bad econo-miſt ; and ſometimes abſented himſelf from Court when he could not pay his debts. On one of theſe occaſions, the Great FREDERIC called for him, and found him in his garden, employed in pointing paper cannon at 1500 pins of wood in different directions, ſo as to diſcover how he might pour the greateſt quantity of fire upon them, as their poſition changed. The King paid his General's debts, was delighted with the diſcovery of his amuſement, and augmented the number of pins to 12,000; after which, he and his general had many a *keen engagement* in the garden, which proved of great ſervice afterwards in the field.

Antiquities.—As this parifh has, for upwards of 500 years, been only a part of a larger eftate, and never divided into fmall properties, we cannot expect to find ftately manfions here. Some peices of ftone and lime are to be met with, hard by the mouth of the Ugie, where it falls into the fea, and here, it is faid, was the ancient refidence of the family of Cheyne. They afterwards built another caftle, to which they alfo gave the name of INVERUGIE, * at the diftance of more than a mile weftward, on the fame fide of the river. The fite of this caftle does honour to the judgement and good tafte of its founder. Here the Ugie forms a femi-circle before the caftle, and the area of this femicircle is ter-minated, by *Mount-Pleafant*, a fteep rifing ground on the op-pofite fide of the river. The caftle is now in ruins, but the two courts are almoft entire ; part of them ferves as a gra-nery, and part is ufed as a brewery for porter and beer. Within a few paces of the wall of the North court, are the remains of an *ice-houfe*, which perhaps was the firft of the kind in this country.—On an eminence N. W. from the caftle, there is an artificial moat, where, it is probable, the ancient proprietors held their courts for the diftribution of juftice.

Character and Manner of Living.—The people in general are very hofpitable, kind to ftrangers, intelligent and conten-ted. They have fuch an attachment to their native foil, that few of them chufe to leave it. From Buchan there never were any emigrations, and indeed there can be no reafon for

any,

* This continued to be the refidence of the fucceeding proprietors, until the attainder of Lord Marifchal, who unfortunately engaged in the rebel-lion 1715. The precife time when this caftle was built is not known ; but as one part of it, now in ruins, was called the *Cheyne's-Tower*, it is probable that it was built by that family.

any, as every man, who is difpofed to work, can always have good employment and good wages, either as a mechanic or a labourer. Although few of the farmers have leafes, from many years experience, they confider themfelves as perfectly fecure, and in no danger of being removed, while they live peaceably and are punctual in the payment of their rents, which are very moderate, when compared with thofe of the neighbouring eftates. They are fenfible the heritor could have more rent than he draws from them. He has abolifhed all cuftoms and fervices ; and, if any of them build good houfes, a proper allowance is made. The kind and indulgent manner in which they are treated by the proprietor, has ftrongly attached them to him. They are fenfible that he is happy in beholding their profperity, and will not from thence take any advantage to raife their rents above what they can bear. The manner of living here is greately changed within the laft thirty years. The farmers now appear at church and market dreffed in Englifh fuperfine cloth, and many of their wives and daughters in cloaks and bonnets. The man-fervant is as expenfively arrayed as his mafter, and the drefs of the maid-fervant is little inferior to that of her miftrefs. The food of the inhabitants formerly confifted chiefly of oat meal, and fometimes of fifh, but thefe generally falted and dryed ; owing to this caufe, the fcurvy was a common difeafe. They raifed few vegetables, and turnips were often brought by fea from Aberdeen. Every cottager now has his turnips, cabbages, potatoes ; and many of the farmers have their mutton, fed by themfelves for fummer food, and the greateft part of them kill a fed ox or cow, for winter provifion. †

---

† From the middle of November 1792, to the firft of January 1793, 40 fat cattle, weighing from 14 to 24 ftone, were killed in this parifh for food during the winter, befides a confiderable number of fheep.

MORAY

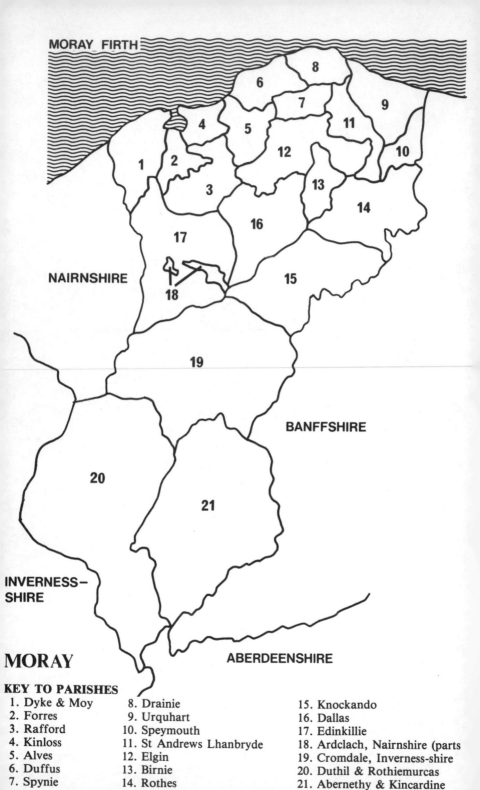

MORAY FIRTH

NAIRNSHIRE

BANFFSHIRE

INVERNESS-
SHIRE

ABERDEENSHIRE

MORAY

KEY TO PARISHES

1. Dyke & Moy
2. Forres
3. Rafford
4. Kinloss
5. Alves
6. Duffus
7. Spynie
8. Drainie
9. Urquhart
10. Speymouth
11. St Andrews Lhanbryde
12. Elgin
13. Birnie
14. Rothes
15. Knockando
16. Dallas
17. Edinkillie
18. Ardclach, Nairnshire (parts
19. Cromdale, Inverness-shire
20. Duthil & Rothiemurcas
21. Abernethy & Kincardine

UNITED PARISHES of ABERNETHY AND KINCHARDINE.

(Counties of Murray and Inverness *, Synod of Murray, Presbytery of Abernethy.)

By the Rev. Mr John Grant.

Name, Extent, Soil, Surface, Climate, &c.

THE name is defcriptive of the fituation of the church, with refpect to the river *Nethy*, being near the entrance of it into the Spey. Abernethy, or the *Inver*, or termination of Nethy, is in Gaelic, Abetneich. The meaning of the name *Nethy*, or *Neich*, is not known; that of *Kinchardine*, or *Kinie-chairdin*, is the " Clan of Friends." In what follows, both parifhes muft be frequently mentioned

---

* About one half of it in the county of Murray, the other half in the fhire of Invernefs. The middle part being in Murray, and the two extreme parts of it in Invernefs-fhire It is a little remarkable, that at the fouth eaft point of this parifh, between Glenlochy and Glenbrown, the fhires of Invernefs, Murray and Banff meet; fo that when ftanding on the Bridge of Brown, one may throw a ftone into any of the three counties.

tioned under the name of Abernethy. It is 15 miles in length, and from 10 to 12 in breadth, and about 30 miles f om the ſea at Inverneſs, Nairn, or Findhorn. The ſurface is very much diverſiſied with corn-fields, woods, and mountains. The ſoil is various ; ſome parts deep, others thin and dry, ſome wet and cold. A ſtretch of about 3 miles of low deep land and meadow, on the bank of the Spey, is often overflowed in times of floods. The Spey here runs ſmooth and ſlow, and of courſe the overflow is ſo too. Although many hundreds of acres are in this ſituation, and would increaſe greatly in their value, if free of this encroachment ; yet it appears doubtful if embankments could ſave the ground ; and ſtill more problematical, whether the acquiſition would be worth the expenſe, which behoved to be very great, on account of the great height to which Spey riſes at certain times. What increaſes the difficulty is, the great body of water which, in time of floods, comes from the mountains in the Nethy and ſmaller rivulets, and which would come in behind the embankments ; beſides, the proprietor has a great deal of land on the other ſide in the ſame predicament, ſo that double embankments would be neceſſary. The arable ground bears but a ſmall proportion to the uncultivated. A great proportion of the ſurface is covered with woods, much of it in hills, mountains, and rocks. The ground riſes towards the mountains, and the air and climate vary accordingly. Healthy every where. The people in general enjoy health to a degree that is not exceeded in many parts of the kingdom. The ſmall-pox is the only diſeaſe that is remarkably fatal. Inoculation is not general, though, upon the whole, peoples prejudices againſt it are much removed *.

Rivers

---

* *Longevity.*—A Donald Cameron is 98,—A Marjory Grant 101. It is to be regretted, that ſuch perſons are obliged to beg or be ſupported in
their

Rivers and Lakes.—The only river of any note, befides the Spey, is the Nethy, which, rifing in the high hills, interfects the parifh, running through or near the fir-woods, for above 7 miles, and empties itfelf into the Spey. In dry weather, it is very inconfiderable ; but after rains or thaws, it fwells fo as to bring down loofe all the timber that is cut in the woods, either to the faw-mills or to the Spey, whence it is fent in rafts to the fea at Gar-mouth. There are feveral lakes in Kinchardine ; the moft confiderable of which, is the oval bafon in Glenmore. near-ly two miles diameter. It is in the bottom of the glen, furrounded with fir-woods, rifing gradually towards the mountains. Here is a pleafant fcene in a fine fummer day. In Glenmore likewife, there is a green loch, in extent about one acre, full of fmall fat green trout. At the foot of Cairn-gorm, is Loch Aven, from whence the river of that name iffues, containing plenty of trout, but dry and indifferent ones to eat.

Cave and Mountains.—At one end of this loch, furround-ed with vaft mountains, is a large natural cave, fufficient to hold a number of men fecure from fnow, rain, or wind. People often lodge here for nights, fome from neceffity, others when hunting or fifhing. It is commonly called Chlachdhian, or the " Sheltering Stone." Of the whole range of mountains in view of the parifh, the *Cairngorm*, (or blue mountain), is the moft remarkable. Stones of va-lue are fometimes found at and near it, but rarely now, and
that

their quarters by the neighbours. A James Stuart, keeper of the Duke of Gordon's forefts and game, is 93, a blooming, correct fenfible man, and comes to church the coldeft day in winter. The laft incumbent, Mr William Grant, who was 60 years minifter of the parifh died in 1764, aged 96 ; and Robert Grant of Lurgg in 1772, 97 years old.

that ſometimes by chance or accident ; at other times, by digging for them. Some pretend to know the vein where they may moſt likely be. It is an employment not worth following. Numbers of ſtones of variegated colours, and regular ſides, as if cut by the lapidary, are found above ground, particularly after thaws or floods, which waſh off the ſurface, but when examined, ſeldom worth any thing. Theſe high mountains, to the ſouth of the pariſh, occaſion much cold and froſt. Cairngorm is ſeldom free of ſome ſnow any time in ſummer. On the tops of theſe high mountains, there is very little paſture, but a downy foggy cover on the rocks. The fir-woods never grow up the ſides of theſe high hills, or approach the regions of cold. Cairngorm commands an extenſive view. Roſs, Sutherland, and Caithneſs, are ſeen from it.

Woods, and the Progreſs of Manufaɛlure.—Beſides a great deal of birch and alder, there are two very large fir-woods in theſe pariſhes, almoſt meeting in one place. The fir-wood of Abernethy, belonging to Sir James Grant, is of great extent, and of an exceeding good quality, and very thriving ; but is kept from coming to a great ſize, by a conſtant manufaɛlure, for about 60 years backward. Before then, the making of deals by ſaw-mills was little known, and leſs praɛliſed. The firſt and early method of making deals, was by ſplitting the wood with wedges, and then dreſſing the boards with the ax and adze. A high room in Caſtle Grant appears to be floored with deals made in this way, and never planed. The marks of the adze acroſs the boards are ſtill viſible. And though this floor appears to be of great antiquity, ſuch is the ſuperlative quality of the timber, that it may continue as found as it is now hundreds of years hence. This floor has another mark of antiquity, the

nails

nails appear all to have been made by a country-fmith, according to the times ; the bonnets being as broad as a fmall halfpenny. Afterward the country-people got the fmall-framed faw. There being no demand for deals, neither did they know how to fend them out of the country, the heritors took any thing they could get for the wood that was manufactured. It is not a very long time back fince the Laird of Grant got only a merk a-year, for what a man choofed to cut and manufacture with his axe and faw ; people now alive remember it at 1 s. 8 d. a-year, afterwards it came to 3 s. 4 d. and then the Laird of Rothiemurchus, commonly called *Maccalpin*, brought it up to 5 s. a-year, and 1 lb. of tobacco. Brigadier Alexander Grant, (who died in 1719), attempted to bring fome mafts from his woods of Abernethy to London. But though a man of great enterprize in his military profeffion, did not perfevere in this, owing to the many difficulties he had to encounter, fuch as the want of roads in the woods, fkill in the country-people, and all kinds of neceffary implements. About the year 1730, a branch of the York-building Company, purchafed, to the amount of about L. 7000 of thefe woods of Abernethy, and continued till about the year 1737 ; the moft profufe and profligate fet that ever were heard of then in this corner. This was faid to be a ftock-jobbing bufinefs. Their extravagancies of every kind ruined themfelves, and corrupted others. Their beginning was great indeed, with 120 working-horfes, waggons, elegant temporary wooden houfes, faw-mills, iron-mills, and every kind of implement and apparatus of the beft and moft expenfive forts. They ufed to difplay their vanity by bonfires, tar-barrels, and opening hogfheads of brandy to the country-people, by which 5 of them died in one night. They had a Commiffary for provifions and forage, at an handfome falary ; and, in the end, went off in debt to the

proprietors

proprietors and the country. But yet their coming to the country was beneficial in many reſpects; for, beſides the knowledge and ſkill which was acquired from them, they made many uſeful and laſting improvements. They made roads through the woods. They erected proper ſaw-mills. They invented the conſtruction of the raft, as it is at preſent, and cut a paſſage through a rock in Spey, without which, floating to any extent could never be attempted. Before their time, ſome ſmall trifling rafts were ſent down Spey in a very awkward and hazardous manner, 10 or 12 dozen of deals, huddled together, conducted by a man, ſitting in what was called a *Currach*, made of a hide, in the ſhape, and about the ſize of a ſmall brewing-kettle, broader above than below, with ribs or hoops of wood in the inſide, and a croſs-ſtick for the man to ſit on; who, with a paddle in his hand, went before the raft, to which his currach was tied with a rope. This rope had a running-knot or loup round the man's knee in the currach, ſo that if the raft ſtopt on a ſtone, or any other way, he looſed the knot, and let his currach go on, otherwiſe it would ſink in a ſtrong ſtream; and when, after coming in behind the raft again, and looſing it, he proceeded again to make the beſt of his way. Theſe currachs were ſo light, that the men carried them on their backs home from Speymouth. There is one of them now in the pariſh of Cromdale below this. The York-building Company had 18 of theſe currachs in their employ at firſt, with which they made little progreſs, till Mr Aaron Hill, one of their number, conſtructed the large raft, as it is at preſent, conſiſting of two or three branders of ſpars in the bottom, joined end to end, with iron or other loups, and a rope through them, and conducted by two men, one at each end, who have each a ſeat and oar, with which they keep the raft in the proper direction. It is
pleaſant

pleafant to fee a number of them going down at once ; each
of them carry down varioufly, according to the quality of
the timber, from L. 10, L. 15, to L. 20 worth ; and at an
average, the expenfe of each raft to Speymouth, is about
L. 1, 10 s. At prefent, there are 4 faw mills in Abernethy.

Glenmore Wood.—About 8 years ago, the Duke of Gordon fold his fir-woods of Glenmore, in the barony of Kincardine, for L. 10,000 Sterling to an Englifh Company.
There were fome inferior companies tried it formerly, but
were not fuccefsful. It appears pretty certain now, that
this Company will fucceed in bringing away all the wood
within their contract, before their leafe is out, which was
26 years ; and it ought to be the wifh of every well-think-
ing perfon, that they may have profit in the end, as they
do much good to the country. They are regular and juft,
and carry on their bufinefs in every department of it with
much exertion and propriety. This was the oldeft, the
largeft, and the beft quality of fir-wood in Scotland,
and the beft accommodated for water-carriage to the
Spey, by means of the loch before defcribed, that is
in the heart of it, and out of which a river iffues, that
brings down even their mafts loofe to Spey, a diftance of 5
or 6 miles. The quantity of fpars, deals, logs, mafts and
fhip-timber, which they fend to Garmouth or Speymouth
yearly, is immenfe, and every ftage of the procefs of manufactory, brings money to the country ; generally once a-
year, they fend down Spey a loofe float, as they call it, of
about 12,000 pieces of timber, of various kinds ; whence
they fend it to England, or fell it round the coaft. For
fome years, they have fent great numbers of fmall mafts or
yards to England to the King's yards, and other places, and
have built about 20 veffels of various burdens at Garmouth

or

or Speymouth, all of Glenmore fir. Among others, there is one now on the ftocks, above 500 tons. Without doubt, thefe manufactures raife the price of labour and other articles, and make fervants for the farmer more difficult to be got. The fir-woods of this country exceed all the natural fir-woods in Scotland put together, without comparifon. Sir James Grant's woods of Abernethy, of many miles circumference; next, the Duke of Gordon's, in Glenmore; then Mr Grant of Rothiemurchus's, who is fuppofed to have more trees than either of them; then the Duke's again; after that, the Laird of M'Intofh's in Glenfifhy, all in a line, of about 20 miles in length, on the fouth fide of Spey, and all having the advantage of abundance of water to bring them to Spey. Befides, Sir James Grant has another wood, of an excellent quality, on the other fide of the country, on the river Dulnan *.

Population.—According Dr Webfter's report, the population then was 1670. The exact number in this parifh at prefent is 1769, of which 262 are below 7 years of age. Births, at an average for 6 years paft, 45; marriages, 10.

Produce, and State of Hufbandry.—The animal productions confift of black cattle, fheep, fome goats and horfes. The principal proprietor does not encourage great fheepfarms, nor are there any large tracts laid wafte for fuch flocks. It is computed, that two or three farms in Abernethy which are wholly given to fheep, and what the Englifh Company have in their own poffeffion in Kincardine without tenants, had about 200 inhabitants when let in

fmall

* *Quadrupeds and Birds*, &c.—Red-deer, roe, foxes, hares, moorfowl, partridge, tarmakan, eagles, hawks, and the other birds common in the Highlands of Scotland, abound here.

{mall farms. However, the sheep are greatly increased of late years, and the farmers endeavour to keep as many cattle as formerly; so that, like Pharaoh's kine the one consumes the other. The sheep are almost all of the black-faced kind, though few have the breed genuine, but crossed. By the tenants increasing their number of sheep, and still striving to keep up their former number of black cattle, neither the sheep can be expected to be fold fat, nor the cattle in general in decent marketable condition; by which means they must always be fold at prices inferior to what they would fetch if properly grazed; so that the parish in general is only a nursery for raising lean cattle and sheep, to be fattened elsewhere *.—The crops here are, barley, oats, rye, potatoes, chiefly the small black oats; on some farms peafe and a good deal of white oats. The crops here are often precarious, and frequently misgive to a very distressing degree. There are only 5 farms in the parish

* The cattle being often half starved in the winter, owing to having too many for the straw, and sent in summer to hills covered with sheep, are often presented to the drovers in August and September with the former year's hair on them. Such in the parish as do justice to their cattle in strawing them sufficiently, and grazing them well in summer, have very comely good cattle. But these are the fewest, the tenants in general keeping their numbers of black cattle while the sheep are insensibly increasing around them. The promiscuous pasturage of sheep and black cattle is unnatural, and must be a losing game; people see the error but do not mend it. This mismanagement is not peculiar to this district; many neighbouring parishes and counties go on in the same tract. While people follow the sheep system as they do, common sense would seem to dictate to them, that they ought to let the whole hill-pasturge go with the sheep, and only keep as many cattle as their inland farms would graze properly in the summer. By these means fewer beasts would exceed in value the present number. Few horses are reared in this parish, and great numbers of small ones used in it by the generality of the tenants, which takes a great deal of money yearly out of it, and which might be much remedied, if every farmer were to rear a foal every second or third year. Proprietors ought to attend to this and encourage it.

pariſh in any degree of improvement: On theſe there are good houſes, offices, and ſome good encloſures, limed and prepared with green crops for graſs, which anſwers well. Peaſe grow well in limed fields here. Theſe farms have the advantage of the beſt climate in the pariſh. They are ploughed with Engliſh or Scotch ploughs, according to the ground. Upon theſe, there are good horſes, oxen, carts, and the other modern implements. The want of hard wood in the country is a drawback; becauſe, without it, there can be no durable inſtruments of huſbandry. There are ſeveral neat farm-houſes built of late through the pariſh; but the farms themſelves in general are in no better ſtate than they were 100 years ago. The braes, or Highland parts of the pariſh, are not ſubjects for the modern improvements in huſbandry, but they might be much benefited by liming, the limeſtone and peats being near their fields in one quarter, but hitherto that has not been attempted. The abſurd ridiculous method of run-ridge ſtill takes place in a great part of the pariſh.—The produce of the pariſh is corn and potatoes; it never maintains its inhabitants, and often, when a failure happens in the crop, falls far ſhort; ſome often buy meal for 6 months in the year. After a pretty exact calculation, it is found, that only about 6 firlots of meal grow at an average of years, in the two pariſhes, for each perſon in them. It is ſhown thus: There are 7 mills in theſe pariſhes, 2 of them ſuperior to the reſt; and, upon ſure information, computed, at an average of years, at 20 bolls multure for each, *i. e.* for both, - 40 bolls

5 ſmall mills, at 8 bolls each, - 40

Total multure, 80

The multure here being the 33d part, gives the whole produce, except ſeed and horſe corn, namely 2640 bolls.

1 boll

1 boll to each perfon of the number of inhabitants, is   -   -   -   1769
½ boll to each, is   -   -   884
                                        ─────
                                        2653 bolls.

This fhows what attention ought to be given to incieafe
the value of cattle, becaufe all depends on the returns from
cattle, fheep, wool, butter, and cheefe, for paying rent, fervants, &c.

Language.—The common living language of the people,
in which they converfe, do their bufinefs, and are inftructed, is the Gaelic ; and the names of places are all Gaelic
ones.

Rent and Heritors.—The valued rent is L. 1553, 16 s.
Scots ; the grofs land-rent of the two parifhes, befides the
woods, is about L. 1500 Sterling.—The heritors are two,
Sir James Grant and the Duke of Gordon. The Earl of
Moray has the fuperiority of thefe lands in the parifh, of
Sir James Grant's, which are in the county of Elgin,
one of the many inftances of feudal abfurdity, which fepa-
rates the fuperiority from the property.

Stipends, Schools, Poor, &c.—Sir James Grant of Grant
is patron. The ftipend is only L. 64 ; a procefs of augmentation is now depending. The glebe about 5 acres of
middling land. The manfe and offices lately repaired.
The church of Abernethy is elegant, and the church
of Kinchardine, 8 miles from Abernethy, a very good
fufficient plain houfe lately repaired ; both church-yards
well enclofed with a wall and hedge, and a belt of wood
about 3 yards broad.—There are two fchools in the pa-
                                                    rifh,

rifh, and a catechift from the Royal bounty. The parochial falary is 200 merks, and a good fchool-houfe. The Society's falary in Kinchardine is L. 9, and one of the beft fchool-houfes in the Highlands.—There is no parochial fund for the poor, but the weekly collections in the church, which will not exceed L. 6 a-year at an average, there being no refiding heritors. Thefe collections are not fufficient to buy fhoes for the poor, for the half of the year. They live on the farmers, by begging from door to door. It is in this way the parifhioners give their charity chiefly, which they do very liberally. To keep within bounds, the parifhioners beftow 100 bolls of meal a-year on the poor that beg, and other donations fent to fuch as, by age or infirmities, are confined at fome home. This calculation is within the truth, and eafily made : A family that gives regularly to fuch objects, will, in the common way, confume a peck of meal each week, which exceeds three bolls in the year to fuch a family. This is a heavy burden upon the tenants, and calls upon heritors to contribute to their relief *.

Antiquities.—There is a large oblong fquare building near the church, called Caftle-Roy, or the Red-Caftle, one fide

* *Wages, Fuel, &c.*—Men fervants get from L. 2, 10 s. to L. 3 in the half year, women 18 s. and L. 1, and fome more; men labourers generally 1 s. the day; women, 6 d. when engaged for the day at peats, &c. Servants are only engaged here for the half year, which is attended with great inconveniencies and much lofs of labour to the farmer. In fhort there are hardly any regulations for fervants in the north of Scotland, which is feverely felt. The fuel of the parifh is peat and wood, with which all, upon the whole, are well fupplied; tho' the cafting, winning, and leading of them, makes them much more expenfive than coals are to fuch as have eafy accefs to them. Befides, there not being fuch a comfortable conftant fire, there is much wafte of time, cattle, and carts in all the operations of them; and after a rifk of being ill fired after all, or getting few of them home, and thefe in bad order in rainy feafons.

fide 30, the other 20 yards, the height about 10. It never was roofed, has no loop holes, and only one entrance to the infide. Neither hiftory nor tradition give any fatisfying account of it.

Eminent and Remarkable Men.—The Honourable John Grant, late Chief Juftice of Jamaica, was a native of this parifh. At Knock of Kinchardine, in the other extremity of the parifh, was born in the 1700 John Stuart, commonly called, and well known by the name of John Roy Stuart. His mother was 55 years old when he was born. The one of thefe gentlemen was as remarkable for certain talents, as the other was eminent in the ftation which he fo lately filled. John Roy Stuart, ferved for feveral years as lieutenant and quarter-mafter in the Scots Grays, till the year 1740, when he applied for a company in the 42d Regiment, which being denied him, he left the kingdom, went for fome time to the continent, and afterward to France, where he died in the year 1752, only a captain. By thefe means, his talents were loft to himfelf and to his country. He had education, without being educated; his addrefs and his figure, fhowed his talents to great advantage. He was a good poet in Gaelic and Englifh.

Roads and Bridges.—It was only about the year 1764, when the prefent proprietor Sir James Grant entered to the eftate, that roads were begun in this part of his eftate, called Strathfpey, which is about 30 miles in length. Since which period, he has made above 130 miles, when the whole is added together. The roads in this parifh, are remarkably good, and going on yearly, by means of the ftatute-labour. The great roads are made through thefe parifhes by Sir James Grant and the Duke of Gordon. Crofs roads

roads are now going on, which will prove highly serviceable. The Duke of Gordon has made one uncommonly good crofs-road, from Glenmore to the Spey, for his Englifh Company. There is one excellent bridge, built about 25 years ago, by Sir James Grant on the river Nethy, at his own expenfe, and 2 fmaller bridges to the eaft by him, with fome affiftance from the county of Invernefs. Another bridge is begun, on a very troublefome rivulet, near the church of Kinchardine on the Duke of Gordon's property, with affiftance from the county of Invernefs. The heritors of the county of Invernefs affefs themfelves, with much fpirit, for building bridges, &c. which cannot indeed be faid for the proprietors of the low parts of Elgin. Sir James Grant has lately made about 7 miles of a very difficult and expenfive road, from Caftle-Grant, paft his own march in the hills to fhorten the way, at leaft to open new communications with Forres and Elgin, and this at his own private expenfe *.

Manufactures.—There are no maufactures in thefe parifhes, but that of wood, as has been already mentioned. A woollen manufacture, for Scots ferges, ftuffs, tartans, &c. might be tried with a profpect of advantage in fome part

of

* And yet, the people concerned in the trade of thefe towns, and the numerous proprietors of the lower eftates, feem to be in danger of forgetting to come forward to meet him. They have hitherto done nothing of their part of it ; and while they continue fo inactive, his great expenfe and labour will be loft. The time was when Highlanders were faid to be averfe to have any roads made in, or to their country. But it is a little fingular to fee the inhabitants of the weft of Morray, who always pretended to fuperior civilization to the highland people, fo outdone here. It is hoped therefore they will come forward next feafon to fave their reputation. The advantages and fatisfaction of the private roads here, and of the King's high road from Fort George to Perth, through the eaft end of the parifh, with its numerous bridges, are fo many and fo fenfibly felt, when contrafted with the ftate of the country fome years ago, that it is unneceffary to take up room here in relating it.

of this country, where the women underſtand the ſpinning of wool very well for ſuch purpoſes; and where there is plenty of wool. Something of this kind, and the ſpinning of flax, would be of the greateſt ſervice for procuring ſubſiſtence to poor people, and keeping them from begging, which numbers are obliged to do, for want of employment of this kind *.

Miſcellaneous Obſervations.—The ſize of the people is generally very good; at an average 5 feet 6, 8, and 10 inches, and many above that height; handy and active in their perſons; generally ſagacious and well informed according to their ſtation; frugal and economical, and in general very ſober. There is no whiſky ſtill in the pariſh, becauſe there is no grain for it. None have been condemned for a capital crime, ſince the days of the regality juriſdiction. They make hardy, clean, tractable ſoldiers when in the army; numbers of them are excellent markſmen. Their chief attachment is to Highland corps, which Government ought to make always as provincial as poſſible; this would increaſe their attachment, and their ſpirit to a degree that none can underſtand but ſuch as know their tempers. A man that

is

* Raiſing of flax has been and is tried, but has not come any great length as yet, owing to ſeveral cauſes. Several parts of the lands near the Spey, are very well adapted for ſuch a crop: but it never can be expected to anſwer in the braes or highlands of the pariſh; the ſoil and climate being totally againſt it. Furniſhing ſuch people as are unacquainted with the kind of crop with ſeed, without any price paid for it, or at a very low rate, might, with proper directions given them, bring this a greater length and do much good. The want of employment, and the large tracts of land laid under ſheep in many parts of the Highlands, has increaſed the number of beggars much. And if the price of leather advances a little further, beggars will not be able to travel for want of ſhoes; as they will not be able to get as much as buy them. Such highland ſhoes as the people here wear, have increaſed within theſe 20 years from 10 d. and 1 s. to 3 s. and 3 s. 6 d. the pair.

is harſh and auſtere, and fond of ſeverity and puniſhment, is not fit to command a Highland corps; but their officers, do them juſtice, ſpeak to them in a diſcreet friendly manner, and encourage them by a little familiarity, and they find them reſpectful, attached and obedient. The vaga-bonds that are recruited in cities and towns, ought never to be allowed to mix with them. The method adopted by Government of late, in making their Highland Fencibles provincial ones, is a wiſe meaſure, and will anſwer the end propoſed. It is peculiar to this pariſh to have two heri-tors, who have got each a Fencible regiment. The Duke of Gordon and Sir James Grant, and who have not only raiſed them in three weeks and a few days, but have each of them ſupernumeraries, for additional companies, in form-ing a conſiderable part of ſecond battalions, if Government ſhould need them; and all recruited in an eaſy, diſcreet, ſmooth manner, without force or compulſion. Men ſo plea-ſantly got, and ſo content when well uſed, cannot miſs of giving ſatisfaction to their officers, and may be relied on by the nation. The people here are loyal to a degree that cannot be ſurpaſſed; amazingly attached to their King, be-cauſe they like his character and his virtues, and that he is a good man. Political or religious fanaticiſm have got no footing here; of courſe it is very eaſy to live in peace a-mong them. There are no religious ſectaries here, the peo-ple being all of the Eſtabliſhed Church. Their language, their garb, their ſocial ſituation, their climate and modes of huſbandry, have kept them hitherto a people different in character and manners, from the inhabitants of the low country, and from being miſled by the doctrines of thoſe itinerant fanatics that infeſt the coaſt. The poiſonous doc-trines of political pamphlet writers, have made no progreſs among them; yet many of the people here ſeem often much diſſatisfied with their condition in ſome reſpects.

What

What they complain of chiefly is, the method followed in letting their farms when their leafes are expired. It is feldom that the tenants are called on to renew, till within a few months of the term of removal, and then perhaps, left for years in fufpence, before they are fettled with, and tried for fome addition every year; and every year receiving a fummons of removal. The offers received are generally kept private ; and when they get a leafe, it is only for 15 or 19 years, which they think too fhort. The effects of this method are very bad, both for mafter and tenant. For during the laft 2 or 3 years of the leafe, they are under apprehenfions of being removed, and of courfe plough up what they ought not, or would not, if they were certain of continuing ; and all this while, carelefs about the repairs of their houfes and buildings. By thefe means, they either hurt themfelves, if they continue, by renewing, or their fucceffor if they remove, and the proprietors intereft in either cafe. Befides, that while people are kept long in fufpence, it occafions much unhappy anxiety, and reftleffnefs of mind *.

Cattle,

* The following or fome fuch rules, if attended to, might be beneficial both to mafter and tenants. 1*ſt*, That tenants ought to be fettled with, at leaft a year before the expiration of their leafes. 2*d*, That no private offers ought to be admitted at all. They are often, when injudicious, unfafe for the mafter and precarious for the tenant. Becaufe a tenant is at a lofs how to act, when he knows not what is offered by others, and of courfe may offer different times above himfelf. A public roup would be fairer than private offers, becaufe then a perfon fees what he is doing. Befides that when people are preffed by neceffity, or hurried by their paffions, it is dangerous to rely on their offers. The method of encouraging people to offer privately or publicly upon each other, is moft hurtful to the very effence of Chriftianity, by deftroying friendfhip and good will, and introducing much ill will, revenge and quarrels. It is common to hear of peoples threatening to offer for their neighbours

Cattle markets.—The people here, as well as in many parts of the Highlands, have but too much cauſe to complain

neighbours poſſeſſions ſeveral years before they expire. In ſhort the ill temper produced by theſe unlucky interferences, ſometimes lives longer than the leaſes. It is hard, therefore, to throw unneceſſary temptations in the way of people; and therefore what might remedy all this and anſwer better, is, 3*dly*, That the maſter, after being well informed, and due conſideration of the nature, quality, climate, advantages and diſadvantages of each farm, ſhould ſet a ſpecific rent on it, as high as he thinks it can bear, and then offer it to the poſſeſſor, and to none other, if he does not reject it, paying due regard at the ſame time to abilities, induſtry, character and principle; and if the poſſeſſor declines it, then to give it to ſome other proper perſon, who may think it worth that rent. 4*thly*, That when a proprietor gets good tenants, he ought to give two or three nineteens, with a certain riſe of rent at certain periods. This would make their minds eaſy, and induce them to act with ſpirit, becauſe of their having a pretty ſure proſpect that they or theirs might reap the fruits of their induſtry. Fifteen or 19 years leaſes are very bad for people of circumſtances and induſtry; becauſe when an induſtrious man upon a ſhort leaſe puts his farm in the beſt order he can, he makes it the greater temptation for others to offer for it and remove himſelf. There is another thing which the tenants of the principal proprietor complain of much, and which they reckon a grievance, tho' it is only the conſequence of their agreement by their leaſes, that is, the paying for the building or reparation of church, manſe and ſchool-houſe. This was no doubt introduced in time of wadſets or mortgages, of which there are none now on the eſtate. It would be equally for the intereſt of the heritor to take this all on himſelf, as is generally done over all Scotland, and ſubſtitute an addition to the rent in place of it. This would likewiſe be moſt pleaſant to any incumbent; becauſe, when any thing is wanted in that way, the people murmur and complain, and look upon themſelves as diſtreſſed by the miniſter.

Cottagers.—Their is a claſs of people much neglected, at leaſt very little attended to, not only here but in moſt countries in the Highlands, *i. e.* the cottagers. They not only have their houſes from ſubtenants, but ſometimes from the ſubtenants of ſubtenants; and few of them allowed to keep a milch cow or a horſe, even for paying for them. This, in a country where there is not conſtant employment for ſuch, by daily labour, muſt of courſe keep them miſerably poor, and force them often to beg

or

complain of loffes fuftained by the failures of little drovers. It is thought by fome, that this might be prevented from being fo frequent. The common method of
buying of cattle is, for any one that attempts droving, to
call a market for himfelf when he fees proper. The neceffity, ignorance, or greed of many, induce them often to
venture their cattle, for a fhilling or two more a-head, with
a man that would be ruined if he loft a crown a-piece by
his parcel at Falkirk. Sales are by thefe means often partial, and feldom general,—picking a few beafts here and
there out of parcels. It is thought, a few public markets
in centrical places, correfponding to the fairs in the fouth,
would anfwer better; that heritors ought to attend to this,
and that they and their factors fhould get the beft information in their power of the prices of the times, and get men of
character and fubftance to come as buyers; that the factors
fhould attend them, and perfuade the tenants to fell in a
reafonable moderate way, according to the times: This
might make the fale more general, and often prevent much
money from being loft to tenants, and, of courfe, to heritors. For, furely, confidering what a fatiguing, hazardous
bufinefs droving is, men that pay well ought to be much
fought after, and much encouraged *.

Progrefs

or tempt them to pilfer. If heritors were to affign fmall fpots of land
for them in centrical places, near the principal farms, from whence labour
might be expected moft, and let each of them have a houfe and garden,
and about two acres of ground for corn and potatoes, this would maintain
a cow, and perhaps a fmall horfe; and they might join about ploughing
their fpots. Four or fix would be enough together; crowding a number of
poor people together might defeat the defign. This might anfwer well
for fmall tradefmen, fuch as country fhoemakers, tailors, weavers, &c.
and promote their comfort, honefty and ufefulnefs to the neighbourhood.

* *State of Glebes.*—Here, though out of place, a few obfervations occur
to be made on the original and general defignation of minifters glebes, the
legal

Progreſs of Civilization.—It is worth obſerving, what change there is in the modes of thinking of the people within theſe laſt 45 years. Two events have contributed, in a remarkable manner, to a better way of thinking, and ſubmiſſion to order and government. The rebellion of 1745-6 in its good effects, and the ſubſequent abolition of the juriſdiction-act. Previous to that period, property was chiefly protected by force, and the exiſting laws known in theory, but little regarded in many parts of the Highlands. Thieving was a trade in many countries, and carried on on a large ſcale, with much contrivance and ſagacity, and countenanced ſometimes in private by thoſe who undertook, for a certain pay called *black meal*, the protection of neighbouring diſtricts. Preſident Forbes of Culloden paid his proportion of this aſſeſſment, before the 1745, to

legal quantity being four acres and a little graſs. It would appear that it was thought then, that miniſters were to live abſtracted from this earth altogether. There is ſuch a difference between four acres in ſome places or countries and others, that there was no juſtice in the general rule. What purpoſe can many glebes of four acres of poor land in many parts of the Highlands anſwer? Will ſuch a glebe maintain cattle to plough itſelf, or two horſes to lead the miniſter's peats? Which way is his family to get fuel brought home, or meal carried from the low country, at the diſtance of 30 or 40 miles or more? Was it ſuppoſed, that miniſters would be able, at any rate when old, to go on foot through their large pariſhes, from one preaching place to another, at many miles diſtance, through froſt and ſnow? Therefore without regard to quantity, every glebe ought to maintain two cows, and two good horſes for ploughing, for the miniſter's riding, for leading his peats and meal from any diſtance neceſſary. It is ſaid heritors reckon it a great hardſhip that the Court of Seſſion ſhould decern for victual to miniſters in pariſhes which pay no victual-rent, and perhaps when enough is not produced for the inhabitants. Some heritors grudge every thing that is given to their clergy, as if they had no right to any thing. But, beſides that victual is the only payment that keeps pace with the times, does it not appear a greater hardſhip, that a miniſter ſhould ſend to to a certain perfon to the weft of him, whofe power and influence were fo great, that he would have ruined his e-ftate if he had refufed to comply. The land of Moray being, it feems, always a land of plenty, feems to have been devoted to be plundered. The people to the weft appear to have claimed a right to a fhare of the productions of it. They ufed to regret, that their corn-ftacks would not drive like their cattle *.—The humiliation produced by the defeat

to a great diftance for what his family requires, and therefore it would feem equitable, that at any rate 20 or 24 bolls meal and bear fhould be ordered ; which, with the produce of the glebe, might be fuppofed to anfwer for the confumption of the houfe.

* There is a remarkable correfpondence between Allan Cameron of Lochiel, and the Laird of Grant about 140 years ago, wherein the principles of the times are clearly feen. The correfpondence is publifhed in Sir John Dalrymple's Collection of original papers and letters. The ftory is briefly thus : a party of the Camerons had come down, to carry a *fpreath* of cattle, as it was called, from Morray ; they unluckily carried off the cattle of Grant of Moynes in Nairn-fhire. Moynes complained to his Chief, the Laird of Grant, and he fent a party after them, and after a fharp conflict, brought back the cattle. Lochiel writes a letter to his friend the Laird of Grant, regretting the misfortune, afferting that when his *friends went out*, they did not intend to trouble his Honour's land ; nor did they know that Moynes was a Grant, otherwife they would not have gone near him, or troubled him more than any man in Strathfpey, but they went to Morayland, he fays, " where all men take their prey." Lochiel mentions the number of killed and wounded of his friends in the fkirmifh ; and fays, they were all fo much taken up about the curing of their friends, that they could not attend to any bufinefs for the time. But when that was over, he was willing to refer the whole to their mutual friend Seaforth, which was done ; and it does not appear, that Seaforth had much difficulty in making the two chieftains as good friends as they were before. A little after this period, the Laird of Grant was obliged to build a ftable within his court, to prevent his own brother from taking away his beft horfes. This ftable was taken down about 40 years ago. The incumbent remembers when the people of this country kept out a watch in the fummer-months, for protecting their cattle, and thefe watches kept up by a round of duty, and reliefs at certain periods. In this country, where that bufinefs was not followed

defeat of the undertaking of 1745-6, and the wise plan of
employing the Highlanders in 1757 in the public cause,
contributed by degrees to introduce loyalty and submission
to the laws into the very seats of disaffection and rapine.
The conduct of the people, when employed in support
of the nation, showed that they were only misled at
home. It is to be regretted, that so many thousands
of these now loyal brave people have been forced to a
foreign shore by necessity, for want of employment,
habitation, or ground to subsist on. However advantageous the sheep-farming may be, it is possible it may be o-
verdone ; and if ever that happens, it will be found to be
impolitic in every sense, as it is cruel in many places at
present. It is dangerous in these times to drive poor people to desperation, as it may make many disposed to join
in tumults and riots, who would never think of them if they
had a home and the common necessaries of life. To increase
our gratitude for the protection afforded by our constitution
to the lives and properties of individuals in these countries
at present, we will mention the blessings we enjoy by the
abolition of the jurisdiction-act in the year 1748. That
delegation of feudal power was dangerous in the extreme,
because it was generally abused. When we consult the
traditional history of the country for a century and upwards past, and the extraordinary conduct of some of these
despots, the bailies of regality, and the precariousness of
life and property often within their jurisdiction, one is ex-
cited to grasp with fondness the Government that has anni-
hilated their dangerous power. They often punished
crimes,

followed professionally for some time past, the people in several places and
passes were often obliged to be discreet and hospitable to these intruders, as
they went to the low countries, and no doubt there were connivers and aid-
ers among them, who knew very well for what they were so.

crimes, by committing greater ones themfelves. They often, no doubt, tried by jury; but fome of them, at other
times, in a fummary, arbitrary, and extraordinary manner *.

* A few inftances will be enough to mention, in cafe the reader fhould
imagine, that thefe things were lately done in Tippoo Sultan's dominions. One of them lived in this parifh, named Robert Grant, commonly
called Bailie More. It is faid, he ufed to hang people for difobliging
him. He feldom called juries : He hanged two brothers on a tree within
a thoufand yards of this town, and buried both in one grave, on the road-
fide. The grave and ftones above it are ftill vifible. Another, named
James Grant, commonly called Bailie Roy, who lived long in this parifh,
hanged a man of the name of Steuart, and after hanging him, fet a jury
on him, and found him guilty. The particulars are too long to be inferted here. The Bailie had many reafons for being in fuch a hurry. The
man was, unluckily for him, wealthy, and abounded in cattle, horfes,
fheep and goats, all of which were inftantly driven to the Bailie's home;
Stuart's children fet a-begging, and his wife became deranged in her mind,
and was afterward drowned in a river : It is not very long fince. This
fame Bailie Roy, on another occafion, hanged two notorious thieves, parboiled their heads, and fet them up on fpikes afterward. At another
time, he drowned two men in facks, at the bridge of Billimon, within
a few hundred yards of this manfe, and endeavoured to compel a man from
Glenmore, in the barony of Kinchardine, to affift him and the executioners
he had with him in the bufinefs; which the man refufing to do, the Bailie
faid to him, If you was within my regality, I would teach you better
manners than to difobey my commands. This Bailie bought a good eftate.
There was another of them, called Bailie Bain, in this country; who became
fo odious, that the country-people drowned him in Spey, near the church
of Inverallan, about 2 miles from hence. They took off his boots and gloves,
left them in the bank, and drove his horfe through a rugged place, full
of large ftones. The tract in the fand, boots, &c. difcovered what had
become of him; and when a fearch was made for him down the river, a
man met the party near the church of Cromdale, who afked them, what
they were fearching for? they anfwered, for the Bailie's body; upon
which, he faid, " Turn back, turn back, perhaps he is gone up againft
" the river, for he was always acting againft Nature." As their power
was great, and generally abufed, fo many of them enriched themfelves.
They had many ways of making money for themfelves; fuch as, 1. The Bailie's

lie's Darak, as it was called, or a day's labour in the year from every tenant on the estate. 2. Confiscations, as they generally seized on all the goods and effects of such as suffered capitally. 3. All fines for killing game, black-fish, or cutting green wood, were laid on by themselves, and went into their own pockets. These fines amounted to what they pleased almost. 4. Another very lucrative perquisite they had, was, what was called the Herial Horse, which was, the best horse, cow, ox, or other article, which any tenant on the estate possessed at the time of his death. This was taken from the widow and children for the Bailie, at the time they had most need of assistance. This amounted to a great deal on a large estate. This practice was abolished by the late Sir Ludovick Grant in this country, in the year 1738.

Containing fome additional information, received after the account of Abernethy and Kinchardine was gone to Prefs.

LIST of Vessels built at Kingfton Port, or Speymouth, of Glenmore Timber, by Meffrs Dodfworth and Ofbourne, fince the year 1785.

	Tons.
The brig *Glenmore*, burden - -	110
The fhip *Duchefs of Gordon*, - -	330
The brig *Kingfton*, - - -	140
The fhip *Effay*, - • -	350
The floop *Succefs*, - - -	54
The fhip *Sally and Ann*, - -	200
The brig *Speedwell*, - -	120
The fhip *Yucatan*, - -	260
The fchooner *Difpatch*, - -	34
The fchooner *Neptune*, - -	70
The fchooner *Good Intent*, - -	55
The floop *Harriot*, - - -	25
The floop *Friendfhip*, - -	54
The fhip *Lord Alexander Gordon*, - -	350
The *Lady Charlote Gordon*, - -	180
The *Marquis of Huntly*, - -	380
The *Duke of Gordon*, - -	500
The *Collingwood*, - - -	300
The floop *Jane*, - - -	70

Tons, 3582

Attefted by Thomas Seal, clerk to the Company.

PARISH OF ALVES.

(County and Preſbytery of Elgin——Synod of Moray.)

By the Rev. Mr. WILLIAM M'BEAN, *Miniſter.*

━━━◆━━◆━◆◆━◆━━◆◆━◆━

Extent, Surface, Soil, and Climate.

THE pariſh of Alves is about 5 Engliſh miles in length, and nearly the ſame in breadth. The Moray Frith waſhes its coaſt on the N. The face of the country preſents a moſt agreeable mixture of hill and dale ; and the plantations lately made by the Earl of Moray, will, in a ſhort time, add not a little to its beauty. The ſoil is diſtinguiſhed for its fertility, being generally a deep loam on a clayey bottom ; though, in a few places, it is of a lighter quality. From the nature of the ſoil, the crops are rather late ; but from the happy climate of the county of Moray, this is attended with no material inconvenience to the farmer.

Cultivation and Produce.—The tenants are very induſtrious, and their labours are amply rewarded by excellent crops. For centuries paſt, they have raiſed wheat ; and, until lately,

a

a confiderable proportion of their rents was paid to the Earl of Moray in that grain. This his Lordfhip has now converted into money, as the tenants found it more advantageous to cultivate barley : But wheat is ftill fown, though not to fo great an extent. They are now making a rapid progrefs in the modern ftyle of agriculture. Grafs feeds are laid down on a large fcale. Beans are planted in drills. Many acres of turnips are fown both in drills, and in the broad caft way, with great fuccefs. Potatoes are alfo raifed in very confiderable quantities, both by the plough and fpade. The general fucceffion of crops is three plowings for barley; the firft in autumn, the fecond, after dunging, in April, and a feed furrow in the beginning of May. The fucceeding crop is commonly oats, if grafs feeds are not laid down with the barley. Occafionally, grafs feeds are laid down with the oats ; and, when that is not the cafe, the following crop is peafe, and barley with grafs feeds thereafter. The oats, that grow in Alves, are about a fortnight later in ripening than thofe produced in the neighbourhood, and therefore are in requeft for feed in the light and fandy grounds in this country, and, on trial, are found to produce an excellent quality of grain, and fuperior quantity of fodder.

Leafes.—It would be of material confequence to the intereft, both of proprietors and farmers all over Scotland, but efpecially in this corner, that long leafes were introduced. They would animate the farmers to fuperior induftry and profitable fpeculation, as they would afcertain to them the fruits of their induftry, and prevent their having recourfe to exhaufting crops, under the apprehenfion of being foon removed. It is with pleafure that the writer of this article can add, that in this parifh, upon Lord Moray's property, there

are

are many farms, that have been continued in the poſſeſſion of the ſame families for ſeveral generations *.

Ploughs, Cattle, &c.—The number of ploughs in this pa-riſh may be ſtated at 115 : the number of horſes at 560 ; moſt of them are of a pretty large ſize, and ſo ſtout, that 2 of them draw a plough. The number of black cattle is about 1100. The cattle are not now ſo numerous as they were formerly, but conſiderably increaſed in ſize, from their being fed with artificial graſſes and turnips. The number of ſheep is about 2500. They are of a very ſmall ſize, excepting a few of the large Bakewell breed.

Prices of Labour.—The price of labour is conſiderably ad-vanced within theſe few years. The wages of men ſervants, employed in huſbandry, are from 6l. to 8l. when they live in the family, and 2 pecks of meal in the week when they do not. Women ſervants have generally from 30s. to 40s. per annum, with ſome perquiſites. The wages paid to reapers, during harveſt, are from 18s. to 1l. 10s. They are gene-rally hired for the ſeaſon, except in thoſe caſes when the farm-ers have cottagers : To cut down their corn is a part of their ſtated labour ; and, for this and other ſervices, the cottagers have a free houſe and a garden.

Minerals,

* It is a circumſtance that deſerves particular notice, as it points out what induſtry and a ſteady economy can produce, and at the ſame time proves the laudable foſtering care and attention of ſome proprietors, that a family, of the name of ANDERSON, have occupied a farm in this pariſh, on the eſtate of the Earl of Moray, for upwards of 400 years. The preſent tenant, having produced to the late Earl of Moray receipts for rents as far back as the time of Earl Randolph, obtained from his Lordſhip a renewal of his leaſe on the moſt indul-gent terms.

Minerals, Fuel, Inns, &c.—The E. end of the parish a-bounds with inexhauftible quarries of excellent freeftone, very fit for either building or mill-ftones.—This parish was once abundantly accommodated with peats for fuel ; but the moffes are now almoft exhaufted, and many of the country people are neceffitated to purchafe coals.—There is but one inn or public houfe in the parifh. It lies on the county road from Elgin to Forres, which paffes through Alves.

Heritors and Rent.—The heritors are, the Earl of Moray; the Earl of Fife ; William Brodie of Windyhills, Efq.; Peter Rofe Watfon of Callfield, Efq.; Mifs Brodie of Lethen ; John Spence Munro of Kirktown, Efq.; and George Forteath of Newton, Efq.—two of whom only have their refidence in the parifh. It is not pretended to give an accurate ftatement of the real rent, as that muft depend upon the price of grain ; but, at an average, it may be eftimated at upwards of 3000l. Sterling per annum. Land, in general, here lets at from 20s. to 30s. per Scotch acre. The rents are paid, partly in mo-ney, and partly in grain ; that is, oats, at 5 firlots per boll, and barley.

Population *.—By every information, the population of this parifh is very confiderably diminifhed. This is ftill far-ther confirmed, by comparing the return to Dr. Webfter in 1755, which was - - - - 1691
with the prefent population, in 1793, - 1111

Which fhews an evident decreafe †, within thefe 50
 years, of - - - - 580
              Of

---

* The parifh regifter has been fo irregularly kept, that the number of births, marriages, and deaths, for fome years paft, cannot be afcertained.

† This decreafe may be afcribed to two caufes, that appear fully adequate to
                  the

Of the preſent inhabitants, there are,

Under 7 years of age,   -   -   -   -   128
And above that age,   -   -   -   -   983

Church, School, and Poor.—The Earl of Moray is patron
of the pariſh of Alves. A new and ſubſtantial church was
built in the year 1769. The manſe is ſaid to have been built
in the year 1690, and has ſince undergone frequent repairs.
The ſtipend is 80 bolls of barley, 300l. Scotch, with 60 merks
for communion elements. The ſalary of the ſchoolmaſter is
10 bolls of bear, and 33l. 6s. 8d. Scotch. The quarterly
payment for reading is 1s., for reading and arithmetic 1s. 6d.,
and for Latin 2s. The ſchoolmaſter is always ſeſſion-clerk,
for which he has a ſalary of 1l. 12s. per annum, together
with the caſual perquiſites ariſing from the regiſtration of baptiſms and marriages. In the year 1715, GEORGE DUNCAN,
late merchant in Inverneſs, mortified (ſunk) 3000 merks for the
benefit of this ſchool; the intereſt of which is applied to the
education of 6 boys, not above 10 years of age, each of them
enjoying this for 4 years. Theſe burſars are named by the
miniſter and kirk-ſeſſion.—The funds, for the ſupport of the
poor, ariſe from the weekly collections, fines from delinquents, mortcloth dues, and ſome mortifications. The late
Rev. Mr. ALEXANDER WATT, who was once incumbent at
Alves, and died miniſter of Forres, mortified the principal
ſum of 30l. Sterling, for behoof of the poor of this pariſh.
Theſe funds afford a comfortable relief to our poor, who are
not very numerous.

Antiquities.

the effects: The ſcarcity of fuel, ariſing from the moſſes being worn out; and
the crofts and ſmall poſſeſſions being converted into very extenſive farms. This
laſt meaſure is peculiarly hoſtile to population, and in the end will appear very
much againſt the beſt intereſts of our country at large, as well as the permanent
advantage of the proprietors.

Antiquities.—Under the head of antiquities, there is little that deserves notice, but a prodigiously large cairn of ftones, in a moor on the N. fide of the poft or county road, where tradition fays a battle was fought ; but no circumftances are handed down concerning it. Some Lochaber and Danifh axes, of a particular figure, have been dug out of the mofs of Earnfide, in the neighbourhood of this cairn. An infcription on a grave-ftone in the church-yard, dated in the year 1590, records a very uncommon circumftance. It runs thus: " Here lies ANDERSON of Pittenfere, maire of the earldom of " Moray, with his wife MARJORY, *whilk him never difplicit.*"

Character of the People.—The people, in general, are very fober and induftrious, regular in their attendance upon public worfhip, and fully equal to their neighbours in point of knowledge and information. They have lately acquired a tafte for greater neatnefs in their houfes, furniture and drefs, than formerly prevailed.

PARISH of BIRNIE,

(County of Elgin, Synod of Moray, Presbytery of Elgin.)

By the Rev. Mr Joseph Anderson.

Name, Extent, &c.

THIS parifh was named *Brenuth* about the beginning of the 13th century : A name probably derived from *Brae-nut, i. e.* " High land abounding in nuts ;" for many hazle trees once grew upon the fides of the hills and banks of the rivulets, and the general appearance of the parifh is hilly. The natives pronounce it *Burn-nigh, i. e.* " A village near the burn or river." This etymology is defcriptive enough of the particular place now called *Birnie.* The remoteft houfe is 7 miles from Elgin, where the poft goes thrice eaft and weft every week. The figure of the parifh is irregular, but comes neareft to an oval fhape ; the diftance from the N. to the S. extremity being about 5 miles, and from the E. to the W. about 2.

Surface and Soil.—The greateft part of the furface confifting of feveral high hills covered with heath, makes in general

neral a bleak rugged appearance ; the cultivated foil, however, in the valleys, and on the fides of hills, and the
feveral falls of water in the rocky channel of the rivulets,
have formed fome beautifully diverfified fcenes. The uncultivated foil confifts of moor and peat-mofs, with fome
interjacent plots of green pafture. The arable land in general is fandy, fhallow, ftony and fteep, lying either on a
bed of rock, or of compacted gravel. Some fields contiguous to the Loffie, confift of loam either upon a clayifh or
fandy bed. Several plots of a mofly and moory nature are
to be found both among the high and low lands.

Rivulets, &c.—The parifh is adorned with the three rivulets of Lennock, Barden and Rufhcroock, which flow into the river Loffie. The Loffie taking its rife in the parifh
of Ediakillie, and gliding through Dallas, begins at its confluence with the burn of Lennock, to run by part of the
weft fide, and then through the north end of this parifh,
and after a courfe of about 18 miles from its origin to its
mouth, flows into the fea at the harbour of Loffie-mouth.
The river abounds in burn trouts and eels. Some falmon,
finnacs *, and white trouts fwim up the river about Lammas, which give fine diverfion to the angler. The moft
remarkable inundations happened in the years 1768 and
1782. Three-fourths of the farm of Over-bogs have been
deftroyed by land floods, which have hurled from the hills
an immenfe quantity of ftones and fand, and left them upon
that plain field, where the river fometimes parts into two
or three ftreams.

Climate.—

* Finnacs are a fpecies of fifh in colour and fhape like a falmon. They
weigh from 2 lb. to 4 lb. White trouts are of a lefs fize. but of a whiter
colour. They are fuppofed to be two fpecies of fea trouts. In April,
fhoals of the fry of each fpecies fwim down to the fea, from which they
do not return fooner than July.

Climate.—The air is pure along the banks of the Loffie, but rather moift among the hills. They rife to a confiderable height above the Loffie, and attract more fhowers than the low land. The inhabitants, however, in each of thefe places, are equally healthful, and free from any diforders, but fuch as are common all over this country.

Minerals, Trees, Animals, &c.—A large chain of rocks extend eaft and weft through the middle of the parifh. The greateft part of the country houfes are built with moor ftones, which abound in every hill. Some ftrata of freeftone, of flate and limeftone, have been lately difcovered. The freeftone and flate have been ufed in repairing the church and manfe. There are fome oak, birch, hazle, afh, and plane trees; but they are not fufficient for fupplying the implements of hufbandry. Some large trunks of oak and fir are dug out of the moffes. Of thefe the inhabitants make very ftrong couples and lath for their houfes. Fruit trees are fcarce. The fhrubs of broom, furze, juniper, floes, hips and brambles, are innumerable. The water-lilly is the only herb, which perhaps is peculiar to this parifh, it grows in the Gedloch. Moorfowl, partridge and hare are the principal game. The Earl of Moray, as tradition relates, ufed often to hunt and fhoot on thefe hills. That he might have accommodation during the fporting feafon, he allotted a croft of land to the vintner, and another to the blackfmith ; for which the one paid a rofe, and the other a horfe fhoe, yearly, if required. The crofts ftill retain the names of Brewer's-croft and Smithy-croft. The lapwing appears in March, the cuckoo in April, and the fwallow in May; they all begin to difappear about the end of fummer.

Agri-

Agriculture, &c.

Number of acres in Scotch meafure, - -	5000
—— — —— arable, - - - -	850
—— of which under oats, - - -	450
—— — —— under bear and barley, -	200
—— — —— under wheat, rye and peafe, -	40
—— — —— under ley or natural grafs, -	120
—— — —— under clover and rye grafs, turnip, potatoes, flax and cabbage, -	40
Total value of produce at L. 3 the acre, L. 2550 o c	

Number of horfes 140, valued at L. 4 each,	L. 560	o o
—— — cattle 360, at L. 3 each,	1080	o o
—— — fheep 1500, at 5 s. each,	375	o o
—— — fwine 5, at 15 s. each,	3	15 o

Total value of live ftock, -	L. 2018	15 o
Valued rent in Scotch money, -	L. 734	13 6
Real rent (1791,) in Sterling, - -	360	o o
Feu-duty payable to the Earl of Moray, bolls 8,	1	4 2
And bifhops rents, - - - -	3	10 10

Number of farms above L. 50 yearly, -	2
—— — ditto under L 50, - - -	40
—— — grafs farms poffeffed by non-refiding tenants,	2
—— — carts, - - - -	100
—— — ploughs, - - -	45

Wheat and rye are fown in November. Several attempts have been made to prevent *fmut* in wheat without fuccefs. By a few recent experiments, however, there is ground to think that fmut may be prevented by drying the feed wheat on a kiln with a flow fire of peats. Ten firlots of wheat may be reduced by the heat to about eight. Nothing

thing would be more agreeable than to hear that others
are equally fortunate in making similar experiments.—Oats
and peafe are fown from the 13th of March to the middle
of April; barley from the middle of April to the begin-
ing of June; turnip feed from the 25th of June to the
middle of july.—Harveft begins about the 12th of September, and ends about fix weeks afterward.

The late Earl of Findlater and Seafield, a nobleman of
diftinguifhed character, induced his tenants to make confiderable improvements in agriculture, by encouraging them
to fallow their fields, to fow grafs and turnip feeds, and
plant potatoes. All which are obvioufly of great advantage to the farmer. He promoted alfo the manufacture of
flax and wool, by giving fpinning wheels to the farmers
wives and daughters. They now manufacture the whole of
the wool of their own fheep. Of a ftone of wool they make
from 36 to 40 ells of excellent plaiding, which they fell for
about 1 s. the ell. When they have done with manufacturing the wool, fince the foil does not produce flax to perfection, they employ themfelves in fpinning flax imported
by the merchants in the neighbourhood, who allow them
3 d. for each hank of the coarfeft, and 6 d. for each hank of
the fineft yarn which they fpin.

Population, &c.—According to Dr Webfter's report, the
number of fouls was then 525.—The numbers in 1781
were 460; in 1791, were 402. To explain the decreafe,
befides 24 perfons who have emigrated to America, two
farms are poffeffed by tenants who do not refide in the parifh, for the purpofe of pafture, where 4 tenants formerly
lived. Befides there are 4 tenants who poffefs as much
land as 8 did before. There were 6 heritors in 1766, fince
that period the Earl of Findlater has purchafed all the lands
except a croft of about 5 acres.

Average

Average of births for			Members of the Eſta-	
8 years preced. 1791,	9		bliſhed Church, -	400
Ditto of deaths, ditto,	8		Seceders, - -	2
Ditto of marriages, ditto,	2		Schoolmaſter, -	1
Under 10 years of age,	101		Young perſons taught	
—— 20, - -	85		to read and write,	16
—— 50, - -	113		Ditto, taught Latin,	4
—— 70, - -	85		Weavers, - -	8
—— 90, - -	16		Carpenters, - -	2
—— 100, - -	2		Blackſmith, - -	1
Houſes inhabited, -	85		Shoemakers, - -	6
Married perſons, -	128		Tailors, - -	4
Average children from			Miller, - -	1
each marriage, -	5		Day-labourers, -	2
Widowers, - -	10		Male farm-ſervants, -	22
Widows, - -	20		Female ditto, -	17

The farms in general being of ſmall extent, are managed by the tenants themſelves, and their children. They only need the aſſiſtance of reapers in harveſt.

Stipend, Church, Poor, &c.—The money-ſtipend is L. 41, 16 s. 4$\frac{10}{12}$d. Sterling; the victual, 18 bolls 2 pecks 3$\frac{1}{4}$ lippies bear; and, 20 bolls 1 firlot 3 pecks 1 lippie oat-meal. Patron, the Earl of Moray. The glebe, graſs incloſure, and garden, contain about 9 acres. The church, built with hewn freeſtone, conſiſts of a nave and choir. Part of the walls was repaired in 1734, as appears from the date on the bell-houſe. The late Mr Shaw, a learned and reſpectable clergyman of this preſbytery, who publiſhed the hiſtory of this province in 1775, ſays, that it is probable, that the bi-ſhop's firſt cathedral in this dioceſe was ſituated in Birnie, and that Simeon de Tonei, one of the biſhops of Moray, was buried in Birnie in 1184. It is held in great venera-

tion

tion by many in this county. They ftill, in fome meafure, entertain a fuperftitious conceit, that prayers there offered up three feveral Sabbaths will furely be heard. Info-much that when a perfon is indifpofed, or of bad behaviour, this common faying obtains, ‘ You have need to be pray-ed for thrice in the church of Birnie, that you may either end or mend."

There are 18 poor now inrolled, who have nothing to depend upon for their fupply but the weekly voluntary collections, and a fhare of a mortification, which amount on-ly to about L. 7 a-year. That fum is diftributed among them every year, and goes but a fhort way towards fupply-ing their wants. The aged and infirm, therefore, muft tra-vel beyond the bounds of the parifh, and implore alms from the charitable. It is remarkable, however, that 20 years ago, there was but one common beggar in the parifh. He was blind, and led from door to door. To the poor who are not able to work, nor go from home, the parifhioners prove their charitable difpofition, by putting fome meal in-to bags, hung up in the mill, for the purpofe of their relief, when they are grinding their corn there, or by fending them at other times fuch quantities of meal and of fuel as they can fpare.

Mifcellaneous Obfervations.—The talleft man in the parifh is 6 feet 2½ inches. The general fize of the people is fup-pofed to be 5½ feet.—The year 1782 was very remark-able for the latenefs and coldnefs of the harveft, which on-ly began the 15th October that year. At a moderate com-putation, one half of the corn was damaged by the froft and heavy falls of fnow. The fcarcity and high price of meal that enfued was truly alarming; and had not Pro-vidence put a ftop to hoftilities in America and Europe, and given the Britifh Parliament time to mind the ftate of

North

North Britain at that period, thousands must have perished for want of bread. Happily, in consequence of some supply of meal from Government, and by importing corn and meal from the Continent of Europe, none died for want of the necessary means of subsistence. At that time potatoes were often used in place of bread by many. A family, consisting of 9 persons, had nothing else to eat for a whole week, and yet they looked pretty well.—There is plenty of heath, furze, broom, turf, and peat. Peats are the best fuel. A great many, besides the parishioners, are supplied with peats from the mosses of Birnie. Two hundred loads of peats are requisite to keep a good fire in a room, and another in the kitchen, for a year. They cannot be cast, dried, and carried home, at the distance of 4 miles, for less than 1 s. the load.—The people are industrious, temperate, and cheerful, though poor. Music is their favourite diversion. Some of them can play on the bagpipe, and others on the violin. Ferocious manners have given place to civilized. There has been no instance of suicide or murder during the last 26 years. Neither has any one been banished, or suffered capital punishment. They speak English, in the Scotch dialect. It is remarkable in this, as well as in other parishes of this county, that when the consonants *r* and *s* meet, as in the words *horse, curse,* &c. the letter *r* is quiescent, and the common people pronounce these words as if they were written *hoss, cuss* *.

Antiquities and Natural Curiosities.—A stone baptistery, and an old bell, made of a mixture of silver and copper, of

an

* As to the price of grain, and other provisions, for 10 years preceding 1791, the price of a boll of wheat, on an average, is L. 1; of barley, 16 s.; of oats and oat-meal, 14 s. 6 d.; of pease and barley meal, 13 s. 4 d.; of the best beef, mutton, veal, pork, and salmon, 3 d. the pound; of a hen, 7 d.; of a chicken, 3 d.; of a pigeon, 1 d.; of a dozen of haddocks, 6 d.

an oblong figure, named the *coronach*, are still kept as the remains of antiquity. Tradition relates that the bell was made at Rome, and confecrated by the Pope.—The *bible-ftone*, having the figure of a book diftinctly engraven, lying about a mile eaft from the church, on the fide of the road leading from Birnie to Rothes, has probably been laid there as a land-mark.—The Cairn of Kilfoeman, of a conical figure, 300 feet in circumference at the bafe, has been probably placed over the remains of a brave man, whofe exploits are now forgotten.—The cave in the middle of a fteep high rock, near the Gedloch, was, according to tradition, haunted about 100 years ago by a gang of armed ruffians, who had no vifible way of obtaining the means of fubfiftence, but by theft and robbery. The happy conftitution we now enjoy has fuppreffed all fuch lawlefs banditti.—All who have feen the falls of water in the Lin of the Shoggle, and the Eats of Glenlaterach, much admire them, and the adjacent wilds. There is about 20 feet of a fall of water in each of thefe places.—Some veftiges of an incampment can be traced in a well-aired dry fituation, watered on the weft fide by the burn of Barden, and fortified on the E. and N. by a valley. It commands a profpect of the Moray Frith, from Speymouth to Cromarty Bay. Probably the Danes, after invading this part of the country, had a camp there.

Advantages and Difadvantages.—The pafture for cattle and fheep annexed to the feveral farms in the Highlands, is of great advantage to the tenants ; but the arable land being much expofed to the north, the corn growing there is late in ripening, and frequently damaged by froft.—From the winter folftice to the vernal equinox, heavy falls of fnow often cover the face of the earth, and deprive the fheep of convenient pafture. They, having nothing but

ftraw

ſtraw to eat in the folds, become lean and feeble; inſo-much, that when the ewes yean, many lambs die; becauſe their dams have not milk enough for them. The owners would therefore do well to provide a ſufficient quantity of turnip and hay for the ewes.—Materials for the implements of agriculture are ſcarce. An aſh tree coſts the artificer himſelf from 1 s. 6 d. to 2 s. Sterling the foot. It would therefore be equally advantageous to the proprietors and tenants, that ſuch an extent of waſte ground were incloſed, and planted with aſh, birch, and alder, as might furniſh the farmer with every neceſſary utenſil of timber.

PARISH OF DALLAS.

(COUNTY OF ELGIN.)

By the Rev. Mr DAVID MILNE.

Name, Situation, Extent, Soil, &c.

THE name of this parish is derived from *Dale uis*, *i. e.* 'Watered Valley.' Dallas is in the prefbytery of Forres, Synod of Moray, and county of Elgin. It is 12 miles from E. to W. and 9 from N. to S.; the form is o-val. It is bounded by the parishes of Rothes and Birnie, on the S. E. and E.; of Elgin, on the N. E. and N.; of Bafford and Edenkillie, on the N. W. and W.; and of Knockando and Cromdale, on the S. W. and S. It is fur-rounded by hills, fo as to form a valley or ftrath, almoft equally divided from S. W. to E. by the fmall river Loffie, and interfected by feveral burns or rivulets, falling from the furrounding hills into Loffie. Thefe burns partly bound the parifh on the E. and N. and partly fall into Loffie within the bounds of the parifh. The furrounding hills are cover-ed with heath. The foil is black and moffy, excepting fome fields or haughs on the Loffie banks.

Fine fmall trout are found in Loffie during the fummer. In September and October, finnac or white trout are got, from 1 lb. to 3 lb. and a few fmall falmon.

The fields on Loffie banks are very fubject to inundations. Thefe do much damage, by breaking through and carrying away the beft of the foil, notwithftanding the attention and exertions

exertions of the proprietor and his tenants. In fummer alfo, and harveft, the corns and grafs within reach, are hurt by gravel and fand left upon them. The moft remarkable in-undations were in 1768, 1782, 1786, and 1789.

Population.—Shaw's Hiftory of Moray, publifhed 1775, reckons the catechifable perfons about 500. Dr Webfter's ftatement, about 40 or 50 years ago, is 700. The prefent incumbent found the number of fouls in July and Auguft 1778, to be 917 : Of whom 84 were under 6 years of age; 434 were males, 483 females. In 1788, the number amount-ed to 888, of whom 426 were males, 462 females.

TABLE.

Annual average of baptifms for 20 years, from the
    year 1770 to 1789, is   -   -   -   -   25
Annual average of males baptized, about   -   13
————————— of females   -   -   -   -   12
Annual average of marriages from the end of the
    year 1774, till that of 1782, is   -   8
Annual average of deaths in the fame period   -   15
Annual average of males who died, about   -   8
——————————— females, nearly   7

A man and woman, married 63 years, died here, the huf-band in the 95th year of his age, and the wife aged 93. Up-wards of 20 young men, fince the year 1778, particularly fince the years 1783 and 1784, have emigrated to America and other foreign parts. A few have gone into England. Some families and fingle perfons to the fouth of Scotland, and families alfo and unmarried perfons into the neighbour-ing towns for employment. There are not above fix or eight uninhabited houfes at moft, fince the year 1778, and only a few erections have been made fince that period; but a great many fome years before.

Produce,

Produce, &c.—Potatoes are raifed for family ufe, and a few garden and field turnip, principally for the fame pur-pofe. Natural oaks, birch and allar, apple, pear, plum, gean and cherry trees grow in feveral places, and fome large inclofures of planted firs, of a pretty old ftanding, large enough for deals, farm-houfe couples, &c.

Barley, rye, and oats, are raifed in the parifh. Very lit-tle flax is cultivated, and a few fields are laid down in grafs.

Ever fince the prefent incumbent was fettled, (1778,) un-lefs in a few inftances, the crops have been found infufficient to maintain the inhabitants or their cattle. Living, how-ever, in the vicinity of Elgyn and Forres, they are em-ployed in carrying peats twice a-week to market. This enables them to purchafe fome additional provifions for their families, and alfo corn, or corn and fodder in the feafon, when a deficiency at home requires a fupply. Sow-ing does not become general till towards the middle of April. The climate admits not of it earlier: And the tenants, doubtlefs, owing to the poverty of the foil, think they have the cleaner crop the later fown. Of courfe, it is the middle or rather the end of November before all the corns are got in. From 1s. to 15s. may be the rent of each acre, from the leaft improved miur to the higheft cultivated field. Every parifh in the north of Scotland, doubtlefs, fuffered by the failure of crop 1782; among which, it may be conceived, this parifh had its me-lancholy fhare. A liberal fhare of bounty-meal was, at that period, allowed for the indigent in the parifh. The firft and fecond moieties, *gratis*, came moft feafonably in fum-mer 1783, or before the corns were ripe. The third and laft moiety from Government, at 6½ d. a peck, came alfo feafonably a fhort time thereafter.

Mifcellaneous

Miscellaneous Observations.—The air is sharp and dry. The inhabitants are generally healthy. The small-pox is become less fatal by means of inoculation.

There are some chalybeate springs, but seldom resorted to.—The parish abounds in grey slate quarries. There is likewise a freestone quarry of excellent quality.

Towards the top of the east gable of the church, in a niche on the outside of the wall, stands a stone weather-beaten effigy, of about 4 feet high and 2 broad, of a saint, called Michael, to whom the church is said to be dedicated. In the middle of the church-yard, there still remains, entire, a neat erect well cut stone pillar, anciently the cross, to which are still brought the cattle and effects of some bankrupts. A large square stone, above ground, is the pedestal. The capital a *fleur de luce*, covered with moss, emblematical of a hoary head, and the whole height from the ground 12 feet.

Each tenant has a horse, for the most part, bought at market; many have 2, some 3 or 4. Several farmers have a flock of goats for the accommodation of tender people in summer. The parish is sufficiently stocked with black cattle of the common Scotch breed. There are a great many flocks of sheep of a very hardy kind and tolerable size, commonly called Badenoch, from whence every year a supply of lambs is brought. The lambs are bought for about 4s. 6d. or 5s. a-piece, and, when 4 or 5 years old, are sold from 8s. to 12s. each.

The lateness of the harvest, the scarcity of grain, and the overflowings of Losse, may be reckoned among the greatest disadvantages of Dallas. Among its advantages may be ranked the salubrity of the air, inexhaustible mosses, the vicinity to Elgin and Forres for the sale of peats, and to markets for the sale of cattle : Good pasture for sheep, goats and black cattle : Timber from the woods for many imple-

ments

ments of hufbandry, and for building farm-houfes : Fuel for their families, and minds ftrangers to luxury and extravagance. The cart-load of peats on the ftreet brings only from 8 d. to 10 d. in fummer, and from 10 d. to 14 d. in winter. They are of an excellent quality, but the load is fmall. Thefe bring always ready money, and enable the people to buy the family neceffaries when required, and to pay the landlord at the term.

The Englifh language is fpoken throughout the parifh ; yet, as is the cafe in many other places, the names of the farms appear to be of Celtic derivation.

The inhabitants are much inclined to induftry and frugality. They are alfo difpofed to acts of humanity. A good many weavers are conftantly employed in making coarfe cloth, commonly called *plaiden*, from the produce of their fheep, which, in the fummer markets, is fold for from 9 d. to 1 s. the Scots ell. By that, and other fources of induftry, they are enabled to fupport their families and pay their rents. There are fome cart and cart-wheel wrights, with fome carpenters for making flakes or paling for folding cattle in fummer, and inclofing fields.

Their drefs and manners are confiderably improved within thefe few years. It is thought, and earnefty to be wifhed, that their condition may be meliorated. This, it is believed, might be done, by introducing and encouraging a ftocking manufactory, or fome fuch ufeful and accommodating employment, efpecially to occupy the young.

Laft fummer a petition was tranfmitted from the inhabitants of Kellas to the Honourable the Society at Edinburgh, requefting a Society School for that quarter. Thefe families lie at a great diftance from the parochial fchool. Accordingly, a fchool was appointed to be fettled there,

and

and a teacher entered at Martinmas laſt, who, ever ſince, has had a full attendance, and is aſſiduous.

There is great occaſion for a bridge over the impetuous river Loſſie. In particular, over that river, where a public road from Forres and the low country croſſes, leading to the pariſhes of Knockando, Aberlour, Inveraven, &c. The roads are in bad repair. The ſtatute-labour is but irregularly called for, and ill executed, as there are no gentlemen of property reſiding in the pariſh. Turnpikes would be altogether inefficient in Dallas.

PARISH OF DRAINY.

(COUNTY OF ELGIN.)

By the Rev. Mr LEWIS GORDON.

Situation, Extent, Name and Soil.

THE parish of Drainy is situated in the Synod of Moray, the county and presbytery of Elgin, and about 6 measured miles from the royal borough of that name. It is a peninsula, stretching E. and W. along the coast, about 2 measured miles in its greatest breadth, and 4 in its greatest length; bounded on the N. by the Moray frith; on the S. by the lake of Spynie, which separates it from the parish of Spynie; on the E. by the river of Lossie, which divides it from the parishes of St Andrew's and Urquhart; and on the W. by the parish of Duffus. Drainy consists of the 2 ancient parishes of Kinneddar and Ogstown, which were united soon after the Restoration. It obtained its name from a new centrical church being built, in consequence of this annexation, on the lands of Drainy, which probably were called so from draining the neighbouring swamps and marshes. In general, this part of the country is low and flat. There are only two small eminences that deserve the name of hills. Scarcely one half of the surface is arable, the greatest part consisting of barren moorground, covered with short heath, or coarse benty grass. The land under cultivation is very fertile, part of it being

3

a rich loam or clay, and part a light, black, or ſandy ſoil.

Rent, Manufaƈtures, &c.—The valued rent is L. 3044, 17 s. 4 d. Scotch ; and the real rent may be eſtimated at about L. 1200 Sterling, though this muſt depend on the price of grain. There is only one reſiding heritor, who poſſeſſes two-thirds of the property ; the remaining third belongs to the only other heritor. It is a great misfortune that no manufaƈtures have been eſtabliſhed here, as ſcarcely any part of Scotland is better adapted for them. The. women ſpin linen-yarn ; by which, with the greateſt application, they can only earn from 2 d. to 3 d. a-day ; and even this yarn, except what is neceſſary for our own conſumption, is exported (unwrought) to Edinburgh, Glaſgow, or the N. of England. The 2 hills, mentioned above, abound with excellent quarries of white and yellow free-ſtone, which is not to be found any where elſe in the Moray frith. About 20 maſons, including apprentices, and nearly double that number of labourers, are conſtantly employed in quarrying and dreſſing ſtones, to ſupply the demand for that article from this and the neighbouring counties.

Village of Loſſiemouth, Imports and Exports.---The principal village here is Loſſiemouth, a ſea-port belonging to the town of Elgin. It contains from 150 to 200 inhabitants. There are no veſſels belonging to the place, except 1 ſloop and 2 fiſhing-boats. But during the laſt year 49 veſſels, from 55 to 60 tons burden, at an average, entered this harbour. The imports and exports were as follow :

IMPORTS.—English coals,	-	20 veſſels.
Scotch coals,	-	6
London goods,	-	10

Carried forward, 36

IMPORTS.—   Brought forward,   36 veſſels.
              Leith goods,   -   4
              Tanners bark,   -   3
              Native ſalt,   -   2
              Bottles,   -   -   1
              Slates,   -   -   1
              Iron,   -   -   1
              Lime,   -   -   1
                                        ———
                             Total   49

EXPORTS—were 20 cargoes barley and oats, at an ave‹
rage, about 400 bolls each, and an inconſiderable quantity
of peltry. The quantity of corn formerly exported from
this county, was reckoned, at an average, 20,000 bolls
yearly. But it is probable this exportation will, in future,
be ſomewhat reduced, as the ſmuggling of foreign ſpirits is
now, in a great meaſure, ſuppreſſed, and whiſky is ſubſtituted in their place. Twenty licenſed ſtills are at preſent employed in this county; and a conſiderable quantity
of the ſpirits is manufactured, and conſumed in the highlands of Moray and Inverneſs-ſhire.

Fiſhing Towns.—There are other 2 creeks in the pariſh
that admit boats, Cauſea and Stotfield; at the latter there
are at preſent 3 fiſhing-boats, which, with the 2 at Loſſie-
mouth, are a vaſt benefit to the town of Elgin, and to the country at large, in ſupplying white fiſh. The rent derived from
theſe fiſhing-boats is L. 5 Sterling each yearly: But the
proprietors are obliged to furniſh a new boat every ſeventh
year, which coſts, when rigged and complete, from L. 18
to L. 20 Sterling. The fiſh commonly taken on this coaſt,
are cod, ſkate, hollibut, haddocks, whitings, ſaiths or eud-
dies, with plenty of crabs and lobſters; but none of them
                                                         in

in greater quantity than to anſwer the demand for home conſumption.

River and Lakes.—The river Loſſie has its ſource in the hills of Dallas ; and, after a courſe of near 26 meaſured miles, diſcharges itſelf into the ſea at the town of Loſſie-mouth, in the N. E. corner of this pariſh. It is too ſmall to be navigable beyond its mouth, and its bed too ſandy to be favourable to ſalmon ; yet about 3 or 4 ſcore of that fiſh have ſometimes been taken in a ſeaſon, at its entry into the ſea. It abounds with excellent red ſpotted trout, from 1 lb. to 3 lb. and even ſometimes 4 lb. in weight, called here phinnocks.—The loch of Spynie is a beautiful piece of freſh water, about 1 mile broad and 3 miles long, which diſcharges itſelf into the river Loſſie, about a mile from the ſea. It abounds with eel and pike, and water-fowl of various kinds ; ſuch as, ſwans, geeſe, duck, teal, &c. This loch, at ſome former period, appears evidently to have form-ed a bay of the ſea, and to have been connected with ano-ther loch in the pariſh of Urquhart, called Cotts, which is only half a mile diſtant. The mouth of this bay is formed by 2 banks of hard gravel about 500 yards aſunder, and the water of Loſſie paſſing through this opening, ſeems, in a ſeries of ages, to have carried down ſuch a quantity of ſand, as to have at length ſeparated theſe lochs from each other, and ſhut up their communication with the ſea. The beds of ſhells all around the loch of Spynie, and the names of places in the neighbourhood, clearly prove that it has formerly been connected with the ſea ; and there are alſo ſome written evidences of the ſame fact.

Church, Stipend, Poor, School, &c.—The church was built more than 100 years ago, and looks tolerably decent without, but is very naked and ill finiſhed within. Our

churches

churches are, in general, exceedingly cold and dirty, and there is little hope of this evil being soon remedied. The patronage belongs to the family of Gordonston. The stipend is 72 bolls of barley and oats, and L. 50 Sterling of money, with L. 2, 10 s. for communion-elements. The manse and offices are new; the glebe and gardens contain about 5 Scotch acres. The old church of Ogstown is now converted into a burying place for the family of Gordonston, and was rebuilt some time ago with great taste, in the ancient Gothic style. The vestiges of the old church are to be seen in the church-yard at Kinn_ar, and adjoining to these the remains of an old palace or castle belonging to the Bishop of Moray, where he resided before the castle of Spynie was built.—The parochial funds are very inconsiderable, the whole income not exceeding L. 20 Sterling; and this sum, out of which the salary of the session-clerk, beadle, and other parochial charges, must be paid, is all the provision for 40 or 50 poor.—At the parish-school, about 30 or 40 children are instructed in Latin, English, writing and arithmetic. The salary of the schoolmaster is 12 bolls barley, besides the emoluments arising from the office of session-clerk, which is commonly conjoined with that of schoolmaster, and amounts to L. 3 Sterling, exclusive of a few trifling perquisites.

Population, &c.—The return to Dr Webster was 1174 souls. At the beginning of the year 1791, there were—

Males,	—	—	—	480
Females,	—	—	—	560
Total,	—		—	1040

Farmers,

Farmers,	—	—	—	68
Seamen,	—	—	—	37
Mafons,	—	—	—	13
Weavers,	—	—	—	5
Tailors,	—	—	—	5
Smiths,	—	—	—	3
Joiners,	—	—	—	4
Merchants,	—	—	—	3
Labourers,	—	—	—	35

The remainder being widows, married fervants, and perfons of mixed profeffions, were   57

Male-fervants,	—	—	87
Female-fervants,	—	—	95
Apprentices,	—	—	15
Married couples,	—	—	159

Children of the above, and refiding with their parents,   —   —   —   334

Widowers and widows,   —   —   64

In the above lift, thofe only are reckoned farmers who live folely by that occupation : But feveral other people in the parifh rent a few acres of ground for the accommodation of their families.

Births, Marriages and Burials, for thefe laft eight years.

Years.	Births.	Males.	Females.	Marriages.	Burials.
1783	29	18	11	8	16
1784	34	18	16	11	25
1785	32	12	20	9	19
1786	31	12	19	9	27
1787	31	19	12	13	15
1788	34	20	14	9	24
1789	35	18	17	14	30
1790	35	21	14	6	23
Sums	261	138	123	79	179

The

The number of inhabitants has not varied much for thefe laft 20 years; vibrating generally from 1020 to 1050.

In general, the climate of this country is mild and whole-fome. There is more dry weather in the narrow flip a-long the Moray-fhire coaft, than in moft other parts in Scotland, owing to the land being very low and plain, and the clouds being attracted by the high hills to the fouthward; fo that often in fummer, when this parifh is burned up with drought, rain falls in abundance in the high country. One happy confequence of this pe-culiar fituation is the goodnefs of the harvefts; even in 1782 the greateft part of the crop here was got in without damage.—There are no extraordinary inftances of lon-gevity here, nor are there any difeafes peculiar to this di-ftrict. Agues were very common about 25 or 30 years a-go, in the marfhy parts of Drainy and Duffus, but have for fome time paft totally difappeared. The complaints that prevail moft among the lower claffes of people, are obftinate coughs and colds, attended with pain of the breaft, difficulty of breathing, and fwelling in the extremities, ef-pecially in the winter-feafon, and are very fatal. They feem to be occafioned by the coldnefs and dampnefs of the houfes, and the great fcarcity of fuel, for there are no peats nearer than the diftance of 10 meafured miles. If the attention of Government could be awakened to the many evils arifing from the impolitic tax on coals, and could be prevailed upon to fubftitute fome other revenue in its ftead, it would be of effential benefit to the North of Scotland in general, and to this province in particular.

Produce, Rent, &c.—All the kinds of grain raifed in Scotland fucceed here; but barley is the principal crop. Flax is alfo cultivated, but to no great extent. Potatoes thrive admirably well in our light ground, and ferve for

the

the fubfiftence of the poor, at leaft a third part of the year. Agriculture is the chief employment of the people; yet the modern improvements in hufbandry are only in their infancy. Inclofures are yet far from being general. The introduction of turnips and fown graffes promifes to be of infinite advantage, as proper food for our cattle was fcarce both in fummer and winter. There are in the parifh in all about 96 ploughs; the number of horfes is from 300 to 400; the black cattle about double that number; fheep from 1500 to 2000, and from 20 to 30 fwine or hogs.—The rent of land, when paid in grain, is from a boll to a boll and a half of bear or oats, Linlithgow meafure, the Scotch acre; but it is the practice here to allow 5 firlots of oats to a boll, being nearly equal to an Englifh quarter. Lands, when fet for money alone, give from 15 s. to 20 s. and 21 s. the acre.—In fome part of this parifh the teinds are drawn in kind, that is, the tenth fhock or fheaf is carried off the field before the corns are ftacked, and this is commonly reckoned equal to a third of the rent actually paid.

Prices, Wages, &c.— The price of bear and oats for thefe laft 10 years, has not been lefs than 15 s. the boll, at an average. Beef and mutton commonly fell in the Elgin markét from 3 d. to 4 d. the lb. Amfterdam weight; geefe from 1 s. 6 d. to 2 s.; hens and ducks from 8 d. to 9 d. each; eggs 1½ d. the dozen.—The ordinary wages of male day-labourers here, without victuals, are 8 d. in fummer, and of females 4 d.; but both get higher wages in harveft. Menfervants employed in hufbandry commonly get from L. 5 to L. 8, and women-fervants from 30 s. to 40 s. a-year, and their victuals. Victual at the Reformation was converted at half a merk Scotch the boll.

Minerals,

Minerals, Rocks, &c.—In the Coulart hill, between Loffiemouth and Stotfield, there are appearances of lead : Many detached maffes of ore are to be feen in the rocks. Some adventurers, however, lately came from England, and after fpending above L. 500 Sterling, could difcover no vein of ore worth the expence of working. The hill of Caufea, or Cave-fea, confifts of one uninterrupted mafs of free-ftone, more than a mile long, divided into horizontal ftrata of different degrees of thicknefs and hardnefs, but generally foft and friable. This hill forms a very bold fhore ; and the violence of the winds and furge, has cut and excavated the free-ftone rock fo as to form many curious arches, caves, and pyramids, of various fizes and figures. Thefe rocks are covered, in fummer, with different kinds of plants of variegated colours, and are frequented by crows, pigeons, gulls, and other birds, in prodigious numbers. In the fummer time, the noife of the fea below, the varied cries of the birds, the beauty of the flowers, and the grandeur of the rocks, all heighten the fcenery of the place. There was alfo at Loffiemouth, in a natural cave, a fmall hermitage, not exceeding 10 feet fquare, called St Gerardine's Cave, which commanded a view of the fhore as far as Cullen, and was adorned with a handfome Gothic door and window; but thefe artificial decorations were pulled down about 25 years ago, by a rude fhipmafter ; and in the courfe of working the quarries, the whole cave has fince been totally deftroyed. There was a fpring in the rock above the hermitage, called St Gerardine's Well ; but neither this, nor any other fprings in the parifh, have acquired fame for their medicinal virtues.

Mifcellaneous Obfervations.—The inhabitants of this parifh, like all others employed in hufbandry, are robuft and healthy. Their general character is that of a fober, honeft,

peaceable

peaceable people, regular in their attendance on the ordinances of religion, rather grave than lively, ſeldom in-
dulging themſelves in any relaxation or diverſion, excepting the young people, who ſometimes take a dance at
Chriſtmas, or at a penny-wedding*. Crimes of great e-
normity are unknown here. There has not been an inſtance of ſuicide during the 22 years of the preſent miniſter's incumbency; nor has any native of this pariſh
been hanged or baniſhed, in the memory of man. This
regularity of conduct muſt in part be aſcribed to the
poverty and depreſſion of the people; for the ſituation
of the ſmall tenants in this country, in general, is far from
being comfortable. Few of them have any capital to begin the world with; and fewer have any inclination to a-
dopt the modern improvements in huſbandry, while the
rents of their farms, and the wages of their ſervants, have
of late been conſiderably advanced. The laſt article, in
particular, is nearly doubled within theſe 20 years paſt.
One advantage they derive from their vicinity to the ſea,
in being ſupplied from the ſhores with a conſiderable quantity of ſea-weed, which is a valuable manure.

It is perhaps a ſingular circumſtance, that, in this pariſh,
there is no lawyer, writer, attorney, phyſician, ſurgeon,
apothecary, negro, Jew, gipſy, Engliſhman, Iriſhman, fo-
reigner of any deſcription, nor family of any religious ſect
or denomination, except the Eſtabliſhed Church.

There are 4 ale-houſes, and fewer would hardly accommodate the neighbourhood, as there is generally a reſort of
ſtrangers to ſea-port towns. There can be no doubt but

an

---

* A penny-wedding is when the expence of the marriage entertainment is not defrayed by the young couple, or their relations, but by a
club among the gueſts. Two hundred people of both ſexes, will ſometimes be convened on an occaſion of this kind.

an increafe of them would prove a real nuifance, and contribute materially to corrupt the morals of the people.

The only language here is Scotch ; but the pronounciation is gradually approaching nearer to the Englifh*. Gaelic is not fpoken nearer than 20 miles; and very few of the names of places here feem derived from it.

There are no bridges in this parifh, excepting a fmall one of 3 arches on the outlet from the loch of Spynie ; nor is there any on the river Loffie below Elgin, though much wanted. The roads here are all made by the ftatute-labour ; and though better than they were formerly, are ftill far from what they ought to be : And this is the more inexcufable, as they are more eafily made here than in moft counties in Scotland. On the highland road to Edinburgh, a traveller meets with no turnpikes or tolls till he arrives at Perth.

I have often thought, that the deftruction of grain by pigeons was much greater than commonly fuppofed. There are 4 pigeon-houfes here; each of which, at a moderate computation, confumes 20 bolls of corn annually.

---

* The greateft peculiarity of the Moray dialect is founding Wh like F ; What, Where, When, for inftance, are pronounced by the vulgar, Fät, Fär, Fän.

PARISH OF DUFFUS.

(County and Synod of Moray.—Preſbytery of Elgin.)

By a FRIEND *to* STATISTICAL INQUIRIES.

Extent, Surface, Soil and Produce.

DUFFUS extends 5 miles in length, from E. to W. along the S. coaſt of the Moray Frith, and in breadth from 2 to 3 miles S. and N. It is one continued plain, ex‑cepting a riſing ground, of no great height, near the middle of the pariſh, which is every where arable. Along the coaſt, all the length of the pariſh, and more than half a mile of the breadth of it, the ſurface is a meagre, green, benty paſture. All this ground had formerly been a rich cultivated ſoil; but for many years, has been overblown with dry ſand, from the weſtern beach. The ſand has for ſome time ceaſed to blow, and a great part of this ſpace may again be brought into culture, by the application of the ſpade or trench plough. There have already been ſome ſuccesful experiments of this kind, and in many places, there is but little depth of ſand upon the top.

All

All the reft of this parifh is one continued arable plain, capable of producing every thing that will grow any where in Scotland. The eaftward diftrict is a deep rich clay, refembling the Carfe of Gowrie, and is remarkable for fuperior crops of wheat, and of peafe and beans. The weftern diftrict is a black earth, in fome places fo much mixed with fand, 4s to render it of inferior quality; but in other places fo remarkably rich, as, without any application of modern hufbandry, to produce crops, particularly barley, for quality and increafe not to be furpaffed in Scotland; and reaped as early as the fame crop on the coafts of Lothian, where fowing is in general earlier, and where agriculture is underftood. The barley of this diftrict, when fent to the Frith of Forth, yields as good a price as the beft Stirlingfhire or eaft Lothian barley. Along the coaft of this parifh, there are quarries of fine freeftone, and, a little way up from the coaft, quarries of lime-ftone; a treafure in agriculture, locked up from us for want of fuel, and which nothing but the abolition of the COAL TAX can open. The plain of Duffus, together with the ground of the adjoining parifhes, is often (perhaps more from richnefs than fituation) called the *Heart of Morayfhire,*

Coaft.—The coaft of this parifh is generally flat. At the weft end, the land is at prefent only 4 feet above the level of the water. At this quarter, during the courfe of this century, the water has increafed confiderably on the land. Should it ever rife 4 feet higher than it does at prefent, it muft fall into the lower grounds to the eaftward, and overflow a great proportion of the extenfive plains of Duffus, Drainy, Leuchars, Spiney and Innes. Yet this *poffibility* is fo little regarded, that perhaps no one ever bought or fold the property of thefe diftricts, a farthing lower from this confideration. How far it is expedient or practicable, to ward off fo great an evil,

by

by erecting mounds and bulwarks on the ſhore, is left to thoſe immediately concerned to determine.

Climate.—The ſuperior earlineſs, fertility, and warmth, of the plains of Morayſhire, are facts more certain than eaſy to be accounted for. It is known, that we are in a very northern latitude. The mountains of Sutherland and Caithneſs, ſeem to be at too great a diſtance from us, to afford us ſhelter from the north winds, which blow over a great ſurface of water before they reach us. To the E. we are alſo open to the German Ocean. It is true, that we have leſs rain than elſewhere, which is ſaid to be accounted for by the flatneſs of our county; but other counties of Scotland, equally flat, have more rain. Our ſurface alſo inclines to the N., and the only near hills we have, are thoſe on the S., ſeemingly more calculated to overſhadow and hurt us, than to give us warmth. It is ſaid, our ſoil is light, and therefore warm: it is ſo in many places; but there are alſo large diſtricts of deep black earth, and of rank clay, where the ſame earlineſs appears. After all, were we merely to conſult taſte and imagination, in the choice of a reſidence, many would prefer what are often to be met with in the ſouth of Scotland, green hills, with leſs fertility, and warmth in the valleys, to our dryer, earlier, and richer plains, with the proſpect of black gloomy hills on the upper landſcape.

Diſtempers.—Pectoral complaints, rheumatiſm, and fevers, are the moſt frequent diſeaſes. The king's evil is not uncommon; and of late madneſs ſeems to be increaſing, even among the common people. Upwards of 20 years ago, agues were frequent near the lake; but were confined to that ſituation. None of the ſea-faring people are ever ſeized with agues. The itch is become much more rare than it was formerly. It is a truth, which no mere *Engliſhman* will readily believe, that

that in this comparatively rude part of Britain, the itch, at prefent, is lefs frequent, in proportion to its population; than in the Britifh capital. With us, it arifes from want of cleanlinefs in our perfons and clothes; but in London, confined fituation, ftrong feeding, and a thronged population, are the co-operating caufes.

Woods.—Upon the fouth border of this parifh, a common was lately divided by the different proprietors, and planted with Scotch firs. Planting here is doubly meritorious, as wood is needed equally for timber and for fuel. It may be obferved, that the planting of foreft trees is the only branch of improvement, in which our country has of late kept pace with the improving diftricts of Scotland. Within the laft 25 years, confiderable plantations have been made. In the eaftern diftricts of the county, Scotch firs chiefly appear, even in many places where it is prefumed the ground would have nourifhed better wood. In the weftern diftricts of our county, Scotch firs have been employed in the plantations, as they ought to be where the foil and climate require it, merely as nurfes in tender years, to more beautiful and valuable trees, as oak, elm, afh, &c.

Orchards.—Buchanan fays, "that Moray, for pleafantnefs, and the profit arifing from fruit trees, furpaffes all the other counties of Scotland." In modern times, we have much neglected this culture; and our orchards are at prefent often found about deferted caftles and religious houfes, nearly as much in decay as the buildings they furround.

Draining of Lakes.—The art of draining lakes, fo as to render grounds fit for agriculture, feems to be here, as it is indeed throughout Scotland in general, but in its infancy. The

The lake of Spiney has been allowed to ſpread for miles, be-yond its original bed, and to cover, in whole, or in part, a large portion of very rich ground. A few years ago, an im-perfect attempt was made to draw off the water from the up-per grounds, by which ſome hundreds a-year were gained to the proprietors; but a complete draining, which is very prac-icable, and would be deemed eaſy in other countries, would produce thouſands.

Cultivation.—Agriculture, with a few exceptions, is here in a very low ſtate. The old plan of inceſſant tillage, with-out reſt to the ground, or without having any ſufficient pro-portion of it ſown out in graſs, or other green crops, ſtill pre-vails. Graſs, on the little ſpots where it is ſown, thrives re-markably well. Our tenants are either without leaſes alto-gether, or have leaſes too ſhort for anſwering any valuable purpoſe. No wonder then that farming has not advanced. Our farms are ſmall, and we have no ſubtenants. The pa-riſh is totally open, excepting ſuch incloſures as are round gentlemen's places. Various are the evils incident to open fields. One of the moſt teaſing, and not the leaſt hurtful, is the devaſtation inceſſantly made by our half ſtarved cattle, upon the adjoining corn fields, whoſe hunger impels them to break from the range of graſs, to which they are ſtaked, or from the charge of careleſs boys and girls ſet to watch them.—Sea-weed is much uſed for a manure.

Services.—Some ſervices are ſtill continued here; and upon one eſtate, the *tenth ſheaf* is drawn in teind from the field, as part of the rent. Rent is paid chiefly in grain, often at the rate cf a guinea per acre,—a price not too high for the quality of the ground; but too high without leaſes, ſtrength or ſkill to cul-tivate it. The abject ſpirit of feudal habits, has made our tenantry

tenantry undervalue their labour, and give to the fuperior fuch a proportion of their earnings, as leaves them without a decent maintenance ; and renders this clafs of men, of all thofe who are able to labour, the pooreft and moft dependant among us. Their poverty has thruft them out of the rank, which it is advantageous to the community, that their profeffion fhould hold.

General Appearance.—Although there is abundance of excellent ftones for building houfes, the people in general are ill lodged. The meannefs of their cottages, the leannefs of their cattle, the open unimproved appearance of the fields, &c. prefent to the eye of a ftranger a very unfavourable view of a country naturally rich. Perhaps it was, with fuch objects before him, that the great living hiftorian of Scotland, while in Moray, faid with furprife, " *Is this the fine province, of which I have heard fo much ?*"

Black Cattle, Horfes, Sheep, and Poultry.—Our mode of farming makes little provifion for black cattle, of which our ftock is not great. We plough all with horfes, and thefe are ftill of an indifferent breed, and ill kept up. They fubfift in winter chiefly upon ftraw ; the farmers have no hay.—There are, in the parifh, about 2000 of the fmall white-faced breed of fheep, fed on the benty pafture already mentioned.—Our poultry have long been remarkable for large fize and good quality ; whether this is to be afcribed to the fuperior richnefs of our grain, or whether there is any peculiarity in the breed, is not afcertained.

Population.—Our population is at prefent 1500. It has not greatly diminifhed for fome years paft, notwithftanding there have been a few emigrations. The return to Dr. Webfter

fter in 1755, however, was 1679. About the end of laſt war, ſome individuals went to North America, a few of whom returned and ſettled at home, bringing bad tidings of the country, which their imaginations had figured to be the *fairy-land* of wealth. Since that time, thoſe who would have gone to America, had the proſpect been favourable, have preferred a *home* emigration to the ſouthern parts of Scotland, particularly Glaſgow, Paiſley, &c. And from this part of the north, there is, and always has been, a conſtant ſucceſſion of adventurers iſſuing forth to the Britiſh capital, the Eaſt and Weſt Indies, and other parts of the empire. There are 6 heritors in this pariſh. By far the greateſt part of the people, are employed in agriculture *.

Trade.—There is a village, called *Burgh-head,* upon the coaſt, containing 400 ſouls, more than two thirds of whom follow a ſea-faring life. Moſt of the reſt are quarriers and ſtone maſons. Here there are a few ſmall boats employed in fiſhing, and 7 large boats are hired to the fiſhing on the weſt coaſt, on board each of which there are ſix people. Five large boats, with ſix people in each, are alſo employed in tranſporting ſtones from the quarries, to different parts of the country. Two ſloops are employed, chiefly in carrying grain to the ſouth of Scotland, and in bringing back coals.

Imports and Exports.—The principal imports are coals, moſtly from Northumberland ; and merchant goods, chiefly from London. Our exports are *men*, grain, linen yarn, and a few black cattle. The firſt and the laſt go chiefly to England, eſpecially to the London market. The grain and yarn go to the ſouth of Scotland.

Fiſhing.

* The wages of a male labourer without victuals, is 8d. per day; of a female 4d. In autumn both are higher. When fed by the employer, men ſervants in huſbandry get from 5 l. to 8 l. ; women ſervants from 30 s. to 40 s. a year.

Fishing.—There is a good white fishing here; cod, skate, ling, &c. are fold at prefent, from 1 d. to 1 ¼ d. the pound. We have alfo hollibut, mackarel, whitings, feath, &c; but although there are turbot on the coaft, our people cannot fifh them. Haddocks have never entirely deferted our coaft, but they are at prefent in fmaller numbers, and in deep water farther from land: Of confequence, they fell fix times dearer than they did lately, being now at the rate of one penny each. They are larger in fize than before. Of late, a lobfter fifhing has been fet a going in the Moray frith by an Englifh company. On the ftation, which included the coaft of this parifh, and of Drainie, there were caught laft fummer, and fent to the London market, 60,000 lobfters. It is faid that no lobfter traps were ever before feen on this coaft. If this be true, it fhews how long mechanical inventions are of becoming univerfal. So little are the people here accuftomed to mechanical operations, that after feveral fruitlefs attempts, they have not yet been able to imitate with fuccefs this fimple invention *.

Propofed Improvement.—At the village of Burgh-head, upon the weft fide of the promontory, nature has pointed out a ftation well adapted for a deep, a capacious, and a fafe harbour. The property belongs to Sir Archibald Dunbar; and this gentleman, as well as the country at large, would be much benefited by fuch an erection. It could be made at a moderate expence, and with proper precautions, fuccefs would be certain. When one confiders, that there is not along the whole fouth coaft of the Moray Frith, from Buchannefs to Invernefs,

(upwards

* In Statiftical accounts, the progrefs of mechanical inventions, ought not to be omitted. The benefit of fuch difcoveries often remains confined to corners, becaufe the public is not made acquainted with them. The improvement of a plough, a loom, a fpade, a wheel, a lever, &c. as well as of the more complicated machinery of a fhip, or of a fpinning jenny, it is of importance to have as generally, and as quickly known as poffible.

(upwards of 100 miles) one good or safe harbour, the pro‑
priety of this undertaking appears in a strong point of view.
Most of our present harbours are at the mouths of rivers,
which are constantly forming bars and shallows. At Burgh‑
head, there is no river ; there is shelter from dangerous winds,
a fine bottom, and water of any necessary depth. Burgh-head is
nearly at an equal distance from Elgin and Forres ; and if
it had a good harbour, would soon become the port of both
towns. Commerce and manufactures would of consequence
soon visit this part of the country, and all the various advan‑
tages, arising from them to the public, would quickly follow
such an important undertaking.

Church, Sectaries, School, and Poor.—The stipend is 8 chal‑
ders of barley, and 22 l. Sterling. Sir Archibald Dunbar is
patron. Till commerce and manufactures arrive, to put money
into the purses of the lower ranks, we cannot expect to see
that multiplicity of religious opinions, and diversity of wor‑
ship, which mercantile wealth, in a special manner, produces.
We have two or three Antiburghers. A small Non-jurant
meeting has existed in the parish, ever since Presbytery was
established. It has been upheld, for many years past, by a
very small number of very poor peasants. Will it be believ‑
ed, 200 years hence, that such a description of people had,
during the whole of their lives, been at the expence of a pas‑
tor and place of worship, chiefly that they might *clandestinely*
offer up their prayers for a *proscribed race of Kings*, whom
they never saw. These people are remarkable for their good
neighbourhood, and Christian fellowship with those of the
establishment around them.—The parochial school here has
no other salary, than 7 bolls of bear, called *Reader's Bear*.
The number of scholars may be from 40 to 50. Of all go‑
vernments, ours requires most, that youth be well educated,

and knowledge univerfally diffufed. In thofe appeals to the people, which it neceffarily produces, nothing fo much as a competent degree of knowledge can guard againft the effects of impofture, and can eftablifh, from age to age, in the public mind, a fteady attachment to its free and unequalled conftitution.— The poor at prefent amount to 60 ; and all the public fupply they have is from the church collection, which is about 5 s. each funday : fcanty provifion indeed ! We received with gratitude our fhare of the bounty in grain, fent to us, in the year 1783, by a wife and humane Legiflature. How ftrange, that the fame humane and enlightened policy, which faved from famine many individuals in one feafon, fhould fhut its eyes for fo many years, againft the operation of a tax (viz. that on coals), which, in its effects, has, every year, embittered the exiftence of thoufands in the northern parts of Scotland, and, at the fame time, has proved an invincible bar to the increafe of population and wealth, by the introduction of manufactures. Thank God, that tax is about to be abolifhed.

Fuel.—The moffes here are utterly exhaufted ; and we depend on Northumberland chiefly for coals, which coft very dear. The expence of a private family, fituated at the diftance of 8 miles from the harbour, and ufing three fires conftantly, is about 24 l. a-year, including the payment of carriage from the fhip. When the odious and impolitic tax on this commodity, at the Red-head, is taken off, then fhall we of the north date *the firft year of equality, and of rational taxation.*

Roads.—We have no turnpikes, nor is the ftatute labour commuted. Road-making here is, as yet, but in its firft rudiments. It feems ftrange, that fociety, all over Europe, fhould have perfected (fo far as it appears capable of perfection,) intercourfe by the watery element, long before general plans have been any where adopted, for perfecting the internal intercourfe of countries, by rendering good roads univerfal.

There

There is now, however, reaſon to expe(t, that the contraſt
which almoſt every quarter of this kingdom at preſent exhibits, between made roads and unmade, between comfortable
motion, and uncomfortable, between quick and ſlow journeys,
muſt operate ſtrongly and rapidly, in rendering good roads
univerſal *.

Eminent Men.—Two of the ableſt men, which this part of
Scotland has produced, were both heritors of this pariſh ; Sir
Robert Gordon of Gordonſton, father of the preſent Sir William, and Mr. Gordon of Clunie, father of the preſent Mr.
Baron Gordon. The former gentleman held a ſeat in the Britiſh Senate; but it is ſaid, that, owing to incumbrances upon
a fortune now remarkably affluent, he was induced in early
life to quit a ſcene, where, from his ſingular eloquence and
profundity of intelle(t, nature had ſo remarkably fitted him to
ſhine. It was afterwards the lot of thoſe two gentlemen, to
be frequently oppoſed to each other in the petty competitions
of private life ; in which they diſplayed an ability that marked them out to all their co-temporaries, as individuals far ſur-
paſſing the common line of human genius. It is not always
the fortune of nations to be able to draw, from the great maſs
of the community, ſtateſmen of ſuch ability as thoſe two individuals poſſeſſed. They have left no literary memorials, however, behind them.

Antiquities.—In Malcolm II's reign, the Danes took poſſeſſion
of Moray. The king headed an army againſt them in perſon,
and was overcome in a pitched battle. " Upon this," ſays Buchanan, " the caſtle of Nairn was ſurrendered to them, which
they

* *Query*, When labourers are in ſuch requeſt, and farmers ſo pinched, by the
high wages they muſt pay their ſervants, why might not the military, in peaceable times, be employed in road-making, and other public works?

" they ftrongly fortified, and of a peninfula made an ifle, by cut-
" ting through a narrow neck of land ; and then they called it
" by a Danifh name, *Burgh*." All our hiftorians are miftaken
in placing this fort at *Nairn*, where there never was any fuch
building. But, in this parifh, the peninfula above mentioned
is fituated ; and upon it, there are large remains of a regular
fortification. The cut made to infulate the promontory is yet
vifible, but now dry and nearly filled up. The place ftill retains its Danifh name, being generally called by the common
people *Burgh*, and fometimes called and written *Burgh-head*.
2. After Malcolm had overcome the Danes, under Camus, in
the battle of Panbride, in Angus, Camus, with his remaining
troops, attempted to retreat to Moray, by the mountains, but
was overtaken, routed, and flain. There is an obelifk ftanding at the weft end of the parifh, conjectured to be the obelifk
which, hiftorians fay, was erected for this victory ; and near
this monument, there is a village called *Kaim*, which is fuppofed to be the village mentioned by Buchanan, as retaining
the memorable name of Camus. 3. Upon the north-weft
border of the lake of Spiney, there are ftanding upon an artificial mound, furrounded with a foffee and draw-bridge, the
walls of a ftrong caftle, called *Old Duffus*. It is known to be
of great antiquity ; but at what precife time it was built, or
who were the original proprietors, cannot be traced with any
degree of certainty. It is furrounded with orchards and foreft trees, and, ftanding in the heart of a charming plain, prefents, at every point of view, one of the moft picturefque and
beautiful objects which the country exhibits. 4. At the village of Duffus there is a fquare, (in the centre of which the
church is placed), furrounded by four ftreets regularly paved,
the workmanfhip of *Oliver Cromwell's* foldiers ‡.

Difadvantages.

‡ Had it not been for fwelling the Statiftical work too much, to have allowed a corner in it, for a felection of fuch epitaphs as are curious, would have fur-

Diſadvantages.—The principal of theſe, are the diſtance from mills, and a ſevere *mill thirlage*,—idleneſs,—little attention to induſtry,—a want of manufactures,—a want of general ſkill

niſhed a pleaſant morſel to readers of a certain taſte. The following epitaph is found on the tomb-ſtone of a ſailor in the church-yard of Duffus.

" Though Eolus' blaſts, and Neptune's waves, have toſs'd me to and fro,
" Yet now at laſt, by heaven's decree, I *harbour* here below :
" Where at an *anchor I do ly*, with others of our fleet,
" Till the laſt trump do raiſe us up, our *Admiral* Christ to meet."

The Gaelic is not ſpoken on the coaſt of Morayſhire. We ſpeak the Engliſh mixed with a large portion of provincial dialect. Our accent is, in the ear of a ſtranger, ſnappiſh and provoking, aſſimilating to that of Aberdeen, but is ſaid not to be quite ſo invincible as theirs, to thoſe who leave the country. It is more diſagreeable and more difficult to overcome, than the accent of our weſtern neighbours of Inverneſs; beſides, that they have an advantage over us in uſing none but modern Engliſh words. The remark, which ſtrangers make of us, that we ſeem unwilling to open our mouths when we ſpeak, is fully confirmed, by finding that of the 16 vocal articulate ſounds which compoſe the Engliſh language, we have totally thrown out in our dialect the two fulleſt and moſt ſonorous, and have ſubſtituted ſhort and ſlender ſounds in their place. No Morayſhire man of the lower ranks ever pronounces broad *a*, or long *o*; for the firſt he always uſes the ſhort and ſlender ſound of *a*, as *lă* for law, *Aguſt* for Auguſt, *ăl* for all; for the laſt he always uſes likewiſe the ſhort and ſlender ſounds of *o*, as, *clŏs* or clōſe, *rŏd* for rōad and rōde, *nŏt* for nōte, *rŏt* for rōte, *nŏ* for nō, *chŏck* for chōke, *pŏſt* for pōſt. This peculiarity is the more remarkable, becauſe, although theſe two full ſounds of *a* and *o*, are very prevalent in England, yet they are ſtill much more ſo in the ſouth of Scotland; inſomuch that the more frequent uſe of them, is that, which (next to the North Britiſh accent) moſt readily diſtinguiſhes the language of a ſouth country Scotchman of education, from the language of England. And perhaps, from this circumſtance, we have received our national nick-name, in the broad ſound of *Sawney*. But, although faſhion is now beginning to force upon our middling ranks here, thoſe two full ſounds, yet they feel, in the endeavour to pronounce them, nearly the ſame difficulty, that would attend the introduction of ſounds altogether foreign. Our diſlike to full ſounds, alſo appears in our preference of the ſlender *ee*, which in the language of the north, uſurps occaſionally the place of almoſt every other vowel, as *meen* for moon, *ſpeen* for ſpoon, *freet* for fruit, *yeel* for yule, *meedow* for meadow, *teetle* for title,

ſkill in agriculture,—a perplexing and inconvenient variety of weights and meaſures,—want of fuel, attended with loſs of health and lives among the poor,—frequent celibacy, or late marriages, occaſioned by poverty and depreſſion,—an oppreſſive coal-tax,—and an inconvenient diſtance from a Cuſtom-houſe, being 40 miles from Inverneſs, which is the neareſt.

Advantages.—The principal are, a ſea-coaſt,—a good ſoil,—a good people,—and a good climate. Whether what hiſtorians remark, of our having in the plains of Moray, about 40 days more of dry weather through the year, than in any other part of Scotland, be preciſely accurate, has never been aſcertained.

Charaĉter and Manners.—Society in this country is as yet chiefly divided into *high* and *low.* The latter claſs, though poor

---

eeſ for uſe, *peend* for poind, &c. Our people ſubſtitute the ſound of f for wh, as *fat* for what, *futch* for which, &c. They pronounce ſuch words as *filthy, fifcal, will, which,* &c. as if ſpelt *fulthy, fuſcal, wull, futch,* &c. They ſuppreſs r in a good many words, as *fiſt* for firſt, *hoſs* for horſe, *puſs* for purſe, &c. This is the more remarkable, as in general the Scotch pronounce this letter much more forcibly than the Engliſh do. The gutturals, *gh* and *ch,* are more frequently pronounced here, than in the ſouth of Scotland. The Scotch and French *e,* which is never heard in England, though not in ſo frequent uſe here as in the ſouth of Scotland, is notwithſtanding ſo prevalent as to have the name of this vowel expreſſed in that ſound : as is alſo the caſe in the reſt of Scotland. Here *w* and *v* are ſounded for one another; but this is alſo the caſe among the illiterate in other parts of Britain. The French *u,* reſembling the Υψιλον ſound, and ſo frequent at Edinburgh and the neighbouring countries, never found its way to the north. It was imported by the Scotch court from France. The Scotch diphthong *ei,* we uſe as frequently as in other parts of Scotland; for inſtead of pronouncing the Engliſh *i* in *life, ſtrife,* &c. we pronounce thoſe words as at Edinburgh ; *leif, ſtreif, kneif,* &c. The ſound of ſhort Engliſh *i,* as in *pit, fit, pick,* &c. is never uſed in our dialeĉt. Its ſubſtitute is a ſound approaching nearer to the ſhort Engliſh *e,* than to the ſhort Engliſh *i,* as if ſpelt, *pet, fet, peck :* this however is common to our lower ranks, with the reſt of Scotland.

poor and depreſſed, are not querulous, but peaceable and well diſpoſed. The higher ranks ſtill retain, comparatively, a conſiderable portion of the manners of the old barons. In ſome inſtances, thoſe peculiarities of behaviour are apparent, which an excluſion from the public eye, and a remote ſituation, are ready to produce. So that we are reminded, at times, of the remark of a celebrated dramatiſt : " In the cities and popu-" lous parts of the empire, there prevails ſuch a uniformity of " level manners, that I have been obliged to beat about amongſt " the out-ſkirts of the country, for charaƈters, at once *natural* " and *ſingular*, with which to fill my drama." Our middle ranks, compared with thoſe of other countries, are yet inconſiderable. They are not fully occupied with buſineſs,—have no ſtile of manners appropriated to their ſtation,—but are fond of the company and manners of their ſuperiors, and converſe more frequently, than is done in other places, about modes and faſhions in dreſs and manners. A ſuperior degree of *ſhrewdneſs*, has been commonly affixed to the charaƈter of a north-country man, which is well expreſſed in the common adage, " you are *too far north* for me." The remark is more applicable to our neighbours of the Aberdeen and Inverneſs diſtriƈts, than to us ; compared to them, we, in Morayſhire, are a blunt and plain people. Our people are as yet ſober, and little addiƈted to the intemperate uſe of ſpirits. The ſuppreſſion of ſmuggling, ſo happily effeƈted of late by the vigilance of government, has baniſhed foreign liquors, and introduced very generally the uſe of whiſky of our own diſtilling, which is both wholeſomer and cheaper. Beer, however, is ſtill too little uſed, for which whiſky is a moſt improper ſubſtitute. It is ſubmitted, whether the price of this unneceſſary article ought not to be kept ſo high, as, if poſſible, to prevent it from being in too frequent uſe among the loweſt ranks. Diſlike for diverſity in religious opinions, and modes of worſhip, together

gether with the illiberal prejudices respecting *Highlander* and *Lowlander*, have greatly ceased amongst the people. They became Presbyterians more from accident than from temper. During the alternations of Presbytery and Episcopacy, which took place after the Reformation, they did not at all discover that decided preference to Presbytery, which marked the western and southern counties. Had not their sentiments been keener than ours on this point, our island would probably at present have had but one national church. At the Revolution, few of the clergy of this province conformed to Presbytery, but availed themselves of the indulgence which the government gave, of allowing them to remain in their benefices for life, upon qualifying to the civil government. And in order to cherish Presbytery, it was necessary, from time to time, to send clergy from the south country to serve the cure. That horror at the name of *holidays*, which was once a characteristic of the Puritans, and *true blue* Presbyterians, never took possession of our common people here: and they still celebrate (perhaps without ever thinking of the origin of the practice), *St. John's* day, *St. Stephen's* day, *Christmas* day, &c. by assembling in large companies to play at foot-ball, and to dance and make merry. It is among the marks of an improving country, to find all the different ranks of society enlarging their sphere of motion. The higher ranks roam chiefly for amusement, and from curiosity; the lower move principally with a view to business and gain. In both cases, the consequences are beneficial to the district to which they belong, by giving rise to a wider comparison of objects and usages. The common people resident in Scotland every where, at present, move more from their native spot than formerly. In the time of our grand-fathers, fewer of the commonality crossed the Spey or the Findhorn, (the two rivers bounding the country), than now visit distant counties and towns, and even fo-

reign

reign regions. The improvement derived from this change, is here, as yet, but beginning to be felt. The dreſs is what is common in the low countries. The women, among the common people, come abroad to church and fair, without caps or bonnets on their heads ; and, inſtead of cloaks or mantles, are often dreſſed in ſtriped blankets ; ſuch as are uſed for beds. The laſt particularly ſtrikes and offends the eye of a ſtranger. An Engliſh woman, who came among us lately, ſaid, this dreſs always put her in mind of M'Beth's witches at Drury-Lane. Sirnames are here more numerous, in proportion to the population, than in the Highlands, but leſs numerous than in the ſouthern diſtricts of Britain.

Parish of Duffus.

By the Rev. John Reid, minister of that Parish.

Name, Extent, &c.—Duffus, i. e. Dubuist, signifying the 'black lake,' is from 3 to 4 miles broad from N. to S. and from 6 to 7 long from E. to W.; contains about 1800 souls, young and old. This parish seems rather to increase than decrease in numbers, owing to small farms, and a populous fishing town.

The soil here is of various kinds. From 200 to 300 acres, lying on the side of the Loch Spynie, is a rich fertile clay; and produces excellent wheat, pease, beans, and oats, but not so fit for barley. The N. and W. parts of the parish are of a light, sandy, black mould, very fit for barley, which in this parish is preferable to most in Murray.

There is a great extent of waste grounds lying on the sea coast, covered with a kind of grass called bent, only fit for sheep pasture, bottomed with a rich clay, but lying too deep for improvement.

About 50 years ago, several hundred acres of the best ground on the sea coast were covered with sand, blown from the western coasts. Some parts of this ground is 3 feet deep of sand, and by trenching has been made fit to produce corn of all kinds; but the expence is too much for the returns, so that it must continue in a barren state. In one night, I am told, more than 14 inches of sand were laid on some fields by the west winds.

There are some limestone quarries in this parish, but, owing to the scarcity and dearth of fuel, cannot be turned to account. There is no moss, but a kind of sulphureous turf, which, when used in the houses of the tenants, destroys all the fire

fire irons; even the locks and hinges of the doors are confumed by the fmoke. The fcarcity and dearth of fuel will in a fhort time render this and feveral neighbouring parifhes defolate, if not prevented by taking off the duty from coals carried coaft-ways.

The people here are poor in general, having no manfactures; though no country is better calculated for them, as it is very populous, and great quantities of corn are raifed and exported.

Farming, which is the only means they have of living, is now become fo expenfive, that unlefs a man can with his own children manage the farm, he cannot afford to pay the rent and fervants' wages. Their whole fummer's employment is to carry their fuel the diftance of 10 or 12 miles, to the great deftruction of horfes and carts. There is no wood within 10 miles, except fome firs lately planted by fome neighbouring proprietors; thefe, in the fpace of 20 or 30 years, will be of great fervice for fuel.

The people here are very temperate and induftrious, confequently healthy. The only local difeafe is the fcrophula, with which many of them are infected, owing, as fome fay, to the quantity of peafe-meal and fifh they feed on; others affirm it never was feen here till Oliver Cromwell's foldiers brought it under another name.

Natural Curiofities.——The moft remarkable curiofities in this parifh are fome extenfive caves on the fea fide, where there are abundance of freeftone quarries; and in thefe rocks are fome very extenfive grand caverns, reaching under ground farther than can be fearched : fome 100 yards, others more, in breadth, and from 60 to 100 yards in height; others fmaller, but very prettily fcooped out by the frequent wafhings of the fea.

There

There is in this pariſh an old caſtle called the Caſtle of Duffus, concerning which, both tradition and hiſtory ſay little. It ſeems to have been built for a place of defence; the walls in ſome places are 6 or 7 feet thick, ſituate on a riſing ground, ſurrounded with a ditch 30 feet broad, with a drawbridge, the only place of acceſs to it. Within the ditch or foſſe, there is a fine orchard and garden, ſtocked with the beſt kind of fruit trees. The foundations of a number of houſes are yet to be ſeen.

A ſtory prevails among the country people that it was built by the Danes in the time of King David I.; others, that a family of the name of Cheyne came from France, got a grant of the ground from King David, and built the caſtle in this defenſive ſtate, becauſe they had been guilty of ſome crime in France that expoſed them to proſecution. The caſtle gave title to Lord Duffus, who about 60 years ago poſſeſſed theſe lands with many others in this country.

Broughead, or Burgus.—There is in the weſt end of the pariſh a place called Broughead, a village containing 400 people who live chiefly by fiſhing.

Here there is a ſmall promontory jutting into the Firth, riſing above low water about 20 yards on the weſt and north ſides, fenced by perpendicular rocks on the eaſt; the aſcent is very ſteep, and now covered with graſs nouriſhed by the rubbiſh of the houſes that have fallen to that ſide. On the ſouth, the aſcent is more eaſy, and was defended by three ſeparate foſſes, through which the ſea was allowed to paſs, arched over with draw bridges. The area on the top formed a rectangular figure; in length 150 yards, in breadth 50. This area ſeems to have been ſurrounded with piles of large oak trees, drove deep into the earth, forming a kind of rampart. Pieces of theſe piles are yet to be found among the rubbiſh
when

when digged into, and appear to have been deftroyed by fire. On the weft there was a place of worfhip, the remains of which ftill appear; alfo a burying ground, which the people of Broughead ufe to this day. The whole feems alfo to have been furrounded on the top of the rocks with a very thick ftone wall. From all that I can learn, this fort was built by the Danes, as a place of fafety for their arms and other effects in times of danger, alfo a place of refidence to fome of their families. When, or by whom it was burnt I cannot learn. A fabulous ftory prevails among the country people, that a daughter of the King of Scotland was married to a Danifh prince who ufed her ill, upon which the Scots King threatened revenge for the affront; and therefore, immediately after, the Danes came over, brought a number of pigeons and other birds, befmeared their feathers with tar and oil, fet them on fire, and let them loofe to fly through the different parts of the garrifon; and how foon the Danes faw the flames, they fled with what valuables they could tranfport with them.

Some fay this was a Roman fort; but from their progrefs northward, it is hardly credible they would have built fuch a place of defence.

The bay to the weft of thefe rocks forms the fafeft and moft extenfive roadftead for fhips in all the North Seas; and the fhipmafters fay there is not a place north of Leith that is fo well calculated for a fea port. Ships of any burden could come in and lie in fafety in the moft violent ftorm, being defended on the north and eaft by the rocks; and the bottom of the bay confifts of clay and mofs; and if a few hundred pounds were well laid out, it would be the beft harbour in Scotland; and, in the prefent fituation of this country, it would be productive of the moft advantageous effects, both in getting coals, and all mercantile goods imported, and the

the corn, and other products of this country exported. Such a situation deserves the notice of government. There are at present 14 small sloops belonging to it; but, for want of a harbour, they are obliged to go elsewhere in winter. These sloops are employed in fishing and transporting freestone, victual, &c. to different parts north and south. ——The Society for promoting Fisheries seem to have neglected, or been ignorant of this place, else they would have erected some of their villages here.——The property is Sir Archibald Dunbar's, of Northfield, to whom the greatest part of the parish also belongs.

There are few different opinions here as to religious matters. A meeting house, at a place called Keam, has been a long time frequented by a small number of nonjurors; but these are equally well affected to government as the others who attend the church.

Poor.——The poor in this parish have no other funds but the weekly collections in the church, which amount to 15l. or 16l. yearly, which is given among them according as the minister and elders see need.

The stipend here is 128 bolls barley, and L. 22 : 15 sterl. including communion elements. Sir Archibald Dunbar is the only residing heritor, and is patron of the parish. There was in this parish a free chapel, called Unthank, which had its own minister and stipend; also one at Broughead. But now the whole parish attend worship at Duffus, except about 100 who meet at Keam; but of this 100, there are none but attend at the church when there happens to be no sermon, or a vacancy at Keam.

Schoolmasters.——The school, here like those in many other
parishes

parifhes, is neglected ; the falary only 7 bolls of barley ; and the fchool fees fo fmall, that no body thinks it worth their while to accept of it, unlefs fome young lad for a year or two. It feems the prefent generation of landholders wifh to extirpate learning altogether, in order to introduce ignorance and flavery among the lower clafs of people, elfe they would give fome encouragement to fchoolmafters ; and the oppofition given to a late application to Parliament for augmenting the fchoolmafters falaries by the landed gentlemen, clearly marks their intentions.

Cattle, &c.—There are few fheep in this parifh. About 500, of a fmall fize, are maintained on the benty hills near the fea coaft, but when fed are moft delicious eating.

The farmers ufe horfes chiefly for labouring and draughts of all kinds.

There is little or no meadow pafture, therefore black cattle are neglected ; though about 20 years ago, they were more numerous, and confequently the crops of corn more plentiful : but as horfes can be ufed with fewer fervants, the farmers find it neceffary to prefer them to oxen.—There is no market in the parifh. At Elgin and Forres there are feveral fairs ; from thefe the people are fupplied with their neceffaries, and to thefe they muft carry every article they can afford to fell, which occafions much lofs of time. There are no diftillers of fpirits here. There are 5 or 6 houfes in which ale and whifky are fold ; to thefe the people refort when they are to tranfact bufinefs either in felling or buying.

There is a remarkable circumftance in this parifh of a farm called Crofshill. It has been occupied by one family, of the name of Falconer, for 450 years back ; and the tenant's name was James and Alexander, alternately. The laft of them died only two years ago : this I can atteft by fome receipts for rents,

that

that fell into my hands after the death of the laſt tenant. The farm belongs to Sir Archibald Dunbar of Northfield.

The people here are well affeᴄted to the preſent king and conſtitution. The only grievances they complain of are the taxes on Engliſh coal, ſo neceſſary for them, on leather and ſalt.

There have been 13 Proteſtant miniſters in this pariſh ſince the year 1569. The preſent incumbent has been miniſter ſince 1780.

UNITED PARISHES of DUTHIL and ROTHIE-
MURCHUS.

(COUNTIES OF MURRAY AND INVERNESS.)

By the Rev. Mr PATRICK GRANT.

D U T H I L.

Name, Situation, Surface, Soil, &c.

THE ancient name of the pariſh of Duthil was *Glen-
chearnich*, ſignifying, in Gaelic, " Glen of Heroes ;"
from various exploits of the inhabitants in expelling the
Cummins from that part of the country, as well as from
their obſtinate defence of it, afterwards againſt the depredations of the Highlanders. The modern name Duthil is
from *Deogh-dhall*, " excellent valley ;" the Kirk-town being ſituated upon a riſing ground, commanding the pro-
ſpeЄt of a valley about 1000 acres. The pariſh is in the
county and Synod of Murray, and preſbytery of Abernethy ; extends 14 miles from E. to W. and is 10 miles
in breadth, is bounded by the pariſh of Moy on the N.
by Alvey on the W. by Abernethy on the S. and by Inverallen on the E. The general appearance is hilly, with
fir,

fir, birch and alder, on the fkirts of the hills ; but beyond them it is covered with heath, and rs rocky. It is divided nearly into two equal parts by the river Dulnan, fignifying in Gaelic, " floody," running from W. to E. about 14 miles. On both fides of which lies a great part of the arable ground. The foil towards the lower end of the parifh, which widens into a flat for feveral miles, frequently overflowed by the Dulnan, is deep. Towards the upper end, and at a diftance from the river, fhallow, vet fertile through the whole. The climate is extremely healthy, and the moft common diftempers are nervous fevers, and fwellings in the joints, occafioned, moft probably, by the viciffitudes of heat and cold, which occafion too frequent and imprudent changes of warmer clothing for the Highland garb. There are feveral mineral fprings in the parifh, two of which have been ferviceable in the gravel.

Animals, &c.—The quadrupeds are of the common kind in the Highlands. Some of the horfes are of the large labouring fpecies. The Highland garrons, as they are called, though not fo fufficient for labour, are more adapted to the lower clafs of people, eafily fupported, by running out in the fields moft part of winter. This country, once ftored with the fineft woolled kind of fheep, has for fome years been over-run with the coarfe Linton breed, which ought to be extirpated from every country. The parifh abounds with groufe, partridge and blackgame, and a vaft variety of the fmaller kind of birds. The wood-cock appears in October, and difappears in April.

Population.—At the time of Dr Webfter's report, the umbers in Duthil and Rothiemurchus were 1785. In
the

the earlier periods of ſociety here, when only the ſkirts of the hills were inhabited, the lower grounds being covered with wood, and infeſted by wolves and other ravenous animals, the population bore a nearer proportion to what it now is than it did for a ſeries of years previous to the rebellion in 1745. Since that memorable period, the population has decreaſed conſiderably, owing chiefly to two cauſes. The opportunity afforded young adventurers to traverſe the field of fortune, and throwing land into large farms. The amount of the preſent population of Duthil is 830, all of the eſtabliſhed church ; males, 372 ; females, 458 ; annual average of births, 70 ; deaths, 15 ; marriages, 15 ; ſouls under 10, 150 ; from 10 to 20, 244 ; from 20 to 50, 295 ; from 50 to 70, 98 ; from 70 to 100, 43 ; farmers and families, 54 ; houſehold ſervants, 3 ; labouring ſervants, male and female, 230 ; one ſtudent at college. Formerly moſt. of the gentlemen's ſons and of farmers ſtudied at college ; but for 40 years paſt, they have become adventurers abroad. Number of perſons born in other pariſhes in Scotland, 141 ; number of gentry, 5. About 20 years ago there was a conſiderable number of very creditable gentlemen with families in this pariſh, moſt of whom have now become extinct ; and the few remaining are ſoon likely to become ſo, their ſons preferring various purſuits abroad ; batchelors, 3 ; each marriage, at an average, produces 7 children ; inhabited houſes, 166 ; perſons at an average to each inhabited houſe, 5.

Agriculture, &c.—Cattle, at an average, are 1022 ; ſheep, 3424 ; horſes, 315 ; ploughs of the Scotch kind, and a few Engliſh, 105 ; carts, 260 ; arable acres, 2183 ; all under corn and potatoes, excepting a few under cabbage, turnip and ſown graſs ; acres in meadow-graſs, 2467 ;

2467; acres in mofs and moor adjoining to the arable and meadow, 4650. What quantity of ground lies wafte, or in common, being the hilly part of the parifh, I cannot afcertain. At leaft a third of the parifh is under wood. The parifh fupplies itfelf abundantly with provifions. The only articles of export are black cattle and fheep. The real rent of the parifh is about L. 1100 Sterling. There are but a few inclofures in the parifh. The people murmur exceedingly at inclofures, their cattle having been accuftomed to range promifcuoufly through the year, excepting in the fummer feafon, and while the corns are on the ground.

Stipend, School, Poor.—The value of the living, including 2 glebes, is L. 67. The church was built in 1400, repaired in 1770. The manfe was built in 1704, rebuilt in 1763. Sir James Grant is patron, and the only heritor.—There are 2 fchools, a parochial one, and the other eftablifhed by the Society for propogating Chriftian Knowledge. The falary of the parochial fchool is 100 merks. The falary and perquifites will amount to about L. 12 Sterling. The number of fcholars during the winter feafon is about 30. In former years, when a number of gentlemen's families refided, there were ufually about 70 fcholars, fome of whom were fent yearly to the Univerfity. But the falary is now fo inadequate to the expence of living, that no proper fchoolmafter can be had; fo that the gentlemen are obliged to fend their children, at a great expence, to diftant counties to fchool. The falary of the Society fchool is L. 9 Sterling, with fuitable conveniencies, furnifhed by the tenants, in whofe diftrict the fchool is ftationed. The number of fcholars, at an average, does not exceed 20.—The number of poor receiving

ving alms is 16. The annual contributions for their relief do not exceed L. 5. There is no eſtabliſhed fund.

Prices, Wages, &c.—The price of beef, for a few years, has
ſtood at $3\frac{1}{2}$ d. the lb. formerly at $1\frac{1}{4}$ d. ; mutton now at 3 d.
formerly 1 d. ; butter, 12 s. formerly 5 s. the ſtone ; cheeſe
from 4 s. to 6 s. formerly 2 s. 6 d. Days wages of labourers in huſbandry, and common labourers, when married,
1 s. which is ſufficient to maintain a family. The fuel uſed
is wood and peat, and is the moſt expenſive fuel in any
part of Scotland, requiring the labour of the whole ſummer. Thus the farmer is under the neceſſity of neglecting the proper buſineſs of the farm. The uſual wages of
male domeſtic ſervants are L. 6 a-year ; female ſervants
L. 3. They are entitled to ſeveral articles beſides wages,
and engage only for a half-year, which is very diſtreſſing to
the farmer. If ſome mode is not adopted to regulate the wages of ſervants, ſuch as reſtricting their wages to a reaſonable ſum, by the univerſal conſent of counties, the farmer
muſt unavoidably fail. Servants during the ſummer, ſtroll
about idly, and live upon their former half-year's wages,
knowing that the farmer muſt yield to the higheſt terms
when the harveſt approaches. The idea of preventing, or
even diſcouraging ſervants from going to the ſouth country, ſo univerſally ſuggeſted, approaches too near to oppreſſion. Servants confeſs that their wages are beyond
the profits of their labour, but when 1 or 2 farmers are
neceſſitated for labourers, they are obliged to give high
fees, and from this view numbers of ſervants lie in waiting.
The increaſe in value of ſaleable articles might ſeemingly
admit of an augmentation of rent. But letting the Hill-
improvements to ſeparate poſſeſſors, having diminiſhed
theſe articles, by reducing the number of cattle, and theſe
too pinched in their paſture, ſtill the ſame number of ſervants

vants is neceffary. It would therefore be of infinite advantage to the poffeffors of low farms to have the Hill-improvements alfo in their poffeffion, or portioned out upon
the common pafture, though they fhould pay the addition
of rent. This obfervation, if applicable only to a particular diftrict, would be foreign to the purpofe; but it extends to a vaft track of country; to the weftern diftricts of
Aberdeen, Banff and Murray fhires; and a great part of
Invernefs and Perth fhires, which properly comprehend
the Highlands of Scotland. Servants wages having increafed fo prodigioufly, it is more advantageous to the farmer to employ cottagers or day labourers, for the purpofes
of hufbandry, where fuel and other neceffaries can be conveniently had; but where it is otherwife, the difficulty
of collecting fuel for the tenant's own ufe, and alfo for the
cottagers, which would be neceffary, if employed in his
fervice, would be unfurmountable. Employing cottagers
or day labourers univerfally in this way, being generally
married, would have the good effect of increafing population, as well as fubjecting fervants to more tolerable behaviour, where they muft neceffarily be had. Still there
is one particular abfolutely neceffary to be obferved,
which, if not attended to, will be an unfurmountable bar
to the farmer's induftry. It is the proper regulation of
the price of corn and meal; when meal can be had under
16 s. a boll, (144 lb. Averdupois,) the different claffes of
labourers become idly difpofed. The wages of 1 half-year
will maintain them idle a great part of the year.

Roads and Bridges.—The roads and bridges have for
fome years been kept in repair, by ftatute labour exacted
in kind. The road from Grantown to Aviemore, 13
miles in length, was repaired in 1779 to 24 feet in
breadth, being formerly 12 feet, by the country people,

at

at the requeſt of the proprietor Sir James **Grant**, without affecting the ſtatute labour of the year. Of which road there are 9 miles extending through the ſouthern limits of the pariſh, therefore, of no material advantage to the people of this country, chiefly accommodating the public. The bridges were originally built at the expence of the proprietor, one of which, a ſtone bridge of one arch, over the water of Dulnan, built in 1700, having now fallen into diſrepair, is completely ſupplied by a bridge built laſt ſummer, 1791, cloſe by it. A military road being projected by Duthil to Dulleybridge, than which, if executed equal to what of it is finiſhed, no road can be more complete. For the proper line of this road, the public are much indebted to the aſſiduity and attention of Colonel Montgomery, Inſpector General of military roads ; having traverſed on foot a vaſt track of very rugged ground for that purpoſe, and thereby rendered the line at leaſt 4 miles ſhorter than that univerſally adopted, before Colonel Montgomery inſpected it, at the ſame time avoiding the expence of bridges, and the inconveniency of riſing ground. The objection to this line, which appeared to other inſpectors, aroſe from moſſes of immenſe depth intervening.

Miscellaneous Observations.—The general ſize of the people is 5 feet 6. The greateſt height which any individual in the pariſh has attained to, is that of a gentleman alive at preſent, being 6 feet 7, handſome and well proportioned.—They are extremely induſtrious, more properly laborious, in the cultivation of their poſſeſſions, ſuperſtitiouſly treading in the footſteps of their anceſtors, diſregarding every new mode of improvement, in which, unfortunately, this country is not ſingular. To emancipate from

a

a prejudice fo univerfal and deeply rooted, will require ftrong and uncommon exertions. The efforts of a native have hitherto had fo little effect, that they only ferve to verify, ' That a prophet has no honour in his own coun-' try.' The only effectual mode would be, by one or more ftrangers of experience fettling in fuch diftricts, as a neceffi-ty of this kind requires. Though proprietors, for a num-ber of years, fhould give the higheft encouragement, the advantage in time would be immenfe.—Until of late, the people were very fond of a military life; but the wages of fervants increafing fo exceedingly, that fpirit is almoft to-tally overcome. Formerly none would inlift but in the Highland corps. Bounty-money now determines the choice. The people are fufficiently œconomical, yet ex-tremely hofpitable and well difpofed. They enjoy the comforts and advantages of fociety, as much as an inland country, and a fevere climate, will admit of.—The fitua-tion of the parifh in 1782 and 1783 was truly diftreffing. Had it not been for Government bounty, and Sir James Grant's large fupplies from diftant countries, the poorer clafs of people would have perifhed. So great was the de-ftruction of the crop in 1782, by the froft fetting in fo ear-ly as the month of Auguft, that the moft fubftantial corn which was fent to fome of the mills in this parifh, was a crop of wild oats from a piece of ground which had been ploughed, but not fown. From various obfervations made upon this kind of grain, it appears to be a fpontaneous pro-duction; fo that fhould oats, by fome calamity, be fweeped off from the face of the earth, it might be regained by a proper cultivation of this fpecies of grain, offenfive as it is. It will naturally occur to thofe unacquainted with a fevere climate, that early fowing would, in fome degree, prevent the fatal effects of froft. This may anfwer in a favourable

climate,

climate, but impracticable, where for moſt ſeaſons the ground is bomb proof in the middle of March, and mere puddle for ſome time thereafter. In 1680, as nearly as can be recollected, there was a famine in this and the neighbouring counties, of the moſt fatal conſequence. The poorer ſort of people frequented the church-yard, to pull a meſs of nettles, and frequently ſtruggled about the prey, being the earlieſt ſpring greens, which they greedily fed upon, boiled without meal or ſalt. So many families periſhed from want, that, for 6 miles in a well inhabited extent, within the year there was not a *ſmoke* remaining. Nurſing women were found dead upon the public roads, and babes in the agonies of death ſucking at their mother's breaſts. Numbers, to avoid the horror of their bodies being expoſed, finding the near approaches of unavoidable death, crawled to the church-yard, for the purpoſe of more immediate interment, that the earth, which denied them ſubſiſtence, might piouſly receive their remains into its boſom.—An augmentation of rent, the prodigious increaſe of ſervants wages, and letting ſmall improvements towards the ſkirts of the hills, called Hill-improvements, all concur as cauſes of great alteration in the cuſtoms and ſtyle of living of the inhabitants, within theſe 20 years. That emigrations, to an extenſive degree, have happened from a country where ſuch oppreſſion prevails, is not to be wondered at. Still emigration is no criterion to judge by, of the ſituation of a people. Whole tribes, who enjoyed the comforts of life in a reaſonable degree, have of late years emigrated from different parts of Scotland, from mere humour, and a fantaſtical idea of becoming their own maſters and freeholders.—The language principally ſpoken is the Gaelic, and the names of places are derived from that language; as *Craig-Elachie,* ' Rock of Alarm.' There are 2 rocks

rocks of the fame name, one at each extremity of the country called Strathfpey, about 30 miles diftant. Upon the approach of an enemy, the fignal was fent from the one to the other, for all fit to bear arms to appear at an appointed place. Hence the Grants motto, ' Stand faft Craig-' Elachie.'—The only principal inn in the parifh is at A-viemore. There are no ale-houfes. The number of houfes in which whifky (a beverage which feems fit only for dæmons) is fold, is 10. There were many more, until of late, when they were fuppreffed by the proprietor, upon finding the very bad effects on the morals of the people.

ROTHIE

ROTHIEMURCHUS.

Name, Situation, Soil, &c.

THE pariſh of Rothiemurchus was united to Duthil in 1625. Sir James Grant of Grant is patron. The name in Gaelic is *Raat-mher-ghiuiſh*, ' great plain of fir.' It is ſituated in the county of Inverneſs, Synod of Moray, and preſbytery of Abernethy; extends 7 miles from E. to W. upon the ſouth banks of Spey; 4 miles in breadth. Bounded by the pariſh of Duthil on the N. from which it is ſeparated by the river Spey; on the W. by Kinguiſich; on the S. by Athol and Braemar; on the E. by Aberne-thy. The nature of the ſoil near the banks of Spey is deep and fertile; but, in general, is ſhallow. There is an inexhauſtible quarry, more properly a mountain, of lime-ſtone, in the centre, with abundance of fuel. There are 2 ſmall lakes, abounding with char. Lochnellan, one of them, exhibits a ſcene moſt picturefque and romantic, and by the ſituation of the ſurrounding hills are formed 5 very remarkable echoes. Upon a ſmall iſland in Lochnellan, is a caſtle, built time immemorial; the walls of which are ſtill entire.—To the birds common in this country may be added, in the pariſh of Rothiemurchus, tarmagans, the only inhabitants, through all ſeaſons, of the tops of the higheſt mountains.

Population.—The amount of the numbers at preſent is 280, all of the eſtabliſhed church. Males, 130; Females, 150. Annual average of births, 30; of marriages, 5;

deaths,

deaths, 12. Of fouls under 10, 48; from 10 to 20, 63; from 20 to 50, 92; from 50 to 70, 46; from 70 to 100, 31; farmers and families, 9; houfehold fervants, 3; labouring fervants, 46; gentry, 5. Each marriage, at an average, produces 5 children.

Agriculture, &c.—Number of cattle, 180; fheep, 2300; horfes, 95. There being a number of wood manufacturers, the parifh does not fupply itfelf with provifions. The land-rent is L. 300; wood, at an average, L. 300.

School, Poor, &c.—The only fchool is that eftablifhed by the Society for propagating Chriftian Knowledge. The falary is L. 10 Sterling. That, and the perquifites, amount to about L. 15. The number of fcholars feldom exceeds 30.—The number of poor is 7. The annual contributions for their relief do not exceed L. 3; and there is no other fund.

Pariſh of Duthil.

Supplement to the Statiſtical Account of the united pariſhes of Duthil and Rothiemurchus ; by the Rev. Patrick Grant.

It is highly gratifying to view a ſpirit of induſtry and improvement, of late years, prevailing in this country in general. During the late ſcarcity of grain, ſo univerſal, the inhabitants of this country were able to afford large ſupplies to their neighbours; and would in all ſeaſons do ſo, did the froſt in Auguſt and September keep off. By attention to ſmall binding and packing about wood, a rainy ſeaſon does not in the leaſt alarm them. To the mere habit of large binding, and allowing corn to remain upon broad band for a day, perhaps longer, without diſcrimination of a wet or dry ſeaſon, may, in a great meaſure, be aſcribed the late ſcarcity ſouthward. If the top of the ſheaf is dry, it matters little ſhould the bottom be taken out of a puddle. If properly packed about wood, the whole will be perfectly ſafe. But it requires judgment and practice.—Among many arguments in favour of large plantations of wood in uncultivated ground, this is not the leaſt conſiderable. A ſupply of wood for the above purpoſe, would perhaps be a mean of preventing a famine.

But, it is matter of regret that, in a ſituation far from the ſea-coaſt, the market, for the moſt part, is precarious ; in which caſe, even great exertion and expence will ſeldom reward the labours of induſtry. Hence numbers are induced to repair to diſtant countries in queſt of various occupations. —Still that local ſituation rarely exiſts attended with diſadvantages

vantages which admits of no remedy. They exist more in idea than in reality; and are owing, for the most part, to inattention to proper means of industry.

The writer of this article has long contemplated with pleasure the advantages that would arise, not solely to this country, but also to all Britain, were manufactories of linen and woollen cloth carried on individually; that is, a loom, or looms, established in each farm-house, in proportion to the farmer's abilities. In this parish there are at least 600 acres perfectly adapted for flax. The objection, that this mode of manufacture would interfere with the business of the farm, vanishes, by the possibility of making them distinct and separate objects, so as that the one party should at no time interfere with the department of the other. Add to this, that a source of gain is of all others the most powerful source of industry; the produce of labour being easily transported to a ready market.

It will be said, that establishing villages in proper situations would be a preferable mode of carrying on manufactories. The writer of this article is unfortunately singular in his idea of the utility of villages. They are ornaments to a country, but too frequently nurseries of political disquisition. —Villages, it will be argued, afford a ready market even for trivial articles from a farm. But the profits arising therefrom are only seemingly advantageous. The farmer's wife or daughter repairs to the village to dispose of her basket of eggs. This is one advantage arising from the neighbourhood of a village. But, what is the consequence? She returns loaded with tea, sugar, a bottle of wine as a cordial or medicine, some yards of fine muslin, silk and satin: articles she never would have dreamt of, had she not been ensnared by the glare and show of a fine shop, and unfortunately forgot the most necessary petition, ' into temptation lead me not.'

But,

But, allowing the utility of villages in its utmoſt extent; ſtill the eſtabliſhment of private manufactories can be no embarraſsment upon that utility, or upon the buſineſs of farming. To corroborate which, we need only look to our neighbouring country Ireland, crowded with cities and villages, and farming alſo carried on to a great extent.

Hence this meaſure, among many other advantages, would be a vaſt ſource of population. What crowds of both ſexes, in different corners of the kingdom, leave their native ſoil in queſt of employment! thouſands of whom, by a ſudden tranſition of living, and other caſualties, are hurried to an untimely grave. Had they ſufficient employment in their native country; few would think of going in queſt of that ſubſiſtence they might find where they drew their firſt breath, and fewer ſtill would viſit foreign ſhores. Thus would Britain quadruple its numbers by a race of hardy ſons, attached by the fruits of ſober induſtry, and bid defiance to every uſurping foe! France would not then even dare to menace her well-guarded ſhore.

In Ireland, experience, long experience, has ſanctioned this mode of manufacture, and given her the ſuperiority in the linen market. What has not nature done, what would not induſtry do, in that well-ſituated iſle? Proſperous and happy might ſhe be, were not that happineſs abuſed. The Iriſh lord, wallowing in luxury, is conſequently regardleſs of the ſhameful abuſe committed by the deſtructive mode of wadſetting, or nearly ſo, his fruitful ſoil, by renting it to a few, who are denominated reſpectable farmers. Theſe ſubſet to a ſecond claſs; the ſecond to a third; and ſo on, to a ſixth. From the ſecond claſs, what ſtrides does oppreſſion make! By remedying this ſource of grievance, Ireland would become happy, proſperous and peaceful.

To this mode of oppreſſion, how ſtriking the following contraſt!

contraſt ! This country, in common with others, long laboured under the ſame deſtructive grievance. But, the preſent proprietor, Sir James Grant, ſo ſoon as he got poſſeſſion of his property, ſtruck at the root of this baneful evil,
by paying off the wadſets, under which hardſhip a great part
of his property laboured ; and thus unfettered the hands of
induſtry, which he has invariably encouraged. But, induſtry, when long cramped and diſcouraged, becomes ſlow and
tardy in recovery : People get into habits and modes of culture, which time, long time, can hardly induce them to relin-
quiſh. Thus Sir James Grant's property in this and the other
pariſhes ſtill admits of improvement. And, over what ſoil
will the traveller caſt his eye where this does not hold true ?
Still, Sir James Grant, by an uniformity of conduct, in giving every proof that it is his earneſt wiſh to render his people happy and comfortable, has the ſatisfaction of being poſſeſſed of the ſincere attachment of a numerous and induſtrious tenantry, with every individual of whom he is perſonally
acquainted : A proof of which was given in recruiting the
1ſt Fencible Regiment ; and in this hour of aid and exertion, they with one voice declare their readineſs to take
the field, ſolicitous, in that event, that Sir James Grant may
be their leader.

Arming the Highlanders.——In the preſent hour of alarm
and urgency, it is matter of ſurprize that exertion has hitherto been ſo ſlow, when every individual is threatened in
his perſon, family and property, by an inſulting and rapaci-
ous foe.

All able to bear arms throughout Sir James Grant's property, and that of Rothiemurchus, ſcouting the idea of individuals being picked out, or ſerving within the limits of certain counties, are eager to a man to be trained to arms, and
follow

follow their leader, Sir James Grant, wherever the enemy dare to trample on Scottish ground.

His Majesty has not more zealous, faithful or loyal subjects, than ' the sober-minded' Highlanders, throughout the whole of the vast extent of country they possess. At a distance from nurseries of vice, and fashionable, but destructive luxuries of life ; prosperous and happy under indulgent masters ; sensible of the privileges they enjoy under a mild government ;——they are eager to defend and preserve these invaluable blessings. Of the disaffection and disloyalty of some individuals southward, they talk with detestation. Of French fraternity and equalization, they express themselves with horror, as a measure under which society could not subsist. Not from individuals only, but from many of the inhabitants of the parish of Duthil and Rothiemurchus, has the writer of this article heard, with much satisfaction, the following just and proper idea, cloathed in the forcible language of a sagacious Highlander :——' That, from the Almighty, to the low-
' est reptile, a regular chain of subordination exists ; and
' praying God to preserve that chain, and prevent horror
' and confusion ; and for that valuable purpose, to bless and
' counsel the judges of the land to administer justice and equi-
' ty betwixt man and man.'

Woods.——A considerable extent of ground in this parish lies under aller wood, the most useless for manufacture, and yet occupies the most fertile soil. How preferable would it be, how pleasing to the eye, how much more profitable to proprietors and tenants, to see fields of corn and flax alternately in its stead, surrounded with rows of beech, elm, &c. ! The present proprietor of Rothiemurchus has the merit of introducing this piece of improvement, among many others, into his property.

Muir-burning.

Muir-burning.—The fportfman exclaims, nay, thunders out execrations and anathemas againft the fhepherd as an enemy to game. Burning of heath is in fome degree a fcience, executed partially, with confideration and caution; feldom done but from the 1ft of October to the month of March, and at no time until the heath begins to decay. The benefit of it to fheep is immenfe, in point of feeding and medicine. To the game, efpecially groufe, it is luxury. The heather bells from the young growth, pregnant with honey, the variety of mountain berries, and the richnefs of verdure, which continues for feveral years until the heath becomes rank and begins to decay, afford a plentiful fubfiftence to the game. Could the feathered tribe articulate, they would blefs the hand which was the mean of fo plentiful a ftore. In effect, in hoarfe and fonorous notes they do fo.—The idea that heath, if never burned, would in time decay and be eradicated, fcarcely deferves a reply.

Turnip and Potatoes.—The culture of turnip has in moft countries been carried to perfection; that of potatoes, of late years, has made great progrefs, but, in point of feeding cattle, not fo univerfally attended to. Turnips are dangerous to cows before calving, and many fuffer thereby; but they improve even by a few handfuls of potatoes a-day, and no quantity will injure them. Beef fed upon turnips is far inferior in quality to that upon potatoes; three bolls of which, with ftraw or hay, and a fheaf of corn each a day, for the laft two or three weeks, will completely feed an ox of an ordinary fize. Peat and turf afhes, if kept dry, and laid in drills, fo as to go a greater length, will yield excellent turnips, and feeding cattle upon the field will fufficiently manure it. Thus the manure commonly ufed for turnips may be allotted for potatoes; no matter how rich for fuch as are
intended

intended for cattle. But manure for potatoes to be used in the kitchen, requires great attention. The difficulty of preserving potatoes in winter will be an objection, by some people, against the culture of them to any great extent. This objection arises from mere indolence. The immense benefit of them to man and beast, if properly attended to, will more than repay the labour required in preserving them in pits, vaults and mill-leads, that is, in plain Scots, the sheelings of the corn ; a small quantity of which thrown among a number of bolls of potatoes, but covered foot deep upon the surface, will secure them, under a roof, from the severest frost, and render them more dry and mellow, and preserve them fit for use during a great part of summer.

Eminent Characters.——Dr. William Grant, physician in London, was son to James Grant of Rothiemurchus. Having taken his degree of M. A. at the College of Aberdeen, he commenced his medical studies in the University of Edinburgh, under the celebrated Drs. Monro, Rutherford, Alston, Whytt. Having received the most ample testimonials of his character and abilities from his several masters, he entered the University of Franeker, in Friesland, where he studied for two years. He then removed to Paris, where he remained for six months ; when hearing of a very mortal fever, which the French physicians thought new, had broke out at Rouen in Normandy, he repaired thither on purpose to attend the hospital where it prevailed. At Rouen he continued three months, and then returned to Paris, where he soon after took the degree of M. D. He thence returned and settled in London, in 1755, where he practised physic for about 36 years. His several medical publications speak superior abilities in his profession ; and the estimation he was held in abroad is conspicuous from the correspondence

of

of eminent phyſicians upon the continent, copies of which, in Latin, are to be ſeen at the end of the 2d edition of his Treatiſe on Fevers. His chief correſpondents were Kauffman, Tiſſot, De Haen, and Stoll; the latter of whom dedicated a medical work to him, and pronounces him to be a bleſſing to mankind. Finding his heaſth impaired, he reſolved to retire to his native ſoil; where he devoted his whole attention to the improvement of his paternal property, and tendering medical counſel and aſſiſtance to the ſick and diſabled. Finding a diſorder in his ſtomach becoming obſtinate, he repaired to Edinburgh; where having lingered, with becoming and exemplary reſignation and fortitude, under a ſevere illneſs for three months, notwithſtanding the united efforts of the ableſt phyſicians, he reſigned his laſt breath.———Dr. Grant, in ſocial intercourſe, rendered himſelf the delight of all his acquaintance. Never was there a man who, with ſo much knowledge, and ſo much energy of expreſſion in converſation, rendered himſelf more pleaſant in company, or was more regretted when he died.

Alexander Cumming, ſon to Mr James Cumming late in Aviemore in the pariſh of Duthil, gave ſtriking proofs of mechanical genius at an early period of life, when a boy at ſchool. Being patroniſed by John Duke of Argyle, he reſided under the patronage of the Duke at Inveraray for ſeveral years. From thence he ſettled in London, where his inventions and improvements in the mechanical line recommended him to the favour of the late Earl of Bute, and the notice of his preſent Majeſty. Having, by his merit and induſtry in the mechanical department, acquired a ſufficient independency, he now enjoys the fruit of his labour in his villa near London.

PARISH OF DYKE, INCLUDING THE ANNEXED PARISH OF MOY.

(COUNTY OF ELGIN AND FORRES, SYNOD OF MORAY, PRESBYTERY OF FORRES.)

By the Rev. JOHN DUNBAR.

SINCE the union of theſe pariſhes in 1618, cuſtom has comprehended the annexed pariſh of Moy under the name of the other, both pariſhes now reſorting to one church at Dyke. The ſeparate pariſhes had their names from the villages where their reſpective churches were firſt erected; and theſe being of Gaelic derivation, are ſufficiently deſcriptive of local circumſtances.

Names and their Derivation.—Dik, or Dyk, as it was written of old, is from *Dig*, a water drain or ditch. Leſly Biſhop of Roſs, in the 9th book of his Hiſtory, calls this village

village a municipium; but no traces of any municipal privileges now remain.

Moy is from *Maigh*, a plain; which being remarkable
for its fine level extent and fertility, is, by way of diſtinction, called the Moy, and formerly the Mey. In this plain
were two diſtinct contiguous eſtates, now veſted in one proprietor, called the Eaſter and Weſter Mey. Each of theſe
had a villagè of its own name. In the village and lands of
Eaſter Moy * ſtood a prebendary church. The burial-
ground around it is yet in uſe.

Bearing and Situation.—This united pariſh, by an obſervation taken at the ſhore, is in 57° 26′ 21″ north latitude.
It lies in the ſynod of Moray, the preſbytery of Forres, and
county of Elgin and Forres; being ſituated on the ſouth
coaſt of the Moray Frith, and on the weſt ſide of the river
Findern, excepting only the lands of Upper and Nether
Buchtalies, and the lands of Moy Carſe, on the right ſide, or
eaſt of that river. It is the moſt weſterly coaſt pariſh in the
preſbytery or county to which it belongs; being weſt of the
pariſhes

---

* Eaſter Moy is one of thoſe inſulated diſtricts which has been append-
ed to a different county from that wherein it lies, and is ſubject to the juriſdiction of the county of Nairn, becauſe it had belonged to the Thanes of
Calder while they were hereditary Sheriffs of Nairn. There are many inſtances, both in South and North Britain, of particular ſpots ſo connected
with diſtant counties, that are in ſome caſes very remote. Such appendages
were made *per annexationem*, after the introduction of the feudal ſyſtem,
to gratify the haughty ſpirit of the feudal Barons, who would neither reſide,
nor let their vaſſals live, under any other juriſdiction but their own. If the
act veſting heritable juriſdictions in the Crown has not already made ſuitable
proviſion, expreſs or implied, for a more near and ready adminiſtration of
juſtice, againſt the inhabitants of lands and tenements annexed to remote
counties, the aforeſaid encroachments of the feudal ſyſtem, on the former di-
viſions of the kingdom, may be productive, in ſome caſes, of inconveniencies,
not undeſerving the notice of the Legiſlature.

parishes of Kinlofs and Forrefs; north of Edinkellie; and eaft of the parifh of Auldearn and county of Nairn. It is an irregular four-cornered figure, running up the Frith for about 6 miles along fhore, from that corner oppofite to Findern harbour, till it reaches the mouth of the Ellands Bourne, over againft the opening into Cromarty Bay. From thence another of its boundaries ftretches up through the eafter end of the Hardmoor *, in a foutherly direction, for a great way into another heath, called the Broad Shaw. This boundary, from the fhore, feparates the barony of Brodie and Torreftry lands, in this parifh, from the lands of Infhough, Boghole, and Moynes, in the parifh of Auldearn, and county of Nairn. The other boundaries are too irregular for defcription.

Extent and Contents.—The fuperficial extent of this irregular figure may be about 21 fquare miles; containing 2697 Scots acres of corn-field, 1191 acres of natural and planted wood, and the reft in pafture, heath, and exhaufted moffes, with a fandy defert all along the fhore; which defert is a full half of the whole contents. There are evident marks of an early population in different places of this extenfive and deferted track, which has been entirely flat, till overwhelmed by fand from the fea. On the outfide of this fandy defert there is a high bank, which may be traced almoft

* Where this boundary croffes the heath called the Hardmoor, there lies fomewhere a folitary fpot of *claffic ground*, unheeded here, but much renowned in Drury, for the Thane of Glammis's interview with the Wayward or Weird Sifters, in what fome editions call the *Harmore* fcene of the tragedy of Macbeth. Here the inventive genius of Shakefpeare, fo predominant in the fupernatural and fublime, catching the hint from old tradition, has conjured up a night-piece of infernal horror, well adapted to fuggeft the hellifh purpofe, and forward the bloody work, that fet the Ufurper on the throne.

moſt to Invernefs.   This bank has, in many places, limited the inundation.

Above this bank, to the ſouth-eaſt, there is another extenſive plain, of mooriſh ground, which has been turfed to
the gravel.   Though unfit for culture, it is well adapted to
the production of firs.   It has been tried with ſuccefs ſince
the commons were divided, and will now be encloſed and
planted without delay.

Surface.—In the eaſter end of the pariſh, the cultivated
lands are uncommonly flat and ſmooth ; but, upwards from
the moor laſt mentioned, the cultivated land, in the weſter
end, riſes in a gentle acclivity toward the ſouth.

The ſurface of the cultivated parts, is agreeably diverſifi-
ed with flats and eaſy ſlopes, and beautified by the windings of running-water, ſkirted with natural wood.   There
are clumps upon eminences ; trees about farm-ſteads ; gentlemens ſeats finely ſituated, with gardens, orchards, and
hedged incloſures around them ; and the whole is ſurrounded with thriving plantations, riſing one above another, with
a variety of ſhade and proſpect, which gives the inland parts
an appearance that may be called picturefque.

Soil.—The ſoil, which has been much exhauſted by an
early culture, and a long continuance of inceſſant cropping,
is in ſome places a brown, and in others a black loam, generally light, kindly, and of eaſy culture.   At preſent it is
more remarkable for ſure and early crops of well filled
grain, than for many returns of the ſeed, which is liberally
beſtowed at a boll or upwards *per* acre, to keep down
weeds ; ſo that the average of crops cannot be ſtated at more
than 3½ or 4 returns.   The ground is not enough retentive
of moiſture, and conſumes dung quickly.   Under ſome of
the thinner ſoils, there lies, about 6 inches from the ſurface,

face, a tawny or browniſh coloured ſand, which adheres in large maſſes. It muſt be carefully avoided by the plough, as deſtructive of vegetation. A judicious uſe of lime, which could be had from Sunderland at 4 d. *per* meal firlot, would, by attracting the dews, bring a more copious ſupply of nightly moiſture; and a plentiful uſe of the lighter clays, even in compoſt dunghills, would give a firmer texture to the ſoil, to retain the moiſture which it receives, and would enrich the ground that has been injudiciouſly empoveriſhed, by intermixing the barren ſurface of turfed moors, and by heaping on ſand where there is already more than enough.

Nature and Extent of the Sea Coaſt.—The coaſt, though it be every where flat, ſhallow, and ſandy, is ſeldom prejudicial to ſhips, which, in paſſing up and down, can keep the deep water, under cover of the bold coaſt and mountains of Roſs; and Cromarty Bay is a harbour of ſafety, which is never inacceſſible. Here are no kelp rocks, nor is ſea-weed caſt out in any quantity for manure. The coaſt, of about 6 miles extent in this pariſh, preſents no ſituation for an harbour; nor does it afford productions of ſponges, corals, or weeds, worth notice.

At the back ſhore, behind Cullen, there are beds of cockles of the beſt quality. They are the perquiſite of the poor, who rake them out of the ſand at ebb of tide, both for ſuſtenance and ſale. The muſcles on this ſide are conſidered as property, and carefully looked after, being in requeſt as bait for white-fiſh. There was formerly a boat and crew for white-fiſhing at Hill of Findern, in this pariſh, which was a great convenience, and often furniſhed hands for the navy. It was ſuppreſſed by a former proprietor, and the fiſhers ſet adrift, becauſe the coſt of upholding the boat ſeemed to exceed the rent. But, at the increaſed prices of

fiſh

fifh fince that time, it might yet be an object for the new proprietor, to fet the white-fifh bufinefs afloat again.

It would alfo be a great convenience, if a quay were to be erected on the weft fide of the river mouth, below Benf-nefs, where fhips from Findern harbour might come over and lie to, for unlading lime and coals for the ufe of this pa-rifh, and for receiving the grain and wood wherewith it a-bounds. This would fave a long carriage round the Bay, and prevent the detention of corn fhips by the fwells of the river, which wind raifes as well as rain, to be frequently im-paffable. This might be done without any prejudice to the dues of Findern harbour.

Lakes.—There are no lakes of any confiderable magni-tude. We have feveral fprings impregnated with iron ; but none of any remarkable ftrength or efficacy.

Rivers and Streams.—Our only river is the Ern or Find-ern, not navigable, but of confiderable value for its fal-mon fifhings ; and there are four fmall ftreams befides, that water the parifh, containing nothing but trout.

Iflands, Rocks, and Caves.—There are no iflands, rocks, or caves ; but there are remarkable hills of fand, for which, and for the old bar, fee the Appendix.

Woods.—Few coaft parifhes are fo well provided with va-riety of natural and planted trees. The larger allars are in requeft for building boats and fmall floops. Birch finds a ready fale for peat-carts, and other implements of hufbandry of the cheaper kinds, to fupply the neighbouring markets. Afh, elm, beech, plain-tree, and fuch oaks as can be had, are taken off by water-carriage ; and firs, for roofing, fark-ing, and flooring of houfes, are fawn out here, and carried

off

off by the like conveyance. Ships, with coals and lime from Newcaſtle and Sunderland, may ſhortly carry back cargoes of fir-deal and ſlabs, for boxing the ſhafts of mines. It has probably encouraged the plantation of wood in this pariſh, that the Earl of Moray has a thriving beech at Earlſmill, that meaſures 14 feet 7 inches; and an aſh meaſuring 14 feet 10 inches in the girth. Experiments were made before the middle of the laſt century, of planting a few aſhes in the vicinity of great houſes; but for the firſt judicious and ſpirited exertion on a larger ſcale, in planting and improving an eſtate, this pariſh and county has been much indebted to the example of a Lady, of moſt reſpectable memory, Mary Sleigh *, the wife of Alexander Brodie of that Ilk, Lord Lyon.

Orchards.

* This excellent Lady, who had full liberty to manage matters at home, while her huſband attended his duty in ſeveral different Parliaments, had acquired liberal and comprehenſive views of the benefit and mutual relations of agriculture, manufactures, and commerce. She had ſeen much of the world before ſhe came here. When ſhe ſaw the ſituation of the country, ſhe pitied it; ſhe knew the value of people on an eſtate, and ſtudied to make them induſtrious, by contriving work, and giving them wages and bread for their ſervices. The men ſhe employed in levelling, trenching, draining, and raiſing fences; and trained the women to induſtry, by eſtabliſhing a ſchool for ſpinning, and for diſpenſing premiums. She raiſed quantities of flax, encouraged her tenants to cultivate it, and built them a mill, for bruiſing and ſcutching it. She encloſed and ſubdivided an extenſive mains ſubſtantially; trained up the hedges with uncommon care, and, further, ſheltered the encloſures, with belts planted with great variety of trees. Her gardens, orchards, and nurſeries, ſurpaſſed every thing, but Dunkeld and Blair, benorth Tay. From theſe, ſhe was fond of providing her neighbours *gratis*, who had a mind to make experiments in planting. She made new roads; ſtraightened old ones, planting them on both ſides; put trees in the gardens of every farm-ſtead, and raiſed ſylvan ſcenes all around her. The profit of this has been already realized, and will endure for many years to come. Planting has now become a favourite object. The Earl of Moray is doing great things, and has improved, upon her method. He intermixes all kinds of trees, with pines for ſhelter. His plantations about Darnaway are uncommonly thriving. He cuts out the firs whenever they can be diſpenſed

Orchards.—There are 4 orchards in the parish. The early blow is often blasted by easterly winds *. The later kinds thrive best. The crop of apples and pears are seldom plentiful.

Air.—The air, which is dry and healthy, is not productive of local distempers. There are a number of old people, but no instances of remarkable longevity.

Diseases.—The most frequent disorders are vernal and autumnal fevers, which, here, as well as elsewhere, have changed their nature, and become nervous and lingering. Though they be visibly infectious, an ill-judged sympathy brings many young people into danger, who, while they cannot profit the sick by their personal attendance, do a prejudice to themselves and others, by carrying home the infection. The natural small-pox are less fatal, since they have been less an object of solicitous care. Fresh air and cool regimen have saved the lives of many. Inoculation is not yet general, nor is it much relished, among the lower ranks.

Climate.—The climate is not inferior to that of Lothian. By the shelter of a wall it ripens apricots and peaches in the open air. Stone-fruit of every kind thrives better than in richer soils ; apples and pears not so well.

State

dispensed with. The weedings are a good succedaneum for peat-moss, which is scarce, by affording a comfortable firing, from 4 d. to 6 d. *per* load ; and trees will in time generate both soil and moss where there was none, and make way for the plough at length, in places where it might have long laboured in vain.

 * They should follow the plan here, adopted in Denmark, of covering the trees, in the spring, during the day, and uncovering them at night; which keeps the blossom back, till the season becomes genial.

State of Property.—Having yet no ſalt-pans, lime-works, nor mines of coal or metals, the property conſiſts of lands, woods, and ſalmon fiſhings.   There are ſtell fiſhings on the ſea, and cobble fiſhings on the freſh-water of Findern.   Some of the freſh-water fiſhings belong to the pariſh of Forres. Such fiſhings as have been repeatedly aſſeſſed with ſtipends, I preſume, may belong to this pariſh, and theſe are, the two halves of the Long-pool fiſhings, one belonging to the Dalvey eſtate, in this pariſh, and the other to a landholder of Forres pariſh, who has no property but fiſhings here. Two-eight parts of the Nether Water, *i. e.* two-eighths belonging to Dalvey, and two-eighths of the ſame belonging to Birdſ-yards, who has no lands in this pariſh ; (the remaining four-eighths of the Nether Water belonging, as I preſume, to the pariſh of Forres. All the freſh-water fiſhings, as deri-ved, at ſome period, from the Abbots of Kinloſs, and inde-pendent of the adjacent lands, have right to draw nets indif-ferently on either ſide. The ſtell fiſhings ſpecially men-tioned in the decreets of the miniſters of Dyke, are, Eth ſtell, Elven ſtell, the Sheriff's ſtell, and the Eaſter and We-ſter ſtells of Culbin.

Number of Proprietors, Reſident and Non-reſident.—The number of proprietors, in the laſt century, were at leaſt 12 or upwards. For 50 years back, the greater part of the pro-perties have been rather fluctuating. The proprietors, in 1793, are but five ; four landholders, whereof two have fiſh-ings in the pariſh, two have no fiſhings in it, and one has fiſhings without lands.

The reſident proprietors are, James Brodie, Eſq; of Bro-die, and Hugh Grant, Eſq; of Moy. The Earl of Moray retains a family of ſervants at Darnaway, where he occupies the Mains, and keeps his caſtle in repair, for the ſake of a ſhort reſidence when his occaſions call him to the north.

He

He keeps a factor here for his northern properties, who refides at Earlfmill. The proprietor of Dalvey is refident in London.

Mode of Cultivation.—The mode of cultivation is not yet, in the general practice, reduced to eftablifhed rules, or a regular fucceffion of crops ; and all attempts of binding down the mode of procedure upon tenants, by articles, are either fpurned at, or prove abortive. The general prepoffeffion is in favour of whatever mode of cultivation gives the quickeft returns, with leaft expence and trouble. Their practice (as it ought to be) is more the refult of obfervation and experience, than of theory * and fyftem ; yet it is gradually, though flowly, changing for the better. Nobody doubts any longer of the profit of fown graffes, with, or even without, enclofing. Small patches of grafs are fown, and enclofed with flakes or paling by the poorer fort ; and clover and rye grafs, to greater

er

* Such proprietors as are bent on agricultural improvement, are too apt to complain of the flow progrefs of new methods among their farmers, which they erroneoufly impute to ftupidity or obftinacy ; but, confidering how many richer people have fuffered deeply, by new experiments and fpeculations in hufbandry, it is a lucky circumftance for landlords that tenants are not fo venterous as proprietors in thefe particulars. With a heavy rent hanging over them, and their living and credit at ftake, it behoves them not only to fee before they believe, but to be fomewhat eafy before they hazard upon fchemes of enclofing, fallowing, and liming ; and it is not to be expected, that they fhould haftily lofe fight of thofe cautious habits, which have enabled them to keep credit from the beginning. Perhaps the fpeedieft and moft effectual way, of introducing ufeful alterations in their method and management, would be, for proprietors to make farmers of the moft judicious and thorough bred of their farm-fervants. When thefe could be obferved to profit by the new methods they had been bred and accuftomed to, hundreds would copy from a thriving farmer, who has no refources but his plough and better management, for one that will venture to imitate a monied landlord ; whofe crops his tenants may admire, while they remain doubtful and fufpicious how far the profit will repay the expence.

er extent, are ſown in the open fields, which is bringing winter herding more into uſe ; and the quantity of ley-graſs is
much increaſed.

After 3 years reſt, they have 2 good crops of oats before
barley, with the benefit of better ſummer feeding for their
cattle, an increaſe of milk, and enlargement of the breed, in
conſequence of reſting the ground. Potatoes were little
known before the year 1745, and, when tried, yielded no
crops but in lazy beds, or new ground that ſent up no
weeds. It was long before they learned to keep them properly clean. Now, nobody miſſes plentiful crops ; and they
are the beſt improvement in the cultivation of our corn
fields, where, by ſome, they are trenched down, with dung,
by the ſpade, but many have diſcovered, at length, that,
with clean keeping, the beſt crops are after the plough.
The farmers give ground to every cottager for his dung and
culture, which has greatly leſſened the conſumption of grain,
and is the chief ſubſiſtence of the labouring poor. The potatoe crop is ſucceeded by wheat or barley, with ſown graſs ;
and where graſs is not ſown in potatoe-ground, they have 2
crops of oats after the wheat or barley ; then they take
barley, peaſe, and 2 crops of oats again. Flax is commonly
ſown after barley ; and wheat ſometimes after ſown graſs,
when broke up.

The tillage is much better ſince the introduction and general uſe of Engliſh ploughs. There is one indiſputable fact,
which I can only aſcribe to the potatoe culture, and increaſe
of graſs and reſting, that the barley crops are not nearly ſo
much choked as formerly by the gool or yellow gowan,
which is almoſt baniſhed here, in compariſon of former times.
But, with our ſown graſſes, we have got a plentiful importation of ragweed.

Liming, ſummer-fallow, or drill-huſbandry, whether of
turnips

turnips or potatoes, have got no footing yet but among gentlemen-farmers.

Implements of Hufbandry.—All the implements of ordinary hufbandry, are now made more fubftantial and commodious than formerly. Box-carts are coming in ufe for kellochs, and fingle draughts are preferred to double, which ill fuit the ftrength of our fmall horfes.

Manures.—There are no manures in common ufe but compoft dunghills, in which they intermix earth, clay, or water-fand from the burns, with ftable-dung and afhes: They now make very little ufe of moorifh earth.

Seedtime.—Wheat and rye would fhoot before winter, if fown as early in warm as in cold or ftiff foils, and would not be eafily kept from cattle if they were not fown late; they are laid down from Martinmas to the end of December. Oats and peafe from 12th March to 12th April. Oats are fhort, and peafe a poor cover, when early fown here, being too forward to have the full benefit of the July rains. Barley is fown from 10th May to 10th June. Of late, it has been fown in February and March, in dry feafons, and grounds in high order, which gives the weightieft grain; but, in other cafes, the lateft is the thickeft and moft plentiful crop. Flax is fown in April,—and pulled; and potatoes are moftly planted in that month.

Harveft.—Harveft commonly runs from 20th Auguft to 12th October, new ftile.—A ftate of the crop and live-ftock, of 1793, is fubjoined here, being the amount of particulars noted down at every houfe, on the report of the people, comprehending the mains of proprietors, and not omitting the flax and potatoes of trades-people and day-labourers; by
which

which it appears, that, omitting fractions on the ſums total of every kind, the ſowing of 1793 was, of rye, oats, and barley, *in cumulo*, the oats at 5 firlots, 1511 bolls.

Wheat *,	- -	15
Peaſe and beans,	-	46
		1572 1572
Average return at 3½ or 4,		3.5
		7860
		4716

Produce.—Produce reckoned from 5502.0 to 6288 bolls.
Potatoes planted in 1793, 228 bolls, at 8 returns, 1824.
Lintſeed, 1893 Scots pints, ſowed about 12 acres.

Turnips,	- -	60
Fallow,	- -	38
Sown graſs under hay and paſture,	543	543
Infield paſture unſown, or ley-graſs,	- -	340 beſide out-paſture.

Live Stock.—The live ſtock of all ages in 1793 ſtood thus :

Sheep, including lambs, and generally of ſmall ſize,	1533
Black-cattle, including calves, -	1047
Horſes of all kinds, including foals, few of the common ſort reaching 13 hands, -	384
Swine omitted, but may be reckoned at, -	40

Of the value of live ſtock I am no competent judge.

Valued

---

* The ſowing of wheat, in 1793, was a mere trifle, becauſe of low prices and ſtock on hand, and becauſe barley had been riſing for ſeveral years. Wheat is ſown here according to the appearance of demand. In the year 1795, every one ſowed wheat largely.

Valued Rent.—Valued rent by the county books, L. 5674, 6 s. 6 d. Scots.

Real Rent.—Real rent in victual, money, fishings, mills, customs, and wood, L. 2900 Sterling *.

Average of Rents.—The average of rents cannot be stated under 19 s. *per* Scots acre, for corn fields.

Prices of Grain.—The average of grain, for several years prior to 1793. Wheat, 20 s.; oat-meal, weighing 9 stone Dutch,

---

* It is but a small proportion of the present rents that are paid in victual. The bolls have been mostly converted into money-rents, and these money-rents, at different times, augmented. But I have seen a computation of the land-rents and fishings, made by the last minister, about 40 years ago, where the victual-rents are valued at L. 5 Scots, equal 8 s. 4 d.; and the salted salmon at L. 32 Scots, equal L. 2 : 13 : 4 Sterling *per* barrel, of 4 cwt. By this calculation, including but very little money-rent, the amount of the rents of the parish are computed at L. 14,866 : 13 : 4 Scots money, or L. 1238 : 17 : 9 $\frac{4}{11}$ Sterling. Since that time, till now, the rents, computed on a money scale, appear to be more than doubled. But, computed on the scale of produce, their increase appears far less considerable, in regard the number of bolls and fishes then paid, would, according to their present value, fetch the double of what they were then worth. And, in general, it is evident, that in corn parishes along the coasts, where every soil fit for corn was brought under culture many centuries ago, the rents paid in kind, whether of corn or fish, being a proportion of the produce, must have nearly reached their *ultimatum* at a very early period, so as to admit of little rise, except it were on the money scale. In such maritime parishes whose payments were made in produce, the rents would seem to have been heavier about 1633, than at any period since that time. When the valuation of tithes was then introduced, the substitution of one-fifth of the rent, as an equivalent for one-tenth of the produce, seems to warrant a supposition or inference, that the proprietors (whom the Legislature wished rather to ease than to injure) had, in those days, to the amount of value of half the produce on account of rents.

Dutch, 16 s. ; peaſe and rye always the ſame price with oat-
meal, 16 s. ; oats, at 5 firlots *per* boll, 16 s. ; barley, 18 s. *.

Prices of other Proviſions in 1793.—Potatoes *per* boll, of
32 ſtone Dutch, 6 s. 8 d. ; beef from 2 d. to 4 d. ; mutton
3 d. ; ſhot lamb 3 d. ; veal from 3 d. to 4 d. ; pork 3 d. all
Dutch weight; turkies 4 s. 6 d.; geeſe 2 s. 6 d.; ducks 9 d.;
hens 8 d. ; eggs 2 d. *per* dozen; butter 12 s.; and cheeſe
4 s. *per* ſtone, of 22 lbs. Dutch ; ſalmon from 4 d. *per* Dutch
lb. groſs weight, to 2½ d. at different ſeaſons; haddocks
from 1 s. 4 d. to 1 s. 6 d. *per* dozen; cod from 8 d. to 1 s.
2 d. apiece; ſmall ſkate from 6 d. to 8 d. ; flounders from
2½ d. to 4 d. *per* dozen, according to ſize ; herrings, from
Nairn, from 1 d. to 3 d. *per* dozen ; crabs 2 d. ; and lobſters
from Nairn 4 d. apiece.

Wages.—The wages of labouring ſervants, in the houſe,
was, 50 years ago, at 16 s. 8 d. the man, and 7 s. 8 d. the
woman, half-yearly, with a pair of brogues, or apron, value 1 s. : now, they are from L. 3 to L. 4 for men, and from
20 s. to 25 s. for women, half-yearly. Men-ſervants not
domeſtic, get a free-houſe or lodging, and 52 ſtone of meal
for aliment. The number of married ſervants has much
increaſed of late, which is very convenient for rearing up
ſervants in ſucceſſion.

Wages of livery-ſervants from L. 6 to L. 12 ; houſe-maids
from 25 s. to 30 s.

Day-

---

* By a contract of wadſet in 1702, wherein the ſeſſion of Dyke were
creditors for a ſhare, 42 bolls of farm bear are pledged, redeemable in 5
years, for the uſe of 5000 merks Scots, or L. 277 : 15 : 6 $\frac{8}{12}$ Sterling ; by
which contract, the price of barley muſt have been 6 s. 8 d. Sterling *per*
boll.

Day-labour.—Summer and harveſt wages for men 1 s. ; for women 9 d. Winter wages for trenching, ditching, or planting, 8 d. to 9 d. ; all without victuals. Hay-cutting 2 s. 6 d. *per* acre. Journeymen maſons from 1 s. 3 d. to 1 s. 6 d. Carpenters 1 s. to 1 s. 3 d.

Services.—Services of tenants are very generally aboliſhed.

Manufactures.—Of manufactures there is nothing to ſay, but that the harn, tweeling, coarſe linen, and plaiden, made by individuals, are readily bought up at faiŕs by dealers, for high prices, and carried away. The quantities of each kind not known.

Articles of Commerce.—The chief articles of commerce are, grain, black-cattle, iced and barrelled ſalmon, linen-yarn of the coarſer kinds, and wood.

Grain.—The ſurplus of grain for export is very conſiderable ; of wheat ſometimes, of oats and barley always. Oats are ſold at 5 firlots *per* boll, wanting only (according to Bald's Tables) 1 lippy and .5206 of an Engliſh quarter. Barley or farm bear, at 4 firlots, weighs from 17 to 19 ſtone Dutch, wanting 1 firlot 1 lippy and .579 of a lippy, of an Engliſh quarter. A regulation for ſelling all grain by weight would do juſtice to good farmers, make bad farmers better, and render purchaſers by commiſſion more ſecure. It would be convenient, at the ſame time, to regulate the weight of hay, wool, butter, and cheeſe, and bring the different counties to one ſtandard, that buyers and ſellers might have nothing to differ about, or ſettle, but the price.

Cattle.

Cattle.—Runts, and yell or dry cows, are the chief articles in the cattle trade : we ſpare ſome of every kind, and ſtots ſell deareſt ; yet they ought rather to be wrought out. It would be more profitable to carry on the farm-work altogether with oxen, which are fit for every work except riding, are much more eaſily maintained, are far leſs liable to ſudden diſeaſes, and, in the end, fetch a good price for beef: when old, horſes muſt be given to the dogs. Some have eſtimated the difference of working a farm with horſes, and with oxen, to amount, all things conſidered, to the value of the rent : the ſaving upon oats is great.

Fiſhings of Salmon.—Freſh ſalmon are ſometimes ſent to London in ice; but are moſtly kitted at Findern. The trade has been much monopolized by an Aberdeen company, who took leaſes of all the fiſhings they could get throughout the north, and bought up the fiſh caught by other leſſees. The boil-houſe prices, allowed by that company, were, in the firſt of the ſeaſon to the 1ſt of May, 4 d. *per* lb. groſs weight ; from 1ſt May to end of May, 3 d.; thence to the end of June 2¼ d. and while they continue to kit. Three fiſhes of 10 lib. ſuffice for one kit; this, at the early price, comes to 10 s. The kit, boiling, and curing, with freight, and other coſts, bring up the charges to 13 s. *per* kit; which fetches, at London, from 18 s. to 31 s. 6 d. The profit, therefore, on kitting fiſh, bought at the above prices, runs from 94 to 135 *per cent.* nearly.

In times of ſcarcity, they kit as long as it is allowable to fiſh. But, generally, after the 1ſt of June, the raw fiſh are cured in barrels, with one-half boll of foreign ſalt to each barrel. From 30 to 40 well ſized fiſh make a barrel, of 4 cwt. The ſalt and barrel coſt from 12 s. to 13 s. The freight is 3 s. to London, and 4 s. 6 d. to Holland. The barrel,

rel, of 4 cwt. formerly fold for L. 4, and fometimes for L. 5, now it fetches only 50 s.

Cod.—Cod are fometimes caught in great abundance, by Nairn and Findern boats, in the beginning of winter, when the weather cannot ferve for drying them. An adventurer, from this parifh, cured a quantity in barrels, like falted falmon, carried them to London, and made no lofs by the adventure, though they fold heavily, and muft have been but unpleafant food. But had thefe cod been parboiled, and cured with vinegar at the boil-houfe, like ketled falmon, it is believed, fuch foufed fifh would have excelled the falted, as much as the kitted falmon exceeds the falted, in quality and price.

Seals.—There are alfo fea-calves or feals on the coaft of this parifh, whereof one man has killed 130 in a year, worth 4 s. apiece, for their oil and fkin. The matter of feal-fifhing is the more deferving of attention, becaufe, befide the intrinfic value of feals, they lie in wait for falmon, and frighten them away from a fhallow coaft.

Yarn.—The yarn-trade has fallen off greatly fince the ufe of cottons hath become almoft univerfal. There are yet 3 yarn factors in the parifh, who buy up yarn fpun from home flax, and give out foreign flax to be fpun, from $2\frac{1}{4}$ d. to $3\frac{1}{2}$ d. *per* hank. They were in ufe to expend about L. 500 a-year for the fpinning and purchafe of yarn; now they do not exceed L. 300 in whole. From the number of weavers in the parifh, I fuppofe the high prices for coarfe cloth makes the fpinners manufacture their own lint for the fairs. From 20 cuts to $2\frac{1}{2}$ hanks is the common grift of fpinning here.

Wood.

Wood.—The wood market has already begun briſkly, and will ſhortly be great. One heritor draws a hundred a-year, for 7 years, for the cutting of one fir park, which will be planted again when it is cleared. He has another ready for felling down, and ſeverals riſing in ſucceſſion. So that moderation in cutting, and diligence in planting again what is cleared, will bring the buſineſs to a very conſiderable ſtanding rent.

Villages, Inns, and Still.—There are villages at Broom of Moy, Kinteſak, and Dyke; at which laſt there is an inn, near the poſt road, and another inn at the Ferry Boat, on the eaſt ſide of the river; and no other inns or alehouſes. One licenſed ſtill, of 38 gallons, has ſupplied this pariſh; I believe one of 30 might ſuffice.

Roads, and Statute Labour.—The roads being naturally good, there are no turnpikes, nor any need or wiſh for them. The ſtatute labour is exacted, which keeps the roads in tolerable repair. Commutation was attempted, but it raiſed diſcontent, and was dropped.

Bridges.—Three ſtout wooden bridges, floored acroſes, railed, and painted, have been built, at Moy, Dalvey, and Barley-mill, near the fords of the Beg-Bourne, at the coſt of L. 114, 7 s. Sterling, out of 5¼ years of the ſtipends accruing at the laſt vacancy.

They admit no carriages, nor even the poſt-cart; but the horſe and mail can paſs. Three ſmall ſtone bridges were alſo built on the public road, out of the ſame fund, for L. 30, 14 s.

State of the Church.—A new and commodious church, of 66 by 33 feet, inſide, was built in 1781, at the expence of the heritors, for the ſum of L. 525, beſide the carriages performed

formed by the parish. It is neatly plastered and ceiled, well lighted, paved in the areas, and regularly seated. It has a geometrical stair in each end, with galleries quite round ; and none are allowed to bury in it. The plan has been adopted by other parishes.

Manse.—The manse and offices were completely rebuilt and slated in 1790, and garden-walls built, of stone and lime, for L. 321 : 18 : 3, out of the above mentioned vacant stipends. L. 101 : 8 : 7 of these stipends went to the payment of interim assistants, during the vacancy ; and the remnant, to other necessary purposes within the parish.—On the 19th January 1795, a still fire broke out, near mid-day, with inextinguishable vehemence, in a room that had been deafened with straw and shavings of wood, instead of clay, whereby the manse, but not the offices, was rapidly consumed. The walls remained entire, and the heritors completely repaired the dwelling-house, for L. 170 : 18 : 3, in 1795-6.

Stipend, Glebes, and Patronage.—The living, which had not been augmented since 1650, was made better in June 1795, by an addition of 16 bolls more barley, and about L. 15 more money. It stands now at 106 bolls 1 firlot barley, 7 bolls 2 firlots oat-meal, at 9 stones, with L. 40 : 15 : 2 Sterling of money-stipend, and L. 5 more for communion-elements. There is a glebe of 6 acres at Dyke, and a small one in the other parish, for which the proprietor of Moy pays a rent of 6 bolls of barley. The minister has L. 1, 13 s. 4 d. for grass-money. The living, with its accommodations, according to present prices, may be reckoned at L. 150.

The patronage has been lately declared a vice-right, between the Crown and the heritor of Easter Moy, Hugh Grant, Esquire.

The

The incumbents, ſince the annexation, in 1618, have been, Mr William Dunbar, prebendary of Moy before 1618, and afterwards miniſter of the united pariſhes, till 1624; Mr William Falconer ſenior, from 1625 to 1674; Mr William Falconer junior, from 1674 to 1689; Mr A-lexander Forbes, from 1689 to 1708; Mr James Chalmers, from 1709 to 1726; Mr Robert Dunbar, from 1727 to to 1782; and, Mr John Dunbar, tranſlated from Knock-ando, in 1788, a widower, with three ſons, and one daugh-ter.

Poor.—Aſſeſſments for the maintenance of the poor have never been attempted here. They are believed, and not without reaſon, to encourage idleneſs and inconſiderate ex-pences. The charity of the pariſhoners would afford ſuffi-cient aid to the pariſh poor, if it were not ſo much fore-ſtalled by vagrant and ſtrolling beggars, recommended, out of their own pariſhes, to the public at large, by canting cer-tificates, deſerving of no regard.

The average number of enrolled poor, for the 7 years from 1789 to 1795, incluſive of both years, is 61. Among theſe, the church-ſeſſion diſpenſes all the caſh in hand by half-yearly diſtributions; the one in February; the other in Auguſt; which laſt includes the meal of 3 bolls of bear : L. 5, deſtined for clothing 12 children, is divided each No-vember.

Funds.—The parochial funds, from which theſe diſtribu-tions are made, are, the Sabbath collections, with ſmall fines for illicit amours, and the dues of a velvet pall ; all which are booked, as they come in, both in the treaſurer's ac-counts, and in thoſe kept for a check by the ſeſſion-clerk. The average of theſe three articles, for the ſeven years
aforeſaid,

aforefaid, appears, by the cafh-book, to have been *per an-*
num, - - L. 25 7 8 Sterling.

Add the annualrents of L. 66 : 13 : 4,
which has accrued, either from legacies or favings of former times,
and lies at intereft, for bettering
the diftributions, - 3 6 8

Add 40½ ftone or more, barley-meal,
from 3 bolls barley, paid out of St
Ninian's Croft, by a mortgage of
Mr William Falconer fenior, one
of the former minifters, value, 2 14 0

Add the intereft of L. 100, deftined
by Henry Vafs, for yearly clothing to 12 fatherlefs or deftitute children, which is difpenfed each November, - 5 0 0

The average of the yearly amount of
the funds is, - L. 36 8 4

Deduce 20 s. to the precentor, and
15 s. to the officer, yearly, as their
fees, - - 1 15 0

Remains the yearly average of diftributions, for the above 7 years, L. 34 13 4

This 7 years average of receipts and expenditures for the
poor, which includes occafional fupplies in times of ficknefs,
is a fmall pittance among fuch a number. But, in fevere
feafons, or times of fcarcity, the refident proprietors fometimes ftep forward, and fend meal, to be divided among the
labouring poor, which is not entered in the feffion accounts.
And there is a lodge of free mafons in the parifh, who
have

have a laudable fympathy for the poor, and give fupply to feveral from their own funds.

The collections, which are far from liberal, are but a fmall proportion of the charity given by houfe-holders. But, every one has a right to difpenfe his own charity to his own mind.

The feffion has a right of recommending patients from this parifh, to be received *gratis* in the Infirmaries of Edinburgh and Aberdeen, in confequence of a bequeft, by the above mentioned Henry Vafs, made upon that condition, to each of thefe charitable inftitutions. Every heritor has a right to a vote in the management of the poor's funds; and the books are open at all times for infpection of all concerned. The accounts of receipts and expenditures, kept by the clerk and treafurer, are every year revifed and compared, and being found to agree, the treafurer is formally acquitted of his intromiffions, by a minute entered into the book of difcipline, and takes charge again, *de novo*.

On thefe occafions, an edict is ferved 10 free days before, notifying the meeting for infpecting and paffing the treafurer's accounts, and warning heritors and all concerned to attend.

Schools and Scholars.—There is another parochial fund, deftined for two fchools in the village of Dyke; the one for boys; the other for girls. It confifts of the intereft of 3500 merks, $= $ L. $194:8:10\frac{4}{12} \div 20 = $ L. $9:14:5\frac{8}{12}$ Sterling; the intereft of 1000 merks, payable to the parochial or grammar fchoolmafter, $= $ L. $2:15:6\frac{8}{12}$; and the intereft of 2500 merks to the miftrefs of the woman-fchool, $= $ L. $6:18:10\frac{8}{12}$.

The grammar fchoolmafter has alfo L. 1 out of the collections, and 16 bolls bear, one-half paid by the heritors,

tors, and the other half by the parifhoners. He teaches Englifh and writing for 1 s. 6 d. *per* quarter; arithmetic for 1 s. 8 d. *per* ditto; Latin for 2 s. 6 d. *per* ditto; menfuration and land-furveying for 4 s. 6 d. *per* ditto; geometry for 7 s. 6 d. *per* ditto; and book-keeping for 10 s. 6 d. and 15 s. He receives 1 s. 6 d. for proclamation of bans; 6 d. for recording baptifms; and 4 d. for extending certificates : and has 40 fcholars at an average. The falary and emoluments amount to L. 33, befides his lodging, in the fchool-houfe, which was rebuilt and flated in 1785, with a floored fchoolroom, and 2 fmall chambers, for the mafter's accommodation.

The woman's fchool is a joint foundation, in the year 1702, refting on a bequeft from John Anderfon, writer in Edinburgh; and a further deftination by James Brodie of that Ilk, the truftee, who added 500 merks to Anderfon's donation of 2000 merks, gave off ground, and built thereon a flated houfe of 2 floors, with garrets, for the accommodation of the miftrefs and fcholars; and gave alfo a garden at his own expence. His heirs, though conjoined with the heritors and feffion, are managers *fine quibus non.* The falary, at the beginning, in 1702, was 21 bolls bear, mortgaged for a capital of L. 138 : 17 : $9\frac{1}{12}$ Sterling, or L. 2500 merks, belonging to this fchool. At the redemption of the mortgage or wadfet, the falary was reduced to L. 6 : 18 : $10\frac{8}{12}$ Sterling, the legal intereft of the capital. The fchool-houfe, though ftill in ufe, is ruinous, and in urgent need of immediate repair *.

Averages

* There was once a great refort from Caithnefs, Sutherland, Rofs, &c. to this boarding-fchool, where young gentlewomen were taught reading, knitting ftockings, marking, plain and coloured feam, and mufic, by the miftrefs; and writing and arithmetic by the parochial fchoolmafter. Many daughters of men of property were educated here, without reforting for accomplifhments any where elfe.

Averages for ascertaining the ancient Population.—Finding no lists of the ancient or modern population, prior to 1788, nor any list of deaths or burials, I subjoin, from the registers of births and marriages, what follows:

Years.	Marriages.	Births.	Males.	Females.
1671	17	69	42	27
—72	16	64	39	25
—73	14	59	25	34
—74	10	70	41	29
—75	18	81	50	31
—76	8	61	30	31
—77	10	69	58	41
	—— Average.	—— Average.	—— Average.	—— Average.
	7)93(13.286	7)503(71.857	7)285(40.714	7)218(31.143
1694	17	71	40	28
—95	24	59	31	42
—96	15	94	52	31
—97	9	69	40	29
—98	14	97	52	45
—99	15	39	26	23
1700	9	36	22	14
	7)103(14.714	7)465(66.13	7)253(36.14	7)212(30.285
1765	11	43	21	22
—66	12	41	25	16
—67	8	35	22	13
—68	7	39	20	19
—69	11	40	22	18
—70	17	36	18	18
—71	10	41	22	19
	7)76(10.857	7(275(39.286	7)150(21.43	7)125(17.857
1787	10	21	8	13
—88	9	30	10	20
—89	6	31	18	13
—90	6	21	12	9
—91	10	41	21	20
—92	16	40	21	19
—93	12	34	15	19
	7)69(9.857	7)218(31.143	7)105(15.	7)113(16.143

Present

Prefent Population, and other Statiftical Particulars.—At a parochial vifitation and enrollment, in 1788, the population was found to be 1564 fouls. At another enrollment, in 1793, (when the numbers had become 35 lefs), the various informations then obtained, and committed to writing, afford materials for the Tables of Population and other Statiftical particulars that follow :

Population Table for 1793.

Souls in 1793,	-	-	1529
Families,	-	-	345
Average number in *per* family, $\frac{1529}{345}$ = 4.432			
Males,	-	-	728 $\Big\}$ = 1529
Females,	-	-	801
Aged below 10,	-	-	375
From 10 to 20,	-	-	360
—— 20 to 50,	-	-	537 $\Big\}$ = 1529
—— 50 to 70,	-	-	206
—— 70 to 100,	-	-	51
None exceeding 83,			
Uninhabited houfes,	-		0
Houfes inhabited by 1,		39	39
———————— 2,		63	126
———————— 3,		56	168
———————— 4,		43	172
———————— 5,		49	245
———————— 6,		27	162
———————— 7,		22	154
———————— 8,		19	152
———————— 9,		5	45
———————— 10,		8	80
Carried forward		331	1343

Brought

Brought forward 331		1343
Houſes inhabited by 11,	5	55
———— ———— 12,	3	36
———————— 13,	1	13
———————— 14,	1	14
——_———— 15,	2	30
———————— 17,	1	17
———————— 21,	1	21

Families 345   1529 Souls.

Inhabitants variouſly claſſed.

Married perſons, - -	459
Widowers, - -	26
Widows, - - -	53
Unmarried men, from 50 to 70, -	5
Unmarried women, from 20 to 50, -	141
Male-ſervants in whole, - -	122
Ditto married, - - -	27
Female-ſervants in whole, -	111
Ditto married, - -	2
Large farmers, as from L. 50 to L. 100 and upwards,	12
Leſſer farmers, under L. 50, - -	75
Pendicles in the hands of tradeſmen or crofters having ploughs, - -	28
Ploughs in whole, - -	115
Reſident proprietors of lands, -	2
Non reſident ditto, - -	3
Non-reſident ditto of fiſhings, - -	1
Factors, - - -	2
Eſtabliſhed clergy, - -	1
Other clergy, - -	0
Diſſenters, all but 2 of the Seceſſion, -	39

Parochial

Parochial fchoolmafter, - -	1
Ditto fchoolmiftrefs, - -	1
Other private teachers, - -	9
Scholars of all kinds, - -	179
Students in divinity, - -	2
Private tutors, - - -	1
College ftudents, - -	1
Half-pay lieutenant, - -	1
Ditto navy furgeon, - -	1
Ditto mafter and commander, -	1
Penfioners of artillery, - -	1
Out-penfioners of Chelfea College, -	4
Millers, - - -	6
Ferrymen, with 2 boats, on Findern, -	1
Farriers and blackfmiths in whole, (apprentices included), - - -	7
Mafons, (apprentices included), -	27
Slaters, - - -	2
Plafterers, - - -	1
Carpenters for country work, -	23
Weavers, - -	31
Shoemakers, - -	12
Tailors, - -	16
Mantuamakers, - -	2
Cartwrights, - -	18
Turners, - - -	2
Coopers, - - -	2
Midwives, - - -	3
Tinkers, - - -	1
Country merchants who are yarn factors, -	3
Salmon fifhers, - -	28
Day-labourers, - -	42
Gardeners, (2 paying rent), - -	5

Other

Other Matters

Flour-mills,	2
Meal-mills,	5
Barley-mill,	1
Saw-mill,	1
Wind-mill, for pumping a quarry,	1
Pigeon-houſes,	5
Ale-houſes,	2
A ſtill of 38 gallons,	1
A hot-houſe for fruit,	1
Oxen wains,	15
Double draughts,	16
Peat-carts,	291
Coach,	1
Chaiſe,	1
Servants paying tax,	10
Saddle and carriage horſes,	13

Cauſes of the Decline of Population.—The population of this pariſh, as far as can be gueſſed by multiplying the average of births by 31⅓, would ſeem, from the above Tables, to have been, in 1677, as high as 2200. From that period there are three viſible cauſes of its ſubſequent decline.

1. One unavoidable cauſe, was the overwhelming of the populous barony of Culbin *, by a violent drifting of ſand from the Maviſton hills ; and, excepting a ſmall remnant
fartheſt

---

* The ſand had been making great encroachments before it overwhelmed the mains and garden of Culbin. But that event, which completed the buſineſs, muſt have happened conſiderably earlier than the date aſſigned in Shaw's Hiſtory of the Province ; becauſe it is ſpecially mentioned in the Act of Parliament, againſt pulling of bent, paſſed in 1695, intitled, for Preſervation of Lands adjacent to Sand-hills, and is mentioned as one of the reaſons for paſſing that act, K. Wil. III. 1 Par. 5 Seſ. Act xxx.

fartheft from the coaft, the depopulation of that barony
was completed before the clofe of the laft century.

2. Another caufe, affecting all the other eftates in the parifh, is the change that has taken place fince the rebellion,
1745, in the fize and number of farms. Formerly they
were very fmall and numerous, running from 4 to 16 bolls
of rent; now they are larger, and not half fo numerous as
they were. A multitude of fmall farms is very favourable
to population; yet the enlargement of farms, to a certain
degree, was needful in this parifh, where the grounds fo
much needed reft, and where milk, butter, and butcher-
meat were fo fcarce; and, had there been manufactures
fufficient to employ the hands fuperfeded from tillage, the
enlargement of farms might have been favourable to agriculture, without diminifhing the population. But this not
being the cafe,

3. The neglect of manufactures may be ftated as a third
caufe, and the greateft of any, affecting the population of this
parifh. The prefent poffeffors, finding that there are not
fo many rooms as formerly for farmers, breed their children to handicrafts; and thefe, not finding employment at
home, pufh their way to Edinburgh, Glafgow, Paifley, or
London, from whence they feldom find their way back to
fettle here. This caufe affects moft of the northern diftricts,
where manufactures do not meet with the attention and encouragement that they deferve. This is what occafions
yearly emigrations, during the feafons of fummer and harveft work, to places where there is more employment and
higher wages; and thefe fhort excurfions frequently end in
a removal to manufacturing towns at the laft.

Remedies.—The remedies are pointed out by the caufes
of emigration, or decreafe of people.

1. To

1. To divide the larger farms when the leaſes have run, and bring them into proper compaſs. Evils are generally correĉted by their effeĉts; and wiſe proprietors begin to diſcover, that ſmall farmers make better payments than the great, eſpecially when they pay in produce. It is beyond doubt, that more corn was raiſed when farms were ſmaller than at the preſent time.

2. The introduĉtion and patronage of manufaĉtures would not only prevent further depopulation, but would give new life and ſpirit to agriculture, bring an increaſe of people, by promoting and providing for marriage, and form a ſolid and ſatisfaĉtory baſis for increaſing rents. If manufaĉtures were firſt eſtabliſhed, rents would quickly riſe of courſe, and the enlargement of farms would occaſion no diſtreſs. But it is a ſhort-ſighted policy, that aims at an increaſe of rent, by a decreaſe of people, whoſe labours can at once be made profitable to landlords, and comfortable to themſelves. A more timely attention to fiſheries and manufaĉtures, and particularly to the manufaĉturing of wool, in the Highlands of Scotland, might have prevented the emigrations to America, and even increaſed the ſources of public proſperity and national defence. It is a ſpeculation equally mean and hazardous, to diſpoſſeſs brave and attached Highlanders, to make way for a population of ſheep. The maxim, that it is lawful for a man to do what he will with his own, has already miſled too many; it is ſo far from being univerſally true, that it has its limitations in every kind of property. *Quia intereſt reipublicæ ne quis re ſua malè utatur :* He who uſes his own to the detriment of the public, incurs juſt blame and obnoxiouſneſs. One's right to diſpoſe of his own money, does not extend to a right of melting down the current coin ; and more eſpecially, in all feudal tenures, there are reſerved rights of the Sovereign, as head of the community, whereby proprietors

ſtand

ftand amenable for fuch abufe of property as is prejudicial to the common-weal. For though ftatute law never has, and probably never will, intermeddle with a fubject fo delicate, complicated, and difficult, as fixing limitations on the ufe of property, it ought to be more generally underftood than it would feem to be, that malverfations and abufes of power, in the ufe of property, iffuing in public detriment and alarming depopulation, have already been brought under the lafh of the common law, at the inftance of the Crown, even in South Britain. A lawyer of the laft century, Mr Robert Powel, of Wells, publifhed a treatife, in 1636, intitled, Depopulation Arraigned, where, at page 84, he narrates a trial and fentence, at Michaelmas term, decimo Caroli, *anno* 1635. The judgment againft this depopulator, for converting fo much arable into pafture, was accompanied with heavy penalties, and with circumftances of humiliating difgrace. Such as wifh to be more fully informed, may have recourfe to the records of the times, not omitting thofe of the Privy Council of England.

Quarries.—There are 2 free ftone quarries in this parifh, both of the harder kind. And there is a limeftone rock on the weft fide of the river, at the Boat-pool, but, for want of fuel, it is more eligible to purchafe lime, than to burn it here.

Fuel and Coals.—Peats are very fcarce, dear, and of little ftrength. The parifh would have been in uncommon diftrefs for want of fuel, long fince, had it not obtained a feafonable fupply from the weedings of fir plantations, and an eafement of the duty upon coals, which begin to be ufed by the lower ranks, becaufe they afford light to fpin. Newcaftle coal are bought from 1 s. 10 d. to 2 s. *per* barrel.

Antiquities.

Antiquities.—At Darnaway, the feat of the Earls of Moray, of the Randolph, Dunbar, Douglas, and Stewart race,
ftands an old caftle, nobly elevated, with great range and
variety of profpect, which has been built at different periods, adjoining to a princely hall, that had been erected by
Thomas Randolph, Regent of Scotland, during the minority of King David Bruce, for the reception of his numerous vaffals. This hall is by much the oldeft and moft remarkable part of buildings, which are now altogether a
venerable pile. After all the changes it has undergone, it
is ftill a pleafing monument of ancient hofpitality and magnificence. The length is 89 feet, and breadth 35. It has
yet from 18 to 20 feet of fide wall, though it wants about
12 of its original height, by reafon of a range of vaults conftructed on its ground-floor, for cellars, with a ftone pave-
ment above them. It has a battery in the outer end, and
above that a mufic gallery, from fide to fide. There was a
large chimney in the oppofite end, and another fpacious
fire-place in one of its fides.

The roof is fupported by diagonal couples and rafters of
maffy oak, more fuperb than any modern ceiling, and refembles that of the Parliament Houfe of Edinburgh, and
Guildhall of London. Earl Randolph's hofpitable board, of
thick oaken plank, curioufly bordered and indented, ftanding on 6 pillars, draws out at one end to double length.
His oaken chair, on which are coarfely carved the bearings
of his office and arms, weighs about 60 libs. avoirdupois,
and differs little from the coronation chair in Weftminfter
Abbey.

Coins.—In digging the foundation of the new church, behind the old one, a day-labourer found a depofit, as he was
working alone, before the arrival of his companions, and, covering it up, contrived to employ himfelf and the others,
till

till night, in digging the foundations in a different quarter. Before morning, he had fecured the contents of an earthen pot, of old coins, which, at convenience, were fold as bullion, for about L. 46. They were all of one fize, broader than a fixpence, and very thin; but the filver was fine and unfullied. Such as had been unavoidably fcattered, were found, by the teft of Anderfon's Numefmata, to be groat pieces; with a rude impreffion of a head, hand, and fceptre, upon each. They had been ftruck, at many different places, both in Scotland and England, as appeared by the one fide; on the other fide, they bore the impreffion and name of one or other of thefe contemporary princes, Henry II. of England, or King William of Scotland. Some, that had been ftruck at Striveling, had the words RE VILLAM; *Re* being the Gaelic word for King. I faw fome of both kinds.

Records.—The oldeft parifh record now extant, goes back as far as 1610. It is very ill to read. In fome periods, the records feem very exactly kept; in others, they are very much deranged and confufed. No record of burials has ever been regularly kept; as there are two burial grounds, and two grave-diggers, it is the more difficult to be exact. At prefent, there are three records carried on at once. A regifter of baptifms and marriages; a cafh-book; and a book of difcipline, for recording the proceedings of the church feffion. This has frequent references to the cafh-book, and the cafh-book to it. All of thefe new records commenced in 1788.

Mifcellaneous Obfervations.—In the laft century, James Brodie of that Ilk, and his brother-in-law, Sir Robert Dunbar of Grangehill, had each of them 9 marriageable daughters, who were coufin-germans; and 8 out of each family were married.—A rape, committed by a foldier, about 50 years
ago,

ago, was punished by his public execution.—A murder was committed, in 1780, on a strolling packman; the perpetrator never was discovered.

Character of the People.—The people are, very generally, decent, quiet, and well affected to the religion and government under which they live. They are neither addicted to a seafaring or military life; yet the frequency of recruiting parties reconciles them, when that business is accompanied with music, mirth, and drink. They can live poorly, to dress neatly; but few think of laying any thing up. On public occasions, there are not a few who will spend, what they can ill afford, in vying to be neighbour-like, with others who are either more rich, or more inconsiderate than themselves. In general, they are better fed and clothed, and have greater variety of convenient furniture, than they had 40 years ago. But the use of tea makes rather an alarming progress among many, who need a better nourishment, at less expence.

Means of bettering their Condition.—The best means to meliorate their situation, would be manufactures, for which this parish, with such a soil and climate, and so near the port of Findhorn, is no unpromising situation. Having plenty of flat grounds, well watered, and being very fit for the cultivation of flax, it seems by nature best adapted for the linen manufacture, in all its branches, of flax-dressing, spinning, weaving, bleaching, and thread-making.

Cotton manufacture is now going forward at Skibo and Spinningdale, where L. 4000 a-year is now circulated, in Sutherland, for which branch this parish would be no less commodious.

Of

Of woollen manufacture, knitted stockings seems the best, as requiring most manual labour, and affording the best recompense for it.

A stone bridge over the Findern, and another over the Big-bourne, on the post-road, would be of great advantage to this parish, for an open communication to all the villages and towns west of the river, with Forres and Elgin. For want of this, the daily posts are often long detained, lives are frequently endangered, and sometimes lost. In 1781, 11 were lost by the oversetting of the ferry-boat on the day of a Forres market. On such occasions, there is no preventing the people from overloading the boat.

The servitude of thirlage, remains yet a dead weight upon agriculture. It retards all improvements in the machinery and art of grinding, occasions great waste of time, indifferent service, and vexatious debates and law-suits, about abstracted multures. A conversion of all multures, and a consequent freedom to grind wherever people found themselves best served, and the acceptance of an equivalent, for buying off the astriction of one heritor's lands to another heritor's mills, would bring every thing to rights, and make a great change for the better. This measure, adopted by general consent, would be a laudable concession to public utility; and, on supposition of full indemnification, could do no prejudice to any. This measure was long since adopted in the county of Clackmanan. Its happy effects were soon observed, in an emulation among the millers, to excel in their machinery, and art, and promp service; and the corn yielded considerably more meal than ever it had formerly produced, in consequence of an improved management.

The sale of all grain by a common standard of weight, will be generally approven.

APPEN-

A P P E N D I X.

Cauſes, Antiquity, and Effects, of the Maviſton Sand-hills, &c.

IN paſſing through the pariſh of Dyke, no object ſtrikes
the attention ſooner, or more excites the curioſity of travellers, than the ſand-hills, piled up along the coaſt. Some
account of their cauſes, antiquity, and effects, may be expected in a publication of this nature.

Theſe hills contain no different ſtrata, or other marks of
an original ſtate. Nor could they receive their formation
from the ſea, as is commonly ſuppoſed, having no mixture
of ſhells, pebbles, or ſea-weeds. They are an immenſe accumulation of a pure white ſand, of the ſmalleſt grit.
Doubtleſs the ſea has, at ſome time, ſupplied the material;
but the winds have always been the arbiters of their form,
ſituation, and ſize. They riſe gradually on the ſouth-weſt,
and are ſteep on the ſouth-eaſt ſide. This is the tract of our
ſtrongeſt winds here, which further appears, by the bent and
falling of trees in the ſame direction. The ſmalleſt particles are always the firſt ſuſpended, and the laſt that are depoſited by water, after which, they lie neareſt to the winds,
and are eaſily ſwept away, while ſtones, pebbles, ſhells, and
ſand of a larger grit, are left upon the beach. This accounts for the ſhape of theſe hills, and for the fineneſs and
purity

purity of their fand. It muft have been a prodigious agitation of the ocean, that could fo affect an inland frith, as to throw out, within reach of the wind, fuch accumulations of fand, as are now contained in the parifhes of Kinlofs, Dyke, and Auldearn. But the wide opening into the Moray Frith, from Buchan-Nefs to Dungfbay-Head, has made it liable, wherever the coaft was flat, to a wider inundation, and deeper load of fand, through the confinement of a large body of water, forced up into a narrowing channel. But the violent commotions of the German Ocean, are vifible on the coaft of Holland, and all along the eaftern coaft of Great Britain, from the Goodwin Sands in Kent, to the Pentland Frith.

Though the era of the fand's arrival here, is beyond the reach of local tradition, hiftory takes notice of feveral inundations, when large quantities of fea-fand, might have been lodged, and augmented upon our flat and early cultivated coaft. The deluge, in later times, that feems moft likely to have had the greateft effect, in this way, upon our ifland, is that inundation of the German Ocean which fwept away the princely eftate of Earl Goodwin, in Kent, and left the Goodwin Sands in its room. Such a commotion of the waters as could produce that effect, muft have reached all the friths, on the eaftern coafts, as far up as the falt-water could flow, and muft have affected the navigation, as well as the agriculture, of the coaft, upon that fide.

The era of this calamitous event, was in the clofe of the 11th century, in the reign of King William Rufus of England, and near the demife of King Malcolm Canmore of Scotland.

1. Trufsler, who has probably followed Blair's Chronology, and the Englifh hiftorians, in this matter, refers the origin of the Goodwin Sands to the year 1100.

2. To

2. To the like devaſtation in Scotland, and the ſupera-
bundant lodgement of ſand upon our coaſt, Buchanan ſeems
clearly to allude, at the end of the Life of Malcolm Canmore; and though he avoids ſpecifying the exaᵭ year of
King Malcolm's demiſe, it is clear, from his deſcription, and
his uſe of the word *prodigia*, that he has, in this matter,
grounded on the authority of Boethius. The indefinite expreſſions of Buchanan, " Inter prodigia hoc tempore nume-
" ratur, maris Germanici tam inſolita inundatio, ut non
" agros modo dimeiferit, et arenis obruerit, ſed et vices,
" oppida et arces everterit."

3. Boethius, according to whom King Malcolm died in
1097, comes within three year's of Truſsler's date, and extends this commotion of the ſea expreſsly to the Moray
Frith. " Incidit Malcomi mors anno redemptionis ſupra
" milleſimum ſeptimo & nonageſimo, idibus Oᵭobris;
" Regni vero ejus trigeſimo ſeptimo. Eodem vero anno,
" Albion multis graviſſimisque prodigiis territa eſt. Nam
" exundatione Germanici maris, multi vici, caſtella, op-
" pidaque, & maximæ ſylvæ ſubrutæ ſunt, in Scotia pariter
" & in Anglia. Qua tempeſtate ſedeta, Agri Godovini,
" cujus ſuperius mentionem fecimus, haud procul a Thami-
" ſis fluminis oſtiis, arena obruti ſunt, quæ & noſtra me-
" moriᴀ Godovinæ Arenæ appellantur, vulgo Godvin Sands.
" Nec parum Agri Moraviani in Scotia eodem tempore a
" mari eſt devaſtatum, ſubrutis a fundamento Caſtellis, de-
" letisque urbibus quibuſdam, cultuique effeᴔum humano,
" (ob arenas a mari egeſtas) ineptum. Tonitrua faᴔa tam in-
" gentia, tamque immani fragore horrida, ut multi homines
" in agris iᴔi, & animantia quædam perierint. Turres
" quoque eorum impetu proſtratæ. In Laudonia, Fifa et An-
" guſia, arbores et ſegetes multis in locis ſponte incenſæ."

4. In the ſame year which Boethius mentions as ſo de-
ſtruᴔive to Moray, John of Fordun, in his Scotichronicon,
B. vii.

B. vii. ch. 50. takes notice of the appearance of a comet, which feems, at leaft, to have much affected the atmofphere; and poffibly its approximation to the earth, in its aphelion, might have occafioned an unufual fwell of tides, and contributed, in that year, to make the commotion of the waters more violent and deftructive. " Anno Dom. 1107, incepit " ordo Trinitatis, & eodem anno, imperii Henrici Quarti " quadragefimo primo, (i. e. in the 41ft year of the Empe- " ror Henry the IV.), cometis in occidente apparuit, a pri- " ma hepdomade Octobris. Nimia aquarum inundatione " autumnalis falio impeditur, & fterilitas frugum terræ fe- " quitur." The " inundatio aquarum" feems not more applicable to the clouds than to the fea, overwhelming the beft and warmeft cultivated lands on the coaft, beft adapted to the production of winter grain. For thefe two laft quotations, I am indebted to Profeffor Macleod, Sub-principal of King's College, Aberdeen ; and there feems to be no doubt, that all the above quotations relate to the era of the Goodwin Sands.

There is another paffage in Fordun, B. x. ch. 22. quoted in Lord Hailes's Annals, that feems to relate to an after inundation, about 1266, being more than 160 years later than the above dates. " Sed in profefto undecem mille virgi- " num, tempeftas permaxima, ab aquilone fuborta eft, unde " mare in rabiem concitatum, fines debitas miro modo " tranfgrediens, domos, villas, arbores, complanavit, et " damna plurima intulit multis locis, fed maxime inter flu- " mina de le Tay & Tweed. Tempeftas talis non eft vifa, a " diebus Noæ ufque ad diem illum, funt adhuc veftigia ma- " nifeftant."

I have alfo been told, upon good authority, that there is a paffage in the Red Book of the Priory of Plufcardin, now lying in the Advocates Library, at Edinburgh, that would feem to refer to an earlier inundation than thofe above mentioned,

mentioned, provided there be no miſtake about the date, viz. that the whole laigh of Moray had been covered by the ſea in the year 1010. A tranſpoſition of the two middle figures, (which would be no ſurpriſing ſlip of memory), would bring the year 1010, mentioned by my informer, to correſpond exactly with Trufsler's date of the origin of the Goodwin Sands, in 1100. Such as have accefs, may have recourſe to that book.

Many of the beſt lands in this pariſh, which, from their ſituation, could not eſcape being overflowed in the 11th century, ſtill continue in ſafety and great fertility.

The effects of the lodgement of ſand then made, have ſpread conſiderably during the laſt 700 years, and overwhelmed, with a deep cover of dry ſand, many grounds which the ſea had, at its reflux, left tolerably clear. The north corner of this pariſh, in which was comprehended, with other lands, the large and populous barony of Culbin, was, in the laſt century, called the Granary of Moray; but the depoſited ſand, which had been piled up by the winds into three enormous hills, and eſpecially below Maviſton in Auldearn pariſh, has long continued to affect the neareſt cultivated lands. From this great reſervoir, the ſand has been in a conſtant progreſs, from the ſouth-weſt to the north-eaſt; and a very large proportion of the three Maviſton hills, have, in my remembrance, been blown away, and lodged in the north extremity of this pariſh. The barony of Culbin, lying neareſt to the Maviſton hills, and moſt in the tract of the ſtrongeſt winds, was moſt expoſed, and for many years ſuffered gradual encroachments, and diminutions of rent and population. It was only in the end of the laſt century, that the manſion-houſe and gardens were overwhelmed, by an uncommonly violent drifting of the ſand, and the meſſuage-houſe removed to Ern-hill, a remaining corner of that eſtate, quite out o the tr act of the winds. Yet, ſince that time,

the

the lands of Drumreach, and Lake, and even fome part of Binfnefs, have been covered. But, from the tract of the winds, it can do little more damage in that quarter than has been done already. About 20 years ago, a march-ftone was placed on the top of a fand-hill, from 40 to 50 feet in height, to make it more confpicuous ; fome faid, the march would tumble down ; others, that it would fink out of fight, in the fand. But the ftone always remained vifible, finking gradually, with the hill, till the hill had entirely forfook it, and fled. From the north-eaft corner of this parifh, where the fand has been long accumulating, it is by ftrong winds carried into the fea, and fometimes is carried acrofs the river mouth. At the town of Findern, in a blowing day, one may feel the fand fharply ftriking on his face, from the weft fide.

Another effect of the fand-hills, is a change made, in the laft century, of the bed and mouth of the river, which has now got a fhorter paffage to the fea, and occafioned an en-tire removal of the harbour and town of Findern, for more than half-a-mile down the frith. There is a narrow neck of land, belonging to the parifh of Kinlofs, and barony of Meurton, to which it lay contiguous, while it was on the right fide of the river. It ftretched up the frith, for about 3 miles, towards the Mavifton hills. On this neck, now co-vered with fand and bent-grafs, and fit only for fheep pa-fture, and fummer huts, for ftell fifhings, ftood the town and harbour of Findern, three-fourths of a mile weft of where they now are. At the wefter end of this neck of land, now called

The Old Bar, lay the mouth of the river, which then run between this bar and the eftate of Culbin, in the parifh of Dyke. The old bed of the river is yet vi-fible, and the old bar is yet infulated during the flood of fpring tides, except at its wefter end, where the ground is

higheft,

higheft, in a place where the river had formerly run. This fhews, that the river has been damed up by the drifting of fand; and that this had moft probably happened during the high winds in the laft century, which gave the finifhing ftroke to the depopulation of Culbin. As the river then entered the frith fo near to Mavifton hills, it is prefumable, that the fand had then choked and filled up the mouth and bed of the river, and this, with concurrence of the firft land fpet, has made the river cut its way through the eafter end of the flat and narrow neck before mentioned, fo as to leave it, with the old town and harbour, on the left fide.

People alive 40 years ago, remembered to have feen the ftones of old Findern removed to the eafter fide of the new channel, and applied in building the firft houfes of the prefent town, on the Meurton fide, from which the old bar, now contiguous to the parifh of Dyke, had been completely disjoined.

Since the former channel was deferted, both ends of the old bar have been confiderably wafhed away and fhortened by the tides. Some of the ftones of the old town, which have fubfided, are yet to be feen at ebb of tide, in a clear day, lying at the bottom of the falt-water, when boats are paffing over them. And thefe remnants of the old houfes, are more than half-a-mile weft of where the prefent town ftands.

But though the river forced a direct paffage into the fea, it has not been able to keep a clear channel into the deep water. A new bar, oppofite to its prefent mouth, is ftretching weftward, between which and the old bar, the fafeft accefs into the prefent harbour is from the weft.

PARISH OF EDENKEILLIE.

(*Prefbytery of Forres—Synod and County of Moray.*)

By the Rev. Mr. JOHN MACDONNEL, *lately Minifter of that Parifh, now Minifter of* FORRES.

Origin of the Name.

THE name of the parifh is clearly of Gaelic origin; *Aodincoillie* fignifying *the faoe of the wood.* It is defcriptive of the nature of the parifh, which contained two royal forefts, *Ternway*, or *Darnway*, and *Drummine*. In the public records there is preferved a charter, by King David Bruce, granting to RICHARD COMYNE, a predeceffor of Cumming of Altyre, an heritor in this parifh, the office of forefter of the king's foreft of *Ternway*, in the earldom of Moray. And there is an after grant, in 1478, to THOMAS CUMMYNE of Alter, of the office of forefter of the foreft of *Drummyne*. The remains of natural wood, and the great quantities of oak and fir, found in the moffes of this parifh, prove that the whole face of the country was formerly covered with wood. The names of many of the places in the parifh, fhew, what indeed might naturally be fuppofed, that it once abounded with deer. *Drummyne*

574

myne ſignifies *veniſon hill ; Boganſheigh* and *Auchindair*, the places frequented by deer in the rutting ſeaſon, &c.

Extent, Erection, Surface, &c.—This pariſh is very exten-ſive, being, from N. to S., about 12 miles ; and, from E. to W., about 10. It is ſometimes called *Braemoray* ; and it was anciently a vicarage to Forres, the ſeat of the Archdeacon of Moray, and comprehended Ardclach, which was not erected into a ſeparate pariſh till the year 1638. The face of the country is in general hilly, but not mountainous: The higheſt hill in it, is called *the Knock of Braemoray.* The height of this hill, which is not conſiderable, has not been aſcertained by meaſurement. Upon the banks of the rivers Findhorn and Divie, there are ſome of the moſt romantic rural ſcenes, which wood, water, rocks, and variety of ground can produce.

Proprietors and Rent.—There are 5 proprietors ; of whom only 1 reſides conſtantly in the pariſh, and another occaſionally. The valued rent of the pariſh is 1945l. 8s. Scotch : The real rent cannot be ſtated with any degree of accuracy.

Rivers and Lake.—The Findhorn, already mentioned, is the principal river in this pariſh. It takes its riſe in the hills, betwixt thoſe diſtricts of Inverneſs-ſhire called Strather-rig and Strathearn, above 50 miles from the ſea ; after traverſing, with amazing rapidity, a tract of mountainous country, in a courſe nearly from S. W. to N. E., it diſcharges itſelf into the Moray Frith, about 4 miles below Forres. Over this dangerous river, from its ſource to the ſea, there are only at preſent 2 bridges * ; one upon the military road, from Avie-more

* Near to Relugas, the river Findhorn runs between two rocks, which are only 7 feet diſtant from each other. A plank is here placed over it, which ſerves for a bridge,

more to Invernefs ; and another at Dulfie, upon the military
road from Granton to Fort-George. This river crosses the
great post road to Nairn and Invernefs, &c. And although
it often detains the mail for many hours, and notwithstanding the lofs of many lives every year, no aid has yet been
procured from Government to build a bridge over it*. The
other river, called *Divie*, or *Black Water*, falls into the
Findhorn, and is perhaps one of the most rapid rivers in
Scotland, rifing often very fuddenly to a great height. The
principal branch of it rifes among the hills which lie betwixt
this parifh and Strathfpey. The other branch flows from a
pretty confiderable lake, in the S. W. corner of the parifh,
called Lochindorb. This branch is called *Dorback*, till it joins
the Divie, about a mile below the church.

Roads and Bridges.—The road, from Forres to Granton,
crosses the Divie by a ftone bridge. The fame road crosses
the Dorback twice, and at both places there are ftone bridges.
In the year 1783, another bridge was built over the Divie,
near its junction with the Findhorn. The arch is 62 feet
wide, fpringing from the rocks on each fide. The expence,
about 220l. Sterling, was defrayed by a grant of 100l. from
the

a bridge, and affords accefs from a confiderable part of the parifh, lying on the
weft fide of the river, to the church. Owing to the river being confined fo much at
this narrow pafs betwixt the rocks, it rifes, in floods, to a prodigious height, fometimes more than 30 feet above its ordinary channel.

* Mifs Brodie of Lethen, having procured fome aid from the county
funds, and fubfcriptions from her neighbours, engaged in building a bridge
over this rapid river, about a mile below the houfe of Coulmony. An agreement with workmen was entered into, to execute this ufeful undertaking ; and,
in a fhort time, a moft elegant arch, 72 feet wide, was thrown over the river.
But, through fome unlucky defect in the work, within lefs than a month after
it was paffable, this ufeful bridge gave way, and, in one night, fell into the
river.

the Commiſſioners of the Annexed Eſtates, 25l. from the county funds, ſome ſubſcriptions from the neighbourhood, and the remainder by Mr. Cumin of Relugas, who took the whole charge of the work. It is a moſt uſeful bridge for this part of the country, opening a ſafe communication, betwixt the lower part of it and the higher, at a place where many lives were formerly loſt.—In addition to the above road, from Forres to Granton and Aviemore, Sir James Grant, with a view to ſhorten the diſtance from Elgin to Edinburgh, through Strathſpey, has planned out a new road, on the eaſt ſide of the Knock-Hill, intended to paſs through the valley of Pluſcardine. This road is already made, with great labour, and at much expence, from Strathſpey to the extremity of this pariſh. When completed, it will ſhorten the diſtance from Elgin to Granton no leſs than 8 miles. The gentlemen of this pariſh are very attentive to the roads, and call out the people to perform the ſtatute labour, with great exactneſs, every year; but the roads are of ſuch extent, and ſo difficult to make, that it is impracticable, upon the preſent ſyſtem, to keep them in very good order.

Fiſhing.—There is a conſiderable ſalmon fiſhing upon the Findhorn, within this pariſh, the property of the Earl of Moray. It is let to a company in Aberdeen, at 90l. Sterling of yearly rent. The 2 laſt years, 1791 and 1792, have been very favourable. The Sluie Pool, where moſt of the fiſh are caught, has been celebrated, from the moſt ancient times, for the great number of fiſh taken there. By a letter, dated 7th June 1648, from James, then Earl of Moray, to the Counteſs, it would appear, that the fiſhing was greatly more abundant in thoſe days than in latter times; for he writes, that " in " one night, on this pool, 1,300 ſalmon were taken; and, at " one draught, ſix and twenty ſcores." This curious letter is

in

in the prefent Earl's poffeffion. Whence the great difference in modern times can arife, it is not eafy to explain; unlefs from the fuperior fkill and induftry of the fifhermen nearer the fea, which prevents fo great a number now getting up the river. Above the Sluie Pool, the channel of the river is fo rocky, that boats and draught nets cannot be ufed; and the fifhers are obliged to ufe hang nets, and other devices of that kind. Among the rocks, long iron hooks, here called *clips*, are ufed for catching the fifh. So confiderable is the number caught by thefe devices, and by the rod, that the price of falmon, during fummer, is fometimes fo low as three halfpence per pound, and feldom above twopence.—Salmon are alfo fometimes caught in the Divie ; and both rivers afford excellent fea trouts and finnocks, and a variety of other trouts of inferior quality.

Woods and Plantations.—The natural woods in this parifh are very extenfive. The banks of the river are in general covered with trees. Along the weft bank of the Findhorn, the ancient foreft of Darnway, or Ternway, already mentioned, ftretches, for upwards of 5 miles, covering about 900 acres of ground, and confifting of oaks, afhes, elms, birches, allers, hollies, mountain afhes, and a few venerable Scotch firs ; with beeches, geen trees, poplars, and almoft every kind of tree produced in Scotland. Among thefe the weeping birch makes a diftinguifhed figure ; many of them being fo large as 9 feet in girth. Some of the oaks, at the fide of the Findhorn, are upwards of 10 feet in girth, at 3 feet from the ground. They are frefh vigorous trees, without the fmalleft appearance of decay. Farther up the river, is the wood of Dunduff, which is of confiderable extent, and likewife the property of Lord Moray. And there is alfo a good deal of natural wood upon the eftates of the other proprietors. But the plantations in

this

this pariſh, are ſtill more extenſive than the natural woods. About the year 1767, the preſent Earl of Moray began to fill up the vacancies in the old foreſt of Darnway, and has ſince gone on every year, extending his plantations all around his ancient Caſtle of Darnway, and near to Caſtle-Stewart, in the pariſh of Petty. The quantity of ground planted by his Lord-ſhip, including the ancient foreſt, is conſiderably above 3,400 acres. Part indeed lies in the neighbouring pariſh of Dyke, and part in the pariſh of Petty, in Invernefs-ſhire, but by much the greateſt part in this pariſh. The nurſeries from which theſe plantations have been made, except a little at the begin-ning, have been all raiſed at Darnway. Scotch firs, planted out at two years old, from the ſeed-bed, are uſed as nurſes ; and as ſoon as they are fit to afford ſhelter, the more valuable kinds of foreſt trees, principally oaks, are planted amongſt them. Theſe oaks, at two years old, are planted from the ſeed-bed into the nurſery, where they remain three years; and then, as above mentioned, are planted among the firs. When the oaks, and other deciduous trees, are ſufficiently advanced, the whole of the Scotch firs are to be cleared away ; and ſome of the earlier plantations are ſo well grown, as to admit of the firs being completely cut out. Others of them are only clear-ed of the firs in part ; and this operation of clearing goes on gradually and regularly. The Noble Planter has already the ſatisfaction of beholding his public-ſpirited plan fully anſwer-ing his moſt ſanguine expectations ; to which he is well enti-tled, as every part of the plan, which is extremely ſimple, has been carefully and accurately executed ; and proper atten-tion paid to the preſervation of the plantations, which are all in the moſt flouriſhing condition, and already greatly beautify the face of the country. Having obtained an accurate account of the number of trees planted by the Earl of Moray, ſince

the

the year 1767, the public will, doubtiefs, be much gratified with a copy of it, which is here fubjoined.

Oaks planted between November 1767. and autumn 1791,   -   596,000
Afh, beech, elm, fycamore, Spanifh chefnut, fpruce firs, and
    larix, during the fame period,   -   1   -   -   -   308,000
Scotch firs, between November 1767, and autumn 1787,   -   -   9,687,000

                            Total,   -   10,591,000

It will ftill require many years, before thefe very extenfive plantations can be filled up with oaks ; but there is at prefent, in the nurferies, a very large ftock of young plants coming forward. The other proprietors have not been deficient in carrying on this improvement. On the eftate of Logie, there are confiderable plantations of Scotch firs, and a confiderable number of afhes, planted by the prefent proprietor's father, fome of them near 100 feet in height. One of thefe afhes was lately fold at 5l. 13s., at the rate of 1s. 6d. per foot ; a ftrong proof of the profit of planting. And on the eftate of Relugas, about 200 acres have been planted, upon a plan fimilar to Lord Moray's, and upwards of 60,000 oaks planted out. Upon the eftate of Dunphail, there are fome old fir plantations, which have been cutting down, and felling for the ufe of the country, for feveral years paft.

Climate, &c.—The air and climate of Moray, from the moft diftant times, have been celebrated, as of the pureft and moft falubrious quality, by all the writers who have defcribed that country ; and it has been a common faying, that it enjoyed 40 days more of fair weather, than moft other places in Scotland. In Whitelock's Memorials, a book of great authority, there is a curious teftimony in favour of the country, in *Oliver Cromwell*'s time : He fays, " Afhfield's regiment was
                                    " marched

" marched into Murrayland, which is the moſt fruitful country
" in Scotland, and the common proverb is, that it hath fifteen
" days more of ſummer than any other part of the nation." *
It is unneceſſary to mention the praiſes given to it by Buchanan and others. The ſuperior degree of dryneſs, perhaps
applies more to the level plains of Moray, along the ſea ſide,
than to this pariſh, where more rain falls than in the lower
parts of the country. But no place can enjoy a healther air
than this pariſh does, being hardly ever troubled with fogs,
or pernicious exhalations ; and the rivers, ſo far from being
hurtful, rather tend to purify the air, by the rapidity of their
courſe. There are no diſeaſes peculiar to this part of the
country.

Fruit, Orchard, &c.—In the valley of Logie, which is the
warmeſt part of the pariſh, ſtandard and wall fruit trees grow
well. Mr CUMMING of LOGIE, beſides an excellent garden,
a good many years ago planted 4 Scotch acres of ground with
fruit trees. This beautiful orchard is cloſe to the Findhorn,
expoſed to the ſouth ; but on all other ſides well ſheltered by
higher grounds, and tall foreſt trees. In favourable ſeaſons,
it already richly repays the expence of planting and incloſing.

Soil, Cultivation and Produce.—The ſoil of the lower part
of the pariſh, near the rivers, is of a light dry quality, rather
tending to ſandy ; but, when properly managed, very fertile
and productive. A very great proportion of the pariſh conſiſts of muir and moſs ; great part of which might be improved, if lime, of which there is none in this pariſh, could be procured. For though there is ſome in the pariſh of Forres, it is
too expenſive an article for common tenants to purchaſe, and
hitherto

* Lond. Edit. Anno 1732, p· 517.

hitherto has not been furnished in any sufficient quantity. The only kinds of grain raised in this parish, are barley, Scotch bear, oats, and some rye. Every tenant plants a few potatoes for family use; but no great quantity is raised. In the upper parts of the parish, they prefer sowing the black or grey oats; a species much inferior to the white; but the black are thought more productive of straw for fodder; an article much wanted, as a considerable number of cattle are bred in the parish. Farming is in a very wretched state in this part of the country. They give all their dung to their bear crop; after which they take repeated crops of oats, sometimes 4 or 5 successively, till the land hardly returns the seed; and then it is left ley for some years. Although the great benefit of green crops, and a proper rotation, has been shewn by some of the gentlemen, the example has not hitherto had any effect to improve the practice of the common farmers.

Black Cattle, Horses and Sheep.—A considerable number of black cattle are reared in this parish, somewhat larger in size than the Highland kind; and many of them are used in the plough. The horses are small, and of a very indifferent quality. Most of the tenants keep a few sheep; but the management of that animal is not well understood here. They had no other kind, till of late, but the ancient breed of the country, with white faces, affording fine wool, and most excellent mutton. The best of the wool of this species, sells for 18s. per stone; and, though generally a small animal, from poor feeding, it may, when better kept, be brought to the size of 13lb. or 14lb. per quarter. This part of the country, abounding in woods and rocks, affords too much harbour for foxes; it is therefore necessary to house the sheep at night in cotts, which makes the constitution of the animal rather delicate, and has been the reason of introducing the black faced Tweeddale breed;

breed; which, though rather hardier, is much inferior, both as to wool and mutton. *It will be a great loss to the country,* IF OUR ANCIENT BREED SHOULD WEAR OUT, *of which there is great danger.*

Population.—The register of births, marriages, and deaths, having been irregularly kept, previous to the settlement of the writer, which was only in 1791, he can say little upon the population of the parish. The number of souls, in the return to Dr. Webster in 1755, was 1443; it is now 1800: so that the increase is 357; and the population appears to be still upon the increase, as a good deal of the waste land, in the remoter parts of the parish, has lately been brought into culture, by families settling in these wilder parts of it.—Many of the people live to a great age. There are two women, now alive, whose ages amount to 180.

Occupations.—The chief employment of the inhabitants is agriculture. The farms are very small, from 3l. to 10l., and a very few go the length of 20l. a year, which fully accounts for the low state of farming.—There is little industry among the men, except in the poor employment of preparing and carrying peats to the town of Forres, at the distance of 10 or 12 miles from the mosses, of which there is an inexhaustible quantity among the hills. The women are diligent spinners; a branch of manufacture, introduced into this parish, by the late Dr. PATRICK CUMING of Relugas, who obtained a number of wheels and reels from the Society for Propagating Christian Knowledge, and a salary to a schoolmistress. But there is still much room for improvement in this branch.— The people, in this part of the country, have such frequent intercourse with the town of Forres, that they buy the greatest

part

part of their neceffaries at the markets there †. This like-wife gives them an opportunity to get their own manufactures difpofed of, which are but very few. There are a fufficient number of weavers and tailors, for manufacturing the ftuffs worn by the inhabitants. There are 2 fhoemakers, 4 coopers, and 10 riddlemakers ; and almoft every man in the parifh is a cartwright. They make their carts of aller and birch tim-ber, and fupply the Elgin and Forres markets. The price of them, in general, is from 6s. to 12s.

Diftilleries.—There are no lefs than 4 diftilleries for mak-ing whifky in this parifh, which confume a great quantity of barley ; and, what is aftonifhing, they fell thefe fpirits as faft as they can run them ! The inhabitants of this parifh are, however, in general, fober. Their whifky they fend up to Strathfpey and Badenoch. To account for the conftant de-mand for whifky in the north of Scotland, we muft reflect, that, of late years, a total ftop has been put to fmuggling, by the great attention of the revenue officers, in the weft and north coafts of Scotland, which formerly fupplied the whole country with foreign fpirits. It muft, however, be allowed, that there is more of this liquor ufed by the common people, than is good for their health or morals.

Church, &c.—The church is fituated upon the banks of the Divie, about 8½ miles fouth of Forres. It was built in
1741,

† The prices of provifions are much regulated by the neighbouring town of Forres. Hens are fold for 6d. a piece, chickens 3d., ducks 5d., geefe 2s.; eggs, per dozen, 1½d.; fweet milk, per pint, 1d.; fkimmed ditto ½d.; butter, per pound, 8d.; and cheefe, per ftone, 4s.: get farm fervants, from 1l. 10s. to 2l. in the half year, with 6½ bolls of meal in the year, or victuals in the houfe: women fervants from 15s. to 1l. in the half year, with victuals, or 3 ftones of meal: day labourers 7d. or 8d. in fummer, and 6d. in winter.

1741, and, with some repairs, might be made a very commodious place of worship. The manse, which is of an older date, is not in good condition. The stipend is 41l. 2s. 2¾d. Sterling, and three chalders of victual, half bear half meal, with a glebe of eight acres, and a good garden. The Earl of Moray is undoubted patron.

Schools and Poor.—There is an established school in this parish, the salary only 100 merks Scotch. The number of scholars is about 30. Reading English, writing and arithmetic are the branches of education commonly taught. There is at present only 1 school in this parish, supported by the Society for Propagating Christian Knowledge, though there is a *claim for three*, in consequence of a donation by Dr. Duncan Cuming, son of James Cuming, Esq. of Relugas*. This school, however, is of great utility, being situated in a part of the parish, altogether detached from the church and the parish school.—The poor's funds are very small, not exceeding 5l. Sterling annually, arising solely from the collections at the church ; but the deficiency is made up by the charitable disposition of the inhabitants, who never refuse to assist those in distress.

Antiquities.—In the upper part of the parish, among the hills, between Strathspey and Braemoray, stood the *Castle of Lochindorb*, built on an island, situated in the middle of a lake of the same name. It appears to have been a very considerable place, and a fortress of great strength. *Catharine de Beaumont*, widow of *David de Hastings*, Earl of Atholl, who
was

* This gentleman was physician to King William III. at the battle of the Boyne, in 1690, and afterwards settled as a physician in Dublin. In 1714, he sent the sum of 261l. 13s. 7d. Sterling to the Society, with a recommendation, that they should keep always 3 schools in this pari

was killed at the battle of Kilblaine, anno 1335, refided in this caftle, which was blockaded by Sir Andrew Moray, the regent during King *David Bruce's* captivity. In the follow-ing year, Edward III. of England led his army northward, the length of Invernefs, and, on his way thither, raifed the fiege of this caftle. It feems afterwards to have been convert-ed into a ftate prifon ; for, in the year 1342, the famous *William Bullock*, who was a great favourite of King David Bruce, was imprifoned there, and died through extremity of cold and hunger †. The remains of this caftle cover a fpace of ground, not lefs than 100 fquare yards.

The *Downe Hill of Relugas* feems to have been a fortrefs of ftill greater antiquity, and ufed as fuch far beyond the period of authentic hiftory. It appears to have been a place of ftrength, to which the inhabitants of the country retired, with their cattle, upon the invafion of the Danes, to which this country of Moray was fo frequently expofed. It is a conical hill, round a confiderable part of which runs the rapid river of Divie, in a deep rocky channel ; and, where not de-fended by the river, it is encircled by a deep foffee, or ditch, with a ftrong rampart on the outfide, moftly compofed of ftones, fome of which have the appearance of vitrification ‡.

About a mile higher up the fame river, ftands the *Caftle of Dunphail*, upon a rock of a very fingular appearance, fur-rounded

† *Vide* Lord Hailes's Annals, vol. II. p. 189, 190, and 209.

‡ Upon the fummit of this hill, which is 220 feet of perpendicular height above the river, there is a level fpace, in the form of an oblong fquare, about 60 yards in length, and 20 in breadth. This level piece of ground has been converted into a nurfery for trees. In digging the ground, a quantity of human bones, afhes and charcoal were found. When the country was covered with wood, this place, from its difficulty of accefs, and the fteepnefs of the hill itfelf, muft have been of great ftrength, and eafily defended by a handful of men againft great numbers.

rounded by a deep *gully*, or narrow glen, formed probably by the river, which, at a very remote period, ſeems to have run in this channel. The rock is of a conſiderable ſize, with a level area upon the ſummit of it, ſimilar to the Downhill, of good ſoil, covered with graſs, and ſeveral trees growing upon it. The ſides are ſo ſteep, that it is altogether inacceſſible, except upon that next the river, where there is a narrow road leading up to the caſtle. It formerly belonged to a family of the name of Dunbar; it is now the property of Mr Cumming of Altyre *.

Character of the People.—The inhabitants are all of the eſtabliſhed religion, there being no ſectaries. In the lower part of the pariſh, the Scotch dialect of the Engliſh language is only ſpoken; but, in the upper part, the Gaelic is ſtill much in uſe. About 50 years ago, the miniſter preached the one half of the day in Engliſh, and the other half in Gaelic. The people are rather gloomy in their ideas as to religion; but they are of a peaceable diſpoſition, ſober and honeſt in their dealings, and very ready to extend their charity to the poor.

* The very ſingular *Bridge of Rannich* ſhould alſo here be taken notice of. It is certainly of great antiquity; for tradition ſays, that it derived its name from the illuſtrious RANDOLPH, Earl of Moray, who was regent of Scotland, after the death of King ROBERT BRUCE.

STATISTICAL ACCOUNT

OF

SCOTLAND.

PARISH OF ELGYN.

(COUNTY OF MORAY.)

By the Rev. Mr JOHN GRANT, *one of the Minifters of Elgyn.*

Origin of the Name.

IT is eftabifhed by records, prior to the 1226, that the ancient name of the town, which communicates its name to the parifh, was *Elgyn*, or *Helgyn* *. Various etymologies, and interpretations of it, have been fuggefted. Whitaker fays,

---

* Ca tularium Moravienfe, Fol. 5. v. Befides the town, there is an extenfive country parifh, about 10 Englifh miles in length, and fix in breadth.

ſays *, that *Elgyn* ſignifies a peninſula or cherſoneſus; and Bullet aſſerts †, that *El* is a town, and *gin* agreeable. But were theſe derivations juſt, the ſame name would have been applied to an infinite number of places, in ſimilar ſituations, which is far from being the caſe. It is more probable, therefore, that it derives its origin from Helgy, general of the army of Sigurd, the Norwegian Earl of Orkney, who, about 927, conquered Caithneſs, Sutherland, Roſs and Moray. It is ſaid, that he built a town in the ſouthern part of Moray, which, it is probable, was Elgyn, particularly as it is ſituated to the ſouth of Duffeyrus, or the burgh in Duffus, where the Norwegians had a harbour for their ſhipping ‡. Many Norwegian princes were alſo named Helgy, and the inſcription upon the town ſeal is, " *S. commune civitatis de Helgyn,*" engraved in Saxon characters, in a ſtyle earlier than the middle of the ſixteenth century.

Caſtle.—In thoſe ages a caſtle was always neceſſary to protect any town, and one was probably built, at an early period, for the defence of Elgyn. In the reign of William the Lyon of Scotland, there was a royal fort on a riſing ground, now called Ladyhill ‖; the ruins of which are ſtill viſible.

The Borough.—At what particular period, Elgyn was erected into a royal borough, does not appear. The firſt
charter

---

* Hiſtory of the Britons Aſſerted.
† Bullet Memoires ſur la Langue Celtique, vol. 1. p. 397.
‡ Rerum Orcadenſium Hiſtoria, a Thormodo Torſæo, p. 12. 13. 28 31 113.
‖ Cart. Morav. fol. 17. v.

charter, in the archives of the town, is from Alexander II. *anno* 1234, who grants to the burgeſſes of Elgyn, a guild of merchants, with as extenſive privileges as any other borough enjoys in Scotland.

It was the policy of the ſovereign, in the middle ages, to give great privileges and immunities to the towns, for the purpoſe of balancing the dangerous power, which had been acquired by the nobles. But when the regal government became at any time feeble, theſe towns, unequal to their own protection, placed themſelves under the ſhelter of the moſt powerful lord in their neighbourhood. Thus the town of Elgyn found it neceſſary at various periods, between the years 1389 and 1452, to accept of many charters of protection, and diſcharges of taxes, from the Earls of Moray, who held it in ſome ſpecies of vaſſalage. At laſt, Charles I. in 1633, eſtabliſhed and confirmed all the grants of his royal predeceſſors, in favour of the borough ; and the ſet, or form of its government, was ratified by the convention of boroughs, in 1706 *.

Biſhoprick.—At the beginning of the eleventh century, the biſhops in Scotland wore blue gowns, with their hair tucked under a cap †, and, having no particular dioceſe aſſigned them, were itinerant. The preciſe time, that Moray was erected into a biſhoprick, is uncertain, the chartulary going no farther back than the 1200 ; but it appears, that before that period, the biſhops occaſionally employed the churches of Bruneth or Birney, of Spyny and Kinnedor,

as

---

* Elgyn has been frequently deſtroyed by fire ; but, for hiſtorical facts, Shaw's Hiſtory of the Province of Moray, muſt, in general, be referred to.

† Hiſt. Orcad. Th. Torfæi. p. 113.

as cathedrals, and refided near them *; and that bifhop
Briceus, foon after the 1200, had the cathedral eftablifhed
at Spyny. In 1224, Bifhop Andrew tranflated it to the
church of the Holy Trinity near Elgyn. This building
was deftroyed by Alexander, Lord of Badenoch †. About
1397, however, it was begun to be rebuilt, but it was not
finifhed till after the 1414. From the ruins which ftill remain, it appears to have been a large and fplendid edifice,
in the Gothic ftyle of architecture, in length above 260
feet, and above 34 feet broad, and was not furpaffed in
beauty, by any building, of that nature, in the kingdom ‡.

The revenues of this bifhoprick, were not contemptible,
even prior to the 1239; but afterwards, in confequence
of royal grants, and private donations, they became very
confiderable indeed. On the eve of the Reformation,
feveral eftates were feued off at low ftipulations, yet the
remainder would now produce a yearly income of above
L. 4000 Sterling. In 1565, the rents were, L. 273 : 16 : 2
Sterling, 10 bolls of wheat; 41 chalders, 7 bolls, 2 firlots
farm bear; 23 chalders, 3 bolls dry multure; 13 chalders,
11 bolls of oats with ftraw; 60 marts, or fat beeves; 162
fheep; 166 lambs; 206 dozen of capons; 42 dozen of
poultry,

---

* Cart. Mor. Fol. 1. r.
† Ibid. Fol. 62. r.

‡ A large fpace of ground was furrounded with a high wall, in many
places yet entire, which inclofed what is now called the college, and contained, not only the cathedral and burying ground, but the houfes or manfes, with the fmall gardens, that belonged to the twenty two canons, and
dignitaries of the fee. All thefe have now come into lay hands, but feveral
of the manfes are inhabited, and diftinguifhed by the names of the canonry
they belonged to. Within this boundary the bifhop alfo, had a large houfe,
which was repaired by Bifhop Hepburn, as his arms are carved on it, with
the initials of his name, P. H.

poultry, 166 geefe ; 66 horfe fhoes ; 8 fwine ; 11 lafts, and 8 barrels of falmon. *

Surface and Soil.—The furface of this parifh is flat, with little variety from rifing grounds, except towards Black-hills, where the fields gradually afcend. The foil varies ; here, a rich loam, there, a clay, but, in general, it is fandy, abounding with calcareous particles, and, on the whole, is fertile, producing plenty of grain, and of good quality. Within thefe few years, the quantity of pafture is enlarged, and abundance of hay raifed, by the introduction of artificial graffes. This is greatly promoted by a climate friendly to vegetation, which, at the fame time, gives fo little interruption to the operations of the hufbandman, that, it is reckoned, there are about three months more, of fair weather here, than in many places of the neighbouring county of Banff.

Agriculture.—Even in very remote times, the cultivation of the foil feems to have been properly attended to, in this part of Scotland : Our hiftorians, it is true, chiefly employ themfelves in retailing legendary ftories, or giving inaccurate accounts of foreign or domeftic wars, and political contefts, overlooking unfortunately, the more important details of induftry, trade, and population. In an inveftigation of this nature, therefore, fcattered facts muft be collected, and cafual and contingent fources of information relied on ; the refult of which, however, is, that this country was anciently well cultivated and productive.

In

* Rentale Epifcopatus, Mor. in A. D. 1565. Mro. Archibaldo Lindfay Camerario.

In the reign of William the Lyon, lint paid teind [1].
In 1232, there were gardens of pot-herbs [2]; about 1225
there were carts in ufe [3]; before 1369, oxen were yoked
to waggons [4]. Arable lands were meafured prior to
1240 [5]; and water-mills for grinding corn were common
prior to the 1200 [6], and high multures paid [7]. Private
gentlemen, in 1225, had breweries [8]; there were royal
breweries before 1199 [9]. Leafes were granted for five
lives in 1378 [10], and for three lives about 1390 [11]; as alfo
for three lives in 1383, under conditions to have the farms
properly inhabited, and to preferve the woods in them [12].
In 1550, a perpetual annuity, from land-rents, was bought
at 15 years purchafe [13]. There were falt-works in the
neighbourhood of Elgyn before 1226 [14]. In 1369, their
grain appears to have been principally bear and oats [15], *.

Thefe

1 Cart. Morav. Fol. 15. v.	2 Ib. Fol. 18. r.
3 Ib. Fol. 42. Col. 2. v.	4 Ib. Fol. 8. v.
5 Ib. Fol. 49. r.	6 Cart. Mor. Fol. 14. r. 17. v.
7 Ib. Fol. 19. v.	8 Ib. Fol. 14. v. 79. v.
9 Ib. Fol. 37. Col. 1. r.	10 Ib. 34. v.
11 Ib. Fol. 73. r.	12 Ib Fol. 90. v.
13 Ib. 75. v.	14 Ib. Fol. 21. v.
15 Ib. Fol. 81. r.	

* To thefe facts, and the rental already mentioned, of the Bifhop of
Moray's eftate in 1565, may be added the following evidence, arifing from
the teftament of James Ogilvie of Findlater, dated 15th September 1565.
In the inventory of his moveables, there are the following articles, " 50
" drawing oxen; 28 fteers; 48 cows; 16 ftirks; 18 calves; 400 fheep,
" whereof 11 fcore ewes, and four fcore lambs: *Item*, fown on his Mains,
" of oats, 21 fcore of bolls, eftimate to the third corn; of bear, four fcore
" bolls, eftimate to the fourth corn; of wheat 21 bolls, eftimate to the
" fourth corn; of peafe, feven bolls: *Item*, in the barn-yards, three ftacks
" of bear, extending to fix fcore bolls bear; one ftack of oats, extending to
" fix fcore bolls of oats; one ftack of wheat, extending to 30 bolls wheat:
" *Item*, five work horfes." The original is among the Earl of Findlater's
papers.

These facts tend to prove, that tillage, in those early periods, was attended to, and indeed confiderably advanced. It was probably in an improving ftate, until the acceffion of James VI. to the throne. During his minority, and thence to the year 1620, Scotland in general, and the northern parts of it in particular, were torn by facti ns, and laid wafte by rapine and bloodfhed, more than any other country in Europe. When beginning to recover, the civil wars in the reign of the unfortunate Charles I. the perfecutions under Charles II. and the famine in the reign of King William, materially affected the induftry of the people ; fo that the nation did not breathe, in peace and quiet, till the beginning of this century. Nor was it cured of its languor, till after the 1746, when the people awoke, as it were, from a profound flumber. Within thefe laft 30 years, their induftry has become active, and, in general, has been directed by intelligence.

The prefent practice of farming, and fucceffion of crops, varies, according to the nature of the foil, and the genius of the farmer. Three plowings are generally given to a field for bear ; one after harveft, another in March, and a third in May, with the manure. The fucceeding crop is oats, with grafs feeds, or peafe, and next year it is dreffed for bear, with a fprinkling of dung. Others, fallow, or have turnips or potatoes, which is followed by oats or bear, fowed down with grafs feeds. In very light foils, rye is fown after bear to great advantage, and the next crop is bear with manure and grafs feeds. Sometimes old leys are broken up in Auguft, and after another plowing in fpring, the crop is oats, and the fucceeding feafon bear, after three plowings and dung.

This is the general rotation of crops. Fallows are daily becoming more univerfal, as are turnips, which feveral

farmers

farmers begin to raiſe on a large ſcale, either to feed cattle for the butcher, or, which is found to be more advantageous, to give them to their young cattle, as it greatly improves their ſize.

The practice of ſowing clover and rye-graſs, is daily gaining ground. Six pounds of red clover ſeed, and from 8 to 10 of white, with 2 buſhels of rye-graſs, is the general quantity to an acre. Hay is taken for two years, and paſture the third, and then the field is broken up for oats or barley, according to its ſtate. A few ſow red clover alone, at the rate of about 20 pounds to the acre.

Sowing wheat was much run upon, about 20 years ago, in this pariſh and the neighbourhood, but now is juſtly on the decline ; for the returns from the wheat, however high the price, did not compenſate for the injury done to the ſoil, by ſo exhauſting a crop.

Potatoes were introduced into the fields, about 60 years ago, and are now planted in great quantities all over the country. Their quality, from the dryneſs of the ſoil, is excellent, and the produce conſiderable. Sometimes they are exported to Newcaſtle, and other places.

Mr Leſlie of Balnagight, a very accurate obſerver, has lately adopted a method of managing a potatoe crop, which many imitate with ſucceſs. It is this : He plows his po-tatoe field before winter, and, if the ground is full of weeds, propogated from the roots, he plows again before he plants. If not, he dungs as for barley, and plants early in March, putting the ſeed in every furrow after the plough, and harrows well immediately after. As ſoon as the weeds get up, and the potatoes begin to appear, (perhaps one in a ſquare yard or two,) he gives it a third plowing and harrowing, about the firſt of May, according as the plants are advanced. This culture, with one hoeing when

the

the weeds appear again, never fails to produce a good crop. But what is alfo of great advantage, it leaves the ground cleaner and mellower, and in a fitter condition for wheat, or any other crop, than a complete fallow. Thofe who grudge the few feeds, that may be turned up by the plough or the harrow, have only to caufe a boy replace the plants, on the face of the furrow, where it may be neceffary.

A confiderable quantity of grain, of different kinds, has been annually exported from Moray in general, principally from the ports of Findhorn, Loffiemouth, and Germach, to London, Leith, and the mouth of the canal at Carron. Laft year, above 10,000 bolls were fhipped from thofe ports. This is almoft the firft export in any quantity, fince 1783, when by the failure of the crop in 1782, about 100,000 bolls of corn and meal were imported to both fides of the Moray frith.

The whole low part of the county of Moray is fruitful in corn, and the parifh of Elgyn, among the reft. Befides what is exported by fea, and fent to the Highlands, the licenfed ftills in the county, confume a great quantity. There are 19 of thefe ftills, meafuring in all 635 gallons, which, by law, are intitled to diftill 3863 bolls of bear annually, and a brewery, eftablifhed of late in this town, malts above 1500 bolls. Were the fmuggling of foreign fpirits into this country effectually fuppreffed, the exportation of corn would probably greatly diminifh, if not total‐ly ceafe.

Many years ago, the land was tilled by 6, 8, or 10 oxen, in a plough, and fometimes by 2 or 4 oxen, with 1 or 2 horfes. The late Sir Robert Gordon, of Gordonftown, about 30 years ago, introduced the practice of plowing with only two horfes, managed by reins, without a driver. This mode

mode is now generally adopted, and, within thefe 12 years, 2 oxen in traces, are alfo ufed by feveral farmers, and in the light foils, with fuccefs. For this reafon, and as the pafture is improved by artificial graffes, and green food being occafionally given them in winter, the breed of black cattle has been greatly improved, though in the country at large, the numbers on the whole are diminifhed. L. 12 Sterling is often paid for an ox raifed in this neighbourhood, and above L. 20 has been given for a fatted ox. Farmers, however, prefer in general, horfes for the plough, particularly when they are bred on their own farms, which is done by many. The ftyle of farming utenfils is greatly improved, in regard to ploughs, as well as carts and waggons. Two-horfe carts are coming into ufe. The average rent of the Scotch acre of arable land, in the immediate vicinity of the town, is from L. 1, 10 s. to L. 2 Sterling, and in the country part of the parifh, it is from 15 s. to 18 s. Sterling; but this varies, as a great proportion, perhaps too great, of the rents, is paid in bear and oats. Rents are advancing daily. The price of labour is amazingly raifed within the laft 30 years. Then a plowman had from 40 s. to 50 s. a-year; and now they receive from L. 5 to L. 7 Sterling, and other fervants are paid in the fame proportion. There is no fuch thing as fervices exacted by any of the proprietors, in this parifh.

The moft confiderable heritor is Lord Fife, next the Earl of Moray, &c. There are great numbers of proprietors, in the immediate vicinity of the town, who have only fmall pieces of land belonging to them, and, in general, moft improperly feparated, and detached; fo that they cannot cultivate their grounds, to the fame advantage, as if they were more contiguous to each other. From this caufe, there are but few inclofures or hedges about the place.

Commerce.

Commerce. When King Alexander gave Elgyn the charter of guildry, there doubtlefs exifted fome foreign, as well
as domeftic trade. It is certain, that in 1249, a French nobleman, (the Count de St. Paul and Blois,) had a fhip of war
built at Invernefs, at no great diftance from Elgyn *. It appears, that in 1383, the burgeffes of Elgyn had a trading veffel, named Farcoft, that failed up the Loffie, which then had
direct communication with the loch of Spynie, at that time
an arm of the fea †. This veffel was loaded with barrels of
beer, tallow and flour. In thofe days, alfo the bifhop's fifhing boats failed from the town and caftle of Spynie, to the
Moray Frith ‡. In regard to the more recent commerce of
Elgyn, about 40 or 50 years ago, it was principally carried
on with Holland; but now the trade is chiefly with London,
Leeds, Manchefter, Birmingham, Newcaftle, Carron, &c. &c.
for the importation of manufactured articles, rather more than
the country can well afford; as the exports, independent of
cattle, a few horfes and corn, are but confined, and moftly
confift of dreft fkins for gloves, to the amount of between
L. 300 and L. 400; and of linen yarn, to the value of about
L. 2000 Sterling. There are now 44 fhops opened in this
town, principally for the fale of imported goods.

In the end of laft century, and about the 1722, there was
a confiderable export of malt, from this place to Norway.—
There were then above 30 malt barns, always employed,
but the people at Dunbar fupplanted them greatly, and the
malt tax completed its ruin. Gloves were made here, fome
years ago, in great perfection, and a number fent to different
markets. That trade is much on the decline. The fpinning
                                                        of

* Lord Hailes's Annals of Scotland, vol. 1. † Cart. Mor. fol. 93, r. ‡ Ib.
fol. 93, r.

of lint has prevailed over a manufacture of woollen stuffs, which formerly existed in this town and parish, to a considerable amount. The great number of sheep, then in the neighbourhood, did not supply the demand, so that it was necessary to purchase wool from the highlanders in Strathspey, &c. The plantations of wood, and sown grasses, have thrown sheep so much out of the low country, that thirty years ago, more hundreds were annually sold out of it, than there are now scores in it. The wool was then of a very fine staple, from a small white faced breed, and indeed approached in quality to that of Shetland. Now the large bodied, black faced sheep, whose fleeces are of a very rough and inferior nature, are in request among us.

That some estimate may be formed of the occupations in this parish, it may be proper to observe, that in the country part, there are 9 tailors, 19 weavers, 9 wrights, including mill-wrights, 5 shoemakers, and 7 blacksmiths. In the town are 16 blacksmiths, 70 weavers, 70 wrights, including makers of ploughs and waggons; 55 shoemakers, 32 tailors, 8 glovers, 3 tinmen, 6 barbers, 4 bakers, 2 surgeons, and 2 physicians. There are also 2 tanners, who carry on their business, though not on a large scale; and a soapery, in which the partners propose to manufacture a considerable quantity.

Funds of the Town.—The gross amount of the public revenue of the town, is about L. 200 Sterling, arising from lands, feu-rents, petty customs of the markets, &c. and from the village of Lossiemouth, of which the magistrates acquired the property, from the family of Brodie, in 1694. They possessed it many years, without any advantage. At length some public-spirited members of the magistracy, proposed to improve the harbour, at the river mouth. From the funds of the town, and voluntary contributions of the in habitants,

habitants, with a grant from the Convention of Burghs, and other liberal donations, one jetty head has been erected, and another carried out a confiderable way, but not completed. This has rendered the harbour more commodious, fo that veffels of 80 tons can now enter with a fpring-tide. The harbour could, without doubt, be much more improved, but this partial amendment has already encouraged a fpirit of building at that place. The town can give in all, 180 feus on their property there, of various meafurement, at the rate of from 5 s. to 1 guinea each, of yearly feu-duty. Sixty of thefe feus are already granted, more are daily taken, and many are actually built on.

Charitable Funds.—The guild-brethren, in 1714, began the eftablifhment of a fund, for the widows of their decayed members. The yearly contribution, from each individual, is 23 s. but by their care and œconomy, they have pur-chafed lands, in the vicinity, to a the mount of L. 76 Ster-ling, of yearly rent; and they have alfo fome money at inte-reft. But of this revenue, they diftribute L. 40 annually in penfions to widows, and the remainder is added to the ca-pital. The fix incorporations of fmiths, glovers, tailors, fhoemakers, weavers, and wrights, have alfo, each of them, various capitals, arifing from yearly affeffments, on their re-fpective brethren, for the aid of their poor, and decayed members and widows. Thefe capitals are from L. 100, to L. 300 Sterling, and they have very properly followed the example of the guildry, by laying out their favings in the purchafe of lands and houfes. There are alfo two charitable foundations in the town, begun in 1785, and fubject to cer-tain regulations. The one is called the *Friendly*, and the other the *St Giles's Society*. The members of each contribute 7 d. a month, and the funds of the firft amount to a-

bout

bout L. 350, and of the other to about L. 230 Sterling. The town, from mortified money, diftributes yearly about L. 18 Sterling, which is under their management. They have alfo four beidmen, eftablifhed on the preceptory of Meffindew, in their gift. Provoft Cumming alfo mortified lands, with houfes, for four decayed guildbrethren, to which his heir, and the magiftrates of Elgyn, prefent alternately. Each of thofe, fo prefented, have L. 2 Sterling, quarterly, with a houfe and a fmall garden. Here alfo, it may be mentioned, among the other fources of charitable donations, that there are two mafon-lodges, one of which is opulent. The Sunday collections amount to about L. 45 a-year, and the intereft of the money, under the management of the kirk-feffion, is L. 8, 11 s. Sterling. Altogether, what is fet apart for charitable purpofes, in this town and parifh, amounts to no contemptible fum.

Schools.—In confequence of fome Royal grants *, the magif-trates have been enabled to build two fchool-houfes, which are

kept

* Andrew, Bifhop of Moray, between the years 1225, and 1237, founded a *Domus Dei*, near the brook Taok, and Leper-houfe at Elgyn, and eftablifhed fome brothers'and fifters in it, for charitable and pious purpofes; and endowed it, for that defign ; as did alfo King Alexander II. On the Reformation, the Crown feized it; and 22d March 1594, King James, by a grant, gave the magiftrates of Elgyn the lands and fuperiorities, belonging to this hofpital, or *Domus Dei*, vulg. *Meffindew,* for fupporting fome poor, agreeable to the defign of the original foundation. The magiftrates were appointed patrons. This was confirmed by a royal charter, 5th December 1599. On the laft day of February, 1620, the magiftrates obtained another charter, under the great feal, confirming the original grant, and appointing them; not only to maintain a few poor out of thefe lands and fuperiorities, but, to fupport a fchoolmafter, " *ad docendum muficam, aliafque liberales* " *artes, intra dictum noftrum burgum in pofterum.*" The original charters are in the archieves of the town. Agreeable to this, the magiftrates have built, and kept in repair, a houfe for lodging four beidmen ; and give each of them four bolls of bear yearly, with a gown, and a fmall piece of garden ground. The reft of the fund is applied to the maintenance of fchools.

kept in proper repair. To one mafter, who teaches church-music, writing, reading, and arithmetic, they give L.10 yearly. They have alfo eftablifhed a fchoolmafter for claf-fical learning, the teacher of which has L. 21 Sterling of fa-lary, arifing partly from this endowment, and partly from mortified money; to which the heritors of the town or country, contribute nothing; fo that it is not a legal paro-chial fchool, though it anfwers that purpofe.

The magiftrates, and feveral refpectable inhabitants, wifh-ing to have the plan of education in the town enlarged, and that the children might be inftructed in fome additional branches of learning, immediately under their own eye, have propofed a plan, for an academy in the town, in which, not only reading Englifh, arithmetic, and claffical learning, is to be taught, but Greek, French, geography, book-keeping, and various branches of the mathematics, with land-furveying, and drawing. The magiftrates have fubfcribed, for carrying this plan into effect, L. 42 Sterling a-year, and the inhabitants have contributed already about L. 500 Sterling; and, depending on the liberality of the pub-lic, have addreffed their friends at home and abroad to af-fift them.—There are alfo Sunday fchools eftablifhed in the town, and with fuccefs.

Population.—The population of the parifh of Elgyn, in the country part of that diftrict, is, from various caufes, confiderably on the decline. The town, indeed, has increa-fed in the number of its inhabitants, but not of late in pro-portion to the decreafe in the country. The number of fouls, in the country parifh is 1614, divided into 377 fami-lies, among which are 43, that have but one perfon in each. In the town are 2920 fouls, divided into 658 families, of which 140 contain one perfon in each. The total number is is 1035 families, and 4534 souls, which is nearly 4¼ to a family. The return to Dr Webster, from this parish, being 6306, fully proves to what an extent depopulation has been carried.

The annual average of baptisms, for the last 7 years, is, by the register, but 89. At least 15 more may be added, to supply the deficiencies in the register, or those baptised by sectaries. The annual average of marriages, for the same period is 33. No accurate state of burials can be given *.

Stipend.—The stipend victual of the parish of Elgyn to each minister, (it is a collegiate charge,) should amount, by the decreet in 1714, to 104 bolls of bear, but the actual payments are only 103 bolls 2 pecks. The money stipend to each, is L. 49, 9 s. Sterling, but in this are included L. 6, as the rent of half of the glebe, and L. 2, 2 s. as his share of the rent of the ground for a manse and garden. But from this sum is to be deduced 11 s. 1 d. as the vicarage of the college, which does not now exist. There is no manse, though the ground for building on, had been set apart, with a suitable garden. The Crown is patron of both livings. The congregation in the parish church, is numerous and respectable.

---

* In 1643, a Mr Douglas, town-clerk of Elgyn, by order, and at sight of the magistrates, and upon their credit, attests, that, by the rolls at their muster, there were only aucht score, (one hundred and sixty) able bodied men, fit for bearing arms in the town, and to pass six months, in such business; and of these only fourscore could be furnished, with *muscaths, pickes, gunnis, halberds, denfaixes*, or *Lochaber aixes*. This bears, to be taken up, by the direction and warrant of the Committee of Estates. There is another attestation in 1645, signed by the same Douglas, and the Provost and Council of Elgyn, that bears there were only fourscore fensible men within the burgh, many having fled from the town, for fear of their enemies. In this attestation, the Provost, after his name, adds *Provost of Helgeyne*.

refpectable. There is alfo a feparate meeting, confifting partly of perfons belonging to this parifh, but principally from the neighbouring ones. They contribute L. 40 Sterling a-year to the maintenance of their clergyman. The Seceders have one, and the Epifcopalians two meeting-houfes. None of thefe are numerous; neither are the Roman Catholics, nor Methodifts.

Difeafes.—The difeafes moft prevalent, in this town and parifh, are fluxes, confumptions, and the King's evil. Children have the common routine of chincoughs, meafles and fmall-pox. The type of fevers is much changed within thefe laft thirty years. Before that period, the pleuritic and inflammatory kinds prevailed. Now, they are low, lingering, and nervous. This alteration may arife, from our wanting the hardinefs of our forefathers. Every thing cold is in difufe. Clothing is warmer. Warm liquors, as punch, tea, &c. are the fafhion, even among the lower claffes. On the whole, we are become more effeminate; and labour more fevere, whilft the mind is depreffed, from the anxieties of life, and the difficulty of procuring a fubfiftence.

The progrefs of the fcrophula is alarming, by intermarriages, and the imperfect cure of the lues, with a low diet. Confumptions are frequent among the young. Manufacturers and tradefmen, in particular, are fubject to them, from the nature of their employment. The women lead fedentary lives in fpinning, from which arife obftructions, &c. that often terminate fatally; and from the fame caufes, difficult labours are more common than formerly.

Borough Lands.—There is a large field of arable land, to the weft of Elgyn, through which the Loffie runs, divided into what are called *auchteen parts*, but confifting of *fixty-four*, which

which vary in extent from 4 to 6 acres each. Originally, they belonged to 64 diſtinct proprietors, burgeſſes of El- gyn. The ſoil of a great part of this ground is good, being a rich loam, over a clay bottom ; and the whole might be greatly improved, were the ſeparate parts thrown into one connected field; but they lie in run-rig, and ſo disjoined, that different portions, of the ſame lot, may be almoſt an Engliſh mile aſunder. The Loſſie is making great encroach- ments on ſome of them ; and as they ſtill are the property of a number of different perſons, though many of them have been acquired by one individual, no common meaſure has been adopted, to imbank the river, which might be done by piles, at a ſmall expence. Theſe havocks of the river, have diſcovered in different places, a foot or two thick of excel- lent peat moſs, buried from 4 to 6 feet, under the loam and clay. It is uncertain, who originally granted theſe lands to the 64 burgeſſes of Elgyn. Tradition has uniformly re- ported, that they were given, as a compenſation, to the fami- lies of men who had fallen in battle, on ſome important oc- caſion *.

Pluſcarden.—The ruins of the priory of Pluſcarden, in the weſt end of this pariſh, are truly magnificent. The church was never completed, as the foundations of the weſt part of the croſs were only laid. There are ſmall pieces of freſco painting, that remain under an arch in the church, which are tolerably accurate in the deſign, and the colours lively. The mill for grinding their corns, was within the high free-ſtone walls, that ſurrounded their burying-ground, &c. Their gardens were excellent. A fig-tree was there

a

* See Robert Gordon's deſcription of Scotland, in Bleau's Atlas, anno 1647, vol. 6. p. 105.

a few years ago, which annually produced fruit. The Glen of Plufcarden, after paffing through the hands of many proprietors, has become the property of Lord Fife.

Mifcellaneous Obfervations.—In the year 1754, a fhip loaded with coals, came to Loffiemouth. The demand was then fo fmall, that the importer could not difpofe of 100 Barrels. Now, the demand is fo great, that upwards of twenty fhips arrive with Englifh coals, and fix with Scotch, and it is daily encreafing. It is particularly unkind in government, not to fay *oppreffive*, that thofe who are neceffarily fubjected to a high freight, and an inland carriage, fhould pay an exorbitant duty on that indifpenfible accommodation of life, from which thofe at the pit mouth are exempted. It is an odious difcrimination of the fubjects of the fame kingdom, and, in its effects, it is equally hoftile to the agriculture and the manufactures of the country.

The inhabitants of the towns, in the northern parts of Scotland, are tolerably induftrious; but, in general, they have not as yet eftablifhed any manufacture, for employing young children, and giving them early habits of induftry, which would operate greatly in their favour through life. A pin-work, or any fuch employment, that demands no great capital, and yet requires a number of feeble hands, would be of the greateft confequence, and produce happy effects.

Throwing a bridge over the Spey, would open the communication between the north and fouth, would facilitate the land-carriage of goods, and would prove of fingular advantage to the traveller; fo that it is, in fact, a national object, to have this fpeedily accomplifhed.

The hiftory of a plantation of common firs, made by the late Lord Fife, many years ago, deferves notice. It is in the vicinity of the boat of Bog, near the Spey. It was twice

planted

planted over, and as often failed, from its northern exposure, the neighbourhood of the sea, and a sterile soil. A sagacious country gardener raised a nursery on the most exposed place of this plantation, from which he took the plants, and they throve well. By this mode, were it uniformly adopted, plantations might be raised, even within the reach of the sea spray, or on any exposure, the plants being habituated, in early life, to their situation. There is moss, in many parts of Scotland, at flood-mark; and, in North America, trees grow within the reach of spring tides.

It may not be improper, to conclude this paper, with some observations on the causes of depopulation, in some parts of Scotland, by which this district in particular seems to be distinguished.

1. Our standing armies, from dissipation and other causes are hostile to marriage, and the rearing of children; nor are the children produced, in general, either healthy or long lived. A great navy, and multitudes of sailors employed in foreign commerce, must have the same effect.

2. Increase of manufactures. It is allowed, that where manufacturing families are scattered over a country, and each of them has a few acres of land, in the culture of which they are occasionally employed, a numerous and healthy breed is the necessary consequence. But when numbers are cooped up, in ill-aired. low, damp houses, neither the parents, nor the children are healthy. Besides, a sedentary, and confined situation, is adverse to longevity, and to a healthy progeny.

3. Sheep farms in the Highlands of Scotland, and in other places, have obliged numbers to emigrate; and when once a country becomes depopulated, by the removal of it's native inhabitants, it requires ages to recruit them.

4. In the Lowlands, the spirit of the times, has introduced a system, of converting many small, into one large farm.

The

The individual, who occupies such a farm, having fewer mouths to maintain, can afford, perhaps, a greater rent, than what many families, on the same surface of ground, could pay at once. But the population being thus greatly diminished, the value of the property may, in procefs of time, suffer by it. Numbers, made superfluous by this measure, flock into towns, where with difficulty, they earn a scanty subsistence. They, no doubt, increase the population of these towns; but towns, on almost any scale, are adverse to either the keeping up, or the increasing of numbers. A country life was the original destination of man, is the most favourable to wealth and population, and ought, on every account, to meet with all possible encouragement and protection. The most favourable size of farms to make a country populous, is from 15 to 40 acres of arable land. The occupiers of such farms marry early, as they have the prospect of bread, if they are industrious. But when farms are overgrown, they are mostly inhabited by servants and day-labourers; and every measure is tried to keep wages and the price of labour low, by which marriage is discouraged. Day-labourers then become afraid of marrying, and servants very seldom can; and thus the numbers of a healthy peasantry are daily diminished.

5. These circumstances also lead to emigration, and to this it may be added, that incited by the prospect of making a fortune, as it is called, the flower of our young men, of every class and description, go abroad; and for one, who returns in a comfortable situation, and raises a family, how many hundreds, I had almost said thousands, drop by the road. Their wealth, however accumulated, cannot surely compensate for the loss of so many citizens; indeed, scarcely repaying the original expence of fitting them out.

Lastly,

Laſtly, luxury and its certain attendant, an exorbitant expence of living, moſt materially affeﬅs population. It dif-
courages marriage, until perſons acquire an income, adequate
in their eﬅimation, to that ﬅate; or, in other words, until they
are advanced in years, and then a puny helpleſs race of children is produced. Hence, how many men of every deſcription remain ſingle ? and how many young women of every
rank are never married, who, in the beginning of this century, and even ſo late as the 1745, would have been the
parents of a numerous and healthy progeny ?

PARISH OF FORRES.

(COUNTY OF BANFF.—PRESBYTERY OF FORRES.—
SYNOD OF MORAY.)

By the Rev. Mr JOHN M'DONNEL, *Minister.*

***

Situation and Name.

FORRES, a royal burgh, situated upon the Moray Frith, gives name to this parish. It lies in the synod of Moray, and is the seat of the presbytery of Forres. Forres, as antiently written, is of Celtic origin, signifying its situation upon the sea.

Extent and Boundaries.—The form of this parish is irregular, approaching nearest to a triangle, with a stripe of moorish and hill ground, about three miles in length, stretching from one corner. It is four miles in length, and about two and one half in breadth; bounded upon the north by the bay of Findhorn, a large bason of shallow water, formed by the meeting of the tide and the river Findhorn; on the northeast by the parish of Kinlop; on the east and south by the parish of Rafford. On the south-west and north north-west, by the river Findhorn, which divides it from the united parishes of Dyke and Moy.

The

The fouth and fouth-eaft parts of this parifh are hilly, co-vered with fhort heath and furze. The reft is one continued rich arable well cultivated field.

Climate and Profpect —Forres, in point of fituation and climate, is inferior to no part of Scotland. The air is dry, ferene, and healthy. The town, being built upon a rifing ground, about a mile from the Bay of Findhorn, commands an extenfive profpect of a rich and well cultivated country, interfperfed with the feats and improvements of many of the neighbouring proprietors. Lefs rain falls here than in moft other parts of the kingdom, the fhowers being attracted by the Moray Frith on the north, and on the fouth, by the hills which divide Moray from Strathfpey.

Church and Stipend.—The value of the living is 98 bolls of bear, 20 bolls of meal, and 490 pounds Scots, a glebe of 4 acres, and manfe and office-houfes. The Earl of Moray is undoubted patron. The church was built in 1745. Its dimenfions, within walls, are 72 by 36 feet; and it contains 1800 people.

The heritors of the parifh are the Earl of Moray, Sir James Grant of Grant, Robert Urquhart of Bandfyards, Alexander Penrofe Cumming of Altyre, John Gordon of Grufhop, Dunbar of Grarye, Leflie of Balnegeith, Urquhart of Tannachy, and Mr Strahan of Druimduan, with fome fmall proprietors, holding of the town of Forres.

All thefe, except Lord Moray and Sir James Grant, have their refidences within the parifh.

Population.—From an actual furvey lately made, the number of inhabitants was found to be 2987; of which number there are,

Males

Males	1341	2398 reside in the town
Females	1646	589 reside in the country.

2987   2987

The number of inhabitants in 1774, appears, from actual surveys, to have been 2793, so that there is now an increase of population of 194.

The number of births, during a period of 11 years, from 1779 to 1789 inclusive, is 895; 453 males, and 442 females, being in the proportion nearly of 41 to 40, and the average $81\frac{4}{11}$.

Upon an average of the last 11 years, the number of marriages of persons residing in the parish is 15 annually.

There are many persons now living in the parish of 80, but none whose age exceeds 92.

There are 18 farmers residing in town, and 43 in the country, many of whom, especially those in town, hold very small possessions.

56 Shoemakers   4 of whom reside in the country.
33 Weavers   8 ditto.
25 Taylors   2 ditto.
 6 Blacksmiths
58 Journeymen and apprentices.

Trade.—There are in Forres 60 merchants and shopkeepers. These were formerly principally supported by travelling and vending their goods in all the villages and market towns to the west and north, particularly Sutherland, Caithness, and Ross, and as far as Orkney. But this intercourse is in a great measure now rendered unnecessary, as in all these countries they have got stationary shopkeepers, who

can

can retail their goods nearly upon as low terms as the merchants of Forres.

Manners.—About 50 years ago there were only 3 tea-kettles in Forres: at present there are not less than 300. The blue bonnets of Forres were then famous for good credit, and at that period there were only 6 people with hats in the town; now above 400. Happy for our country did we keep pace in virtuous improvement, with the extravagant refinement adopted in dress and manners. About 30 years ago, 30 s. would have purchased a complete holiday suit of clothing for a labouring servant; according to the present mode of dress, it will require at least 5 l. to equip him.

Rate of Wages.—About the year 1750, a servant engaged for harvest had 4 d. a day with his victuals; now 10 d. with two meals. For the whole time of harvest then, he had 10 s. now 25 s. A journeyman mason had then 1 merk Scotch, without victuals, now 20 d. A labouring man servant had, at the above period, 15 s. 4 d.; now from 2 l. 10 s. to 3 l. 10 s. in the half year. A woman servant then had 8 s. and 4 d. and some 10 s. half yearly; now from 18 s. to 21 s.

Ecclesiastical State.—There are no sectaries in Forres, except a few Seceders. They are not upon the increase.

Productions of this Parish.—The soil and climate of this parish will produce any crops that can be raised in any part of Scotland. Harvest begins the first week of August, and towards the end of that month, even during the late rainy seasons, it becomes general. It is no uncommon thing, in
this

this neighbourhood, to cut down barley in 12 or 13 weeks after the time of fowing it.

Poors Funds.—About 125 perfons receive charity from the church and poors funds, many of whom are heads of families. Amongft thefe there is annually divided about 40 l. arifing chiefly from the collections made at the church doors. But the poors funds have been lately confiderably augmented by a donation left by the Rev. Mr Alexander Watt, late minifter of this parifh, of about 200 l. Befides the above fums, there is 15 l. annually divided amongft the poor of Forres, being the intereft of money left under the direction of the Town Council.

Price of Provifions.—About the year 1750, beef and mutton fold in the markets at 1 d. per lib. and fifh for 1 d. per dozen ; oat meal for 8 s. per boll of 9 ftone ; wheat for 11 s. and barley for 10 s. Our market is plentifully fupplied with every article of provifion, beef and mutton at 3 d. ; fifh, at an average, at 6 d. the dozen of haddocks, and falmon at 4 d. the lib. ; pork, from 3 d. to 4 d. ; lamb and veal from 4 d. to 4¼ d. ; butter, from 7½ d. to 9 d. per lib. ; and cheefe 4 s. to 4 s. 6 d. per ftone. The lib. of butter 24 oz. and 16 lib. to the ftone.

Schools.—In the town of Forres there is a grammar fchool, with a falary of 20 l. ; and, from the abilities and attention of the prefent teacher, it has acquired a great character. Latin, Greek, French, and the various branches of the mathematics, are taught with great fuccefs ; and a young gentleman may have board and education for 20 l. *per annum.* Befides the falaries given to the public teachers, the Magiftrates give fome fmall donations to thofe who keep private fchools, ſchools, to encourage them in their attention to their charge. There is likewiſe an Engliſh ſchool, ſeparate from the grammar ſchool; the teacher has a ſalary of 15 l. *per annum,* and every encouragement from the magiſtrates that can render his ſituation comfortable. The price of education in this town, as in every other part of Scotland, is very low. The learned languages are taught for 2 s. 6 d. per quarter; Engliſh for 1 s. 6 d. per ditto.

There is likewiſe a boarding-ſchool for young ladies, where the various branches of needle work, muſic, and other parts of female education, are taught with great ſucceſs. The miſtreſs has a ſalary of 16 l. *per annum* from the town; and a young lady may have every accommodation for 15 l. a year. Dues per quarter, muſic, 10 s. 6 d.; plain work, 2 s. 6 d.; tambour, 5 s.; gum flowers, a guinea. Particular attention is paid to the morals of youth in theſe different ſeminaries of learning; and from the abilities of the preſent teachers, and attention paid to the ſchools by the Magiſtrates, and the healthy ſituation of the town of Forres, there is not, perhaps, a more eligible place for the education of youth any where.

Rivers and Fiſh.—In this pariſh there are no freſh water lakes, and the river Findhorn and the burn of Forres are the only ſtreams in the pariſh. The fiſh found in the river and bay of Findhorn, are ſalmon, trout, eels, flounders, and abundance of haddocks are taken in the Frith, which ſupplies the town of Forres and the neighbourhood. The quantity of ſalmon exported from Forres, upon an average of 10 years, from 1773 to 1783, was about 300 barrels annually, beſides the home conſumpt, which is not very conſiderable. Since the 1783, the quantity of ſalmon taken is conſiderably leſs; but laſt year, 1792, the fiſhing of the Findhorn has been

been much more productive than for several years preceding. The price of salmon is 4 d. and for trout 5 d. per lib.

Navigation, &c.—The river Findhorn is navigable for boats no farther than the tide flows. But did the increase of commerce and manufactures require it, there is no place where a canal might be more easily made. From Forres to the mouth of the Bay of Findhorn, which is the sea-port of Forres, the distance does not exceed 3 miles, and the tide flows in the bason more than half that distance; and the level of the ground, at the foot of the eminence on which the town of Forres stands, does not exceed the level of half tide by 14 feet; and that depth of a canal would carry boats and lighters at high water to the town; and such a canal would have the advantage of the burn of Forres to keep it clear. The bason already mentioned is a triangular piece of low ground, partly of that kind of stiff clay soil, called carse ground; and partly of fine compact sand, mixed with light particles of earth washed down by the floods. It is all dry at low water, except the channel of the river, and a little space at the inlet at high-water. Its circumference will be at least 7 miles, and contains more than 2 square miles of ground, all of which might be recovered from the sea, except what is necessary for a channel to the fresh water streams. A bar of sand, which stretches across the mouth of the river, prevents any surge from entering the bason; so that an embankment would have no weight of water to sustain, but the small fetch of the lake itself.

Limestone, &c.—In all this parish there is only one quarry of limestone, upon the estate of Mr Cuming of Altyre. It is not used in any great quantities. There is only one small patch of coarse moor-stone; and no detached stones are

found

found of any confiderable fize, either above or below ground.

Inundations.— The lower part of this parifh is very much fubject to be flooded by the rivers. In September 1768, and Auguſt 1782, there were a remarkable inundation. The river Findhorn rofe to fuch a height, that more than a mile in bread.h of the fineſt lands was laid under water, and the crops either carried away or deftroyed.

Manufactures.—The inhabitants in general are difpofed to induftry. No manufactures of public importance are carried on in or about Forres, except what fupplies the town and its vicinity. The fpinning of linen yarn has for 20 years back brought a confiderable fupply of money to this country. The fpinning of yarn and manufacturing fuch of it as may be neceffary for domeftic purpofes, has employed a confiderable number of women, whofe earnings have been of great advantage to themfelves, and beneficial to the public. The merchants are in the ufe of buying the yarn, and fending it to Glafgow, where there is generally a ready fale, unlefs the market is overftocked with Irifh yarn, which, only on account of its cheapnefs, at certain times is preferred. But fince the year 1784, the yarn trade has been gradually declining, owing to the increafe of machines for fpinning cotton in the fouth country, and the great quantities of yarn from Ireland imported into Glafgow, by which the price of yarn in this country has been greatly reduced. Many of thofe formerly employed in fpinning yarn for fale have of late taken to the fpinning of Dutch flax for the manufacturing companies at Aberdeen and Invernefs.

A merchant of this town, in the year 1784, fent to Glafgow 23,290 fpindles of yarn, which was collected near this place.

place. The other dealers in that article fent at leaft 47,000 fpindles, which, at the rate of 2 s. per fpindle for fpinners, produced 7029 l. Sterling. The Truftees for Manufactures and Improvements have given fome encouragement for the erecting of lint-mills in this neighbourhood, and thefe promife to be of great utility; and while they provide a proper and expeditious mode of manufacturing the flax, they will at the fame time encourage the raifing of that article in the country. Too much attention cannot be paid to this ufeful branch of trade, which employs thofe, and makes them ufeful to fociety, who would otherwife be a burden to the ftate.

Rent.—In the neighbourhood of the town, land let fo high as 50 s. and fome of the fields clofe to the town at 3 l. an acre. Thefe are farmed by horfe-hirers, who lay them down in grafs; and, by the high wages they get for letting out their horfes, are enabled to pay this enormous price for the land.

Plantations.—To the fouth of this town, upon a rifing ground, commanding a view of Forres and Findhorn, and the Moray Frith, ftands the houfe of Burdfyards, reckoned one of the beft fituations which any country can afford. Upon this eftate are very extenfive plantations of firs, in a very flourifhing condition, planted by the prefent proprietors and others, and which now yield a profit of 100 l. a year. There are likewife confiderable plantations of firs upon the eftate of Cuthall, belonging to Alexander Penrofe Cuming of Altyre, fituated to the fouth-weft of the town, about 3 miles upon the road leading from Forres to Yverttown.

PARISH OF KINLOSS.

By the Rev. Mr JOHN HOYES.

Name, Situation, Extent, Soil, &c.

THE antient and modern name of this pariſh is Kinloſs, derived from *Kain*, a Head, and *Loch ;* i. e. the Head of the Loch ; Kinloſs being ſituated on the head of the Bay of Findhorn. This pariſh is in the ſhire of Elgin and Forres ; in the preſbytery of Forres, and ſynod of Moray. It is of a ſquare form, being between three and four miles long and broad. It is bounded on the eaſt by the pariſh of Alves ; on the ſouth and ſouth-weſt by Rafford and Forres ; and on the north by the Moray Firth. It is a very flat level country. The ſoil is various ; in ſome places light and ſandy ; in others a rich and deep clay, moſs, and loam, make up a conſiderable part of the ſoil ; and all of it, when well managed, produces good crops of grain of every kind. This pariſh, being flat, is but poorly ſupplied with good water ; and moſt of the ſprings taſte of minerals. The ſhore is flat and ſandy. The fiſh caught here are moſtly haddocks and whittings, and, in the ſeaſon, cod, ſkate, and ling, which are all ſold in the country, and at Forres, at about 1 d. or 1½ d. a pound.

Climate

Climate and Diftempers.—The air is fharp, dry, and healthy. The moft prevalent diftempers are cutaneous difeafes, fcurvy, and rheumatifm ; owing, perhaps, to hard labour, the fharpnefs of the air, a fpare or fifh diet, and want of cleanlinefs.

Population.—The amount of the inhabitants of this parifh is 234 families, which contain 1031 perfons, being nearly 4½ to each family. There are 4 heritors, 40 farmers, 56 fifhermen and failors, 9 fhoemakers, 6 weavers, 6 carpenters and wrights, 2 taylors, 2 fmiths, 2 millers, 2 mafons, 2 coopers, 1 merchant, 1 brewer, 1 thread manufacturer, 10 day labourers, and 6 traveling beggars. Dr Webfter's ftate of the inhabitants is 1191. The annual average of births from 1700 to 1720, is 25 males and 21 females ; from the beginning of the year 1779 to the beginning of 1789, is 29. In this laft period were born 147 males, and 145 females. The decreafe of population is owing to the fpirit of traveling, and the engrofling of farms.

Church and Stipend.—The manfe was built in 1751 ; the church in 1765. The value of the living is uncertain ; a procefs of augmentation having been carried on fince the year 1781. The patrons are Lord Moray and Mifs Brodie of Lethen.

Mifcellaneous Obfervations.—There are no rivers in this parifh but the Findhorn, which runs fouth and weft, and falls into the Moray Firth at the town of Findhorn. This river abounds with falmon, which, in the fpring, and beginning of fummer, are boiled at Findhorn, and kitted and fent to the London market. Frefh falmon is fold here at 4 d. a pound.

The

The only harbour in this pariſh is Findhorn, which has a bar that is continually changing, and prevents ſhips of great burden from entering; ſo that the trade is carried on in ſmall merchant veſſels, or ſloops. The imports are merchant goods, ſugar, wine, porter, bark, &c. The exports, oats and barley, ſalmon, linen yarn, &c.

PARISH of KNOCKANDOW,

(COUNTY OF MORAY.)

By the Rev. Mr FRANCIS GRANT.

Name, Situation, Extent, Soil, &c.

KNOCKANDOW has its name from two Celtic words, *Knock*, ſignifying 'hill,' and *Dow*, 'black.' It is ſituated in the county of Moray, preſbytery of Aberdour and Synod of Moray, about 10 miles in length, and, at an average, 2 in breadth. It is bounded on the S. and S. W. by the pariſhes of Inveraven and Aberdour, from which it is ſeparated by the river Spey, one of the moſt rapid in Scotland; on the E. by Rothes, on the N. by Birnie and Dallas, on the W. by Edinkilly and Cromdale.—The country is hilly; the ſoil either deep moſs or ſandy gravel; the air dry and healthy.—Spey is the only river connected with the pariſh, which produces ſalmon; but owing to cruives, few of them get up this length. The hills are covered with heath, and the river-ſide with birch, oak and alder. The many ſmall rivulets that deſcend from the hills, are frequently in the months of February and November ſwelled by the rains, overflow their banks, and do conſiderable harm. This happened particularly in 1783, when

622

when a water-fpout, there is reafon to believe, fell in the adjacent hills.

Population.—-According to Dr Webfter's return, the numbers were 1267. The population is rather lefs than about 25 years ago, many having gone to Aberdeen. The number of all ages at prefent is about 1500; of whom 600 are males, and 900 females. The annual average of births is 40, of marriages 12. The number of fouls under 10 is 460, and from 70 to 100 is 36.

Agriculture.—The grain principally cultivated is black oats, big, or Scotch bear, fome rye, turnip and potatoes. There is very little artificial grafs. Seed-time generally begins in the end of March, and continues through the whole of April. Harveft here is in Auguft, September and October. The land-rent of the parifh is about L. 2000. The fifhings produce about L. 10 a-year. The number of horfes 300, of cattle 3000, of fheep 5000. There may be about 150 ploughs, all of the Scotch kind, except one. The laft in general are very bad. The very beft arable land is 14 s. the acre; the general fize of farms about 30 acres.

Stipend, Poor, &c.—The value of the living, including the glebe, is L. 85 Sterling. Sir James Grant of Grant is patron. The church was built in 1757, and the manfe in 1767. There are 4 heritors.—The number of poor is 20. The collections for their relief are about L. 3 ; and the fines of delinquents, with what arifes from a mortification, may amount to L. 7.

Prices and Wages.—Provifions formerly were very cheap. A fat ox might have been got for L. 1, 5 s. and a fheep for 3 s. 4 d. ; a boll of oat-meal for 6 s. 8 d. Now, beef and
mutton

mutton fell at 3 d. the pound, meal at 14 s. the boll, and fowls, which fold at 2 d. coft 6 d. and 7 d.—A labourer will earn 6 d. a-day in fummer, and 4 d. in winter, including victuals. A wright 8 d. a mafon 10 d. and a tailor 4 d. befides victuals. A common labourer, when married, could never maintain his family, if he had not a fmall croft. This defcription of men, in general, is in great poverty. A man fervant earns from L. 4, 10 s. to L. 5 a-year, and a woman L. 1 : 13 : 4.

Miscellaneous Obfervations.—The Gaelic was generally fpoken here till about 50 years ago.—Peats are the only fuel. —The general fize of the people is about 5 feet 6 inches, and their complexion black. Many of them are very deficient in induftry, but œconomical. They are fond of a military life, and prefer the Highland regiments.—The roads in the parifh were formerly well made, and kept in good repair; but, for fome time paft, they have been greatly neglected. The people, fenfible of this neglect, pay the ftatute-labour in kind, and work, it may be fuppofed, as little as poffible. Were a more liberal plan of management adopted, and the ftatute-labour commuted, it would be more agreeable, and of much advantage. The people here have no idea of turnpikes, or their advantages. —In 1782, there was neither a fufficiency of feed nor bread, and had not Government interfered, numbers muft have ftarved; but the fupply granted, relieved, in a great degree, their wants.—The parifh, in general, is uninclofed. The people are fenfible of the advantage of inclofures, but they are little encouraged, except by one of the heritors. The condition of the people might be much meliorated, by granting them leafes for 38 years, and a lifetime, by encouraging inclofures, and giving them good examples of hufbandry.

PARISH OF RAFFORD,

(SYNOD OF MORAY, COUNTY OF ELGIN, AND PRESBYTERY
OF FORRES.)

By the Rev. Mr WILLIAM STEPHEN, *Miniſter.*

Name.

IN the courſe of time, the name of this pariſh has undergone ſome variation. About the beginning of the 13th
century, in a charter from Pope Innocent to Bricius biſhop
of Moray, it is denominated *Ecclefia de Ruffus.* How long
this had been the received orthography, ſeems not very
clear; but from the commencement of our preſbyterial
record in 1651, I find it written, at ſucceſſive periods, *Raf-
fart, Riffard,* and for about 60 years back, almoſt invariably *Rafford.* Being no adept, however, in the ancient
Celtic or Gaelic languages, I will hazard no conjecture a-
bout its true etymology.

Situation,

Situation, &c.—It is fituated in the county of Elgin, prefbytery of Forres, and Synod of Moray; extends from N. E. to S. W. above 8 Englifh miles in length, and from 5 to 3 miles in breadth. On the E. it is bounded by the parifhes of Alves and Elgin; on the S. by thofe of Dallas and Edinkillie; on the W. by the river Findhorn, and the parifh of Forres; and on the N. by that of Kinlofs.

Soil, &c.—The face of the country is much diverfified; part of it being low, flat, and fertile; part of it elevated, moorifh, and rocky. The complexion of the foil, too, is various; confifting of a deep and rich clay, a hot and blowing fand, a black and fhallow mould, bottomed with rock; though the greater part is compofed of a rough brown gravel, where the bottom is a continued ftratum of fmall pebbles, fo clofely compacted that no ploughfhare almoft can pierce it, and having the appearance of calcination.

Climate, &c.—The *air* can hardly be faid to poffefs any fpecific quality; it is rather dry than moift, rather healthy than otherwife. The moft prevalent *diftempers*, at leaft fuch as generally prove moft fatal, are fevers, confumptions, and afthmas; thefe may partly be owing to the heat and drynefs of the foil, to the clofe and fmoky air of the dwellings, as well as to the nature of the food, efpecially potatoes, on which, for feveral months of the year, many of the poorer clafs are almoft wholly fuftained.

Hills.—The *hills*, none of which are remarkable for height, are chiefly covered with heath, furze, whins, and juniper. They produce abundance of excellent peat, turf, fallen fir, and other fuel, and afford **extenfive** pafturage for fheep and black cattle.

Minerals.

Minerals.—Here are two valuable *quarries*, the one of freeftone, the other of grey flate, both of which are deemed inexhauftible. The accefs to both is eafy, and the materials are much efteemed in building, for their eafinefs in working and durability.

Cattle.—The native breed of cattle is fmall ; an ordinary ox or cow feldom outweighing 70 or 80 lbs. a-quarter. The horfes are very indifferent, except with the beft farmers. Sheep are numerous, fmall fized, and moftly white ; their wool is fine, and the mutton very delicate.

Population.—According to Dr Webfter's report in 1755, the population of Rafford then amounted to 1313 fouls. From an accurate lift taken in 1791, the number of parifhioners did not exceed 1072 ; of thefe 488 were males, and 584 females ; about 840 were found examinable, *i. e.* above 7 years old. The number of houfeholders was exactly 238 ; of whom 136 were married, and had iffue ; 16 were married, and had no iffue ; 18 were widowers ; 48 widows ; the remaining 20 unmarried, and 5 of them bachelors. The annual medium of births for the laft 7 years, as they ftand on the record, may be computed at 32 ; of marriages, at 8 : But of the deaths no exact regifter has been kept, owing chiefly to that reluctance with which the tax on burials was paid by country people *.

Poor.—About 40 poor are fupplied from the parifh funds. Our capital ftock is L. 50 Sterling, and our weekly collections amount from 2 s. 6 d. to 3 s.

Longevity.

* The late taxes on births, baptifms, marriages, burials, &c. are now repealed.

Longevity.—Few of the natives are remarkable for longevity. There are now only about three individuals in the parish whose ages exceed 80, and the generality of old men seldom attain that period.

Agriculture.—The bulk of the people are employed in agriculture, and some have pretty extensive farms, though few have begun to inclose their grounds, or to lay down green crops. This defect may be partly owing to want of due encouragement, as well as to ancient prejudice, to which last cause it is perhaps too often ascribed. Of late, indeed, several of the farmers have built decent houses, for which they have an allowance from the landlord, and a spirit of improvement begins to prevail. Those whose farms are in good order, yoke two horses only in a plough, with which an expert hand will make very neat and excellent work ; but the greatest number discover a predilection for oxen, of which they generally couple 6 together, and in the hilly parts, (or as they are called provincially *the braes*), where the farms are small and the tenants poor, the yoke is frequently composed of two cows, and two horses to lead.

Occupations, &c.—Spinning flax is the great occupation of the females, most of which they raise at home, and make into sheeting, diaper, and sackcloth ; for little of the native growth is fine enough for shirting. Many of the poorer class, too, support themselves by spinning to yarn-merchants, who allow them from 10 d. to 1 s. *per* spindle.

Of *handicraftsmen* weavers are the most numerous class, amounting to 16 or 17, including journeymen and apprentices. There are 4 tailors ; 3 blacksmiths ; 3 millers ; 5 joiners, and some of the farmers work in wood, and make
their

their own ploughs, harrows, carts, and other implements of huſbandry.

Religion.—All the pariſhioners, (excepting two or three families, who belong to the Seceſſion), profeſs the Eſtabliſhed Religion, and are very punctual in their attendance at church. Viewed in this light, they appear, upon the whole, a ſenſible, decent, and ſerious people. In former times, indeed, the high and myſtical doctrines of Calviniſm being univerſally taught, and admired as the only ſyſtem of orthodox belief, had diſſeminated among the ignorant a ſpirit of wildneſs and bigotry; but this, for more than half a century paſt, has been gradually ſubſiding; and it is humbly hoped, that the rigid and fallible dogmas of men will no longer be ſubſtituted for the pure and rational truths of the goſpel. On the other hand, as no earthly community is perfect, the moſt prevalent vices I have had occaſion to remark in this, are falſehood, intemperance, ſenſuality, and petty thefts; theſe perhaps will be found moſt congenial to mild and temperate climates.

Heritors, &c.—The heritors are the Earl of Moray, proprietor of Tarras and Cluny; the Honourable Lewis Duff of Blervie; Alexander Penroſe Cumming of Altyre, and Joſeph Dunbar of Grange, Eſquires. The valued rent of the pariſh amounts to L. 2612 : 18 : 10 Scots; and the annualrent, of which a great part is victual, may be eſtimated, *communibus annis*, about L. 1600 Sterling.

Eſtates, &c.—The Earl of Moray, though he has no family ſeat, holds ſome of the fineſt lands in the pariſh; his people, too, ſurpaſs moſt of their neighbours in the decent appearance of their houſes, and the order in which they keep their grounds. In Tarras they raiſe plentiful crops of wheat,
barley,

barley, oats, peafe, beans,—flax and potatoes; thefe laft
are found an ufeful mean of improvement. The mode of
preparation is this: An exhaufted field is let out in parcels, rent free, to poor people in the neighbourhood, who
on their part furnifh the manure, labour the ground by trenching it with the fpade, plant and reap the crop. In this
manner, the bottom foil, which is a ftrong clay, being expofed and meliorated, acquires a degree of fertility which
it does not lofe for years after. The oats produced here
are of a fuperior kind, and highly efteemed for fowing.
The lands of Cluny, fituated in the hilly part of the parifh,
are fomewhat cold and backward; the foil, however, is
powerful, and the corn pretty good of its quality, and the
whole eftate is accommodated with abundance of fuel and
pafturage. Here is the flate-quarry formerly mentioned,
which is rented from the proprietor by the tackfman of
the farm wherein it lies, and by him let out to the quarriers, at the rate of 40 s. *per* 1000 rough flates.

The barony of Blervie is a valuable eftate, comprehending large and fertile fields of corn, which produce grain of
an excellent quality, efpecially barley, oats, and rye. There
are confiderable tracts of moorifh and hilly ground upon it,
where the pafture in general is very dry and falubrious. It
is alfo well fupplied with fuel; for though in fome places,
by the abufe of thofe who have long had fervitudes upon
them, the peat-moffes have fuffered dilapidation, yet in
others they ftill remain unbroken; and wherever the proprietor's people find a deficiency of peat, they have recourfe upon the moors, which furnifh them with turf fufficient to make up their annual complement. Mr Duff
has built a very neat modern houfe, which he has greatly
ornamented, by planting the adjoining hills, improving his
farm, and laying out his fields to advantage. The ancient
family

family ſeat belonging to the Dunbars, is moſtly demoliſhed ; all that remains of it being a high tower, which, ſtanding on elevated ground, commands an immenſe proſpect,
including almoſt the whole Moray Frith, with a great part
of the counties of Elgin, Nairn, Inverneſs, Cromarty, Roſs,
Sutherland and Caithneſs.

Eaſtward from this about two miles, ſtands the caſtle of
Burgee, the ſeat of Dunbar of Grange. It is a large and
beautiful fabric, conſiſting of a ſquare tower of ſix ſtoreys,
built in 1602, and an adjoining manſion founded about a
century later. The gardens occupy ſeveral acres, contain
a variety of fruit-trees, and are ſkirted with double rows
of fine ſpreading beeches. In approaching this place,
which is very conſpicuous, the mind is powerfully impreſſed with an idea of ancient magnificence. Here is the
freeſtone quarry alluded to page 340. from which, though
great quantities of materials are conſtantly taken, the proprietor derives almoſt no pecuniary advantage. It is further remarkable, that though Mr Dunbar's rental has ſu
ſtained little or no alteration for more than 80 years ;
though the whole of his lands are very improvable, and
abound with every needful accommodation ; yet his people are not affluent, their farms are poorly cultivated, and
their houſes mean. Theſe defects muſt doubtleſs in ſome
meaſure be attributed to want of leaſes, which, on account
of certain family embarraſſments, that gentleman is not
diſpoſed to grant them. Being reſtricted, too, from cutting peat in the moſſes of Burgie, they conſume a great
part of the ſummer in providing their fuel, which they
muſt bring from the moſſes of Altyre in the oppoſite extremity of the pariſh, where Grange has a ſervitude. This
inconvenience ſtill further aggravates the want of agricultural improvement in his eſtate.

Altyre

Altyre was formerly a diftinct parifh, belonging to the parfonage of Dallas, and was annexed to Rafford by act of Parliament 1661. The walls of the old church remain entire, which till of late, that Mr Cumming erected a new tomb, had been the burying-place of his anceftors time out of mind. The Cummings of Logie, who are a branch of this family, and moft of the ancient refidenters, ftill continue to bury here. The foil of Altyre is generally thin, but fharp and productive. It commands a prodigious extent of hill and pafturage, and the peat-moffes are inexhauftible. The prefent proprietor has brought his farm into the higheft order, and obferves a judicious rotation of green and corn crops, which feldom fail to be rich and abundant. He has planted about 1000 acres, with fir and other timber, which are advancing rapidly and decorating the place. The family feat is an old plain building, with two neat modern wings, and though well fitted up and commodious, is not fuitable to that ftyle difplayed by its ingenious owner everywhere around it. Of late, however, he has adopted the idea of building a new manfion, on a very fuperb and elegant plan. Here is a fpacious garden, abounding with a variety of excellent fruit and culinary ftuffs. On the north and eaft it is inclofed with a high wall, which is covered with a number of fine efpaliers, confifting of apples, pears, cherries, plumbs, apricots, nectarines, peaches, &c. all of the rareft kinds, and moft exquifite flavour. For fome time, Colonel Cumming has refided, with his family, in Tarres, where he has a fine houfe and a confiderable property.

Church, Stipend, &c.—The church is nearly centrical, being fituated about 3 miles fouth-eaft from Tarres ; it was rebuilt in 1754 ; and the manfe in 1746. In the times of Dioceſan Epiſcopacy, this was the ſeat of the ſubchanter of Moray. Miſs Brodie of Lethen is patron. The ſtipend, by decreet in 1752, is 76 bolls 3 firlots barley, and L. 349 : 13 : 4 Scots, including 100 merks for communion-elements. A proceſs of augmentation is now depending before the Court of Teinds.—The ſalary of the ſchool is 16 bolls of bear; it has long been in a flouriſhing ſtate. By his unremitting attention to the morals as well as proficiency of his pupils, during a period of more than 40 years, the preſent teacher has acquired a juſt degree of celebrity. Many characters now reſpectable in the literary, the commercial, the civil, and military departments, among others the learned Rector of the High School of Edinburgh, who is a native, received their claſſical education here.

Obeliſk.—The only piece of antiquity worthy of remark, is the ſtanding pillar near Tarres, commonly called Sueno's Stone. It is allowed by all journaliſts who have viewed it, to ſurpaſs, in elegance and grandeur, all the other obeliſks in Scotland, and is ſaid to be the fineſt monument of the Gothic kind to be ſeen in Europe. Some time ago, when it was like to fall, Lady Anne Campbell, late Counteſs of Moray, cauſed it to be ſet upright, and ſupported with ſeveral ſteps of freeſtone. The height of this ſtone cannot now be eaſily aſcertained; it riſes about 23 feet above ground, and is ſaid to be 12 under it. Its breadth is about 4 feet. What is above ground is viſibly divided, on the eaſt ſide, into ſeven parts, containing a variety of military ſculptures. The greateſt part of the other ſide is occupied by a ſumptuous croſs, under which are two auguſt perſonages in an attitude of reconciliation.

The

The Reverend Mr Cordiner of Banff, in his letters to Mr Pennant on the antiquities and scenery of the north of Scotland, has exhibited a fine drawing of this monument, and his remarks on it appear to be more satisfactory than any I have read. He supposes it to have been erected in memory of the peace concluded between Malcom and Canute, upon the final retreat of the Danes from the kingdom. This event is said to have happened about the year 1012.

But to whatever transaction it may allude, it can hardly be imagined, that in so early an age of the arts in Scotland as it must have been raised, so elaborate a performance would have been undertaken but in consequence of an event of the most general importance. It is therefore surprising, that no more distinct traditions of it reached to the æra when letters were known.

PARISH OF ROTHES.

(*County of Murray.*)

By the Rev. Mr G. CRUICKSHANK.

Situation, Soil, &c.

THIS pariſh lies along the bank of the Spey, on the north ſide, and is in a great meaſure ſurrounded with hills, which are all covered with heath. The ſoil is generally dry and ſandy, and the crops are, for the moſt part, oats and bear. The culture of green crops is not very extenſively practiſed. There is neither lime nor marle in the pariſh. Salmon are caught in the Spey, and commonly ſell for 4 d. a pound, during the months of March, April, and May, and afterwards from 3 d. to 2 d. *per* pound.

Population.—In the old pariſh of Rothes there are 1000 ſouls, and in that part of the pariſh of Dundurcas, which was annexed to Rothes about ſeven years ago, there are about 500, ſo that the pariſh of Rothes, at preſent, contains about 1500 ſouls. In Dr Webſter's report, previous to the annexation, the number is 746. The population has greatly increaſed of late, owing to a village that is built at Rothes, which contains about 300 young and old,

Heritors.

Heritors.—There are four heritors in the parish, namely, Lord Findlater, who has about two thirds of it ; Sir William Gordon of Gordonston, Baronet, who has the lands of Inchbeary and Gerbety ; the Honourable Arthur Duff of Orton, who resides at Orton, and Mrs M'Dowal Grant of Airndelly, who has the lands of Ackenway.

Antiquities.—There are the ruins of an old Castle, which gives title to the noble family of Rothes, which was once the residence of the Earls of Rothes, from whom all the Leslies are descended.   It now belongs to Lord Findlater.

PARISH OF ST ANDREW's, LHANBRYD,

(COUNTY OF ELGIN, SYNOD OF MORAY, PRESBYTERY OF ELGIN.)

By the Rev. Mr WILLIAM LESLIE.

Geography and Natural Hiſtory.

L*HANBRYD*, ſignifying in the original, " St Bridget's Church," was united to St Andrew's, to which laſt, two other chapels had alſo been joined before the Reformation. This pariſh meaſures about 3 Engliſh miles from W. to E. along the highway from Elgin to Spey ; and from S. to N. about 4, excluſive of an improvement in the hill 1 mile diſtant, on the S. disjoined by an intervening ſkirt of the pariſh of Elgin, to which it pertains. It was originally the moor where the cattle were collected for drawing part of the teinds of both pariſhes, before they were converted into money, from which it retains the name of *Teindland* ; and on account of its diſtance from Elgin, the inhabitants have in general ranked themſelves in this pariſh. The general appearance of the country is a plain, in which ſeveral low hills riſe, ſo arranged as to appear connected

with

with each other, and all covered with corn or grafs, or with plantations of wood. The foil in general is fandy, yet fertile where it is low and damp. The air is healthful and dry; not productive of any prevalent diftemper; although the inhabitants are not diftinguifhed for longevity. There is one mineral fpring in the Teindland, of a ftrong chalybeate kind, as yet of no celebrity; though it has given relief to all who have made proper trial of its effects. There are three lakes on the confines of the parifh; the largeft, that of Spynie from 4 to 6 feet of water on a deep rich mould, inviting its proprietors to drain off its fhallow water. Several years ago, one of them carried on this operation at a confiderable expenfe, and with the moft encouraging profpects; but when he had nearly completed the improvement of the old canal, he was retarded by a litigation before the Court of Seffion, with his neighbour on the other fide of the lake, who wifhed to retain all the water. This oppofition being at laft unfuccefsful, the undertaking was completed; by which, although not effectual, many acres were regained, where the courfe of ridges, the formation of artificial roads, and every token of ancient and unknown cultivation, moft evidently and unexpectedly appeared. The neighbouring loch of Cots, originally a part of that of Spynie, at firft a ftrait of the ocean, defcribed in the chartulary of Moray as a bay, in the 13th century, is on the fame level, and offers equal encouragement to drain off its water, in proportion to its extent; and being fupported by two confiderable rivulets, the mouth of the canal would afford a profitable falmon-fifhing. Lochnabee, in the S. E. corner of the parifh, is about 3 miles in circumference, and has an ifland covered w th wood. There is a foreft round this lake planted by the Earl of Fife, fo extenfive and thriving, as to have already induced a fcore or two of red deer to make their refidence in its cover. Thefe lakes abound

with

with trout, eel and pike, with a great variety of wild ducks, and at one ſeaſon of the year with wild geeſe and ſwans; but neither the proprietors, nor their tenants, avail them in any degree whatever of theſe advantages. The only river is Loſſie, which, entering the pariſh at the N. W. corner, divides it there from the town of Elgin, and ſhaping its courſe in the form of a parabola, leaves it near the ſea at the north, including within the parabola about one third of what was the pariſh of St Andrew's; having its church in the apex, at which there is a ſubſtantial timber bridge[*].

Population.—According to Dr Webſter's report, the numbers then were 690. The number of inhabitants was conſiderably greater than now about 30 years ago. Several farms which were each poſſeſſed by 12 or 16 families, are now let to one man; and of late ſeveral are occupied by inhabitants of the town of Elgin, and by farmers of other pariſhes, ſome of whom have no reſident ſervant, and others only one or two, where numerous families dwelt. At preſent, the number is 777, including the improvement of Teindland, making 140 families, of which 106 are wedded pairs; the number of males 345; females 412. The yearly average of births is 16, which muſt be multiplied by 48 or 50, in order to produce the population; although a note in the 17th chapter of Gibbon's Hiſtory of the Roman empire,

[*] A great part of St Andrew's is expoſed to land-floods, by the overflow of Loſſey on both ſides. The higheſt now remembered was in 1768; a very deſtructive one in 1782; and much damage was done by two, during the harveſt of 1789. This calamity might be prevented at no great expenſe, by a little concert among the proprietors, and taking out the dam of a mill, which has no thirlage, and gives but a trifle of rent. The extent of the ſea-coaſt is only about one mile; a low ſandy ſhore, pertaining to one farm; upon which ordinary tides riſe from 7 to 8 feet perpendicular; at preſent it affords nothing but an inconſiderable quantity of ſeaweed for manure.

empire, bears, " That the annual proportion of births to the whole people, is about 1 to 26 in the province of French Hainault." The number of Seceders is 34, Methodists 7, Episcopalians 2, 736 may be accounted of the Established Church, although nearly 30 of them prefer more generally a kind independent preacher, supported by the magistrates and elders of Elgin *.

Agriculture, &c.—Grain, eatable roots, and the whole class of cultivated brassica, the ordinary fruits, and almost every tree known in Scotland, are raised in the parish, which has always produced more grain than requisite for the inhabitants. The victual rents disposed of by the proprietors to Highland counties of crop 1782, greatly overbalanced the supply of meal granted to the poor that year by the State. Since the excise on tanning leather obliged the poorer families to give up making their own shoes, no hemp has been cultivated; but there is still flax raised, though only for domestic accommodation. There are 252 horses, each pair in general managing a plough; 750 black cattle, a very small number of which are labouring oxen,

a

* This meeting was established about 20 years ago, by one of the ministers of Elgin, who was prejudiced against the presentee appointed for his colleague; for the support of which, he bequeathed a capital of L. 100 Sterling. They assemble in an old edifice on the end of the church, built for the week-day worship of the town's people, in compliance with their prejudice for holydays, on the abolition of Episcopacy. The managers let such seats as have not been claimed; but a subscription by the hearers is also requisite for the support of the preacher, who has little other connexion with the Church, but that he must be licensed by a presbytery of the Synod of Ross: While the people of this meeting are content with the ministration of their respective parishes, unless in the article of ordinary public worship, which some attend from all quarters, at the distance of 10 or 16 miles.

a few pairs only being employed in the plough and wag-
gon; there are 1060 ſheep, a ſmall number of which are
accounted here of the Bakewell breed. They are without
horns, and have long wool; the fleece weighs from 7 to
12 pounds; about a fifth-part are of the Linton breed,
the reſt are a white faced breed, that have always been in
the country, much diminiſhed in bulk by ſcanty paſture;
as yet there is no idea of improving the quality of the
wool.—Tenants of the rank of gentlemen have all their
graſs of ſown clovers, rye and rib graſs; the poor tenants
depend on natural ley graſs, with a patch of clover in their
gardens. The rent by the acre on moſt farms is varied e-
very year, by the difference of the price of grain, of which
a portion of the rent of every farm has been in general
paid. When grain ſells at 14 s. cr 15 s. the boll, the a-
verage rent by the acre is about 15 s.; but a great proportion of almoſt every farm can be only valued at 5 s. the
acre; and a part of each, if let ſeparately, would bring a
guinea the acre. There being little or no common paſture
pertaining to any farm, the land, conſidering the quantity
of grain produced from the acre, muſt be reckoned high
rented.

Miſcellaneous Obſervations.—The poſſeſſors of the landed
property are 7. The Earl of Fife has the whole of what
was the pariſh of Lhanbryd, and the ancient barony of Kil-
malemnock, in St Andrew's; the Earl of Findlater holds
Linkwood and Linksfield, in the weſt; the Hon. George
Duff, Barmickity, in the middle of the pariſh; John Brander, Eſq; holds Pitgaveny, in the north; William King,
Eſq; has Newmill, and the lands in the vicinity of Elgin;
and John Innes, Eſq; writer to the Signet, has Dunkinty,
towards the eaſt; and a ſmall farm was, in the laſt generation, given by Gordon of Cairnfield, for the ſupport of
the

the Epifcopal chapel in Elgin.—The only language of the parifh is Scots. The names of the places, in general, are of that language; fuch as Hornhead, Hairftones, Hollow-wood, and Cockftown. Thefe are beauties peculiar to this language, in energy, brevity, and animation; which would be more natural ornaments in the Englifh tongue, than any of its exotic importations. Thefe, therefore, as well as the Scoticifms, might be alfo collected and publifhed.—The people, over all this country, are moft ftrictly œconomical, and as little expenfive or luxurious as poffible. They are difpofed to every kind of humane and generous action, as much as their circumftances will admit of. The lower rank of farmers and labourers, though not content perhaps with their fituation, and though they do not enjoy all the comforts of life, yet do not complain more than their opulent neighbours. There are numbers of them, however, who are generally without fmall beer and milk, and almoft none of them have meat, butter, cheefe or fpirits, and all their poultry and eggs are fold in the Elgin market. Their drefs, furniture and habitations are ftill of the cheapeft kinds which can be procured. They ufe no candles; and urine they fubftitute for foap. Funerals are conducted without expenfe; there is no company or dancing on the occafion of a wedding; nor at baptifms, in general, is there any kind of entertainment. Almoft the only pleafure they indulge in, is meeting occafionally, to the number of 15 or 25, for the purpofe of converfing about fome of the abftrufeft doctrines of Calvinifm, in which they difplay their eloquence in the only kind of fpouting of which they have any notion, that of a theological oration and a prayer, varied by occafional reflections on the degeneracy and oppreffions of the age. It is probable, the anceftors of the prefent generation of peafants poffeffed at no period, a much larger ftock of knowledge; but fince, by the alteration

tion of the times, the ſalaries of ſchoolmaſters can in no way ſupport a family, that office has fallen altogether into the hands of mere ſchool-boys, which they abandon as ſoon as their own education is ſuppoſed to be completed, or into that of bankrupt tenants, ſtill leſs qualified for the duties of it. So that a thicker cloud of ignorance muſt be ſettling over the lower ranks of people, than that which covered their fathers. And while the reputation for learning, which Scotland has ſo long ſupported among the nations, muſt in a ſhort time be loſt, thoſe numbers, who, by means of that mediocrity of literature acquired in the pariſh ſchools, roſe from the loweſt ſtations of life to *merit, wealth,* and *rank,* muſt be henceforth ch ined down, hopeleſs and inglorious, to the miſerable ſphere of their humble birth. Pariſh ſchools are peculiar to Scotland. The idea of this inſtitution was originally ſuggeſted as proper for reconciling the minds of the people to the adminiſtration of Charles I. And, in a ſimilar view, they were eſtabliſhed in their preſent form by the firſt Parliament of King William. For ſeveral gene-rations, while the example of country gentlemen, and the ability of ſchoolmaſters, ſupported the labours of miniſters, the ſchoolmaſter's connexion in the pariſh being equally permanent, and their learning in general on a reſpectable par, the people were preſerved loyal to Government, and ſteady to the Church ; but after the gentlemen withdrew their countenance, and ſlighted the ordinances of their na-tional religion, and the office of ſchoolmaſter became inef-ficient, by the diminiſhed value of its appointment, the mi-niſters were wholly unſupported, the people blind to the ſignal advantages of their Government, and feeling the pref-ſure of its manifold exactions ; while their minds, relating both to Church and State, as much perverted now by vagrants in the character of diſſenting preachers, as they were then by trafficking prieſts, are, in as great a degree, diſpoſed

for

for innovation, if it fhould elfewhere fpring up, as in any former age ; with this difference, that the band of religion which tied the people fo ftrongly to their fuperiors, being now broken, they would be very little controlled by their influence. Perhaps it would be wife, therefore, in the State, to augment the living of fchoolmafters to the fame value which it comparatively bore in the reign of William ; which would not at prefent require, in all, above L. 5000 Sterling a year, which might be tranfmitted to the Sheriffs, or paid by the Collectors of Excife.

By thefe means the condition of the kingdom would be meliorated ; for while fome knowledge of writing and arithmetic is now indifpenfable to every mechanic, mafon, carpenter, weaver and tailor, nothing can be more abfurd than to allege, that a man makes a better farmer, is more content with his fituation, or a more ufeful member of fociety, becaufe he can neither read or write ; on the contrary, ignorance of itfelf occafions difcontent, and expofes thofe who are under its gloom to be more eafily mifled by the crafty, which the members of every mob, and the fmalleft obfervation of the fentiments of that condition fufficiently demonftrate. The parifh having no advantages nor difadvantages peculiar to itfelf, the means by which its condition might be meliorated, would alfo influence that of all the country. Granting long leafes, has, in general, been accounted among the means of meliorating the condition of tenants, and of improving the country ; yet their being no other advantage from this, but that the tenant is encouraged to improve by the certainty of reaping its profit, it would be eafy, by the conditions of the leafe, to give equal encouragement for temporary or permanent improvement, if the tenant fhould be removed in fuch circumftances, as to give the landlord the profits of it. On moft farms there are corners inacceffible to the plough, the bank of a ditch,

er

or the winding margin of a brook, where trees wouid be ornamental, and promote the growth of graſs, by their ſhade and their ſhelter. The tenant at preſent has ſeldom any encouragement to plant ſuch ſpots, as, by act of Parliament, all the growing timber is the ſole property of the landlord. But were ſome arrangement made between the landlord and the tenant, to encourage the latter, either to plant ſuch ſpots himſelf, or to take care of the trees therein planted, every farm, in the courſe of the riſing generation, would be provided with timber ſufficient for its own accommodation.—For many years paſt the agricultural induſtry of this part of the country has been conſiderably diſcouraged, by the difficulty of procuring and managing farm-ſervants, occaſioned by an emigration of many of that rank to the manufacturing and commercial places of the ſouth; while, by a pretty widely extended combination among themſelves, they have raiſed their wages here, as high as in any part of the kingdom, it is certain there is leſs work accompliſhed by equal numbers. They inſiſt on being regulated in all circumſtances, by the faſhion or practice of other farms, which themſe ves have by this means eſtabliſhed; and if any perſon contends any particular with them, he thereby incurs the imputation of being a bad maſter, and muſt thereupon, at the next term, give an advance of wages, or ſome conceſſion ſtill more humiliating. How far this may or does affect the land-rent, is not aſcertained, nor have the gentlemen of the country yet felt the evil; an additional ſervant or two is of little conſequence to them, and their influence ſecures in general a preference to the moſt diſcreet, ſo h t they rather foſter than check the extravagance. It w uld, nevertheleſs, be proper n them to extend their care a little to the concerns, in this reſpect, of their poorer neighbours, and to the ſtate of the country in general; and it is yet practicable, by a little concert among them,

them, gradually and filently, to introduce practices more beneficial to all concerned.—This country fuffers alfo fomewhat from a fpirit of litigation, which the landholders feem rather to foment, than take any care to fupprefs ; for having univerfally relinquifhed their legal ancient privilege of warning out tenants by their own authority, great numbers are yearly brought together in the fheriff-court, upon an act only of the Court of Seffion, to fee themfelves decerned to remove, where they acquire notions concerning the rights of men, no way favourable to induftry, concord or thrift. Befides, the depreffing influence of the tax on water born coal, which is above the fixth part of the price, this country moreover feels the partiality of the tax on Scots coal carried north of the Redhead, of which it now requires a confiderable importation, and befides the freight, fhore-dues, and other unavoidable expence of conveyance, this tax alone increafes the original price at the pit one-fourth part by the ton *.

This country in particular, and the whole ifland, would be greatly benefited by a bridge on the river Spey, at the ferry of Fochabers. The improved fyftem of agriculture in fowing grafs and other green crops, inftead of the uninterrupted cultivation of corn, has naturally turned the attention of the people to the increafe of black cattle. The county of Banff, and the adjoining parts of Aberdeenfhire, where Banff is only 8 or 10 miles broad, are by climate

* Numbers alfo in this country are mortified by another inconvenience. The ports of Findhorn, Loffie, and Spey, belong to the diftrict of the Cuftom-houfe of Invernefs. Befides the trouble of obtaining the clearance, on the arrival of every veffel, an exprefs muft be difpatched thither, before they can begin to unload ; by which a delay of three days, befides much expenfe, is unneceffarily incurred. But no inconvenience could refult from a deputation to proper officers at Elgin ; yet the gentlemen of the country fubmit to this diftrefs, with a patience and felf-denial which at leaft does honour to their Chriftian refignation.

mate adapted to paſturage, therefore, during ſummer and autumn, cattle markets have been eſtabliſhed in ſome place of that country every week ; croſſing the cattle over this rapid and generally unfordable river, and bringing home under the night ſuch as may not be ſold, is attended by a moſt forbidding inconvenience, which it is not neceſſary here particularly to deſcribe. The application of lime as a manure has of late been practiſed in this country, and much greater quantities of it are now uſed in building than in any former age. Banffſhire abounding in limeſtone and fuel, furniſhes the whole quantity required for both pur- poſes. Beſides hard labour, and much time in loading and unloading the boat, the freight alone adds a fifth part to the price. How far Government may be intereſted in this bridge, needs not be here ſtated ; but it may be obſerved, that experience hath now proved, that the opening of pro- per roads, has alone civilized and improved the rudeſt cor- ners of the Highlands, while the forts which were erect- ed there, and are ſupported at ſo great expenſe, have in this reſpect been found entirely nugatory ; although they could not be intended for any other purpoſe in a country which, nature having interdicted from being the theatre of war, can only at any period exhibit the ſcene of a ſlight ſkirmiſh, or one ſhort engagement.—The eaſy practicabili- ty, and the advantages of making a canal through the loch of Spynie, and the N. W. corner of the pariſh from Loſſie- mouth, to within a mile of Elgin, navigable without a lock for any veſſel that can get into the harbour, might be point- ed out.—But it only remains rather to ſuggeſt the advan- tage of eſtabliſhing a corn-market ſimilar to that of Had- dington. The county, at an average, diſpoſes of from 10,000 to 16,000 bolls, by the agency only of 3 or 4 perſons, who, in general, purchaſe by commiſſion from their correſpondents in the ſouth, and they alone are often

able

able to fix the price for the year. Although the city of Edinburgh, and the distillers, may be suppoſed to purchaſe the whole grain of the Haddington market, yet, ſince the eſtabliſhment of ſmall ſtills in the north, it is evident the ſituation of this country would admit of ſuch a weekly market on a ſmall ſcale at Elgin, and it would require no great exe.. a'or t.e ing auity, or attention of the country gentlemen, to form and ſupport an eſtabliſhment ſo obviouſly patriotic —Although the people of Teindland are at liberty to chooſe any church moſt convenient, they are bound to a mill in then own pariſh of Elgin, and beſides it, there are 8 mills with which the pariſh is connected.—By the quantity of potato, and alterations in the mode of living, it is certain there is not ſo much meal conſumed in the country as was formerly. The people in general murmur greatly on account of mill exactions and ſervices ; perhaps, therefore, it would be more advantageous for the proprietors of mills to apportion their preſent ent on the lands of their thirlage, than it may be at any future period, when this meaſure, according to the practice of more highly cultivated countries, may be univerſally adopted.

PARISH of SPEYMOUTH.

(COUNTY AND SYNOD OF MURRAY, PRESBYTERY OF ELGIN.)

By the Rev. Mr. JAMES GILLAN.

Situation, Extent, &c.

THE parish of Speymouth is bounded by the Murray Frith on the N., and by the river Spey, which separates it from the county of Banff, on the E. It extends about 6½ miles in length from N. to S., and about 1½, at an average, in breadth from E. to W. It is composed of the 2 old parishes of Essil and Dipple, which were united in the 1731, when the present name was given to the united parish, from its situation at the mouth of Spey. The harbour, or mouth of Spey, is, according to observation on the spot, W. longitude 3 deg. 6 min., latitude 57 deg. 41 min. *

---

* A few of the names of the places appear to be of Gaelic extraction, as Dipple, the name of one of the old parishes, is said to signify the " black

of

Face of the Country, Soil and Climate.—At the diftance of about half a mile from the fea, the ground rifes
fuddenly to a fmall hill. Beyond this, there is almoft
one continued plain for 3¼ miles in length, and about
1¼ in breadth, bounded on the fide towards the river by
a fteep bank from 40 to 50 feet in height. At the end
of this plain, the ground again rifes and terminates in a
high hill to the S. The foil is for the moft part light.
About one half of the arable ground is good fertile foil,
being a light loam, of fufficient depth, on a bottom of
black earth or clay ; the other half is a thin, gravelly,
fharp foil, on a hard gravelly bottom ; in fome parts it
is fandy. The grounds below the bank above mentioned, and between it and the river, are almoft all very
good foil, efpecially that part towards the S., called the
Haugh of Dipple, extending about a mile in length, and
3-4ths of a mile in breadth. The cultivated ground lies,
for the moft part, on the fide towards the river ; but
towards the two extremities, it falls back nearly the
whole breadth of the parifh. About the middle alfo,
there are 2 pretty extenfive farms near the boundary to
the W. The cultivated ground is equal to about one
third part of the whole extent of the parifh : the pafture
ground will be about 530 acres : there are about 300
acres in plantations of wood : about 50 acres of mofs
ground : 110 acres of pebbles, or bare beach, along the
river

or deep pool," viz. in the river Spey. Effil, the name of the other, is
faid to fignify " low." Garmouth, or, as it is commonly pronounced, and
probably fhould be written Garmach, a town or village fituated at the
mouth of Spey, is faid to fignify the " rough outlet," either from the rapidity of the river, or the roughnefs of the beach near its mouth. Balna-
coul, the " town of Gaul ;" Lunan, a " low lying place on the fide of
a river."

river and sea side : all the rest, equal to about the half of the whole extent of the parish, is moor.

The air is pure, the climate comparatively temperate and mild, and the situation consequently healthy. The most prevalent complaint seems to be rheumatism, which may proceed chiefly from an inattention to wet clothes, and from the cold N. E. winds in spring. It has been long said, that the low part of Murray has 4 : days more of fair weather in the year than any other country in the N. of Scotland ; and this part of it towards Spey is reckoned the driest part of the country. And there is no doubt, that from April to October, we have generally much more dry weather than the countries in the neighbourhood. Indeed, what the farmer fears most, in the low part of Murray, is the droughts that often take place here in the month of July. But it may be observed, that the lightness and thinness of our soil in general renders it particularly liable to injury from drought. For the same reason, a showery summer is very favourable to it, and even that quantity of rain, which is very hurtful in most parts of Scotland through the summer, and especially in the higher parts of the country in this neighbourhood, is beneficial through the greatest part of the low country of Murray, and especially in this parish. Accordingly, in the year 1782, when there was such a failure in the crop through the greatest part of Scotland, from the excessive rains, it is believed, there was a sufficiency here for the consumption of the country ; and that many of our farmers made more profit than usual by that crop, from the high prices. It has been observed by many, that the summers have been more rainy since the year 1782, than for a considerable time before, and that the crops in our

dry

dry light grounds have confequently been better. The medium depth of rain water fallen in a year, will be about 24 inches.

The moſt prevalent winds all along the coaſt of Murray are from the S. W. They may be faid to prevail for two-thirds of the year. Perhaps the greateſt defect in the temperature of our climate is the cold N. E. winds, that commonly prevail in the months of April and May, which often retard the growth of the corns, and efpecially of the grafs, and are very fevere on delicate conſtitutions. This is an inconvenience that is felt over almoſt all the E. coaſt of Britain ; but is particularly fo in fituations like this, which are open, and expofed to the N. and E. Perhaps it might tend to leffen this inconvenience, if ſtrips of wood were planted at certain diſtances where the country is level.

Population, &c.—According to Dr. Webſter's report, the population in 1755 was 994. The number of fouls in this pariſh, according to an accurate liſt taken in 1792, is 1347.

Males,	- - 655	From 20 to 50, -	512
Females,	- 692	From 50 to 70, -	216
Under 10 years of age,	304	From 70 to 80, -	86
From 10 to 20,	- 210	From 80 to 90, -	19

Two or three of which laſt are 90, or on the verge of it. The number of houfes inhabited is 310. The number of perfons to a family is 4⅓, at an average.—The regiſter of baptifms, deaths, and marriages is not complete for many years paſt, as the people will not always be at the trouble and expenfe to have them recorded. This has been the cafe, efpecially fince the duty was impofed. But, from notes taken by the miniſter for fome
time

time paſt, the average number of marriages for a year appears to be 10 ; of deaths, 28 ; of baptiſms, 43. The number of the males baptiſed is to that of the females as 17 to 16 *.

There are in this pariſh at preſent 12 Engliſh and 2 Iriſhmen. There are 5 of the Epiſcopal perſuaſion ; 40 Roman Catholicks ; all the reſt are of the Eſtabliſhed Church.—There are 71 farmers, 8 weavers, 7 tailors, 5 blackſmiths, 3 coopers, 10 joiners, 32 ſhip carpenters and blockmakers, 20 ſawers, 8 ſaw millers, 3 corn millers, 30 ſeamen, 6 ſhopkeepers, 45 ſalmon fiſhers, 8 ferrymen, 5 inn and ale-houſe keepers ; the reſt are ſervants, cottagers, day-labourers, carriers, &c.

Agriculture.—This cannot be ſaid to be yet in a ſtate of great improvement in this pariſh in general. Some of

---

* The pariſh regiſter was kept by a former miniſter, from the 1731 to the 1750; and as it has every appearance of uncommon accuracy, it may be proper to inſert ſome notes from it here.

The number of ſouls in the pariſh in the year 1736, is ſtated to be 994, of which the examinable perſons are 844 ; the children not examinable 150. The average of baptiſms for a year, of 9 years, of which the above year (1736) is the middle, that is, from 1732 to 1740, incluſive, is 35 7-9ths. The number of males baptiſed during all theſe years is 162 ; of females, is 160. The average of marriages for the ſame time is 8. The average of burials is 24 1-9th ; of which there is about 1-5th more of females than males; viz. males 10 8-9ths, females 13 2-9ths. A greater number of years is not taken, becauſe the regiſter is not complete before the year 1732, and becauſe, in the 1741 and 1742, there is an extraordinary number of deaths, no leſs than 112 for theſe 2 years. This uncommon mortality is to be accounted for, partly from the ſmall pox which raged at that time. But it may probably be alſo accounted for, in ſome meaſure, from the great failure in crop 1740. It is ſaid in the pariſh record, that a faſt was appointed by the ſynod in November 1740, on account of the threatened famine. From the ſame cauſe, perhaps, the baptiſms are ſo few in 1742.

of the better fort of the farmers raife turnips and artificial graffes, but not to the extent that could be wifhed.
Their general mode of cropping is, 2 crops of oats after
grafs ; then barley or bear (big) with dung ; or, inftead
of this, turnips, potatoes, and peafe, and then bear ;
next oats with grafs feeds, or peafe and rye after the
bear ; and then oats with grafs feeds. The grafs is cut
for hay the firft 2 years ; is paftured on for a year or
2 more, and then broken up for oats as before. The
proportions for grafs feeds generally ufed are, 12 lb. red
clover, and 5 lb. of white, with 2 bufhels rye grafs.
They generally find profit in adding 2 lb. more of red
clover, and half a bufhel, or even a bufhel of rye grafs.
They have begun to add 2 or 3 lb. of rib grafs, for the
fake of the pafture. In the low grounds, near the river,
they raife fome wheat, and this generally after turnips
or potatoes. The proportion of ground under grafs in
fuch farms, will not generally be above 1-fourth of the
whole.

This mode of farming will appear faulty from the
great proportion that is under crop. But the practice
of the leffer farmers, who are by far the greateft number, is ftill more objectionable. Their common method
is to take 2 or 3 crops of oats after ley ; then bear with
dung ; then a crop, partly oats, partly rye ; then 2 crops
more of oats ; and when the ground is now fufficiently
exhaufted, to leave it out in ley or natural grafs. Sometimes they fow a little peafe the fecond crop after the
ground has been dunged for bear ; and this gives them
an additional crop of oats, which is their great object.
It is very common here to mix about a fourth or fifth
part of rye with the oats, the firft or fecond crop after
bear ; and this they account a very profitable method,

as they fay they have the rye over and above what they would otherwife have in oats. They allow the ground to reft in ley, fometimes 4 years, but generally no more than 3 : The proportion of fuch ley is not above a fifth, or even a fixth of their farm. This frequency of cropping will no doubt appear ftrange ; yet it is not peculiar to this place. It was pretty much the univerfal practice over the N. of Scotland, not very many years ago, and is ftill pretty general among the fmaller tenants : They feem to acknowledge the error of this practice here, but fay, they cannot do otherwife, as they muft raife fo much corn, for bread to their families, and fodder to their cattle. Oats is the ftaple produce of the parifh, and feem to anfwer beft with the foil in general. The oats here generally ufed are of a kind peculiar to the place, called Haugh or Dipple oats ; and when fown in ground properly prepared, are of an excellent quality. They are a middle kind, between the early and late oats ; and are beginning to be in requeft in the neighbourhood. Rye fucceeds very well in our light foil. In fome places, barley is ufed ; but in general Scots bear or big is preferred, as a richer crop. Neither the one or the other are found to fucceed very well in the upper parts of the parifh ; nor are peafe or red clover found to anfwer well, except in the grounds below the bank or nigh the Spey. To produce grafs fit for making hay, or peafe, or even barley or bear, in any proportion, lime is found neceffary in moft parts of the ground above the bank. But with the affiftance of lime, all thefe crops fucceed very well : and, from the experience of the beft farmers in this neighbourhood, it is found, that lime is particularly adapted to light, thin, dry foil, efpecially fuch as has been originally improved

out

out of moor, and is confequently of a moorifh nature. On fuch a foil, it is found to have the moſt powerful effect, and to make it produce the above mentioned crops, viz. grafs, peafe, and bear or barley, in abundance, which it would not do before, even with the beſt dreffing and dunging. This effect it muſt produce, not only from its acting as a ſtimulus, but from its power alfo of deepening the foil, and efpecially of retaining the moiſture ; a circumſtance of the firſt importance in thin, light, dry ground. Our farmers here are fenfible of the great benefit of lime to their grounds ; but fome cannot afford, and others grudge the expenfe ; and thus not a great deal is yet ufed. It is to be had from the diſtance of about 6 or 7 miles, in the parifhes of Boharm and Keith, in the county of Banff, of the beſt quality ; and when carried by the owners, as it generally is, it coſts about 9d. the boll ; that is, 3 Wincheſter buſhels pretty nearly : when brought only to the other fide of the Spey, it coſts generally 7d. or 7½d. The trouble and expenfe of ferrying it over the Spey is a great and almoſt unfurmountable bar to the general ufe of it here. Among the many advantages that would refult from a bridge over Spey, the removing of this difficulty would be one of the moſt important, not only to this parifh, but to all the eaſtern part of Murray.

Turnips and potatoes anfwer extremely well in our light foil, even without lime. But as our grounds are almoſt all unenclofed, and cattle and fheep, for the moſt part, go at large duing the winter, there is a great difcouragement in raifing turnips, and little are therefore yet raifed. There is nearly the fame inconvenience with refpect to fown grafs ; the fheep either pluck it up by the root, or eat it fo bare, as to prevent its coming

ing

ing to any perfection in the ſummer. Even our leſſer farmers are ſenſible of the great advantage of turnips and ſowa graſs ; but as they have almoſt all ſome ſheep, and are unwilling to keep them during the winter, they chooſe rather to forego this advantage. The better ſort of farmers endeavour to enforce winter keeping ; but the attempt is generally very unpopular and trouble-ſome, and oft-times ineffectual. It is to be hoped, that it will ſucceed better by degrees.—Every family raiſes a certain quantity of potatoes. The farmers raiſe them often without dung, and even in the grounds that are moſt exhauſted. They plough the ground 3 or 4 times, and plant them after the plough in the end of April or beginning of May. They harrow them at different times ; and ſometimes give them a very ſhallow plough-ing before they begin to ſpring above ground. This they find leſſens the trouble of hoeing but it renders them ſomewhat later. Planting them without dung, has alſo this effect ; nor is the crop ſo rich as it would be with dung ; but it is ſtill tolerable, if the ground be kept clean, and the potatoe is thought better in quality.

For barley or bear, it is the practice here and through all Murray, to give 3 ploughings ; one after harveſt, one in April, and the laſt, with dung, from the middle of May to the 8th of June, which is thought the beſt time for ſowing this grain here. For oats after bear, they give one ploughing in ſpring : for oats, after ley or graſs, they plough after harveſt, or after the firſt ſtrong froſt. Sometimes they give a rib furrow to the ley in harveſt, or early in autumn, in order to rot the ſward in due time. For a ſecond or third ſucceſſive crop of oats, and for a crop of rye, they almoſt always give a rib furrow after harveſt ; and this is found to

anſwer

answer well. Oats are sown in the month of April; peafe about the fame time; rye after harveft, or in March. The produce, at an average, will not be above 4 bolls the acre. The parifh will fupply itfelf for common. The plough generally ufed is of the fmall kind, here called the Englifh plough. In fome of the ftronger grounds, they ufe the Scotch plough, fomewhat lefs and lighter than of old; and this, when properly conftructed, is perhaps the beft form of any, in every kind of foil.

The number of horfes in the parifh will be about 194; of black cattle about 636; of fheep about 2000; of fwine or hogs about 40. The better fort of farmers keep horfes of a good fize, 2 of which are able to draw a plough; but the generality of the horfes are of a fmaller fize, but ftrong and hardy. The cattle are generally of a fmall fize; fuch as when fed for the butcher, will weigh from 20 to 22 ftone. A mixture of the Highland breed is now generally preferred and adopted all over this country, as being the handfomeft and moft hardy. The fheep are generally of a very fmall kind. Some time ago, the Linton breed was fought after, as being of a larger fize. But their wool was found to be much coarfer, and they were not found to thrive fo well with our pafture, as the old native breed of the country; nor was their flefh thought fo delicate. The old native breed is therefore now preferred here, and almoft all over Murray. Their wool is of the fineft quality, approaching, it is faid, to the Cheviot and Shetland wool. They will generally weigh, when fed for the butcher, about 7 or 8 lb. the quarter. The better fort of farmers ufe ploughs drawn by 2 ftout horfes. Some few ufe 6 or 8 oxen in the plough. But the moft common

draught

draught for the plough in this pariſh is 2 horſes of a moderate ſize, with 4 oxen, or a mixture of oxen and cows behind them ; ſometimes 2 horſes with 2 oxen ; and ſome are now beginning to plough with 2 oxen only. There are about 140 carts in the pariſh, almoſt all of 1 horſe draught ; and this is found to be the moſt convenient mode.

There are 3 corn mills within the pariſh, to one or other of which all the lands in the pariſh are aſtricted. The multure, or the proportion paid for grinding the corns, will be about an eleventh part of the quantity ground. The tenants are likewiſe bound to ſupport the mill-houſe and dam, and to carry the mill-ſtones. It were better that mills were generally laid open, and that, inſtead of high multures and mill-ſervices, a proportionable additional rent were paid by the tenant to the landlord directly.

Extent of Farms, Rent of Lands, &c.—The farms in this pariſh are generally of very ſmall extent. There are about 6 from 60 to 80 acres in extent, and from 40l. to 50l. of rent, which employ 2 ploughs ; about 3 or 4 from 40 to 50 acres, and from 20l. to 30l. rent; about 15, from 20 to 35 acres, and from 10l. to 20l. rent. All the reſt, being nearly double the number of the former, are from 10l. down to 5l, or even 4l. rent, and of a proportionable extent in acres ; and moſt of theſe have a ſeparate plough. The rent of the lands in the country part of the pariſh, is from 15s. to 5s. the acre. The average will be very nearly 10s. the acre on the whole. The lands belonging to the town of Garmouth, are let at from 20s. to 30s. the acre, and ſome ſmall parts as high as 50s : But the average will be about 25s. the acre. This

higher

higher rent arifes from the populoufnefs of the town of
Garmouth, and the confequent greater demand *.

The

* The above account of the fmall extent of our farms, will appear
furprifing to moft people. But it is to be obferved, that the greater
part of the North of Scotland, about 30 years ago, was let in fmall
farms. And there can be little doubt, that farms, of a moderate
extent, are the moft favourable to the population of a country. The
farmers of this parifh, who only labour from 14 to 20 acres, and pay
only from 6 l. to 9 l. of rent, fupport families of healthy children, have
them taught to read, and generally to write a little, and train them
to induftry and virtue. They will alfo perhaps accommodate a cottager with a houfe on their fmall farm, fome poor or infirm relation,
or a tradefman, or day-labourer. Six fuch farms may fupport perhaps 40 perfons, young and old, befides accommodating cottagers and
their families. But all thefe together, would be reckoned but a fmall
or moderate farm in many places, and would not probably fupport
above a dozen of perfons. If, then, the number of the people be the
ftrength of a nation, there feems little room to doubt, in anfwering the
queftion as to the propriety of large or fmall farms, that in a public or
political view, as well as that of humanity, the latter are to be preferred
to the former. The mode of cultivation, and of laying out the lands, will
not probably be in fo improved a tafte in fmall as in large farms; but the
produce, on the whole, it is probable, will be equal, and even much greater in the article of grain, which is the moft valuable. And even as to the
cropping and laying out of the ground, the proprietor may take care
that this be done in a proper manner, by a little attention in laying down
regulations in the tenant's leafe, and feeing that thefe regulations be followed. And as to the improvement of new grounds, he may alfo fecure
that point as effectually, by binding the tenant in the fame way. And
even with refpect to the proprietor's intereft, which muft always be a
leading confideration, it is prefumed, that fmall tenants can afford to pay
as high a rent as greater ones, from their fuperior induftry and attention;
and if one fhould now and then fall in arrears, the rifk is not fo great as
when the fame thing happens to a greater tenant; or if the proprietor's
intereft fhould fuffer a little, for it cannot be a great deal, yet he has the
fatisfaction of giving fupport to a greater number of people, which, it is
hoped, will always be an object of no fmall confideration with many.
The extent of farms fhould vary, according to the quality of the foil,
and the circumftances of the country. The beft general rule feems to
be,

The real rent of the whole lands of the pariſh cannot be exactly aſcertained, as one part (the lands of Garmouth) is feued out, and is moſtly in the poſſeſſion of the feuars themſelves. Beſides the lands, there is a very valuable ſalmon fiſhing on Spey, belonging to this pariſh, from the ſea for 4¼ miles up the river. The real rent of this fiſhing is conſiderably greater than that of the lands in the pariſh. The valued rent of the lands is 2771l. 17s. 1d. Scotch money. The valued rent of the fiſhery is 2541l. 17s. 8d. Scotch.

Heritors.—The Duke of Gordon is proprietor of the greater part of the lands of this pariſh, and ſuperior of the reſt. Of the fiſhery on Spey in this pariſh, he is proprietor of 7-9ths. The Earl of Murray is proprietor of the remaining 2-9ths. There is a conſiderable number of ſmaller heritors or feuars, who have feus of different extent of the lands of Garmouth, all holding of the Duke of Gordon as ſuperior. The greater part of them reſide in Garmouth, and poſſeſs their own feus. Several of them are in opulent circumſtances. One keeps a carriage.

Church,

be, to allow as much ground to a farm as can be laboured with one plough ; much leſs than this, would be a loſs to the tenant. Here and there, however, there ſhould be larger farms, and farmers of greater ability and ſkill, to give examples of new and more improved modes of culture, and thereby introduce improvements into the country at large. The Duke of Gordon, agreeably to that humane ſyſtem which he follows on all his eſtates, on renewing, of late, the leaſes in this pariſh, continued almoſt all the ſmall tenants in their poſſeſſions ; and ſuch of the farmers as had ſubtenants, he took bound to continue them alſo in the grounds they had before, or to allow them an equivalent in ſome other part of their farm, if that were more convenient, according to the judgment of men mutually choſen. This is an example that ought to be generally followed, as it tends to prevent ſubordinate oppreſſion, and to keep the people in the country.

Church, Schools, Poor, &c.—The church was built in the year 1732, foon after the annexation of the parifhes, in a centrical fituation for the united parifh ; but though of fo late a date, is in very bad condition. The manfe was built about the fame time, at a little diftance from the church, and lately underwent a thorough repair. The offices were rebuilt of late. The ftipend, by decreet of annexation 1731, is 77 bolls 1 firlot 2 pecks bear, 32 bolls 1½ peck oatmeal, at 8¼ ftone the boll, and 34cl. Scotch. The glebe is about 25 acres, being given as an equivalent for the two glebes of the annexed parifhes. The Earl of Murray and Sir. William Gordon of Gordonftown, prefent *per vices.* Our boll in Murray is very near the Linlithgow meafure, and 1¼ boll, nearly equal to the quarter Englifh, is generally allowed for a boll of oats. The parochial fchool, was fome time ago fixed at Garmouth, though at one extremity of the parifh, as being the moft populous place. The fchoolmafter's falary is 8¼ bolls meal, and 2⅛ bolls bear. He has alfo 100 merks as the intereft of 2000 merks, mortified by a Mr. Patrick Gordon, watch maker in Edinburgh, for the behoof of a fchoolmafter in this his native place *.

The

* He has 2l. Sterling as feffion clerk ; 1s. for every proclamation of marriage ; 4d. for every baptifm recorded ; 4d. for every certificate granted by the kirk-feffion, and as much for every extract. The fchool fees are, 1s. the quarter for teaching reading ; 1s. 4d. for reading and writing ; 1s. 8d. for arithmetic ; and 2s. for Latin : For book-keeping, half a guinea. The number of fcholars is generally from 40 to 50. The number of Latin fcholars is now much lefs than it ufed to be here, and at all our fchools in the N. We have lately got another fchoolmafter at the other end of the parifh, from the Society for propagating Chriftian Knowledge. He has 10l. Sterling a year from the Society. The Duke of Gordon gives him a houfe and kail yard, and 2l. Sterling ; and he has 25 merks mortified for the fchoolmafter of one of the old parifhes, by one of the anceftors of the Earl of Fife. The number of fcholars at this fchool
may

The number on our poor's roll is generally about 40.
The poor's funds are the collections at the church, which
will amount to about 20l. Sterling in the year, dues for
the mortcloth, and 4l. 3s. 4d. Sterling a year, mortified
for the poor of this parish by the above mentioned William Duff, Esq. of Dipple, ancestor of the Earl of
Fife, and paid by his Lordship. That gentleman, much
to his honour, made similar charitable donations to several parishes in this neighbourhood *.

Prices and Wages.—Beef and mutton are sold at from
2d. to 4d. the pound Dutch. The average price will be
about 2¼d.; a hen 7½; a duck 8d.; eggs 2d. the dozen;
butter 6d. the pound Dutch, of 17½ oz. The boll of
bear or barley, nearly the Linlithgow measure, has for
these 10 years past, been generally from 15s. to 18s.;
oatmeal at 8 stone, 13s. 4d.; wool 18s. the stone of 21
lb. Dutch. The wages of men servants have been tripled
within

may be about 30, at an average; and there are sometimes as many more
at an evening school, kept in the winter by this schoolmaster. There is
another mortification of 25 merks, for the schoolmaster of the other old
parish, left by the same ancestor of the Earl of Fife, and now enjoyed
by a supperannuated teacher. Besides these, there are 2 or 3 poor women in the parish, who teach children to read. Even the poorest of the
people take care to have all their children taught to read, and most of
the boys learn a little writing and arithmetick.

* The session-clerk has 2l., and the kirk-officer 1l. a-year of salary out
of the poor's funds. There are commonly two general distributions in the
year, and occasional supplies are given to the most necessitous. Poor's rates are
not known in this part of the country, and perhaps the poor are on as proper a
footing. The supplies granted from the session-funds, and by the private charities of the people at large, are sufficient to preserve the poor from suffering
much from want, and there is less danger of abuse, and of encouraging idleness. In populous cities, where the conditions of the poor cannot generally be
so well known, and in countries in a very different situation, poor's rates are,
no doubt, very proper and even necessary.

within thefe 40 years. A ploughman, or qualified man fervant, will now have from 3l. 10s. to 4l. in the half year; a fecond rate fervant, or a lad from 17 to 20 years of age, who can drive horfes, from 2l. to 3l.; a woman fervant about a farm houfe, 20s. for the half year; a man for the harveft 1l. 5s.; a woman for the fame 16s.; a day labourer 9d. a day, or 6d. with his victuals, for 9 months in the year, and 5d. with 2 meals during the winter months. In harveft he will have 1s. a day, or 10d. and 2 meals; a woman has 3d. a day and victuals, and 7d. and 2 meals in harveft *.

Garmouth.—The only village that deferves notice is Garmouth, or, as it is commonly pronounced, Garmach. It is fituated at the mouth of Spey; contains about 620 inhabitants; is a burgh of barony, and has an annual fair. The lands belonging to this place, extending to about 240 acres, with a right on an extenfive common, are held by a confiderable number of feuars of the Duke of Gordon. The feus are of different extent. Moft of the feuars refide in Garmouth; poffefs their own feus, and live comfortably; and feveral, from fuccefs in va-rious

---

* The wages of men fervants for the half year, have rifen above one third within thefe 7 years; and feem rather too high for this part of the country. It is alfo a pretty general complaint, that they do lefs work than when they had much lefs wages. To remedy this inconve-nience, the beft method feems to be, to employ married fervants more than has been done in this part of the country for fome time paft, and to accommodate them, and day-labourers and tradefmen, with houfes and other conveniences on the farms. This will encourage them to fettle in the country. The greater farmers are beginning to fee the conve-nience of having fome married fervants. As they cannot fo eafily re-move their families, they are lefs given to change, and, by confequence, more ftudious to pleafe. Their children, too, by encreafing the number, will leffen the wages of fervants.

rious purfuits in life, are in opulent circumftances. The greater part of the houfes in this place are of mud. The mud, when made into mortar, is well mixed with ftraw; and the more ftraw, it is thought the better. For about a foot from the foundation, they think it better to build ftones with the mud. After this, the only pre-caution that feems neceffary is to make a ftop at every 2 or 3 feet more height, that the wall may dry, and be-come firm before they proceed further. Thefe houfes, if well thatched, are very dry, clofe, and comfortable, and laft a very long time. They are fometimes built the height of 2 ftoreys. It adds to the look and dura-bility, if the walls are harled with lime on the outfide.

The river of Spey and Harbour.—The river Spey rifes on the borders of Lochaber, and runs through Badenoch and Strathfpey, until it comes within about 8 miles of the fea, nearly in the direction of N. E.; it then runs due N., and falls into the Murray Frith at Garmouth, after a courfe of about 85 miles. It is faid to derive its name from a Pictifh word, fignifying *froth*, from the rapidity of its ftream. It is the moft rapid river in Scotland, and, except it be Tay, is the largeft; and though it does not ordinarily appear fo large as Tay, it is thought by fome to run as much water in the year. Its fall from the Boat of Bog, nigh Gordon Caftle, to the fea, the diftance only of 3 miles, is 60 feet. Below this, it runs in a flat of about a mile in breadth, between the Bank of Bellie on the one fide, and that of Spey-mouth on the other, which there is every appearance that it has formed *. From the great fall towards the

fea,

* The fimilar appearance of the rock and clay on both fides, being both of a red colour, naturally leads to the conclufion, that they were once
joined,

fea, the tide does not flow above half a mile up the river. The ordinary depth of water on the bar at neap
tides, is from 8 to 9½ feet.

The greateft inconvenience of the harbour is, that the
ftream, by its ftrength and rapidity, fometimes brings
down in a flood fuch quantities of gravel as fhift the
channel a little, efpecially at the entrance of the harbour. But there are always good pilots at the place ;
and many veffels belonging to the Englifh Company at
Garmouth. Some of them of 350 tons burden, have been
going and coming for thefe 7 years, without any particular detriment or inconvenience. There has never
been any attempt to build a pier ; and, from the above
caufe, it is to be feared that it would not fucceed, or
that the expenfe would exceed the value of the trade.
The fhore on both fides, all along the bay of Spey, is
foft gravel, for 5 or 6 miles, excepting one rock, which
runs out a little into the fea, about 3 miles W. from
Spey, and is hidden at high water ; fo that a veffel will
be in no great danger, if there be a neceffity, in running
afhore

joined, and that the river once run 50 feet above its prefent level, along the
extenfive plain which begins at Orton, about 8 miles from the fea, and
runs nearly the whole length of the parifh of Speymouth to the fea. The
fmall ftones and pebbles in this plain, which have the appearance of being
rounded and fmoothed by running water, and the bank behind which has
the appearance of being formed by the fame, feem to ftrengthen this conjecture. But at this time, far beyond all the hiftorical records of the
country, the appearance of the furface of the earth muft have been very
different from the prefent. The river, at prefent, runs ftraight into the
fea. But there is a tradition, and indeed a plain evidence, from the appearance of the ground, that it has once taken a fudden turn within a few
hundred yards of the fea, and run weftward in a narrow cut of hollow
ground, parallel to the fhore, now called the Lin, and entered the fea
about 3 miles to the W. of its prefent mouth, oppofite to a hill yet
called Spey's Law.

afhore at high water, within this fpace, keeping clear only of this one rock : and accordingly feveral have here run afhore without much damage.

Salmon Fifhing on Spey.—The fifh in Spey are, the falmon ; a trout, called here the white trout, of about 2 or 3 lb. weight, which comes in March, and continues for fome months, and is very delicate : the grilfe, which begins about the middle of June, and continues until the end of Auguft ; this is here believed to be the young falmon : the finnic, which comes about the end of Auguft, and continues to the end of October. There is alfo a fmall fpotted trout found near the mouth of the river. All thefe afford excellent diverfion to the angler. But the falmon is the chief object ; and of this there is a very valuable fifhing on the river, and along the fhore near it. This fifhing, for the whole extent of this parifh, and fome diftance above it, belongs to the Duke of Gordon, excepting 2-9ths of what is in this parifh, which belong to the Earl of Murray. The fifhing belonging to this parifh extends for about 4¼ miles up the river from the fea. Mr. Richardfon of Perth, and Mr. Gordon of Portfoy, have it in leafe. The fifhing here begins on St. Andrew's day, and ends the 26th of Auguft. There is feldom, however, any regular fifhing until about the beginning of February. Until about the beginning of May, the greateft part of the fifh is fent frefh in ice to London. From that time, the greateft part is boiled, and fent to the fame market. Very little is now falted for exportation, as there is a fufficient demand at the London market ; and the countries to which the falted falmon was formerly fent, are now fupplied in a great meafure from America. The price of falmon

at

at the river fide is 4½d. the lb., which is thought very high. The fending of falmon frefh in ice to London, is but a late difcovery, and adds greatly to the value of our falmon fifhings, as the fifh fetches a much higher price in this way than in any other. Mr. Richardfon of Perth is faid to have the merit of introducing this practice. The fifhing is carried on with fmall boats, called Cobles, with 8 men and an overfeer, here called a Kenner, to each. The crew is changed every 12 hours. Our fifhers are reckoned uncommonly fkilful in this bufinefs. This arifes from the difficulties attending the fifhing on Spey, from the rapidity of the river and other circumftances. The fifhers have about 1l. 15s. of fixed wages, each man, for the feafon. They have 6d. each, when they catch 6 fifh or more within the 12 hours, and 3d. when they catch only 4.: when they catch beyond a certain number, they have a ftill farther allowance. In this way, they will make from 4l. to 6l. in a feafon. They have bread and beer, as much as is neceffary, while they are working, and a bottle of fpirits among the crew for the 12 hours they are employed *.

Wood-Trade.—At Garmouth, or the mouth of Spey, there is a wood-trade, the moft confiderable, it is fuppofed, of any in Scotland, for home wood. The wood is moftly fir, with fome little oak and birch. It comes from the extenfive forefts in Strathfpey and Badenoch, belonging to the Duke of Gordon, Sir James Grant of Grant,

Mr.

---

* The hardfhips which thefe people undergo, without any inconvenience, in wading in the water, often above the knee, during the winter and fpring, and remaining in wet clothes perhaps for 12 hours, will appear almoft incredible to thofe who have not witneffed it. Yet fuch is the wonderful effect of habit.

Mr. M'Intosh of M'Intosh, and Mr. Grant of Rothie-murchus; and is floated down the river Spey in deals, planks, logs, and spars. The medium prices of the best timber are as follows: Spar wood, from 16 to 24 feet long, and from 5 to 8 inches square, at 7d. to 8d the solid foot; logs, in the round form, 10 to 20 feet long, and 12 to 18 inches diameter, at 1s. the solid foot; 3 inch plank, 12 feet long, and 10 inches broad, at 3s. the piece; 2 inch plank, 12 feet long, and 10 inches broad, at 2s. the piece; 1¼ inch deals, 12 feet long, and 8 inches broad, at 1s. the piece; 1¼ inch deals, 10 feet long, at 10d. the piece; scantling, cut to any dimensions the timber will allow, at 1s. and 1s. 2d. the solid foot. The wood is partly sold at Garmouth, to the people of the adjacent country; but the greater part is carried coastwise by shipping. There are several persons engaged in this trade at Garmouth; but, for some years past, the greater part of it has been carried on by an English Company. Two capital wood merchants, Mr. Dodsworth of York, and Mr. Osbourne of Hull, about 8 years ago, purchased of the Duke of Gordon, the extensive forest of Glenmore, in Strathspey, about 50 miles from the sea; and since that time, they have carried on the trade with great spirit. They employ a great many hands, at the forest of Glenmore, in felling the trees, and manufacturing them into plank, deals, masts, &c., and in preparing the floats. The plank, deals, and masts are sent down the Spey in rafts, conducted by 2 men, at the rate of 30s. the raft. The logs and spars are, for the most part, floated down the river loose, to the number, perhaps, of 20,000 pieces at a time, with men going along the side of the river with long poles, to push them on, as they stick on the banks. These men have 1s. 2d.

a-day,

a-day, befides whifky ; and there will fometimes be from
50 to 80 employed at once in the floating. At Garmouth, this company has built 2 faw-mills, for manufacturing the timber after it comes down. The one is
a windmill, and works from 36 to 40 faws. The other
goes by water, and works from 30 to 36 faws. The
wood belonging to this company is fent partly to Hull,
and to the King's yards at Deptford and Woolwich, in
their own fhipping ; but the moft confiderable part is
fent coaftwife, all along the N. coaft, from Aberdeen to
the Ifle of Sky, or fold at Garmouth to the people of
the country around, or employed in fhip building. The
greateft part of this wood is of the very beft quality,
equal, it is faid by competent judges, to any that is imported from the Baltic, and inferior to that only in point
of fize. The largeft mafts are 60 feet in length. This
company has built, fince the 1786, befides a good number of boats, 23 veffels from 500 to 25 tons burden ;
the greater number about 200 tons, and amounting in
all to about 4000 tons ; and all of their own fir wood of
Glenmore, both the plank and timbers. Some of thefe
veffels they have fold ; others they employ in their own
trade from Spey, and in the Baltic trade, and one was
bought for the trade to the Bay of Campeachy. Thefe
veffels, though wholly of fir, are thought by good
judges to be equal to thofe of New-England oak, from
the excellent quality of the fir. There are generally
about 28 fhip carpenters and blockmakers employed by
this company at Garmouth ; about 16 or 18 fawers ;
and 8 faw millers, befides feveral other workmen. They
build veffels by contract. Befides the above veffels,
built by the Englifh company, feveral floops have been
built at Speymouth, during the fame time, by others ;

and

and ſeveral have been repaired ; and from the ſatisfaction they give, it is expected the trade will continue
and increaſe.

Exports and Imports at Speymouth.—The exports
from Spey conſiſt chiefly of wood and ſalmon ; and there
are generally 4 or 5 cargoes of grain or meal exported
in a ſeaſon, of 400 or 500 bolls each. The imports
conſiſt chiefly of coal, and this, for the greateſt part,
Engliſh coal, from Sunderland.

The exports and imports, from 1ſt October 1791 to
1ſt October 1792, were as follows :

Veſſels ſailed from Spey with wood in that time, from
   350 to 20 tons burden, average 50 tons, for different
   places,   -   -   -   -   82
Touched at Spey, and took in ſalmon for London ;
   having taken in part of the ſame at other ports,   24
With yarn,   -   -   -   1
With oats and meal,   -   -   2

              Sailed with cargoes,   109

ARRIVED IN SPEY.

With coals,   -   -   -   11
With empty kits, ſtaves, and hoops,   -   5
With ſalt 1 ; with iron and goods 6,   -   7

              Arrived with cargoes,   23
The average burden of theſe veſſels will be 50 tons.

A Bridge on Spey at the Boat of Bog.—This is an object of the firſt importance to this pariſh, and to all the
                      country,

country, to a confiderable diftance on both fides of Spey;
and in regard to one common objeƈt, it may be ftated
as the moft important improvement that could be made
to all the extenfive and populous counties W. and N.
of Spey, as well as to the counties of Banff and Aberdeen to the S. and E. It is of importance in a publick
view, as the judges muft pafs this way to and from the
circuit at Invernefs, and the troops to and from Fort
George, Fort Auguftus, and Fort William; and it is
an objeƈt of importance to every traveller that vifits
this country. The road that paffes the river Spey at
the Boat of Bog in this parifh, is, and from the fituation
of the country ever muft be, the only great poft road,
and great line of communication from the S. to the
counties of Elgin, Nairn, Invernefs, Rofs, Cromarty,
Sutherland, Caithnefs, and Orkney. Spey can very
feldom be forded with fafety. The boat here is indeed good, and well ferved. But a paffage by boat is
inconvenient at the beft; and when a river, fo great and
rapid as the Spey, is higher than ordinary, or, in a
flood, as is oft-times the cafe, it muft be highly inconvenient, and fometimes dangerous. When the importance of a bridge at this place to fo confiderable a part
of the kingdom is confidered, it muft naturally excite
furprife, that it has not long ago attraƈted effeƈtually
the attention of the publick. The internal improvements of a country claim the firft care of the publick;
and of thefe, roads and bridges, for facilitating communications, are held the moft effential. If fo, then, a
bridge over the Spey, at the great poft road, which is
fo important an objeƈt to the whole of the North of
Scotland, has a high claim on the publick attention.

There

There is nothing impracticable in the undertaking, if the publick will lend the suitable aid. An experienced architect, Mr. Stevens, who built the bridge at Dublin, and is now building that at Montrose, surveyed the river at that place 2 years ago, and found the work perfectly practicable, and that the rock, at the W. side of the river, run acrofs the whole way, at a moderate depth below the bed of the river. The breadth of the river at that place is about 98 yards. This he propofed to cover with 3 arches. The expenfe he eftimated at 14,000l. at the higheft. No fuch fum as this, even for an object of the greateft utility, can be expected to be raifed in the country, either by fubfcription, or by a toll, or by both. This could only be expected in the neighbourhood of a great town. It is only by the effectual aid of government, that a work of fuch magnitude can be undertaken in the country, and efpecially in fuch a diftant part of the country as this. And to that effectual fupport, this work appears to have the jufteft claim, not only from its great utility to fo confiderable a part of the kingdom as above mentioned, but likewife for reafons in which government is more immediately concerned. At prefent, a flood in Spey may very materially affect the adminiftration of juftice, by ftopping the judges in going on the circuit to Invernefs, or in returning from thence to Aberdeen : Or the troops may, by the fame caufe, be retarded in their march to or from Fort George, or the other forts in the North, or from the country on the one fide of the Spey to the other ; and cafes may occur, in which this may be of very bad confequence to the peace of the country, to the protection of the fubjects, and to other purpofes of

good

good government. Hence may appear, the interest of government in this matter *.

Character

---

* If the sense of the country on this subject can be of avail in drawing the attention of government, this may be gathered from the most unequivocal expression of it lately given, and affords the strongest argument for the effectual interposition of government in this matter. Last year a subscription was set on foot by the Duke and Dutchess of Gordon, for building a bridge on Spey at the Boat of Bog, near Fochabers, and in a very short time upwards of 3000l. was subscribed in this neighbourhood, or by persons connected with it. A good deal more would have been subscribed; but as the subscription was undertaken in the confidence that government would give an effectual aid in seeing the sense of the country as to the utility of the work, so fully expressed, and as it was soon after found, that this expectation could not be realised at that time, from the breaking out of the war, as was said, the subscription was given up for the time, because of itself it would never be effectual. It seems there was the like flattering prospect of a bridge at this place before the American war; but that war, in like manner, banished it. It is hard that war should so materially affect the internal and essential improvements of a country. It is hoped, that such a small aid can still be spared for so useful and necessary a work. But if this cannot be otherwise granted, it might be done by means of a small temporary tax on the northern counties. It is presumed, that they would readily submit to some small additional burden for such a purpose; and it is supposed, that an additional duty on home spirits in these countries, would be the most proper in itself, the least felt, and the most readily agreed to. It has been proposed to build a bridge over Spey at the Boat of Brig, about 5 or 6 miles above the Boat of Bog. A bridge could be built there, it is said, at a much less expense, and would, no doubt, be very useful to that part of the country. But with regard to publick and general utility, it could never answer the purpose of a bridge at the Boat of Bog, or supersede the necessity of another there. The road which leads to the Boat of Brig from the S. and E., is often impassable, and always inconvenient during the winter, so that it is impossible that it can ever become the post road, or the great line of communication between the S. and N. On the other hand, the road which passes at the Boat of Bog, being the coast road, is always passable, and for this reason is, and ever must be the post road, and the great line of communication from S. to N. Nor from the situation of the ground does it appear possible to make a patent road between the two places on the S. side of Spey. However useful, then, a boat may be at Boat of Brig, it can never supply the place or supersede the necessity of one at the Boat of Bog. A bridge over the river Findhorn

also,

Charaƈter of the People, Mode of Living, Dreſs, &c.—
The people of this pariſh are, in general, honeſt, peaceable, and induſtrious ; very charitable to the poor, and, in caſes of diſtreſs, very much diſpoſed to aƈts of humanity. They are generally rather above the middle ſize, aƈtive and hardy. Few go into the army. The greateſt part apply themſelves to huſbandry, to the ſalmon fiſhing, or a ſeafaring life. The young men of the part of the pariſh next to the ſea, and eſpecially of the town of Garmouth, are much diſpoſed to this laſt ; and many of them go to ſea, and become excellent ſeamen. There are about a dozen natives of this place who are now maſters of veſſels. The people ſeem to enjoy the comforts of ſociety in the ſame degree, as thoſe of their ſtation throughout the kingdom in general, and are contented with their ſituation. The kindneſs and indulgence of their landlord, the Duke of Gordon, contributes in no ſmall degree to their contentment, as well as comfort. The diet of the labouring people here, and in general, all through the Lowlands of the North of Scotland, is porridge, made of oat meal, with milk or beer, to breakfaſt ; ſowens, (that is, a kind of flummery, made of oat meal, ſomewhat ſoured), with milk or beer, to dinner ; and kail, that is, greens or cabbage, boiled with oatmeal, to ſupper. With all theſe, they uſe bread of oat meal, or what is called houſehold meal, that is, ſome
mixture

alſo, where the poſt road paſſes it, would be extremely convenient and uſeful. But if one were built over Spey, that over Findhorn would follow of courſe. And if there were bridges over theſe two rivers at the places mentioned, there would not be one ferry to paſs on all the great poſt road from Queensferry to the Ferry of Dornach in Sutherland ; a circumſtance which would be moſt conducive to the convenience and comfort of travellers, and to the commerce and proſperity of the country.

mixture of barley, rye, and peafe. On Sundays, they have generally barley broth, with fome meat in winter, and butter in fummer. In places near the fea-coaft, they have fometimes fifh. Turnips are fometimes ufed in place of cabbage or greens ; and potatoes dreffed in different ways, with butter, milk, onions, &c., is commonly one-third part of their food from the beginning of September to the end of March. This is the general run of diet of the labouring people in this part of the country, that is, of leffer farmers, farmers fervants, and people of that clafs ; and all the above they have in fufficient plenty. The oat meal, which forms fo confiderable an article in the above, is of the very beft quality throughout all Murray ; and, notwithftanding the objections made againft the ufe of oat meal by fome, it is known to thofe who are beft qualified to judge, to be, when properly dreffed, one of the moft wholefome and nourifhing articles of food. The cottagers and poorer fort of the people have not always what is called kitchen, that is, milk or beer, to their meals. In the view of patriotifm and humanity, it is a pity that the article of beer cannot be rendered more attainable by the poorer fort of people. This might be effected, at leaft in fome meafure, by lowering the duty on malt, and impofing it on fpirits ; and this would have the double happy effect of affording to the poor a comfortable and ftrengthening beverage, and checking the ufe of that which is noxious. Such a meafure deferves the attention of thofe who are able to carry it into effect.

The better fort here, as elfewhere throughout the N., ufe cloth from England or the fouthern parts of Scotland ; and many of the farmers, and tradefmen, and fome even of the fervants, ufe the fame on Sundays, and on

occafions

occaſions when they are in dreſs. But the common farmers, and the poorer ſort of the people, uſe cloth made at home. In this pariſh, moſt of the common tenants have as many ſheep as ſupply wool for their own and their childrens clothing. This is ſpun in their families, and manufactured and dyed in their neighbourhood Almoſt all raiſe as much flax likewiſe as ſupplies their families with ſhirts, &c , which they ſpin alſo in their houſes. The induſtry of the women in ſpinning is very commendable. In many families they make a little of woollen and linen cloth, eſpecially the latter, for ſale ; and the poorer women ſpin a good deal of linen yarn for ſale. The bonnet is ſtill commonly uſed by the men. A watch is no uncommon thing among the ſervants.

Miſcellaneous Obſervations.—It would add greatly to the value, as well as to the appearance of the country, if part of the moor-grounds were brought into cultivation, and part planted. Some parts of the moor in this pariſh might be cultivated to advantage with the aid of lime. In other parts, clumps or pieces of plantation, properly diſpoſed, would be a great improvement. Extenſive plantations have been made on the W. ſide of this pariſh, by the Duke of Gordon and the Earl of Fife, which are already a great ornament, and will ſoon be of great uſe to the country. There is no doubt that the plantations will ſoon be continued on each ſide of the highway all along to Spey. As our moſſes are nearly exhauſted, it is of great importance to extend plantations for a ſupply of fuel. Firs, and ſome other kinds of wood, grow on our hardeſt ſoil to the ſea ſide.—The *piḷularia,* or, pepper graſs, is the only uncommon botanical

tanical plant that has been obferved here. It is found
in fome low damp places in the moor, that have been
under water in the winter.—The common fuel through
the greateſt part of the pariſh is moory turf. In Garmouth, and near the fea, they ufe coals, the greateſt
part from Sunderland. Since the duty has happily been
taken off, they have fold at from 22d. to 2s. the barrel ;
which ſhould be equal to 3 Winchefter buſhels heaped.
There is fome moor ſtone in the upper part of the pariſh, which is ufed in building. The ſtone that is principally ufed, is taken out of a rock that runs along the
Spey for about a mile, where the poſt-road paſſes. It
is of a red colour, and is altogether of the nature of
lime-ſtone. It becomes harder according to its depth ;
and it is only what is at fome depth, that is hard and
durable enough to be fit for building. Towards the top,
it is foft, and of a marly nature ; fome parts of it pretty
rich, and when expofed to the air and weather, it diffolves. The clay that is mixed with this rock, or between the different ſtrata of it, is alfo of a red colour ;
and in many parts, of a marly nature, and of confiderable ſtrength. Both the foft ſtone and the clay are laid
on the lands, by thofe in the immediate neighbourhood,
to great advantage. But the quantity neceſſary to produce any confiderable effect, has hitherto prevented thofe
who are at the diſtance of a mile, from ufing it. It
feems, however, to be worth the trouble ; and it is probable, it will be more ufed as its value is known. The
great poſt road enters this pariſh at the Boat of Bog,
and paſſes through the middle of it to Elgin. The fare
for the paſſage here over the Spey is for a fingle perfon ½d. ; for a man and horfe 2d. ; for a chaife and
pair 2s. 6d. ; for a horfe and cart 2d., &c. When the
river

river is in a flood, the fare is raiſed. There is another ferry at the mouth of Spey. Another road leads from Garmouth, or the mouth of Spey, along or near the ſide of the river to Rothes and the Highlands. A third road leads from the ſame place to Elgin. All theſe roads are in pretty good condition. Like the other roads in Murray, they are, from the lightneſs of the ſoil, and the dryneſs of the climate, eaſily kept in tolerable repair. Turnpikes would not ſuit the ſtate of this country, nor would they, it is believed, be at all reliſhed. The expenſe would be too great for the general condition of the people. It would be better to convert the ſtatute-labour into money, at a low rate. There is reaſon to think, that 1s. 6d. for every man for the year, would, if properly applied, go farther in keeping the roads in repair, than the ſtatute-labour itſelf, as at preſent exacted.

This pariſh has the honour of a connexion with the celebrated family of Chatham, which, though ſomewhat diſtant, is not to be omitted *. Jane Innes, wife to Governor Pitt, and great grandmother to the preſent Chancellor of the Exchequer, was daughter to James Innes, Eſq. of Redhall, a place within a few hundred yards of the preſent church of Speymouth, on the bank of Spey, immediately oppoſite to Gordon Caſtle. The family of Redhall was a branch of the family of the Inneſes, Baronets, of Coxtoun.---From the ſituation of this pariſh on the river Spey, it has been the ſcene of ſome actions of fame in our hiſtory †.

There

---

* Vide Edmondſon's Peerage, Family of Chatham ; and the fact is known in this country.

† Near the mouth of this river the rebels of Murray, Rofs, and Caithnefs, made a ſtand in the year 1078, to oppoſe the paſſage of King Malcolm III.

with

There are no remains of antiquity within the parish
that deserve notice. The language here spoken is the
English;

with his army over the Spey, and here they made their submission at the intercession of the priests, and on seeing the resolution of the Royal army, in attempting and passing through the river.—(*Buchanan.*)

Another army of rebels, in the year 1110, halted at the mouth of Spey, with
a determination to dispute the passage of King Alexander I., who was pursuing
them. The king forced the passage, and ordered Alexander Scrimger to attack the enemy with a part of his army, who routed them, and put them to
flight.---(*Ibid.*)

In the year 1160, near the mouth of the same river, and on the moor between Speymouth and Urquhart, as is supposed, a rebellion of a still more serious aspect was quelled, by a victory gained by Malcolm IV. over the people
of Murray, when the whole army of the rebels was cut to pieces, after
which the chief families of the province, and all who were concerned in the
rebellion, (as being, according to Buchanan, " a people of a turbulent dif-
position,") were removed and dispersed through other parts of the kingdom; and others from different parts were transplanted into Murray in
their room.——(*Ibid.*) King Charles II. landed at Speymouth from Holland
in the year 1650. Some say, he arrived first at Cromarty. It is certain,
however, he came by sea to Spey, as the descendents of a man of the
name of Milne, who carried his Majesty on shore, are still in Garmouth,
and are distinguished from others of that name, in the same place, by the
name of King Milnes, from that circumstance. He was here received by
the Laird of Innes, and other gentlemen, and dined with the factor of
Lord Dumfermling, who lived in Garmouth, in a house which was only lately taken down; and here it probably was, that he was made to sign the cove-
nant. In spring 1746, the rebels, on their return from the S., collected in
great numbers on the banks of Spey, and the manse of Speymouth became, for
some time, according to an account left by the minister of that period, their
head quarters on Spey; and several of their principal officers, as Lord John
Drummond, the Duke of Perth, Lords Kilmarnock, Balmerinoch, Secretary
Murray, put up in it, and many others frequented it. This, the minister ob-
serves, was expensive to him, but they used him very civilly, and gave him no
disturbance in point of principle; only there was no public worship during
their stay. It appears from this, as well as from what they themselves gave
out at the time, that they meant to have made a stand at Spey against the
King's army; and this the Duke of Cumberland expected. And there is no
doubt, that it was the place for them to have tried their strength; but a want
of

Engliſh, if the broad Scotch that is ſpoken throughout the greateſt part of Murray, Banff, and Aberdeenſhires, be thought entitled to that name. Erſe is not the common language within 20 miles of us. Formerly there was a good deal of ſmuggling carried on, on this coaſt ; but, by the late regulations, that is now in a great meaſure ſuppreſſed. By the ſame means, the private diſtilling of whiſky, which was formerly pretty generally carried on in this quarter, is now almoſt entirely brought to an end ; and in conſequence of both theſe, the uſe of ſpirituous liquors is greatly and happily leſſened.

of concert among their chiefs, and of ſubordination among the men, prevented this, and they went off in great haſte on the approach of the King's army. On the 12th of April, the Duke of Cumberland, with his army, paſſed the Spey, at a ford directly oppoſite to the church of Speymouth, with the loſs only of one man, and encamped between the river and the church, and ſlept himſelf that night at the manſe ; and on the 16th, the battle of Culloden was fought ; and thereby an end was happily put to the Rebellion.

PARISH of SPYNIE, or NEW SPYNIE.

(County and Synod of Moray.—Presbytery of Elgin.)

By the Reverend Mr ABRAHAM GORDON, *Minister.*

Name, Lake, Fish, &c.

THE LOCH of SPYNIE, which has given this parish its name, is the first object in a statistical account which claims attention. This lake is more than 3 miles in length, and about 1 in breadth. It bounds the parish along its N. side, and appears to have been a Frith of the Sea, though it is now shut up by a long extent of valuable land at each end, both on the E. and W. Accordingly part of the country, between the lake and the sea, still retains the name of ROSS ISLE; and there is a place near its western end called KINTRAE, (in Gaelic, *Cean Traidhe,*) which signifies, *the Head of the Tide.* Besides which, beds of shells, principally oysters, which are not now found on the coast, are frequently discovered on the banks of the lake, several feet below the surface of the earth *. This lake abounds with swans; and

---

* It appears, from the *Chartulary of Moray,* that, in the 13th century, small boats were sent from the village of Spynie to fish in the sea; in testimony of which, a heap of shells, collected by the fishers, was lately discovered, under a thin covering of earth, on the ground where the village stood. It also appears, from

and FORDON, in his Hiſtory, remarks it as a curioſity. There are alſo perch and trout in this lake.

Palace.—The BISHOP'S PALACE is the next object to which the attention is moſt naturally called. It is ſituated in the eaſtern extremity of the pariſh, on the bank of the lake;

from the chartulary, that, in 1451, the biſhop got this village erected into a burgh of barony, and the next year into a burgh of regality; but there is now no other veſtige of it than a market croſs. But although it is evident, that, at a period compa- ratively not remote, the ſea flowed into the ſpace which the lake now occupies, and covered, beſides, a large extent of land at each end of it; yet it is alſo obvious, that, at a ſtill more re- cent period, the bounds of this lake were more limited than at preſent. For, a few years ago, when the canal, which had long been neglected, was cleaned out and enlarged, a cauſeway was diſcovered, ſtretching from this pariſh quite acroſs the lake, in which there were ſeverai paſſages for the water, each about 3 feet wide, and covered by a thick flag-ſtone; and, upon its ap- pearance, a tradition was recollected, that this cauſeway was cal- led *the Biſhop's Steps*, and had been formed by his influence, for the accommodation of the miniſters of St. Andrew's, who officiated alſo in the church of *Ogueſton*, (ſince united to *Drainy*,) both having been menſal churches before the eſtabliſhment of Preſbytery. Biſhop Falconer told the author this; and that the Biſhop's prieſt, who officiated, had prayers in the forenoon in the one, and in the afternoon in the other, and thereafter his dinner in the Caſtle every Sunday. This cauſeway was ſoon converted, by Mr BRANDER of PITGAVENY, into a ſubſtan- tial road, by which a more direct communication was opened between Elgin and the ſhore. And as he is now farther im- proving the canal, ſo as to gain nearly two feet of additional fall, it is expected, when this work is completed, that the lake will be again reduced to its ancient narrow limits. It may be farther obſerved, that it has been conjectured, that the vaſt qnantity of land waſhed up by the ſea, on the coaſt between Nairn and Find- horn, and drifted eaſtward by the wind over the eſtate of Cu- bin, deſtroyed the oyſters on the coaſt, and ſhut up the lake on the weſt, which, preventing any current, permitted the alluvion of the river Spey to cloſe it in at the eaſt, as the appearance of the ground ſeems ſtill to ſhew.

lake; and near to it, where the water is deepeft, a fmall artificial ifland emerged, upon clearing out the canal, of an oval form, about 60 by 16 paces, appearing to be compofed of ftones from the quarry, bound together by crooked branches of oak, and as if the earth, with which it was completed, had been wholly wafhed off during its fubmerfion. The palace itfelf was a magnificent and fpacious building, round a fquare court, having the gate on the eaft fide, and fortified by towers at the corners, and a dry ditch on the weft and fouth, containing lofty halls, deep vaults, a chapel, ftables, and other offices *. The remains of paintings, on a part of the

* Spynie Palace has been fo often defcribed by antiquarians, that it would be ufelefs to recapitulate the fubject at large. It may, however, be obferved, that although there is no certainty when the palace was firft founded, yet the bifhopric was erected by MALCOLM CANMORE, anno 1057; and we are authorifed to fay, that GREGORY was appointed bifhop here, in the year 1107, by the Cartulary of Drumferling, when King WILLIAM confirmed to that monaftery the cell of Urquhart, in this neighbourhood, and renewed the privileges and gifts to this abbacy, made by MALCOLM, and the worthy ST. MARGARET his wife. King JAMES II. anno 1450, by his charter in the public records, refers alfo to the gifts made by that King's fucceffors, DUNCAN, EDGAR, ETHELRED his brother, ALEXANDER, and SYBILLA his Queen, DAVID, MALCOLM, WILLIAM, and ROBERT BRUCE, fucceffively. Hence we may infer, that the fame King Malcolm Canmore erected this diocefe, at this period, and the bifhops occupied the church as a cathedral; and made their refidence here, as well as at Birnie and King-edward, where they lived in Caftles, which are ftill remaining in ruins. This church continued to be the domicil of the bifhop till the Revolution: It ftood where the cathedral was eftablifhed, till the year 224; when King ALEXANDER II's mandate authorifed its tranflation to Elgin. It is dated the 10th year of his reign, and the deed is granted, *Apud Mufkylbr. quinto die Julii.* The cathedral of Elgin was founded by ANDREW MURRAY, fon of William Murray of Duffus. The Murrays of Duffus had the lands of Kintrae and Leggat, in this parifh, from King DAVID I. along with the great eftate of Duffus and Ogfton. Of this great family are defcended the Sutherlands, the Douglafes, and the Murrays, in the fouth.

The

the walls, were ſo diſtinct, a few years ago, as to ſhew, that a
landſcape with trees, and ſeveral repreſentations of ſcriptural
hiſtory,

The boundaries of eſtates were early attended to. There was a
diſtinct march, dividing Spynie and Findraſſie from Kintrae and
Quarrywood, by agreement, in 1226, between Hugh de Moravia, and his brother the biſhop, and eſtabliſhing the road to
Sherriffmiln, Auchter-Spynie, and Elgin, the march of property, declaring the muirs to the eaſt neutral ground The
pariſh conſiſted of church lands and King's lands. Thoſe
of the church were *Spynie, Myreſide, Biſhopmiln, Murrayſton,
Burrowbrigs, Aughter-Spynie,* and *Auldrochty.* Thoſe of the
Crown were *Leggat, Kintrae,* and *Quarrywood,* and *Barony* of
Weſtfield.

The earlieſt feu of the biſhop is that of a ſtance for a miln upon Auchter Spynie, (Sherriffmiln,) in a donation of the ſaid
Andrew, biſhop of Murray, to Walter of Duffus, his brother, anno 1237. As on this ſtance alone, a miln is built, a
few rigs along with it, though 6 miles diſtant from the barony, continued the miln of that eſtate 500 years, and lately were
purchaſed, from Mr Arthur Duff, by the proprietor of Duffus,
whoſe grandfather ſold them to Lord Braco, in 1740. The lands
themſelves were feued before the year 1309, in favour of Adam
Steven, burgeſs of Elgin ; and the ſaid ſtance of a miln is there
reſerved. They were in the perſon of Thomas Urquhart of
Burdſyards, in 1390. The lands of Auldrochty belonged to Robert Sibbald, in 1398 Findraſſie was fewed by the biſhop to
John, *Dominus de Toilres,* and Margaret his wife, anno 1378.

The remaining lands of the church continued with the biſhop
till the eve of the Reformation, when Biſhop Hepburn made
great havock. What of them were ſaved from his prodigal
hands, with the feu-duties and patronages. were granted by
James VI. in favour of Alexander Lindsay, who was created
Lord Spynie, and the biſhopric erected into a temporal Lordſhip to him; and his heirs and aſſignees, and to Jean Lyon,
Counteſs of Angus, his wife.

This Alexander Lindſay, a brother of the Earl of Craw-
furd, was a great favourite of this Prince, who wrote him from
Denmark, adviſing him to the marriage of Jean Lyon, in
theſe words : '. Dear Sandy, marry her—your young *tout* will
' blaſt her old *horn.*'—About the year 1605, Lord Spynie diſ-
poned the biſhopric to the Dunbars of Weſtfield, who afterwards ſold it to the family of Grange.

Burrow-

hiftory, had been the defign *. Adjoining to it alfo were gardens, though of no great extent, now diftinguifhable only by

Burrowbrigs and Myreside were feued out by Alexander Douglas bifhop of Murray, in 1609, to his fon. Alexander, and Mary Innes his wife, who was proprietor alfo of Spynie and Murrayfton, and died provoft of Banff about 1669

In this parifh lived the Dunbars of Weftfield, a family which flourifhed 400 years in Murray, and the different branches of which poffeffed a great part of the country. A century ago, there were 26 heritors in the fhire. of whom only two now remain. Of the family of Weftfield, and not of Mochrum, or Aimach, (as feveral authors narrate,) was Gavin bifhop of Aberdeen, fon of Alexander Dunbar of Weftfield, and Elizabeth Sutherland, daughter of William Sutherland of Duffus, and laird of Quarrywood and Leggat, in this parifh. This Alexander fhould have been Earl of Murray in 1446, being the only fon of James, Earl of Murray, and laird of Frendraught. The faid Bifhop was Lord Regifter in 1503; Bifhop of Aberdeen in 1518, and built the bridge of Dee. which Bifhop Elphinfton began, and mortified the lands of Ardlair in Garioch, in 1529, to its fupport, under the management of the Provoft, (Menzies,) and Council of Aberdeen. He endued an hofpital for 12 poor men at Old Aberdeen, and mortified 50 merks Sterling to two chaplains, payable out of the lands of Quarrywood and Leggat, in which he was infefted; and the deed was confirmed by King James V. proceeding on the faid William Sutherland's contract to the Bifhop, dated *Apud Quarrywood, die quinto menfis Augufti*, 1529, in which this remarkable condition is inferted: ' *Provifo infuper, quod fi contingat monetam regni* ' *Scotiae, feu ejufvis alterius regni, in Scotia curfum habentem, ad al-* ' *tius praetium levari quam ut nunc in folutione capiunt, unde reve-* ' *rendus ipfe pater, aut heredes, feu affignati, feu quicunque pauperioris* ' *aut deterioris conditionis officientes, in eo cafu obligo et aftringo* ' *praedictas terras meas, de Quarrywood, et Leggat, poffeffionibus* ' *quibufcunque dicti annui redditus. ad folvendum pro qualibet* ' *Marca et viginti duabus denariis, unum unciam puri argenti* ' *quod creat ad minus* Alewyne Penny Fyne. *vel ejus verum* ' *valorem, in ufuale Moneta Regni Scotiae. pro quibus licebit ipfis* ' *poffefforibus dicti annui redditus, ipfas terras, pro fe aut fuos officia-* ' *reos, aut factores, diftringere et namare.*'—Inftead therefore of 2l. 15s. 6 8/12 d. Sterling, the *reddendo* ought to be about 9l. 12s. Sterling.

* It is hardly poffible to furvey thefe ruins of ecclefiaftical magnificence,

by the ruined walls, in which was the beft fruit, faid to be reared from plants of foreign countries. The whole pre-cincts, which do not exceed 10 acres, are now the property of the Crown, and are let by the Court of Exchequer to the Earl of Fife, the adjoining heritor, at the rent of 12 l. Sterling.

Situation, Extent, Surface, Wood, Minerals, &c.—A great part of this parifh lies pleafantly fituated along the banks of the Loffie, within view of Elgin, including *Auchter-Spynie*, called alfo *Upper Haugh*, Murrayfton, called, in 1378, *Middle Haugh*, (then feued by the Bifhop to John Dallas, fon

of

magnificence, without reflecting upon the almoft unlimited influence which the clergy, for a long period, poffeffed over the minds of men. In this enlightened age, we can hardly think, without indignation, of that fpiritual bondage in which our anceftors were held ; but, perhaps, a philofopher, in viewing the ftate of fociety in this country, during the times of Epifcopacy, when the police was extremely imperfect, and the government too weak to enforce obedience to the laws, would confider the great afcendency of Ecclefiaftics to have been a happy circum-ftance for the people, feeing it was often exerted to prevent and to redrefs injuries from powerful layman ; and thus ferved to mitigate thofe evils, which could only be cured by the wifdom and energy of a better government.

Although no perfon, in the catalogue of the MORAY BISHOPS, made any confpicuous figure as a ftatefman, yet, both in the Roman Catholic and Proteftant Churches, they appear to have been men of very refpectable characters, and to have poffeffed the regard and confidence of their refpective contemporaries, having been often chofen as the arbitrators of their difputes. Several eftates are ftill bounded according to the decreets arbitral of COLIN FALCONER, the laft bifhop who inhabited this palace, who died, anno 1686, much efteemed. The late PHESDO, and WILLIAM CUMING of Craigmiln, were at his burial, and heard often to fay, that the whole country, *gentle* and *fimple*, attended his funeral. Neither of his two fucceffors, (ALEXANDER ROSE and WILLIAM HAY,) had any perfonal refidence in their official character.

of William Dallas of Strathardel,) and *Wester Haugh*, now called *Burrowbrigs*. From the eastern precincts of the palace, a ridge of moor stretches the whole length of the parish, nearly 4 miles, rising gradually towards the west into a pretty high hill, and clothed almost throughout its whole extent with thriving plantations of fir, interspersed with other forest trees. The medium breadth of the parish is nearly two miles. On the south side of the highest part of this ridge, about a mile westward from Elgin, on the post road to Forres, there is a large extent of very flourishing natural oak wood, the property of the Earl of Fife, who has inclosed it with a substantial stone wall, and keeps it properly thinned and clear of underwood, so that, when fully grown, its value must be very considerable. Under a thin stratum of moorish soil, the whole of this ridge seems to be a mass of excellent hard free stone ; of which there is a quarry near the summit of the hill, that supplies a large extent of country with mill-stones, and the town of Elgin and the neighbourhood with stones for building. When the intended BRIDGE OVER THE SPEY at Fochabers comes to be erected, it will, no doubt, occur to those concerned, that they can no where be supplied with better stones, or at a cheaper rate, than from the Earl of FIFE's quarry in this parish.

Soil, Climate, River. &c. —Upon each side of this ridge lies the whole of the cultivated land, in which almost every variety of soil is to be met with, from the heaviest clay to the lightest sand. The air is healthy, and, on the south side of the hill, peculiarly soft and warm, during a great proportion of the year : On the north side, the climate is not so pleasant, the soil being wet and cold, and the lake often emitting a very thick and disagreeable fog. These disadvantages do not, however, seem to have any bad effects upon

upon the health of the inhabitants, no diſeaſe being more prevalent here than in any other part of the country.—This pariſh is bounded on the S. throughout the greateſt part of its length, by the river *Loſſie,* excepting that oppoſite to the town of Elgin there is a fine field of about 40 acres, called *Brrough-bridge,* which belongs to this pariſh, though on the ſouth ſide of the river : The reaſon of this is, that the Loſſie formerly run cloſe by the town, as appears from the title deeds of the properties in the adjoining quarter of the burgh, which ſtill bound them by the river, although this valuable field, the property of the Earl of FINDLATER, has been, from time immemorial, interjected between them. The re-verſe of this has happened a little lower down, in a ſmall ſe-micircular field, called *Dean's Crook,* which has been evident-ly cut off from the Cathedral lands of Elgin, by the river occupying the diameter inſtead of the periphery, which ſtill remains a reedy pond.

Produce.—The productions of the pariſh are in no reſpect different from thoſe of the country around. Grain, includ-ing peaſe and beans, is the article on which the tenants chiefly depend for the payment of their rents, and the pur-chaſe of the neceſſaries of life. On the larger farms, which are rented by gentlemen, turnips and ſown graſs have their places in the rotation of crops ; but, on the ſmaller, none of the modern improvements in agriculture have yet been a-dopted *. Every farmer, however, raiſes hay, the ſoil being

very

* Thirty years ago, neither turnips nor potatoes were known in this pariſh, except a few in gardens. The principal farmers have now both in abundance in the open fields, and partake of the profits of theſe uſeful productions. Graſs ſeeds, ſuch as rye-graſs and clover, were equally unknown 40 years ago. A few families of rank, in the neighbourhood, began to raiſe graſs ; and

very productive, and the fmall poffeffor finds it his advantage, as o.c ..re will produce 300 ftones, when properly cultured, which anfwers for the food of cattle in fummer, and prevents their fending them to the Highland Glens, 40 miles diftance, which was their former practice, and ftill partly prevails. In this parifh and the neighbourhood, within 4 miles of each other, there are 9 *pidgeon houfes* well ftored ; a fign of the good grain of the parifh, which, upon an average, weighs from 18 to 20 ftones, per boll, of barley ; 15 ftone, per boll, of oats ; and 16 ftone. per boll, of wheat. The wheat is meal meafure. That of the other grain exceeds the Linlithgow boll about a peck.

Cultivation, Farm Rents, &c.—The farm of Sherriffmiln, rented by JAMES WALKER, Efq; M. D. claims particular notice in an account of this kind. This gentleman, in the early part of his life, entered, with all the ardour of enthufiafm, into the horfe-hoeing hufbandry, on the plan of JETHRO TULL ; in which he has ever fince perfevered with unfailing fteadinefs, raifing crops of wheat, barley, and beans, in drills without a particle of dung, always following the intervals, (about 3 feet,) for each fucceeding crop ; and thus compleatly demonftrating the effect of cultivation without the ufe of *manure.* Although every operation has been performed with the niceft accuracy, and in its proper feafon, and though the foil of Sherriffmiln feems to be well calculated for this kind of hufbandry, being light and fandy, yet the refult has not been fuch as to encourage imitation. The corn is indeed fuperior in quality to any in the country ; but the quantity by the acre *much lefs* than is raifed in the

broad-

and a gardener in Elgin, who had been bred in London, was employed to cut the grafs, and overfee the hay, for the fcythe was then little known, and could not be ufed.

broad-caſt way, on the ſame kind of ſoil, well plowed and manured. The average rent, per acre, is about 15 s. the clay land letting at 1 l. the ſandy ſoils at about 10 s. and thoſe of the intermediate qualities from 14 s. to 17 s. the acre *. Although the clay land in general produces large crops, yet, on account of the additional expence which attends the management of it, it is not by many reckoned the moſt profitable ; as the labour of this ſoil is often ſuſpended for a great part of the winter, and in the beginning of ſpring, while all the neceſſary operations of that ſeaſon are diligently proſecuted on the drier lands.

Improvements.

* In this pariſh, and generally in the whole pariſhes of the country, the land-lords drew a victual rent ; and this practiſe continued till Lord Fife introduced a converſion at 12 and 12 s. 6 d, per boll. If the ancient rents were exacted, *ipſis corporibus*, it would be found, that, on the average value of grain, the preſent rents would not much exceed the rents eſtabliſhed 170 or 200 years ago. For, by the valuation of teinds, anno 1629, Spynie, on the one end of the pariſh, is then rented at 108 bolls, and now pays the heritor, excluſive of the precinct or biſhops part, 72 l. Sterling. The farm of Sherriffmiln, then rented at 50 bolls, now pays 48 l. In the vicinity of the town of Elgin, and in the other part of the pariſh, Kintrae was given up, anno 1629, at the yearly rent of 130 bolls of victual, and recently ſet by Lord Fife at 118 l. 14 s. of money, and 20 bolls of wheat. This, reckoned with the firſt quality of ſoil in the country, is about 20 s. per acre ; which, eſtimating the value of a boll at 16 s. proves, that the preſent *reddendo* ſcarcely exceeds the ancient exaction ; and likewiſe ſhows, whether the farmer has improved the method of cultivation, for he has no other ſource, but the prices of cattle, which, in the memory of man, have been tripled in value. If the caſe were otherwiſe, the tenant ſtill could not pay, nor the land-lord receive, the ſtipulated rents exigible 170 years ago.—It alſo proves that victual, then valued at 5 l. Scotch the boll, has not been doubled, when every other article of life has been doubled, tripled, and quadrupled. Servants wages, in this pariſh, 40 years ago, were, for a ploughman, 10 l. Scotch half yearly, now 30 l. ; and exceeding it in many parts of the country.

Improvements.—The induftry of the farmer will often in-creafe the value of a farm, where the fluggard will ftarve. A remarkable inftance of this occurs in the improvement of the farm of Murrayfton, which was poffeffed by Mr James Dun-can, and held by 4 tenants, at the low rent of 70 bolls, in the year 1764, when they all became bankrupts. The land-holder then adapted his converfion for 19 years to Mr Do-naldfon, who exerted much induftry, and improved the farm greatly. On his refignation, Mr Duncan entered at an advanced rent of 10 l. He lives as comfortably as Mr Donaldfon did; and now, befides the profits of his crop, by attention to the dairy alone, draws, for milk and butter, 150 l. yearly.—It may be obferved, that the farm of Burrow-brigs was, 170 years ago, only rented at 18 bolls of victual*; but now it rents at 100 l. Sterling, owing to its vicinity to the burrow lands of Elgin. As a farther evidence of what the grounds, by proper cultivation, may produce, Mr Ruf-fell, the proprietor of Weftfield, has let his eftate in lots of from 20 to 40 acres, and built houfes for the inhabitants, whereby he gets a rent of from 30 s. to 40 s. per acre. So that

* By the Sherriff Court records it appears, that the price of a boll of victual was 8 l. anno 1635, 6 l. 13 s. 4 d. in 1636, 7 l. in 1642. 6 l. in 1644, 12 l. in 1647, and 9 l. in 1649; and bear given in charity 10 l. per boll. that is, a peck to the boll; and 8 l. for the meal. Country cloth was 10 d. per ell; half a merk for a pair of hofe; a merk for a pair of fhoes; and 8 l. for the ftone of wool, in 1649 A white horned wedder was fold for 2 l. Scots, and a young gimmer for the fame; a cart of peats for 4 s; 8 tups for a boll of houfehold meal; a good horned cow for 18 l. Scotch; a grey horfe to the Laird of Innes 20 dollars; falt 5 l. per boll; and a pound of onion feed for 4 l. A man fervant's fee was 4 l. 3 s. 4 d. for the half year, in the year 1649; and in a procefs at the inftance of Robert Gutherie in Speyfla againft Beffie Douglas, good wife of Leu-chers, fhe is decerned in 20 merks for ilk boll of victual oats, that is, 5 firlots, (fcarcely 6 firlots of Linlithgow meafure,) crop 1649.

that this eſtate, bought ſome years ago at 6000 l. draws now more than 400 l. annually.

Cattle.—There are 201 horſes and 560 black cattle in the pariſh, beſides 14 large oxen, which go in pairs either in the plough or wain. Before the moor was planted, almoſt every tenant had a ſmall flock of ſheep; but now there are not above 200 ſheep in the pariſh : And theſe are chiefly of a ſmall white-faced breed, which has been in this country from time immemorial. There is little attention paid to the breeding or improvement of black cattle, except by a few of the gentlemen, who alone turn this branch of huſbandry to any account.

Rent and Proprietors.—The valued rent is 3055 l. 3 s. 8 d. Scotch *, which is divided among 5 heritors, excluſive of the precinct of Spynie, belonging, as was ſaid, to the Crown. Beſides the farm of Spynie, the Earl of FIFE holds all the lands in the north and weſt, except the eſtate of Weſtfield, the property of FRANCIS RUSSEL, Eſq; of Blackhall, Advocate. The Earl of FINDLATER holds the lands of Burroughbridge, lying between the Loſſie and the town of Elgin; as well as the lands of Greenhall, Myreſide, and Biſhopmiln, in the eaſt, between Spynie and Elgin; JAMES MILN, Eſq; having only the milns of Biſhopmiln, with a ſmall contiguous property. And the LESSLIES of Findraſſie have long poſſeſſed that eſtate, on the ſide of the lake, between the properties of the two Earls.

Population.

* By the old valuation roll of this county, in the year 1667, the real rent is ſaid to have been 198,217 l. 13 s. Scotch, (16,518 l. 2 s. 9 d. Sterling,) and the valued rent 66,672 l. 11 s. 11 d. Scotch.

Population.—The population feems to have decreafed in the courfe of the laft 30 years. Although there are no very large farms in the parifh (there being only one that exceeds 100 acres), yet there are feveral, in which, within that period, one tenant has fucceeded to 405. It is probable, that the population may be ftill a little farther diminifhed, as nearly one half of the parifh confifts of farms from 20 to 40 acres, which the proprietors may through time fee proper to lay out in larger tenements.

The return to Dr Webfter, in 1755, was   865 fouls.
The number of fouls at prefent is,

Males	-	-	-	289
Females	-	-	-	313

                                     602

                    Decreafe   263

Of thefe there are, of the Epifcopal perfuafion, 5 families, confifting of about   30 perfons.
The annual average of births *. for 7 years, is 12
Ditto of marriages *   -   -   -   -   6

Manufactures.—The only manufactory of this parifh is that erected by Mr John Ritchie, merchant in Elgin. In the eaftmoft part of this parifh, on the river of Loffie, within a half mile of the town of Elgin, he has built on a feu belonging to him, a mill for the manufactory of tobacco, a wauik-mill, a flax mill, and bleaching machinery, which has brought to great perfection the bleaching of linens and thread ; and he is, with great affiduity, giving every hope of bringing thefe ufeful and laudable inventions to perfection.

                                             Fuel.

* Thefe averages are taken from the parifh regifter, from 1784 to 1790, inclufive, a period in which it appears to have been very exactly kept.

Fuel.—Coals may now be had at ſo moderate a price, and in a few years there will alſo be ſuch abundance of wood, that it is hardly neceſſary to notice the preſent ſcarcity of fuel for domeſtic accommodation.

Eccleſiaſtical State.—The church and manſe were moſt pleaſantly ſituated at the eaſtern extremity, in the vicinity of the Caſtle, until the year 1736, when they were removed to *Quarrywood,* a more centrical, though more bleak ſituation, nearly under the higheſt part of the north ſide of the hill. Both are at preſent in pretty good repair; and the glebe and garden, conſiſting of about 6 acres, are both ſubſtantially incloſed with ſtone walls. The ſtipend, including 60 merks for communion elements, is 30 l. Sterling, and 64 bolls of bear.

Antiquities—The remains of a Daniſh camp * are ſtill very conſpicuous on the hill of *Quarrywood.* It would appear that thoſe Danes, who inhabited the burgh *(burges)* in this neighbourhood, had erected it as an aſylum for their families. It commands a view of the whole county, and a pleaſant proſpect into the counties of Caithneſs, Sutherland, Roſs, Inverneſs, Nairn, Banff, and Aberdeen. It is worthy of Lord Fyfe's notice, and becoming his taſte, in beautifying the county, to renew this monument, and perpetuate its antiquity.

Advantages.

---

* Both FORDON and BUCHANAN give account of the Danes landing in Murray, about the year 1008, when Malcolm II. marched againſt them, fought, and was defeated at Forres. In the career of their ſucceſs, they ſent for their families, who enjoyed the land till they were repeatedly defeated at Gamerie in Banff-ſhire, and Cruden in Buchan, where the Daniſh camps are ſtill to be ſeen.

Advantages.—One great advantage, which this parifh in a peculiar manner enjoys, is the abundance of ftone fo well adapted both for building and inclofing; of which, however, the inhabitants have not yet availed themfelves in any great degree. Befides this, no part of the parifh is inconveniently diftant from either of the harbours of Lofliemouth or Findhorn, or the markets of Elgin, to which laft there is at all times an uninterrupted accefs by a handfome ftone bridge, where the poft-road to Forres croffes the Loffie, about the middle of the fouth fide of the parifh.

Language—The language of the parifh is the Scotch dialect. Some of the names of places are evidently Gaelic, fuch as *Kintrae, Infhagarty**, (*Innis-ant fhagairt*), the *Leggat,* (*an lag-fhad*), &c. And it is highly probable that many more of them are of Gaelic origin, though they are now corrupted or difguifed fo much, by having been fo long in the mouths of Lowlanders, that it is hardly poffible for a Highlander to recognize them for his native tongue.

Character, &c.—The people are induftrious and frugal, poffefling alfo other virtues, not fo much the neceffary confequence of their fituation; being in general honeft, benevolent and friendly, and entertaining a high refpect for the ordinances of religion. The drefs of the poorer tenants and day-labourers is of the cheapeft kind, chiefly of home manufacture; that of the more fubftantial farmers, and their fervants, is purchafed from the fhops of Elgin.

* The Prieft's Ifland.

PARISH of URQUHART,

(County and Presbytery of Elgin, Synod of Moray.)

By the Rev. Mr William Gordon, *Minifter.*

Name, Extent, and Situation, &c.

THE etymology of the name cannot be afcertained with precifion. If it be of Gaelic extraction, fome information may be received from thofe quarters where that language is underftood. There are other two parifhes of the fame name, the one a few miles from Invernefs, and in that county ; the other in Rofs-fhire. This parifh extends about 4 miles from E. to W. and 3 from N. to S ; and lies at an equal diftance from Elgin on the W. and the river Spey on the E ; the poft road paffing along it on the S.

Surface, Sea Coaft, Fuel, &c.—That part of the parifh which lies to the N. W. is flat and low, rifing a few feet on-ly above the level of the fea, and has probably, at fome for-

mer

697

mer period been covered by water, as there are evident
marks of the sea having receded from the coast : The rest
is a good deal more elevated, and of an unequal waving surface.   The sea coast, which is about 4 miles in extent, is
low and sandy ; it contains no creek nor landing place of
any kind.   Our grain, which is our only article of exportation, is shipped from Speymouth or Lossiemouth ; and our
great article of importation, which is coals, is imported at
the same harbours ; the former of which is at the distance of
4 miles, and the other of 6.   It is proper here to mention,
that this, as well as several other neighbouring parishes, was
formerly ill supplied with fuel ; but now, that article is rendered much less expensive, by taking off the high duty on
coals, that was laid on with little attention to political e-
conomy, and which has lately been abolished by the exertions of a great statesman ; to whom this country is more
obliged on account of that measure, and many others, than
to any other native of this part of the united kingdom.

Climate, &c.—The air is dry and salubrious, and the people in general healthy ; there are, however, few instances of
remarkable longevity to be met with.   The climate here, like
that of all that narrow tract of land, which lies along the south
side of the Moray Firth, is mild and temperate to an extraordinary degree : Its superiority, in that respect, over the
high country, is most remarkable in the spring months.   Often in that season, while all the operations of husbandry are
going forward in the low parts of Moray, there are many
places in the high country, distant only a few miles, where
these operations meet with a total interruption, from the in-
								tenseness

tenfenefs of the frofts, and from deep falls of fnow. * Our winters likewife, in general, are fo open, that feveral plants commonly ranked amongft the hot-houfe divifion, ftand throughout that feafon in the gardens of Innes, expofed to the open air, and lofe little of their verdure.

Soil and Cultivation, &c.—The foil is various, and, though in general light and fandy, is of a kindly and fertile nature, exceedingly well adapted for raifing turnips, potatoes, barley, and all kinds of artificial graffes. And a confiderable part of it would be extremely fit for wheat, if there were any opportunity of procuring fufficient quantities of manure. Notwithftanding the mildnefs of the climate, and the kindlinefs of the foil, agriculture has made but flow advances. Some patches of turnips are indeed to be feen, and a few acres are fown with grafs feeds; but the fields in general are rather in a ftate of bad cultivation. This feems to be occafioned, in a great meafure, by the expence and difficulty of conftructing fufficient inclofures; there being no ftone quarries in the parifh, nor any ftones in the fields fit for this purpofe; and thorn hedges are fo long of coming to perfection, and fo difficult to be fenced when they are young, that no tenant, on a leafe of ordinary endurance, can attempt them with any profpect

---

* It may likewife be obferved, as a farther proof of the excellency of this climate, that in the end of the laft, and beginning of the prefent century, while there was fo great a deficiency in the crops, in many parts of Scotland, as bordered on a famine, owing to the cold and wet feafons; in Moray, at that period, the land was fo productive, as not only to fupply its own inhabitants, but alfo to fpare confiderable quantities of grain for the fubfiftence of their neighbours. And it is a fact well afcertained, that in thofe years of fcarcity and dearth, people came from the fhire of Angus, to purchafe oat meal in this country, for which they paid at the rate of 30 s. *per* boll.

proſpeĉt of ſuccefs. The farms alſo are of too ſmall extent
for carrying on any ſubſtantial improvements in agriculture.
There are a few that may contain from 60 to 100 acres;
but the common run is from 20 to 30.

Farm Rents and Ploughs, &c.—The rent of land varies
according to the nature of the ſoil; there are ſome fields let
for 20s. *per* acre, while others are below 10s.; the average
rent may be from 10s. to 15s. The ploughs, of which there
are above 100, ſome of Engliſh, ſome of Scotch conſtruĉtion,
are drawn chiefly by a pair of horſes. In this branch of
farming, an improvement has been introduced about 20 years
ago, which now begins to be pretty generally adopted; that
is, plowing with two oxen, harneſſed in the ſame manner as
horſes. This method is warmly recommended, and the advantages of it fully explained by the late Lord KAIMES, in his
book called *The Gentleman Farmer*.

Produce, Exports, &c. The produce of this pariſh, conſiſts principally of barley and oats; beſides ſupplying the inhabitants, it exports annual y a conſiderable quantity of grain;
which muſt increaſe yearly, partly by the increaſing improvements of agriculture, but chiefly by the uſe of potatoes, which
are now almoſt univerſally cultivated, and during a great part
of the year, are, in a manner, the principal ſubſiſtence of a
conſiderable number of the inhabitants. This food, which
at firſt was not in general uſe, becomes more and more ſo e-
very day, from the various modes that have been diſcovered
of dreſſing it, by different ſeaſonings, at little or no expence.
They make an excellent diſh with milk, but above all with
onions, which are raiſed in abundance in this county, and
ſold at ſuch a moderate price, as to come within the reach
of the pooreſt inhabitant.

State of Property, Plantations, &c.—Four fifths of this parish are the property of the Earl of FIFE *, whose plantations are executed with uncommon taste and judgement, and add much to the beauty and ornament of the country. In some places, he has planted moors and hills of great extent, but what makes the most beautiful appearance, is a number of little rising grounds, all of which he has covered with singular good taste, and so as to make their appearance with relation to each other extremely beautiful. In all these plantations, the Scotch fir at present predominates; but his Lordship every year causes a great many of these to be cut down, and the voids to be filled up with beech, oak and other deciduous trees §. Besides these plantations, Lord FIFE has planted hedges, and hedge rows in particular places along the high ways, that shew much fancy, and will afford considerable utility and warmth; the hedge rows, before they were planted, were pollards of a considerable size, and are thriving exceedingly well. A small plantation, at the place where the road to the house of Innes leaves the high road, two miles east of Elgin, from the beauty of its lines, must strike every traveller, and the hedge rows are continued a considerable length along the high road. In mentioning the high road, it is but justice to Lord FIFE to let it be known, that

---

* About 26 years ago, his Lordship purchased the estate of Innes; and being at that time proprietor of considerable estates in the adjacent parishes; the estate of Innes, and the lands of Urquhart, lately acquired by an exchange with the family of Gordon, he became possessed of so large a tract of property all contiguous, and comprehending a great variety of ground, that he has been enabled to execute plantations of very large extent.

§ Previous to the year 1779, at which period about one half of these plantations were formed, there were always planted in each acre 3000 Scotch firs: Since that time the proportion has only been 1200 to each acre.

that ſince he became proprietor of Innes, all the highways within the pariſh have been properly attended to, judiciouſly directed, and, by a regular application of the ſtatute labour, kept in a ſtate of good repair †. The only other heritor is Mr INNES of Leuchars ‡, who has about one fifth of the real rent of the pariſh. He is at uncommon pains to raiſe and fence hedges ; he has planted ſtripes and belts about the ground round his houſe to a very conſiderable extent, beſides ſeveral clumps ſimilar to thoſe executed by Lord FIFE. Theſe clumps, like his Lordſhip's, at preſent conſiſt chiefly of Scotch firs ; but the plantations around his farm, and about his houſe, are all deciduous trees of the beſt kinds ; oak, aſh, and witch elm, with a proper mixture of larix, which are all uncommonly well preſerved, beſides being kept under the hoe for ſeveral years after they are planted. The water of Loſſy runs through the property of this gentleman ; that river ſwells ſometimes to a great height, and frequently flooded the low ground on each ſide ; but of late, with great induſtry and merit, embankments have been conſtructed, that will contain the river, and in a great meaſure prevent future inundations : By this circumſtance the value of his lands is conſiderably raiſed.

Lakes,

† The houſe of Innes, one of Lord Fife's numerous ſeats, had been many years ago partly deſtroyed by accidental fire. Since his Lordſhip became its poſſeſſor, it has been repaired at a very conſiderable expence, and fitted up in the moſt faſhionable ſtile ; a large addition has been made to the gardens, and the grounds about the houſe have been laid out in the beſt taſte ; the whole makes now one of the moſt pleaſant and elegant places of reſidence in the North.

‡ Before Mr INNES ſucceeded to this eſtate, it had been in the poſſeſſion of a gentleman who paid very little attention to improvements of any kind. Since the preſent gentleman became proprietor, it has undergone a very great alteration to the better.

Lakes, Fiſh, Water Fowls, &c.—There is one lake in this pariſh called the *Loch of Cotts.* Pike is the only fiſh it contains : In winter it is frequented by a conſiderable number of ſwans, and, in the ſpring and autumn, by flocks of geeſe, ducks, and other water fowls. At the upper part of the pariſh, there is another lake called *Lochnabeau,* partly in this pariſh, and partly in Lhanbryd. Lochnabeau is in the middle of what was formerly an extenſive bare moor ; about 20 years ago Lord FIFE planted the moor, and particularly carried his plantations round the verge of the lake. Theſe plantations are now far advanced, and by their vicinity to the water, which is uncommonly limpid and clear, form a moſt beautiful and delightful ſcene.

Stags.—This improvement, however, has been attended with one inconvenience. In ſome ſevere winters, ſeveral years ago, a few ſtags and hinds came down to the low country from the Duke of Gordon's foreſts of Glenfiddich and Glenavon ; of late years they have taken up their reſidence in the neighbourhood of Lochnabeau, and the plantations around it, and are become ſo fond of their new habitation, that they have never returned to their native foreſts ; on the contrary, they increaſe every year, by breeding, and by the addition of freſh emigrants. Theſe animals make a very fine appearance, and afford much pleaſure and amuſement to the ſportſman ; it is therefore to be regretted that they are ſo hurtful to plantations and agriculture. Throughout the ſummer, they paſture in the night time on the corns ; in the winter on turnips ; and in the ſpring, as the winter crops of rye and wheat are then fartheſt advanced, they are particularly deſtructive to them ; but the ſtems of potatoes ſeem to be their favourite food, as they are known to paſs through fields of corn in order to brouſe on them. Upon the whole, it were much

much to be wiſhed, that they were either driven back to their antient habitation, or utterly exterminated. The laſt meaſure has been ſucceſsfully followed by a worthy nobleman in the weſtern part of this county, celebrated for his extenſive and flouriſhing plantations, who kept hounds for the ſole purpoſe of extirpating thoſe deſtructive animals. I need hardly ſay that the nobleman I mean is the Earl of MORAY. If theſe plantations have attracted the deer to this corner, it has been remarked that they have not been favourable to the increaſe of hares and patridges : this may be owing to the protection which they afford to beaſts and birds of prey. Were gentleman to give ſmall premiums for the deſtruction of theſe vermin, it would prove more effectual in preſerving the game and increaſing its numbers, than all the game laws that ever were, or ever will be enacted.

Church, School, and Poor.—The preſent incumbent, who is a bachelor, had his preſentation from the Duke of Gordon ; but the patronage of the church has ſince been conveyed to the Earl of Fife, at the time that the exchange of lands took place between his Lordſhip and the family of Gordon. The ſtipend, by a decree obtained February 1793, is 8 chalders victual and 40l. Sterling, including 5l. for communion elements. The glebe conſiſts of 5 Scotch acres. Some years ago, the miniſter entered into a contract with the heritors, for keeping the manſe and offices in repair during his incumbency, for which he receives an annuity of 15l. Sterling, beſides 30l. paid per advance. The church was completely repaired about 18 years ago.—A new ſchool-houſe was then built ; the ſchool-maſter's ſalary is 12 bolls of oat meal, and 6 bolls of barley.—The average number of poor in this pariſh is about 20. The funds for their ſupport ariſe from the weekly collections at church, which amount to 10l.

yearly

yearly, together with fome mortifications that produce 2l.
11s. 4d. of annual intereft.

Population.—The number of inhabitants has decreafe𝗍
within thefe 40 years, as appears from the following ftatement :

STATISTICAL TABLE OF THE PARISH OF URQUHART.

No. of fouls in 1755, as returned to Dr Webfter, - 1110
Ditto, in 1793, males 506, females 544. - - 1050

			Decreafe	60
Annual average of baptifms,		-	-	30
CONDITIONS, PROFESSIONS, &c.		Diffenters † from the Eftablifhed		
Proprietors,	-	2	Church, - -	20
Minifter,	- -	1	LIVE STOCK, RENTS, &c.	
School-mafter,	-	1	Horfes, - -	310
Gardeners,	- -	6	Black Cattle, -	900
Smiths,	- -	3	Sheep, § -	1570
Tailors,	- -	5	Valued rent in Scotch mo-	
Joiners,	- -	6	ney, - L. 5567 : 15 : 6	
Mafons,	- -	6	Real ditto in Sterling,	
Weavers,	- -	6	about 1800 : 0 : 0	
Shoemakers,	- -	3	No. of acres, planted by the Earl	
Millers,	- -	5	of Fife, - 2478	
Ale and fpirit dealers,	-	8	—— Deciduous trees, 230,835	

Manner of Living.—Though the progrefs of agriculture
has not been fo rapid as might be wifhed, the increafing comfort of the people is very obfervable. Within thefe 20 years,
a great

† Thefe confift chiefly of Seceders, of the Antiburgher perfuafion.

§ Since the moors were planted, the number of the fheep has confiderably decreafed, there having been formerly in the parifh more than double
the above number. The farmers are every day becoming more reconciled to
the want of thefe animals, which cannot be kept with any advantage in an
improving country, without fufficient inclofures.

a great difference to the better may be remarked in their clothing, their cleanlineſs, and every other circumſtance that tends to make life more agreeable. Their habitations have likewiſe been very much improved ; within leſs than the period above mentioned, there have been upwards of 50 neat farm houſes built in this pariſh, either by the landlord or the tenant.

Character.—Though the number of ale-houſes, mentioned in the table, may, at firſt appearance, ſeem to bear hard upon the ſobriety of the people, it is to be remarked, that only two of theſe houſes retail any conſiderable quantity of ale or whiſky. The people in general are very ſober, and diligent in their ſeveral occupations ; their efforts of induſtry being as well directed as their ſituation and circumſtances will permit.

Antiquities.—The ſite of the old priory ¶ has lately been converted into an arable field ; and the name of *Abbey-well*, which the country people ſtill give to the fountain that ſupplied the Monks with water, is the only memorial of it that now remains.

Propoſed

¶ In the 11th century, the whole of this pariſh was King's property. As early as the year 1125, a priory, dependent on the Abbey of Dunfermline, was erected at Urquhart. It was very liberally endowed ; all the lands now called the Lordſhip of Urquhart, the lands of Fochabers, as well as ſeveral others in this county, together with a part of the fiſhing on Spey, appertained to it. It appears that about the year 1345, this cell, as well as that of Pluſcardene fell into diſorder ; and the Roman Pontiff having commiſſioned the biſhops of Scotland, to enquire into thoſe irregularities, it was ſoon after ſeparated from Dunfermline, and conjoined to Pluſcardene, with which it continued united till the Reformation. At and before that period, the priors began to feu out the lands, reſerving only in their own poſſeſſion the manor places and mills ; the revenue which by that method they drew from thence, if we take into the account the teinds, multures, and ſervices, would even at this

day

Propoſed Bridge.—This account ought not to be concluded, without mentioning the ſatisfaction entertained in this pariſh, and the reſt of the country, at the late proſpect there was of a BRIDGE acroſs the Spey. At preſent the ferry is extremely troubleſome, attended with ſome danger, and neceſſarily very expenſive to travellers. If there were a bridge thrown acroſs that river, the commerce and intercourſe of the country would be very much increaſed; travelling would be rendered much more eaſy and comfortable; and, above all, it would be ſingularly uſeful for the march of the King's troops; this, in the winter, being the only road by which they can paſs either South or North. For theſe reaſons it is univerſally hoped, that meaſures for a bridge acroſs the Spey, which have been begun, and generouſly promoted, by a moſt illuſtrious family ‡ in the neighbourhood, will be taken up by government, and aided by the ſubſcription of every perſon

day be nearly adequate to a moderate rent. The priory was ſituated a little to the eaſt of the preſent church, in the midſt of a moraſs, and probably went to ruin ſoon after its union with Pluſcardene. In the year 1654, the greater part of the materials were carried off to build a granary near the ſhore at Garmouth; the remainder, ſoon after that period, was employed in repairing the manſe, and incloſing the church-yard.

In the year 1162, the *Moravienſes*, or inhabitants of Moray, (for what cauſe is not now known) took up arms; they were met in the moors of Urquhart by the King's army, which was ſent to quell the inſurrection, and, as we learn from ſome of our hiſtorians, were, after an obſtinate reſiſtance, defeated there with great ſlaughter. As the inhabitants of Moray were at that period, according to Buchannan, of a reſtleſs and turbulent diſpoſition, all the families engaged in this rebellion were diſperſed through the different provinces of Scotland. It is ſaid that thoſe who were then removed into the Northern Counties, received the name of SUTHERLAND, which their deſcendents ſtill retain, and that thoſe who were ſent to the South, aſſumed the ſurname of MURRAY, which they likewiſe have tranſmitted to their poſterity.

‡ The family of GORDON.

ſon who wiſhes well to his country.   A great part of
the ſaid road, from that to Elgin, will, in a ſhort time, be
bounded with wood on each ſide.   The large plantations
of his Grace the Duke of Gordon begin where Lord Fife's
end, and are likely to be continued Eaſt-ward to the river
ſide.

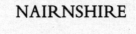

NAIRNSHIRE

NAIRNSHIRE

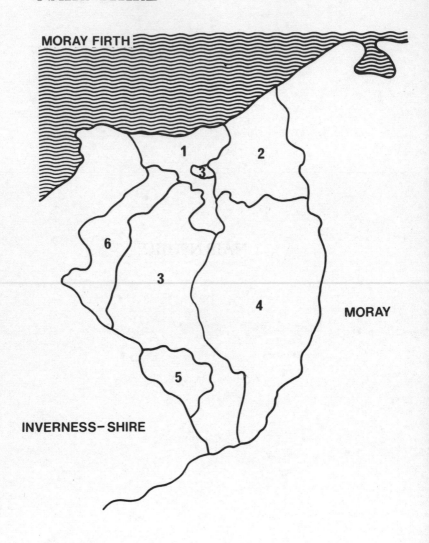

MORAY FIRTH

MORAY

INVERNESS-SHIRE

KEY TO PARISHES
1. Nairn
2. Auldearn
3. Cawdor
4. Ardclach
5. Moy, Inverness-shire (part of)
6. Croy, Inverness-shire (part of)

PARISH of ARDCLACH,

(COUNTY OF NAIRNE.)

By the Rev. Mr DONALD MITCHELL.

Name, Situation, River, Surface, &c.

THE name Ardclach is Gaelic, and fignifies ' a ftony ' high ground.' The parifh is fituated in the extremity of the county of Nairne, and lies S. E. of the town of Nairne, in the prefbytery of Nairne, and Synod of Moray. It is bounded by Auldearn, Nairne, Calder, Moy, Duthel and Edinkelly, and reckoned about 10 or 12 miles long, and between 7 and 8 broad, divided by Findhorn river, which is not navigable; neither is there a poffibility of rendering it fo. During the fummer months, fome falmon pafs up from the fea, feveral miles above Ardclach, in this water. No other kind of fifh, but trout, is to be found in it. This river is rapid, and frequently impaffable every where, excepting at Dulcy bridge, on the highland road leading from Fort George to Edinburgh. There are two boats on this water within the parifh, and one on the poft road; but owing either to the mifmanagement of the boatmen, or temerity of the people, many lives are loft. During the incumbency of the prefent mi-

niſter,

nister, no lefs than 23 perfons have been loft between Dulcy bridge and the poft-road. The lofs of lives from this
caufe claims attention; and the only method that can be
pointed out, to prevent it, is to erect a bridge between the
two boats, which would render the communication both
fafe and eafy. This parifh is a hilly mountainous diftrict,
covered with heath, and furnifhes little of any other kind
of pafture. There is much wood in it, confifting of firs,
birch, and what is called weeping birch, alder, hazel, afh
and fome oaks. The birch, alder and afh, are manufactured for labouring utenfils. The woods and hills abound
with moor-fowl, wood-cock, partrides, hares, foxes and
fome deer. The otter and wild cat are frequently feen on
the water's fide.

Agriculture, &c.—The quantity of grain produced, generally ferves the people; but in the years 1782 and 1783, they
felt the effects of thefe feafons of fcarcity; however, none
perifhed from want. The principal crops are black and
white oats, Scotch bear, rye and potatoes. The foil feems
to be unfit for any other kinds, being fhallow and thin,
covered with ftone, with a hard gravelly bottom. There
is feldom above the third return, and the crop is much expofed to froft. It is fuppofed lime might improve the foil;
but the tenants are in general fo poor, that they cannot afford the expence of it. Attempts have been made to difcover limeftone within the parifh, without fuccefs. The
method of labouring feems to have undergone little alteration for centuries back. The farmers ufe the fmall Scotch
plough, drawn by 4 or 6 black cattle, and 2 fmall horfes,
or by 4 horfes and 4 black cattle. From the moft accurate
accounts, there are about 300 horfes, 1000 black cattle,
and 2000 fheep, of the fmall Scotch breed; a larger kind
of thofe laft have been tried, but it is generally thought a
mixed

mixed breed anfwer beft.—The rental produced before the Court of Teinds, in a procefs of augmentation in the year 1786, was 283 bolls victual, and L. 543 : 8 : 5 in money. Since that period, there has been an increafe of rent in feveral parts of the parifh, and the heritors propofe giving leafes in general for 19 years. The fole dependence of the tenants is on their cattle. From their want of leafes, as well as the barrennefs of the foil, they found it their intereft to rear as many black cattle as they poffibly could. It is fuppofed there are about 2000 acres of arable land, and 4000 acres confifting of mofs and moor, a very fmall part of which feems to be improvable for corn-lands.

Manufactures.—The principal manufactures are plaiden, which is reckoned the beft in the country, and coarfe tartan, with a kind of broad cloth and duffle. Within thefe 5 years wool has fold at 18 s. the ftone. Attempts have been made to raife flax, without fuccefs. There are no lefs than 5 licenfed diftilleries, which are fupplied with barley and malt from the low country. Their licenfes are below L. 40. It might be thought that the diftilling of fo much whifky, would be attended with the worft of confequences to the morals of the people; but this has not proved to be the cafe. As this parifh abounds with mofs for peats, and mofs-fir, a confiderable number were in ufe of making whifky in a fmuggling way, and fo had an opportunity of drinking more than was proper for them; but fince the eftablifhment of licenfed diftilleries, this practice has been checked, and the people are become more fober than formerly. There is no inn within the parifh, but one at Dulcy bridge, on the highland road to Edinburgh.

Prices and Wages.—The neareft markets for butchermeat are Forres and Nairne, about 12 miles diftant from

this

this place, and meat of all kinds is commonly fold there at
3 d. and fometimes 4 d. the pound. Fowls are fold within
the parifh at 6 d. the loweft, and eggs at 2 d. the dozen.
The wages of domeftic men-fervants are L. 5 and L. 6 in
the year, of women-fervants L. 1, 16 s. and L. 2. Day-labourers have 8 d. a-day, with their victuals; and till of
late they were fatisfied with 6 d.

Population, &c.—The air appears to be healthy. Many
ftill alive are paft 70, and fome paft 80 years of age; and it
is faid there have been inftances of a few arriving at 100.
From the lift given to Dr Webfter, the number of fouls
then was 1163, in 1781 it was 1167, at prefent 1186.
The proportion of males to females is as 18 to 20. There
are 4 heritors, none of whom refide. No Diffenters. Many
perfons emigrated from the parifh a fhort time before the
American war. There are no uninhabited houfes; the
houfes in general are built of feal, and of fome ftones in the
foundation. As the people have feveral burying places
without the parifh, deaths cannot be exactly afcertained;
but for fome years back, it is believed they have not exceeded 24 in the courfe of the year, and births are between
30 and 40. St Anthony's fire is a difeafe peculiar to the
people of this place, both young and old. The fmall pox
is frequently fatal here as in other places, and has been remarkably fo this feafon, to children and fome advanced in
years. The moft effectual way to remove their prejudices
againft inoculation, would be for the heritors to defray the
expence for a limited period.

Church, Stipend, Poor, School, &c.—The church is faid
to have been built in 1626, and was rebuilt about 30
years ago. The manfe was built in 1744. The ftipend
is L. 55 : 16 : 9 Sterling, and 31 bolls, 3 firlots, 3 pecks oat-
meal.

meal. The glebe is between 4 and 5 acres arable, with little grafs. Mifs Brodie of Lethen has the right of patronage.—There is no fund for the poor, excepting the weekly collections, which amount to about L. 3 or L. 4 yearly. The number of poor on the roll is 35, though many more might be added. This fum, joined to the collections made when the Sacrament is difpenfed, furnifh but a fcanty allowance. The ordinary method by which the poor in this country procure a fubfiftence is by begging.—The falary of the parifh fchool is L. 10 Sterling, and the number of fcholars in winter is about 40. There is befides a Society fchool in a diftant part of the parifh, for reading and writing, where the number of children this winter have been upwards of 40, and another called a Spinning-fchool, to which Mifs Brodie of Lethen pays about half the falary, the reft is paid by the Society, making in all L. 10 Sterling. Mifs Brodie likewife gives the perfons who have charge of this fchool fuel *gratis*.

PARISH OF AULDEARN,

(COUNTY OF NAIRN, SYNOD OF MORAY, AND PRESBY-
TERY OF NAIRN).

By the Rev. MR JOHN PATERSON.

AULDEARN is ſaid by Mr Shaw's hiſtory of Moray to be compoſed of two Gaelic words, importing the iron-coloured brook, from a ſediment of that colour occaſionally thrown out by the brook, which runs weſtward of the village. By other gentlemen ſkilled in that language, it is ſuppoſed to denote the brook covered with alders, from the abundance of the trees ſo denominated, which grew along the ſides of it, and which ſtill grow near it. It was formerly a place of much greater conſideration than at preſent, and the ſeat of the Dean of Moray, who preſided over ten canons, and in the biſhop's abſence preſided in the chapters and in ſynods. From a grant of the " lands of Penie (Pethenach juxta Erin per ſuas rectas diviſas)" in this pariſh to the Priory of Urquhart, by David I. its ancient name ſeems to have been ſimply Erin.

The

The church and manse are pleasantly situated on a rising ground, which commands an extensive prospect of the
Moray Firth, and Bay of Cromarty, of part of five different
shires, and a landscape of many thousand acres of cultivated
lands. They are situated in the centre between Elgin and
Inverness, 20 miles from each. On the north the parish
extends four miles along the coast of the Moray Firth, 6
miles from south to north, and the same from east to west;
bounded on the south by the hills of Ardlach, on the west
by the parish of Calder, and on the east by Dykes and
Edinkaillie. The south-east part of the parish is of a rich red
mortar soil, of difficult cultivation, but producing luxuriant
crops of barley, oats, and pease. The south-west division is
of a mould darker, and not so fertile as the former, and in
late seasons the corn is liable to much damage. Around the
village of Auldearn the soil is light and dry, in showery
seasons recompensing the labours of the husbandman; but in
those of an opposite description is parched, and the crop deficient. The north part is of a cold and heavy loam, extremely difficult in wet weather to labour in winter. The
east and west sides are of a similar mould, producing weighty crops of oats, but not so favourable for barley, although
barley, in general, is the grain most congenial to the soil of
the parish, and vies in excellence with any in the northern
part of this island. In that quarter of the parish which is
the property of Lord Cawdor, the ground is so encumber-
ed with stones, that if his estate was cleared of them, it is
computed it would rise one-fifth in value.

Climate.—The climate is mild and serene, at least in the
lower and level parts of the parish. No diseases peculiar
to the place are prevalent. Notwithstanding the immoderate
use of spirituous liquors, the ravages which dropsical and
consumptive distempers have made elsewhere, are here happily

pily unknown; very few have fallen a ſacrifice to the ſmall-pox, though the people are in general averſe to inoculation, from the general gloomineſs of their faith, which teaches them, that all diſeaſes which afflict the human frame are inſtances of the Divine interpoſition, for the puniſhment of ſin; any interference, therefore, on their part, they deem an uſurpation of the prerogative of the Almighty.

State of Property.—The valued rent of this pariſh, a-mounting to L. 7255, 7 s. Scots, is divided among ſix heritors. Miſs Brodie of Lethen has an elegant ſeat in the ſouth part of the pariſh, ſituated in a hollow betwixt two hills, ſheltered on the eaſt, weſt, and ſouth ſides, by plantations of trees; among which the majeſtic ſize of ſome venerable beeches, with their luxuriant diffuſion of boughs and branches, muſt attract the notice of every beholder.—North of the church, in a delightful plain, beautifully variegated with wood and water, lies the family-ſeat of the Dunbars of Boath. The garden and pleaſure-grounds, with the ſeveral incloſures adjoining, are laid out with the utmoſt elegance of taſte. The family of Boath have been proprietors of that eſtate upwards of 250 years.—Mr Gordon of Braid has a ſummer lodge at Kinſteary.

The valued rents of the ſeveral heritors, as ſtated in the ceſs-books, are as follow, viz.: Charles Gordon's, Eſq; of Braid, confiſting of Kinſteary Park, and Auldearn, L. 2322, 14 s. 4 d. Scots money. James Brodie's, Eſq; of Brodie, eſtates of Inſhoch, Lochloy, and Penich, L. 1599, 11 s. Lord Cawdor's eſtates of Bogholl, Moyneſs, Earlſeat, Black-hills, Laylands, and Raitlone, L. 1493 : 19 : 6. Miſs Brodie of Lethen, L. 1100. Alexander Dunbar, Eſq; of Boath, L. 652 ; 15 : 9. Knockowdie, L. 96. The real rent confiderably exceeds L. 3000 Sterling yearly.

Population.

Popalation.—In 1755 the population is faid to have a-
mounted to 1951 fouls. This ftatement, however, is liable
to the fufpicion of exaggeration ; for the laft incumbent, in
his unfuccefsful application for an augmentation of ftipend
the preceding year, 1754, reprefented them as amounting
to only 1600 fouls. In an accurate lift taken fpring laft
year (1796), the parifh was found to contain 1406 inhabitants ; 661 males, and 745 females.

The total of thofe who follow the profeffion of agriculture is 127. Several mechanics and tradefmen poffefs fmall
crofts, in order to augment the means of fubfiftence for
themfelves and families. Of day-labourers there are 43,
11 fhoemakers, 7 fmiths, 15 weavers, 8 taylors, 7 millers,
11 mafons, and 9 fquare-wrights ; and there are 3 inns, and
4 merchants, in the village of Auldearn, which contains 41
houfes, and 185 inhabitants. There are about 97 fece-
ders of the Antiburgher perfuafion, who, in conjuction with
fome others, attached to that fect in the neighbouring parifhes, contrive to fupport a clergyman of their own in Bogholl, in the fouth-eaft corner of the parifh; and confines of
Edinkaillie.

This feceffion from the communion of the eftablifhed religion began about 40 years fince, and is now rather on the
decline. All the reft belong to the eftablifhment, and join
with it, at leaft in religious ordinances, although their attachment to puritanical doctrines makes many of them wander
miles to hear popular and applauded preachers.

Abftract of births and marriages for 12 years, preceding
1797 :

		Males.	Females.	Total.	Marriages.
1785	-	12	19	31	13
1786	-	15	14	29	19
1787	-	12	9	21	10
1788	-	19	15	34	16
Carried over		58	57	115	58

	Males.	Females.	Total.	Marriages.
Brought over	58	57	115	58
1789 -	15	14	29	14
1790 -	13	20	33	15
1791 -	17	14	31	13
1792 -	10	13	23	10
1793 -	12	7	19	8
1794 -	9	16	25	8
1795 -	21	14	35	13
1796 -	21	15	36	9
	176	170	346	148

Average of births nearly 29, of marriages $12\frac{1}{3}$.

Abſtract of births and marriages for 5 years, previous to 1749 :

	Males.	Females.	Total.	Marriages.
1744 -	28	26	54	16
1745 -	18	20	38	7
1746 -	18	23	41	7
1747 -	29	31	60	13
1748 -	23	36	59	6
	116	136	252	49

Average of births $50\frac{2}{3}$, marriages $9\frac{4}{5}$.

By reaſon of the negligence of the ſeſſion-clerk of that period, the liſt of baptiſms for 5 years previous to 1755, which would have afforded the faireſt point of compariſon, has been very inaccurately kept. From the above view it appears, that the population has decreaſed conſiderably, owing, as in other places, to the enlargement of farms, and flocking of young men to manufacturing towns.

Advantages and Diſadvantages of the Pariſh, and Miſcellaneous Obſervations.—There are few natural woods of any

any extent, but one of birch on the eftate of Infhock, the property of Mr Brodie of Brodie ; and from this wood the neighbourhood are generally fupplied with moft of their implements of hufbandry. Here likewife are fome valuable firs, equal in quality to thofe of Glenmore, and which fell at a fhilling a foot cubic. There are, however, large plantations of firs interfperfed with laryx, and every fpecies of hard wood known in Scotland reared on the eftates of all the proprietors ; but the moft confiderable on that of Mr Gordon of Braid. The exertions of this gentleman, in the improvement and embellifhment of his eftate, by planting of trees and hedges, draining of marfhes, burfting of ftones by gun-powder, and inclofing of his grounds, and thus furnifhing conftant employment to the induftrious poor in this quarter, deferve much praife. The extent of ground covered by Mr Gordon's plantations, including the clumps and belts of his pleafure-ground, exceed 600 acres; and their thinnings have already been very ferviceable for firing, and various other country purpofes.—From the appearance of the dips and rifes of the various ftrata of metals betwixt the houfe of Boath and the fea, it has appeared probable to fome perfons of fagacity and obfervation, that coal might be procured at an expence nowife inadequate to the object, by means of a fire-engine planted near the fea-fhore. And on that property there is a quarry of dark-blue ftone, which mounts like coal into a blaze by the operation of fire, but is not confumed thereby, nor diffolves in water like limeftone.

An almoft inexhauftible fund of marl may be found in Loch Lity, upon Lord Cawdor's eftate, covering about 40 acres of furface, to the depth of from 16 to 20 feet ; the lake might be drained by a fmall fire-engine of L. 60 or L. 70 value. Few of the parifhioners have made application to Lord Cawdor in order to avail themfelves of this valuable manure. The moft confiderable mofs belongs to Mr Brodie

of

of Brodie. Some other proprietors pretend to have ſervitudes on it, though with the origin of their claims the preſent writer is unacquainted. The tenants are occupied during the greater part of the ſummer in digging, preparing, and bringing home their peats. If there was regular ſupplies of coals brought to Nairn, this labour might in a good meaſure be ſuperſeded, and the attention of the huſbandman might, to much better purpoſe, be directed to his proper employment during that ſeaſon. Large planks of fir are contained in the bottom of this moſs, which ſerve for couples and lath to houſes. Trees have been found 60 feet long, and 3 feet ſquare. On the coaſt, on the north part of the pariſh, lies an inconſiderable lake called Loch Loy, of a mile in length, and a quarter broad, rather below the level of the ſea. It has formerly undoubtedly been much larger than its preſent extent, but gradually contracted by the blowing of the ſands in its neighbourhood, in which are two of thoſe hills of fluctuating ſand deſcribed more at large in the account of Dyke.

Theſe hills have ſhifted eaſtward within theſe 20 years 500 yards, ſtill preſerving their magnitude and relative diſtance. The largeſt of theſe hills is about 100 yards perpendicular.—There are three markets held annually in this village; one upon the 21ſt June, called St Colm's market, in honour, it is ſuppoſed, of St Columba, the founder of the monaſtery of Iona.

The State of Agriculture.—The inhabitants are tenacious of antiquated practices, and admit of the improvements of enlightened experience by ſlow degrees. The mode is not materially altered from that in uſe 30 years ſince. When the corns are got clear off the ground, they begin to give a rib-furrow acroſs the field intended for barley or peaſe; when that is over, if the ſeaſon prove favourable, they give a
clean

clean furrow to their laſt year's barley-ground, for oats, which are begun to be ſown the 28th of March, and finiſh- ed the 5th of April; then they begin to ſpread their dung, and give a clean furrow to their barley-ground; a third fur- row precedes the ſowing of the barley ; begun the 8th May, and finiſhed towards the concluſion of that month.

The harveſt, in indulgent ſeaſons, begins 10th Septem- ber, and ends about the laſt days of October. The common mode of preparing their dung for barley, is one half dung, and the other half mortar, but more frequently ſand.

The better ſort of tenants have ploughs of the Engliſh conſtruction, drawn by a couple of horſes ; others are the old Scots plough, drawn by 6 or 8 oxen, where the ground is ſtony and of hard culture. The former makes uſe of box-carts, and the latter of kellocks, for conveying the compoſt which they uſe for manure. The kellock is of a co- nical figure, conſtructed of twigs of broom or juniper, interwoven in the manner of baſkets ; the fabrication of which furniſhes employment to ſome of the labouring poor. It is ſuſpended by two ſhafts, in which a ſingle horſe is placed, and ſet on a clumſy two-wheeled carriage. The kellock is in value 1 s. and ſlider and wheels 4 s. The common rotation of crops after breaking up the graſs-field is, 1ſt, Two of oats, in ſucceſſion; 2d, Barley ; 3d, Oats ; 4th, Peaſe ; and thereafter barley, with clover-ſeeds, both white and red. All kinds of clover are ſown here, though but lately introduced ; they are uſed here even only by the more opulent, little hay being raiſed by the pooreſt ſort. The labouring cattle are weak and ſtarving in the ſpring, for want of fodder, and are fed on ſtraw. They are thus often under the neceſſity of ſending their cattle to the High- lands in ſummer, whence they return in as wretched a con- dition as they are ſent. Potatoes, forming the ſubſiſtence of the people one-third of the year, are planted by every

rank ;

rank; by the more fubftantial they are drilled, by the poorer they are planted in every furrow. The latter, though
not fo productive as the other, yet are efteemed better food.
The ordinary return of an acre of drilled potatoes is about
16 bolls, but that of the other fort is not fo abundant. The
barley of this parifh is in high demand among diftillers, and
weighs between 17 and 19 ftone, Amfterdam weight. A-
bove 2000 bolls of barley, and an equal quantity of oats,
befides what is neceffary for the maintenance of the inhabitants, are annually exported. No peafe are raifed but for
home confumption, and little wheat, till laft year, that,
alured by the high prices of that grain, fome farmers have
begun to direct their attention to its cultivation, and, it is
hoped, will find their account in it. The beft cultivated
fields let from 25 s. to 36 s. *per* acre; but in the hilly parts
rarely above 15 s. The moft extenfive farmers rent from
L. 60 to L. 80 Sterling; the fmalleft from L. 10 to L. 26.
Sterling. None of the proprietors have inclofed any of
their grounds, nor give encouragement to their tenants to
do fo, although moft of them would give chearfully an advance of rent to have them inclofed, as their neighbours
feed their cattle promifcuoufly from the end of harveft to
the firft of April, which prevents improving tenants from
raifing turnips, wheat, or fown-grafs to advantage.

The horfes in this parifh, about 370 in number, are of a
fmall fize, from L. 6 to L. 10 a-piece in value; thofe poffeffed by the more opulent from L. 10 to L. 20 Sterling. The
black cattle, in number 910, are of a mixed breed; Lan-
cafhire, Dutch, Fifefhire, and Highland; though the laft
mentioned fpecies furpaffes the others in number. The fmalleft will weigh from 50 to 60 lb. *per* quarter, $17\frac{1}{2}$ oz. Amfterdam weight: The middling fize from 70 to 80 lb. the
quarter: The largeft fize from 100 to 140 lb. the quarter.
The fheep, about 1200, are of the fmall white-faced kind;
the

the ewes weighing from 6 to 10 lb. *per* quarter, and the wethers from 8 to 12 lb. *per* quarter. Their wool is efteemed, and reckoned preferable to that of the large blackfaced.

No manufacture, flax-mill, or bleachfield, have yet been eftablifhed here, though the parifh is fuppofed to be poffeffed of fingular advantages for them all, and likewife for fome branch of thread or ftocking manufactory.

The ftipend, by decreet 1755, was fixed to be 6 chalders of victual, half barley, half oat-meal, 400 merks Scots, with L. 60 Scots for communion-money, 14 wethers, and 11 fhillings feu-duty for the Dean's Crook near Elgin. But by an interlocutor of the Court of Teinds, 24th February 1796, the minifter's ftipend is augmented L. 21 Sterling annually; and the meal altered from 48 bolls of the meafure ufed and wont, to 54 bolls, at 8 ftone *per* boll.

The church was built in the year 1757, and is ftill in good repair; the manfe was built in 1751, was refitted laft fummer, and is now well finifhed, at the expence of above L. 200 Sterling.

The fchoolmafter's falary is 16 bolls barley. The fchoolhoufe is decent; about 30 fcholars attend, who are initiated in the elements of Latin, Englifh, writing, and arithmetic; his fee as feffion-clerk is variable, arifing from the fines of delinquents. The funds for the fupport of the poor arife from the weekly collection and mortcloth-money, amounting to the fmall fum of between L. 8 and L. 9 Sterling yearly, with the intereft of L. 94 Sterling, accumulated by the attention of the late incumbent. The number of poor on the roll are 56. Mr Brodie of Brodie is patron of this parifh.

The inhabitants are fufficiently turned to the devout virtues; but their zeal not being of that fort which is founded in knowledge, and which adds ftrength and ftability to virtue,

tue, is conceived by them to imply ſuch a degree of merit as to emancipate them in ſome meaſure from the reſtraints of morality. There are not wanting inſtances of petty thefts, yet they have never been diſgraced by any crime of ſo flagrant a nature as to ſubject them to a trial before a criminal court ; and their faults are in general the offspring of ignorance and illiberal prejudice, rather than of a corrupted heart.

There are veſtiges of two Druidical temples, but not ſo entire as to merit particular deſcription. Hard by the church is a green mount, in form almoſt perfectly circular, commonly called Caſtle Hill, which has all the appearance of artificial formation, and was probably one of thoſe places which antiquarians conjecture to have been deſtined for the purpoſe of holding aſſizes.

Pariſh of Auldearn.

Additional Communications, by the Rev. John Paterſon.

The ground adjacent to the village of Auldearn, on the weſt, is diſtinguiſhed as the ſcene of a ſignal victory, obtained by the forces of Charles I. commanded by the renowned James Marquis of Montroſe, over the Covenanters, in the time of thoſe civil commotions by which this kingdom

was

was agitated laft century, and which terminated fo fatally to its unfortunate and mifguided monarch. In the early part of his life, with that ardour which feems to have formed the prominent feature of his character, Montrofe had embraced the caufe of the Covenanters; and was now won, by the careffes of his fovereign, to lend his ftrenuous fupport to the interefts of monarchy *. Alarmed by his rapid career of victory, the two leaders of the Covenanters, Baillie and Urrie, thought it expedient to divide their forces againft him. Having defeated the Campbells at Inverlochie, and being joined by Lord Gordon, who had efcaped from his uncle Argyle in Mar, with 1000 foot and 200 horfe, Montrofe marched directly to the Spey, in fearch of the republican army, if poffible to compel them to an engagement. He had now approached within fix miles, before Urrie imagined that he had paffed the Grampians: with fuch aftonifhing rapidity he had advanced, as to anticipate all accounts of his movements. Urrie, finding him fo near, croffed the Spey without delay, that he might not be obliged to fight before he acquired a reinforcement of auxiliaries, of which he entertained expectations; and having appointed Invernefs the place of convention for all his forces, proceeded thither through Elgin and Forres with all expedition: Montrofe ftill advancing in his rear, and purfuing him fo clofely, that with difficulty, under protection of the night, he reached Invernefs.

Montrofe then encamped at Auldearn. Urrie found at Invernefs, as he expected, the Earls of Seaforth and Sutherland,

---

* For the detailed hiftory of this engagement, we are indebted to the Memoirs of Montrofe, by Dr. George Wifhart, his Lordfhip's chaplain, who enjoyed his confidence, and attended him in all his expeditions, till he was taken by the Covenanters. He was afterwards Bifhop of Edinburgh.

land, the clan of the Frafers, and feveral from the fhires of
Moray and Cairhnefs, all convened in arms to the appointed
rendezvous. Having added fome veterans in the garrifon
of Invernefs, he marched directly againft Montrofe, with an
army now confifting of 3500 foot and 400 horfe. Montrofe's army was far inferior, and confifted only of 1500
foot and 250 horfe : he was therefore more inclined to retire, than engage with fuch inequality of force. But Urrie
preffed after him fo hard, that to retreat with fafety was impracticable; and Baillie, with an army yet more powerful,
and more formidable for cavalry, had now far advanced on
this fide the Grampian Hills. Montrofe was therefore reduced to the alternative, to give Urrie battle on unequal
terms, or expofe himfelf to the more hazardous fituation of
being hemmed in betwixt two armies. He refolved therefore, without delay, to try the fate of war; and began to
chufe the moft advantageous ground, there to await the enemy. The village then ftood upon high ground covering the
neighbouring valley. Here he drew up his forces, entirely
out of the view of the enemy; placing a few chofen foot
before the village, where they were covered by fome newly-
formed dykes. On his right he fet Alexander M'Donald,
ftationing him in a fpot fortified with dykes and ditches *, and
interfperfed with bufhes and ftones ; commanding him on no
account to quit the advantage of his ground, fortified alike
againft the impreffion of the foot and cavalry of the enemy.
To them alfo, with a penetration which reflects the higheft
honour on his abilities as a commander, he entrufted the
royal ftandard, which was wont to be carried before himfelf;
judging, that, upon fight of it, the oppofite army would direct their forces againft that wing, where, by reafon of the
difadvantageous

---

* A place called Newmills ftill correfponds exactly to this defcription.

disadvantageous ground, they would be of no avail. All the rest of his men he conveyed to the opposite wing; putting the horse under the command of Lord Gordon, and himself conducting the infantry. He had thus no main army, but the shew of one under covert of the dykes.

The army of the Covenanters, as Montrose had happily conjectured, no sooner saw the royal standard displayed, than they dispatched their choicest cavalry, with their veteran troops. Montrose, unable to adopt this course, from the limited number of his troops, resolved to make an assault at once with all his men on the left wing. No sooner had he projected this, than some person, on whose fidelity he could confide, came and whispered in his ear that M'Donald with his forces, on the right, were discomfited and put to flight. Not alarmed with the tidings of this disaster, to prevent the dejection of his soldiers, he, with admirable self-command, exclaimed to Lord Gordon, ' My Lord, M'Donald has al- ' ready routed the enemy on the right : shall we merely look ' on, and let him win all the honour of the day ?' Instantly he led on to the charge. Urrie's horse could not withstand the shock of Gordon's, but immediately wheeled about, leaving the flanks of their army bare and defenceless. The foot, though deserted by the horse, while at any distance, maintained the combat with the most obstinate valour, by the superiority of their number, and the excellence of their armour ; but coming at length to close combat *, they threw down their arms, and betook themselves to flight.

The

---

* We are informed by Spalding, commissary-clerk of Aberdeen, (whose manuscript history has been lately published,) that this defeat was attributed by the vanquished, to one Crowner or Major Drummond, who unskilfully wheeled about upon their own foot, and thereby broke their ranks, and so occasioned many of them to be killed; for which he was afterwards condemned by a council of war, and shot.

The fuccefs with which this ftratagem was defervedly crowned, could not render Montrofe forgetful of the perilous condition of the right wing, and he haftened thither to its relief with all the men he could collect. M'Donald, (a man of the greateft perfonal intrepidity, but endowed rather with the qualifications of a mere foldier than of a general, bold even to rafhnefs,) moved with indignant fcorn at the infults of the enemy, and difdaining to fcreen himfelf behind the dykes and bufhes, withdrew from the ftrong ground, where he was fecure from all danger, to face the enemy on the open field. He had nigh fallen a facrifice to his rafhnefs. The Covenanters, fuperior to him both by their horfe and number, and many of them experienced foldiers, foon threw his troops into diforder, and repulfed them in great confufion ; and had he not quickly retired with them into a neighbouring inclofure, they had all been cut to pieces, and the royal ftandard fallen into the power of the enemy. This rafh miftake, M'Donald abundantly redeemed, by the fingular courage he difplayed in bringing off his men. He himfelf was the laft man who quitted the field, and alone covered the retreat of his men ; defending his body with a large target, and oppofing himfelf to the thickeft of the enemy : fome foldiers came fo near him, as to fix their fpears in his target, which he is faid fucceffively to have cut to pieces by a fingle ftroke of his fword.

When the detachment with whom M'Donald was engaged, in the inclofure, faw Montrofe coming to his affiftance, and perceived that their own men on the left were fled, the horfe ran with precipitation ; but the foot, principally frefh foldiers, fought with the utmoft defperation, and fell almoft every man in his rank. The conquerors continued the chace for fome miles.

There were flain of the Covenanters about 3000 foot, among

among whom the veteran ſoldiers fought with uncommon bravery; but almoſt all the horſe eſcaped, by a well-timed, but inglorious flight. Of the Covenanters, the moſt eminent perſons ſlain, were, Campbell of Lawers and Sir John and Sir Gideon Murrays. Montroſe loſt, on the left wing, only one private ſoldier, and on the other, where M'Donald commanded, 14 ſoldiers; but there were many more wounded. Mr Shaw, (Hiſtory of Moray), mentions M'Pherſon of Invereſchie among the ſlain on the ſide of the Royaliſts. This battle of Auldearn was fought May 4th, 1645.—Spalding's remarks on this engagement are characteriſtical of his age. ' It was ' miraculous, and only foughten with God's own finger, as ' would appear; ſo many to be cut down on the one ſide, ' and ſo few on the other: yet no thanks was given to God ' for this great victory.'

After this victory, Montroſe gave directions to burn the lands and houſes of Campbell of Calder in Nairn, and plunder all his goods. The Earl of Moray being in England, his ground was plundered, alſo that of Kinſterie and Lethen, and ſeveral other lands in the county.

PARISH of CALDER,

(COUNTIES OF NAIRN AND INVERNESS.)

By the Rev. Mr ALEXANDER GRANT.

Name, Situation, Soil, Surface, Rivers, &c.

THE old name of the parifh was *Borivon*, fuppofed to be derived from the Gaelic, *Brae Ewen*, or, ' Ewan's ' high country.' Calder is derived from *Coille*, a ' wood,' and *Dor*, ' water.' It is fituated chiefly in the county of Nairn; a fmall part of it lies in that of Invernefs; it is in the prefbytery of Nairn and Synod of Moray. The form of the parifh is not unlike the letter T. Its extent is about 4 miles from S. W. to N. E. The general breadth is not above 2 miles, but a part of it from the centre runs up to the high country about 7 or 8 miles. The parifh is at the diftance of 2 or 3 miles from the fea; bounded by Nairn on the N. by Auldearn and Ardclach on the E. by Moy and Duthil on the S. and Croy on the W. The low part of the parifh is flat and level, the higher part hilly and mountainous, abounding with heath, mofs and fome wood.—The foil is fharp, fertile and friendly, but not wet or deep. The mountains which divide Calder from Moy to the S. are

very

very high; are covered with heath, and abound with moſs. There is a good deal of hilly and rocky ground in the lower parts. A part of the low lands has ſometimes been laid under water, by the overflowing of the burn of Calder, and the water of Nairn. The moſt conſiderable inundation happened in 1782. The wood of Calder, and particularly the burn that runs through it, offers to the view the moſt delightful ſcenery. It runs in a dark and deep channel, ſo as to be loſt to the ſight, with high, ſteep and rocky banks on the eaſt ſide, covered with trees of all kinds, and the moſt beautiful ſhrubbery. The rapid river of Findhorn runs through the higher part of the pariſh, as does the river of Nairn waſh it below. Both theſe rivers abound with ſalmon and trout. Salmon about 12 years ago, and leſs, ſold at 1 d. and 1½ d. the pound, of late it has got up to 3 d. and even 4 d. The ſalmon is in high perfection in May.

Population.—There is every reaſon to believe that the pariſh is better peopled now than it was ſome years ago. Although the farms are enlarged, ſeveral ſmall ones being thrown into one, yet the number of improvers of moor and waſte lands is increaſing. Tradeſmen are more numerous, and ſo are cottagers. Dr Webſter's ſtate is 882. The pariſh may now contain about 850 perſons, above the age of 6; of which 400 may be males, and 450 females. The annual average of births is 23½ for the laſt 10 years; of deaths, 14; of marriages, about 9. There are about 20 perſons between 70 and 100 years of age. The number of farmers, and their families, is upwards of 60; of traders, dyers, carpenters, ſhoemakers, wheel-wrights, tailors, ſmiths, maſons, &c. upwards of 40, and about 20 apprentices. There are upwards of 150 labouring ſervants, including

both

both fexes ; 2 ftudents at the Univerfity ; 1 perfon a native of Wales, and 1 of America.   There are fcarce above
20 here born in any other parifh or diftrict of Great Britain.   There are 3 or 4 gentlemens families, only 1 Seceder, and 1 Epifcopalian.   The proportion between the
annual births and the whole population, is about 1 to 37 :
Between the annual marriages and the whole population, a-
bout 1 to 94 :   Between the annual deaths and the whole
population, about 1 to 60.   Each marriage, at an average,
produces 6 children.   There has been no emigration of confequence from the parifh ; but every other year there are
fome young lads, in the character of adventurers, fervants,
and apprentices, who go to America, London, Edinburgh,
and other parts.   There are about 160 inhabited houfes,
and about 5 or 6 to a family.   Only 1 perfon has been banifhed from this parifh in the memory of man.

Produce, &c.—Almoft all kinds of vegetables and plants
that are produced in the north of Scotland, are to be found
here.   Trees are the oak, alder, birch, mountain-afh, afh,
elm, beech, larix, and other pines in great numbers.   Horfes,
about 420 ; black cattle, 2100 ; fheep, 6300 ; goats, 400.
There was a furvey and map made of the greateft part of
the parifh in 1782 ; by which it appears, that the number
of acres may be about 26,000, making a reafonable allowance for what has not been furveyed.   Of the above, 18,000
acres, at leaft, confift of moor and mofs.   There may be a-
bout 1000 fown yearly with barley, 2600 with oats and
rye, 400 under potatoes, turnip, and flax, 500 let out in
ley, without fown grafs, there being little grafs-feed fown
in the parifh ; and the remaining acres under wood, broom,
green mofs, and common pafture.   The parifh does more
than fupply itfelf with provifions, and furnifhes a great deal
                                                              of

of oat-meal, in particular, to the neighbouring towns of Invernefs, Nairn, and Fort George. It fells a good many
cattle and fheep to the butchers in thofe towns, and to
drovers. It affords much barley to the diftillers, of whom
there are 2 in the parifh. The rent of the parifh is about
L. 1200 Sterling. Some acres of arable land are let at 15 s.
an acre, and fome fo low as 2 s. 6 d. The fize of the farms
is very different, fome confift of upwards of 100 acres, and
others below 40. There are not as yet many inclofures,
but the tenants are fenfible of the advantage of having their
land inclofed, and fome of the more opulent have begun to
inclofe and fence. The fituation of the parifh in 1782 and
1783 was furely bad enough, though not fo ill as in many
places. The corns were not fo much hurt by the froft, of
courfe, the crop was better, and few of the cattle died, having been maintained chiefly on the tops of whins, cut and
threfhed, of which there are great quantities almoft in eve -
ry part of the parifh. Oats are fown the latter end of
March, barley generally before the 20th of May ; and they
are begun to be reaped between the 1ft and 12th of September.

Prices and Wages.—Beef, mutton, veal, and pork, are
from 2¼ d. to 3½ d. the pound. Hens 6 d. geefe 1 s. 6 d. to
2 s. ducks 8 d. turkies 2 s. 6 d. butter 12 s. cheefe from 4 s. to
6 s. the ftone ; barley has not been under 15 s. for many
years ; meal is variable. It is to be obferved, that in all thefe
particulars, there has been a prodigious rife of price fince
the 1780. A day-labourer may receive 6 d. and perhaps
7 d. a-day throughout the year, with fome other advantages ; fuch as a houfe and garden, time to gather and prepare his fuel, an extraordinary allowance in harveft, with·
liberty to plant potatoes, as far as any dung he can gather
will

will go. This is found very fufficient to maintain a family of 5 or 6 perfons, if the wife has any indultry at all. Male farm-fervants get from L. 4 to L. 6 in the year, and female fervants from L. 1, 10 s. to L. 2. Domeftic fervants get a little more. A labourer in hufbandry gets 6 d. a-day, with his victuals. A carpenter, mafon, or other tradefman, about 1 s. 4 d. or 1 s. 6 d. without victuals.

Stipend, School, Poor, &c.—The church was built in 1619. The value of the living is about L. 80. Mr Campbell of Calder is patron. There are 2 heritors, but neither of them refide. The manfe was built about 1730.—The fchoolmafter's falary is a chalder of victual, half meal, half barley. The meal is paid by the tenants, and the barley by the landlord. The fchoolmafter receives alfo L. 1, or L. 1, 5 s. Sterling, as feffion-clerk and precentor, 1 s. for every marriage, and 6 d. for every baptifm. The fchool-fees are 1 s. a-quarter for Englifh fcholars, 1 s. 6 d. for writing, and 2 s. 6 d. for Latin and arithmetic. In winter the fchool is generally very throng, between 3 and 4 fcore of boys and girls attend. The parents in general wifh their children to read, write, and get fome knowledge of arithmetic, but fhow little defire for the learned languages.—The number of poor is about 40. The annual contributions for their relief are only about L. 12. The poor have certificates to beg from door to door in the parifh.

Mifcellaneous Obfervations.—The parifh has fome very peculiar advantages. It is well furnifhed with water, wood, and fuel. It has within itfelf, or is in the clofe neighbourhood, of mills of many kinds, not only meal-mills, but flour-mills, waulk-mills, lint-mills, barley-mills, and malt-mills. It is well ftocked with tradefmen of every kind,

and

and withal the landlord is the moſt indulgent of maſters. The air is remarkably ſalubrious. The rents of cottagers houſes, with a ſmall garden, are from 15 s. to L. 1, when paid in money, but are generally exacted in ſervices. It is found convenient to have cottagers in the neighbourhood· They are employed as day-labourers, and are extremely uſeful, particularly in the more buſy ſeaſons of the year. But the tenants would not chooſe to truſt to them alone for the whole work of the farm, preferring ſervants hired from term to term, as the moſt ſteady and fixed. But few ſervants can be prevailed upon to engage for a longer ſpace than half a-year at a time, which is often a great inconvenience. As to perſonal ſervices, they are almoſt in diſuſe, being only preſerved on a ſmall eſtate, and a wadſet held by a gentleman in the pariſh. Where they are ſtill continued, they conſiſt of various attendances and carriages· The tenants or ſubtenants aſſiſt their maſter in caſting and leading his peats; in cutting his corns, and bringing them home; in repairing his offices, in carrying his victual to market, &c. But Mr Campbell of Calder, the principal proprietor, has of late, in a moſt generous and humane manner, aboliſhed all ſuch ſervices and carriages on his eſtate, commuting them with the tenant at a very eaſy converſion; and has included the rent, ſtipend, ceſs, cuſtoms, in one ſum, payable by the tenant at 2 different terms, obliging him only to aſſiſt in leading materials for the church, manſe, and offices, ſchool-houſe, and for keeping the old caſtle in repair.—There is 1 inn in the pariſh, and 2 or 3 ale-houſes; but it does not appear that the morals of the people are in the leaſt corrupted by them. They are convenient for travellers, there being ſeveral public roads through the pariſh, but they are very ſeldom viſited by the pariſhioners. It muſt be allowed that the people are

very

very induftrious in their way.   Their great induftry in the
fummer, lies in preparing dunghills and their fuel, and in
winter, in threfhing out and milling their corns.—There is
no eftablifhed manufacture in the parifh, but ftill a great
deal of work is done in the web-way in their families, both
for home-ufe and for fale.   A number of the women are
alfo occupied in fpinning lint, given out by manufacturers
in towns, for which they receive from 2½ d. to 3 d. the
hank.—The inhabitants difcover no particular propenfity
for the military life, and very few inlift in the army or
navy.   Luxury, in point of drefs, feems to have crept in
very much of late, owing to the high wages.   The people
in general are humane, moral, and religious.   There are few
quarrels or law-fuits among them, and horning has fcarcely
been executed againft any one in the parifh for many
years.   They feem to be very much contented with their
fituation, and, as a proof of this, fhow little or no defire to
leave the parifh.   But ftill they would find the felves more
at eafe, were their leafes permanent, and the caprice, the
wantonnefs, and high demands of fervants, in fome meafure checked.—The roads are in a tolerable ftate, being
kept in repair by the ftatute-labour, which is exacted in
kind.   The bridges are in good order, being fo kept by
Government, as the military road paffes through the parifh.—Erfe and Englifh are equally fpoken.—In place of
fome of the more obnoxious taxes of fmall confideration,
laid on, or now laying on by Miniftry, a ftamp might
be propofed of a 6 d. on certificates to fervants, from their
mafters or miftreffes, when they leave their fervice ; to
journeymen and fhopkeepers, (not apprentices), clerks in
offices, and the like, when they leave their employment ;
to all day-labourers, adventurers, handicraftfmen, and o-
thers, when they leave one parifh and county, and go to
another,

another, teſtifying, (where there is reaſon to do ſo), their honeſty, ſobriety, and peaceable behaviour ; to be ſigned by the Miniſters, Juſtices, Sheriffs, or Magiſtrates ; and that all theſe deſcriptions of perſons ſhould be obliged to carry along with them ſuch certificates upon every remove, otherwiſe be conſidered as ſuſpected perſons. Something of this kind, it is imagined, would be very productive, and would have a happy tendency in preſerving good order, and preventing many miſchiefs in ſociety. The ſtamp might likewiſe be extended to certificates to ſtudents, when they leave the Univerſity, from the profeſſors, atteſting not only their progreſs ·in literature, but their general good behaviour while there ; to patrons, when they preſent, certifying their having qualified for that purpoſe ; and to probationers alſo, when they accept, of their having taken the oaths to enable them to accept ; in ſhort, to all who are by law obliged to qualify to Government, on their acceptance of any place or office ; to all certificates, proving the identity and exiſtence of perſons, ages, marriages, degrees of propinquity, and the like. From the above might be excepted certificates granted to widows and orphans of all ranks and denominations ; alſo thoſe granted to the poor, either recommending them to charity at home, or to hoſpitals, infirmaries, and any public donation ; alſo certificates granted to perſons in ſickneſs, preventing their attendance at courts, aſſizes, or in any other way and place where their preſence is required by law.

All the ploughs are of the old Scotch kind. About 70 are in conſtant employment, and occaſionally in the ſpring there are more. The tenants have not as yet got any of the large ſhod-wheel carts and waggons ; they uſe the ancient and ſtill common ſort of ſledges and carts.—A ſmall

village

village was begun at Calder some years ago, but not improved to any height. It may contain about a score of families, confifting chiefly of tradefmen, labourers, and the
fervants who have the charge of the cattle.—Peat is the
moft common fuel. Wood, furze, broom, &c. are alfo
ufed.

PARISH of NAIRN.

(COUNTY OF NAIRN, SYNOD OF MORAY, PRESBYTERY OF NAIRN.)

By the Rev. MR. JOHN MORRISON.

Name, Extent, Soil, and Appearance.

THE parish of Nairn derives its name from the river which runs through it, called in Gaelic, " Uifge Nearne," or Water of Alders, from the great quantity of trees and fhrubs of that fpecies of wood which grows upon its banks. Some are of opinion that Invernearne implies the influx of the weftern, as Inverear, or Findhorn, does that of the eaftern river into the fea. From E. to W. it meafures 6 miles, and from N. to S. upwards of 8. The figure fomewhat refembles the letter X. In the environs of the town, and along the coaft by Delnies, as alfo about Kildrumie, the foil is light and fandy. On the river fide, fand mixed with a kind of mortar or clay. The S. fide of the parifh is rather

of

of a rich and heavy mould. On the N. side of the river, the ground is flat and level; and on the S. it rises with a gradual ascent, terminating at one corner of the parish in the hill of Urchany, the only eminence in the parish deserving the name of a hill.

Town.—The town is a royal burgh. In conjunction with Invernefs, Forres, and Fortrose, it returns a member to serve in parliament. At what period it was erected into a royal burgh, is uncertain *. The immunities of Nairn originally appear to have been very extensive; however, in the lapse of time, these have been greatly lessened; so that the common good now consists only of a few moors, which of late have been let on various leases, and which, in process of time, will be of considerable advantage to the community. There are likewise some lands, besides the burgage lands, which pay eques and feu-duties to the town; therefore, though the public revenue be now but small, yet it is increasing, and in a few years will be considerable. The town originally, being situated in a different place, probably, from where it now stands, was defended by a castle. As far back as the time of King Malcolm the First, Buchanan informs us that this castle was taken by the Danes, and that by them the *custodes* or keepers thereof were cruelly used. Since that period,

---

* The first charter, of which any copy is extant, was obtained from James the Sixth of Scotland, in the year 1589, being the renewal of one granted by Alexander, perhaps the first of that name who swayed the Scotch sceptre, as it is only said to have been granted by Alexander. There is also another charter by Charles the Second, in confirmation of the abovementioned one, dated 1661. The town-council consists of 17 members, viz. the provost, 3 bailies, dean of guild, and treasurer, with 11 counsellors, 9 of which make a quorum. The 3 bailies, the dean of guild, and treasurer, in consequence of a late decision of the House of Peers, must be resident. The whole trades make but one corporation.

riod, however, the fea has made great encroachments, and the courfe of the river is greatly altered. Where the caftle then ftood, is entirely covered with water, and the river which then run hard by the caftle, now flows into the Moray Frith nearly half an Englifh mile to the E. of that place. Neverthelefs, there are fome perfons ftill alive, who at ftream or fpring tides, remember to have feen fome veftiges of the foundation of the ancient caftle *.

Agriculture, Heritors, Rents, &c.—Improvements in hufbandry are here as yet very little known. The fowing of clover and rye-grafs feeds, though introduced many years ago, yet for want of enclofures, turns out to little account. The field around the town, comprehending fomething more than 400 acres, is fo remarkably pleafant, that perhaps there is nothing like it in the north of Scotland. The lands of which this field is compofed, and which are all contiguous, were formerly runridge, or acre and acre alternately ; but owing to an excambion which took place about 4 years ago, the different proprietors will now have it in their power, if they pleafe, to enclofe their lands, which heretofore, conveniently, they could not have done. The grounds of 2 or 3 of the proprietors are now enclofed with ftone and feal fences or funk fences ; and 1 has fubdivided part of his lands in the neighbourhood. The ordinary crops raifed about the town,

and

* In the town there are 2 very good inns, commodioufly fitted up, and well kept. The one is of a long ftanding, and the other, which is a very large houfe, was lately built by Mr. Davidfon of Cantray, at his own expenfe ; fo that perfons travelling through this country, may, at this ftage, expect to be well accommodated. There are, befides thefe inns, fo many alehoufes and whifky fhops in the town, that to mention the number, might, to ftrangers, perhaps appear incredible. It were fincerely to be wifhed, that thefe tippling houfes were entirely abolifhed, as they are a nuifance in any place, and highly detrimental to the health and morals of the people.

and throughout the parish, are barley, oats, and peafe ; potatoes in great quantities are likewife reared. Thefe laft mentioned, make up the food of the common people for nearly two-thirds of the year. In the neighbourhood of the town, oats are a very unprofitable crop, feldom yielding the third feed in return. In the parifh there are about 50 farmers. The farms fmall; few of them exceeding 20 l., and only 2 amounting to about 50 l. Sterling a-year. In this parifh are 10 heritors and 1 wadfetter. 4 of the heritors only refide. The valued rent of the parifh, as taken from the cefs-books of the county, amounts to 1106 l. 8 s. Scotch money, exclufive of the burgage lands, which may be nearly half as much. The prefent real rent, is about 1300 l. Sterling, befides about 200 bolls of victual. The rent of lands has rifen greatly of late years, both in the town and country diftricts of the parifh. In the immediate vicinity of the town, the acre lets at 35 s., a little farther diftant, at from 18 s. to 30 s., and in the country from 5 s. to 20 s. the acre. Of old, the greateft part of the rent was paid in victual ; but now it is moftly all converted into money. Few cuftoms or carriages are exacted. And it is to be hoped, that every remain of feudal fervitude will foon be entirely abolifhed.

Ecclefiaftical State, Schools, Poor.—Nairn originally was a menfal church attached to the Deanry of Auldearn. The prefent kirk, manfe, and offices, had a partial repair 1789, and are juft now in a tolerable ftate. The ftipend is 5 chalders of victual, and 27 l. of money, exclufive of the fum allowed for communion elements, which is only 5 l. ; fo that at the ordinary converfion, the ftipend does not exceed 67 l. Sterling. Brodie of Brodie is patron.—The grammar fchool is, and has been in a very flourifhing condition for many years back. The prefent incumbent, who is extremely attentive

and

and affiduous, has been remarkably fuccefsful in his line. The number of fcholars is feldom below 80, and often exceeds 100. Gentlemen from all quarters of the country, and fome from England, fend their children to be educated here. Every branch of education, which now makes fuch a noife in the academies, is taught at Nairn, in perfection. Several fcholars are annually fent to fome one or other of the univerfities; and many gentlemen who now make a figure in diftant parts of the world, and not a few who are an ornament to their country at home, in the learned profeffions, received their education at Nairn within thefe 25 years from the prefent teacher. The falary is only a chalder of victual; and even that paid in pecks and lippies by the tenants *.—The poor are extremely numerous, and many of them very indigent indeed. The roll contains upwards of 150 names; and therefore, any relief they can receive, muft be but very inconfiderable. The funds for their fupport, arife from the church collections on the Sabbath days, a fmall mortification, and the intereft of fome money laid up by the feffion in good years for the behoof of the poor. A public diftribution is only made once a-year; but they who are greatly reduced, and very needy, receive occafional fupplies. None, even in 1783, died for want. Independent of the victual beftowed by Government, the feffion advanced a confiderable fum for the wants of the neceffitous. The weekly collections are but trifling, feldom exceeding 3 s. Sterling of good copper. Many of thofe who receive

---

* What a pity, that men of abilities and character, who dedicate their time and labours to the improvement of youth, fhould be fo poorly rewarded, as the generality of the fchoolmafters of Scotland are! It is truly melancholy to think, that grooms and footmen fhould receive fuch extravagant wages, whilft a body of men, on whofe labours the welfare of fociety doth fo much depend, fhould, in a manner, be neglected and overlooked. There is alfo in the town a fchool for girls, with a houfe for the miftrefs, and 10 l. of falary.

receive ſome aſſiſtance at the annual diſtribution, work alſo for their own livelihood. The heritors never have been aſ-feſſed for the maintenance of the poor.

Population.—According to Dr. Webſter's report, the num-ber of ſouls in 1755, was 1698. From an accurate liſt taken of the catechiſeable perſons in this pariſh, in the years 1789 and 1790, by the preſent incumbent, from 7 years old and up-wards, the total number amounts to 1780. But as there are ſeveral families of Antiburgher Seceders in the pariſh, and ſome of the Epiſcopal perſuaſion, whom the miniſter at that viſitation did not ſee, the number of catechiſeable perſons, at the loweſt computation, excluſive of the ſcholars at the gram-mar ſchool, cannot be below 2000 ; ſo that eſtimating ⅕ be-low 7 years of age, the number of ſouls in town and pariſh is, at leaſt, 2400. From the foregoing liſt, it appears, that in the town there are ſomewhat more than 1100, and in the country part of the pariſh, ſomewhat leſs than 1300 ſouls. It is ſaid, that about 40 years ago, there were only 600 inha-bitants in the town ; ſo that the increaſe is very conſiderable. Some time ago, there were 2 Antiburgher clergymen in this pariſh : One of them is now ſettled in Perthſhire. Seceſſion, in this country, is not gaining ground. The proportion of males to females, is nearly as 30 to 27.

ABSTRACT of BIRTHS and MARRIAGES *for* 13 *years paſt.*

| | BIRTHS. | | | MARRIAGES. |
	Males.	Females.	Total.	
1780	24	24	48	25
1781	38	31	69	18
1782	38	23	61	17
1783	30	19	49	17

BIRTHS.

	BIRTHS.			MARRIAGES.
	Males.	*Females.*	*Total.*	
1784	27	18	45	14
1785	24	20	44	17
1786	30	39	69	15
1787	29	22	51	12
1788	23	36	59	18
1789	21	27	48	31
1790	32	30	62	14
1791	30	33	63	13
1792	22	23	45	16
Totals,	368	345	713	227

Average of births nearly 55, and of marriages 17½.

ABSTRACT of BIRTHS and MARRIAGES *for 5 years previous to* 1755.

	BIRTHS.		MARRIAGES.
	Males.	*Females.*	
1750	28	16	7
1751	19	15	12
1752	32	29	21
1753	22	35	21
1754	28	24	24
	129	119	
		129	
Totals,	248		85

Annually, there are perhaps from 6 to 10 children of seceding parents, whose names are not inserted in the session records. No register of deaths. In the town, there are a-
bout

bout 16 merchant ſhops ; only about 6 or 8 any thing conſiderable.

Fiſhings, Boats, &c.—The ſalmon fiſhing on the water of
Nairn is the property of Lord Findlater, and of Mr. Davidſon
of Cantray; and alſo a ſtell fiſhing at the mouth of the river.
Theſe fiſhings are let to tackſmen (36 l. each), two in number, who drag or draw the river and ſtell fiſhings alternately,
or day about. James Brodie, Eſq. of Brodie, has a ſtell fiſhing on the E. ſide of the river mouth. The greateſt part of
the ſalmon caught in this pariſh is carried to Findhorn, and
ſold there to a company of merchants from Aberdeen, who
cure and export it either to the London or a foreign market.
There are 6 fiſhing boats in the town, and 2 in the country
part of the pariſh, in each of which about 7 men are employed. Formerly there were from 10 to 12 boats ; but on account of greater encouragement, ſeveral of the fiſhermen, particularly young lads, have removed to other parts of the
kingdom. Haddocks, ſkate, cod, flounders, and ſome ling,
&c. are caught in the Murray Frith. Some herrings are likewiſe, in the ſeaſon, found on the coaſt ; but for this laſt ſpecies of fiſh, the fiſhermen muſt frequently go as far to the W.
as the Ferry of Keſſock, and even to Beauly. In this Frith,
fiſh of all kinds are much ſcarcer ſince 1782 ; previous to
that year, they were caught in abundance, juſt oppoſite
to the town, but ſince that period, the ſeamen are ſometimes obliged to go to the coaſts of Sutherland and Caithneſs
for them *.

                                                          Roads

* *Prices of Proviſions, Labour, &c.*—Within theſe 30 years back, the price
of proviſions has riſen almoſt beyond belief. Moſt articles are tripled in value,
many quadrupled, and ſome far exceed that proportion. Mutton, beef, and
pork, which, at the forementioned period, ſeldom drew more than 1 penny a-
                                                          pound.

Roads and Bridges.—The great military road leading from Forres to Fort-George, is in very good repair. The Highland road from Nairn to the Bridge of Dulfie is remarkably bad. Statute labour is not commuted, and therefore cannot be fuppofed to be fo well executed. The only bridge in the parifh worth mentioning, is that of Nairn. It was built in the year 1631 or 1632, as appears from an infcription on a ftone of the bridge, now fallen into the river. The infcription is, " Gulielmus Rofe de Clava." The motto, " Non eft falus, nifi in Chrifto." " Soli Deo Gloria." In the year 1782, nearly one half of the bridge was carried off by a flood or fpeat in the river. In that fituation it continues to this day; and were it not owing to the attention of the magiftrates and council, who have made a temporary repair with timber, on many occafions, the river would be impaffable. It is exceedingly ftrange, that an affair of fuch public utility fhould have been fo long neglected and overlooked; for furely it is well known to every traveller, that a bridge over the water of Nairn is much more neceffary than either over the Spey or the Findhorn, becaufe the two laft mentioned rivers have eftablifhed paffage-boats. It is therefore earneftly to be hoped, that Government will foon take a grievance of fuch public notoriety

pound, now fell at an average from 3 d. to 4 d. the pound. Fifh, even 25 years ago, could be had commonly at 3 d. the fcore of haddocks, 26 to the fcore, now they commonly fetch from 1S d. to 2 s. and fometimes 2 s. 6 d. a fcore. Hens fell at 6 d. and 7 d. each; ducks ditto; and fo on. Men fervants hired during the year, receive from 4 l. to 6 l., with victuals in the houfe. Lads and boys in proportion. Maid fervants from 12 s. to 20 s. in the half year. Labourers engaged by the day receive different wages at different feafons of the year. In fpring, fummer, and harveft, a man receives commonly 1s. a-day, without meat; in winter, from 8 d. to 10 d. ditto. At cafting peats, women get 6 d., and in harveft 8 d. without meat.

notoriety into confideration, and grant aid for building a new bridge at this place.

Antiquities, &c.—On the N. fide of the hill of Geddes are to be feen the veftiges of an old edifice, about 26 yards long, and nearly half as broad. It is called *Caifteil Fionlah*, i. e. Finlay's Caftle. It has been built with run, or burnt lime, and furrounded at fome yards diftance with a ditch. The ditch is drawn round the middle of the detached hill, or rifing ground on which the houfe was built, and is ftill very vifible. At the bottom of this little hill, on the S. E. there appears to have been a funk, or draw-well for the ufe of the caftle. Even tradition does not fay by whom, or for what purpofe this e-difice was erected. A little to the E. on the fide of the fame hill of Geddes, are the remains of the Caftle of Rait, built probably by Rait of that ilk, but at what period is uncertain. It was, for fome time, the refidence of one of the Cummines; and confidering the time at which it feems to have been built, it appears to have been a houfe of great ftrength. A little below this caftle, is a place called Knock-na-gillan, i. e. the hill where the young men or lads were killed. Here, it is faid that 18 of the Mackintofhes were deftroyed by the Cum-mines, who then lived at Rait, on account of fome grudge that fubfifted between the families. At the place of Eafter Geddes, are the remains of an old chapel, with a burying ground around it. In this chapel is the burying place of the family of Kilravock; and here they have been interred for many generations back, perhaps ever fince the Rofes came to this part of Scotland. How long the Rofes were in poffeffion of the lands of Geddes, previous to the marriage of the Laird of Geddes with Mary de Bofco, lady and heirefs of Kilravock, cannot now, with certainty, be afcertained, as the writs of the family relative to that eftate were deftroyed in the cathedral

churc

church of Elgin, when it was confumed by fire. Lady Kilravock, and her hufband Hugh Rofe of Geddes, obtained a charter (pofterior to the lofs of the writ. above mentioned) from King John Baliol in the year 1293, confirming to them and to their heirs, the lands of Geddes and Kilravock *.

Advantages and Difadvantages.—The climate here is remarkably good. No difeafes peculiar to the place. Rheumatifms and nervous complaints are perhaps the moft prevalent. This town was, of old, greatly renowned for the cheapnefs of all forts of vivres. All the neceffaries of life, till within about thefe 20 years, fold very low. An excellent peat-mofs, at little more than a mile in diftance from the town, was a great inducement for bringing numbers of people

* Concerning the family of Kilravock, it would be needlefs, on this occafion, to fay any thing particular. The figure they have made in the world, in various departments in life, their tafte for the fine arts, for literature, for politenefs, hofpitality, &c. is too well known to require the pen of a panegyrift. Geddes probably derives its name from Geelda, a Pictifh Saint, to whofe memory, on this fpot, it feems a place of worfhip was dedicated.

The charter of foundation of the Chapel of Eafter Geddes, part of the walls of which is ftill extant, and granted by Hugh Rofe of Kilravock, bears date 1473. This chapel was dedicated to the Virgin Mary, and endowed with 5 l. Scots of ftipend, together with a fmall croft, as a glebe, and on which to erect a manfe. The prieft or chaplain was to perform daily offices, not only for the foul of the founder, but alfo for the fouls of his predeceffors, and of his heirs and fucceffors for ever. The buil of privileges for faid Chapel is dated at Rome, 26th April 1475, in the 4th year of Pope Sextus the Fourth.

The fite of the Conftabulary is ftill vifible in the town of Nairn. The Lairds of Calder were, for a feries of time, high conftables, and heritable fheriffs of the county. Notice is taken of the Kebback-ftone, in the ftatiftical account of the parifh of Arderfier. In the N. E. corner of this parifh is a place called the King's Steps. Even tradition doth not fay on what account this royal appellation was affixed to this fpot of ground. There is an excellent quarry of freeftone below flood mark, eafily wrought, and of no contemptible quality. There are fome chalybeate fprings of water, but not of fuch confequence as to deferve a particular defcription.

ple to reſide here. But the prices of proviſions of every kind
having riſen greatly of late, and the moſs being almoſt entirely exhauſted, have contributed to increaſe the number of men-
dicants who infeſt the place, and added conſiderably to the
poor's roll. Beſides the bridge before mentioned, there are
two other great diſadvantages, which bear hard upon the town
and country, and theſe are, the want of ſome manufacture,
and the want of a pier. Both theſe might, it is ſuppoſed, be
removed at no very conſiderable expenſe, and to the great e-
molument of Nairn and the neighbourhood. By altering the
preſent courſe of the river, many people ſay that a pier might
be built, capable of receiving ſhips of conſiderable burthen.
Were a ſpirit of improvement once introduced, either a linen
or a woollen manufacture might be eſtabliſhed, which, if well
conducted, would add greatly to the advantage of proprietors
of ſhares, and to the country in general. The number of people who apparently want employment in the town and its
vicinity, is abſolutely incredible. If induſtry, which in a
great meaſure ſeems to be dormant, were arouſed, there is
little doubt but Nairn might become a flouriſhing place.

Miſcellaneous Obſervations.—The people, in general, are
about the middle ſize, affable enough in their manners, with
a few exceptions, pretty regular in their attendance on the
ordinances of divine inſtitution, and rational, without an over-
heated zeal, or too much coldneſs in their religion. Thoſe
of the Eſtabliſhed Church, ſome few of the Epiſcopalian perſuaſion, and the Antiburgher Seceders, live in good terms
with one another. * Few perſons from this pariſh have been
criminally

* Unfortunately, however, this ſpring two lads were tried and condemned
at Inverneſs for ſhop-breaking and theft. One of them was hanged. It is ſurely much to be wiſhed that his fate may prove a warning to others, to avoid the
like

criminally tried before the Court of Jufticiary for many
years.

like crimes. The other young man (brother to the lad who was executed), has
been reprieved. The writer of this account is forry to obferve, that petty
thefts are not fo feverely curbed by parents in the lower ranks in life, as they
ought to be; and he is alfo forry to fay, that the fatal effects of fpiritous liquors become more apparent every day. Nairn is remarkably well calculated
for fea bathing. For the accommodation of perfons who require the benefit of
the falt bath, Mr. James Brander, one of the innkeepers, has a bathing machine
provided.

INDEX

Index

Index

Index

Index

Peat, peat mosses, 50, 105, 108, 113, 130, 139, 140, 147, 149, 153, 161, 172, 191, 194, 202, 219, 242 – 243, 245, 249, 254, 332, 357, 359, 362, 389, 397 – 398, 402, 440, 457, 461, 467, 473 – 474, 496, 515, 562, 583, 605, 624, 626, 630, 650 – 651, 677, 721 – 722, 740, 752

Pigeon-houses, 388, 486, 690

Pigs, 463

Placenames, 1, 15 – 16, 40, 79, 89, 99, 106, 110, 113, 121, 134, 145, 153 – 154, 166, 183, 193, 198, 200 – 201, 233, 244, 247, 256 – 257, 264 – 265, 315, 319, 333, 355 – 356, 361, 406, 415 – 416, 429, 431, 460, 470, 474, 504, 511, 519, 531 – 532, 574 – 575, 588 – 589, 619, 622, 625, 637, 642, 649 – 650, 665, 682, 698, 711, 716, 732, 741

Ploughs, 27, 83, 216, 239 – 240, 249, 329, 387, 412, 456, 483, 513, 557, 623, 640, 658, 700, 712, 723, 739

Poor, poor rates, 6, 13, 32 – 34, 65, 86 – 87, 93, 104 – 105, 107, 117, 126 – 128, 139, 154, 174 – 175, 176, 188, 196, 199, 224 – 227, 236, 257 – 258, 317, 340, 358, 381, 384 – 385, 404, 418, 440, 458, 466, 480, 496, 508, 514 – 515, 522, 551 – 553, 585, 601, 614, 623, 627, 663, 704 – 705, 715, 725, 736, 745 – 746, 752

Population, 4 – 5, 11 – 12, 40 – 42, 84 – 85, 91, 103 – 104, 107 – 108, 112, 118, 124 – 125, 139 – 140, 149, 151, 172 – 173, 187 – 189, 195, 198, 206 – 211, 235 – 236, 245, 251 – 252, 272 – 273, 316 – 318, 325 – 329, 357 – 358, 385 – 387, 401 – 403, 413 – 414, 436, 457 – 458, 464 – 465, 471, 480 – 482, 492 – 493, 504, 512 – 513, 521 – 522, 555 – 562, 583, 602 – 603, 611 – 612, 620 – 621, 627, 635, 652 – 653, 694, 714, 719 – 720, 733 – 734, 746 – 747

Post, post offices, 54, 130, 259 – 260, 345, 361

Potatoes, 4, 22, 82, 114, 141, 152, 188, 214, 330, 356, 364, 412, 426, 437, 455, 463 – 464, 467, 471, 482, 513, 528 – 529, 541 – 543, 545, 582, 595, 623, 626, 630, 648, 654, 656 – 657, 676, 689, 699 – 700, 723 – 724, 734 – 735

Quarries, 116, 137, 147 – 148, 186, 194 – 195, 219, 401, 409, 457, 473, 477, 484, 488, 493, 504 521, 559, 562, 627, 630, 688, 751

Religious denomination—Antiburghers, 495, 705, 719, 746, 752
 —Dissenters, 13, 211, 640
 —Episcopalians, 31 – 32, 85, 104, 107, 125, . 149, 151, 198, 209, 211, 245, 334, 358, 383, 402, 495, 508, 604, 640, 653, 694, 734, 746, 752
 —Established Church, 5, 13, 31 – 32, 85, 104, 107, 117, 125, 140, 149 – 151, 176, 198, 209, 211, 234, 245, 251, 334, 353, 358, 382 – 383, 402, 465, 485, 495, 508, 513, 587, 604, 613, 629, 640, 653, 694, 705, 714, 719, 734, 746, 752
 —Methodists, 358, 604, 640
 —Relief Church, 31 – 32, 151
 —Roman Catholics, 5, 31, 33, 85, 104, 107, 117, 125, 140, 150 – 151, 198, 209, 211, 234, 236, 238, 251, 272, 279, 318, 334, 358, 383, 402, 604, 653
 —Seceders, 85, 104, 107, 117, 149, 151, 198, 209, 211, 251, 318, 334, 358, 465, 613, 629, 705, 734

Index

Index